Professional IBM WebSphere 5.0 Application Server

Tim Francis

Eric Herness

Rob High Jr.

Jim Knutson

Kim Rochat

Chris Vignola

Wrox Press Ltd. ®

Professional IBM WebSphere 5.0 Application Server

First Printed January 2003

Published by Wrox Press Ltd.,
Arden House, 1102 Warwick Road, Acocks Green,
Birmingham, B27 6BH
United Kingdom
Printed in the United States of America
ISBN 1-86100-581-4

Trademark Acknowledgments

Wrox has endeavored to provide trademark information about all the companies and products mentioned in this book by the appropriate use of capitals. However, Wrox cannot guarantee the accuracy of this information.

Credits

Author
Tim Francis
Eric Herness
Rob High Jr.
Jim Knutson
Kim Rochat
Chris Vignola

Technical Reviewers
Andrew Bates
Scott Bonneau
Chadi Boudiab
Frédéric Dutreuil
Willy Farrell
Thorsten Millhoff
Steve Parker
Dr P.G. Sarang
Larry Schoeneman
Matt Staples
Prabu Swamidurai
Andre Tost

Managing Editors
Matthew Cumberlidge
Kalpana Garde

Commissioning Editor
Craig A. Berry

Technical Editors
Nilesh Parmar
Aliasger Talib

Project Manager
Emma Batch
Cilmara Lion
Abbas Rangwala

Production Coordinators
Sarah Hall
Manjiri Karande

Cover
Natalie O'Donnell

Indexer
Seth Maislin

Proofreader
Chris Smith

About the Authors

Tim Francis

Tim Francis is a Senior Technical Staff Member, Tech Lead, and Development Manager working on the WebSphere Studio product at the IBM Canada Toronto Lab. He has been one of the lead architects for the Eclipse-based WebSphere Studio since it was first conceived, and has played a key role in its evolution and development since then. Tim currently leads the development of the WebSphere deployment tools, including the EJB deployment codegen and the server tools unit test environment.

Previously Tim has led development teams for a number of different products, including VisualAge for Java, and the Component Broker Object Builder. Tim holds a Bachelor of Applied Science in Electrical Engineering and Master of Mathematics in Computer Science, both from the University of Waterloo (Canada).

For Karolyn, Kimberlee, and Gavin; You make it all worthwhile.

Eric Herness

Eric Herness is a Distinguished Engineer with IBM in Rochester, Minnesota. He is currently the lead architect for WebSphere Application Server Enterprise. Eric has also been involved in implementing the EJB 2.0 specification in the base application server, especially those parts that enable container-managed persistence.

Eric has been involved in object technology and servers that host objects since the late 1980's. In the early years, he drove work on object analysis and design methods, defining how to practically leverage these concepts in large-scale software projects within and outside IBM. Eric played a lead role in the implementation of Component Broker and in the associated component model definition work that planted many of seeds we now see flourishing in J2EE.

Eric holds a Masters in Business Administration from the Carlson school of Management at the University of Minnesota. He has also been an adjunct computer science faculty member at Winona State University in Rochester, MN.

I would especially like to thank my wife Kate for her patience and support during this adventure. Thanks also to my children Hans and Heidi. Finally, thanks to the people in the BringUp lab (past, present, and future) for helping out with the unexpected.

Rob High Jr.

Rob is a Distinguished Engineer and the Chief Architect for the WebSphere Application Server product family. He has 26 years of programming experience and has worked with distributed, object-oriented, component-based transaction monitors for the last eight years, including SOMObject Server and Component Broker prior to WebSphere. He helped to define, and then later refine the basic concepts of container-managed component technology, which is now intrinsic to the EJB specification and implemented by WebSphere and other J2EE application servers.

Rob started his career with IBM in 1981 in Charlotte, NC. During his 12 years in Charlotte, Rob primarily worked in Finance Industry as a developer on the 4700 controller, in 4730 and 4736 ATM microcode development with responsibility for the device access methods, led the development of Application Foundation PC software for Retail Branch computing, and culminating in responsibility for the Financial Application Architecture. He moved to Austin, TX in 1993 to lead IBM's participation in the Open Software Foundation's Object Management Framework, which lead eventually to his involvement in SOMObjects, and later Component Broker and WebSphere.

Rob has a bachelor degree in Computer and Information Science from the University of California at Santa Cruz. He graduated from UCSC in 1981.

With tremendous gratitude to my parents, and all my love to Cindy, Jamie, and Jordan.

Jim Knutson

Jim Knutson is WebSphere's J2EE Architect. He has been responsible for delivering EJB and J2EE technology in IBM products such as Component Broker and WebSphere since the technology's inception and his accomplishments include the first CORBA-based EJB server.

Prior to this, Jim led IBM's BeanExtender project, a rapid development environment for JavaBeans component-based distributed applications, and has been building distributed object systems for over ten years.

Kim Rochat

Kim is a Senior Software Engineer at IBM's WebSphere development lab in Austin, TX. He was the project leader for the Web Services Technology Preview and participated in the JSR-101 and JSR-109 standards efforts. Prior to WebSphere Web Services, he implemented Java and CORBA support for WebSphere's predecessor, Component Broker. He has worked for a number of companies in his 27 years in the industry, and joined IBM in 1994.

Chris Vignola

Chris Vignola is a senior software engineer with IBM in Poughkeepsie, NY. He is presently a lead architect for the WebSphere Application Server product, specializing in WebSphere integration on the z/OS and OS/390 platform and systems management. His experience with WebSphere includes work in the areas of EJB persistence, EJB Container, and JNDI. Chris has been working on distributed, object-oriented, transaction systems since 1995, including work on Distributed SOMObjects and Component Broker, where he lead the team that first brought WebSphere EJB technology to the z/OS and OS/390 platform. His prior experience includes ten years developing the MVS operating system, where he worked on operations console, sysplex, and workload manager. Chris joined IBM in 1984 after graduating from the State University of New York with a Bachelor of Science degree in Computer Science. Chris lives and works in New York state, where he resides with his wife and three children.

All my love and thanks to Teresa – my inspiration. And to Kathy, Jonny, and Thomas – my hope and my joy.

Table of Contents

Table of Contents

Table of Contents

Table of Contents

Table of Contents

Table of Contents

Table of Contents

Table of Contents

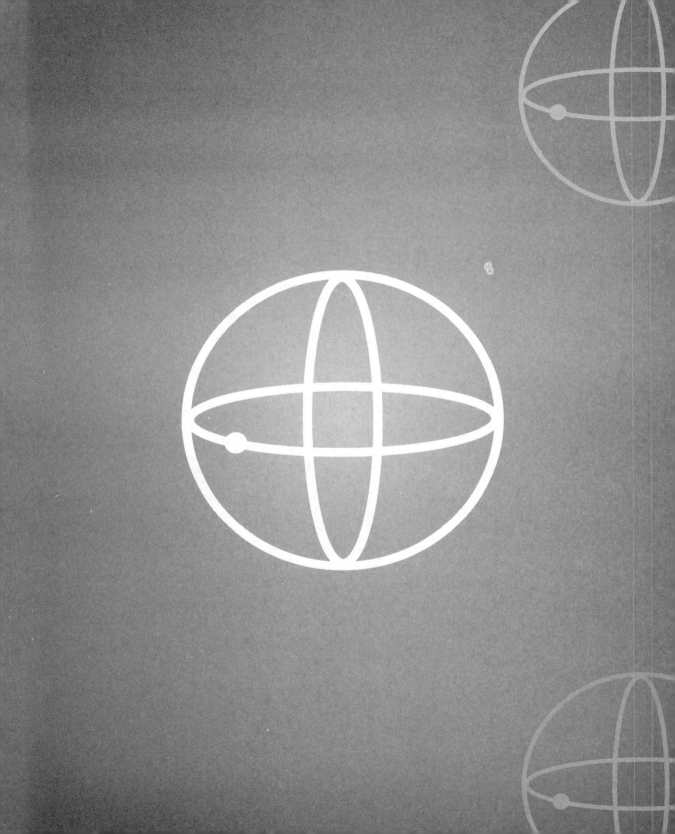

Foreword

The real story behind WebSphere probably goes back to the 60s and 70s – the development of CICS and IMS as application platforms, hierarchical and relational data management, transactional integrity and security, the entry of object-oriented concepts, distributed computing, and virtualization.

However, in 1995 there were three major concerns: how to build a business-value proposition around a small, but interesting technology called SOM (System Object Model); how to get 10^9 scalability out of the CORBA persistence framework; and how to build a hosting environment for system and application objects. The answers to these problems coalesced to form what was then referred to as Component Broker (CB) – a product for hosting component-based business applications in a distributed, container-managed environment. In essence, the value proposition was supposed to (and still does for WebSphere) put application developers back into the business of writing business applications – letting the component broker handle the complexity of the underlying information system and focusing the business application developer's attention on creating reusable object-oriented parts (components based on what was then referred to as the Managed Object Framework). Don Ferguson was brought in from IBM's Research division to lead the development of CB and every one of the authors of this book were founding architects (along with several others). From conception to delivery, CB took less than 18 months to put into the market – shipping in May 1997.

Then, in 1998, the World Wide Web and Java really started to take off. IBM built an extension to the web server for hosting Java-based presentation components. By the end of 1998 there was enormous synergy in a common hosting platform for presentation and business components and thus was forged a marriage between these two servers. IBM began work with SunSoft and others to form the J2EE specification for building Java-based business components – Enterprise JavaBeans (EJBs) – drawing from our experience with MOFW in CB and combining that with the already emerging specifications for servlets and JavaServer Pages (JSPs).

WebSphere Version 3.0 (the name was new, but the numbering sequence borrowed from the predecessor products) was brought to market in October 1999 with a crudely formed alliance between Component Broker, web-based computing, and J2EE. The architecture fully converged with WebSphere Application Server Version 4.0 in August 2001 and that lay the foundation on which IBM could build the WebSphere brand as an entire suite of products that extend the value proposition of the base application server.

With the release of WebSphere Version 5.0 in December 2002, WebSphere has become the most rapidly successful software product in the history of IBM. WebSphere is the leading application server in the industry, and continues to grow market share faster than any other commercial application server. Some of the largest web sites on the Internet are hosted by WebSphere. e-Bay, a common reference for IBM, is driving on the order of 8,000 transactions a second with around-the-clock operations and availability on WebSphere. To say the least, we are enormously proud of the WebSphere product and having been a part of its creation.

This book is about the WebSphere Application Server and its tooling partner the WebSphere Studio Application Developer.

In this book, you will find some perspective on the philosophy and rational behind WebSphere. You will be taken through the programming and deployment model and become familiar with the WebSphere Studio Application Developer tool set. You will learn how to use the application server to build business applications, and how to integrate your business. You will find specifics on how to build presentation and business components, how to interconnect your applications through messaging and adapters, and how to build web services to leverage service-oriented architecture. You will be introduced to valuable extensions for building enterprise-enabling business applications and business processes, and provided with an understanding of how to configure, secure, and administer your production systems.

This book has been divided into four parts:

Part 1 will introduce you to WebSphere. It discusses the value proposition, strategy, and philosophical principles that will guide you through the development and evolution of the WebSphere Application Server. The section will spend some time going over the major elements of the programming model, including the things that differentiate the base application server from its programming model extensions. Finally, you will be introduced to the WebSphere Studio Application Developer (WSAD) tools.

Part 2 will focus primarily on the core J2EE programming model – building presentation and business components, including how to assemble and deploy J2EE applications with the WSAD and Application Assembly Tool (AAT). You will learn to use the messaging engine to build point-to-point and pub/sub notification-oriented communication between your applications and how to use the Java 2 Connector architecture to build adapters to integrate with your non-J2EE applications. Finally, you will see the process of building web services with WebSphere.

Part 3 then takes you beyond J2EE and basic web services. This part will refine your knowledge of how the container can efficiently manage the persistent state of your business components – incorporating Access Intent policies, and Application Profiles. The details on how to use the WebSphere workflow manager, how to incorporate business rules into your application, and how to use the internationalization service, workmanager, workareas, and the startup service, will be covered.

Part 4 shifts your focus to the production environment. It describes the various topologies that you might exploit in your enterprise. It details how to secure your applications in the production environment. These chapters will take you through the process of administering your environment – including, how to install an application, how to configure application servers, and how to manage the operational state of your system. This section also describes how to write administrative applications using the JMX interfaces supported by WebSphere. A later appendix on this topic lists the command-line, scripting, and ANT tasks that you can use to build operations automation routines for use in your production environment. This section concludes with a summary of other features of WebSphere that you might explore on your own.

This book was conceived from the passion that all of us share about this product. WebSphere represents more than just an outlet for our creative energies – we truly believe that WebSphere will add value to your business. It will help you harness the complexities of your information systems and, in doing so, let you exploit the advantages of your computing infrastructure to improve the way that you do business. It will change the way that you think about programming your applications. We hope that you enjoy reading this book as much as we enjoyed writing it.

Rob High, Jr., Eric Herness, Jim Knutson, Tim Francis, Chris Vignola, and Kim Rochat
Architects of the WebSphere Application Server and WebSphere Studio tools

What you Need to Use this Book

Over the course of this book, we cover the use of a number of different WebSphere Application Server and WebSphere Studio editions:

❑　For Chapters 4-8, you will need WebSphere Studio Application Server version 5.0 and WebSphere Application Server version 5.0

❑　For Chapters 9 and onwards, you will need WebSphere Studio Integration Edition version 5.0 and WebSphere Application Server Enterprise version 5.0

❑　Some of the clustered topology will also require WebSphere Application Server Network Deployment version 5.0

On the CD

Accompanying this book there are two CDs that contain the following:

❑　An evaluation copy of WebSphere Studio Application Developer version 5.0 for Windows (Disk 1 and 2)

❑　The Web Services Technology Preview for WebSphere Application Server version 5.0 (Disk 2)

❑　EAR files for the sample code developed over the course of the book (Disk 2)

❑　The PLANTSDB database used by the Plants-By-WebSphere application in this book (Disk 2)

The installation of WebSphere Studio should launch automatically upon inserting Disk 1. For the Web Services Tech Preview and sample code you will need to browse the disk and retrieve these items manually.

Refer to the readme files on the disks for more instructions.

Conventions

To help you get the most from the text and keep track of what's happening, we've used a number of conventions throughout the book.

For instance:

> **These boxes hold important, not-to-be-forgotten information, which is directly relevant to the surrounding text.**

While the background style is used for asides to the current discussion.

As for styles in the text:

❑ When we introduce them, we **highlight** important words

❑ We show keyboard strokes like this: *Ctrl-K*

❑ We show filenames and code within the text like so: `<element>`

❑ Text on user interfaces and URLs are shown as: Menu

We present code in two different ways:

```
In our code examples, the code foreground style shows new, important,
    pertinent code
while code background shows code that is less important in the present
    context or has been seen before.
```

Customer Support

We always value hearing from our readers and we want to know what you think about this book: what you liked, what you didn't like, and what you think we can do better next time. You can send us your comments, either by returning the reply card in the back of the book, or by e-mail to feedback@wrox.com. Please be sure to mention the book title in your message.

Errata

We've made every effort to make sure that there are no errors in the text or in the code. However, no one is perfect and mistakes do occur. If you find an error in one of our books, like a spelling mistake or faulty piece of code, we would be very grateful for your feedback. By sending in errata you may save other reader hours of frustration, and of course, you will be helping us provide even higher quality information. Simply e-mail the information to support@wrox.com; your information will be checked and if appropriate, posted to the errata page for that title or used in subsequent editions of the book.

To find errata on the web site, go to http://www.wrox.com/, and simply locate the title through our Search or title list. Click on the View errata link, which is below the cover graphic on the book's detail page.

E-Mail Support

If you wish to directly query a problem in the book with an expert who knows the book in detail then e-mail support@wrox.com. A typical e-mail should include the following things:

❑ The **title of the book**, **last four digits of the ISBN (5814)**, and **page number** of the problem in the Subject field.

❑ Your **name**, **contact information**, and the **problem** in the body of the message.

We won't send you junk mail. We need the details to save your time and ours. When you send an e-mail message, it will go through the following chain of support:

❑ Customer Support – Your message will be delivered to our customer support, and they will be the first people to read it. They have files on the most frequently asked questions and will answer anything general about the book or the web site immediately.

❑ Editorial – Deeper queries are forwarded to the technical editor responsible for that book. They have experience with the programming language or a particular product, and are able to answer detailed technical questions on the subject.

❑ The Authors – Finally, in the unlikely event that the technical editor cannot answer your problem, they will forward the request to the author. We do try to protect the authors from any distractions to their writing; however, we are quite happy to forward specific requests to them. All Wrox authors help with the support on their books. They will e-mail the customer and the editor with their response, and again all readers should benefit.

The Wrox support process can only offer help on issues directly pertinent to the content of our published title. Answers to questions that fall outside the scope of normal book support may be obtained through the community lists of our http://p2p.wrox.com/ forum.

p2p.wrox.com

For author and peer discussion, join the P2P mailing lists. Our unique system provides **Programmer to Programmer**™ contact on mailing lists, forums, and newsgroups, all in addition to our one-to-one e-mail support system. If you post a query to P2P, you can be confident that many Wrox authors and other industry experts on our mailing lists are examining it. At p2p.wrox.com you will find a number of different lists to help you, not only while you read this book, but also as you develop your applications.

To subscribe to a mailing list just follow these steps:

1. Go to http://p2p.wrox.com/

2. Choose the appropriate category from the left menu bar

3. Click on the mailing list you wish to join

4. Follow the instructions to subscribe and fill in your e-mail address and password

5. Reply to the confirmation e-mail you receive

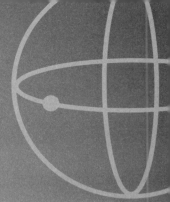

Part 1: A WebSphere Perspective

Part 1: A WebSphere Perspective

This book is divided into four parts, each with a story to tell.

One of WebSphere's primary objectives is to put you back in the business of writing business functions that add value to your business; that enable a high return on your investment in application development; and that help you sustain the value of the investment. WebSphere is intended to hide, or at least reduce, the complexity of information systems by abstracting the computing infrastructure from the application-programming model. This enables you to build efficient and durable application functions that address your business concerns. WebSphere incorporates a substantial arsenal of techniques and component facilities to address a broad range of scenarios and computing concerns.

The first part of this book is designed to create a view of the landscape that we call WebSphere. We won't teach you how to program WebSphere in this part, but we will help you put WebSphere in perspective. We will introduce you to the set of business problems that WebSphere can help you with. We will sort out some of the jargon that IBM typically uses when talking about WebSphere, and why WebSphere is so much more than just an application server – although, it is that too. You will understand the packaging philosophy, the programming model, and tool support for WebSphere, and how it addresses a huge range of computing needs – both in terms of scale and sophistication.

This part will help you understand the major pieces of the programming model and how they fit together. WebSphere has a soul that gets its energy from the Java language, but WebSphere has given that energy form and utility – enabling you to leverage its power to make your business more productive and competitive. As with all powerful machines, it is good to understand something about how all the parts work and their use. This survey of the programming model will help orient you; to prepare you for the more in-depth programming information you will receive through the rest of the book.

Harnessing the power of WebSphere is made easier if you have the right tools. We will introduce you to the WebSphere Studio tools because the rest of the book relies on this knowledge when explaining important programming concepts; more importantly we need to convince you that using such a tool is critical to your programming productivity. If you're still using `vi` and `make` for building applications, consider moving into the 21st century – you won't look back.

Having completed this part, you will be equipped to maximize your use of the programming information we provide in the subsequent sections.

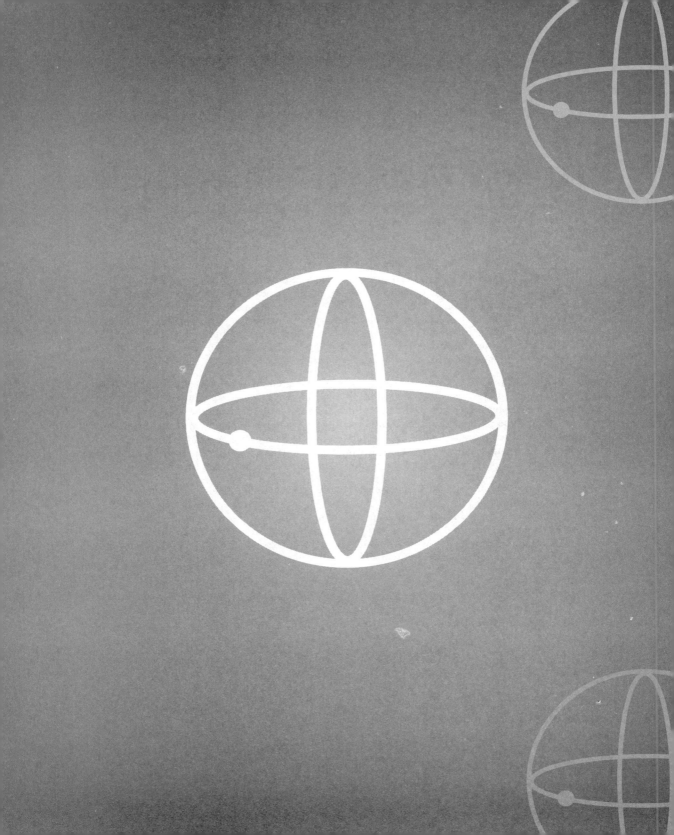

1

Introduction to WebSphere

We are in the early part of the 21st century, where our software challenges have grown and continue to grow faster than our means of dealing with them. Web application servers and the capabilities that they possess represent the component servers being used to solve today's complex business problems. Web application servers combine the best of object technology for clients and presentation (servlets, JavaServer Pages) with the latest technology for representing and implementing the business model in software (web services, Enterprise JavaBeans).

Application servers are also utilizing the latest integration software using connectors and asynchronous communication (Java Message Service) to tie together old and new systems into robust clusters of computing power that meet the ever changing demands of modern e-business and business in general. Many of these application servers rely on Java for implementation technology and basic services.

We are in the application server generation. This phase of the evolution of computing technology is as significant as the introduction of computing models such as the relational database and the transaction monitor. Each of these generations of software has leveraged the newest in hardware technology and in fact has driven hardware and the base operating systems in particular directions. The same applies to the application server, which in many ways is driving our industry forward. Middleware, as a class of software has been traditionally dominated by products based on technologies such as DCE (Distributed Computing Environment) and OMG's CORBA. Middleware now includes the application server as a full member.

What is WebSphere?

The WebSphere brand represents a platform for today's e-business applications. The WebSphere vision and direction represent an ongoing strategy and vision about how software will evolve and meet future application needs.

WebSphere is an application server that runs business applications and supports the J2EE and web services standards. It is a place to host business and presentation logic, which can integrate into the existing computing infrastructure of small as well as large organizations. The following figure provides an overview of where an application server fits into a typical computing environment:

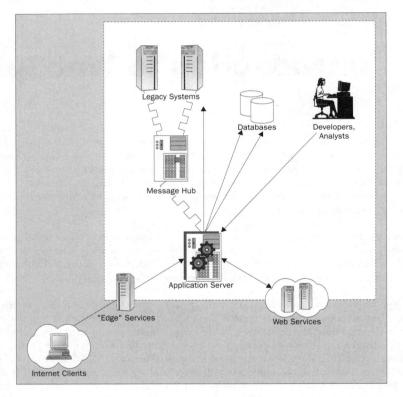

As you can see from the diagram, the application server is the hub of the e-business computing infrastructure. Application servers provide a place to execute policies, to enforce terms and conditions, and to apply business rules. Global clients commonly access these engines using browsers and pervasive devices that operate on both static and dynamic content. The web server sits between the browser and the application server in the most common topologies. Static content is normally served directly from the web server while dynamic content requests are passed on to the application server. Content can be cached at the edge of the network to drastically reduce both network traffic and system load. "Edge Services" refers to the WebSphere capabilities that work in conjunction with the web server to provide this caching at the edge of the network.

Of course, the application servers are not islands, as they typically need to access persistent information stored in one or more databases. In addition, existing systems and applications often need to be leveraged as part of an e-business solution; messaging technology and message brokering are frequently used to drive such legacy system interactions. We complete the picture by showing that developers need an easy way to create and update the applications that are hosted by the application server. Similarly, business analysts need a way to model, monitor, and maintain the various business processes and policies that run there.

How does the application server perform these tasks? The application server, through the services that it provides, handles the presentation and business logic. As the J2EE standards have matured and web services standards have quickly emerged, more services are inherently part of the application server.

Application servers also contain messaging capabilities via the Java Messaging Service (JMS). JMS and the additional messaging features of WebSphere 5.0 provide further evidence for the fact that the asynchronous and synchronous programming models are both required to build next generation applications. The application server provides these features and functions for environments where existing infrastructure is not in place, or where the features need to be more tightly integrated and managed by the application server.

Interoperability, co-existence, and plugability are important themes in the WebSphere Application Server. A first glance at how these themes are leveraged is provided in the next section, where details on the various application server offerings are described.

The WebSphere Application Server

WebSphere Application Server (WAS) represents a set of application server offerings each having its own specific capabilities and functions. This allows WebSphere Application Server to address a broad spectrum of solutions, ranging from the most rudimentary web application to transactional and scaleable e-business applications.

In Version 5.0, WebSphere Application Server has a variety of packages:

❑ **WebSphere Application Server – Express**
   This is a new entry-level offering, which will support servlets and JSP pages. It is targeted to rapid application development and building applications based on associated application-development tooling.

❑ **WebSphere Application Server**
   The generic name, WebSphere Application Server, applies to the J2EE 1.3 certified version of WebSphere that is configured and managed on a single machine. This is similar to the version 4.0 package known as the WebSphere Application Server – Single-Server edition.

❑ **WebSphere Application Server Network Deployment**
   This package is similar to the version 4.0 package, known as WebSphere Advanced or WebSphere Application Server, Advanced Edition. It adds the ability to manage multiple application servers and handle clustered environments. This package comes with a basic WebSphere Application Server.

❑ **WebSphere Application Server Extended Deployment**
   The edition of WebSphere that extends the WebSphere Application Server Network Deployment, with additional features for scalability and manageability. This is a new package for version 5.0.

❑ **WebSphere Application Server Enterprise**
The high-end package for WebSphere Application Server. It introduces additional programming interfaces and supporting run-time capabilities referred to as the programming model extensions. All of the possible capabilities and configurations for WebSphere Application Server are enabled by this package.

❑ **WebSphere Application Server for z/OS**
The application server package delivered for the z/OS environment. The packages described so far apply to all operating system environments except for the z/OS. WebSphere Application Server for z/OS is a special packaging optimized for the z/OS environment that encompasses basically all of the functions described by those packages listed previously that are appropriate for the z/OS environment.

The following diagram positions the various editions of the application server:

```
┌─────────────────────────────────────────────────────────────────────┐
│                        Application Server Editions                    │
│ ┌──────────────────────────────────────────────────────────────────┐ │
│ │ WAS Enterprise                                                    │ │
│ │                        Programming Model Extensions               │ │
│ │ ┌──────────────────────────────────────────────────────┐         │ │
│ │ │ WAS Extended Deployment                               │         │ │
│ │ │         Additional Deployment Optimizations           │         │ │
│ │ │ ┌────────────────────────────────────────────┐        │         │ │
│ │ │ │ WAS Network Deployment                     │        │         │ │
│ │ │ │        Deployment Features                 │        │         │ │
│ │ │ │ ┌─────────────────────────────────┐        │        │         │ │
│ │ │ │ │ WebSphere Application Server     │        │        │         │ │
│ │ │ │ │                                 │        │        │         │ │
│ │ │ │ │ ┌──────────────┐ ┌───────────┐ │        │        │         │ │
│ │ │ │ │ │ WAS Express  │ │           │ │        │        │         │ │
│ │ │ │ │ │              │ │           │ │Distributed│       │         │ │
│ │ │ │ │ │              │ │           │ │Systems   │       │         │ │
│ │ │ │ │ │              │ │           │ │Management,│       │         │ │
│ │ │ │ │ │              │ │           │ │clustering,│       │         │ │
│ │ │ │ │ │              │ │           │ │basic workload│    │         │ │
│ │ │ │ │ │              │ │           │ │management,│       │         │ │
│ │ │ │ │ │ J2EE 1.3 and │ │J2EE 1.3 and│ │monitoring│       │         │ │
│ │ │ │ │ │ Web Services │ │Web Services│ │...       │       │         │ │
│ │ │ │ │ │ Subset       │ │           │ │          │       │         │ │
│ │ │ │ │ └──────────────┘ └───────────┘ └──────────┘       │         │ │
│ │ │ │ └─────────────────────────────────────────────┘              │ │
│ │ │ └──────────────────────────────────────────────────────┘        │ │
│ │ └──────────────────────────────────────────────────────────────┘   │ │
│ └──────────────────────────────────────────────────────────────────┘ │
└─────────────────────────────────────────────────────────────────────┘
```

Now let's look at the features provided by these various editions on more detail.

WebSphere Application Server – Express

WebSphere Application Server Express provides a J2EE and web services subset application server. This is the extension of the Standard Edition concept that was part of WebSphere Application Server 3.5 package. It does not support EJBs; however, there is application development tooling provided as part of the package. WebSphere Studio Site Developer code is provided with the runtime in a single integrated offering. The emphasis is on integrated tooling, with a full Java, servlet/JSP page building, and support for JavaScript and tag libraries. You do not need to be a Java programmer. The secondary focus will be on JSP pages and servlets (but not EJBs). Ease of use, small footprint, and pre-canned applications are all included here.

WebSphere Studio Site Developer is available separately as a tool-only environment. However, even in this configuration, there is an instance of WebSphere Application Server – Express provided as the unit test environment.

WebSphere Application Server (WAS)

The WebSphere Application Server provides a run-time and management environment that can host applications that fully leverage the J2EE 1.3 and web services programming models. This environment is managed through a built-in management capability driven by a web browser. WebSphere Application Server is a single machine execution environment. WebSphere Application Server 4.0 supported J2EE 1.2. The major additions in J2EE 1.3, and thus WebSphere Application Server 5.0, include support for EJB 2.0 and Servlet 2.3. Additional details on each of these are provided in upcoming chapters.

In WebSphere Application Server version 4.0, the environment similar to the WebSphere Application Server (WAS) was known as the WAS Single Server (meant for single machine or single server production applications). The same server is in the test environment of the application development tools offering named WebSphere Studio Application Developer.

WebSphere Application Server Network Deployment (WAS-ND)

This package of WebSphere Application Server is focused on providing a deployment environment for multi-node and multi-server environments. It provides the same programming model support as the base WebSphere Application Server, but adds support for a variety of topologies and architectures consisting of multiple machines and multiple application servers managed under a single umbrella.

WAS-ND provides deployment optimizations mainly in the form of clustering, workload management, and administration. These features allow larger scale deployment than is possible in the base WAS configuration. A deployment manager is introduced as key new concept in an environment that is capable of managing a set of applications from a single console that run across multiple server and multiple machines. More details on this are in upcoming chapters.

WebSphere Studio Application Developer is the associated application development tooling used to construct applications for this execution environment.

WebSphere Application Server Extended Deployment (WAS-XD)

WebSphere Application Server Extended Deployment provides additional optimizations, extending the base and objectives established by WAS-ND. It does this by adding capabilities such as cross-domain failure bypass and dynamic load balancing, in support of enterprise class deployments. Optimizations in WebSphere Application Server Extended Deployment are actually broken into three categories, as follows:

Performance Optimization

This enables the same number of machines to do more work by using a series of workload balancing features. Application server instances will be able to detect variable run-time conditions, and then redirect work dynamically to the machines that are the least busy. These and other examples of performance optimizations will be explained in later chapters.

Availability Optimization

Highly available systems often need to have at least two instances of key run-time components, such as configuration repositories and workload controllers. This allows work to continue in the event of component failure. The more failure bypass that a system offers, including for the failure of internal components, the less that an end user will be disrupted when something goes wrong. Additional features relating to workload management and systems management extend those available in the Network Deployment configuration.

Scalability

Scalability means many things in the context of application serving and WAS-XD addresses all of them. Most traditionally, it means that more work can be handled easily. Effective scaling ensures that all customers receive the service that they request. Effective scaling lets your business expand beyond its traditional boundaries to embrace new partners and suppliers. Features and functions, which support these capabilities, are described in later chapters.

Scaling also means that you can deploy new applications into large environments easily and automatically. This includes applications that extend out to the edge of the network. You can effectively manage those environments, and through plugability, you can leverage the investments that you have made in existing management and security software, as well as operational skills. There is obviously more to come on these topics as well.

Applications that run in a WAS-XD environment will be created with the WSAD tooling. Additional configuration and deployment activity, specific to the XD-enabled runtime will be performed at deployment and installation time.

To summarize, it is expected that WAS-XD configurations, when compared to WAS-ND configurations, will:

❑ Run applications faster based on additional run-time optimizations

❑ Support high availability configurations more directly

❑ Readily handle more machines and more servers in a distributed topology

WebSphere Application Server Enterprise (WAS-EE)

The WebSphere Application Server Enterprise is the next generation of the WebSphere Application Server Enterprise Edition of Version 4.0. The Enterprise product offers some new programming model extensions. A programming model extension is an application programming interface and the association run-time and management features. The application programming interfaces are used by application developers, and these interfaces generally complement the standard interfaces and are used in conjunction with them.

With reference to the packaging described earlier, WAS-EE contains the combined content of WAS, WAS-ND, and WAS-XD, in addition to the programming model extensions. This makes it the most comprehensive WebSphere Application Server offering available. WAS-EE also includes a WebSphere MQ license, enabling construction of applications that leverage WebSphere MQ and WebSphere Application Server.

WebSphere MQ is IBM's flagship messaging product, providing middleware to enable asynchronous communication between various environments, including application servers.

The first set of capabilities provided by the programming model extensions, center on extending and leveraging the EJB 2.0 component model that is part of the J2EE 1.3 specification. The Dynamic Query Service extends EJBQL, enabling query statements to be processed at runtime. This provides a great deal of flexibility and lets applications start dynamic e-business.

Complementing the EJB 2.0 component model is the support for Access Intent via Application Profiles. An example of access intent would be concurrency. The concurrency access intent, for example, can be set to optimistic or pessimistic, depending on the desired behavior of a transaction. Once again, this will make higher performing applications and enable more advanced reuse of components. As this function has both a programming implication and a deployment aspect, portions of this may appear in the Extended Deployment package of the server as well.

WebSphere Enterprise provides strong support for accessing and leveraging existing assets. The WebSphere Studio Application Developer Integration Edition development environment and the WebSphere Application Server Enterprise run-time, work together to provide a service-oriented architecture from which advanced solutions can be constructed. These solutions use services, which represent and encapsulate a variety of resources both within and outside the organization, as the building blocks for complex compositions and choreographies.

The concept of business process choreography is introduced in the enterprise server. This provides for a variety of workflow patterns, including interruptible flows, compensated flows, and micro-flows all to be created with development tools and executed in the runtime. These capabilities are supported by the tool using a Service-Oriented Architecture (SOA). Workflows can drive any service, including intra-enterprise calls to components and connectors and external calls to web services.

For example, you could create basic service definitions through "adapter tooling" that visually connects your Java applications to Enterprise Information Systems. You could then choreograph these basic services into "composed services" that perform higher-level business activities. Wiring these interactions together in a visual fashion makes it easier for developers to create applications, and to preserve the flow structure of the application when underlying service implementations change over time.

Other productivity gains come from the close integration of components and messaging systems. This includes the automated transformation and mappings required between message flows and components to satisfy application needs.

The ideas of messaging and JMS are built upon through the introduction of Extended Messaging Support. These tool-supported APIs are used to program various patterns that are common when dealing with messaging-based interactions to WebSphere and non-WebSphere systems.

Transactions provide a unit of work scoping mechanism for short duration activities, and the compensation support that complements workflow provides a long running unit of work concept. The Activity Session Service and the Last Participant Support service both provide intermediate unit of work and resource management options. The combination of these features offers a comprehensive set of capabilities for properly scoping business activities and handling exceptional conditions that may arise.

Services such as WorkArea and Internationalization allow more flexible and adaptive applications to be constructed. There is a CORBA C++ SDK, to enable C++ clients to EJBs and to provide a basic C++ CORBA Server capability. There is a Scheduler service and Asynchronous Beans delivered as part of WebSphere Application Server Enterprise. These capabilities to allow parallel and asynchronous work to be spawned and managed in the system under prescribed environments.

WebSphere Application Server for z/OS

The z/OS edition of WebSphere is specially optimized to provide scalability and reliability, consistent with that of the z/OS environment. Some of the core application server features have optimized implementations on the z/OS platform, taking advantage of the rich and mature systems services, which are available. Special affinity is provided for the resource managers such as IMS, DB/2, and CICS that reside on the z/OS platform.

WebSphere Application Server applications are portable from a source code perspective and can be easily moved from one of the other application server editions onto the z/OS environment. Additional information on the vision for WAS 5.0 and beyond can be acquired at ftp://ftp.software.ibm.com/software/websphere/partners/TheVisionForWASV5AndBeyond.pdf.

WebSphere is a Platform

WebSphere Application Server is actually just one set of the many offerings that are associated with the WebSphere name. In fact, the WebSphere brand includes a number of products. IBM WebSphere Portal is a label for a set of offerings in the portal market. The WebSphere brand also includes the IBM WebSphere Commerce set of products, IBM WebSphere Host On Demand and Host Publisher IBM WebSphere Translation Server, the IBM WebSphere Voice products, IBM WebSphere EveryPlace products, IBM Transcoding Publisher, and so on. These are complemented by the IBM WebSphere MQ run-time products and the IBM WebSphere Studio set of application development tools.

WebSphere as a platform is essentially about providing three things for users and solution providers who choose this platform:

❑ **Reach and User Experience**
Personalized and streamlined access to content and collaborative services on any variety of devices (including pervasive devices). Note that this also includes the ability to conduct electronic commerce.

❑ **Business Integration**
Integration services both within and between enterprises to promote business agility and to strongly support business-to-business initiatives.

❑ **Foundation and Tools**
An infrastructural underpinning for a whole range of e-business solutions. Application serving and integrated development environments are some of the key elements here.

The WebSphere Application Server provides a fundamental role in the platform. All of the run-time products that are in the platform depend upon the WebSphere Application Server to provide basic services. The Portal server, for example, depends upon servlets and business rules which come from various applications server packages. The Commerce products make heavy use of the J2EE programming model and of many of the extensions introduced in the application server. The consistent usage of the application server by the platform products provides a more manageable solution and a better overall user experience for customers.

WebSphere Product Objectives

WebSphere Application Server has evolved to where it is today because of a few basic product objectives and goals:

- ❏ Provide a platform for enterprise computing
- ❏ Provide a platform for innovation
- ❏ Enable application developers to focus on building applications, not infrastructure
- ❏ Establish and maintain standards leadership
- ❏ Provide a flexible set of product configuration options

The first WebSphere product objective is to provide the platform from which we can really observe and realize the fusion of the web computing world with that of the core enterprise computing world. Properly combining these competencies can provide significant competitive advantage in the marketplace. This is a foundational role, if ever there were one, in the world of middleware and software in general. This objective helps to establish WebSphere as the platform for enterprise computing.

While being a stable and reliable platform from which a company can run the business is important and primary, WebSphere also serves as a platform for innovation. WebSphere is a modern software engineering platform. WebSphere got here by introducing new technologies in ways that were usable, consumable, and palatable to large and small organizations trying to solve business problems. For example, WebSphere has recently begun introducing web services to a heavily J2EE-based environment. The presentation of this implementation has been done in a way that web services are easily adopted and leveraged. There is no leap of faith or step increase in skill requirements to adopt and leverage the new things in a given version of WebSphere.

Innovation is also demonstrated by the Enterprise Edition of the WebSphere Application Server. This package contains a couple of key categories of function. First, there are those functions that extend the programming model available in J2EE and web services. These new interfaces are intended to enable developers to easily solve the more complex problems that are bubbling to the top of lists across the world. These new interfaces are previews of the interfaces that will emerge in future versions of J2EE. Activity Service (JSR-95), WorkArea (JSR-149), and Internationalization Service (JSR-150) are Enterprise Edition programming extensions that really do provide tomorrow's standards today.

This innovation comes in a production-ready platform, so not only are the new capabilities available, but they are ready for production use. A second set of capabilities in the Extended Deployment offering, introduced in WebSphere 5.0, also represent innovation. This set, often referred to as "qualities of service", is provided to deliver WebSphere applications into complex and dynamic environments. These innovations and features do not affect the application programming interfaces, but focus on ensuring that large-scale deployments of applications can be successful in a variety of complex environments.

The third objective of WebSphere that lives in the hearts and minds of the engineering team revolves around the goals of middleware. The objective of WebSphere and perhaps the ongoing quest is to let application developers get back to building applications instead of middleware. The types of applications being built today are increasingly more functional, and thus more complex. It is the job of middleware to keep providing services and capabilities that let the developers build applications, rather than generic middleware that applications are constructed on.

As an example, there has been a perceived need for additional synergy between the synchronous invocation model and the asynchronous model of computing. It is increasingly the case that applications need a combination of both of these programming styles in a single solution. WebSphere Application Server adds some new capabilities in this area in version 5.0 to further encapsulate the differences in the models as they are presented in the application server, while still making these architectural patterns available in the application server. There is also an evolving component model in the form of EJBs that again provides additional abstractions to the application builder and implies the need for more run-time capabilities.

Establishing a platform certainly includes focus on the objectives already described. However, establishing a platform also means establishing and maintaining leadership in standards. This is the fourth product objective for WebSphere Application Server. The J2EE standard, the evolving web services standards, the CORBA standards, and many others are of ongoing interest to WebSphere as a product and to WebSphere as a platform. Not only will WebSphere continue to introduce standards and contribute to the ongoing standards definition activity, but the goal is now to be able to deliver early implementations of these standards, and most importantly be persistent in delivering compliant, robust, scalable, and reliable implementations of those standards.

J2EE 1.3 is a perfect example of the kind of leadership that is important from a WebSphere perspective. The contribution of the IBM team during the formation of the J2EE 1.3 components is significant. WebSphere architects were in on the ground floor of J2EE 1.3 highlights, such as EJB 2.0 CMP support and EJB 2.0 message-driven beans support. Through the timely introduction of WebSphere Technology for Developers version 5.0, WebSphere demonstrated early implementations of the standards by becoming the first major run-time vendor to be certified. Through the introduction of WebSphere Application Server version 5.0 offerings, the J2EE 1.3 loop is being "closed" by delivering run-time implementations of the standard across a variety of platforms that can enable large-scale production usage of these standards.

A final product objective focuses on the product packaging and organization of capabilities into the various WebSphere Application Server editions. While the various configurations of WebSphere have different purposes and function, consistency and structure allows customers to easily upgrade from one edition to another.

This theme is often referred to by the engineering team as the "pay as you go" principle of WebSphere. This principle states that any additional development and management complexity, targeted at complex and large-scale environments, must not be observable until the capability is required. This means that WebSphere does not overwhelm developers starting out with simple applications on simple topologies. This also, however, does mean that WebSphere is customized and specifically architected for a large variety of complex environments.

WebSphere Principles

Beyond a set of product objectives and goals lie a set of values and principles that internally drive the WebSphere Platform. The basic principles, which drive the engineering activities around WebSphere, include:

- ❑ Treating platform as a development principle
- ❑ Leveraging core competencies
- ❑ Robustness
- ❑ Using what we sell

The engineers that work on WebSphere take the platform concept and interpret it with their own set of perspectives and contexts. To the WebSphere engineers, a platform means that they have something that is consistent, works as a single unit, and provides a user experience that is complete, rich, and robust. This is the first and most broad reaching of the WebSphere principles.

We have a platform, what does this mean? To some, it means that WebSphere Application Server is like an operating system. The WebSphere engineering team runs on and abides by many of the principles of operating system development. These are engrained in the team. Many members of the WebSphere engineering team work in development labs in places where operating systems such as OS/400, AIX, OS/2, and OS/390 were invented, delivered, and supported. Today the WebSphere engineers work in buildings alongside many of the teams that continue to be involved in operating systems development. The synergies are too many to describe.

WebSphere is effectively a layer over the top of the operating system that provides all of the programming abstractions (at least in combination with Java) that are needed to build next generation e-business applications. J2EE and application servers are effectively distributed operating systems from an API perspective. WebSphere is a distributed operating system from the perspective of performance, reliability, availability, recoverability, usability, and serviceability. This is a fundamental tenet of WebSphere.

WebSphere is based on a philosophy and value set that runs deep into the history of computing and into the history of IBM. Operating systems were the extent of software that was provided by the computer manufacturers in the beginning, or at least shortly after the beginning. IBM pioneered such concepts as transaction monitors and databases. These provided a layer that shielded, simplified, and expedited solution development. This layering idea has grown to now encompass the rich programming model that is contained within WebSphere. Within WebSphere, this platform-oriented thinking lives on and contributes in many ways to the WebSphere Application Server that exists today.

A second principle revolves around leveraging core competencies. IBM has a rich and varied set of engineering talents, spread across the globe. When specific skills are needed, the team within IBM that has those skills is found and commissioned to become contributors to the application server.

For example, when JMS became part of the J2EE, the WebSphere team went to the messaging team that provides WebSphereMQ and acquired the necessary JMS components of the application server. When object-oriented query entered the J2EE specification, the team that constructed the IBM Component Broker query service was once again called upon to deliver. In general, WebSphere takes a pragmatic approach to constructing the WebSphere Application Server, soliciting and in fact requiring contributions from the IBM Software Group at large.

Robustness is a third key principle. Being robust, WebSphere isolates the execution of customer code from the execution of system code. This is generally not the case in a world where we have no "kernel mode" to rely on for separating and isolating customer-written applications from the system. Through a series of internal components and a set of powerful reliability, availability, and serviceability capabilities, WebSphere does provide the environment of choice for application serving.

For example, our reliability, availability, and serviceability capabilities, which have been improved again in version 5.0, clearly demonstrate a commitment to robustness and reliability. In many cases, the WebSphere runtime will report a problem, point to the actual line of code (customer code and system code alike) that causes an event or failure to occur and suggest a solution. Version 5.0 actually adds an additional First Failure Data Capture (FFDC) capability that allows problems to be diagnosed without collecting additional trace data, or re-running the application to gather logs.

A knowledge base is built into the product. If a failure occurs a second time, the system will remember this and immediately gather the additional data necessary for diagnosis and providing a solution. Keeping the WebSphere JVM alive is a key part of the robustness story. Through careful programming and isolation techniques, WebSphere does everything possible to prevent a rogue piece of application code bring down the entire server.

The fourth and final principle that applies to the application server and the entire platform is that of "Use What We Sell". This principle states that the technology that WebSphere provides is the technology that we use to build some of the components of WebSphere. A good example of this in the WebSphere Application Server is the administration support provided by version 5.0. This is a J2EE application that makes heavy use of servlets and JSP pages. In WebSphere Application Server Enterprise, a number of components, including Business Rule Beans and Workflow, leverage J2EE APIs such as entity EJBs in their implementation.

A Vision for the Future

What is next for WebSphere? Where does the platform go from here? WebSphere Application Server, version 5.0 is one of the strongest and richest modern application server available today. Today is the keyword, as there is constantly a change in technology.

In the months following the general availability of WebSphere Application Server version 5.0, we can expect mostly the usual and maybe a bit of the unusual. There will be service releases and an appropriate introduction of the rest of IBM's WebSphere branded products that leverage and run on WebSphere Application Server version 5.0. With these additional IBM products in place, partners will then complement these offerings with additional run-time and tooling-based offerings. Customers will enjoy a complete platform offering and proceed to deploy large-scale production applications.

In addition to service releases, it is likely that incremental functional capabilities will rollout and the J2EE 1.3 base will be enriched with more capabilities. The openness and flexibility of the WebSphere Application Server in version 5.0 suggests that it will be a production platform, used widely and over a long period by many large customers.

Meanwhile, it is also expected that there will be tactical activity in the standard areas. J2EE 1.4 is already something being defined and WebSphere architects are working on the steps necessary to provide support for this next standard. The version 5.0 architecture has already planned for and has even implemented some of the future J2EE standards. JMX support, for example, is already built into the administration model of WebSphere version 5.0. Another example is in the area of web services. JSR-109 will add web services directly into J2EE. WebSphere Application Server will have early support for this in version 5.0 and will formalize this support as the standards become final. The intention will be to deliver production-ready products supporting these features and others, in a fashion similar to that which was used for the version 4.0 and 5.0 deliveries.

Strategically, the WebSphere Application Server will continue to evolve with the industry, to lead the way as the platform for building that next application which delivers business value. Some of the version 5.0 features and functions clearly represent an initial offering of function in a specific area. This is especially evident in the programming model extensions. Many of these could be enhanced and upgraded as initial usage yields additional requirements and new application types are invented which require additional middleware support.

Internal to IBM, the role of WebSphere Application Server will also grow. The evolving portfolio of WebSphere branded products will come to depend on the application server for a growing number of services and capabilities. These could be called base or basic services, but in actuality, they represent capabilities that are functionally beyond what is evident today in WebSphere Application Server version 5.0. Internal to IBM, the strategy is to continue to achieve engineering efficiencies in middleware product development, by focusing efforts on building high-level business value that extends and leverages the functionality of the underlying application server.

Summary

You should now have an initial understanding of what WebSphere Application Server is. We have defined the server configurations:

- ❑   WebSphere Application Server Express
- ❑   WebSphere Application Server
- ❑   WebSphere Application Server Network Deployment
- ❑   WebSphere Application Server Extended Deployment
- ❑   WebSphere Application Server Enterprise
- ❑   WebSphere Application Server for z/OS

We have also looked at the platform concept and the important role of the application server as part of the platform. A quick visit to the past and some projections for the future has also been provided.

Some key points from Chapter 1 include:

- ❑   Application Servers are central to solving today's and tomorrow's business problems
- ❑   Standards are important to the application server industry and will continue to be so in the future
- ❑   Application Servers represent the results of years of product development and standards evolution
- ❑   Application Servers provide a distributed operating system concept that encapsulates and abstracts details of individual platforms

With this introduction to WebSphere now in place, let's move ahead to the details.

The WebSphere Programming Model

2

We examine many aspects of the WebSphere programming model in this book. However, notwithstanding the breadth of coverage included in this book, the total WebSphere programming model is larger than we can hope to address between a single pair of covers. Fortunately, the majority of the WebSphere programming model is based on open standards, and so, a great deal of what we don't cover here can be learned from other readily available sources – the most important of which is the Java web site at: http://java.sun.com/. Other useful books on the general topic of J2EE programming include:

❑ *Professional Java Server Programming J2EE 1.3 Edition*, Wrox Press, ISBN: 1-86100-537-7

❑ *J2EE Design Patterns Applied*, Wrox Press, ISBN: 1-86100-528-8

❑ *Expert One-on-One: J2EE Design and Development*, Wrox Press, ISBN: 1-86100-784-1

To help put WebSphere in perspective, we provide an overview of the entire programming model in this chapter:

❑ We begin with a discussion of the basic models of computing supported by the WebSphere programming model.

❑ We then proceed with a discussion of the classic J2EE roles and some thoughts about additional roles that can contribute to the development and deployment of applications in your enterprise. This will include a discussion on how these roles play into the overall programming model process.

❏ We follow with an overview and introduction to the additional programming facilities introduced by WebSphere that go beyond the J2EE standard, including the web services programming model.

This chapter will also outline the APIs included in the WebSphere programming model. It will provide some perspective on the value of the functions intrinsic to the WebSphere programming model – hopefully offering you some new ways of thinking about your business applications.

We will, in this discussion, provide some insight on which APIs are considered strategic, which are supported across all of the WebSphere platforms and editions, and which are restricted. We will introduce the idea of privileged code to gain access to otherwise restricted elements of the programming model. By the time you've finished reading this chapter, you will have a base line on the WebSphere programming model, and be better prepared to understand the programming concepts and details presented through the rest of this book.

Models of E-Business Computing

WebSphere is a J2EE-compliant application server supporting the entire breadth of the J2EE specification. WebSphere version 5.0 is certified at the J2EE 1.3 level, and as such, J2EE is at the heart of the programming model. Given the platform portability premise of Java (and J2EE itself), there is a good chance that you will be able to port your conforming applications to WebSphere with little effort.

However, that only tells a part of the WebSphere story. As programmers, our needs for information computing are varied, dynamic, and growing. Most computing scenarios today have to address a variety of issues: end-user delivery channels, development methodologies, business-enablement approaches, legacy protection, and fulfillment goals. WebSphere has excellent capabilities for supporting many of these requirements. To understand these, it would be best to start with a basic understanding of the key models of computing and how WebSphere addresses each of these. Then, you can combine this knowledge to form a solution tailored to your specific situation.

WebSphere provides support for four basic models of e-business computing:

❏ Multi-tier distributed computing

❏ Web-based computing

❏ Integrated enterprise computing

❏ Services-oriented computing

The fundamental structures of application design enable distributed computing for different business and organizational scenarios. Most applications will eventually exploit a combination of these models to solve the needs of the environment in which they will be used. The WebSphere programming model covers the full span of each of these models.

If you are already familiar with the fundamentals of distributed computing, component programming, shared and reusable parts, business process management, and service-oriented architecture then you might like to skip ahead a bit. More so, if you're already familiar with J2EE and the core premise for WebSphere, then skip this section – move on to *The WebSphere Development Model* section. If, on the other hand, you're not sure about these topics or a brief refresher might cement the issues in your mind then read on. Our view is that to best understand WebSphere you need to understand the types of computing models it is designed for.

Multi-Tier Distributed Computing

Multi-tier distributed computing is what motivated the development of many of the core server technologies within WebSphere. The idea of component-based programming is to define reusable and shared business logic in a middle-tier of a three-tier distributed application:

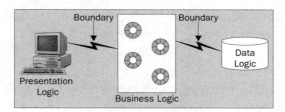

The value of three-tiered distributed computing comes from first structuring the application with a clean separation between the logic elements (presentation, business, and data) and then leveraging the boundaries between these elements as potential distribution points in the application, allowing, for example, the presentation logic to be hosted on a client desktop, the business logic in a middle-tier, and the data logic on a traditional data centre.

Placing the presentation logic on the user's desktop has the benefit of enabling a rich interaction model with the end user. Placing the data logic in the traditional data center allows tight, centralized control over the data and information assets of the enterprise. Placing the business logic in a middle-tier allows for the exploitation of a variety of computing systems and better reuse and sharing of common computing facilities to reduce the cost of ownership that is commonly associated with expensive thick clients. It also means that you don't have to manage large quantities of application logic in the desktop environment.

The boundary between each tier represents a potential distribution point in the application, allowing each of the three parts to be hosted in different processes or on different computers. The J2EE programming model provides location transparency for the business logic, allowing you to write the same code irrespective of whether the business logic is hosted over the network or is in the same process. However, you shouldn't let this trick you into treating your business logic as though it is co-located in the same process – notwithstanding the tremendous improvements we've seen in networking technologies, communication latency will affect the cost of invoking your business logic and you should design your application keeping in mind that such boundaries can carry this expense.

Even if you don't distribute your application components across a network, you can still benefit from the boundary between the tiers. Every boundary that you are able to design into your application becomes an opportunity to 'plug-replace' other components. Thus, even nominal distribution of these components can improve the ease of maintenance of your application. It also becomes an opportunity for the runtime to spread workload over more computing resources (we'll discuss this in detail in Chapter 12).

Through J2EE, WebSphere provides a formalized component architecture for business logic. This component technology has several key benefits to application development. Foremost, the component model provides a contract between the business logic and the underlying runtime. The runtime is able to manage the component. This ensures the optimal organization of component instances in memory, controlling the lifecycle and caching of state to achieve the highest levels of efficiency and integrity, protecting access to the components, and handling the complexities of communication, distribution, and addressing:

Secondly, the component architecture allows the client programming model to conform to well-established rules, which implies that distributed components are shared components – that is, the same component can be used by many different applications simultaneously:

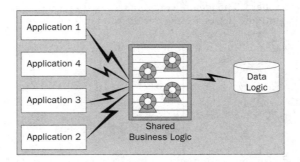

Finally, because the J2EE component model is designed around object-oriented principles, you are able to do a better job of modeling your business in the application design. This will help improve communication between you and your business end users – you can cast your application artifacts in terminology that they recognize, with behavior that is consistent with the conceptual model of the business they are trying to automate. We recommend that you exploit UML or some other standard modeling notation to define your basic business model design, and then use that model to generate the base J2EE artifacts in which you will implement that model. Rational Rose, for example, is one of several products that allow you to build a UML model, and then export that to a J2EE component implementation skeleton.

So, having a single, shared implementation and instantiation of business components in an environment where the developer doesn't have to deal with concurrency issues, not only reduces the duplication of development effort, but also allows you to concentrate more on ensuring the correctness and completeness of your component implementation. It gives you more control over your business processes by ensuring that business entities are adhering to your business policies and practices – you don't have to worry that someone has an outdated or alternative implementation of your business model sitting on their desktop. We have all heard stories about loan officers giving out loans at the wrong interest rate with inadequate collateral because someone had out-of-date rate tables loaded in the spread-sheet. Shared business logic implementations help avoid these costly problems by encouraging fewer implementations of the business logic and therefore fewer opportunities for the business logic to get out of sync.

With the introduction of a component technology for business logic in a three-tiered distributed computing model, we immediately began to see design patterns for the composition of business objects. That is, businesses want to be able to form higher-level business concepts that aggregate previously independent elements of their business. Instead of a customer having multiple accounts, and therefore, multiple relationships with the business, the enterprise could bring together all the individual accounts for a given customer under a single customer object and thus form a better and more enhanced relationship with the business. The business logic could thus be structured in multiple tiers, ranging from general to more specific, all formulated under the same underlying component architecture.

From this was born the idea of multi-tier distributed computing, where the middle-tier of business logic could be composed of an arbitrary number of intermediate tiers all running on a common WebSphere J2EE platform architecture and thus ensuring consistency of programming, deployment, and administration:

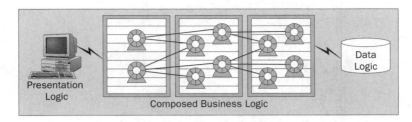

We should reiterate here that the multi-tiered distributed computing nature of component-based programming for business logic enables the integration of distribution points within your application design. It also defines a contractual boundary to your business components that can be leveraged to share your business logic components within many different applications, which in turn may be distributed. However, you don't have to distribute the components of your application to benefit from component-based programming. In fact, distributing your components introduces coupling issues that are not normally found in centralized application designs.

In cases where you know the latency of distributed communication between two components cannot be tolerated in your application design, you can instrument your component with local interfaces that will defeat distribution, but still retain the benefits of component-based programming.

Many of the benefits of component-based programming come from the separation of application logic from concerns of information technology. In particular, the J2EE component model enables a single-level-store programming model, whereby the issues of when and how to load the persistent state of a component are removed from the client.

The component model allows the runtime to *manage* the component in the information system. This same principle of management applies to object identity, transaction and session management, security, versioning, clustering, workload balancing and failover, caching, and so on. In many cases, the runtime has a much better understanding of what is going on in the shared system than any one application can ever have, and thus can do a better job of managing the component and getting better performance and throughput in the information system. Since WebSphere is a commercially available product, you can acquire these benefits for much less than it would cost you to create the same capability on your own.

Web-Based Computing

Web-based computing is, in some sense, a natural extension of the multi-tier distributed computing model whereby the presentation logic has been re-located in the middle-tier of the distributed computing topology, and drives the interaction with the end user through fixed-function devices in the user's presence. We refer to an in-presence, fixed-function device as a Tier-0 in the multi-tier structure of the application. The most common form of the Tier-0 device is the web browser on your desktop. Pervasive computing devices are emerging in the market in other forms as well – from PDAs and mobile phones, to intelligent refrigerators and cars:

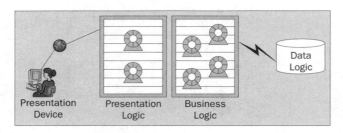

Web applications exploit the natural benefits of component-based programming to enable the construction of web presentation logic that can be hosted on a server platform, and to achieve richer styles of interaction than can be achieved with plain static content servers. The web application server was originally conceived to extend traditional web servers with dynamic content. However, in the course of developing these web application servers, we realized that the issues of serving presentation logic are essentially the same as the issues of serving business logic. As with business logic, the purpose of the presentation logic server is that many clients (in this case, Tier-0 clients) share a common implementation.

When creating WebSphere, IBM found significant synergies in the marriage of web-based application serving and business logic serving. WebSphere uses the same underlying server technology for serving both EJB-based components for business logic and servlets for presentation logic. JSP pages are served as an extension of servlets. HTTP session persistence is implemented with some of the same underlying technologies as EJB essential-state persistence.

An emerging trend in the industry is to further extend the benefits of component-based programming of presentation logic out into the network. This trend is motivated by the need to further reduce the effects of latency on end-user response time. This idea leverages the fundamental nature of how workload is distributed over the presentation logic.

Presentation components that manage simple catalog-browsing logic can be pushed out in the network, closer to the end user, without putting the business at risk. Where the component is hosted in the network, whether at a central data center or out in a network hub, becomes primarily a matter of how the component is deployed and whether the hosting environment can protect the component's integrity to the level required by the component's implementation and value. The result can be a substantially better end-user performance with a moderate increase in the cost of managing the application and almost no increase in the complexity of the application design itself. Hosting parts of your application out in the network is referred to as **edge-computing** – computing is moved to the edge of your enterprise or the edge of your network.

Introducing component-based presentation logic in your application design does not limit you to simply delivering HTML to a browser. Servlets and JSP pages are capable of generating a wide variety of markup languages for a variety of device types. Information about the target device can be retrieved from the HTTP flow, and can be used to customize the output of the presentation logic. Even within the domain of browser-based devices, you have a variety of options like returning JavaScript or even a proprietary XML exchange to an Applet, in addition to HTML.

The servlet and JSP programming model are discussed in more detail in Chapter 4. The role of edge serving in improving the performance of serving the presentation layer to the end-user interaction model is discussed further in Chapter 12.

Integrated Enterprise Computing

Integrated enterprise computing is critical to retaining value in your past investments. Few new applications can be introduced into an established enterprise without some regard to how that will fit with existing applications and, by extension, the technology and platform assumptions on which those applications have been built. If you look into your enterprise you will find a variety of applications built on a variety of underlying technology assumptions. You may have applications built on SAP, CICS, Oracle, IMS, Windows, DB2, Tibco, PeopleSoft, Domino, MQSeries, and other proprietary technology bases. In many cases, you will be asked to integrate these applications into your application implementation.

In some cases you will be asked to create a new application that is intended to essentially replace an existing application – perhaps to exploit the productivity benefits of the J2EE-compliant, object-oriented, componentized or web-based capabilities provided by the WebSphere Application Server platform. It has become common for enterprises to initiate projects to re-engineer their core business processes. This has been largely motivated by the need for businesses to respond to rapidly changing market conditions that require the introduction of new products – **business process re-engineering**.

In our experience, projects that propose massive re-engineering of existing information technologies to enable business process changes run a high risk of failure. This is due, in part, to the complexity of such projects as it is hard to keep the scope of such projects constrained to isolated portions of the overall business process; features and scope-creep push the project towards higher levels of complexity.

Another major risk factor in the case of such projects is the extent to which the re-engineering can disrupt existing business activities. This requires re-education of end users, not just in the new business processes, but also in the underlying interaction models introduced by the new technology. It means fundamental changes to the administration processes and significant changes to the workload of the computing systems, and thus alters our basic understanding of resource utilization and, further, our ability to predict capacity requirements, not to mention the potential to take existing processes off-line during the transition to the new technology bases. While business process re-engineering is essential for enterprise growth and sustainability in our modern global economy, it can also represent a serious business risk.

A more prudent approach to business process re-engineering is a more incremental approach – one that puts together an application framework representing the re-engineered process on the new technology foundation, but delegates the majority of its business function implementations to the business application legacy already being used in the enterprise. Over time, as the foundation and application framework mature and investment opportunity warrants, legacy business implementations can be re-written as first-order implementation artifacts in the new technology base, and the legacy can then be withdrawn. We refer to this as **incremental business process re-engineering**.

Two things are key to enabling incremental business process re-engineering. The first is a good design for the new business application that will serve as a foundation for your business process objectives. This has to incorporate flexibility towards rapid or customized changes in the business processes, including the introduction of new processes, and yet account for the use of existing application artifacts. The second ingredient is the availability of basic technologies that enable communication of data and control-flow between the application framework and the legacy application elements that you want to exploit.

The methodologies for creating a good framework design are a topic in itself. We won't go into that very deeply here. However, the principles of object-oriented design – encapsulation, type-inheritance, polymorphism, instantiation, and identity – are generally critical to such frameworks. To that end, Java, J2EE component programming, and a good understanding of object-oriented programming are vital.

As usual, the issues of cross-technology integration are complicated – in mission-critical environments, you must address concerns about data integrity, security, traceability, configuration, and a host of other administrative issues for deployment and management. However, to support the productivity requirements of your developers, these complexities should be hidden – as they are in the WebSphere programming model.

The key programming model elements provided by WebSphere for enterprise integration are offered in the form of Java 2 Connectors and the Java Messaging Service, both of which are part of the J2EE specification. In addition, WebSphere offers programming model extensions that effectively incorporate these programming technologies under the covers of a higher-level abstraction – for the most part presented in the guise of standard J2EE component model programming. For example, in Chapter 7, we introduce the WebSphere adapter to J2EE Connectors that uses a stateless session bean programming interface.

Messaging-based approaches to application integration are very effective and introduce a great deal of flexibility. The asynchronous nature of a message-oriented programming model allows the applications to be decoupled (or loosely coupled if they weren't coupled to begin with). One popular model is to instrument one application to simply state its functional results as a matter of fact in an asynchronous message. The message can then be routed by the messaging system to other applications that may be interested in that outcome and can operate on it further. In particular, the message may be routed to multiple interested applications, thus enabling parallel processing.

Series of applications designed in this manner can be strung together in various patterns to create a business system. The system can be re-wired in many different patterns to create different effects. No component ever has to know what other components it is wired to and so re-wiring can be accomplished without affecting the component implementations. For example:

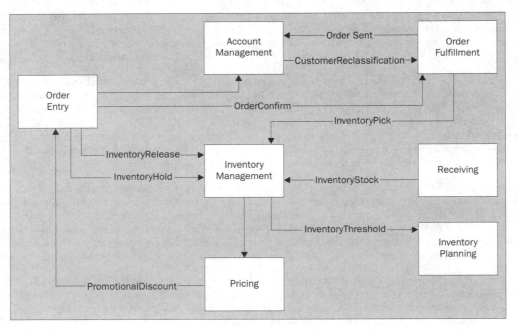

In this sample enterprise information system (composed of several otherwise independent applications), the inventory hold message is sent to the inventory management system to put a hold on the stock for a pending order. Likewise, if the customer cancels the order, an inventory release message is sent to free that stock for another order. An order configuration message is sent to the order fulfillment system to ship the requested items to the customer. That same message is also sent to the account management system to be used to calculate the customer's loyalty to the store. If a customer is reclassified (for example, they've ordered more than a certain amount in the last 12 months) then a message is sent to the order fulfillment system – higher-classified customers received preference over other customers. If inventory (plus holds) drops below a certain threshold, then an inventory-threshold message is sent to the order fulfillment system (orders may be held to allow higher-classified customers to get preferential treatment). The inventory threshold message is also sent to the inventory planning system (to order more stock from the supplier), and to the pricing system (which may adjust prices if demand continues to exceed supply).

The point is that all of these systems are loosely coupled – each responding to the messages they receive based on their own encoding and considered policies. The system continues to work (albeit differently) if message-connections are dropped or added between the parts. For example, if the connection between the order entry system and account management system is dropped, the rest continues to work – you just don't get any assessment of customer loyalty. Likewise, adding a connection to pass the inventory-threshold message between the inventory management system and the order fulfillment could be used to slow down the fulfillment of orders containing items with a low inventory (allowing more higher-priority orders to be fulfilled).

Variations on message-oriented computing include: point-to-point asynchronous messaging, request-response messaging, and publish-subscribe messaging.

Looking at the problem of application integration (or perhaps, more appropriately, lines-of-business integration) from the top, it is important to model your business process flows in a way that allows you to adapt those flows rapidly to new procedures and opportunities – to be able to model and then rapidly modify the order entry process to perform credit checks or to process partial orders, and other similar processes without having to re-write either your order entry or your inventory systems.

Business process management is discussed in greater depth in Chapter 10.

Services-Oriented Computing

Services-oriented computing started out as the definition for the next level of coarse-grained functional composition – the idea being to aggregate interdependencies that you did not want to expose across a network boundary: the next higher aggregation beyond components in a distributed system. Services-oriented architectures (SOA) leverage the relative cohesiveness of a given business service as the primary point of interchange between parties in the network.

SOA has a lot of affinity with business-to-business integration. More recently, SOA has re-emerged with a renewed focus on leveraging Internet technologies, and has been re-branded as **web services**. The idea is to use XML as the basic message-encoding architecture, and HTTP as a communication transport, to provide a very low barrier to driving the programmatic interaction of automated processes between companies. Since both these technologies are pervasive in the web-based computing environment – nearly everyone now has support for HTTP and XML (or at least HTML) in their computing infrastructures – the problem of agreeing to a common technology base as a requisite to inter-enterprise communication could be quickly overcome.

We've come to realize that the fundamentals of services-oriented computing could be exploited to overcome similar barriers between lines-of-business within an organization as well. In fact, the exploitation of web services may, in the end, be more pervasive for intra-enterprise integration than for inter-enterprise integration. When combined with more classic approaches to enterprise integration and gateways, the principles of incremental business process re-engineering can be applied to integrate legacy systems into the services-oriented computing model.

Advances in the field of services-oriented computing are heavily focused on web services now – especially on Web Services Definition Language (WSDL), and to a lesser extent on the Simple Object Access Protocol (SOAP), and Universal Description, Discovery and Integration (UDDI). These technologies combine to introduce business services that can be easily composed with other business services to form new business applications. At some level, web services are just a new generation of technology for achieving distributed computing, and in that sense, they have a lot in common with many of the other distributed computing technologies like OSF/DCE, CORBA, and J2EE's RMI/IIOP that went on before them. However, web services differ from their predecessors in the degree to which they deliberately address a 'loose coupling' model.

We measure the coupling of distributed application components in at least three ways:

- ❑ Temporal affinity
- ❑ Organizational affinity
- ❑ Technology affinity

Temporal Affinity

Temporal affinity is a measure of how the information system is affected by time constraints in the relationship between two components. If an application holds a lock on data for the duration of a request to another business service, there are expectations that the requested operation will complete in a certain amount of time – data locks and other similar semaphores tend to prevent other work from executing concurrently. Tightly-coupled systems tend to have a low tolerance for latency. On the other hand, loosely-coupled systems are designed to avoid temporal constraints – the application and the underlying runtime are able to execute correctly and without creating unreasonable contention on resources even if the service requests take a long time to complete.

OrganizationalAffinity

Organizational affinity is how changes in the system affect other parts of the system. A classic example of this is in the versioning of inter-dependent components. If the interface of a component changes, it cannot be used until the dependent components are changed to use that new interface. In tightly-coupled systems, the change has to be coordinated between the organization introducing the new interface and the organization responsible for using that interface. This often requires direct and detailed communication between the organizations. On the other hand, there is a high degree of tolerance for mismatches between components in loosely-coupled systems.

Another dimension of organizational affinity is the degree to which the system has to be managed from a single set of administrative policies. Tightly-coupled systems tend to require a common set of administrative policies, most commonly handled with a centralized administration facility to ensure consistency of policy. The administration of loosely-coupled systems tends to be highly federated – allowing each party to apply its own administration policies and expressing the effects of those policies only as 'qualities of service' at the boundaries between the organizations. Generally, the invoker of a service in a loosely-coupled system can make choices based on the trade offs of costs, benefits, and risks of using an available service. Different providers with different quality of service characteristics can supply the same service, thus enabling capitalistic marketplace economics to drive a services community.

Technology Affinity

Technology affinity addresses the degree to which both parties have to agree to a common technology base, to enable integration between them. Tightly-coupled systems have a higher dependence on a broad technology stack. Conversely, loosely-coupled systems make relatively few assumptions about the underlying technology needed to enable integration.

Our national road systems represent a very good example of a loosely-coupled system – imposing few temporal or organizational constraints or technology requirements. Transactions of very different duration can travel over roads – from riding your bike next door to visit a neighbor, to driving across town to pick up dinner, to transporting your products to new markets across the country. On-ramps come in a variety of shapes, and can be changed significantly without preventing you from getting onto the highway. While the country may impose some basic regulatory guidelines, states and municipalities can have a great deal of latitude to impose their own regulations and to provide their administrative goals on the part of the system they control. The technology requirements are relatively low – enabling a huge variety of vehicle shapes, sizes, capacities, and utility. Many of these same characteristics can be attributed to the Internet as well.

However, loose coupling also introduces a degree of inefficiency – sub-optimization, based on the desire to maintain the freedom and flexibility inherent in loosely-coupled systems. To maintain the analogy, railroads and airplanes represent more tightly-coupled systems, but exist because of the additional efficiencies they can provide. They are optimized to a set of specific objectives – either to achieve optimal fuel efficiency, or time efficiency, respectively.

> *Messaging systems typically enable a degree of loose coupling. However, the majority of traditional messaging products typically introduce a higher degree of organizational affinity than web services (messages often carry a high-degree of structural rigidity), and a higher degree of technology affinity (requiring both parties to adopt the same proprietary software stack at both ends of the network – or suffer intermediate gateways). web services, on the other hand, emphasize the use of XML-based self-describing messages, and fairly ubiquitous technology requirements.*

WebSphere takes the idea of web services to a new level – centering the elements of web services first on WSDL as a way of describing a business service. One of the things that you will encounter as you enter into the web services world is the realization that web services and J2EE are not competing technologies – in fact they are very complimentary. Web services are about how to access a business service, J2EE is about how to implement that business service. The next thing you should realize is that you will have a variety of access needs.

The industry tends to talk first, if not exclusively, about accessing web services with SOAP over HTTP. While SOAP/HTTP is critical to standard interoperation over the Internet of loosely-coupled systems, it also introduces certain inefficiencies – namely it requires that the operation request be encoded in XML and that the request flows over a relatively unreliable communication protocol, HTTP. In more tightly-coupled circumstances you will want more efficient mechanisms that can be optimized to the tightly-coupled capabilities of the system without losing the benefit of organizing your application integration needs around the idea of a Web Service.

Web Services Definition Language (WSDL) is an XML-based description of a web service containing interface (messages, port-types, and service-types) and binding (encoding and address) information – essentially how to use the web service and how to access it. WSDL is described in more detail in Chapter 8. We can then leverage this separation to maintain a corresponding separation of concerns between development and deployment. Programmers can use the port-type and message definitions to encode the use of a web service, whereas deployers can use the binding and port definition to construct an access path to the web service. The access path can be loose or tight, depending on where the requesting application and the deployed service are, relative to each other.

> *One flaw in the web services specification is that the distinction between Document-oriented and RPC-oriented web services is captured in the binding – even though this distinction has implications on the programming model used by both the web services client programmer and the web services implementation programmer. We hope this issue will be resolved in future versions of the WSDL specification.*

With this as a foundation, you can introduce all your business services as web services on a **services bus**. The services bus represents any of the business services that have been published as web services in your, or anyone else's organization, which you can see and which can be accessed with any of the access mechanisms available to your execution environment. Constructing distributed applications in this fashion is known and supported by WebSphere as **services-oriented computing**.

The web services programming model is discussed further in Chapter 8.

A Comprehensive Application Serving Platform

The WebSphere Application Server supports the classic servlet- and EJB-component-based programming models defined by J2EE in support of both 'thick' clients and web-centered computing. In addition, it supports the following:

- ❑ Control of multiple presentation device types – both traditional desktop browsers and other pervasive devices

- ❑ web services for loosely interconnecting intra- or inter-enterprise business services

- ❑ Message-oriented programming between application components

- ❑ Business process management for scripting the flow of process activities implemented as J2EE components

- ❑ Legacy integration through Java 2 Connectors and higher level adapters

We will discuss all of these models of computing through the rest of this book.

Basic Patterns of Application and Component Design

Given the models of e-business computing supported by WebSphere, we can identify a set of general application and component design patterns that can be mapped on to those e-business computing models. You should treat each of the general design patterns as building blocks – composing them to construct a complete business application based on an application design pattern. We provide a brief overview of the main component patterns here. All of these patterns are discussed in more detail later in this book. References to further discussions are included in each overview description.

It is worth considering how these basic component design patterns can be composed to form different application design patterns. We won't spend time in this book discussing different application design patterns. The Plants-By-WebSphere example referred to extensively in this book uses a self-service pattern. The characteristics of this pattern are:

❑   Fast time to market

❑   Often used to grow from a web presence to self-service

❑   Separation of presentation and business logic.

This particular collection of characteristics has been classified as a **Stand-Alone Single Channel** (aka *User-to-Business Topologoy 1*) application pattern in the ***Patterns for e-Business: A Strategy for Reuse*** book by Jonathan Adams, Srinivas Koushik, Guru Vasudeva, and Dr. George Galambos ISBN 1-931182-02-7. A useful collection of online information related to e-business patterns can be found at http://www.ibm.com/developerworks/patterns. Following the steps in the selection of the design pattern to use for Plants-By-WebSphere will provide useful information about design, implementation and management of the application.

We recommend the use of this site in selecting a pattern for your application. This site does a good job of illustrating the rationale and implication for each pattern and will increase your chances of building a successful e-business application.

Thick Client Presentation Logic

Classic three-tiered computing design puts the presentation logic on the user's desktop – based on the principle that rich user interaction requires locality of execution, and personal computers afford the processor bandwidth needed for the I/O and computational intensity of a Graphical User Interface (GUI).

WebSphere supports this model with the J2EE Client Container. You can write Java-based client applications, including those that exploit the J2SE AWT and Swing libraries for presentation logic, and then connect these clients to EJBs hosted on the WebSphere Application Server either through RMI/IIOP directly, or more loosely through web services client invocations.

There is very little treatment of this model in this book, although there is a brief discussion of it in Chapter 4, and the programming aspects of calling an EJB through RMI/IIOP or through a web service are no different from calling an EJB or web service from within a server-based component hosted on the application server. The deployment and launching processes are slightly different.

Web Client Presentation Logic

The web-client design takes advantage of the four-tier computing model. This model concedes that a rich user interaction model is not critical to a broad spectrum of business applications, and compromises this for the benefit of localizing presentation logic on the application server and rendering the interaction through a web browser.

WebSphere supports this model with the use of JSP pages and servlets. This model is discussed in depth in Chapter 4.

Model-View-Controller

Model-view-controller (MVC) based designs are relevant to both thick client and web client-based application structures. The MVC pattern introduces a clean separation of concerns between the details of how information is laid out on a screen (the View) and the way business artifacts are laid out (the Model) and the control flow that is needed to operate on the model in response to input from the end user (the Controller).

The MVC pattern maps on to the J2EE programming model supported by WebSphere – views are implemented with JSP pages, models are implemented with EJBs, and controllers are implemented with servlets. Further, WebSphere supports the Apache Struts framework – a pre-engineered MVC framework based on JSP pages, servlets and EJBs.

Componentized Business Logic

We generally classify business logic as either representing procedures (for example, account-transfer, compute-shipping-charges, etc.) or as representing things you use in your business (for example, ledgers, accounts, customers, schedules, etc.). These map to session beans and entity beans, respectively. Generally, you will implement all of your high-level procedures (verbs) as methods on session beans, and implement a set of primitive operations on your business artifacts (nouns) as entity beans. The operation primitives that you implement on the entity beans will represent the fundamental behavior of those entities, and enable (or constrain) the kinds of things that a procedure (session bean) can do with the entity.

Encapsulation of Persistence and Data Logic

One of the significant benefits that comes from componentizing business logic – specifically of the modeling of business artifacts as entity beans – is that it encapsulates the persistence of the artifact's state and implementation. This encapsulation hides the specific schema of persistent state, but also allows that certain operations on the entity model be mapped down onto functions encoded in the data system that operate directly on the state of the entity in the data tier. For example, if you have a DB2 stored procedure in your database that computes order status based on the age of the order, then you can simply encode the `getOrderStatus()` method on your `Order` component to push that operation down on the stored procedure in your database.

Encapsulation of persistence and data logic within the entity bean can be done either with bean-managed persistence (BMP) where you're entirely responsible for managing the relationship of the bean's state to the underlying data system, or with container-managed persistence (CMP) where the container takes responsibility for managing that relationship. We recommend that you always use container-managed persistence whenever possible as the container can generally achieve a higher level of throughput and better resource utilization across the system given its knowledge of everything else that is going on.

Encapsulation of persistence and data logic is discussed further in Chapter 5.

Adapter-based Integration

Business procedures (or even entities) represented in your application design model may be actually implemented elsewhere in your information system – based on completely unrelated information technologies. Abstract components can be introduced to your application to represent this function implemented elsewhere. These abstract components are *adapters* – bridging between WebSphere and your non-WebSphere execution environments. In WebSphere, adapters based on the Java 2 Connector Architecture are implemented as session beans and/or web services. Further, interactions within the adapter to the external application may be implemented with micro-flows (a specialization of work flow) that can be used to compose multiple calls to the external program to form the function represented by the abstract component.

Conceptually, the use of adapters does not have to be limited to just encapsulating business procedure functions – adapters can also be used to encapsulate the state of business artifacts. This is generally achieved by implementing entity beans that make use of session beans that in turn are implemented as adapters to the external system.

Adapters and connectors are detailed in Chapter 7.

Request-Response Messaging

Request-response messaging can be used to form a remote-procedure-call (RPC)-like relationship between two components using messaging. Unlike RPC-based communication, the calls from a component to another component are not blocking. Instead, you issue a request message from one component to the other. Control is immediately handed back to your program, allowing you to perform some other work while you're waiting for the response to your request. In the meantime the second component will receive the request message, operate on it, and issue a response message back to your first component. The first component then needs to listen for response messages and correlate them to their corresponding request messages.

Publish-Subscribe Messaging

Another design pattern for message-oriented components is based on publishing and subscribing to notifications. With the pub-sub model you can create neural-network-like designs in your application. A component subscribes to a message topic that it works on. As messages of that type are generated by other components, the component receives the message and operates on it. It may produce other messages – perhaps of different types put on different topic queues. By interconnecting components of this sort, you can compose an aggregate network of otherwise independent components to perform your business application function.

Web Services

The web services design pattern represents an encapsulation of the business component that, having encapsulated the component with the formalisms defined by the web services standards, enables more loosely-coupled access to the business component. Web services do not define a component implementation model per se, but rather borrow from the existing component model for business procedures. However, the result is to present an abstract component definition to clients of that procedure that elevates it to the idea of a business service.

The web services pattern is described in Chapter 8.

WorkFlow

Workflow is a way of composing a set of individual business services and procedures into an overall business process. The workflow pattern is a powerful mechanism for codifying your business. It allows you to visualize your business processes, reason about their correctness and appropriateness to your markets, and quickly adjust your business processes as business conditions change. The design pattern involves capturing your business process in a workflow definition. The business process definition describes the flow of control and information between business activities. In turn, activities are defined in terms of web services – each *activity* in the flow is a call to a web service that implements that activity. In this sense, a workflow is a composition of business services used to perform that business process.

Workflows are discussed in more detail in Chapter 10.

Together, these models form relatively basic definitions of how to construct the components in your application. Your challenge, then, is to compose these components into an organization that fulfills the objectives for your application.

The WebSphere Development Model

The basic model for creating a WebSphere application involves the following steps:

❑ Create a design model for your application – translating your business requirements into a set of design requirements and technology assumptions. A part of this process should consider the technology constraints that you will have to deal with in your deployment environment. On the one hand, you should avoid imposing too many technology assumptions on the implementation of your components – you certainly don't want to hard-code deployment policies into your business logic; these should be expressed through policy declarations during the assembly and deployment steps. On the other hand, the technology constrains of your deployment environment will help you understand which of the several component design patterns will work best for different parts of your application.

❑ Develop the application components and organize them in the web application and module archives that make sense for your application.

❑ Define the deployment policies for your components – indicating the web defaults, transactional semantics, security assumptions, etc. for your application. In WebSphere, you would also specify the extended deployment policies supported by WebSphere at this time as well – such as access intent policies, session sharing policies, and so on.

❑ Assemble these component JARs into Web Application Archives (WARs) and EJB Modules, and then assemble those into a J2EE Enterprise Application Archive (EAR). Assembly is often performed during your bean development cycle using WebSphere Studio Application Developer. It can also be performed as a separate step by an independent Assembler using the Application Assembly Tool shipped with the WebSphere Application Server. In addition, you can use an XML editor to edit the standard J2EE XML descriptor files stored in your WAR, EJB Modules, and EAR.

❑ Generate the deployment code for your components – this often includes creating the mappings from your EJB properties to the schema of your database. If you want anything other than default schema mappings, you will have to perform deployment-generation in the WSAD tool – which also implies that you will have to perform at least partial assembly in the WSAD tool as well. You can still perform re-assembly in the AAT after you've exported your application from WSAD if you want to maintain this separation of roles. Likewise, an independent Assembler can use WSAD as their assembly tool in place of AAT.

❑ Install your application to the WebSphere runtime – either directly on an application server instance (in a standalone environment), or through the Cell Manager (in a multi-server or clustered environment).

This more or less follows the program development pattern prescribed by J2EE. There are variations on this theme, and some of the process will depend on the tooling that you use. We will discuss the entire process in more detail in Chapters 3 through 6.

Development Roles

A programming model should describe the entire model for developing, deploying, and maintaining applications in an information system. We will begin this by defining the roles of the various participants in that process. This section will overview the roles defined by J2EE, and will go on to describe other roles in the overall development process that J2EE does not currently consider.

Roles Defined by J2EE

In case it isn't already obvious, we should (re-)state here that WebSphere fully embraces Java and the Java 2 Platform, Enterprise Edition (J2EE) programming model. WebSphere version 5.0 complies with the J2EE 1.3 specification and, in fact, was the first major application server product to be certified for J2EE 1.3 compliance – that was with the Technology for Developers version of the version 5.0 product that was made available for Internet download in December of 2001.

J2EE defines multiple roles. These are:

❑ Component Developer
❑ Application Assembler
❑ Application Deployer
❑ System Administrator

In addition, the JSP specification defines the role of an *Author* as someone who is responsible for assembling a set of static and dynamic content to build web pages that are relevant to their web site. And, to be complete, J2EE also defines the role of the Web Application and EJB container provider – otherwise known as the WebSphere Application Server for the purposes of this book.

Component Developer

The *component developer* is responsible for codifying business and presentation logic in servlets, JSP pages and EJBs components. The component developer should focus primarily on writing reusable assets that encapsulate specific business functions.

The distinction between the servlet and EJB component models allows a clean separation of concerns between presentation logic and business logic. This distinction corresponds well to the differences in skills required for good encoding of how the business operates, its procedures and policies as encoded in the business components, and how internal users, business partners and customers access and interact with that business function. Consequently, the component developer role may actually be decomposed into several sub-roles corresponding to the different expertise and knowledge captured in different components of the application.

J2EE presumes that many different component developers may contribute their components to an overall application – either in the context of a specific application or, ideally, with an eye to how that asset can be reused in different applications. The developer will make reference to other components and resources that they depend on using symbolic names – mostly expressed as `java:comp/env` names in their code. For example, if you introduce a component that depends on, say, an `Account` object, you will look up that object's home in JNDI with something like `java:comp/env/ejb/AccountHome`.

The component developer should set any deployment descriptors for their component that are needed to convey assumptions or constraints embedded in the component. For example, the developer should declare any symbolic references that they used within their component implementation. If they've coded to make certain assumptions about the transactional integrity of the things that they call, these should be captured as well.

The components built by a particular component developer (or team) are composed into either a Web Application Archive (WAR) or a JAR file containing a set of enterprise beans referred to as an Enterprise Module. These contain either presentation components or business components and their related artifacts, respectively.

Application Assembler

The *application assembler* needs to understand the semantics of the components provided by the component developer(s) and is responsible for assembling those components to form an enterprise application with a particular functional objective in mind. This includes identifying the components and collecting them in an Enterprise Application Archive (EAR) – a JAR file that contains all of the web application and enterprise component modules produced by the component developers, combined with a manifest and deployment descriptor information representing the deployment policies of the assembled application.

The assembler is responsible for setting the deployment policies for application components – filling in any deployment descriptors that were not already set by the component developer(s) for the components in the assembly. In particular, the assembler should look for and attempt to resolve any discrepancies between the component deployment policies. For example, if you have a component that is implemented to make several calls on other components and is written to assume these calls will be commit-coordinated in a single transaction, the assembler should ensure that the components that are being called are set with deployment policies that will allow such external coordination. Any discrepancy between what the calling component expects and what the called component supports can lead to data integrity problems. The tool support for the assembler in WebSphere will be discussed further in Chapter 6.

The assembler is also responsible for mapping the essential state of an enterprise bean to a particular schema in their database. This, of course, requires the assembler to understand the target schema of the data system. If the application will be deployed into an existing system, the assembler should map to that schema – validating that the schema can be mapped reasonably. Often the assembler will have to work with the database administrator (DBA) to ensure the mapping targets are being interpreted correctly. If the application introduces data elements that do not already exist in the database, then the assembler will have to work with the DBA to add these elements.

A side effect of this collaboration is that the DBA may come to the conclusion that the application is not designed to fit efficiently into the existing database. In this case, the assembler may need to work with the component developers to adjust the design of the application to make it more efficient. Given this, the assembler should begin working with the application developers early in the design phase to ensure the highest probability of success.

If, on the other hand, the target database does not already exist then the mapping process can be easier. The schema of the component's essential state can be used to generate a default schema for the data system. Again, the DBA should be consulted to help normalize the data system schema to ensure an efficient data system design.

A big part of what an assembler must do is to set, or validate, the security policies set for the components. This should start with the method permissions – the policies that state what user roles are allowed to access which methods of the component – and should conclude with making sure the relevant user roles are declared from the application. This will be discussed further in Chapter 13.

Application Deployer

The *application deployer* is responsible for installing the application into the runtime, configuring which application server(s) the application is to run in, and resolving the symbolic references to dependent components and resources to actual, physical resources in the configured topology. So, for example, the bean developer may use the reference `java:comp/env/ejb/AccountHome` in their bean source code, and then declare the use of this reference in a deployment descriptor for their bean. If the actual `Account` (and it's `Home`) are defined in the same enterprise application EAR, then the bean developer or assembler may resolve the reference binding to the actual `Account` object's home in WSAD or in the AAT tool. This binding is then captured in the EAR file and will show up as the default binding in the deployment tools. If, on the other hand, the `Account` bean is actually part of another enterprise application EAR, then the deployer will have to resolve that binding during deployment (assuming that the `Account` application has already been installed and configured).

The deployer is responsible for finding an application server that can host the execution requirements of the application – for example, one that provides transactional integrity if this is what the application requires. WebSphere supports the entire J2EE programming model with a wide variety of configuration options. So, you can normally assume that any WebSphere Application Server instance can serve your J2EE application needs.

WebSphere supports a number of programming model extensions for sophisticated enterprise computing scenarios. Some of these extensions are only available to your application if you have installed the extensions provided in the Enterprise edition. You will have to ensure the application server instance supports these extensions if you will be deploying an application that uses them.

System Administrator

The *system administrator* is responsible for configuring the topology of the application server network. With WebSphere, this includes identifying each of the application server instances on each computer and in the network, establishing any clusters, defining the placement and configuration attributes of any resources that will be used by applications in the network, and ultimately, determining which application will run on which application server instance. In most cases you will want to configure your WebSphere network before you install the applications that will be hosted by WebSphere.

Once the application is installed, the responsibility of the system administrator is to monitor the system – watching for failures and performance bottlenecks, and correcting them as soon as possible. This includes watching for system alerts, evaluating the log files, testing the performance metrics, and monitoring the utilization of the system. A common problem that administrators of successful web sites will have to deal with is capacity monitoring and planning – recognizing when growing demand on the web site is starting to encroach on the available capacity of the computing resources, and projecting when additional capacity will be required.

Before the application is allowed to go into production, the system administrator will often want to evaluate the security policies that have been set by the application assembler and deployer. The system administrator may be called on to authorize individuals or groups in your enterprise to perform certain user roles that grant them access to the component functions they need.

In this sense, the role of the system administrator is multi-faceted, involving configuration management, performance management, problem management, capacity management, integrity management and security management. We'll discuss more about the features of WebSphere that enable this management in Chapter 14.

Defining distinct roles for each of the activities that contribute to the application development and deployment process is essential to maintaining a clear separation of concerns, and for ensuring an orderly delivery and setup for the application. However, in many cases, the same person will perform different roles. In this case, you should recognize the deployment phase that you are in, and perform the corresponding role with the tools provided for that role. Doing so will help maintain rigor in the development process.

Additional Roles

It is naïve to believe that the roles defined by J2EE are all there is to the world. In fact, a number of other roles will contribute to the success of your web sites and enterprise applications. We won't enumerate those here as the roles that will be relevant to you will vary depending on your circumstances. Key among these are the various administrators in your operations centers and business managers. Administrators are responsible for defining your topology, setting up your hardware and software platforms, interconnecting your networks, planning for and installing your applications, ensuring failover and recovery procedures, managing and planning the capacity of your systems, and so forth. Business managers are responsible for defining the business requirements for your applications, and for matching those applications to the business processes and policies. You may have other roles that factor into the deployment of your systems in your company.

Programming Features

This section will provide a very high-level survey of the entire application programming suite for WebSphere Application Server, identifying any significant caveats and conditions to their use in WebSphere. This should not be taken as a complete reference to the APIs of the application server, nor a detailed specification of best programming practices. It is merely intended to be an introduction – most of the topics introduced here will be discussed in more detail through the rest of this book.

Java 2 Platform, Standard Edition APIs

WebSphere supports most of the Java 2 Platform, Standard Edition (J2SE) 1.3 APIs on all platforms and editions in both, WebSphere version 4 and version 5. We will summarize each of the major elements of the J2SE platform APIs here, including any limitations and caveats that should be understood.

Applets

Applets are a way of augmenting your browser-based client with functions that you can write in Java. A common use of applets in a WebSphere environment is to build rich-client user interfaces, and then make direct calls back to EJBs running in the WebSphere application server. A key advantage to applets is that the code for the applet is held on the server, and then downloaded to the browser on-demand when needed. This avoids having to administer code at every client that you want your application to run on. While this seems like a promising approach to building rich interaction models, it does have a couple of pitfalls.

❑   Given the differences in support for Java in different browsers and on different platforms, it is hard to build portable applets. You can mitigate this by limiting your clients to a specific browser on a specific platform.

❑   Generally, the applet will be downloaded every time your application client is invoked – depending on how caching policies are set in the browser. Sophisticated applets can be relatively large and the download time for the applet will affect the overall response time experience for your end users. Applets should be kept relatively simple and small to lessen the response time impact.

❑   If you will be communicating directly back to the EJBs of your application in the application server, you have to overcome the communication constraints of your network. If your browser clients are located outside your firewall, for example, your firewall may prevent IIOP-based communication between your browser clients and the application server. You can turn on HTTP tunneling to overcome this. With HTTP tunneling, the IIOP traffic will be wrapped in an HTTP stream and will pass through the HTTP ports of your firewall. You should carefully examine the security implications of this configuration to your enterprise – in effect, you are creating a covert channel through your perimeter protection boundary.

❑   Applets are typically sand-boxed – that is, prevented from accessing vulnerable resources on the browser desktop environment. For example, you generally can not access the file system of the desktop from an applet. Some of these restrictions can be overcome by signing your applets, and then instructing your end users to authorize your applets to access the resources you need.

While WebSphere condones the applet model, it doesn't provide any specific support for it. If you want to build an application that uses applets to improve the interaction model for your end users, you are largely on your own to build the applet, resolve the bindings in your applet, locate it properly, and configure your system to manage them.

AWT and Swing

Swing and AWT offer an alternative to the thin browser-client. You can build thick clients or applets that use Swing or AWT to provide a rich user interaction experience. We've discussed the Applet model above. The variation on that theme is the thick client – a full application client program installed and executed from your end user's desktop computer. WebSphere provides support with a J2EE client container for exactly these types of client programs. You can make use of the full Swing and AWT function set from a J2EE client container.

You cannot, however, drive AWT or Swing-based user interfaces from your applications hosted on the application server, if for no other reason than typically there are no users directly connected to the application servers. Application servers should normally be treated as daemon functions that have no user interface directly associated to them on the platform. The biggest reason for avoiding AWT and Swing is that these packages will spawn additional threads to perform their work. We will go into this in more detail shortly.

Notwithstanding the practical limitations of using AWT and Swing from within WebSphere, J2EE also puts limitations on its use. Not all of the Swing and AWT functions are regulated by Java 2 Security permissions. But of those that are, J2EE only permits the use of the clipboard, Swing events, and showing windows without a warning banner in a J2EE client container. None of these are permitted in an applet, web or EJB container. If your application must use these functions in these containers, or needs any other regulated functions of AWT or Swing, you must request permission to these (see the *Enabling Privileged Code* section at the end of this chapter).

JavaBeans

JavaBeans are a component type that was originally introduced to support presentation artifacts. Programmers have found utility in JavaBeans for a variety of uses – essentially anything for which you want to abstract out properties of your Java object, and manage the object (the bean) around those properties. WebSphere places no restriction on the use of JavaBeans in applications hosted by WebSphere.

I/O (Input/Output)

The I/O classes provide support for importing and exporting Java objects to various data and file streams. WebSphere and J2EE do not place any specific restrictions on the use of these classes, except to the extent that the physical realization of these streams may be restricted by File permissions as described below.

Files

WebSphere allows you to read or write to the file system from either servlets or EJBs in the application server. However, WebSphere will prevent you from accessing any system files or other protected files that make up the WebSphere runtime.

Language Classes

Java offers a rich set of primitive classes that are, in effect, a part of the language. These include support for scalar types (rendered as objects), class management, package, process, runtime, and system manipulation, and threading. Obviously, these classes were intended to be used by Java programmers. However, there are a few gotchas in this list of capabilities – things that could have a detrimental impact on the application server runtime. These gotchas basically fall into two categories – system-related functions, and process-related functions; most notably thread-related functions. Let's discuss this further.

System-Related Runtime Functions

The J2EE security permissions deny an application hosted in a J2EE application server from performing a number of system-related functions. The rationale behind these restrictions is two-fold. First, these functions are generally not considered germane to business functions and thus their use compromises the separation of concerns that the J2EE component models are intending to provide. However, that argument is somewhat philosophical. Much more importantly, the use of these functions can prevent the application server from doing an effective job of managing your components efficiently. To do its job, the application server must make certain assumptions about who is controlling certain resources, and how. For example, competing for control over the ClassLoader will prevent the application server from maintaining a proper level of isolation between applications in the server.

Applications in the application server may not:

- ❑ Create or get the ClassLoader
- ❑ Set the ContextClassLoader
- ❑ Set or create the SecurityManager
- ❑ Register shutdown hooks
- ❑ Create socket factories
- ❑ Set the I/O streams for `stdin`, `stdout`, and `stderr`
- ❑ Modify or stop threads or thread groups
- ❑ Get the protection domain for a class
- ❑ Read or write file descriptors
- ❑ Access or define a class in a package
- ❑ Access declared members of a class

An application may queue up a print job. Web applications and application clients can also link to native code libraries, and application clients can also exit the VM. Most of these restrictions can be overcome by requesting permission to do so in the extended deployment descriptors for the application.

Process-Related Thread Functions

You cannot normally spawn threads using the J2SE threads package from your applications hosted in the application server. The reasons for this are fairly simple: threads that you spawn will not carry the implicit context that the application server normally places on a thread, and WebSphere cannot monitor threads that you create if it does not know about them. Consequently, if you use any part of the J2EE programming model from that spawned thread, including making calls on EJBs, the container will not have the information it needs to manage the request properly. In most cases, your thread will fail, or at least create unexpected results.

45

If your thread should fail, the failure probably won't be detected by WebSphere and so it won't be able to recover it – either to reclaim the resources occupied by that thread or to attempt to restart it to complete the work it was performing.

Since WebSphere is not aware of the thread, it is in turn not aware of the work being performed on the thread, and therefore will not account for the impact that additional thread has on the overall workload being hosted in the server. This will affect its workload balancing decisions – potentially causing the server to over-allocate work to the server and resulting in significant throughput or performance problems with your server.

A major tenet of the WebSphere workload management architecture is the idea that servers in a cluster can serve any request to the applications hosted in that cluster. One request to an application component may be routed to one application server instance, and the next request may be routed to another instance. The application server leverages the J2EE component model to manage component state to ensure that the policies stated for integrity, consistency, throughput, and so on are being met. However, if you have spawned un-managed threads on behalf of your components, any state retained on that thread would not be managed across the cluster. The additional thread may or may not be aware of workload rebalancing decisions, and consequently may not be seeing all that you might want it to see of the subsequent requests made to your application in any given application server instance.

Finally, the threading and dispatching model in the WebSphere Application Server (in J2EE itself) is opaque to your application. The algorithms used for dispatching and threading are refined constantly for improving performance and throughput. The presence of your thread can have a detrimental effect on the dispatching techniques being used by the application server and can undermine any benefit that you might otherwise expect to achieve with WebSphere.

The bottom-line is: you should not be spawning threads within your application.

In prior releases, the WebSphere Application Server on distributed platforms (not including WebSphere for z/OS) did nothing to enforce this constraint. Starting in version 5.0, WebSphere has enabled the Java 2 SecurityManager and applications are not granted access to the Thread APIs.

However, if you absolutely must spawn your own threads – you may have integrated a third-party package that spawns its own threads – there are two things you can do to get around the limitation stated above.

The first involves requesting permission to access the J2SE threads library. The process for doing this is discussed further in the later section *Enabling Privileged Code*. By making this explicit request you are assuming responsibility for the consequences. That is not a legal statement, but is designed to give you control over that decision, and to help avoid cases where you accidentally get into a negative situation. You must avoid using any aspect of the J2EE programming model with threads spawned using this technique – in particular, you must avoid looking up and calling EJBs or web services through the WebSphere client interfaces, you must avoid using any data source or JCA connections that require connection pooling or transactional integration with the rest of your J2EE application.

The second and preferred approach is to use the Async Beans programming model extension provided in the Enterprise Edition of WebSphere. The work manager of Async Beans give you a programmatically safe way of spawning threads. In effect, work manager veneers the threads package, but does so in a way that the application server has knowledge of any threads spawned with this approach. The application server can manage the propagation of context, and can assist in managing state, recovery, and the workload implications of the additional thread. You can program to the full J2EE client application programming model in the thread spun by the work manager. The work manager service is discussed further in Chapter 11.

Other Language Classes

In addition to the language classes discussed above, Java also provides support for references and reflection. WebSphere does not place any specific restriction on the use of these classes in your applications. However, you should be aware that if you attempt to manipulate the behavior of the garbage collector, you could have an impact on the efficiency of garbage collection in ways that are not immediately obvious. For example, WebSphere has its own controls for managing the garbage-collection cycle during periods of idleness. Thus, you should avoid trying to manipulate the garbage collector in your application through the use of references if at all possible.

Math

The math classes are provided to help your application deal with very large or very precise integer or decimal values. WebSphere places no restrictions on your use of these math classes.

Network

You can create outbound sockets and send messages in the WebSphere Application Server. You should not create an in-bound socket listener in your application code. The reason for this is at least two-fold: first, doing so generally requires creating additional threads for handling any in-bound work coming in on the socket. We've already discussed the issues associated with threading above. Second, the work that gets executed as a result of in-bound messages will not be properly conditioned with the context that the application server needs for it to work properly.

In version 5.0, WebSphere will begin enforcing this constraint through J2SE permissions. A language exception will be raised in your application if you attempt to create an inbound socket.

If you absolutely must create an inbound socket, or if you're using a package supplied by another source that does, you can get around this restriction by requesting additional permissions for your application during deployment.

RMI

An application can use RMI/JRMP or RMI/IIOP to make requests on another server environment, assuming the target server supports the appropriate protocols. A CORBA server, for example, can be called using RMI/IIOP. An application may not, however, construct an RMI server in the WebSphere Application Server. WebSphere does provide a standalone C++ CORBA server conforming to the base CORBA 2.1 specification as part of the Enterprise edition.

As an aside, a CORBA client can invoke an EJB over IIOP – although this can be complicated by the Java mappings of EJB types in IIOP, depending on the source language. This, however, is independent of RMI.

Security

The security classes in the J2SE platform are considered a part of the Java 2 Security manager programming model. As we discuss later in this chapter, and then again in Chapter 13, you are discouraged from programming directly to security classes in your application. More than that, though, the J2EE permissions prevent you from using many of these security interfaces – deferring instead to the container to keep your applications protected.

SQL

The SQL classes form the base-line for the JDBC programming model. WebSphere assumes these will be used in the manner described by the J2EE specification. The J2EE permissions will prevent you from setting the log stream for the JDBC driver.

Text

The text classes supplied by J2SE support common functions for formatting text strings, including support for resolving internationalization conventions. WebSphere places no restrictions on the use of these classes.

Utility Classes

The utility classes cover a number of interesting programming functions, including various forms of collections (hash table, sets, lists, maps, iterators, etc.), a variety of date, time, and calendar functions, and other odds and ends such as a pseudo-random generator. J2SE also introduces a set of extended utility functions for manipulating JAR and ZIP streams. The only restriction that J2EE imposes is on the Properties class.

Properties

Application clients, applets, servlets, and EJBs can only read property values. You must request permission to set property values from any of the WebSphere runtime environments.

Java 2 Standard Edition Extensions

In addition to the packages included in the base J2SE, WebSphere packages and ships standard extensions. Let's discuss these extensions in turn.

JCE

The Java Cryptographic Extension (JCE) provides support for encrypting and decrypting data. WebSphere supports the JCE interface and supplies a provider and cipher suites. WebSphere does not, itself, support third-party providers. If you must introduce your own provider to the JCE interfaces for use within your application, you must do so in a way that does not introduce your provider into a WebSphere runtime classpath. If you do use your own provider, it is your responsibility to ensure that the provider conforms to the proper export regulations. See http://home.doc.gov/ and http://www.bxa.doc.gov/ for more information on export regulations for cryptographic functions.

JSSE

The **Java Secure Sockets Extension** (JSSE) provides support for creating secure sockets for SSL version 1 or 2, or TLS v1.0. WebSphere supplies a JSSE provider. As with the network packages of J2SE, you can create an outbound socket with JSSE, but you should not create an inbound socket. Again, you can override this constraint by requesting permissions for inbound sockets.

PKCS

The Public Key Cryptography Standards (PKCS) packages provided by WebSphere are not actually a part of the official J2SE standard extensions. However, they provide a set of useful functions for managing public keys for the standards defined by RSA. They include support for:

- ❑ PKCS #1: RSA Encryption
- ❑ PKCS #5: password-based Encryption; enables encryption of an octet string with a key derived from a password
- ❑ PKCS #7: defines a general syntax for `Data`, `SignedData`, and `EnvelopedData` that may have cryptography applied to it
- ❑ PKCS #8: establishes a standard syntax for private key information
- ❑ PKCS #9: provides standard object types for various security-related attributes, such as a challenge password, counter signature, e-mail address, message digest, and so on
- ❑ PKCS #10: defines a standard syntax for issuing certification requests – such as getting a X.509 certificate signed by a Certificate Authority
- ❑ PKCS #12: describes a transfer syntax for personal identity information

PKCS #11 is covered within the JSSE extensions. Generally, you will only want to use these interfaces if you are programming a public key infrastructure. Otherwise, the majority of reasons for using these functions are already handled for you in the implementation of the WebSphere Application Server and its related administration tools. For more information, go to http://www.rsasecurity.com/.

Java 2 Platform, Enterprise Edition

The WebSphere Application Server version 5.0 conforms to the J2EE 1.3 specification, and as such supports the entire suite of the J2EE-defined APIs across all editions and platforms. With the exceptions noted below, all of the J2EE programming features are available on all platforms supported by WebSphere Application Server – Windows, Solaris, Linux, AIX, HP/UX, iSeries, and z/OS. The following summarizes the J2EE packages and how WebSphere supports them.

Servlet 2.3

The servlet specification defines the component model for servlet-based presentation logic, along with HTTP session state, context, and device information. A servlet is used to generate dynamic content – presentation content that is derived dynamically by executing the logic contained in the servlet implementation. With version 5.0, WebSphere introduces additional support for servlets:

- ❑ **Filters**
  Allow you to externalize processing of request and response messages to the servlet as defined by the Servlet 2.3 specification.

- ❑ **Lifecycle Listeners**
  Can be introduced to receive events that indicate different phases in the application's execution lifecycle as defined by the Servlet 2.3 specification. These include the following new listeners:

  `ServletContextListener`

  `ServletContextAttributeListener`

  `HttpSessionListener`

  `HttpSessionAttributeListener`

  `HttpSessionActivationListener`

  and corresponding event classes to go with these.

❑ **Internationalization Enhancements**
Allow you to control how internationalization context will be handled for your servlet. In particular, the Servlet 2.3 specification introduces a new method on the `ServletRequest` interface, `setCharacterEncoding()`, that can be used to control the character set the web container will use for reading the request's parameters and to post data. In addition, WebSphere further extends the internationalization support for servlets by introducing a pair of new deployment descriptors – `request-encoding` and `response-encoding`. These are described further later in this chapter.

❑ **New Error and Security Attributes**
New error and security attributes are introduced as defined by the Servlet 2.3 specification. These include:

`javax.servlet.error.exception_type`

`javax.servlet.error.request_uri`

`javax.servlet.request.cipher_suite`

`javax.servlet.request.key_size`

❑ **HttpUtils Deprecation**
The `HttpUtils` class has been deprecated (the class will still exist but you will get deprecation warnings from the compiler), and has been replaced with the `getRequestURL()` method on the `HttpServletRequest` class, and the `getParameterMap()` method on the `ServletRequest` class.

❑ **New Context, Response, and HttpSession methods**
Introduction of the following methods as per the Servlet 2.3 specification:

`ServletContext.getServletContextName`

`ServletContext.getResourcePaths`

`ServletResponse.resetBuffer`

`HttpSession.getServletContext`

In addition to the standard interfaces defined by J2EE for servlets, IBM also supports a set of extensions that can be useful for some web application scenarios.

> As always, you have to be aware that if you take advantage of these extensions, you will end up with an application that may not be portable to other vendor's application servers.

The WebSphere extensions include:

❑ `com.ibm.websphere.servlet.cache`
Introduces classes that help you enable your servlet to be used with the WebSphere Dynacache facility.

❑ `com.ibm.websphere.servlet.error`
This is a specialization of `ServletException` that can be used to produce a more detailed description of the error being reported by the servlet.

❑ com.ibm.websphere.servlet.event
Enables you to listen for various events pertaining to servlets and web applications.

❑ com.ibm.websphere.servlet.filter
Defines a mechanism by which you can set up servlet chains to aggregate partial responses from different servlets.

❑ com.ibm.websphere.servlet.request
Extends the standard ServletStream to allow stream manipulation, and introduces a servlet request proxy.

❑ com.ibm.websphere.servlet.response
The corollary to com.ibm.websphere.servlet.request, and also includes support for generating and storing predefined responses.

❑ com.ibm.websphere.servlet.session
Introduces support for managing HTTP session state across clusters.

The servlet model defines deployment descriptors that can be used to describe policies for how the servlet should be managed by the web container. These include policies for how the servlet should be protected, initialized, and loaded, how to resolve references to other resources, and attributes about the servlet.

The following table lists all of the deployment descriptors supported for servlets in WebSphere. All of the J2EE deployment descriptors conform to the definition provided in the Servlet 2.3 J2EE specification available at http://java.sun.com/products/servlet/download.html. In addition, WebSphere supports other extended deployment descriptors. These are marked in **_bold-italic_** and will be discussed further below:

additional-class-path	env-entry-type	large-icon	res-ref-name	taglib
auth-constraint	env-entry-value	load-on-startup	res-type	taglib-location
auth-method	error-code	location	role-link	taglib-uri
context-param	error-page	login-config	role-name	transport-guarantee
default-error-page	exception-type	mime-mapping	security-constraint	url-pattern
description	extemsopm	mime-type	security-role	user-data-constraint
directory-browsing-enabled	**_file-serving-enabled_**	param-name	security-role-ref	web-app
display-name	form-error-page	param-value	**_serve-servlets-by-classname-enabled_**	web-resource-collection

distributable	form-login-config	realm-name	servlet	web-resource-name
ejb-link	form-login-page	*reloading-enabled*	servlet-class	welcome-file-list
ejb-ref	http-method	*request-encoding*	servlet-mapping	welcome-file
ejb-ref-name	home	*response-encoding*	servlet-name	
ejb-ref-type	icon	remote	servlet-config	
env-entry	init-param	resource-ref	servlet-timeout	
env-entry-name	jsp-file	res-auth	small-icon	

All of these deployment descriptors can be specified in the WebSphere Application Assembly Tool – a GUI-based tool for assembling WARs, EJB Modules and their related JARs into a J2EE Enterprise Application or in WSAD.

additional-class-path

If, in your web application, you want to refer to other JARs, classes or other resources that are not included in your J2EE Application (EAR), you can use this element to define the classpath to those resources.

default-error-page

You can specify the default error page in this element, to use in case no other error page is specified in the application.

directory-browsing-enabled

This element can be set to `true` if you want the web application to be able to browse the local directory system. You should set this to `false` if you want the file system to be protected from anyone who may use this application to maliciously interrogate the file system.

file-serving-enabled

If you want to be able to serve static content from this application, you can set this element to `true` – which it is by default.

reloading-enabled

Set this element to `true` if you want to allow the application to be re-loaded. It is `false` by default.

request-encoding

J2EE has clarified the encoding rules for servlet request and response messages. The clarification does not agree with the encoding rules that had been used in WebSphere previously. This element can be used to establish which set of encoding rules WebSphere will use for the web application.

response-encoding

Same as request-encoding.

serve-servlets-by-classname-enabled

Normally, servlets are only addressable by their URI name. This element can be set to `true` if you want to be able to address a servlet by its classname.

JSP 1.2

The **JavaServer Pages** (JSP) specification defines a powerful mechanism for creating dynamic content. A JSP page is essentially a template of the web page that you want generated, but with in-line code or JSP tags that make it easy to condition portions of the page.

The JSP specification describes the use of the Java language for scripting the conditional elements of the JSP. WebSphere uses the extension mechanisms in the JSP specification for introducing support for other scripting languages in the JSP – in particular, JavaScript.

The JSP 1.2 specification introduces:

- ❏ **XML support for JSP pages**
  Allows you to encode your JSP page in fully conformant XML.

- ❏ **Tag-lib Validation**
  Allows you to validate a tag in the context of an entire page and provides better validation messages.

- ❏ **New Tag Support for Iteration**
  Iteration can be performed in custom tags without having to introduce a Body tag. This makes it easier to introduce simple iterators, and improves JSP performance for these cases.

- ❏ **Tag Library Support for Application Lifecycle Events**
  Tag libraries can introduce event listener classes corresponding to the Listeners introduced by Servlet 2.3.

The JSP engine in the web container compiles JSP pages when they are first invoked. The compiled classes form a servlet and so the rest of the JSP processing conforms to the servlet execution model. Since compiling the JSP on the first invocation can be somewhat time consuming and can affect the response time for that JSP page, you can instruct WebSphere to pre-compile the JSP by setting the pre-compile JSP pages flag on the Web Module in the assembly tool for your enterprise application.

EJB 2.0

The EJB specification defines the component model for business logic. The EJB specification introduces three types of enterprise beans: session beans, entity beans, and message-driven beans. Session beans can be both stateless and stateful, and generally represent business functions in your business model. Entity beans are generally stateful and persistent, and their persistence is either managed by the bean implementation or by the container. Entity beans should be used to model entities in your business model – such as `Account` or `Customer` objects. Message-driven beans don't necessarily represent elements in your business model, but can be used to listen for and respond to asynchronous messages that your application may be interested in.

The EJB 2.0 specification introduces several important innovations to the EJB component model, including:

❑ Introduction of local interfaces for EJBs. This allows you to define EJBs that benefit from component management without exposing them to the design implications of those components being potentially distributed – that is, EJB to EJB communication through local interfaces will be dramatically more efficient. Moreover, the local interface support allows you to distinguish between *shared* EJB behavior – methods that you want to be made available to any client – versus *private*, or localized, EJB behavior – methods that you only want made available to other components hosted in the local execution space.

❑ Integration with the Java Message Service (JMS) with the introduction of message-driven beans

❑ Support for container-managed relationships allowing you to model relationships in your business and manipulate and navigate these through application logic. These relationship definitions can also be leveraged in portable queries – you don't have to encode queries with specific knowledge of how these relationships are encoded in the data system in which the EJB state is held.

❑ A common and portable query language for specifying static queries over collections of enterprise beans. EJB Query Language (EJB QL) uses a SQL-like syntax with extensions for the object-oriented nature of EJBs, and can be mapped to any relational-database-specific query syntax.

❑ Custom home methods allow you to introduce the equivalent of static methods to the enterprise bean implementation model.

❑ The run-as security identity element allows you to specify the particular security role that you want the enterprise bean to run with.

❑ The addition of the Common Secure Interoperation V2 (CSIv2) protocol to RMI/IIOP to help ensure secure interoperation between J2EE vendors and with other CORBA vendors.

These additions make EJBs implemented and deployed for container-managed persistence much more effective.

JDBC 2.0 Extension

As its name suggests, the JDBC 2.0 Extension is an extension of the JDBC 2.0 core APIs included in J2SE. The core APIs are included in the `java.sql` package, and the standard extensions are included in the `javax.sql` package. The extension introduces support for:

❑ **JNDI-based data source names**
You can specify the data source that you want to use by JNDI name, thus freeing us from having to hard-code the data source name in our application code.

❑ **Connection pooling**
Connections are obtained and managed from a connection pool. A specific set of connections to the data source can be created and shared among many instances of objects that will use these, thus avoiding the overhead of creating and destroying a connection on each use.

❑ **Distributed transactions**
XA-based global transactions can be created and used to commit-coordinate updates to multiple different data systems in the same transaction.

❏ **Rowsets**
Rowsets represent a set of rows in the database, and essentially cache the contents of those row-tuples. Rowsets use an optimistic concurrency model – extracting the rows from the database and caching them in the rowset, without retaining a lock on the data in the database. On the one hand, this allows concurrent access to the data in the underlying database and in that way improves system throughput. On the other hand, it requires that you handle updates very carefully to ensure you don't invalidate changes that may have been made while you were operating from your local rowset cache. Of course, you will be exposed to these concerns only if you're using Bean-Managed Persistence (BMP). With Container-Managed Persistence (CMP) you will not use the JDBC interfaces directly, and the container will manage these concerns for you.

WebSphere provides support for a variety of databases, including:

❏ DB2/UDB Connect, Workgroup, Enterprise Edition, and Enterprise-Extended Edition v7.2

❏ DB2/UDB for iSeries v5r1 (WebSphere for iSeries only)

❏ DB2/UDB for z/OS and s/390 v6.1 and v7.1

❏ Informix Dynamic Server v7.2 and v9.3

❏ Oracle Enterprise Edition 8i and 9i

❏ Microsoft SQLServer v7.0 and v2000

❏ Sybase Adaptive Server v12

In addition, WebSphere ships with Cloudscape 5.0.3 that can be used for samples and prototyping purposes – it cannot be used in production. WebSphere also ships and works with the Data Direct (previously known as Merant) Connect JDBC Type 4 drivers. This, of course, is just the current support. Any updates to this list are posted at the IBM web site for WebSphere at http://www-3.ibm.com/software/webservers/appserv/doc/latest/prereq.html. Generally, WebSphere works with the JDBC drivers supplied by the corresponding database vendors. JDBC drivers are categorized by how they're constructed.

❏ **Type 1 drivers**
Type 1 drivers are implemented to bridge to ODBC – ODBC binaries must be installed on the platform to use a Type 1 driver.

❏ **Type 2 drivers**
Type 2 drivers use JNI to call into native APIs for the database. While these don't require you to install the ODBC binaries, they may require other native binaries.

❏ **Type 3 drivers**
Type 3 drivers are implemented entirely in Java, but operate to a canonical middleware protocol leaving the middleware responsible for mapping its protocol to the database-specific protocols of the databases it supports. WebSphere does not provide such a protocol, although prior versions of WebSphere shipped Data Direct (Merant) SequeLink supporting such a protocol. This has been dropped from WebSphere version 5, and replaced with Data Direct Connect JDBC Type 4 drivers.

❏ **Type 4 drivers**
Type 4 drivers are also implemented entirely in Java to work directly with the specific DBMS protocols supported by the corresponding database.

The differences between these types should be immaterial to your application's implementation – the semantics of the JDBC interfaces remain entirely consistent across all types of JDBC drivers. However, the differences in these drivers may affect the installation procedures and prerequisites for your application. These differences are handled through the WebSphere administration facilities.

JTA 1.0

The **Java Transaction API (JTA)** provides interfaces that allow you to begin and commit global transactions. If you begin a transaction, initiate a set of updates, and then commit the transaction, the updates that you initiated will be committed as an atomic unit of work – that is, either all the updates will be applied, or none of them will be applied. This will dramatically reduce the complexity of your application. See *Professional EJB* (Wrox Press, ISBN 1-86100-508-3) for more information on global transactions and EJBs.

The transaction manager that implements JTA is built into WebSphere and supports local and global, single-phase, and two-phase commit transactions, depending on the resources used during the transaction. The WebSphere transaction manager will automatically federate other transaction manager instances in the transaction if the method you invoke cascades across other server instances or platforms. For example, if you invoke a method on an EJB on an instance of WebSphere running on a Solaris machine and that method, in turn, invokes another method on an EJB running on a z/OS machine, the resources that you touch on the Solaris machine will be commit-coordinated with the resources you touch on the z/OS machine. All the updates you initiate will be committed, or none of them will, depending on whether any errors were encountered in the transaction.

Further, the WebSphere transaction manager has built-in optimizations for recognizing when only one resource is involved in the transaction, and for when a single-phase commit resource is included in a transaction that involves other two-phase commit resources (only one single-phase commit resource can be combined in a mixed transaction like this).

The WebSphere transaction manager conforms to the CORBA Object Transaction Service (OTS) protocol and therefore is fully interoperable with other vendor application servers also conforming to this specification as required by J2EE 1.3. In accordance with the specification, session-beans can use either container-managed or bean-managed transaction demarcation. Entity beans, however, must use container-managed transaction demarcation.

Limitations

The `javax.transaction.TransactionManager` interface cannot be used by application components hosted in the WebSphere Application Server.

Enlisting and delisting a `javax.transaction.XAResource` is supported for Java 2 Connectors only on the z/OS platform.

Unlike prior versions of WebSphere, the user transaction service can only be obtained from `java:comp/UserTransaction` – it can no longer be got from `jta/usertransaction`. The user transaction service cannot be obtained from the J2EE client container. You must demarcate the transaction with either CMT, or with BMT in the EJB container on the application server.

JMS 1.0.3

The **Java Message Service (JMS)** provides support for exchanging messages between message providers and consumers. The JMS specification defines two different models for exchanging messages.

The first is referred to as point-to-point messaging, where the provider and consumer are explicitly aware of each other and communicate messages directly between themselves – possibly over a messaging network that uses a series of intermediaries to propagate the message over the network.

The other type of messaging defined by JMS is a 'publish and subscribe' model. This is where providers publish classified messages to anyone that may be interested in that classification of message – without any specific knowledge of who that might be. Consumers then register a subscription to a class of messages. The pub/sub model normally involves an intermediate message broker responsible for managing the distribution of published messages to various subscribers. In the pub/sub model, the same message may be re-distributed to any number of consumers that have registered a subscription to that message.

JMS is the only specification for which J2EE requires conforming application servers to supply a fully implemented provider. To that end, the WebSphere Application Server product ships with an embedded JMS implementation supporting persistent, point-to-point, and a high-volume publish and subscribe engine. Like other provider frameworks, such as JDBC and J2EE Connectors, this implementation can be replaced with other providers. In particular, IBM offers the WebSphere MQ product that supports the JMS interface and can be plugged into the WebSphere Application Server.

The integral JMS provider in WebSphere Application Server is largely based on the WebSphere MQ messaging engine. It provides support for the complete JMS programming model, including persistence. However, it does not provide clustering support for its message broker, nor for interoperation with non-WebSphere messaging applications. The WebSphere MQ provider, on the other hand, does enable clustering support, and interoperation with MQ-based applications outside of WebSphere.

WebSphere supports connection pooling of JMS connections, and integration of JMS messaging operations in a global transaction. You can coordinate the commitment of a message to or from the message connection along with other updates to your database. For example, if you want to update an `Account` object, and publish a notification about that update in the same transaction, then you can be assured that the notification is not sent unless the update to the account is actually performed.

J2EE Connector Architecture 1.0

The Connector specification defines a mechanism by which you can create connections to third-party data systems such as CICS, IMS, SAP, Peoplesoft, and so on – thus enabling integration between J2EE and non-J2EE-based applications and components. Since different data systems pose different constraints on how they can be connected, the connector architecture accommodates different connectors with different qualities of service. The architecture puts the burden on the connector to establish its relationship to the application server runtime and containers. The connector is given access to runtime security and transaction context through a connector service provider interface (SPI) from which it can federate in the backend data system in a sensible manner as pertains to that data system.

Applications interact with the connector through either the Common Client Interface (CCI), or through a higher-level abstraction introduced by individual application development tools. Any abstraction introduced by a development tool should be implemented to map down on to the CCI – the abstraction is intended to simplify the programming model for applications as a matter of convenience, not to invalidate the basic programming model offered by the connector specification.

The WebSphere Studio Application Developer Integration Edition provides tooling to create a stateless session bean based adapter for connectors. Applications are written using the stateless session-bean programming model – hiding the nuances and complexities of the CCI.

WebSphere provides support for connection pooling, integrating both single-phase and two-phase enabled connectors and for authenticating a principal in the connection request.

JAAS 1.0

The **Java Authentication and Authorization Service (JAAS)** provides interfaces for creating and manipulating principal credentials. WebSphere does not place any specific restrictions on your use of the JAAS interfaces in version 5.0. Many of the additional classes provided by WebSphere in this space are specific implementations of the abstract classes and interfaces introduced by the standard extensions. In particular, IBM introduces a number of specific credential types. You will only be able to use those specific credential specializations that correspond with the particular authentication mechanisms that you have configured. In general, we do not recommend that you program specific knowledge of the derived credential types into your application – limit yourself to the abstract interfaces of the credential types.

JAXP 1.1

The **Java API for XML Processing (JAXP)** specification defines the interfaces for XML parsing and operating on XML documents. The XML parser support defined by JAXP includes provisions for both Document Object Model (DOM) and Simple API for XML (SAX) styles of parsing. In addition, the specification supports XML namespaces, and XML Stylesheet Language Transformations (XSLT). This API is supported in WebSphere with the Apache Xerces and Xalan packages shipped with WebSphere.

Since these packages have undergone a fairly rapid evolution you may prefer to use your own version of these services in your application. WebSphere can accommodate this – the class-loading facilities in WebSphere allow you to introduce your own version of these types of services in your own application package. Even if the class names collide with those supplied by WebSphere, WebSphere will bind your application to the version that you supply for yourself in your application and will prevent it from interfering with WebSphere's own use of the version that it supplies.

JavaMail 1.2

The **JavaMail** specification defines interfaces for getting and sending e-mail. WebSphere simply ships the Java reference implementation for JavaMail with providers for Simple Message Transfer Protocol (SMTP) for sending mail, and Post Office Protocol (POP3) or Internet Message Access Protocol (IMAP) for receiving mail. You must connect these to your favorite mail service if you want to use these in your application. The WebSphere administration facilities allow you to configure the default mail provider to reference your mail system – the mail provider is a configurable resource.

JAF 1.0

The **Java Activation Framework (JAF)** implements a façade pattern for mapping MIME types to specific commands and components that can operate on those types. The JAF is used by the JavaMail service for handling MIME attachments. See http://java.sun.com/products/javabeans/glasgow/jaf.html for more information about JAF.

Web Services

As we discussed earlier in this chapter, web services technology has grown rapidly as an important mechanism for interconnecting distributed services over the Internet, and more recently, over the intranet. In recognition of the strategic value of web services to the industry, several organizations have begun to standardize various web service definitions – including, among other things, the Java interfaces for invoking a web service. JSR 101 defines the Java APIs for XML RPC (JAX-RPC) and sets the standard for how Java applications should invoke a web service. This standard is embraced by JSR 109, which defines the Implementation of Enterprise web services in a J2EE environment. JSR 110 defines Java APIs for WSDL interfaces for creating, reading, and manipulating WSDL documents. JSR 93 defines a Java API for XML Registries (JAX-R) that can be used to access UDDI.

None of these specifications are currently part of the J2EE specification and so entirely represent extensions to the standard J2EE programming model. None of the interfaces associated with the web services support in WebSphere are considered portable to other J2EE-conforming application servers at this time.

W3C, of course, is in the process of defining standard specifications for SOAP and WSDL, and continues to make progress in the area of context specification and propagation. In addition, recent work between IBM and Microsoft has concluded a strategic direction and de facto standard specification for web services security. In addition, IBM, Microsoft, and several other vendors have formed the WS-I organization (see http://www.ws-i.org) to formulate the baseline for multi-vendor interoperation of web services.

WebSphere version 5.0 remains up to date with the latest and emerging standards. The web services programming model and features for WebSphere are introduced here, and will be discussed in much more detail in Chapter 8.

Invocation Programming Interfaces

WebSphere version 5.0 maintains backwards compatibility to the Apache SOAP 2.2 proxy interface and the WebSphere Studio Application Developer stub interfaces introduced in WebSphere and WSAD version 4. If you wrote applications for version 4 that use these interfaces, you can continue to host these applications in version 5. However, you should realize that these interfaces will be deprecated in a future release and so you should begin to convert these applications over to using the new JAX-RPC interfaces.

JAX-RPC defines a mapping of XML types to Java types and WSDL portTypes to Java interfaces, and in doing so, enables a type-based interface to the web services that you want to invoke in your application. Interfaces conforming to the JAX-RPC specification provide the appearance of local-remote transparency and are used much like EJB remote interfaces. The interface representing a WSDL portType is called a Service Endpoint interface. Of course, as a general rule you should assume that web services are loosely coupled and you should therefore program to them accordingly.

The general model is that you will locate the WSDL of the web service that you want to use. You will import WSDL into your development environment and use it to generate a JAX-RPC Service Endpoint Interface and underlying implementation artifacts representing that web service to your application. You can then simply code directly to this interface to invoke the operations that you want to use. The JAX-RPC implementation is then responsible for converting your Java types into XML, marshaling the result into a web services message and invoking that on the binding and port defined in the WSDL for the target web service.

WebSphere Studio Application Developer adds built-in support for JAX-RPC invoking the web service to a standard SOAP over HTTP binding and port. WebSphere extends that support to invoking web services requests over a variety of binding and encoding mechanisms. The WebSphere binding extensions can be used without changing your application by configuring the JAX-RPC service to return a different implementation of the Service Endpoint Interface to your application.

Web Services Invocation Framework

The multi-protocol support enabled by WebSphere is provided by the **web services Invocation Framework** (WSIF) integrated into WebSphere. WSIF enables communication of web services over a variety of protocol stacks, including the traditional SOAP over HTTP, SOAP over JMS (over WebSphere MQ, for example), and a direct call on a local Java object or EJB that implements the web service.

Protocol selection is managed by the WebSphere runtime. The result is that you can program your application to a type-based interface based on the WSDL definition of the web service, but allow the runtime to resolve the binding to the Web Service based on the quality-of-service requirements of your topology – reinforcing the relationship and separation of concerns enabled by the J2EE Application Developer, Assembler, and Deployer roles.

WSIF also introduces a lower level dynamic invocation interface (DII) exposing the primitives of the invocation process. The DII only deals with XML types and so does not concern itself with the mapping of Java type representations. The same web services Invocation Framework, integrated into WebSphere, has been made available as an Apache open source project – as part of the XML-Axis project (http://xml.apache.org/axis/index.html).

Web Services Security

WebSphere version 5 implements the latest de facto Web Service specification on security – specifically to enable principal authentication, context propagation, and message integrity and protection based on document signing and encryption. The message integrity and protection portion of the web services security specification draws heavily from the SOAP-SEC technology previewed in WebSphere version 4 and so moving to the WS security specification is relatively easy if you did exploit SOAP-SEC in version 4.

In addition, support for propagating principal identity, user name tokens, and X.509 certificates is included in WebSphere version 5. Support for propagating Kerberos credentials should be coming shortly. None of these require any specific programming for applications hosted in the WebSphere Application Server. Anything that you do to establish or manipulate credentials using the JAAS (remembering that these activities should be limited to only those cases where the runtime does not perform credential management in the way that you need for your application) will automatically be applied to the credentials that flow over the web services protocol.

Web services hosted in WebSphere are implemented and deployed in a J2EE enterprise application – generally implemented or wrapped in a stateless session bean. As such, you can apply authorization protection to your web service using the standard J2EE Roles-based authorization mechanisms provided to any J2EE application.

Web Services Gateway

WebSphere version 5 introduces a Web Service gateway. This gateway can be used to represent an aggregation of web services, and as an intermediary for web services message processing in the network. For example, you may have a set of web services that you define in your intranet. If you want to expose only a subset of these to the Internet you can deploy Web Service proxies expose them on the port and bindings for the gateway to the Internet. Thus, all Internet-borne Web Service requests will be directed to the gateway. The web services proxies hosted in the gateway can then re-direct those requests to the real web service implementations in your intranet.

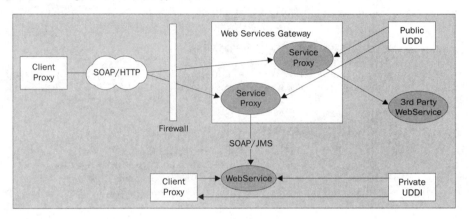

If you want to add other intermediary functions like tracing Internet web services requests, or doing special field checks, you can introduce a filter and extend the Web Service proxies in the gateway.

An additional benefit of the gateway is in enabling you to federate different Web Service middlewares under a single deployment-administration model. For example, you may have a mix of WebSphere and, say, Microsoft IIS-based web services in your data center, but you want to administer a common and consistent authorization and security protection model on all of your web services. You can introduce Web Service proxies in the WebSphere web services gateway that represent your IIS-based web services. Since WebSphere web services proxies are deployed like any other Web Service implementation hosted by WebSphere, you can apply the same procedures for establishing and maintaining security policies as you would for any other WebSphere-hosted Web Service. The result is a common and consistent model for managing your web services across your enterprise – even those that may be hosted in other application execution environments.

Universal Description, Discovery, and Integration Registry (UDDI)

UDDI directories play a key role in the overall web-services lifecycle as a repository of web-services definitions. Web services providers will typically publish the WSDL for their web service in a UDDI directory. Web service consumers then will search the UDDIs for a web service that meets their needs, and then build a web-service client to exploit that service.

IBM, Microsoft, HP, SAP, and others now host public UDDI business registries for exchanging web services definitions in the public domain. You can access the IBM UDDI business registry at https://www-3.ibm.com/services/uddi/protect/registry.html. Anyone can access these UDDI directories to find web services. Subscribers can publish their web services in these registries.

Generally, it's not a good idea to be unit testing your web service by publishing your WSDL in these public registries for reasons that you can well imagine. Also, there are cases where you will want your own UDDI for use within your enterprise, or in a private network of close business partners. WebSphere version 5 provides a private UDDI registry that you can use for these purposes. The WebSphere UDDI Directory is a scalable UDDI implementation that you can deploy in a WebSphere network like a J2EE application. You can set up several directory instances – each representing a different registry need.

The WebSphere UDDI Directory supports the standard UDDI v2 specification. In addition, the UDDI can be accessed via JMS messages, or an EJB Session Bean interface.

Additional Functions of WebSphere

The core WebSphere Application Server provides additional functions that are not part of the J2EE specification, and that haven't been discussed above as extensions to J2EE. These additional functions are discussed here briefly.

Struts and the Struts Tag Libraries

WebSphere integrates and supports the **Struts** programming framework as described by the Apache Jakarta project, which you can check out at http://jakarta.apache.org. Struts is a framework that implements the **Model-View-Controller** design pattern for presentation logic. This framework creates an interworking between servlets (controller), JSP pages (view), and JavaBeans that can then be adapted to EJBs for model elements.

In addition, Struts introduces a standard taglib for various presentation elements and view types, as well as common logic, HTML, and bean constructs such as iteration, links, and parameters.

WebSphere Application Server Extension APIs

Beyond the core extensions shipped in the base WebSphere Application Server, WebSphere also offers a broad set of additional runtime features for enabling a number of enterprise integration scenarios as described in the Integrated Enterprise Computing model discussed earlier in this chapter. These features include:

❑   **Activity Sessions**
Define a unit of work scope that generally aggregates multiple transactions. An activity session may be used to enclose the use of multiple independent resources – enabling a best-effort level of atomicity over resources that otherwise cannot be commit-coordinated that would be hard to create on your own. In many ways an activity session is similar to an HTTP session, except that it is targeted for use by EJBs.

❑   **Application Profiles**
Enable you to define different access intent policies for different clients. This allows the EJB container to manage the same EJB differently for different usage scenarios. For example, one client can get the benefits of container management that is tailored to the set of relationships that client will use, while another client can get equal benefits for the set of relationships it will use, even if the relationships it uses are completely different from the first client.

❏ **Asynchronous Beans and Scheduler**
Provides you with a safe mechanism for spawning parallel work (multiple threads); think of it as asynchronous message processing at a local level. WebSphere ensures the work threads are properly conditioned with context, and monitors the workload on these threads – recovering them if they fail, and accounting for the workload they create. This feature is extended with a Scheduler function that allows you to schedule asynchronous work for execution at some well defined point in time in the future.

❏ **Business Rules Beans**
Continues the tradition introduced by WebSphere Enterprise edition version 4.0. Business Rules Beans can be used to separate the business rules and policies of your enterprise; the relatively dynamic elements of your business logic form the relatively stable and constant aspects of your business functions.

❏ **Choreography**
Builds on the microflow engine introduced in WebSphere Enterprise edition version 4.1 for generalized workflow processing support. This could well be the most important feature of WebSphere Enterprise edition in version 5.0.

❏ **Container Managed Messaging**
Enables a higher level of abstraction for messaging; letting you hide many of the tedious aspects of constructing and interpreting asynchronous messages. This allows your programmers to remain focused on the details of their domain expertise.

❏ **Dynamic EJB Query**
Brings the benefits of object-oriented query and portability associated with the J2EE 1.3 EJB Query Language for use directly by your Java programmers; the equivalent of dynamic SQL for EJBs.

❏ **Internationalization Extensions**
Gives bean developers direct programmatic control over the distributed internationalization context introduced in WebSphere Enterprise edition version 4.0.

❏ **JTA Synchronization Notification**
For those cases where you want to be notified when a JTA user transaction is going through the synchronization phase just before the two-phase commit protocol. The synchronization phase, of course, is the signal to recoverable resources (such as the EJB essential state; data beans) to flush their state out to their respective resource managers.

❏ **Last Agent Optimization**
Enables the intermixing of one single-phase resource with one or more two-phase resource commit-coordination in a single global transaction. If you don't know what this means read about it in Chapter 9.

❏ **Staff Services**
Introduces a concrete implementation of the staff support plug-in of the Choreography service to leverage your LDAP-based directory for organizational information in your enterprise.

❏ **Startup Beans**
Provide you a hook in the application startup process from which you can perform various initialization functions for your application – such as, creating asynchronous beans, performing business notifications, and so on.

❏ **C++ ORB**
Enhances the CORBA, C++ ORB offered in WebSphere Enterprise edition version 4.0 with additional runtime capabilities such as RAS services for logging, portable interceptors, and so on.

These additional features will be discussed in more detail in Chapters 9, 10, and 11.

System Management APIs

Once you've finished building your application you will want to begin to use it. You do that by installing and configuring it to run on a particular WebSphere Application Server instance installed somewhere in your network. The process of installing and configuring your application on a server instance as well as configuring and starting the WebSphere Application Server instance itself is managed through the WebSphere System Management facility. This facility is described further in Chapters 6 and 14.

The WebSphere System Management can be administered through GUI and command-line interfaces provided by WebSphere. The GUI is itself actually a J2EE Web Application that executes in a WebSphere Application Server. The command-line interface can be used with JACL scripting languages. Support for other scripting languages such as Jython and JavaScript will likely be added in the future.

However, there will be cases where you might want to introduce your own application to automate certain WebSphere System Management functions. WebSphere enables you to do so through a JMX interface. The JMX interface is provided through the TMX4J package and is hosted in both individual application server instances, and the Cell manager. You can access the JMX interfaces remotely through either the RMI/IIOP or web services connectors supplied with WebSphere.

Programming Model Durability and Portability

One of the key benefits of using the WebSphere Application Server is the assurance that the programming interfaces supported by WebSphere are durable. A great deal of effort has gone into version 5 of WebSphere to ensure that applications written to the J2EE 1.2 specification to run on WebSphere version 4 will continue to run on WebSphere version 5 in spite of version 5 being now certified to the J2EE 1.3 specification.

The J2EE 1.3 certification test suite includes some 15,000 test cases covering just about every aspect of the J2EE 1.3 specification. In addition, IBM has ported Sun's PetStore reference application to WebSphere in accordance to the portability guidelines for the PetStore application, and participates in various interoperation events such as the J2EE Sun's Java developer conference. All of this is to ensure portability of J2EE applications and interoperation between conforming J2EE application servers.

Likewise, applications written to the J2EE 1.3 specification to run on one of the distributed platforms such as Windows, Solaris, Linux, AIX, HP/UX, or iSeries will run on WebSphere for z/OS as well. Some of the WebSphere Application Server Extension APIs are also available on z/OS, as indicated in the previous section.

To help assure programming durability, WebSphere attempts to be very clear about what APIs are considered strategic, and which are considered tactical or will only be available on certain platforms or for limited releases. We've tried to reinforce that distinction in this book as well by highlighting where we expect a certain interface or programming feature to be deprecated in the future, or limited in some other fashion. In this way, you can decide whether the value of the feature outweighs the risk of having to change your application if the feature is provided in a different form in the future.

Enabling Privileged Code

The J2SE interfaces are subsumed by J2EE – a J2EE conforming application server must also support the J2SE specification. Unfortunately, using certain aspects of J2SE in an application server can impact on the server's ability to provide a robust execution environment for that application. We've discussed some of the implications of generating GUI interactions with AWT or Swing and spawning threads in the *Java 2 Platform, Standard Edition APIs* section, for example. The J2EE specification recognizes this. However, instead of sub-setting the J2SE specification, it simply allows an application server to constrain what an application can do through the use of what it refers to as the J2EE permission set. These are Java 2 SecurityManager permissions to define what an application running in a J2EE environment must be allowed to do. The J2EE permission set for each of the execution environments defined by J2EE is listed in the following table.

Application Clients	Applet Clients	Web Components	EJB components
java.awt.AWTPermission: accessClipboard	java.net.SocketPermission: codebase(connect)	java.lang.RuntimePermission: loadLibrary	java.lang. RuntimePermission: queuePrintJob
java.awt.AWTPermission: accessEventQueue	java.util.PropertyPermission: limited(read)	java.lang.RuntimePermission: queuePrintJob	java.net. SocketPermission: * (connect)
java.awt.AWTPermission: showWindowWithoutWarningBanner		java.net.SocketPermission: * (connect)	java.util.Property Permission: * (read)
java.lang.RuntimePermission: exitVM		java.io.FilePermission: * (read, write)	
java.lang.RuntimePermission: loadLibrary		java.util.PropertyPermission: * (read)	
java.lang.RuntimePermission: queuePrintJob			
java.net.SocketPermission: * (connect)			
java.net.SocketPermission: localhost:1024-(accept,listen)			
java.io.FilePermission: * (read,write)			
java.util.PropertyPermission: * (read)			

Any J2SE class that requires a permission that is not listed in this table cannot be performed. This can prevent you from doing many things that you might otherwise be tempted to perform in the application server. However, in some cases, the need to use a particular disallowed J2SE function is not a matter of temptation, but rather a matter of imperative. One example that we've encountered on several occasions is where an application picks up a third-party library to use and that library spawns its own threads. As spawning threads can undermine the integrity of the application server and is therefore discouraged, disallowing it completely can be overly restrictive. In some cases, a customer will be willing to risk the loss of integrity for the sake of gaining the benefit that comes with such packages.

WebSphere offers a way to overcome the restrictions that would otherwise be imposed by the J2SE permission set. You can request an additional set of permissions in your application through an extended deployment descriptor defined by WebSphere. When deploying and loading your application, WebSphere will consider this request for additional permissions in the context of the application server's constraints and, if possible, grant those to your application, making a record of this with the Java 2 SecurityManager in the application server in which that application will be hosted. The mechanism for identifying a privileged application in this manner is very similar to the approach taken for Java 2 Connector resource adapters that generally have a very similar need stemming from the nature of connecting to different legacy systems.

You should note, however, that the extended deployment descriptors defined by WebSphere for requesting these permissions are unique to WebSphere – if your application creates this sort of dependency, it may not be portable to other application servers. Further, WebSphere is not obligated to grant these permissions in all cases – there may be situations where WebSphere is not able to grant these requests in a particular application server instance.

Most importantly, if you create a privileged application (requesting permissions beyond the standard J2EE permission set) you should recognize that you are exposing the WebSphere execution environment to integrity risks that will, by extension, undermine the assurances that can be claimed for your application and any other application that is located in the same application server instance. You are subject to application execution failures that the application server might otherwise be able to protect you from. So, you should request these additional permissions only if you really are familiar with their effect, and are willing to accept the integrity risk that doing so imposes. In any case, we highly recommend that you isolate any applications that request privileged status – hosting those applications in their own independent application server instance apart from any other application.

The Topology and the Programming Model

Overarching the entire J2EE programming model, web services, and all the extensions supported by WebSphere, is the basic idea that boundaries between components and resources are location-transparent. Wherever you make references to another component or resource in your application, you do so through symbolic references and abstractions that separate you from the physical location of the things you use. Doing so enables the flexibility to place your various application components in the information system where you need them based on capacity, location, and the capabilities of your system, and without being constrained by the actual encoding of your applications. If it becomes necessary over time to place two application components on different machines to address growing demand in your application, you should be able to do so without having to re-implement either component to recognize its new location.

The same principle is exploited by WebSphere to enable the same component to be hosted on multiple application server instances at the same time to achieve a higher level of availability or distribution of workload over multiple processors or machines.

These ideas are key to enabling scalability, high availability, and manageability in your production systems. You can either sustain this or undermine it depending on how you code your application. For example, in your programs you should not encode an assumption that states that other distributed components or resources that you use will be co-located in the same address space. Also, you should not assume that all method requests in different transactions will be routed back to the same component instance, and you should not assume that non-persistent state would be held in memory across transactions or other unit-of-work boundaries.

Contrary to most people's intuition, these principles can actually improve the efficiency of the overall system. While it may seem like having to save state to a persistent store at the end of every transaction is inefficient, WebSphere is able to reduce the impact of this I/O through its caching mechanisms, and in some cases can compensate for any remaining inefficiency by being able to manage the component and its execution lifecycle in the presence of its knowledge about other workload in progress in the system. By retaining these principles, for example, WebSphere is able to distribute workload to where the greatest capacity exists in the system, and thus can improve the response time and throughput for the entire system.

Wherever you need to violate these principles, you should state so explicitly in the deployment descriptors that are provided for this so that WebSphere knows to manage your components within these constraints. However, you should be aware that wherever you impose these constraints, you are limiting the degree to which WebSphere is able to gain optimum efficiency in the execution environment for your application.

The Security Programming Model

WebSphere is designed specifically to protect your application components. The runtime will authenticate end users and enforce authorization policies to prevent unwanted access to your components. You can control how this is done through deployment descriptor declarations associated with your component, and through external policies defined outside your application. WebSphere and J2EE both discourage you from encoding security policies into your application.

Again, this principle is based on the idea that encoding such policies in your application will limit flexibility – if you hard-code a security policy in your application then the security administrators will not be able to change that policy without changing your application. In fact, they may not even be able to see the policy (if your application is compiled and installed as a binary) or be able to evaluate its affect on the overall integrity of the system.

Of course, we also recognize that key capabilities are missing from the J2EE security model that will force you to encode some amount of security function. This is discussed further in Chapter 13.

Summary

The WebSphere programming model is tuned to four basic models of e-business computing. This builds on the J2EE programming model for multi-tier distributed computing. It simplifies the task of leveraging your legacy investments. It provides a solid foundation for modeling your business functions and processes, and integrating your lines of business and business relationships. WebSphere is crystallizing first-class support for service-oriented business structures.

At this point you should have gained a broad view of the entire WebSphere programming model – including the primary models of computing supported by WebSphere, the basic development process, and roles pertaining to components supported by WebSphere. You should now know that the WebSphere programming model consists of the Java 2 Platform, Standard Edition (J2SE) and Java 2 Platform, Enterprise Edition (J2EE) standard features, web services, core extensions, and other programming model extensions covering functions like workflow management, rules processing, threading, internationalization, and so on. Finally, you should have a sense of what to avoid in your programs, and the basic principles of good programming. All of this should prepare you for the detailed discourse offered through the remainder of this book.

3

WebSphere Development Tools

WebSphere Studio is a powerful, yet easy-to-use development environment for an entire development team. The WebSphere Application Server is built around open standards, so there is no technical requirement that WebSphere Studio be used when creating a WebSphere application, but there are significant advantages in doing so. This chapter will introduce WebSphere Studio and will explain the various editions that are available, and the functions that are available with each edition. The later chapters will explore some components of WebSphere Studio in more depth, but the primary purpose here is layout the landscape and provide a general overview of the WebSphere development tools.

We will start with a description behind the WebSphere Studio technology, and explain how the various editions are created and related. Each edition is a superset of the previous one, simply adding a number of new tools each time to provide additional function. Finally, we will discuss most of the key components that compose WebSphere Studio with an aim to provide a brief functional overview of each.

The Platform

The development process for any reasonable sized application includes many stages, with different types of tools required at each step along the way. The previously available tools from IBM, VisualAge for Java, and the old version of WebSphere Studio tool, provided specific support for different development activities.

VisualAge for Java was an integrated Java development environment; it allowed for the easy creation and testing of Java code, and included a WebSphere test environment for the unit testing of WebSphere applications. The previous WebSphere Studio tool was designed to facilitate the creation and editing of web pages, and included a WYSIWYG (What-You-See-Is-What-You-Get) page editor, and the ability to publish the contents of a web project to a remote site.

The problem was that while both these tools were great for their specific tasks, most development projects require more than just Java code or static web pages. Additional types of tools are needed, ranging from different editors, to profiling and performance analysis tools, to integration with multiple source code configuration systems.

IBM does not make tools for every niche market, which in the past led to a very difficult development experience for any project that included more than stand-alone Java and static web pages. Even when tools that are more suitable to the task at hand were available, the experience of exporting and importing projects and transferring data between the different tools was far from ideal. Every tool typically had its own definition of a project, its own user interface paradigm, and its own set of preferences and behaviors.

To address these problems, IBM created the **Eclipse** platform (an integrated development platform for building diverse applications), and then donated it to the open source community. WebSphere Studio is built on the Eclipse platform. As an open source platform, Eclipse has attracted the attention of many tool providers, and Eclipse-based versions of many common tools are already available, with more under development.

Eclipse is designed with dynamic integration of additional tools in mind, and this flexibility means that many industry standard tools can be tightly integrated with WebSphere Studio. The combination of an open source base, IBM's experience with application development tools, the tight integration with WebSphere, and the ability to use other best-of-breed tools in the same development environment, is designed to provide the developer with the best possible development experience.

Eclipse 101

It is beyond the scope of this book to delve deeply into the Eclipse implementation details, but a basic overview is useful to understand how WebSphere Studio is assembled. Additional details along with freely downloadable Eclipse builds are available on the Eclipse web site, http://www.eclipse.org/.

Eclipse is implemented in Java, and provides a number of common services. These include the basic user interface framework, which means that the behavior of the various windows and controls in any Eclipse tool will be consistent. Although the underlying implementation is Java, Eclipse uses its own **Standard Widget Toolkit (SWT)** user interface widget set, which provides a Java interface for the underlying native platform widgets and controls. Thus, Eclipse does not look like a Java application; it looks and feels like a native application on all supported platforms.

Another advantage of the Eclipse framework is that it provides a common definition for things such as resources, projects, and preferences. This means that an Eclipse project is the same project, regardless of which tool or mechanism is used to interact with it. The days of having to export data from one tool, and import it into a different tool (typically loosing your original tool and project settings in the process), are over with the use of Eclipse.

The thing that makes Eclipse so interesting to tool builders, however, is the ability to dynamically add new functions, via the Eclipse plug-in mechanism. Eclipse plug-ins are different from application server plug-ins, although the goal of supporting the dynamic addition of function is the same. An Eclipse plug-in consists a set of Java classes that actually implement the desired function, and a definition file (plugin.xml), which is used to register the plug-in, as well as declare how the plug-in depends on, extends, and interacts with other plug-ins.

Eclipse itself has a very small core, which provides little more than the ability to register, activate, and invoke plug-ins. The majority of the functions that are in the base Eclipse platform, and all functions that are added to form WebSphere Studio, are provided by plug-ins. Previous tools (such as VisualAge for Java) provided limited extension mechanisms that could only add to a single menu item. In contrast, Eclipse allows every aspect of the user interface and the underlying behavior to be defined and extended via plug-ins. The result of this design decision is that it is possible to tightly couple a new plug-in into the existing platform, giving comprehensive UI integration, data integration, and task-flow integration:

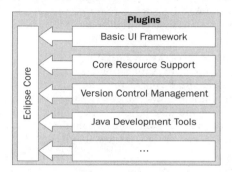

Eclipse dynamically detects plug-ins when it starts, and the plug-in registration mechanism consists of no more than the existence of a plug-in in the right directory and the right form. This means that the assembly of a product based on Eclipse can be done in a very modular fashion as the product is packaged. The entire environment does not need to be re-built simply to add or remove one piece of function; all that is required is the inclusion of the correct set of plug-ins. This is how WebSphere Studio is built, and the result is an entirely consistent family of products; the more advanced configurations simply include more plug-ins, but no changes are required to any of the base plug-ins, and so there is no change to the core behavior as you move from one configuration to another. You get more function as you go, but what is common, stays common.

As WebSphere Studio is built on Eclipse, it also contains all the new functions and features that are being added to the base open source version. WebSphere Studio version 4.0 was built on top of Eclipse 1.0, and version 5.0 is built on Eclipse 2.0. Subsequent versions of WebSphere Studio will continue to use newer versions of Eclipse, and this cross pollination is mutually beneficial – WebSphere Studio requirements will drive new functionality into Eclipse, and other improvements implemented in Eclipse will also appear in the new versions of WebSphere.

WebSphere Studio Overview

The WebSphere Studio family consists of a series of products, with increasing capability for the creation of WebSphere applications. A more detailed description of each product is provided later, but in addition to being built on Eclipse, each edition shares a number of common features and design principles. The different editions offer additional perspectives that provide a role-based development experience. They are:

❑ **Site Developer**
This edition is intended for professional developers of dynamic web applications and sites. It delivers integrated support for open web standards, including servlets, JSP pages, XML, and web services tools. It includes a highly integrated WebSphere Application Server test environment and deployment automation tools.

❑ **Application Developer**
This includes all of the function of Site Developer and adds support for programmers working on business logic (including advanced web services and EJBs). It also adds support for tracing application execution (even across multiple machines), and sophisticated profiling and performance analysis.

❑ **Application Developer Integration Edition**
This includes all the functions of Application Developer, and adds a fully service-oriented development environment for business and enterprise application integration. It provides tools for the creation of micro-flows (which are short lived sequences of different application and function invocations) and macro-flows (which are long running, persistent, and restartable sequences of different application and function invocations). Finally a visual builder is provided to assemble the various flows, and choreograph the complete application.

❑ **Enterprise Developer**
This includes all the functions of Application Developer Integration Edition, and adds tools to aid in the creation of new EIS applications. This includes support for remote editing/compiling/debugging of COBOL and PL/1 applications, and RAD (Rapid Application Development) tools that allow the graphical creation and generation of integrated web applications.

The diagram below shows how all the editions are inter-related:

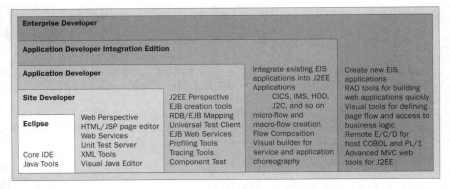

All editions embody the same basic design principles, and all are a proper superset of the preceding product. Eclipse, and by extension WebSphere Studio, stores its resources in the file system, and not in a proprietary repository as VisualAge for Java did. WebSphere Studio extends this model to the metadata that is used to define the various J2EE artifacts as well.

There are multiple editors for manipulating documents, such as web and EJB deployment descriptors, relational schema descriptions, WebSphere server configuration files, and others, but the underlying data is represented as a file. The location and content of the J2EE-defined files is exactly as required by the J2EE specification, meaning that you can go back to the Navigator view at any time, and edit the files with a simple text editor if desired.

WebSphere Studio has been designed with the goal of producing server-side applications, which require a pre-defined specification. What you see on the screen (and in the file system) matches the format required by the applicable specification, and is automatically maintained in the correct structure required for execution on the server.

There are several examples of this, the most obvious being that every J2EE module (WAR/JAR/EAR) is represented as a distinct project in WebSphere Studio. There is a single folder within each such project that represents the contents of the module as required on the server, and specification-required directories (such as /META-INF for EJBs, and /WEB-INF for WARs) are nested in them and populated automatically.

This means that there is no magic required when a project is exported; files need not be moved to a different location, every file that is contained in the folder is exported. The result is an extremely clear distinction of which files should be contained in the resulting application, without the overhead of having to maintain an inclusion or exclusion list. There are typically many more files that are associated with a server-side module than you wish to physically include. Source code, design documents, and test cases are but a few examples of other files that can be easily stored as part of the project as a result of the WebSphere Studio design, with no risk of their accidental inclusion in the resulting application.

Transitioning to a new server version can take some time to implement across your company. WebSphere Studio version 5.0 now includes the ability to work with two versions of WebSphere, version 4.0 and version 5.0. This support ripples across all the tools in WebSphere Studio and will be described in detail below, but the net effect is that you will be prompted for the desired version of the artifacts as you create them. Both J2EE 1.2 and 1.3 project types can exist concurrently in your workbench.

WebSphere Studio User Interface

When you first start WebSphere Studio, you will see a screen that appears very similar to that seen with the base Eclipse. This highlights the fact that Studio is built on top of Eclipse, and every view and function that is available within Eclipse is also available within Studio. Of course, there are many additional functions that are only available as part of Studio, but we will start by introducing the basic Eclipse user interface. The opening screen will appear similar to this:

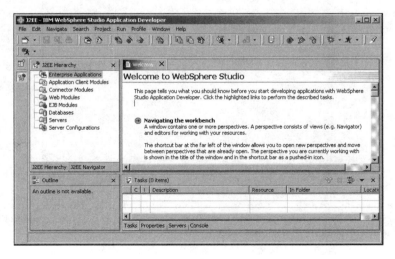

The WebSphere Studio window is both context sensitive and user configurable, but there are some core pieces present in almost every situation. In the top-left is a Navigator view, showing the physical resources in your projects. Each project, contained folder, and resource in the Navigator view represents a directory or file in the file system. There are other views that provide a simplified rendering of the resources, but if you need to see what is really there, the Navigator view will show you.

In the top-right pane is the editor area, although the actual editor that will be used is dependent on the resource. Multiple resources can be edited concurrently, and the filenames will appear in tabs at the top of the Editor view.

In the lower-right pane is the **Tasks view**. An Eclipse "task" is something that is pending to be done. Most tasks are created by Studio for you, and indicate problems in the code that you will need to correct; examples include compilation errors, warnings, and validation messages. You can also add your own tasks on any resource, as reminders of things that still need to be completed. Tasks are associated with a specific file and line number (optionally), so you can double-click on a task and the appropriate editor will be opened. For a large set of projects, the task list can grow quite long, so there is a filtering mechanism available. Clicking on the arrows icon in the title bar of the tasks pane will display the tasks filtering dialog, allowing the tasks that appear in the view to be restricted to those you select:

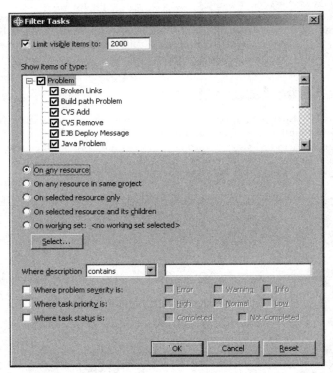

Finally, in the lower-left pane is the Outline view. This can be used to provide a quick overview of the resource being edited. Depending on the editor in question, you can actually navigate the resource from the Outline view, and in some cases make changes as well.

As mentioned earlier, the actual organization of the different panes and views is quite configurable. Each pane can be moved or closed, and different organizations can be saved and reopened. The overall grouping of a set of views, and the actions that are available in that view, is called a **perspective**. The perspective concept allows common views to be easily available, and pre-positioned for a particular set of tasks, or role. The filtering of actions is a useful way to limit the size of menus to only those actions required.

A new perspective can open automatically when you create new resources, or you can manually select a new perspective from the menu in the window. You can have multiple perspectives open at the same time. An icon on the left side of the overall window represents each perspective; here you can quickly switch between them simply by clicking on the appropriate icon.

Source-Code Management

Eclipse provides a pluggable team support mechanism, allowing the use of any Source-Code Management (SCM) system as your underlying repository. Using the defined plug-in points, the normal suite of WebSphere Studio editors can be used without requiring any special team support integration. Since the files that compose a project exist on the file system, catching up with other streams of code, and checking data in and out is easy. The fact that WebSphere Studio uses only textual (and specification-defined) metadata files is also a benefit, as it greatly simplifies the task of comparing multiple versions of the files.

Many SCM vendors are participating in the Eclipse effort, and have compliant plug-ins available that allow use of their system with the product. A complete list of Eclipse-enabled SCM vendors is available at http://www.eclipse.org/community, and the list includes PVCS from Merant, MKS Source Integrity, and Interwoven TeamSite.

However, one SCM is actually included with WebSphere Studio: Rational ClearCase LT, which provides outstanding support for parallel development, and is fully integrated with WebSphere Studio. With automatic branching and snapshot views, ClearCase LT enables multiple developers to efficiently design, code, test, and enhance software from a common code base.

The other SCM that is supported out of the box, is the open source CVS. All aspects of CVS usage are available via the integrated WebSphere Studio team structure. Eclipse supports CVS server version 1.11.1p1 or higher, running on a Linux or UNIX server. Accessing CVS from a Windows client is fully supported, but Eclipse does not officially support running CVSNT on a Windows server (although varied degrees of success have been achieved). In this case, CVSNT version 1.11.1.1 or higher must be used.

The Java Perspective

To highlight the configurability of the user interface, let us examine the **Java perspective**, which is designed for the developer working on Java code, such as a client-side application. The Java tools are also reused in Web and EJB projects, so everything described here is also applicable to those project types. The Java perspective replaces the Navigator view with a Java packages view, in which the nested directories that are used to represent packages in the file system are shown as a single object representing each package. The Editor view is unchanged, but the Java editor (which is available from any perspective when editing Java files) is shown in the following screenshot. The Java editor includes many advanced features, including code assist, syntax highlighting, refactoring, and formatting support:

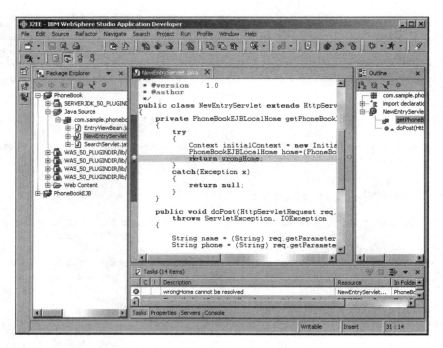

In the screenshot, a syntax error has been shown, which the incremental Java compiler has detected. An x appears in the Packages view on the offending file and in the editor on the offending line, and the Tasks view lists the actual error.

The Outline view is moved to the right of the Editor view in the Java perspective, and an outline of the source file being edited is presented. This makes navigation within the file easy, and several actions (such as searching for references to a method) are available from the Outline view.

Debugger

The Java perspective includes an integrated debugger, allowing you to set breakpoints using the Java editor. All common debugger operations are available, such as the ability to view the call stack, step over or into statements, and view and modify variables. The Studio embedded Unit Test Environment (described later) uses the standard debugger view. You can seamlessly debug client-side or server-side Java applications, even if the application is running on a remote server.

WebSphere Studio Site Developer

In this section, we will describe in more detail the tools and functions that are included as part of WebSphere Studio Site Developer. The purpose of Site Developer is to aid the creation of dynamic web sites, ranging from the creation of static HTML pages through to dynamic content using servlets, JSP pages, and web services. The Site Developer edition also includes the complete Unit Test Environment, and the design of the Test Environment is discussed below.

To highlight the critical pieces of the tool, we will develop a very simple application, which will be used throughout this chapter. The application itself is little more than a J2EE-based "Hello World" sample, but it will provide a consistent base to refer to as we explore Studio. The application is a simple phonebook application, consisting of a web page to input data, a CMP EJB to persist the data, and a JSP page to display the results. The basic flow of this application is a very common J2EE design, and it can be summarised as this:

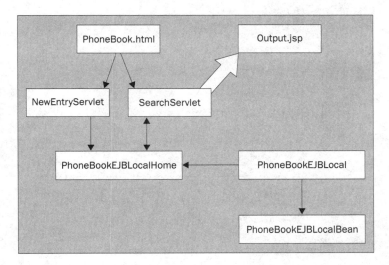

The nodes in the diagram represent the important objects in the flow of the application:

❑ PhoneBook.html is a file used to prompt for data input. The file contains a form, which invokes a servlet when the data is submitted

❑ NewEntryServlet is a servlet that is invoked when a new phone number is created

❑ SearchServlet is a servlet that is invoked when the user wishes to search the phone book

❑ PhoneBookEJBLocalHome, PhoneBookEJBLocal, and PhoneBookEJBLocalBean are the local home, local interface, and the enterprise bean itself, used to persist the data

❑ Output.jsp is a JSP page used to dynamically construct the output of searches

We will now continue with our look at WebSphere Studio, but we will refer to this basic application as we do so.

Web Application Perspective

The primary view for a web application developer is the Web perspective, shown below. In this perspective, the Navigator view is replaced with a Web view, which combines parts of the Java Packages view with the base resources navigator. The Outline view is supplemented with a gallery, allowing the developer to select from many included pieces of clipart, scripts, and icons. There are also several new views added to the tasks area, including a summary of the contained properties and links, and a thumbnail view of the gallery contents:

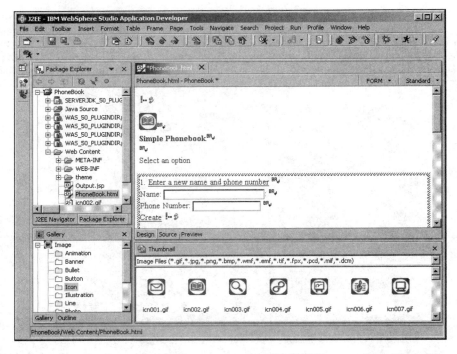

The centerpiece of the web perspective, however, is the HTML/JSP page editor. This editor offers three integrated views of the file being edited, shown as tabs at the bottom of the pane. They are:

❑ **Design**

This allows for the simple creation of even advanced pages. This is not browser specific, but a pseudo WYSIWYG view – it shows the basic structure of the page, but it also includes a visual representation of some data controls (such as JSP pages). The purpose of this view is to allow the rapid creation of web pages, leaving the fine-tuning to the Source view.

❑ **Source**

This can be used for verification of the content created in the Design view, and also to easily change any specific part of the file. The Source view can also be important when integrating business logic (such as JSP pages) into the page.

❑ **Preview**

This is generated by an embedded browser control giving the most accurate representation possible of what the static portions of the page will look like.

In these screenshots, the same page is displayed in both the Design and Source views; notice the tabs at the bottom of the pane:

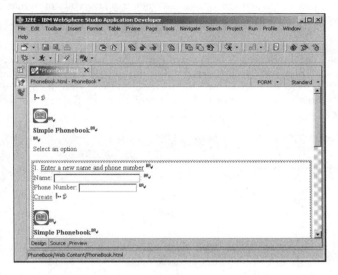

The editor contains a single edit model, meaning that any changes made in any view will immediately be reflected in all other views. There is full content assistance available in the Source view, offering all valid HTML tags based on the current position and context.

In the phonebook application we are developing, we need to gather input from the user. We do that via a form, defined in the `PhoneBook.html` page, as shown below. The form action posts the data to a servlet. Depending on the selected form this will be either the `SearchServlet` or (as below) the `newEntryServlet`. This logic is created in the Studio HTML editor, in the Source view as shown:

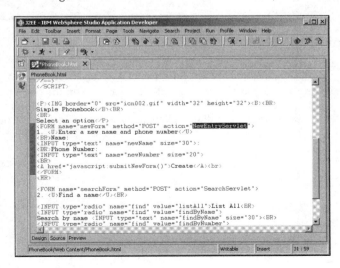

JSP pages are used to display dynamic output, which is what we display after searching our phonebook application. A JSP page is a mix of HTML and Java that can dynamically generate HTML. As shown below, we define a table to represent the output and then use Java code to iterate through the results and populate the table.

The editor really shines when it is used to edit or create JSP pages. The same three views (as described earlier) are available, but the Source view now combines the function of the Java editor. The following screenshot shows two things: the x in the margin indicates the location of a Java syntax error, and the content assist window is showing the list of valid methods to invoke on the highlighted Java variable, and the javadoc for those methods. You would expect both these functions in a pure Java editor, but it is an extremely useful to find them in the HTML editor:

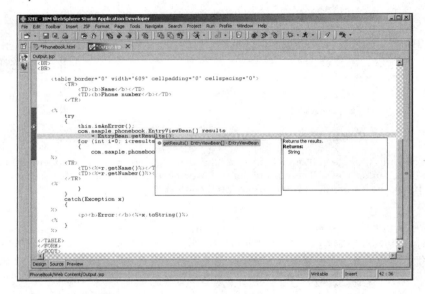

Creating a New Web Project

There are wizards available to create new resources of almost every type in WebSphere Studio. The wizards range from creation of a single HTML file all the way up to a complete J2EE application consisting of multiple projects. Some creation wizards are available on the pop-up menu based on your current context, but you can always select Other from that list as well. This is the same as selecting the File | New menu item, and will result in a dialog allowing you to select from any of the creation wizards:

To create a web application, the first action required is to create a new web project. There are a number of creation wizards available, as shown above. One extremely useful option is the **Java Bean Web Pages** wizard, which will create a web project and populate it with a template web application. Forms are defined to input data, a servlet to gather the data, and a JSP page to display the results. If you are starting such a project from scratch, this application template can save you a lot of time.

Another option is to create just a web project, and provide the content yourself. As shown later, the wizard will prompt to allow creation of either a J2EE web project, or a static web project. The static web project does not add the web project to an enterprise application (and EAR project), and so is simpler, but more limiting. A better alternative is to select J2EE web project. There is limited increase in the complexity exposed to you, but significantly more flexibility in both the short and long term.

As a J2EE application server, all projects in WebSphere run in the context of an enterprise application. If one is not specified, a default enterprise application will be created for you at the application's install time. However, this deprives you of the option of modifying any of the configuration settings in the enterprise application project:

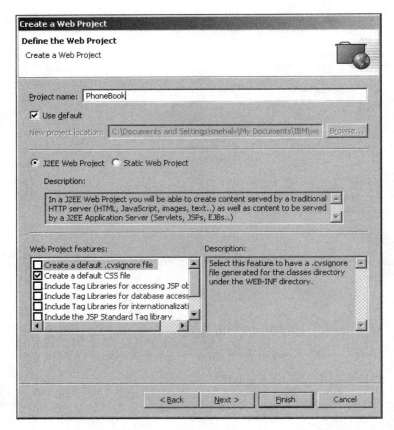

You can also select a number of web project features from this wizard. None of the decisions you make here are irrevocable, but they provide an easy way to configure and populate your project with some common settings. Some options are trivial, such as the automatic creation of a Cascading Style Sheet (CSS) file in your project. Other options will result in additional pages appearing at the end of the wizard to allow you to configure them.

If the J2EE Web Project option is selected, the next page of the project creation wizard will ask you to select the enterprise project to be used. You have the option of creating a new such project, or of selecting an existing one. In either case, the newly created web project will be added to the application.xml file that is contained in the /META-INF directory of the application project, the same action that occurs when you run a normal application assembly tool. In other words, almost behind the scenes, you have already started assembling your resultant project, and are preparing it for execution:

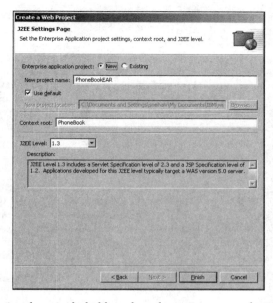

The next pages of the wizard are included based on the options you selected on the first page. All are optional, and in this example we did not select any options that require additional pages. After completing the wizard, the project will be created for you containing two folders, named Java **Source** and **Web Content**. The first is pre-configured to be included on the Java builder's classpath; any Java files you create in this directory will be compiled automatically. The **Web Content** folder represents the contents of the module that will be deployed on the server. It contains a WEB-INF directory, which in turn contains a classes directory where the results of the Java compilation will be placed, as required by the J2EE specification. This directory structure is shown below:

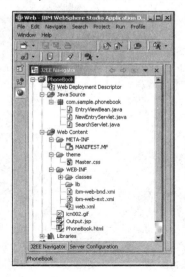

You can store any file you wish in the web project, including requirements and design documents, test cases, and other development-related artifacts. The only files that will be exported into the WAR file, and therefore will be available on the server, are the files that are contained in the **Web Content** folder. Typically, this means that any development-time files (such as design documentation, and so on) would be located in a different folder. It also means that all content for your web site needs to be located in a directory that is contained in the **Web Content** folder. This is also true for Java code; you do not usually want to ship your source code, and so the **Java Source** folder is not contained in **Web Content**. However the results of the compilation do need to be shipped, and this is accomplished by the class files being placed in the `/Web Content/WEB-INF/classes` directory by default.

Validation

WebSphere Studio includes a number of validators to ensure the correctness of files against their respective specification (EJBs, EARs, DTDs, and so on). Each validator included in WebSphere Studio runs against different file types; in general the validators do not need to be manually configured or activated, as they are associated with the different project types. The two most common validators used in web projects are the HTML syntax validators and the JSP compilation validator. Both these validators are configured by default to verify the content of an HTML (or JSP) page is correct when the file is saved; any problems that are detected will be displayed both in the tasks list, and also with an **x** in the editor column when the file is opened.

The validation actions are optimized to only re-validate a file when it has been changed, but even that action can take a few seconds for large files, and so you may not wish to have the validation run on every save action. In this case, you can disable some aspects of the validation from the **Preferences** menu:

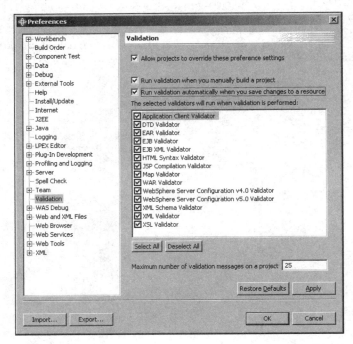

The options include turning off one specific validator entirely, or just disabling the "validate on save" behavior. In the latter case, it is possible to validate a project from the context menu at any time.

WebSphere Studio Server Tools

The primary purpose of WebSphere Studio is to create server-side applications, while providing an easy way to test and debug your applications. VisualAge for Java included a "WebSphere Test Environment", but due to restrictions in the VisualAge infrastructure there were a number of limitations in that test environment, and subtle differences in behavior between the test environment and a production server. The WebSphere Studio test environment is entirely identical in function to a production server. This means that you can be confident about the results of your testing inside Studio; if it works there, it will work on a real server.

One of the most significant features of the new test environment is that multiple server configurations can be defined and stored in the workbench and the underlying configuration system. This provides for a robust test experience. It is possible to ensure that the server configuration used on a tester's machine is exactly the same as that on a developer's machine. Another usage pattern for this support is for testing multiple server configurations. Since the files that form the configuration are saved, and even available via the configuration system to the entire team, even complex differences in configurations can be repeatedly selected.

In addition to supporting multiple configurations of a single server, it is often useful to represent multiple servers, each with a unique configuration. This capability is provided in Studio with the introduction of a server instance object. A server instance represents a specific server with the following information:

- ❑   The identification of the server type
- ❑   The location of the server on the network
- ❑   Information about how to publish files to that server

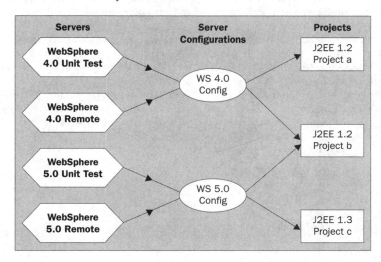

The Studio "server instance" concept should not be confused with the clustering and multiple server support that is available with advanced WebSphere application server editions. The WebSphere run-time clustering support is designed to ensure a scalable, robust, well performing environment. The WebSphere Studio server instance support is designed to provide an easy mechanism to test an application on different servers, ensuring repeatable testing across a variety of server types and scenarios. Server instances are also saved as files in the workbench, and available to multiple users via the configuration system.

Different server instances can represent more than just different physical machines. One of the critical attributes of a server instance is the identification of the server itself. This support is exploited in WebSphere Studio version 5.0, as both WebSphere version 4.0 and version 5.0 servers can be represented in the workbench, configured, started, and used to test code.

The identification of a unit test server, run locally in WebSphere Studio using the embedded server (or a remote server, run remotely on any existing WebSphere installation), is also made via the server instance. Tomcat servers can also be represented as server instances, although Tomcat itself is not included with WebSphere Studio. A project can be associated with one or more server configurations, and a configuration is associated with one or more server instances. The server instances and configurations are stored in a server project.

The usage of server configurations and server instances provides a very flexible test environment, but with this support comes the inherent complexity of having multiple servers, server configurations, and associated projects. Rather than force you to learn the entire structure just to test a simple application, there is a staged introduction to the server environment that starts with a very simple menu click from a web or EJB project to configure and start a server.

All such projects have a **Run on Server** menu item on their context menus. If the project is not associated with a server configuration, a new configuration will be created containing the project. If the configuration is not associated with a server instance, a new instance will be created. Finally, the server will be started with the configuration, and the result displayed with an embedded browser displayed in the editor pane. The net result of this design is a comprehensive test infrastructure that is also easy to use.

Continuing with the phonebook application, the initial page we wish to display is the `PhoneBook.html`. To start the server and execute the application, all that is required is to locate this file, bring up the pop-up menu, and select the **Run on Server** menu action. You do not need to separately define a server project, server configuration, or server instance, as that will be done automatically for you. You do not need to export the project either, or create a WAR or EAR file, as the WebSphere Unit Test Environment will be configured to load the application directly from the workbench. The following screenshot shows the results of the **Run on Server** action:

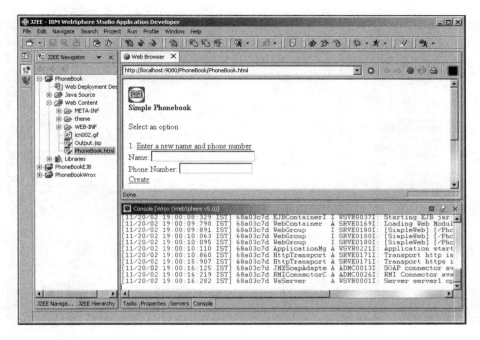

WebSphere Unit Test Environment

The WebSphere Unit Test environment is a specific configuration of the server tools described above. There is an unmodified copy of the WebSphere runtime contained within Studio. The server is run in an external process, using the correct JVM. It is both possible and supported to apply eFixes and formal PTFs to the WebSphere runtime and the WebSphere JVM, further maintaining compatibility between the test environment and the production environment, without impacting on the behavior of Studio.

The other distinguishing feature of the Unit Test Environment is how the server locates the applications being developed. Typically, you would need to publish an application to the server before it could be started and tested. However, the Unit Test Environment generates a specific configuration file for WebSphere, allowing the server to load the various projects directly from the Studio workspace directories.

This eliminates the need for a publishing step, as the files are being developed in the same location as that in which the server requires them. Changes to static files, such as HTML pages and graphics, are therefore automatically picked up when the server next uses them. Any changes made in the Studio Java editor to Java code is automatically re-compiled by the incremental compiler when the file is saved, and the updated class file(s) are then written to disk.

The server configuration ensures that the class files are loaded directly, and do not need to be packaged into a physical JAR. The WebSphere classloader can be configured to automatically detect and reload changes to class files, via an extension in the containing EAR projects' deployment descriptor. The editor for this is shown opposite; the Reload interval text field defines how often the file timestamp should be checked. Note that when a class file changes, the entire module is reloaded:

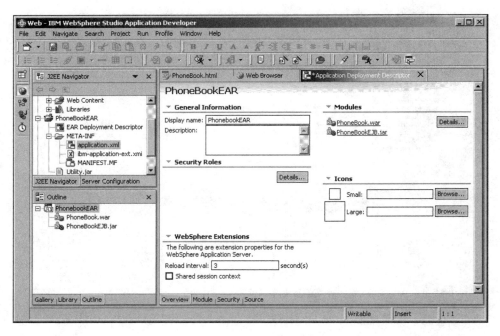

The result of these interactions is a model that allows developers to make changes to all resources under development, while the server is running, and have those changes reflected immediately in the server without an intervening publishing step. WebSphere Studio version 5.0 includes two WebSphere instances for use in the unit testing environment; one version 4.0 AEs server, and one version 5.0 base server.

WebSphere Remote Test Environment

The Remote Test Environment refers to the ability of Studio to publish to, configure, start, and interact with a server defined on a remote system. This capability should not be confused with the production system management function; rather, it is intended to allow testing to proceed on any server other than the one included as part of WebSphere Studio. Examples of this usage would include testing a server on another platform, testing another edition of WebSphere, or just broader system testing performed by a wider audience.

The cost of this additional flexibility is that a publishing step is required before changes made in Studio can be reflected on the server, although this step is automated. In addition, the initial generation of the server configuration, and even the activation of the server process on a remote machine, can be completed by the server tools infrastructure. The first step in defining a remote server includes identifying the server's IP address, and providing some basic information about the server installation (where on the remote system the server was installed, and so on):

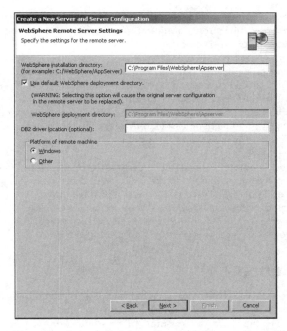

The next part of the configuration is to define how the publishing action will proceed. Studio introduces an abstraction of the publishing step, called a **Remote File Transfer (RFT)**. This abstraction allows for different file transport mechanisms to be defined, including FTP, native LAN file copying, or any other pluggable technique, and then reused in several different scenarios:

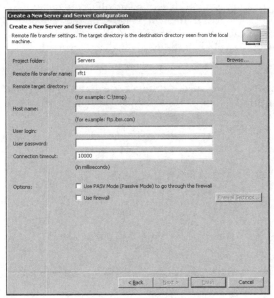

The server definition and RFT information are all saved as part of the server instance. As with all other Studio resources, it is saved to the source configuration system, and therefore broadly available to your entire development team; this file is part of the workbench.

Once the remote server instance has been defined, it can be associated with a project – or more accurately, a project can be added to a server configuration, and then that configuration is associated with a server instance. A remote server is started from within Studio in exactly the same way as the unit test server is started; it can be explicitly started from the server perspective, or implicitly by selecting **Run on Server** for a project that has been associated with it. If a project is associated with multiple servers, you will be prompted for which one should be started.

The mechanics of starting a remote server require that the **Remote Agent Controller (RAC)** be installed on the remote machine (which is included with WebSphere Studio, and also with the runtime on the Application Server Tools CD). This is a service that is used by a number of Studio components to facilitate tracing, logging, and server startup on remote machines. The RAC is typically not installed on a production machine, and must be configured to ensure secure access before it can be used at all, but once activated it allows easy activation and test of remote servers.

Web Services Support

Web Services are an extremely flexible way to create business logic methods (or services) that can interoperate across the web, without regard to the language or platform the service is implemented in. WebSphere Studio includes the ability to consume, or generate code that interacts with an existing web service, as well as the ability to create a new web service. We will describe the function of web services in detail in Chapter 8, and just provide an overview of the support provided by WebSphere Studio here.

The interface to a web service is primarily defined via a **Web Services Definition Language (WSDL)** file. The consumption, or use of an existing web service involves the creation of a Web Services client. This primarily consists of importing a WSDL file, and generating the Java code that is required to invoke the Web Service. A wizard is available that will guide you through this process. The client code will be created in the Web Project that will be used invoke the web service.

> **Note that the client creation wizard will not create a new Web Project. You must have an existing target project before you start the wizard.**

The WSDL file used to create the client can exist within the workspace, but it can also be loaded via any URL, or located via the built-in UDDI browser. The client wizard always generates the required proxy, but it also has the option of generating a sample JSP page that will interact with the proxy. Depending on the state of the application you are writing, the following four JSP pages can provide a quick start to the actual code. The following table describes them:

File Name	Description
TestClient.jsp	The main frame for the test client, run this to use
Input.jsp	Referenced by the TestClient.jsp to gather input fields
Method.jsp	Referenced by the TestClient.jsp to invoke the method
Result.jsp	Referenced by the TestClient.jsp to display the result

When creating a web service, the development flow is to create the application that is being exposed first, and then create a new web service for that application. Many different applications can be used as input to this process, ranging from a simple JavaBean to an EJB:

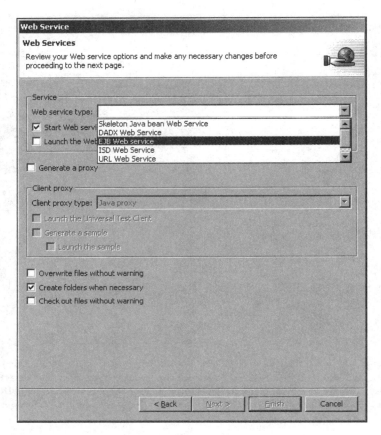

The use of a JavaBean is the simplest form of web service, even though it clearly does not provide the qualities of service that more advanced applications require. EJBs can also be used to implement a web service, and result in a much more robust application. Public methods on the bean are introspected, displayed in the wizard, and can be exposed as methods on the web service. The same structure is followed when creating a web service from a stateless session EJB after prompting for details such as the bean's JNDI name, methods on the remote interface are displayed and can be selected for inclusion on the web service:

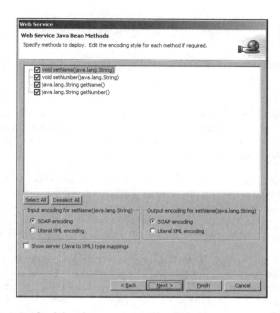

In all cases, the encoding method for the parameters and the return type of each method is selectable; the standard encoding of SOAP and Literal XML are available as radio buttons. However, if you wish further customization, you can select the Show server (Java to XML) type mappings checkbox. This will add an additional page to the wizard, allowing the specific mappings to be defined for each method. Although it is neither required nor recommended for general use, this customization can extend to the provision of your own serialization code, allowing unlimited flexibility for mapping incoming data types to those required by your application:

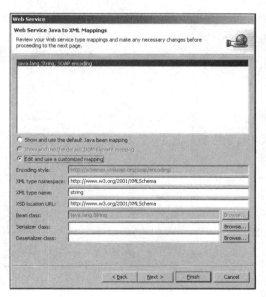

Once the wizard is completed, all required files would be generated into the selected project. The wizard can also optionally generate the same client application described above for a new web service, to facilitate easy testing.

Data Tools

The Studio database support includes the ability to import and export schema definitions via a live database connection, as well as a comprehensive series of editors for all parts of a schema model. There is a data perspective that can be used to consolidate these functions into a single place, but as with all Studio tools, the capability is available from almost every view.

Importing a schema definition from a database connection is best accomplished from the data perspective in which the navigator pane is supplemented with views: DB Servers and Data Definition. In the DB Servers view, the New | Connection menu action will allow the definition of a connection, ranging from the database name and vendor to the JDBC driver and class. Once a connection has been defined, schema definitions can be imported from and exported to the database.

Editing a schema definition is likely the most common database function that will be performed in Studio, and this is best accomplished in the Data Definition pane. The schema definition is persisted as a series of XMI files in the workspace, and these files can be located in any folder, and any project. In an EJB project for example, they are located in the /META-INF/Schema folder. There is a schema editor that can be used to edit or browse the content of these model files, but the Data Definition view also provides an overview in the main pane. There are four unique file types: one each for databases, schemas, tables, and views. When the file is located in any perspective, double-clicking on it will open the correct editor.

In the following screenshot, we are editing the schema definition for the phonebook application. The requirements for this application are very simple; we need a name and a phone number. Both these fields are being defined as VARCHARs. To further simplify the application, the name is being used as the database key:

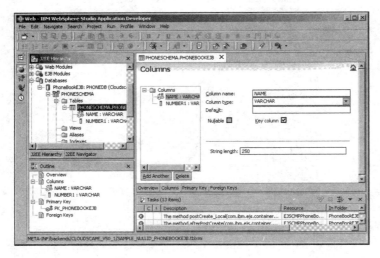

XML Tools

With the ever-increasing importance of XML, it should come as no surprise that WebSphere Studio includes a full complement of XML creation, manipulation, and viewing tools. In addition to a base XML editor, there are editors included for XML Schema, DTDs, and XSL, and also wizards that generate DTDs, XML files, XSL files, code to both read and write XML files from the file system, and JDBC code to both read and write XML data from a database.

The XML editor provides a structured view of any XML file, displaying all current elements and attributes as distinct nodes, and allowing the addition of new elements or attributes. Although all J2EE-defined XML files have their own editors in Studio, the XML editor can also be used to edit them at any time:

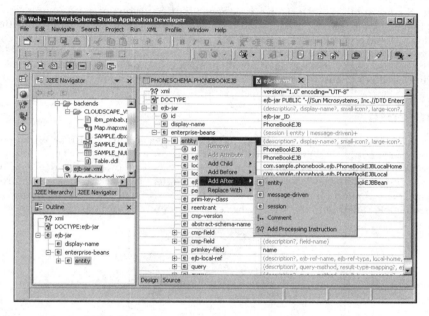

All changes made to the XML file can be are constrained by the file's schema or DTD. Selecting the constraint icon in the toolbar can toggle this behavior.

 This icon indicates that constraints are currently on, and changes to the file must conform to the schema or DTD. Clicking the icon will turn constraints off.

 This icon indicates that constraints are currently off, and any changes at all can be made to the file. Clicking the icon will turn constraints on.

If unconstrained changes are made to an XML file, the Create new DTD wizard (or Create new schema, if desired) can be used to generate a new DTD reflecting the current content and structure of the XML file.

The JavaBean to XML/XSL wizard will take a JavaBean as input, and can generate several different types of XML files. Some of the most useful are a selection of XSL stylesheets, used to dynamically generate a variety of web pages from a passed JavaBean using XSL transforms. The wizard will display the public methods on the bean, allowing you to select which ones should be displayed on the web page for both input and output pages. Upon completion of the wizard the desired XSL stylesheets will be generated, along with servlets that can be used to invoke them. The resulting files can of course be edited by any means, but they provide a great starting point for creating simple dynamic web pages.

WebSphere Studio Application Developer

WebSphere Studio Application Developer is designed for the creation of more complex projects, providing fully dynamic web applications utilizing EJBs. In addition to the complete function of Studio Site Developer, the Application Developer edition adds complete EJB tool support. This consists of the basic EJB tools, CMP and data-mapping tools, and a Universal Test Client that is designed to aid testing of EJBs. Finally, there is a complete set of profiling, tracing, and performance analysis tools included in Application Developer to ensure your resulting application performs and functions correctly.

J2EE Projects

If you have moved beyond simple servlets and wish to create a complete J2EE application using EJBs, the J2EE perspective is likely where you will spend the majority of your time. The primary feature of this perspective is a new view that replaces the Navigator view, and provides an overview of all relevant files in the workspace. The view categorizes the files by content type, listing all the web projects, EJB projects, enterprise application projects, and so on. This is a dynamic view, so any changes made here will be immediately reflected in the underlying resources view, and vice versa:

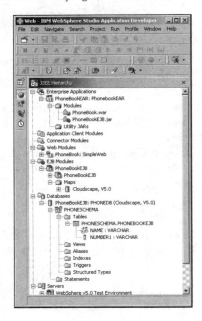

All the J2EE module creation wizards allow you to select an enterprise application project to contain the new module, so the creation and assembly of your complete application should take place almost automatically. However, if you wish to modify the resulting EAR in any way, the J2EE view is the best place to do so. The physical layout of enterprise applications, EJB projects, and web projects in the workbench file system is that all projects are created as peers. You may expect EJB and web projects to be physically children of a containing enterprise application project, but that structure would prevent the use of the same modules in more than one enterprise project.

This approach allows the modules to be created and reused with ease, and the logical containment of EJB web projects in an enterprise projects is represented via the J2EE view. As described with web projects above, the assembly of all projects into their correct file types and containing modules is now strictly a packaging step that can be completed on export if desired. The unit test server can be run, and all development can be completed without having to create the actual archive files.

The structure of an enterprise application project does represent the contents of the resulting archive. There is a /META-INF directory that contains the various metadata files – both the spec-defined application.xml and the IBM extensions. In general it should not be necessary to directly manipulate the content of the files, as the provided enterprise application editor will give a logical view of the data while ensuring the correct files are updated.

The J2EE view also provides an optimized view of your EJB projects; there are many additional files required while executing an EJB. However, the basic premise of the EJB specification is to shield you from the underlying complexity. Therefore, the only source files visible for an EJB in this view are the important, specification-defined, user-created ones: the bean itself, the home, remote, and local interfaces, and the key class. Double-clicking on the EJB node in the tree view will open the EJB editor, allowing changes to be made to the deployment descriptor.

In addition to the modules required to assemble your application, the databases used and server definitions are also available in the J2EE view. This provides an easy way to access the various files, as opening the files from this view will reuse the same editor available in other views.

Utility JARs

Any reasonably sized application will generally include utility code that falls outside the scope of the specification-defined modules, or needs to be reused by several modules. The enterprise application editor now provides the ability to define a Java project as a utility JAR. Once so designated, the Java project will be available as a dependent archive in all projects that are contained in the same enterprise application. If selected as a dependency, the Java builder classpath will be set correctly, allowing the code assist to work correctly, and the actual compilation to succeed.

In addition, the MANIFEST.MF file in the archive will indicate the dependency, ensuring that the code will all work correctly at runtime. As above, the physical assembly of the Java project into a JAR is just a packaging step, and is not required to develop or test the application in the Studio test environment. When you wish to test your application on a remote server, the publishing action will create the required JARs for you. If you wish to deploy the application to a production server, you can export the JARs or EARs using the export wizard:

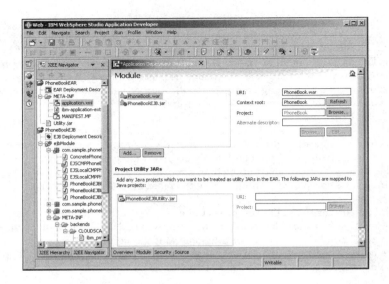

Enterprise JavaBean Tools

EJBs are discussed in depth throughout later chapters, so we will limit this discussion to an introduction to the EJB capability in Studio. WebSphere Studio Application Developer version 5.0 supports the creation and deployment of both 1.1 and 2.0 EJBs. The project type itself must be defined at creation time, as the DTD of the deployment descriptor has changed between versions. An EJB 2.0 project can contain CMP beans with both 1.1 and 2.0 style persistence, although it is not recommended that you mix the two in a single JAR.

The EJB project creation wizard is very similar to the web project creation wizard, prompting first for the desired specification level, and then for any module dependencies. The structure of an EJB Project is also consistent with web projects; there is a single directory (`ejbModule`) that represents the contents of the resultant archive. Any files that are placed in this directory will also be included in the output JAR; any files that are associated with the project, but that you do not wish to distribute should be located in any directory you have created in the root of the project, as a peer to `ejbModule`.

Within `ejbModule` is a `/META-INF` directory, which contains the deployment descriptor and associated metadata files. The WebSphere extensions take the form of several additional files in this directory:

File Name	Description
META-INF/ejb-jar.xml	Spec deployment descriptor
META-INF/ibm-ejb-jar-ext.xmi	IBM deployment descriptor extensions
META-INF/ibm-ejb-jar-bnd.xmi	IBM deployment descriptor bindings
META-INF/map.mapxmi	Mapping information for CMP beans
META-INF/schema/*	Schema information for CMP beans

Note that you can also define multiple schema maps for beans with version 2.0 persistence, but this scenario will result in additional metadata files saved in the META-INF tree.

Despite the fact that the EJB metadata spans multiple files, there is a single EJB editor used to edit the deployment descriptor and associated extensions. The multi-page editor is opened from the deployment descriptor file in the Navigator view, or from the EJB icon in the J2EE view. The specification-defined aspects of the deployment descriptor, and the IBM extensions and bindings aspects are both available in the same editor, avoiding the need to flip between editors when configuring a single bean – although the extensions are clearly marked as such in the editor, and can even be disabled via a preference if desired:

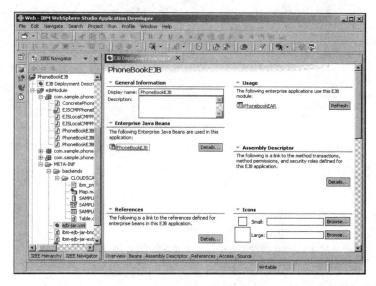

The last page of the editor is a source page, allowing you to view the resulting deployment descriptor. This is a live view, so changes can be made in the source page and they will be immediately reflected in the other pages of the editor.

As described above, the J2EE view shows the critical files for an EJB as nodes in the main Navigator view tree. When editing the bean in the Java editor in this perspective, the Outline view of the file can also be used to add methods to or remove methods from the home or remote interface.

Entity EJBs with CMP require a schema, and a mapping of CMP fields to that schema, to generate the code to implement that persistence. Studio can generate a schema from an EJB definition (known as "top-down"), or you can use the mapping editor to connect an existing schema definition to the entity ("meet in the middle"). These modes of operation can be mixed, allowing you to create a top-down map, and then modify it in the mapping editor. You can also create a new EJB from an existing schema definition, as a so-called "bottom-up" operation.

The metadata files are saved in the JAR, allowing the batch mode EJBDeploy tool to run outside the workbench, and still reflect a comprehensive schema map. When running the top-down schema creation, the database vendor must be defined. The resulting code to implement a particular mapping is type specific, not vendor specific – but the optimum selection of types may vary by vendor.

We want to use a CMP EJB to persist the data for our phonebook application. The resulting EJB is very simple, containing just two fields – a name and a number. The following screenshot shows how this EJB is mapped to the schema we defined previously. The mapping editor provides several views of the components to aid in the correct mapping, but can usually provide most mappings automatically. The upper half of the editor shows the input data, CMP beans and their fields on the left, and the schema, tables and columns on the right. The lower half of the editor, labeled Overview, shows the mappings that have been completed:

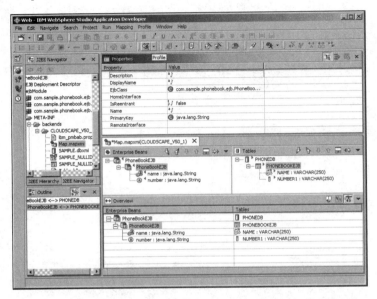

Having completed the mapping operation, the next step is to deploy and execute the bean. The deployment action can be run from the J2EE view, and simply generates the correct code to execute the bean in the container with the desired persistence. To run the EJB, the Run on Server action described above can be selected from the bean's node. This will configure and start the server, and open the Universal Test Client.

Universal Test Client

Testing of web applications is relatively simple, as they are designed with a user (web) interface. You must run the server, and interact with them via a browser, but the method of that interaction is clearly defined. Testing of EJBs is not quite as simple, as they only provide a Java interface. It is certainly possible to create a Java client to test the interaction with the bean, but that client then needs to be configured to interact with the server, and the resulting operation is fairly cumbersome to manage just for a test harness.

To address these issues, Studio includes a web application called the Universal Test Client. This application is optionally included in the server configuration, allowing you to interact with it anytime the server is operational. The testing can also be done from any web browser that has access to the server – the embedded browser within Studio is ideal for this, but you can also an external browser if you prefer.

The test client starts by listing the JNDI namespace. You can either enter the name of the bean you desire, or navigate through the tree to find it:

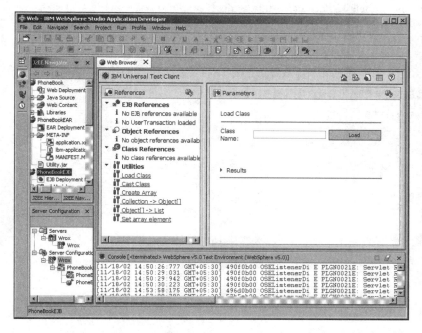

Once you have located the home bean, you will see the methods on the home bean displayed. Invoking a create() or find() method will return a bean instance, which can then be expanded. Any object that is returned can be added to the tree on the left, not just EJBs; objects are dynamically introspected, and so the results can be displayed, and further methods invoked, as required. The same test client can also be used to interact with returned JavaBeans, when working with web services.

Analysis Tools

A complete collection of application analysis tools is available in Studio, including tracing the flow of distributed applications, performance analysis of those applications, and server log analysis and problem determination.

Profiling and Performance Analysis

The distributed trace support requires the installation of the Remote Agent Controller on the remote machines, but this is also required for the remote server support and so may already be installed. To trace an application, you first start the server in profiling mode from within Studio. In the profiling perspective you then attach to the application you have started (which may be on the local or a remote machine), start the monitor, and then just use your application as you would normally. All usage is now being captured, and flows back to Studio, even as the application makes calls to other applications, or across machine boundaries.

When the application is complete, you can close it down, and display the results of the analysis in a large number of different textual and graphical formats. One of the most useful views is the Sequence Diagram, as shown below. This diagram provides a call flow of the application on a UML-style interaction diagram, including the relative performance of the call as a coloured bar on the left of the screen. The brighter the colour, the longer that method took:

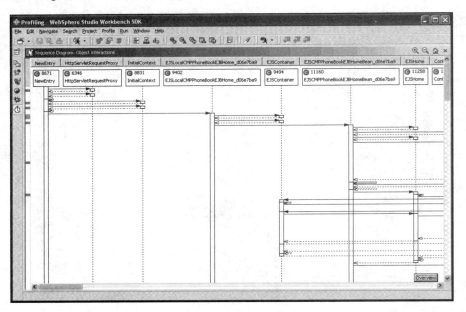

Guided by this overview of the performance, you can then open the details page of the data, which will show the exact time spent in each method, and in turn allow you to focus on the performance bottlenecks of your application.

Logging

The log analyser tool provides a mechanism to import a WebSphere-generated log file, view it graphically, and then compare it with a symptom database. If you are having trouble activating or configuring a WebSphere server, either locally or remotely, the log analyser can help you navigate the different logs that are generated to identify the likely cause. Problems that can be identified by the log analyser range from common configuration errors, to defects in the code for which fixes are available. Suggestions for fixing recognized problems are then displayed in the window.

Updates to the symptom database can be downloaded (in Studio) from an IBM FTP site. This mechanism means that IBM can provide an updated symptom database reflecting the causes of recently discovered problems, and the log analyser tool will always be able to reflect the most recent and commonly encountered problems.

WebSphere Studio Application Developer Integration Edition

WebSphere Studio Application Developer Integration Edition includes the complete function of Application Developer, as well as a new set of tools and wizards collectively referred to as the Enterprise Services Toolkit. The Enterprise Services Toolkit is a fully service-oriented development environment for business and enterprise application integration. A service is a very generic concept, and the Enterprise Services Toolkit uses services to represent various enterprise resources and functions. A web service is a single type of service, which uses Simple Object Access Protocol (SOAP) for its transport protocol. The services toolkit provides support for assembling services of many types, including web services, and services wrapping many other enterprise functions. A comprehensive discussion of the service-oriented architecture is provided in *Chapter 7*.

The toolkit itself allows you to consume and choreograph existing services, such as SOAP, JavaBeans, Stateless Session EJBs, and J2EE Connector Architecture (JCA) services (for example, EIS services, CICS, IMS, HOD, and others). Features like flow composition can be used to compose a new service out of other services. Transformations allow you to map the data from one service to another in a flow composition. Services deployed into the Integration Server can be provided as SOAP services, and via the EJB programming model.

At the heart of the toolkit is the service definition. The tools allow you to create and edit the different aspects of service definitions. They also allow you to create the run-time artifacts for the WebSphere Integration Server and for a service client. The Enterprise Service Perspective customizes the layout of the workbench to facilitate the development of Enterprise Services. The perspective contains views of workbench resources that you would typically use when you develop services.

The Service view contained in the perspective provides you with a view of your service resources. The view presents three folders:

- Service Projects
  This contains your service definitions

- Deployed Services
  This contains the services you have deployed

- Resource Adapters
  These contain the JCA resource adapters added to the workbench

The Flow wizard and editor let you create a service implementation by composing it out of other services. The Flow editor is a graphical composition tool that allows you to script services visually. To use services in your flow composition, simply drag and drop them from the Service view into the Flow editor. The flow of control between the services is expressed by control links, the flow of data by data links, and can contain data mappings when necessary, as shown overleaf:

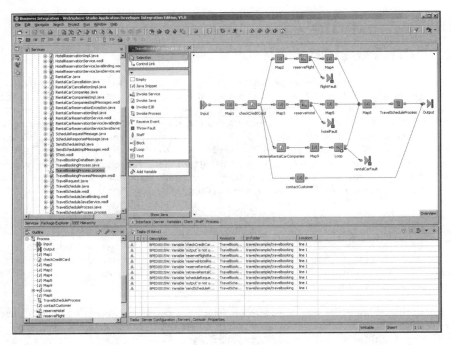

The Transformer wizard lets you create message transformations. You use the Transformer editor to define mappings between service messages. Actually, you can transform (map) multiple input messages to a single output message. The resulting Transformer is itself a service and its operation is implemented using the XSLT specification. The major use of Transformer services is for the data mapping function in the Flow editor.

WebSphere Studio Enterprise Developer

WebSphere Studio Enterprise Developer is an environment for writing sophisticated and large-scale applications, each with numerous run-time components. Those components can arise from different programming languages and can reside on different platforms.

Enterprise Developer contains all the features of Application Developer Integration Edition. As your team designs, codes, and deploys the most complex kinds of business software, Enterprise Developer also provides the following support:

❑ Create ASM, COBOL, or PL/I code, including CICS, IMS, and SQL statements

❑ Edit, test, and compile the source code locally, then recompile the source and build a load module on a remote z/OS system

❑ Transfer CLISTs, REXX EXECs, and USS shell scripts to z/OS; run them and view the resultant output

❑ Generate partially formed JCL, customize it, submit the job stream, and inspect the output

❑ Access z/OS datasets by way of a workstation-like directory structure

Enterprise Generation Language (EGL) provides a Rapid Application Development environment that lets you leverage existing skills to create applications that use the most up-to-date techniques. With this environment, you can implement business processes on a variety of platforms, and can deliver the enterprise-wide data to browsers, regardless of your experience with web or object-oriented technologies.

When you write code with EGL, you use a simplified language that hides the implementation details of CICS, MQSeries, and SQL. In addition to ease, EGL gives you flexibility in that your applications can be re-targeted for use on WebSphere Application Server, CICS, or other environments. You can code with fewer limits on later migration and integration.

EGL is especially helpful for creating web applications because the environment is tightly integrated with the WebSphere Studio Struts tools, and because EGL provides support for using your generated code as a web service.

Summary

This chapter has introduced the WebSphere Studio Development Tools. The tools are available in a number of different editions, targeting developers who are creating increasingly complex applications. Each new edition is a superset of the previous editions, providing a consistent approach to WebSphere application development.

The tools are built on the Eclipse platform, and consist of a variety of editors, resource types, and views. Resources under development in WebSphere Studio are primarily contained in projects that model J2EE modules; web projects, EJB projects, and Enterprise Application Projects. Wizards and type-specific editors are available for all components under development, ranging from XML and HTML editors for web content, to deployment descriptor editors for the different J2EE modules, to mapping editors for EJBs, relational databases, and enterprise services.

There is also support for testing and execution of the application under development; built-in unit test servers allow for execution on WebSphere version 4.0 or version 5.0, with automatic server configuration and activation. The application itself can also be profiled, to analyse its call flow and performance characteristics.

Prior to WebSphere Studio, the development of J2EE applications required separate tools for each stage of the process; design, web page development, business logic development, data design, deployment, application debugging and performance profiling. With WebSphere Studio, you now have a single development environment that spans the complete development lifecycle. One tool means that now there is a single user interface, common configuration system, integrated data and preferences, and a significantly more productive environment for you to create the applications you need.

Part 2: Building Conforming J2EE and Web Service-Enabled Applications

Part 2: Building Conforming J2EE and Web Service-Enabled Applications

We are often asked about how to build applications that can be ported easily to (or from) other application servers. Doing so requires that you confine yourself to the standard programming model defined by J2EE. This part of the book will take you through the major elements of the J2EE programming model for web, enterprise, and service-oriented components. The emphasis in this part of the product is on creating conforming applications that can be ported easily to and from other conforming application servers.

One of our objectives for this book has been to be more than just a J2EE primer. We want to help you understand the relationship between your application and the underlying WebSphere runtime. We believe that doing so will lead you to build more efficient and durable components. This part of the book is no exception, as we show you how the application server functions in the presence of different design practices. In particular, we highlight how you can apply quality-of-service policies to your standard components to cause runtime management of your components in a way that maximizes through-put and minimizes resource consumption.

We spend some time in this part of the book delving into the relationship of J2EE applications with other information-system technologies that are likely to exist in your enterprise. We focus some attention on Java Messaging Services and Java 2 Connectors, and how these can be used both to address asynchronous information flow, and to leverage legacy application functions employed elsewhere in your system.

Web services are quickly proving to be a critical component in distributed computing. The fundamental premise for web services is to enable loosely-coupled integration between distributed parts of the information system. This is essential for bridging the disparity of technologies, time, and organizations that has always stood as an obstacle to broad-based business integration. WebSphere is one of the first J2EE products to support the newly emerging Java standards for web services implementation and deployment. While these standards are not literally required to conform to the J2EE specification at this time, we believe that web services will hold such an important role in application serving, that we have decided to treat them in this part of the book – in anticipation of these becoming a natural part of the J2EE specification and the center-piece for all conforming application servers in the future.

All of the principles discussed in this part of the book are based on the J2EE 1.3 standard and only leverage features of the base WebSphere Application Server runtime and WebSphere Studio Application Developer tool.

When you get done with this part of the book you will have a good understanding of how to build a conforming J2EE application, including the role that web services may play in your distributed computing environment. More importantly, you will understand the inter-relationship between your application and the underlying application-server runtime and the things the runtime does to manage the information infrastructure on which your application is hosted – so that you don't have to.

About the Plants-By-WebSphere Sample

This part of the book makes heavy use of the Plants-By-WebSphere sample application. The Plants-By-WebSphere application is a sample shipped in the WebSphere Application Server, along with source code, to demonstrate a classic J2EE application implementation.

We have substantially modified the Plants-By-WebSphere sample in this book to demonstrate aspects of the J2EE programming model and web services concepts that were not covered in the original example provided by IBM. You will want to use the version of the sample shipped with this book if you are going to follow the discourse in the book.

> **If you are using the WebSphere Application Server, be sure to uninstall the Plants-By-WebSphere example application that ships with WebSphere. Also, you need to remove the data sources that are pre-installed with WebSphere for the Plants-By-WebSphere example. The examples in this book will walk you through creating data sources that are appropriate for the modified example presented here, and the data sources shipped with WebSphere will interfere with those created in this book. Refer to Chapter 14 for more information on un-installing applications and removing data sources.**

The Plants-By-WebSphere application represents a mail-order storefront for plants, trees, and garden tools:

The Plants-By-WebSphere sample in this book is composed of a set of JSP pages, servlets, and EJBs, which are listen below:

❑   **JSP pages**

   ❑   `cart`
        Presents the contents of the shopping cart; the contents of the shopping cart are got from the `ShoppingCart` EJB.

   ❑   `checkout`
        Presents a form for gathering credit-card and shipping information; the contents of the checkout form, along with the contents of the shopping cart.

   ❑   `orderdone`
        Presents confirmation of the completed order submission.

   ❑   `product`
        Presents the a detailed view of the item selected from the main catalog pages.

   ❑   `salesitems`
        Frames the component images of the main home-page logo for the store front.

   ❑   `showcatalog`
        Lists the contents of the catalog; the contents of the catalog are taken from the catalog database retrieved through the `Inventory` EJB.

❑   **Other Pages**

   ❑   `index.html`
        This is the home page for the store; presenting the store front logo and providing navigation to the main features of the web site.

   ❑   `banner.html`
        Presents the standard noteback tab metaphor for navigating the web site.

111

❑ **Servlets**

❑ `ShoppingControllerServlet`
The main point of control for user input to the plant store web interface.

❑ **Model Wrappers**

❑ `CartModel`
A wrapper to the `ShoppingCart` EJB.

❑ `CustomerModel`
A wrapper to the `Customer` EJB.

❑ `InventoryModel`
A wrapper to the `Inventory` EJB.

❑ `OrderModel`
A wrapper to the `Order` EJB.

❑ **EJBs**

❑ `Catalog`
A stateless session bean that collects information from the store inventory that can be used to present a visual catalog to shoppers.

❑ `Customer`
A CMP entity bean representing customers that have purchased items from the store.

❑ `FulFillOrder`
A stateless session bean used to complete the order request processing.

❑ `Inventory`
A CMP entity bean that represents the inventory of items that are available for sale through the plant store. In addition to identifying and depicting the items in the store's catalog, it also retains the price and quantity of stock on hand for each item.

❑ `Order`
A CMP entity bean used to represent a particular customer order.

❑ `OrderIdGenerator`
A CMP entity bean that is responsible for creating unique order numbers.

❑ `OrderItem`
A CMP entity bean that captures the type and quantity of a specific product ordered. `OrderItems` are aggregated by an `Order`.

❑ `OrderSender`
A stateless session bean used to send a message when the order is complete.

❑ `OrderReceiver`
A message-driven bean that receives order messages and calls the `FulFillOrder` bean to complete the order processing.

❑ `ShoppingCart`
A stateful session bean that holds the contents of the shopping cart. The shopping cart is modeled as an EJB to allow it to be retained across different sessions with the user.

❑ **Helper classes**

❑ `CustomerInfo`
A Java holder-object for the `Customer` bean.

❑ `InsufficientInventoryException`
This exception is thrown by the `FulFillOrder` bean if the order cannot be filled.

❑ `OrderInfo`
A holder-object for the `Order` bean.

❑ `StoreItem`
A holder-object for the contents of an item in the `Catalog`. This holder-object is used to pass around the information about the `Catalog` item. It is used in many of the operations on the `Catalog`.

❑ `Util`
It supports a variety of helper functions used throughout the Plants-By-WebSphere application for various repeated activities, such as getting EJB homes, getting the initial JNDI context, and so on.

❑ **Web Services**

 ❑ `PlantsByWebSphereCatalogService`
 This is a web service representing the `PlantsByWebSphereCatalog` port-type with a SOAP binding. This service can be used to get product information from the `Catalog`.

The following diagram depicts the general structure of the Plants-By-WebSphere example produced in this part of the book:

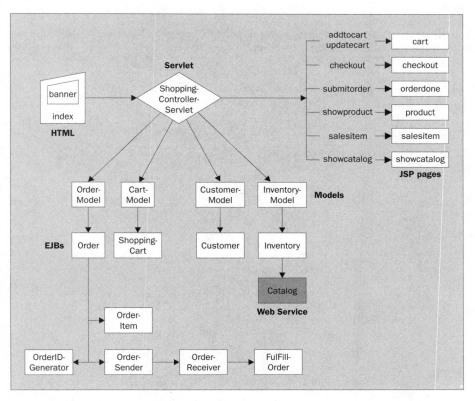

The JSP pages and servlets are developed in Chapter 4. The web application portion of this example is developed to use a set of wrappers to the EJBs in the EJB module. This technique allows the web application to be developed in parallel with the development of the EJBs – the model – wrappers are used as temporary stand-ins to the EJBs during the development of the web application. Later, when the EJBs are completed, these model objects can be mapped or delegated on to the actual EJBs.

The majority of EJBs are developed in Chapter 5. The EJBs in this part of the sample are largely taken from the original Plants-By-WebSphere example that ships with WebSphere, but have been extended to demonstrate the transactional coordination of updates to the database and JMS queues (as demonstrated in Chapter 7), and the use of relationships. To support the latter concept, the OrderItem bean has been introduced – an Order aggregates multiple OrderItems.

This much of the application is assembled and deployed in Chapter 6. To support commit coordination with JMS, the application is deployed in this chapter with XA data sources to the Cloudscape database that ships with WebSphere. For this reason, as the warning above indicates, it is very important that you remove the data sources that are configured by default with WebSphere – the default data sources do not support commit-coordination and therefore, will fail when you introduce the changes discussed in the Chapter 7.

The messaging EJBs, OrderSender and FulFillOrder, are developed in Chapter 7. This chapter discusses the basics of the Java 2 Connector Architecture but does not develop that into the Plants-By-WebSphere, primarily because doing so would require the introduction of a "sample legacy system" and that would be going into too much detail for this book.

Enabling the Catalog as a web service is developed in Chapter 8. This chapter introduces the PlantsByWebSphereCatalogService composed of the PlantsByWebSphere port type (derived from the Catalog bean) and SOAP binding.

The application will be developed further in Part 3 of the book.

Building Presentation Logic with WebSphere Studio

In previous chapters we have seen a description of the multi-tier and web based computing architecture supported by WebSphere and its correlation to the J2EE programming model. We have also seen that the programming model supports various clients types, including web browsers and pervasive devices. This chapter will discuss WebSphere's support for building a presentations layer for the web browser client using WebSphere Studio tooling:

❑ Tier-0 web browsers are the most ubiquitous presentation style used for J2EE applications. Presentation is handled by logic running in the Web Application Server and rendered by the browser. This pattern is useful because it localizes the presentation logic on the server. Distribution and management of a client application is almost a non-issue. Unfortunately, differences in browsers have sometimes forced the presentation logic on the server to be aware of the actual browser in use by the client. The focus of this chapter will be on building web application presentation logic.

❑ Tier-1 clients are commonly used for intranet computing environments. These applications provide a richer set of presentation features, but also tend to rely on direct communication with the business logic, using protocols such as IIOP. This direct communication requirement tends to place their use cases within an enterprise's firewall. A variety of libraries are available for implementing tier-1 client presentations, including the Standard Wideget Toolkit (SWT) (http://www.eclipse.org/articles/Article-SWT-Design-1/SWT-Design-1.html) and JFC/Swing components (http://java.sun.com/products/jfc/).

❏   Pervasive devices are just starting to become an important client for e-business applications. This type of client often has different display characteristics from a web browser on a desktop computer. WebSphere Application Server provides a servlet extension that allows us to detect the client device type and thus select a presentation specific to the device. In addition, WebSphere Everyplace Access provides several transcoding technologies that dynamically convert a single page definition to one appropriate for the client device.

The focus of this chapter is to illustrate how to use WebSphere to build and manage the execution of presentation logic. To illustrate this, we'll build the Plants-By-WebSphere application's web tier using WebSphere Studio tools and discuss the implications of running that application on the WebSphere Application Server.

Building the Web Tier

WebSphere Studio Application Developer simplifies the building of J2EE applications. The previous chapter already provided us with a brief introduction to WebSphere Studio, so instead this chapter will focus on using Studio to build the presentation portion of our application. The basic flow of building the presentation logic will be to:

1.   Create the projects necessary for the application

2.   Create the home page

3.   Create the banner and the navigation menu

4.   Create the controller

5.   Create the model JavaBeans

6.   Repeat for adding additional content and pages and updating the controller

The presentation we will be building will start simple, adding complexity in stages. Eventually, the application will look like the following set of composed pieces:

This screenshot is of the full Plants-By-WebSphere example. In this chapter we will only be building a few parts of it.

An upper frame will contain a common banner and navigation bar. A scrollable lower frame will contain the page being displayed along with a common footer.

Creating the Projects

The easiest way to build the necessary projects is to use the WebSphere Studio wizards. The web application project will need to reside inside a J2EE enterprise application project where all the modules will eventually be assembled.

To create the web application project, select File | New | Project ...

Select **Web** and then select **Web project**. Click the **Next** button. The Create a Web Project wizard is displayed:

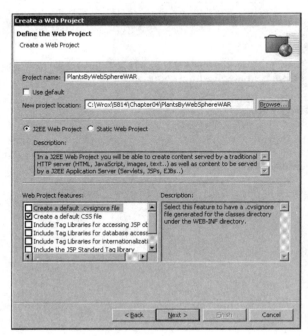

There are two kinds of web projects supported by WebSphere Studio. For simpler uses, a static web project can be used for creating static HTML pages. The Plants-By-WebSphere application will use a J2EE web application project that can be used to create dynamic content using JSP pages and servlets as well as static content.

The **Web Project Features** box allows for some customization of the web project on an as-needed basis. A variety of customizations can be added to the project including:

- ❑ Create a default .cvsignore file
  This can be set when using CVS for source management of the project so that the `WEB-INF/classes` directory is not included in the managed set of files.

- ❑ Create a default CSS file
  Can be used to help provide a common look and feel for the web application project. The Plants-By-WebSphere application uses a common look and feel, so we'll check this feature.

- ❑ Include Tag libraries for accessing JSP objects
  These tag libraries allow you to access the page context of a JSP page and the attributes of a web application or HTTP session. You can also set the HTTP request and response for a JSP page.

- ❑ Include Tag libraries for database access
  This feature gives you a set of beans and a tag library that will help you to access your databases through your web application.

- ❑ Include Tag libraries for internationalization
  Tag library I18N will be added to your project.The I18N custom tag library contains tags that can help you manage the complexity of creating internationalized web applications.

- ❑ Include the JSP Standard Tag library
  This tag library is an implementation of the JSP Standard Tag Library. This provides a set of standard tags for common function. This feature should only be added to a web project with a J2EE level of 1.3.

- ❑ Include utility Tag library
  These tag libraries allow you to handle date- and time-related functions, manipulate strings, and send e-mail. They also include examples that illustrate basic tag library code techniques.

In the **Project name** field, enter the name of the web application project. For instance, enter `PlantsbyWebSphereWAR`. It is recommended that the module type be identified in the project name to prevent confusion and collision of names with other projects. Click **Next**. The J2EE Settings Page will be displayed:

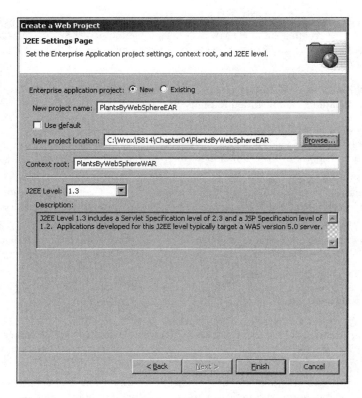

The J2EE Settings Page covers the relationship of the web project to a J2EE application. A choice can be made to include the web project in an existing J2EE application project or to create a new one. We'll create a new one, so ensure the **New Enterprise Application Project** button is selected and enter the name to use for the J2EE application project. For example, enter `PlantsbyWebSphereEAR`. In the context root field, enter `/PlantsByWebSphere`. Make sure the **J2EE Level** is set to 1.3.

> *If the J2EE level option is not displayed, the J2EE preferences may need to be set to enable J2EE 1.3 features. See the Window | Preferences, J2EE settings, Highest J2EE version used for development panel item.*

Click **Next** if it is enabled. Actually, clicking **Finish** would work, but the next panel is important to know about. The module dependencies panel will be displayed. If the **Next** button is not enabled, there are no projects to make this one dependent on:

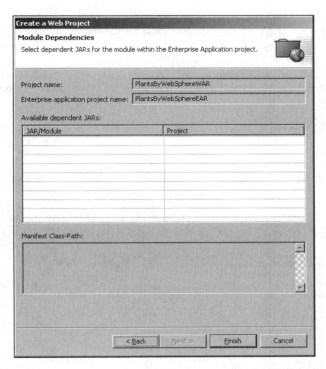

This panel allows other projects to be set up as dependencies. The MVC development pattern allows the development of the presentation and business logic to proceed in parallel and to some extent models the migration of a web-centric application to a more scalable EJB-centric application. When this migration takes place, an EJB project will be added to the application and the PlantsbyWebSphereWAR project will be dependent on it. This could be set up now if the EJB project existed. We'll be developing the EJBs in the next chapter so for the moment just hit **Finish**.

The workbench will now contain a new web application project in the Navigator view, as well as a new enterprise application project:

The organization of the project directory structure follows a J2EE platform role-based scheme. Page developers place HTML, JSP files, and other resources in the Web Content folder. Servlets and other logic are placed in the Java Source folder. The build process will take care of compiling Java code in the Java Source tree and packaging the generated classes in the WEB-INF/classes directory of the WAR file. The WEB-INF directory contains the web.xml deployment descriptor for the WAR file as well as the IBM descriptor extensions (ibm-web-bnd.xmi and ibm-web-ext.xmi).

Creating the Home Page

There's also a wizard for creating HTML pages. The File | New menu is sensitive to the current perspective. The perspective currently in use is the **Web perspective** (as noted by the globe icon on the perspective toolbar on the far left of the screen). The New menu offers selections appropriate for adding to a web application when the Web perspective is selected.

To create the home page, select the Web Content folder of the PlantsbyWebSphereWAR project. Right-click the folder and select File | New | HTML/XHTML File. This displays the new HTML/XHTML File wizard:

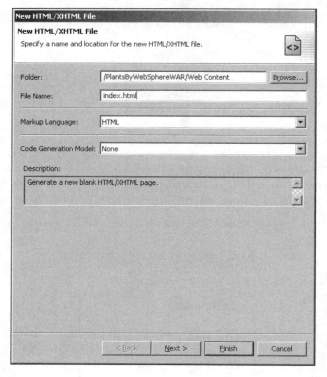

The Markup Language box allows us to select to create either an HTML or XHTML page with or without a frameset.

The Code Generation Model is not used for WebSphere Studio Application Developer.

Enter `index.html` in the **File Name** field. If you click **Next**, you can change the encoding and `DOCTYPE` used as well as select a stylesheet, though appropriate defaults are already selected. Note, the default encoding and `DOCTYPE` can be changed by clicking **Window | Preferences, Web and XML Files + HTML Files**. Click **Finish**. If asked whether or not to save resources, click **Yes**. The workbench will now be editing the home page:

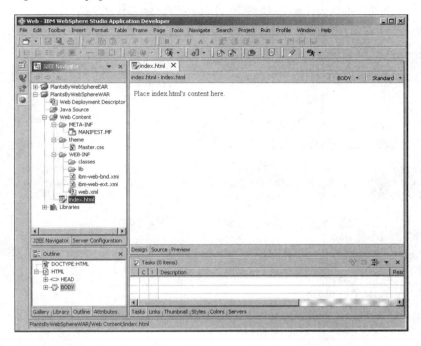

> As more projects are included in the application and different perspectives are used, be sure to check the **Folder** field each time to make sure the new files are created in the correct location. Selecting the destination in the project to create in before selecting **File | New** can help ensure it ends up in the correct place.

Notice that in the J2EE Navigator view, the `index.html` has been placed in the Web Content folder.

To change the title for the home page, switch the HTML/JSP editor to its Source view, then expand the **HEAD** item in the Outline view. Select the **TITLE** element in the Outline view. The HTML/JSP editor should now have the `<TITLE>` element highlighted. Change the `<TITLE>` value from `index.html` to `Plants-by-WebSphere Home Page`. Switch back to the **Design** tab to see the editor's title bar change.

Of course it's not necessary to go through the long winded process of selecting the `<TITLE>` tag in the Outline view and then editing its contents. We could have just gone straight to the source, but the Outline view allows you to easily navigate around your files when they become more complex.

Applying a Style Sheet

For a different look and feel for the web site, a different cascading stylesheet may be used by the web application. WebSphere Studio provides several style sheets that can be selected from by selecting the Style Sheet item on the Gallery tab in the Outline view. Double-clicking the stylesheets that appear in the Thumbnail view will add the style to the currently edited file:

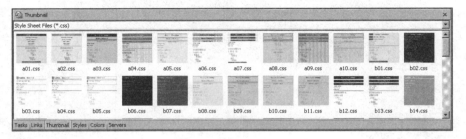

An alternative is to import a new style sheet or create your own. We will use an existing style sheet. Select the theme folder in the PlantsByWebSphereWAR project in the Navigator view. Right-click and select File | Import to bring up the Import source selection panel:

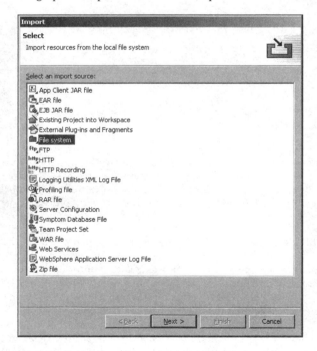

There are many things that can be imported into WebSphere Studio. Importing from the file system allows selection of individual files to be imported into an existing project. Other import sources, such as EAR file, import the entire artifact into a new project. Select File system and click Next. The import wizard will be displayed.

Use the **Directory** field **Browse** button to select the directory containing the `PlantMaster.css` file.

If you have installed WebSphere Application Server (including the samples) then this file can be found in the `<WAS_install_root>/samples/src/PlantsByWebSphere/` `PlantsByWebSphereWAR` directory. Otherwise, you can find this `.css` file as part of the code bundle for this chapter of the book.

Select the `PlantMaster.css` file on the right directory content view. Make sure the destination folder is set to the `theme` directory and click **Finish**:

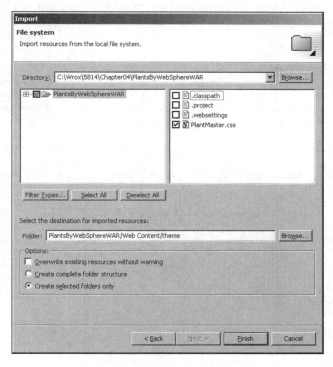

Select the `Master.css` file in the theme folder of the `PlantsByWebSphere` project. Delete it by pressing the *Delete* key. The validation that occurs after deleting the file adds a task. Select the **Tasks** tab in the lower right to display the Tasks view:

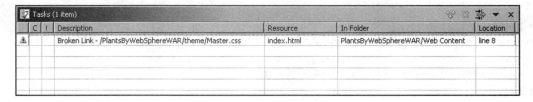

Double-click the task. This will load the `index.html` file into the HTML/JSP editor and show us where the offending broken link is.

Change the link theme/Master.css to theme/PlantMaster.css and save the updated index.html file. The task has been resolved and is removed from the Task view.

Note that WebSphere Studio helps keep projects correct by performing dynamic validation of the project.

Swich to the HTML/JSP editor's Design view. It now displays the text using a new style.

An alternative process that would have prevented the broken link is to use the style editing capabilities of WebSphere Studio to add the new style and remove the old one. For example, edit the index.html file, drag the new style sheet from the Navigator view onto the Design view to add the new style. Select the Styles tab on the lower view, select the style to remove and use the pop-up menu **Remove** item to remove the old style.

Creating the Layout

The home page needs a common banner. The banner will contain the navigation menu as well as the site title. A scrollable region for each page will occur below the banner. A frameset can be used to break the page up into a top banner with a scrollable region beneath.

Start by making sure we're in the Design view for index.html in the HTML\JSP editor.

Then select the Frame | Split Frame | Split Horizontally menu item. The Split Frame selection panel will appear:

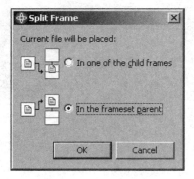

Select the **In the frameset parent** option to keep the index.html file as the frameset parent. Click **OK**. This will not only create the frameset in index.html, but it will also create separate HTML pages for each frame. We will specialize these new HTML pages a little later.

We need to give the frames a name for the later targeting of hyperlinks.Use the pop-up menu on the HTML/JSP editor to select Frame | Frame Attribute. This will display a panel with a frame tree, graphical representation of the frameset below it, and attributes to the right. For the frameset size, use **89 pixels and 1 ***. Set **Show border** to No, and **Border width** to 0:

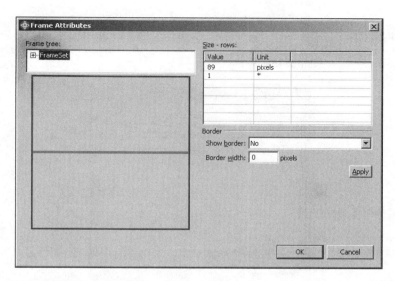

Click on the upper graphical frame to select it. Give that frame a name by entering `banner` in the Frame name field. Set Scrollbar to No, and use 0 for both Horizontal and Vertical margins:

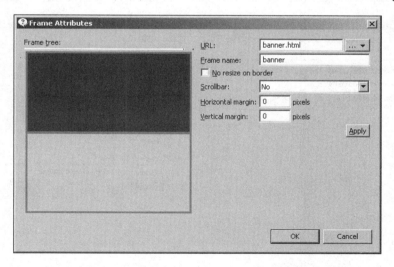

Click on the lower graphical frame to select it. Give that frame the name of `work`. Use **(Auto)** for the scrollbar setting, and 0 for both the margins. Click **OK**.

Save the changes to `index.html`. This will bring up a **Save as** dialog for each of the frames. Change the name of `newpage1.html` to `banner.html` and change the name of `newpage2.html` to `salesitems.jsp`. Later on, `salesitems.jsp` will be updated to display the items that are on sale. The save could be postponed until later, but this may become confusing as stacked sets of changes can cause different dialogs to pop-up and the context for which they are being displayed may be lost.

Open the Web Deployment Descriptor from the J2EE Navigator view to bring up the Deployment Descriptor editor. The `salesitems.jsp` file needs to be added to the descriptor. Find the **Servlets and JSPs** section and click the **Details** button. Now click the **Add** button. A panel will be displayed that allows the selection of a servlet or JSP file:

Select the **JSP** option, then select the **salesitems.jsp** file. **Click OK** to add it to the deployment descriptor.

A URL mapping can be added by selecting the **salesitems** JSP in the Deployment Descriptor editor view and clicking the **Add** button in the **URL Mappings** section:

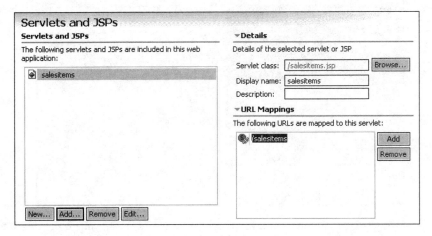

Close the Deployment Descriptor editor and save the changes.

Now let's add some initial content to the page. The `index.html` file should still be displayed in the editor window with the insert point in the upper frame. Start by adding a logo to the home page banner by clicking the **Insert Image File** button from the toolbar (or the **Insert | Image File | From File** menu). Select the `pbw.jpg` file, which can be found in `PlantsByWebSphereWAR/images` directory (either from the sample folder or from the code bundle for this chapter). Click **Open**.

In the bottom frame (that we labeled work earlier), type "Sales Items", as a reminder that the home page view starts with items on sale. Save your changes:

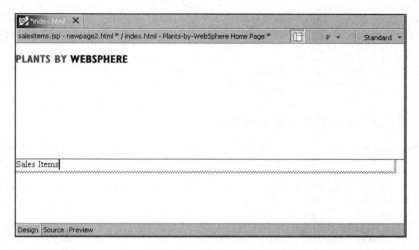

The application will have a lot of images, so we'll organize them by placing them in a common folder. Create the folder by selecting the Web Content folder in the J2EE Navigator view, right-click to bring up a menu and select New | Folder. This brings up the New Folder wizard.

Select the Web Content folder as the parent folder and type images in the folder name field. Click Finish:

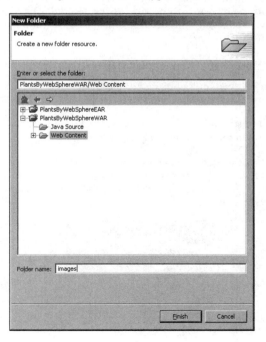

In the J2EE Navigator view, drag-and-drop the pbw.jpg file into the new images folder. This would normally cause a broken link, but WebSphere Studio will automatically update uses of the image file to the new location. Click OK to let WebSphere Studio fix the links. Close the index.html file and save the changes. If you did not save your changes when the image was dropped onto the banner frame, WebSphere Studio will not update the links and you will need to resolve any broken link tasks yourself.

At this point a basic home page has been created and the procedures for creating a new web application have been covered. Adding additional pages is mostly repetition of what has been covered so far. The following sections are going to cover some page-design aspects related to setting up the MVC pattern.

Creating the Navigation Menu

The navigation menu allows you to choose where in the site you want to go. Selection of a menu item sends an input event to the **servlet controller** for processing. The servlet controller processes the input and displays a new screen. To make this happen, a well-formatted set of menu items that generate requests to the servlet controller needs to be created. Navigation will be part of the common banner, therefore the banner.html file needs to be modified to handle the navigation menu. Eventually, the banner should look something like this:

The logo has already been taken care of already. From the above picture, we see that there are two groups of navigation controls; one graphical, one textual. These groups need to maintain some proximity to each other as the browser window is resized. Both the graphical and textual navigation controls need to generate a request to the servlet controller. The graphical portions of the banner can be obtained from the same location as pbw.jpg.

Select the images folder and use the Import wizard to import the remaining images from the file system.

The control of the layout will be handled using a table. Although it is possible to edit the banner.html file through the index.html frameset, it is simpler to edit it directly.

Start by making sure we're using the Web perspective, then double-click the banner.html file in the J2EE Navigator view, to open the file in the HTML/JSP editor.

Place the insert point below the logo by clicking beneath it, then click the Insert Table tool on the tool bar (or the Insert | Table menu). A table size pop-up panel will be displayed. Enter 1 for the number of rows, 7 for the number of columns, and click OK. The reason for the choice of the number of columns will become more apparent shortly:

The table attributes need to be adjusted. If a table cell is not selected, click on a table cell. In the Attributes view (in the lower-left corner of the workbench), select the **Table** tab. Set the **Table width** to 100%, **Cell spacing** to 0, **Cell padding** to 0, and **Border** to 0. Use the image import button (...) to locate the table background image, `images/tabs_background.jpg`:

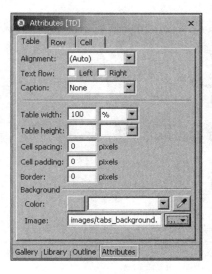

Now, we'll force a fixed padding to be used for the first column by inserting a single pixel image file and setting the width.

Select the first cell of the table. Click the Insert Image File button and select the `images/1x1_trans.gif` file. Select the Image Layout tab in the Attributes view and set the size to a width of 10 pixels and a height of 21 pixels:

Now select the second cell of the table. Insert the `images/tab_flowers_u.gif` image file into the cell. Add "Flowers" as alternative text for the image in the Attributes view. Repeat for the third through fifth table cells with `images/tab_veggies_u.gif`, `images/tab_trees_u.gif`, and `images/tab_accessories_u.gif`. Be careful to make sure the correct cell is selected before inserting each image:

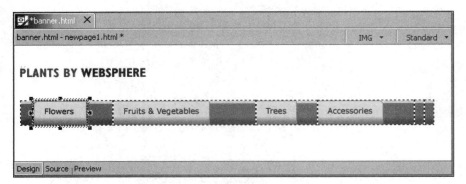

Currently the cells are spaced out along the menu depending on the size of the screen. However, we'd like to keep the four image buttons together. Change the cell width for each of the cells containing the images to match the width of its image. Use the Attributes view to find and set this information.

Now we've got the graphical portion of the menu in place we need to add the text options. So select the last cell of the table and enter the text "HOME : SHOPPING CART : LOGIN : HELP ". The colon separators have two blanks preceding them and one after. These are non-breaking spaces. To enter them, hold the *Ctrl* key down while pressing the spacebar:

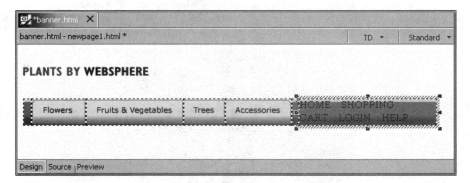

If the text has wrapped in the cell, uncheck the Wrap lines automatically *box on the Cell tab of the Attributes view.*

To apply a different style to the text, first add the stylesheet to the page. Select the Outline tab at the bottom of the Attributes view. Change the HTML/JSP editor view to Source. Select the <HEAD> element in the Outline view, then insert the following just before the </HEAD> element:

```
<link href="theme/PlantMaster.css" rel="stylesheet" type="text/css"/>
```

Change back to the Design tab to see the new text style.

Although it is possible to edit the HTML files directly using the Source view, it would have been much easier and less prone to mistakes to apply the new style by dragging the PlantMaster.css file from the J2EE Navigator view on top of the Design tab.

Now that the style sheet has been applied to the page in general, we will apply a specific style to the banner text. Select the entire text of the last table cell, and choose Insert | Paragraph | Normal. In the Attributes view, set the Alignment to Right. In the Outline tab of the Attributes view, right-mouse click the <P> tag and select Add Attribute | Class. Change the HTML/JSP editor view to Source. Set the class attribute value to "global" as shown below:

```
<TD width="100%"></TD>
<TD nowrap>
<P class="global" align="right">HOME  : SHOPPING
CART  : LOGIN  : HELP   </P>
</TD>
```

Change the HTML/JSP editor back to Design.

The sixth cell is a spacer for adjusting to different browser window widths. Select the sixth cell and set the width to 100% in the Attributes view. Save the changes. Our navigation menu should now match the screenshot from the start of this section.

The banner can be previewed in index.html by using the Preview view of the HTML/JSP editor. More than likely, the banner has wrapped both horizontally and vertically. Adjusting the frameset can be done by right-clicking in one of the frames and selecting Frame | Frame Attributes.

Creating the Sales Items Page

The salesitems.jsp page is quite simple to construct.

Start by opening the the salesitem.jsp file for editing, then replace the "Sales Items" text we added before with a 2x2 table. Change the table properties so the cell spacing, cell padding, and cell border are 0.

Join the two right-most cells of the table by selecting them both and choosing Table | Join selected cells from the pop-up menu.

Find and insert the images/theme_summer_text.gif image in the top-left cell. Find and insert the images/theme_summer2.gif image in the bottom-left cell. Find and insert the images/theme_summer1.gif image in the right-most cell. Save the changes.

Our home page will now look like this:

Now that the input controls for navigation have been rendered, it's time to deal with the controller that interprets the navigation.

Creating the Servlet Controller

Before starting to build the servlet controller, a quick discussion is in order. There are a variety of ways to build the servlet controller. This application will use a single servlet to handle the requests. Another possible pattern is a servlet per request. There are advantages and disadvantages to this. One advantage is that IDEs such as WebSphere Studio can easily detect broken links. The disadvantage is that it doesn't scale well. There are variations in-between as well. In practice, using more than one servlet controller with each controller handling a similar set of functions tends to work the best. For example, account management functions might be handled by one servlet controller, while catalog interaction might be handled by another.

Our servlet controller is going to handle multiple requests, using parameters to distinguish between each request. It will determine the appropriate navigation and actions to perform based on these supplied parameters. The follow steps describe how to set up the servlet and navigation basics.

Select the Web perspective if it is not already selected, and select the Java source folder. Start the Servlet wizard by right-clicking and choosing File | New | Servlet:

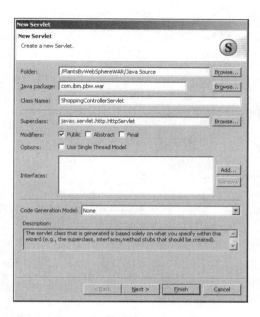

Enter the package name to use for the servlet (we'll use `com.ibm.pbw.war`) and enter the name of the servlet class, `ShoppingControllerServlet`.

The superclass will almost always be `HTTPServlet` unless a common base class is used for developing your servlets. The **Use Single Thread Model** option will add the servlet `SingleThreadModel` interface to your servlet. Click **Next**:

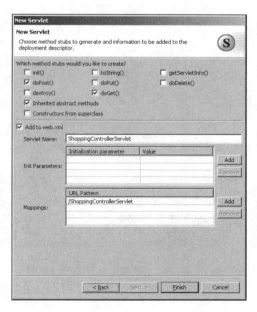

By default only the doGet() and doPost() methods will be created. This stage allows us to specify which additional methods should be created, how the servlet should be initialized, and what URL mapping should be used. The defaults are reasonable for our purposes, so just click Finish.

The servlet will be created, set up to handle both GET and POST requests, added to the deployment descriptor and set up with a default URL mapping. WebSphere Studio will now be editing the servlet:

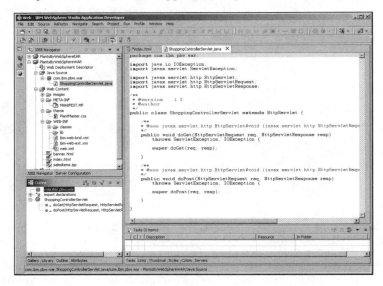

A common pattern to use for building servlets is to use a single method for processing both GET and POST requests. The reason for this will become apparent later on. Add the performTask() method to the servlet using the Java editor. Place the following code at the end of the class. The action parameter will be discussed later:

```
private void performTask(HttpServletRequest req, HttpServletResponse resp)
    throws ServletException, IOException {

  String action = req.getParameter("action");

}
```

Replace the super method call in both the doGet() and doPost() method implementations with:

```
performTask(req, resp);
```

This allows the servlet to process both GET and POST requests using a single method implementation and base a course of action upon a parameter setting. The servlet controller will be able to process requests from links as well as forms. The parameter, action, is part of the command language the servlet controller understands. This will be discussed in further detail below.

Before the servlet can process the navigation request, it must be able to redirect the request to an appropriate page. Add the following private method to the servlet class:

```
private void requestDispatch(ServletContext ctx,
    HttpServletRequest  req, HttpServletResponse resp, String page)
    throws ServletException, IOException {
  ctx.getRequestDispatcher(page).forward(req, resp);
}
```

This method is used by the servlet controller to forward the request to a new page once it has determined what page the servlet controller needs to send the request to.

WebSphere Studio detects and flags problems on the fly. In this case, the method just inserted has a problem:

as indicated by the red squiggly underline, the location marker in the right margin, and the light bulb in the left margin. The fly over help for the problem indicates the ServletContext class cannot be resolved, perhaps due to spelling errors or lack of an import statement. Clicking on the marker in the right margin will scroll the view to the location in the file that has the problem. If WebSphere Studio can provide a Quick Fix, it will be offered by clicking on the light bulb. Click on it to bring up a menu and select the import 'javax.servlet.ServletContext' item to have the import automatically added.

The first action to implement will be to navigate to the pages that display the catalog contents. The application supports partitioning the catalog into groups in order to make the display more manageable (as shown by the different options on the navigation menu). The catalog category to display is a required argument of the showcatalog action command. The action defines the primary behavior and the category defines a specific behavior. Together, they provide enough information to define how the servlet controller and views should perform. The following table illustrates the behavior of the servlet controller with various parameter values:

Parameter		Controller behavior
action	category	
showcatalog	flowers	Forwards request to showcatalog.jsp, which displays flower items in the catalog.
showcatalog	fruit	Forwards request to showcatalog.jsp, which displays fruit and vegetable items in the catalog.
showcatalog	trees	Forwards request to showcatalog.jsp, which displays tree items in the catalog.
showcatalog	accessories	Forwards request to showcatalog.jsp, which displays the accessories in the catalog.

There are two places the code needs to be modified in order to implement navigation to the catalog pages. The first is in the servlet controller, and the second is the navigation menu.

Modify the `performTask()` method of the servlet controller to recognize the `showcatalog` action. Once recognized, we forward the request on to the `showcatalog.jsp` page. Add the following code fragment to the `performTask()` method after the action is retrieved from the `HTTPServletRequest` object:

```
private void performTask(HttpServletRequest req, HttpServletResponse resp)
        throws ServletException, IOException {

    String action = req.getParameter("action");

    if (action.equals("showcatalog")) {
        requestDispatch(getServletConfig().getServletContext(),
                        req, resp, "showcatalog.jsp");
    }
}
```

Now we need to add a link in `banner.html` to the servlet controller for each graphical tab. To do this, double-click `banner.html` in the Navigator view. Switch to the Design view, and then select the Flowers cell. Right-click on it and choose Insert Link. This will bring up the Insert Link panel:

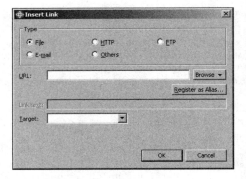

Select the **File** type radio button. From the **Browse** button, select **Servlet**. This will display the Servlet link selection panel:

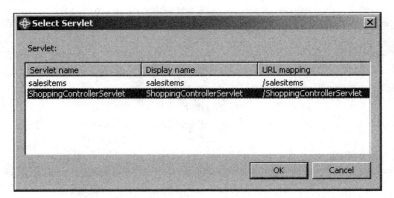

Select the ShoppingControllerServlet and click OK.

In the Target field of the Insert Link panel, type work. This will direct the link to the main frame of the display. Recall that work was one of the frame names assigned when we used the frame split feature earlier. Click OK.

At this point the link has been created to direct a request to the servlet controller, but it does not have any parameters to carry the information necessary for the servlet controller to determine a course of action.

Bring up a pop-up menu for the Flowers cell and select Attributes. If image attributes are displayed, use the change focus pull-down menu on the upper-right of the HTML/JSP editor to select the anchor (A) node. The Link Attributes should now be displayed:

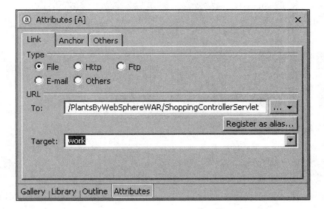

Add the following parameter information to the end of the URL To field:

```
?action=showcatalog&category=flowers
```

This information will be passed on to the servlet as two request parameters. The servlet controller uses these parameters to forward the request to showcatalog.jsp. The JSP page will use the category to determine what to display.

Repeat the last few steps to link up the other naviagation menu buttons with a specific action based on the table shown earlier (changing just the category for the request). Make sure to save all your changes.

Creating the JavaBeans Models

Now that the application supports navigation to the catalog pages, there needs to be data available to display. The JavaBeans model provides an abstract view of the database. It needs to provide enough information to build a view like the following:

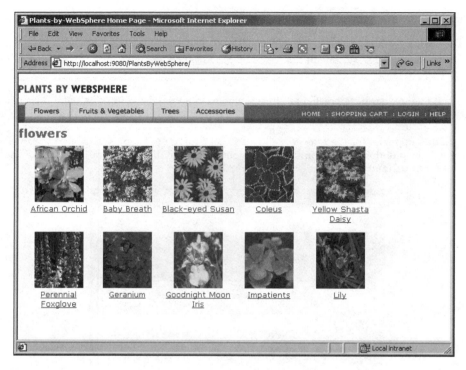

To build this view, the collection of items that form a category (in this screen, all the different products that are flowers) need to be retrieved from the persistent store. Each item will need to at least have an image and a name. The model itself will need a means of retrieving the collection of store items by category. We will create an inventory model that manages a collection of store items.

Create the StoreItem Bean

Select the Java Source folder in the Navigator view. Right-click and choose File | New | Other. This brings up the New selection panel. Click Java in the left-view and Class in the right-view. This brings up the New Java class wizard.

The Source Folder and Package fields are nothing new. The Enclosing type field allows for specification of the outer class of a nested class and will not be used. The specification of other classes the bean extends and implements is handled by the superclass and interface fields. The method stub selection is similar to, though more limited than, the method stub selection for servlets.

Use the Browse button to select the existing package (com.ibm.pbw.war) to create the class in, then enter StoreItem for the name of the class:

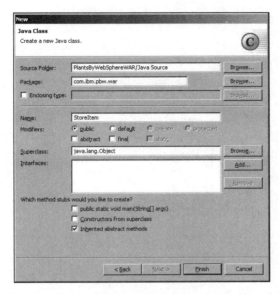

The `StoreItem` class is likely to be used for passing information back and forth to the persistence layer, so this class should be serializable. Click the **Add** button, and type the first few letters of "serializble" in the **Choose interfaces** field. This will narrow the possible choices of interfaces. Select **Serializable** from the **Matching types** list and make sure the qualifier is the `java.io` package. Click **Add** to complete the interface selection, then **Finish** on the main screen.

WebSphere Studio provides a simplified means of creating JavaBean properties. In the Java editor, add the following data members to the new class:

```
public class StoreItem implements Serializable {

    private String id;
    private String name;
    private String imageLocation;
    private float price;
    private String pkgInfo;
    private String descr;
    private int quantity = 1;
    private int category;
    private float cost;
```

Add a constructor that initializes the data members using the following code:

```
public StoreItem(String idString, String nm, String loc,
                 double dollars, String pkg, int category) {
    id = idString;
    name = nm;
    imageLocation = loc;
    price = (float) dollars;
    pkgInfo = pkg;
    descr = "";
    this.category = category;
}
```

Select all of the data members in either the Outline view or the Java editor.

Choose the Source | Generate Getter and Setter menu option to bring up a panel for selecting which getter and setter methods to create:

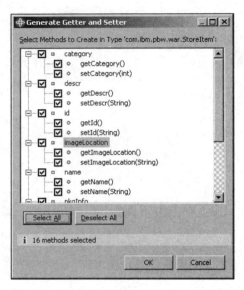

Ensure all of the getters and setters are checked (use the Select All button) and click OK then save the changes.

Create the Inventory Model

For now, the model will be read-only and will be pre-initialized with data. Create a new Java class called InventoryModel in the same package as the StoreItem class that looks like the following:

```
package com.ibm.pbw.war;

import java.util.Collection;
import java.util.Vector;

public class InventoryModel {

  private StoreItem flowerItems[] = {
    new StoreItem("F001", "African Orchid", "flower_african_orchid.jpg",
                  250.0, "per plant", 1),
    new StoreItem("F002", "Baby Breath", "flower_bbreath.jpg",
                  6.0, "2 plants", 1),
    new StoreItem("F003", "Black-eyed Susan", "flower_black-eyed_susan.jpg",
                  9.0, "2 plants", 1),
    new StoreItem("F004", "Coleus", "flower_coleus.jpg",
                  8.0, "4 plants", 1),
    new StoreItem("F005", "Yellow Shasta Daisy", "flower_daisies.jpg",
                  16.0, "2 plants", 1),
    new StoreItem("F006", "Perennial Foxglove", "flower_foxglove.jpg",
```

```
                    12.0, "3 plants", 1),
      new StoreItem("F007", "Geranium", "flower_geranium.jpg",
                    8.0,"per plant", 1),
      new StoreItem("F008", "Goodnight Moon Iris",
                    "flower_goodnight_moon_iris.jpg", 7.5, "5 bulbs", 1),
      new StoreItem("F009", "Impatients", "flower_impatiens.jpg",
                    9.95,"2 plants", 1),
      new StoreItem("F010", "Lily", "flower_lily.jpg", 6.5, "4 bulbs", 1),
    };

    public Collection findByCategory(String category) {
      Vector v = new Vector(flowerItems.length);
      if (category.equals("flowers")) {
        for (int i = 0; i < flowerItems.length; i++) {
          v.add(flowerItems[i]);
        }
      }
      return v;
    }

    public StoreItem findById(String id) {
      for (int i = 0; i < flowerItems.length; i++) {
       if (flowerItems[i].getId().equals(id)) {
         return flowerItems[i];
       }
      }
      return null;
    }
}
```

Use the WebSphere Studio Quick Fix support to fix any problems. This model class will be used by
`showcatalog.jsp` to retrieve the catalog data. Eventually, the implementation of this bean will be
replaced with EJB client code to access data in a database. Isolating the persistence code in the model
allows the model to change over time without affecting the view. For instance, the `Collection` class
returned by the `findByCategory()` method could be a specialized `Collection` class that lazily
retrieves chunks of data from a large result set.

Managing State

In general, there is only one instance of a model in the application. If the model is to be a read-only
model, it doesn't matter if the model is instantiated everywhere it is needed. If the model supports
updates, care must be taken on how many instances of the model exist. In addition, the scope will
become important. A single instance of the inventory model for the entire application, shared among all
clients, is appropriate. However, the shopping cart model needs to be unique per client.

We'll use the servlet controller to create an instance of the `InventoryModel` and share it with
application scope.

Open the Java editor for the `ShoppingControllerServlet`, and add a private `InventoryModel`
data member called `model` to the servlet:

```
public class ShoppingControllerServlet extends HttpServlet {

  private InventoryModel model;
```

In the pop-up menu for the servlet in the Outline view, select **Override Methods**. This will display a panel to add selected parent class methods to the servlet:

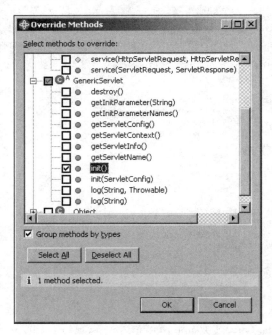

Select the `init()` method of the `GenericServlet` class and click **OK**.

Now use the Java editor to edit the `init()` method and initialize the data member created earlier:

```
public void init( throws ServletException {
    model = new InventoryModel();
}
```

To add the model to the application scope, add the following line:

```
public void init( throws ServletException {
    model = new InventoryModel();
    getServletContext().setAttribute("model", model);
}
```

This line of code will add an application-scoped attribute to allow us to share the model among all components.

Some thought must go into the use of application contexts, particularly if the application will be distributed among multiple servers for scalability. If the deployment descriptor for the web application is marked as `Distributable` (see the **Distributable** check box in the deployment descriptor), then the application context cannot be used to share global information. Instead, state information must be maintained in a persistent store such as a database.

A similar situation exists for state managed at the session scope. State that is maintained across multiple requests is usually contained within the HTTP session. WebSphere Application Server provides both session affinity policies for scalable configurations and a variety of session management policies. Session affinity ensures that multiple requests are always directed to the same server. The session management policies affect fail-over if a particular server fails. HTTP session use is covered in the later section *Stateful Web Applications Using Session Data*, while management issues are covered in more detail in the section on *HTTP Sessions.*

Adding Dynamic Content

It's now time to add dynamic content to the catalog pages. WebSphere Studio provides support for creating both HTML JSP pages and XML JSP documents. The syntax depends on whether or not an XML document is used. HTML syntax will be used throughout the Plants-By-WebSphere application to keep things simple. There are several ways to add dynamic content to a JSP. The simplest form is to use a JSP expression. The syntax for a JSP expression is:

```
<%=expression%>
```

The JSP expression inserts the value of the expression into the output stream. The second form of dynamic content is to insert a scriptlet into the JSP file. The syntax for a scriptlet is:

```
<% script statements %>
```

The script statements are a sequence of statements in the language declared for the page. By default WebSphere Studio uses Java. A script is typically used to control the flow of output for the JSP page. It is used to wrap conditional output or iterate over output in the JSP page. For example,

```
<%
if (funds <= 0) {
%>
    <em>Your account balance is extremely low!</em>
<%
}
%>
```

would output the emphasized text if the funds variable defined earlier in the JSP page is less than or equal to zero.

WebSphere Studio provides some assistance for inserting expressions, scripts and other JSP content into the JSP file (see the JSP menu). The following steps will explore the use of WebSphere Studio in creating dynamic content. The dynamic content will include a category-specific heading and table of all the products in the category.

Start by selecting the Web perspective (if not already selected) and creating the showcatalog.jsp page. This is achieved by selecting the PlantsByWebSphereWAR Web Content folder, right-clicking and the choosing File | New | JSP File:

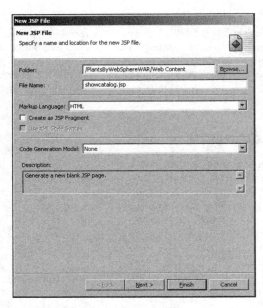

The **Markup Language** field is similar to the HTML/XML page creation wizard markup language field described earlier. If XHTML is selected for the markup language, it will enable the **Use XML Style Syntax** field. If this checkbox is checked, the JSP syntax will use XML namespaces for the specification of the JSP logic as described in the Servlet specification (Chapter 5 on JSP Documents).

The next panel of the wizard allows the selection of additional tag libraries to make available in the JSP. Click **Next** to display the panel for adding page directives:

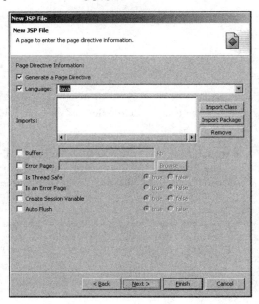

The **Generate a Page Directive** checkbox will force a page directive to be added to the JSP. The language field allows the selection of either **Java** or **JavaScript**. The **Imports** field allows other Java packages to be imported into the JSP file. If these are not known at the time the page is created, they can be added later (as we'll see).

The remaining checkboxes allow us to set additional attributes on the page. Of particular interest is the **Create Session Variable** checkbox. This allows the JSP to access the HTTP session using a session variable. This will be used in later JSP pages we create.

Click **Next** to display the panel for choosing encoding, DOCTYPE, and style sheets.

Click **Next** to display the panel for choosing the stub methods of the JSP page and whether or not to add it to the deployment descriptor. Click **Finish**.

In the Design tab of the HTML/JSP editor, delete the default text ("Place showcatalog.jsp's content here").

Create the dynamic header that displays the name of the category chosen by using the **JSP | Insert Expression** menu item. Then in the Attributes view, enter this expression:

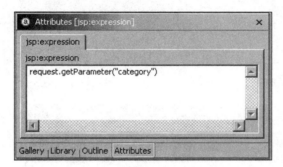

Place the insert point to the right of the inserted expression in the HTML/JSP editor. This will select the paragraph containing the expression (assuming you didn't delete the paragraph when you deleted the text). In the Attributes view, select the Heading 1 paragraph type. This will cause the retrieved category value to be displayed in the H1 heading style.

Creating the dynamic table content is a bit more complex and will require the use of scriptlets. Start off by clicking below the expression in the HTML/JSP editor to set the insertion point so that new insertions will be part of a new paragraph.

To start with, the JSP page needs access to all of the items in the category that need to be displayed. The first scriptlet will declare some variables and initialize them with the set of category items. From the **JSP** menu choose **Insert Scriptlet**. In the Attributes view, insert the following scriptlet code:

```
int count = 0;
InventoryModel model = (InventoryModel) application.getAttribute("model");
Vector invItems=(Vector) model.findByCategory(request.getParameter("category"));
StoreItem inv;
```

Note that `java.util.Vector`, `com.ibm.pbw.war.InventoryModel`, and `com.ibm.pbw.war.StoreItem` are shown with non-qualified names. The scriptlet requires the use of fully qualified type names because no package imports have been declared. In order to solve that problem, the appropriate imports need to be added. The JSP language allows for imports using the JSP page directive.

Right-click in the editor and open the **Page Properties** panel. Switch to the **JSP Tags** tab:

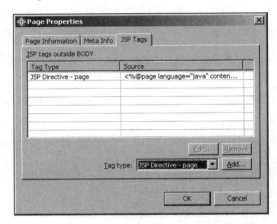

Change the **Tag type** to **JSP Directive – page** and click the **Add** button:

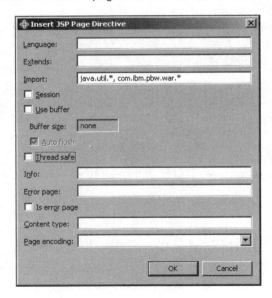

Enter `java.util.*`, `com.ibm.pbw.war.*` in the Import field. Uncheck all the checkboxes and click OK, and then OK again on the Page Properties window.

To create the dynamic table, insert a 1x1 table into the JSP after the scriptlet code. It will be customized and modified later to support the variable content of the categories.

In the Cell Attributes view, set Horizontal Alignment to center and Vertical Alignment to top. In the Table Attributes view, set the Table width to 600 pixels, Cell spacing to 5, Cell padding to 5, and Border to 0.

Fill out an example cell by placing any image in the cell of the table. Click the Insert Image from File button from the toolbar or by selecting Insert | Image File | From File. Select one of the images from the images directory (it doesn't matter which as it will be dynamically changed at run time). Set the image width to 80 and image height to 95 in the Image Layout Attributes view.

Place the insertion point after the image in the cell and choose Insert | Paragraph | Normal. Now insert a new JSP expression (JSP | Insert Expression) and configure the attribute with the following code to display the name of the product:

```
inv.getName()
```

It's not possible to use the Design view for inserting a scriptlet to iterate over content in a table. Switch to the Source view in the HTML/JSP editor to modify the table to handle a variable number of items. Insert a JSP scriptlet between the `<TR>` and `<TD>` elements that looks like the following:

```
<TABLE border="0" width="600" cellspacing="5" cellpadding="5">
    <TBODY>
        <TR>
            <%
              while (count < invItems.size()) {
                  inv = (StoreItem) (invItems.elementAt(count));
            %>
            <TD align="center" valign="top"><IMG border="0"
                src="flower_african_orchid.jpg" width="80"
                height="95">
```

Note that the `while` loop statement does not have a closing brace. Scriptlets can surround arbitrary text/HTML to be displayed, but eventually the statement must be syntactically correct.

Place the following two scriptlets and HTML fragments between the `</TD>` and `</TR>` tags:

```
            <P><%=inv.getName()%></P>
            </TD>
            <% if ( ((count +1 ) % 5) == 0 ) { %>
                </TR>
            <TR>
            <%
                }
                count++;
            } // end of while
            %>
        </TR>
    </TBODY>
</TABLE>
```

These scriptlets set up an iteration around the <TD> element definition that does two things:

❑   Creates a <TD> element for each item in the category
❑   Starts a new row after every five cells in the table

The dynamic item name has already been taken care of in the cell content by the expression inserted earlier. Make the item image dynamic by replacing the static file declaration in the <IMG> element with a JSP expression. The resulting IMG element should look like:

```
<IMG border="0" src="images/<%= inv.getImageLocation() %>"
     height="95" width="80" >
```

To finish off the dynamic table setup, import all the necessary images defined by the InventoryModel class into the images directory (if you haven't already done so).

Testing the Dynamic Content

The Preview view of the HTML/JSP editor provides a means to look at static content formatting, but for dynamic content, something more is needed. WebSphere Studio provides an integrated runtime that can execute the application. In order to test the web application, deployment configuration information needs to be checked and the web application needs to be installed on a server.

Make sure the Web perspective is selected, and select the PlantsbyWebSphereWAR project and bring up the pop-menu for it. Choose Properties to bring up the web application properties panel:

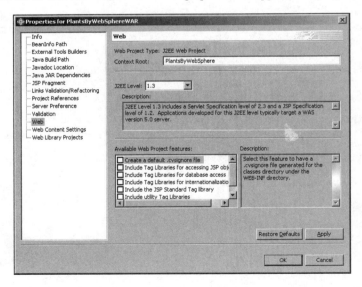

Select the Web node and check the Context Root is set to PlantsByWebSphere. By default, it matches the name of the project. Actually, any value can be used, but the value is what is used to access the application from a browser. Click OK.

Bring up the pop-up menu for the PlantsbyWebSphereWAR project again but this time choose **Run on Server**. If a panel is displayed for creating a new server, give the server a name and select the WebSphere version 5.0 Test Environment for the server type:

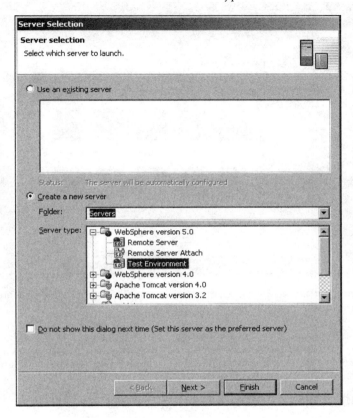

WebSphere Studio can also use a remote application server to run the application instead of the embedded test environment. Other server types provide legacy development and testing capabilities to older versions of WebSphere Application Server as well as non-WebSphere servers.

Wait for the server to start. A Web Browser view will automatically display the web application. Click the Flowers menu image to take a look at the dynamic content:

WebSphere Studio Application Developer in conjunction with WebSphere Application Server supports hot redeploy for rapid edit, compile, and debug cycles.

For example, edit `showcatalog.jsp` and add some text to the page. Save the file changes. Now if you switch back to the Web Browser view and click the Flowers menu item again, you'll notice that the page changes are reflected in the output without having to redeploy the web application to the server.

Stateful Web Applications Using Session Data

For the most part the application is currently stateless. The inventory model is retained across the application, but is read-only. To round out the application, there are two pieces of information that need to be maintained across method invocations on a per-user basis. One is the navigation path, so that a "return to previous page" dynamic link calculation can be made. The other is shopping cart information. This section will explore building stateful functionality into the web application using HTTP sessions.

HTTP sessions provide a means of retaining user state across multiple requests. The state is kept on the server and a minimal amount of information, a session ID, is passed back and forth between the user and the server to identify the session. WebSphere Application Server provides three schemes of session ID tracking (cookies, URL rewrite, and SSL ID) that are in general managed transparently to the application by the runtime. No direct manipulation of the session ID by the web application is required. The most common form used is cookies.

One session ID tracking scheme, URL rewriting, requires some application help. URL rewriting encodes the session ID in the response page sent back to the user. Each link in the page is changed or rewritten to include the session ID as a parameter. For example, a browser might see the following URL:

/PlantsByWebSphere/ShoppingControllerServlet;$jsessionid=DA32242SSGE2

In addition, if a servlet creates an HTML response directly and that response contains a link, the link will need to be encoded. For example:

```
out.println("<a href=\"");
out.println(response.encodeURL(
            "/PlantsByWebSphere/ShoppingControllerServlet"));
out.println("\">");
```

A similar situation exists for JSP pages. For example:

```
<a href="<% response.encodeURL("/PlantsByWebSphere/ShoppingControllerServlet")%>">
```

The drawback is that it only works for dynamic content (Servlets and JSP pages). Static content is not updated. Use of URL rewriting needs to be considered when designing the screen flows to avoid static content while a session is active since the session ID would be lost when navigating to a static HTML page.

The third option tracks the session ID based on the SSL ID. This only works when an SSL connection is used and if the SSL connection is broken for whatever reason, the session ID is lost.

It is possible to use more than one scheme, such as combining cookies and SSL ID, but the process flow for handling multiple simultaneous schemes is fairly complex and should be consulted in the documentation if use of multiple schemes is necessary.

In order to simplify the design, we'll be using cookies for session tracking in the Plants-By-WebSphere application.

Adding Dynamic Navigation

In order to support a link that navigates back to a previous page, information needs to be saved across multiple requests. For instance, we want the user to be able to navigate from the catalog screens to a detail screen to a shopping cart screen and back to the original catalog screen. The showcatalog.jsp file currently uses the request parameter, category, to determine the category to display. This parameter is required in order to determine what to display. However, the category will not be known when returning from the shopping cart screen. In this case, the category will not be supplied and the saved category will be used instead.

Open the ShoppingControllerServlet in the Java editor, add the following line of code in the performTask() method just before the requestDispatch() method call for the showcatalog action to retrieve the HTTP session from the request object:

```
if (action.equals("showcatalog")) {
    HttpSession session = req.getSession();
    requestDispatch(getServletConfig().getServletContext(),
                    req, resp, "showcatalog.jsp");
```

Be sure to resolve any import statement issues created by the use of HttpSession.

Complete the servlet code to place the category in the session object and use it if it is not specified. This will be used by the view JSP pages to determine what to display. The code should look something like the following:

```
if (action.equals("showcatalog")) {
    String category = req.getParameter("category");
    HttpSession session = req.getSession();
    if (category == null || category.equals("")) {
      category = (String)session.getAttribute("category");
    }
    session.setAttribute("category",category);
    requestDispatch(getServletConfig().getServletContext(),
                 req, resp, "showcatalog.jsp");
}
```

Now edit the showcatalog.jsp file and replace the scriptlet code that gets the category from the request parameter to get it from the session. The new code should look like:

```
int count = 0;
InventoryModel model=(InventoryModel) application.getAttribute("model");
String category = (String) session.getAttribute("category");
Vector invItems = (Vector) model.findByCategory(category);
StoreItem inv;
```

Modify the JSP expression used in the heading to get the category from the session:

```
<H1><%=session.getAttribute("category")%></H1>
```

Make sure the JSP is enabled for HTTP session use. Go to the Design view and bring up the **Page Properties**. On the **JSP Tags** tab, select the existing import page directive we created earlier, and click the **Edit** button. This will bring up the JSP page directive panel.

Check the **Create Session Variable** checkbox and click **OK**. Every JSP page that needs access to the Session object will need the session attribute checked in the page directive. Without it, there will be compilation errors using the session "implicit object".

The application should now be functioning as it did before, but using the session attributes to retrieve the category instead of using the request parameters.

Adding the Shopping Cart

The shopping cart support needs a cart model to represent the proposed purchase, an updated StoreItem for additional descriptive information such as total cost, a detail page that allows product items to be purchased, and a shopping cart display page. We'll start with the StoreItem updates since the rest of the code will depend on that.

Open the StoreItem bean in the Java editor, and add a getCost() method which calculates the cost based on price and quantity:

```
public float getCost() {
  return price * quantity;
}
```

Next, we'll create the product detail JSP page. It is a fairly complex JSP page that will look like this:

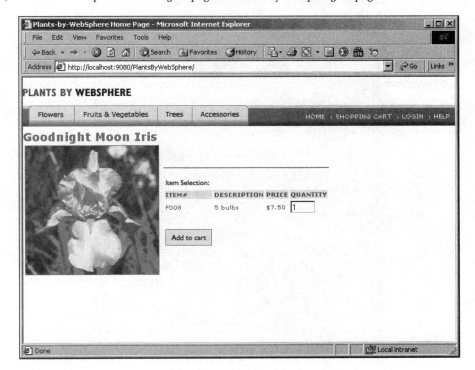

It consists of several nested tables as well as an HTML form. The HTML form will cause an HTTP POST request to be generated to the servlet controller. This differs from the HTTP GET requests that have been used so far. It also validates the choice made earlier in using a common performTask() method in the servlet controller. The next set of steps will describe how to create the complex layout as well as embed a form into the display page using WebSphere Studio.

Ensure the Web perspective is selected, then create a new JSP file called product.jsp with the New JSP file wizard. Click Next twice to get to the Page Directive Information panel of the wizard. Click the Import Package button to add a package to import. This will add a java.lang.* in the Imports box. Edit this value to be com.ibm.pbw.war.*. Make the session available to the JSP by checking the Create Session Variable checkbox:

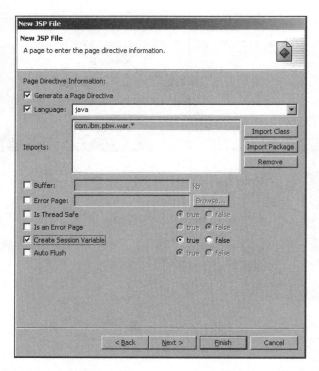

Hit **Finish** to create the file then remove the default text from the page.

Add a scriptlet to the page to access the inventory model and retrieve the item to display (**JSP** | **Insert Scriptlet**). Enter the following scriptlet code in the Attributes view:

```
String id = request.getParameter("id");
InventoryModel model = (InventoryModel) application.getAttribute("model");
StoreItem item = model.findById(id);
```

This allows the `id`, `model`, and `item` variables to be used throughout the JSP page.

Now add a new paragraph heading to display the product name using a JSP expression. Choose **Insert** | **Paragraph** | **Heading 1**, then **JSP** | **Insert Expression**. Enter the following for the expression attributes:

```
item.getName()
```

We'll now create the nested table structure around which most of the product information is based. Start with adding the outer table to the page. Place the insertion point below the heading and **Insert** | **Table**. Set the table size to 1x2 and click **OK**. Set the table border to 0.

Place a temporary image in the first cell (**Insert** | **Image File** | **From File**). Choose one of the existing flower images from the `images` directory. This will be replaced later with an expression to evaluate the proper image to use.

Embed a 3x1 table in the right-most cell (Choose Insert | Table. Set the table size to 3x1 and click OK. Set the table border to 0).

We'll put the item description in the top cell of this newly inserted sub-table. So select the top cell, and choose JSP | Insert Expression. Enter the following in the expression Attributes view:

```
item.getDescr()
```

Put a horizontal line in the second cell. Select the middle-table cell, and then choose Insert | Horizontal Rule.

The bottom cell is where the form will be handled. Select the bottom cell and choose Insert | Form and Input Fields | Form. In the Form Attributes view, set the Method to Post. Set the Action, using the browse (...) | Servlet button, to the ShoppingControllerServlet URL:

```
/PlantsbyWebSphere/ShoppingControllerServlet
```

Switch to the Hidden Fields tab and add the action and id hidden fields and values as shown here:

These will be passed to the servlet controller for operating on the model. In this case, the shopping cart model.

Place the insert point in the form in the lower-right cell. Insert a 5x4 table into the form to display the details of the item. Set the border to 0. Your JSP page design should now be looking something like this:

If you haven't already, import the `item_selection.jpg` and `button_add_to_cart.gif` images into the `images` directory.

Insert the `item_selection.jpg` image in the first cell of the first row of the new table.

Select the first cell of the second row. Enter the text "ITEM#" in the cell. Repeat in the second through fourth cells of that row using "DESCRIPTION", "PRICE", and "QUANTITY" respectively. Select all four cells and check the **Header** radio button in the Cell Attributes view. Set the row's color to #eeeecc in the Row Attributes view.

Use the HTML/JSP editor's Source view to add a `class="item"` attribute to each of the `<TH>` elements on this row. This defines the stylesheet style to use for the headings. The source should look like the following:

```
<TR bgcolor="#EEEECC">
    <TH class="item">ITEM#</TH>
    <TH class="item">DESCRIPTION</TH>
    <TH class="item">PRICE</TH>
    <TH class="item">QUANTITY</TH>
</TR>
```

Of course don't forget to make sure the stylesheet has been added to this page, using one of the methods described earlier, or setting the `class` attribute won't have much effect.

Use the Source view to insert the following JSP expressions one in each cell of the third row to display the item specifics (we could use the Design view as shown previously but this is quicker). Add `class="item"` attributes using the Source view to each `<TD>` element of the row. Set the row color to `#ffffdd`:

```
<TR bgcolor="#ffffdd">
    <TD class="item"><%=item.getId()%></TH>
    <TD class="item"><%=item.getPkgInfo%>()</TH>
    <TD class="item"><%=java.text.NumberFormat.getCurrencyInstance(
        java.util.Locale.US).format(new Float(item.getPrice()))%></TH>
    <TD class="item"></TH>
</TR>
```

The complicated bit of number formatting is simply to take the float price value and display it as a currency value.

We need to be able to specify a quantity in the detail description that can be used as input for adding a number of items to the shopping cart. Insert a text input field into the last element of the third row (**Insert | Form and Input Fields | Text Field**):

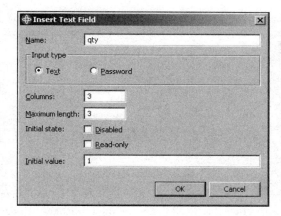

Set the **Name** to `qty`, **Input type** to Text, **Columns**, **Maximum length** to 3 and the **Initial value** to 1.

Insert a non-breaking space into the first cell of the fourth row (*Ctrl* plus the space bar). This preserves the height of the row.

Now we want to insert a form button (but using an image of our choosing). So select the first cell of the last row, then choose **Insert | Form and Input Fields | Image Button**. This will bring up an Insert Image Button panel:

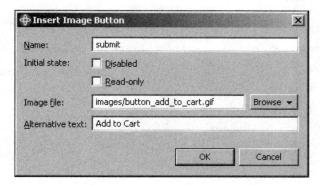

Enter `submit` as the **Name**, and select the `button_add_to_cart.gif` image for the **Image file**. Enter the **Alternative text** and click **OK**.

Now we want to replace the temporary main product image that we added earlier to be dynamically selected. Select the image in the source view. Replace the filename of the image with a JSP expression that looks like the following:

```
<TR>
    <TD><IMG border="0"
            src="/PlantsByWebSphere/images/<%=item.getImageLocation()%> "
            width="220" height="220">
    </TD>
```

161

Make sure to save the changes, and our JSP page design should now look like this:

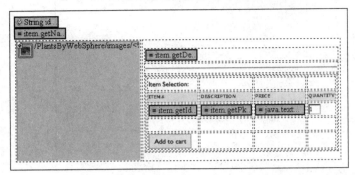

The catalog page and servlet controller need to be modified to make the page available. The catalog page needs a new action to tell the controller to display product details. The controller needs to interpret the new action and redirect the request to the product page.

Open up `showcatalog.jsp` in the HTML/JSP editor. Select the image in the cell and use the pop-up menu to select **Insert | Link**. This will display the Insert Link panel. Select the **File** radio button. Click the **Browse** button and select **Servlet**. Choose the `ShoppingControllerServlet`. Add the following to the `ShoppingControllerServlet` URL:

```
?action=showproduct&id=<%= inv.getId()%>
```

This will tell the servlet controller to display product information for the specified ID.

Repeat for the `getName()` JSP expression below the image and save the changes.

Now we need to edit the `ShoppingControllerServlet` to respond to this new action request. Add the following action processing code to the `performTask()` method:

```
    } else if (action.equals("showproduct")) {
      requestDispatch(getServletConfig().getServletContext(),
                      req, resp, "product.jsp");
    }
```

It's time to create the shopping cart model JavaBean and the page to display it.

Create a JavaBean called `CartModel` in the same package as the `InventoryModel` that looks like the following. It will eventually be replaced with EJB access code. Be sure to fix up the necessary imports:

```
package com.ibm.pbw.war;

import java.util.Vector;

public class CartModel {

  private Vector orderItems = new Vector();

  public void addItem(StoreItem si) {
    orderItems.add(si);
```

```
  }

  public Vector getItems() {
    return (Vector) orderItems.clone();
  }
}
```

Edit the `ShoppingControllerServlet` source. Add this code that recognizes the action command of the `product.jsp` and updates the shopping cart model in the `peformTask()` method:

```
} else if (action.equals("addtocart")) {
  HttpSession session = req.getSession();
  CartModel cart = (CartModel) session.getAttribute("cart");

  if (cart == null ) cart = new CartModel();
  String id = req.getParameter("id");
  StoreItem si = model.findById(id);
  si.setQuantity(Integer.parseInt(req.getParameter("qty").trim()));

  cart.addItem(si);

  session.setAttribute("cart", cart);

  requestDispatch(getServletConfig().getServletContext(),
                  req, resp, "cart.jsp");
}
```

The above code retrieves the model from the application-scoped context. It then retrieves an existing cart model instance from the session scope or creates a new one. A `StoreItem` is created, which represents the item to be bought and its quantity is set to the number specified on the product form. The controller then updates the cart model and the state of the cart is kept in the session for future reference. Finally, the request is dispatched to the cart screen to display the current contents. The cart screen is going to look like this:

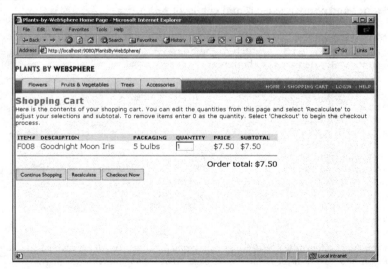

It consists of some static text and a dynamic table similar to the dynamic table created in the catalog view. The dynamic table displays the items in the shopping cart and their current quantity. The quantity can be updated.

Create a new JSP page called `cart.jsp` using the New JSP File wizard that we saw earlier, making sure to support sessions.

Add an new H1 heading for the "Shopping Cart" text (Insert | Paragraph | Heading1) and then a normal paragraph for the rest of the introductory text, as can be seen in the previous screenshot.

Apply our `PlantMaster.css` stylesheet to the page by dragging-and-dropping it from the Navigator view onto our editor. This will update the text we just entered to use the stylesheet.

Add a JSP scriptlet (JSP | Insert Scriptlet) to retrieve the cart model from the session using this code:

```
CartModel cart = (CartModel) session.getAttribute("cart");
```

Now add a form (Insert | Form and Input Fields | Form) to handle quantity updates to the cart. Set the Action to be the `ShoppingControllerServlet` and Method to be Post. Add a hidden field with the Name `action` and Value of `updatecart`. We'll update `ShoppingControllerServlet` later to handle this action.

Add a 4x8 table to the form to display the order items (set the border and cell spacing to 0, and the table width to 75%). This table will work in a similar fashion to the dynamic catalog table created earlier. The data displayed is similar to the product detail information page created earlier, with a row per item in the cart.

On the top row of the table, insert the `1x1_trans.gif` image into the first and eighth cells. Then for the second through to seventh cells, add the header text: "ITEM#", "DESCRIPTION", "PACKAGING", "QUANTITY", "PRICE", "SUBTOTAL", respectively. Select the text in these six cells and change the Cell type to Header and apply a background colour of #eeeecc.

We want the second row of the table to be dynamically generated and populated with data for `StoreItems`. To do this we need to switch to the Source view and enter the following scriptlet between the first and second <TR> elements of the table:

```
</TR>
<%
  Vector items = cart.getItems();
  Iterator it = items.iterator()
  float total = 0.0f;
  while (it.hasNext()) {
    StoreItem si = (StoreItem) it.next();
    if (si.getQuantity() > 0) {
      float subtotal = si.getPrice() * si.getQuantity();
      total = total + subtotal; %>
      <TR>
```

You'll probabaly get a warning about the Vector *and* Iterator *objects not being resolved. To correct this you need to add them to the import page directive statement for the page.*

This code will iterate through the items in the `CartModel` and set up a StoreItem bean that we can use to populate the table. Of course we need to close the `if` and `while` statements after the table row:

```
    </TR>
  <% }
} %>
```

Now we can modify the cells using JSP expressions. Note that the quantity field should be updatable so use a text field. You can either edit the source or use the Design view. Either way the source should end up looking like this:

```
<TR>
  <TD></TD>
  <TD><%=si.getId()%></TD>
  <TD><%=si.getName()%></TD>
  <TD><%=si.getPkgInfo()%></TD>
  <TD><INPUT type="text" name="<%=si.getId()%>" size="3"
            maxlength="3" value="<%=si.getQuantity()%>"></TD>
  <TD>$<%=java.text.NumberFormat.getCurrencyInstance(
          java.util.Locale.US).format(new Float(si.getPrice()))%></TD>
  <TD>$<%=java.text.NumberFormat.getCurrencyInstance(
          java.util.Locale.US).format(new Float(subtotal))%></TD>
  <TD></TD>
</TR>
```

For the third row of the table we want to insert a horizontal rule. However, we can only insert a rule in one cell but we want it to span the table. To do this we need to join the cells. Select the second through seventh cells and from the pop-up menu choose **Table | Join Selected Cells**. Now we can insert the horiztonal rule (**Insert | Horizontal Rule**).

In the the last row of the table we just want to display the order total:

```
<TR>
  <TD></TD>
  <TD align="right"><B>Order total: $<%=total%></B></TD>
  <TD></TD>
</TR>
```

Now we need to add a second table below the first for the three image buttons. Make sure you add this new 3x1 table within the form (if need be just edit the source to move the `</FORM>` tag to after your new table. Set the border and cell spacing to 0.

In the first cell insert the `button_continue_shopping.gif` image. This button will just be a link (unlike the other two in this table, which are input controls) so right-click to insert a link back to the catalog page:

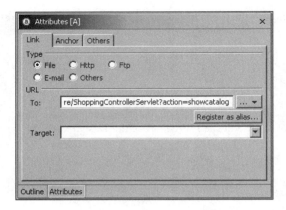

The link should use an `action` of `showcatalog`, but it should not include a category. This will force the previous category to be used.

For the second cell in the table, insert a form Image Button and set the image to `button_recalculate.gif`.

The third cell needs to move the user to the checkout page so insert an image (`button_checkout_now.gif`) and insert a link to `ShoppingServletController` with an `action` of `checkout`:

```
?action=checkout
```

By this point the design of the page should resemble something like this:

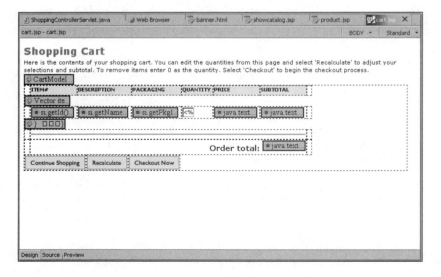

Now we need to update the `ShoppingControllerServlet` with the action handler code for `updatecart`:

```
} else if (action.equals("updatecart")) {
  HttpSession session = req.getSession();
  CartModel cart = (CartModel) session.getAttribute("cart");
  if (cart == null ) cart = new CartModel();

  // Iterate through cart items and update their quantities based
  // on the form fields
  Vector items = cart.getItems();
  Iterator it = items.iterator();
  while (it.hasNext()) {
    StoreItem si = (StoreItem)it.next();
    String idName=si.getId();
    String qtyString=req.getParameter(idName);
    if (qtyString != null) {
      si.setQuantity(Integer.parseInt(qtyString.trim()));
    }
  }
  session.setAttribute("cart",cart);

  requestDispatch(getServletConfig().getServletContext(),
              req, resp, "cart.jsp");
}
```

For completeness, edit `banner.html` and add a similar link for the "SHOPPING CART" text in the banner menu, but set the action to `updatecart`. Be sure to set the target to the `work` frame:

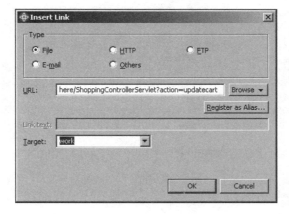

Make a similar link for the "HOME" text in `banner.html`, but set the action to `salesitems`.

Now update `ShoppingControllerServlet` to display `salesitems.jsp` when the `salesitems` action is received:

```
} else if (action.equals("salesitems")) {
  requestDispatch(getServletConfig().getServletContext(),
              req, resp, "salesitems.jsp");
}
```

Save all the changes. At this point you can run the application on a server and test the shopping cart functionality.

Completing the Order Processing

Up to this point, the application has been dealing with local state management or read-only data access. The inventory model is a read-only static set of data, and the cart model is local to the HTTP session. In order to complete the order, we are going to need some information about the individual placing the order and a means of managing placed orders (something more than keeping a shopping cart in the HTTP session).

To do this, we'll create an abstraction using a customer model to represent a collection of customer information and a order model to represent a collection of orders that have been placed. These will be tied to persistent back-end data systems in Chapter 5.

To start, create a bean class to represent the user information that looks like the following (note that it implements `Serializable`):

```
package com.ibm.pbw.war;

import java.io.Serializable;

public class CustomerInfo implements Serializable {
   private String firstName;
   private String lastName;
   private String addr1;
   private String addr2;
   private String city;
   private String state;
   private String zipcode;
   private String phone;
   private String email;
}
```

Use WebSphere Studio's getter/setter generation capabilities (Source | Generate Getters and Setters) to create public getter and setter methods for all of the private data members.

We'll also add another utitlty getter method to facilitate getting a customer's name

```
public String getName() {
   return firstName + " " + lastName;
}
```

Create a customer model that manages the set of customer info beans that looks like the following:

```
package com.ibm.pbw.war;

import java.util.Hashtable;

public class CustomerModel {
   private Hashtable customers = new Hashtable();

   public void addCustomer(CustomerInfo info) {
```

```
      customers.put(info.getEmail(), info);
  }

  public CustomerInfo getCustomer(String emailKey) {
    return (CustomerInfo) customers.get(emailKey);
  }
}
```

Now create the order model abstraction with a class that looks like the following:

```
package com.ibm.pbw.war;

import java.util.Vector;

public class OrderModel {

  public String addOrder(CustomerInfo info, Vector orderItems) {
    return "123";
  }
}
```

Note that the addOrder() method doesn't really do anything at the moment. This will be remedied in Chapter 5 and Chapter 7 when we examine persistence and access to Enterprise Information Systems.

Create a checkout.jsp file that contains a form for collecting the user information required by the UserInfo bean class. It should look like:

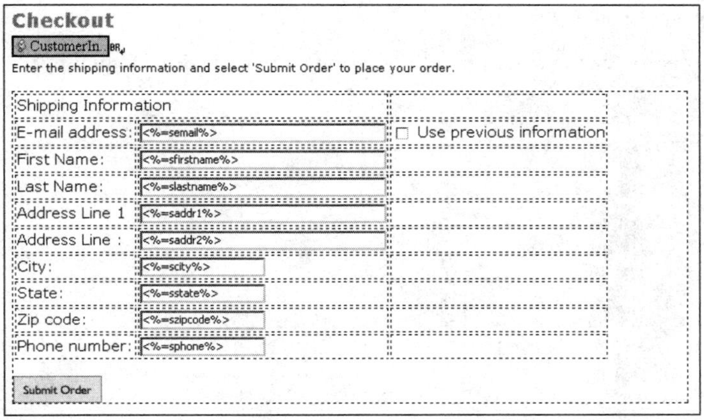

By now you should have a pretty good idea of how to go about creating the above page. If you're not sure then you can look up the code that comes with this book. The non-obvious information that you need to know is that the scriptlet at the beginning is used to set up the field initialization using the following code:

```
CustomerInfo cinfo = (CustomerInfo)session.getAttribute("cinfo");

String semail = "";
String sfirstname = "";
String slastname = "";
String saddr1 = "";
String saddr2 = "";
```

```
    String scity = "";
    String sstate = "";
    String szipcode = "";
    String sphone = "";

    if (cinfo != null) {
      semail = cinfo.getEmail();
      sfirstname = cinfo.getFirstName();
      slastname = cinfo.getLastName();
      saddr1 = cinfo.getAddr1();
      saddr2 = cinfo.getAddr2();
      scity = cinfo.getCity();
      sstate = cinfo.getState();
      szipcode = cinfo.getZipcode();
      sphone = cinfo.getPhone();
    }
```

The input fields are called semail, sname, saddr1, saddr2, scity, sstate, szipcode, and sphone and take their initial values from the Strings set up in the scriptlet; the checkbox field is called useprevious and its value is true; the submit order image button uses the button_submit_order.gif image; and the form has two hidden fields of name action and value submitorder.

To complete the checkout processing, ShoppingControllerServlet needs a checkout action to initiate the checkout processing and display the checkout JSP page. It also needs a submitorder action to submit the order for processing.

Add the following code for the action handling to the performTask() method:

```
    } else if (action.equals("checkout")) {
      requestDispatch(getServletConfig().getServletContext(),
                      req, resp, "checkout.jsp");

    } else if (action.equals("submitorder")) {
      CustomerInfo cinfo;
      HttpSession session = req.getSession();

      String semail = req.getParameter("semail");
      String suseprev = req.getParameter("useprevious");

      if (suseprev != null && suseprev.equals("true")) {
        cinfo = custmodel.getCustomer(semail);
        session.setAttribute("cinfo", cinfo);
        requestDispatch(getServletConfig().getServletContext(),
                        req, resp, "checkout.jsp");
      } else {
        String sfirstname = req.getParameter("sfirstname");
        String slastname = req.getParameter("slastname");
        String saddr1 = req.getParameter("saddr1");
        String saddr2 = req.getParameter("saddr2");
        String scity = req.getParameter("scity");
        String sstate = req.getParameter("sstate");
        String szipcode = req.getParameter("szipcode");
        String sphone = req.getParameter("sphone");
```

```
        cinfo = new CustomerInfo();
        cinfo.setFirstName(sfirstname);
        cinfo.setLastName(slastname);
        cinfo.setAddr1(saddr1);
        cinfo.setAddr2(saddr2);
        cinfo.setCity(scity);
        cinfo.setState(sstate);
        cinfo.setZip(szipcode);
        cinfo.setEmail(semail);
        cinfo.setPhone(sphone);

        custmodel.addCustomer(cinfo);
        session.setAttribute("cinfo", cinfo);

        CartModel cart = (CartModel) session.getAttribute("cart");
        String orderId = ordermodel.addOrder(cinfo, cart.getItems());
        session.setAttribute("orderID", orderId);

        if (orderId != null) {
            session.setAttribute("cart", null);
            requestDispatch(getServletConfig().getServletContext(),
                        req, resp, "orderdone.jsp");
        }
    }
}
```

Note that the request parameter names must match the checkout JSP form field names. In addition, private data members for CustomerModel custmodel and OrderModel ordermodel will need to be added to ShoppingControllerServlet and initialized in the init() method:

```
public class ShoppingControllerServlet extends HttpServlet {

    private InventoryModel model;
    private CustomerModel custmodel;
    private OrderModel ordermodel;

    public void init() throws ServletException {
      model = new InventoryModel();
      getServletContext().setAttribute("model",model);
      custmodel = new CustomerModel();
      getServletContext().setAttribute("custmodel",custmodel);
      ordermodel = new OrderModel();
    }
```

The CustomerModel is also added to the application-level context so that other JSP views can access customer information as necessary.

Lastly, create the orderdone.jsp to display the order ID. The JSP should look like the following:

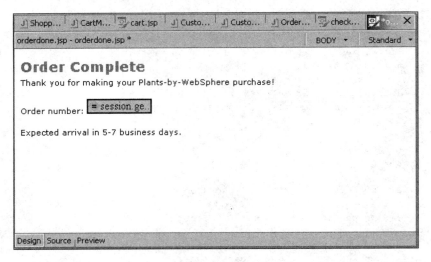

The JSP expression displays the order number picked up from the session. The expression code fragment should be: session.getAttribute("orderId").

Securing the Application

Securing the application is a topic in itself, and is covered thoroughly in Chapter 13. J2EE uses a declarative security model and provides several ways to authenticate (login) a user and check authorization. WebSphere Studio has wizards to simplify the creation of form-based login screens using JSP pages. WebSphere Application Server provides a configurable user registry that contains the set of users that can login and the role privileges that are granted to that user. Resources can be protected using role-based security declarations in the deployment descriptors. The container runtime matches the authenticated user's roles with the declared roles to determine whether or not a user is authorized to access a resource or perform an operation.

For the most part, this J2EE security functionality is sufficient for most applications. One drawback to this model, though, is that it is not completely specified. For example, user registry access is completely unspecified. Any application that needs to directly access or manipulate the user registry must either use a Roll Your Own (RYO) security strategy or use proprietary APIs specific to a vendor to manipulate the user registry. The Plants-By-WebSphere application has chosen to use a RYO strategy.

You'll notice that in our implementation of the presentation layer for Plants-By-WebSphere, we haven't yet touched on registering a customer. We created a Customer model as part of the checkout process but ideally we would want to persist this information to allow the customer to login whenever they return to the site. However, this implementation requires us to configure the security for the application, and as such this functionality will be revisited in Chapter 13.

WebSphere Application Server Extensions

WebSphere Application Server provides a number of extensions to the programming model and administrative model. The extensions that affect the programming model are discussed here. Other administrative model extensions are discussed in Chapter 14.

Extension Packages

WebSphere Application Server provides the following presentation-related APIs in the base application server.

- ❏ `com.ibm.websphere.servlet.session.IBMSession` interface
  Extends `HttpSession`, for session support and increased web administrator's control in a session cluster environment.

- ❏ `com.ibm.websphere.servlet.filter` package
  Provides classes that support the servlet filter object.

- ❏ `com.ibm.servlet.personalization.sessiontracking` package
  Records the referral page that led a visitor to your web site, tracks the visitor's position within the site, associates user identification with the session, and provides session clustering support.

- ❏ `com.ibm.servlet.personalization.userprofile` package
  Provides an interface for maintaining detailed information about your web visitors and incorporating this data in your web applications, so that you can provide a personalized user experience. You can make this information persistent by storing it in a database.

- ❏ `com.ibm.websphere.userprofile` package
  Enhances the user profile.

See http://www.ibm.com/software/webservers/appserv/infocenter.html for a full description of the APIs.

HTTP Sessions

HTTP sessions and HTTP session state management are an extremely important part of web applications. The following sections explore the implications of session extensions to persistence, scalability, and security.

Session Cache

WebSphere Application Server provides cached management of `HttpSession` instances. In certain circumstances, such as exceeding the cache size, the session manager may not manage the session. Instead, a dummy session will be created. An application can check whether or not this has occurred by using the `IBMSession` interface `isOverFlow()` method. It returns `true` if the maximum in-memory session count is exceeded and overflow allowed has not been configured.

Session Persistence

Clustered environments, which need to share state, and failover capabilities all require the ability to persist the state of the session. WebSphere Application Server provides for persistent sessions, but all objects added to the session state must implement the `java.io.Serializable` interface if persistent session state is required. Session persistence also supports persisting the following non-serializable J2EE objects:

173

❑ `javax.ejb.EJBObject`
❑ `javax.ejb.EJBHome`
❑ `javax.naming.Context`
❑ `javax.transaction.UserTransaction`

However, `UserTransaction` objects in the runtime will not persist open transactions and re-establish them across servers. Also, any transaction must be started within the execution of the `service()` method and it must be completed before the `service()` method returns, otherwise the transaction will be rolled back.

Most of the time, the session manager will control when it is appropriate to save the session state. WebSphere Application Server provides a number of policies for controlling this. However, there's also a manual policy that allows the application to control when the session state is persisted. The application must use the `com.ibm.websphere.servlet.session.IBMSession` interface's `sync()` method to tell the runtime to persist the state.

One last consideration is the size of the session state. By default, persisting a session to a database will result in the entire state being serialized to a single row. If the state exceeds 2MB, then a single row cannot be used. WebSphere Application Server provides multi-row persistence capabilities, but not without some overhead cost. Using multi-row session state persistence allows each attribute to be up to 2MB in size and the total size to be unlimited. It also allows individual attributes to be retrieved on demand rather than the full state. Inter-object references should be kept to a minimum, because retrieval of the individual attributes will not reconstruct the object reference graph to the original graph. Each attribute of the session will have its own copy of each referenced object. Cyclic references will be broken causing duplication of objects in memory. One more multi-row persistence policy, Write contents, has an implication on the programming model. A choice can be made of Write changed attributes or Write all session attributes. Single row session persistence ignores these policies and persists everything, but the multi-row persistence honors them. When multi-row persistence is used in conjunction with Write changed attributes, the session manager will persist only those attributes that are placed/replaced in the session using the `session.setAttribute()` method. If an attribute is retrieved from the session and subsequently modified without calling `session.setAttribute()`, it will not be persisted to the session database. Be aware that the combination of large session states, large cache sizes, and long session timeouts can be a deadly combination for an application server. Note, sessions should always be invalidated when they are not needed anymore.

Session Security

WebSphere Application Server performs secure access checks for the session when security is turned on. When the session is created, the current user ID is associated with the session. On subsequent requests, a check of the request ID is made with the session's user ID. If they don't match, a `com.ibm.websphere.servlet.session.UnauthorizedSessionRequestException` is thrown. The session's user ID can be checked with the `com.ibm.websphere.servlet.session.IBMSession` interface.

Summary

In this chapter, we've touched on how to use a variety of aspects of WebSphere Studio Application Developer. This is by no means a complete introduction to the functionality, but it covers the basics of what most developers will run into when developing an application. We've also covered some of the design considerations to use when creating an application and the implications of the design decisions on the presentation. Lastly, we've covered WebSphere extensions related to the presentation. It's now time to consider how to build the business logic and persistence of an application.

5

Building the Business Logic with WebSphere Studio

Chapter 2 advanced the argument for a componentized approach in creating the elements that compose an application. Dividing these elements into the essential categories of presentation, business, and data logic promotes a modularity that can increase the flexibility of the distribution of the application elements; can facilitate independent development of different element categories by different people, departments, or organizations; and can additionally provide new opportunities for logic reuse.

Business logic, generally speaking, is the set of procedures or methods used to perform a specific business function. Applying an object-oriented approach enables the developer to decompose a business function into a set of logical elements or components called **business objects**. Like other objects, business objects have both state and behavior. For example, a customer object has data such as a customer ID, name, address, telephone number, and so on. It has methods for changing the address, or updating lifetime purchases in dollars. To manage a business problem you must be able to represent how such business objects function and interact to provide the desired functionality. The set of methods, business-specific rules, and pre- and post-conditions that must be met as an object exposes its function to the other objects in the system, are known collectively as **business logic**.

The J2EE architecture specifies a component model for each of the major tiers in the application landscape. In the previous chapter, we took a close look at the use of the web component model in building the presentation logic. In this chapter we will use the **Enterprise JavaBean (EJB)** component model to build up the business logic for our sample application, Plants-By-WebSphere.

The EJB component model is a good choice for building business logic for several reasons:

- ❑ **It includes stateless, stateful, and persistent models.**
  This means we have flexibility in choosing the component type that best fits our needs. Stateless EJBs are excellent for organizing into reusable packages business logic that maintains no state of its own. Stateful EJBs satisfy the need for business logic to hold state that is more or less temporary, valid for only minutes, hours, or days. Persistent EJBs are well-suited to model artifacts in the business domain that have state, are long-lived, and have associated business logic.

- ❑ **It is insulated from the presentation and logic tiers.**
  EJBs do not imply your choice for the other tiers in the computing models, increasing their flexibility. EJBs can be driven by presentation tiers on the same system as the EJBs themselves or on a different system. The stateful and persistent EJB models take many of the database programming issues out of the hands of the business logic developers, freeing them to focus on solving problems from their business domain.

- ❑ **It offers powerful declarative transaction and security policy.**
  These and other services are provided by the EJB container, further simplifying the task of creating reusable business components by removing the need for business logic developers to spend time building these capabilities into their components. Moreover, since these services are declarative, they can be adjusted for use in different applications without necessarily changing the component implementation. This further increases component flexibility and reusability.

In the remainder of this chapter, we will focus on using WebSphere Studio Application Developer to build and test the business logic for our Plants-By-WebSphere application. The task ahead of us is to understand the design requirements for the business logic of our application, implement that design using EJBs, and then integrate our EJBs with the web presentation logic that we created in Chapter 4.

Understanding the Design

The Plants-By-WebSphere application follows the Model-View-Controller pattern. In the previous chapter we built the view and controller portions of the application using JSP pages and servlets. There, we created a model façade using simple Java objects in order to create a layer of insulation between the presentation and business logic components. The EJBs we are about to build will "snap-in" to the model objects. The following diagram illustrates the relationship between these components:

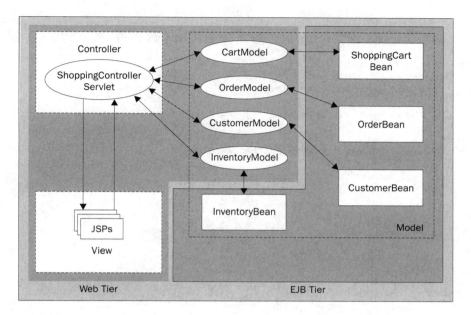

We will therefore create an EJB corresponding to each of the model objects. The model objects implement the following interfaces:

```java
/**
 * CartModel represents a simple shopping cart.
 **/
public interface CartModel {
  /**
   * add a StoreItem to the Shopping Cart
   */
  public void addItem(StoreItem si);

  /**
   * get the list of StoreItem in the Shopping Cart
   */
  public Vector getItems();
}
```

```java
/**
 * OrderModel represents an order placed by a customer.
 **/
public interface OrderModel {
  /**
   * Create an order for the list of StoreItems requested
   * by the specified customer. Return the order ID.
   */
  public String addOrder(CustomerInfo c, Vector orderItems);
}
```

```
/**
 * InventoryModel represents an item in the store's inventory.
 **/
public interface InventoryModel {
  /**
   * find all Inventory items in the specified category
   */
  public Collection findByCategory(String category);

  /**
   * find the Inventory item with the specified ID
   */
  public StoreItem findById(String id);
}
```

```
/**
 * CustomerModel represents a customer making an order through our system.
 **/
public interface CustomerModel {
  /**
   * Add a new customer
   */
  public void addCustomer(CustomerInfo i);

  /**
   * Retrieve an existing customer
   */
  public CustomerInfo getCustomer(String key);
}
```

We will build four primary EJBs:

- ShoppingCart
- Order
- Inventory
- Customer

ShoppingCart will contain temporary state while the customer shops, so we will implement that using a stateful session bean. Order, Inventory, and Customer have long-lived state that we will keep in a database, so we'll use entity beans for those. With entity beans we can either choose to let the EJB container manage our persistent state or we can implement it ourselves. These two persistence models are referred to as container-managed persistence and bean-managed persistence, or CMP and BMP, respectively. We will use CMP because the WebSphere tools and runtime will take care of most of the data logic for us. This built-in persistence support is powerful, but does have its limitations. Highly complex data mappings or certain EIS integration scenarios could force us to implement the data logic ourselves using the BMP persistence model, but that won't be necessary for this application.

Implementing the EJBs

To implement our business logic with EJBs using WebSphere Studio, we will take the following steps:

1. Create a new EJB Project
2. Create the `ShoppingCart` stateful session bean
3. Create the `Order` CMP entity bean
4. Create the subordinate `OrderItem` CMP entity bean
5. Create the utility `OrderIdGenerator` CMP entity bean
6. Create a container-managed-relationship (CMR) between `Order` and `OrderItem`
7. Create the `Inventory` CMP entity bean and define its customer finder methods
8. Create the `Customer` CMP entity bean
9. Create ancillary session beans required by future chapters
10. Map the CMP entity beans to a relational database
11. Specify J2EE references to EJBs and resources required by the EJBs
12. Integrate EJBs with web module model objects

Create a New EJB Project

To add an EJB project to our existing Plants-By-WebSphere application, select menu option **File | New | EJB Project**. This will take you to the first dialog in a series that will step you through EJB project creation. The first dialog window enables you to choose the specification level of your EJB project:

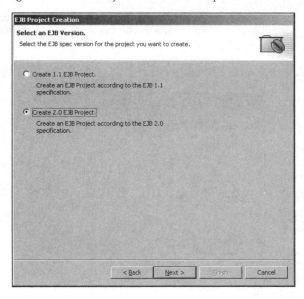

WebSphere Studio version 5.0 supports both the EJB 1.1 and 2.0 standards. We have to choose one now, so we'll choose to create a 2.0 EJB project, because we want to use the EJB 2.0 features such as CMR and EJB Query Language later on. Click Next to continue:

We'll need to name our EJB project, so enter PlantsByWebSphereEJB for the project name.

EJB project are part of an enterprise application project, so we can either create a new enterprise application or add it to an existing one. Since we already have our PlantsbyWebSphereEAR enterprise application, we'll add our EJB project to that.

Click the Finish button to create the EJB project:

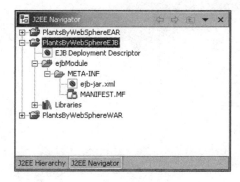

Create the ShoppingCart Bean

Now that we have our EJB project, we're ready to create our first EJB. Select menu option File | New | Enterprise Bean. This will take you to the first dialog in a series that will step you through enterprise bean creation. The first dialog window enables you to designate to which project this new enterprise bean will belong:

Choose the PlantsByWebSphereEJB. Click the Next button to continue. Next choose the type of 2.0 enterprise bean that we want to create. We can choose any of the available EJB 2.0 EJB types:

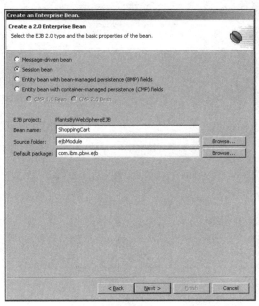

The message-driven Bean (MDB) type, introduced in EJB 2.0 is a new type of EJB that is assigned to a Java Message Service (JMS) message queue. When a message arrives on the queue, the MDB is dispatched to process the message. MDBs are useful for performing asynchronous processing. We won't use an MDB for this part of the Plants-By-WebSphere development. However, in Chapter 7, we will take you through the construction of an MDB.

Naturally, session and BMP entity beans are available choices. We will be using session beans in Plants-By-WebSphere. BMP beans, unlike CMP beans, manage their own persistence, which is necessary whenever the requirements for managing an entity's persistent state exceed the capabilities of available tooling. WebSphere Studio includes powerful relational mapping tools for building CMP entity beans, but it does not address every need. Non-relational data stores and complex mappings demand a BMP approach.

With a CMP entity bean, you have two choices: either CMP 1.1 or CMP 2.0 bean style. The component models of these two specification levels are dissimilar. The 1.1 style places the CMP fields directly in the bean itself and business logic may freely access them. The 2.0 style formalizes CMP field access by declaring the only access to them is through getters/setters, which are created through tooling. The generated code is a subclass of the bean itself. This pattern provides a more standardized structure for tools to add-in persistence support for CMP beans.

On the **Create an Enterprise Bean** dialog, select **Session bean**, specify the **Bean name** `ShoppingCart` and **Default package** `com.ibm.pbw.ejb`. Click **Next** to continue:

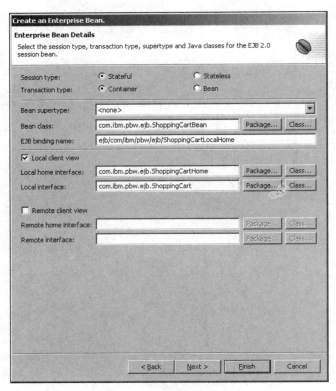

On the preceding dialog, we have a choice of **Stateful** or **Stateless** session bean. We're building a business object to represent a shopping cart. The shopping cart will hold items selected by the shopper either until the shopper checks out, or until the shopper changes their mind and leaves our electronic storefront. Our shopping cart obviously has state, so must be declared as stateful.

WebSphere offers two models for stateful session beans. The first model is strictly in-memory, meaning the session bean's state is maintained in the memory of the application server. The second model stores the session bean's state to the local file system in between transactions. The first model offers the best performance; the second model offers potentially longer availability session bean state, since it can survive across restarts of the application server. The selector for this choice is referred to as **Activation Policy**. This is an assembly-time decision and is discussed in the Chapter 6.

This dialog also gives us the choice of local or remote interfaces for our session bean. We could have either or both. As you would expect, declaring a remote interface enables our session bean to be accessed from another process or machine. A local interface may be accessed only from *within* the application server. While offering more limited access, the local interface offers an important performance advantage. Methods on remote interfaces must support a costly pass-by-value semantic for parameters and return values. Obviously this is necessary if the caller is in another process or machine. However, the EJB specification requires this same behavior for remote interfaces even when the caller is co-located in the same process as the target remote interface. This was a significant barrier for EJB 1.1 beans and discouraged the creation of finer-grained objects due to performance concerns. Local interface methods use simple Java by-value parameter and return value semantics and provide much better performance.

We will specify only a local interface for our `ShoppingCart` session bean. When you choose only a local interface, you are making a design decision that affects the distribution capability of your components. In our case, since the Plants-By-WebSphere web components will interact with our EJBs through the local Java model objects, we are constraining our web and EJB components to be co-located in the same application server. That is acceptable for our purposes. Depending on your application architecture, that may or may not be acceptable. A natural way to remove that constraint is by providing a remote interface to your EJB.

OK, that was a bit of a side trip! The remainder of the work for us to do on this dialog is to specify the names of our EJB artifacts: bean class, its local interface, and the local home interface. You'll notice that WebSphere Studio suggests names that include the word "Local" as part of the artifact name, since we indicated we want a local client view. However, we'll modify these names to be `ShoppingCartBean`, `ShoppingCart`, and `ShoppingCartHome`, respectively, since we don't have a remote client view and therefore don't need the "Local" qualification for our names. Note that the default JNDI lookup name is formed from the fully qualified home interface name. Click the Finish button to move on.

At this point, let's switch our view from the J2EE Navigator to the J2EE Hierarchy. This view more clearly shows the organization of our components in their containing modules, which is consistent with packaging terminology described in the EJB specification. By expanding our `ShoppingCart` EJB, we can see its constituent parts: local home interface, local interface, and the bean itself. Double-click on the `ShoppingCart` bean to open the EJB Deployment Descriptor editor. We will do more work with the deployment descriptor further on, for now let's just modify the JNDI name for our `ShoppingCart`. In our application we will use a simple two-part naming convention: `plantsby/<home interface name>`. So enter `plantsby/ShoppingCartHome`:

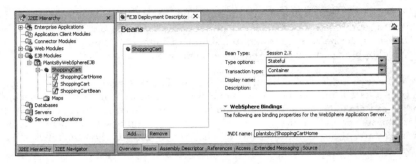

Implement the Business Methods

Now that we've created the basic parts that compose our ShoppingCart stateful session bean, let's add in our business methods. Business methods, as the name suggests, are those methods that provide client access to the business logic encapsulated in the bean. Business methods may provide varied degrees of functionality; for instance, methods that:

❑   Enable a client to manipulate the state of the EJB; such as adding an item to a shopping cart.

❑   Perform transformations against the state of the EJB; such as calculating a purchase total based on the items in the shopping cart.

❑   Apply business rules to the EJB, possibly involving interaction with other EJBs. For example, although not a part of our design, implementing a business rule that requires maintaining a statistic of the 10 most frequently selected shopping items.

Methods declared on any of the remote home, local home, remote interface, or local interface constitute the public client interface to the EJB. Methods declared on any of these interfaces require an implementation in the EJB's bean class. While you probably already know this, it may be helpful to visualize these relationships before diving into the code. The following diagram depicts how the interfaces and bean class relate to one another:

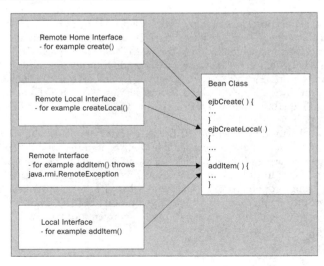

Each interface pair: remote and local home interface, and remote and local interface, may declare the same or different methods. As depicted in the preceding diagram, uniquely named interface methods, such as `create()`, and `createLocal()` on the remote and local home interfaces, respectively, map to correspondingly unique implementation methods in the bean class. However, if the same method is declared on both interfaces of an interface pair, such as `addItem()` on the remote and local interfaces, then both method instances map to the same named implementation method in the bean class.

In the case of our `ShoppingCart`, we have no methods on our local home, and only the `addItem()` and `getItems()` methods for our local interface. These were the ones introduced on the `CartModel`, as described earlier in this chapter. To add our methods, we'll need a code editor. We'll do the local interface first. From the J2EE Hierarchy view, double-click the `ShoppingCart` local interface to open a code window:

Next, add the method signatures for `addItem()` and `getItem()`:

```
public interface ShoppingCart extends javax.ejb.EJBLocalObject {

    public void addItem(StoreItem si);
    public Vector getItems();
}
```

We'll also need the `import` statements necessary to resolve the types we reference. Add an `import` for `java.util.Vector`. We also need to resolve the reference to `StoreItem`, but this class presents a new challenge.

com.ibm.war.StoreItem and com.ibm.war.CustomerInfo

`StoreItem` is a simple helper object that represents a simple, non-persistent view of a single inventory item in our Plants-By-WebSphere store. `CustomerInfo` provides the same function for customers. They were introduced in the presentation logic back in Chapter 4 as part of the model layer so there would be insulation between the presentation and business logic, enabling the two to be developed independently of one another. These two helper classes end up being shared between J2EE modules – between our web and EJB modules.

Since we introduced these helper classes in our web module, we now have a visibility problem between our web and EJB modules. We expected our web module to reference our EJB module, but not the other way around. This would create a circular dependency, which detracts from our ability to use business logic in another application – an application with a different presentation, for instance. This dependency would force us to drag our web module along with our EJB module as its shadow. This is not something we want to have happen. We'll fix this now by moving `StoreItem` and `CustomerInfo` from the web module to our EJB module. We will also change the package name from `com.ibm.pbw.war` to `com.ibm.pbw.ejb` to be consistent with the packaging rules we've been applying thus far in our Plants-By-WebSphere development.

Relocating `StoreItem` and `CustomerInfo` from the `PlantsbyWebSphereWAR` module to the `PlantsbyWebSphereEJB` module will leave behind a number of unresolved references in the presentation logic's servlet and JSP pages that simply adding `import` statements alone will not satisfy. To establish visibility between these two modules, we must update `PlantsbyWebSphereWAR` project properties.

To update project properties, select the project in the J2EE Hierarchy, right-click, then select **Properties** from the pop-up menu. This will bring up a dialog that contains options for a number of project-related options. Among the more interesting ones are:

OK then, to fix our `StoreItem` and `CustomerInfo` visibility problem, we need to update the Java Build path. Select **Java Build Path** on the left, and the **Projects** tab on the right. A list of available projects is displayed. At this point, we only have two: the EJB project we're working on, and our web module project. Check the **PlantsByWebSphereEJB** checkbox to add that project to our build path. Click **OK** to save and continue:

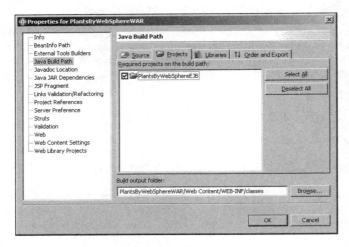

Then to move the two model classes, in the J2EE Navigator view simply select `com.ibm.pbw.war.StoreItem` and `com.ibm.pbw.war.CustomerInfo` from under the **Java source** folder and drag-and-drop them into the `com.ibm.pbw.ejb` folder of the `PlantsByWebSphereEJB` project. Studio can automatically correct all the references on your behalf:

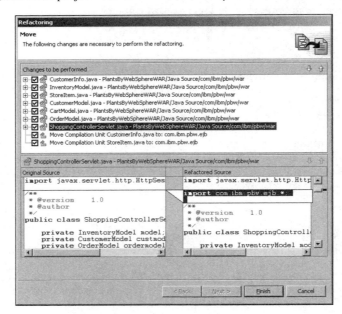

You will also need to update the JSP files manually to change any references to `StoreItem` or `CustomerInfo` to be fully qualified with their new package structure. For example, on `product.jsp`:

```
com.ibm.pbw.ejb.StoreItem item = model.findById(id);
```

With our build problems solved, we can get back to our `ShoppingCart` EJB and implement the bean methods.

In the J2EE Hierarchy view, find and double-click `ShoppingCartBean` to open the bean class in a code window. A good way to get started with in the bean class is to cut and paste the imports and method signatures from the local interface.

Since the local interface methods operate on a vector – `addItems()` adds to it; `getItems()` returns it – let's define a local instance variable of type `Vector` to satisfy that need.

The items variable requires initialization. Nothing special, let's just assign a new `Vector` instance to the variable in the `ShoppingCartBean` `ejbCreate()` method, since that will receive control each time a new `ShoppingCart` bean is created:

```java
package com.ibm.pbw.ejb;

import java.util.Vector;

public class ShoppingCartBean implements javax.ejb.SessionBean {

   private Vector items = null;

   public void ejbCreate() throws CreateException {
      items = new Vector();
   }
```

To finish out our work on this bean, we need to add the implementations for `addItem()` and `getItem()`. For `addItem()`, we'll add some simple logic to ensure that if the caller attempts to add the same item to the `ShoppingCart` more than once, that we detect the duplicate and merely update the quantity in case it is different. The `getItem()` method is trivial, as it merely returns the `items` vector:

```java
/**
 * Add an item to the cart.
 *
 * @param new_item Item to add to the cart.
 */
public void addItem(StoreItem new_item) {
   boolean added = false;
   StoreItem old_item;

   // If the same item is already in the cart, just increase the quantity.
   for (int i = 0; i < items.size(); i++) {
      old_item = (StoreItem) items.elementAt(i);
      if (new_item.equals(old_item)) {
         old_item.setQuantity(old_item.getQuantity() + new_item.getQuantity());
```

```
        added = true;
        break;
      }
    }
    // Add this item to shopping cart, if it is a brand new item.
   if (! added)
     items.addElement(new_item);
  }

  /**
   * Get the items in the shopping cart.
   *
   * @return A Vector of StoreItems.
   */
  public Vector getItems() {
    return items;
  }
```

Create the Order EJB

The `OrderModel` contains only a single method:

```
public class OrderModel {

  public String addOrder(CustomerInfo info, Vector orderItems) {
    return "123";
  }
}
```

Since an order is actually a collection of order items (the things *being* ordered) and some additional information about the order itself, such as name/address of customer and shipping name/address, we'll have to design a scheme for handling the list of items contained in the order. When we only had EJB 1.1, we might have done something like represent the item list as a serializable object and would have mapped it to a BLOB field in the database. While that approach would work, it makes it difficult to fully exploit the strengths of the database, with regard to queries over the order items.

The EJB 2.0 specification offers additional capabilities that are useful for modeling master-detail type business abstractions, such as order-orderItem. Container-managed-relationships (CMR) and EJB query language (EJB QL) are two EJB 2.0 features that are helpful in these cases. We will use both of these before we are finished with the `Order` EJB.

So while building our `Order` EJB, we'll create an additional CMP EJB, which we'll call `OrderItem`, to model the detail portion of the `Order` abstraction. Entity beans are key-referenced persistent objects. We'll need a way to generate key values for our `Order` EJB. Order numbers are not user-assigned; they are generated as part of the application. For our purposes, we'll define a simple `OrderIdGenerator` EJB, which will also be a CMP EJB. This will provide a simple way to manage a persistent "next order ID" value. The following diagram depicts the relationship of our `Order` EJB and the other EJBs that support it:

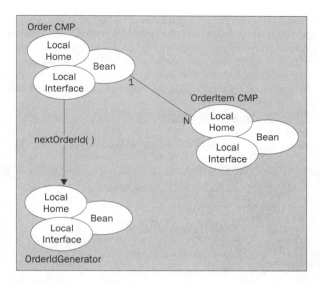

We'll start by creating the Order EJB itself. Select menu option File | New | Enterprise Bean to bring up the Create an Enterprise Bean dialog again. This time we'll create a 2.0 CMP entity bean, and name it Order:

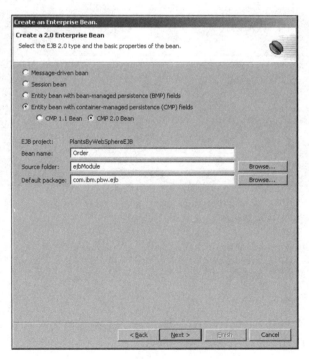

Click **Next** to continue. For the same reason we outlined for `ShoppingCart`, we'll define only local interfaces for our `Order` CMP bean. We could always add a remote interface to our `Order` implementation if requirements demanded such a thing in the future. For now, we'll stick with local. Again, let's remove the term "`Local`" from the default names that WSAD generates for us automatically. In keeping with our Plants-By-WebSphere naming convention, let's also change the JNDI binding name from `ejb/com/ibm/pbw/ejb/OrderHome` to just `plantsby/OrderHome`:

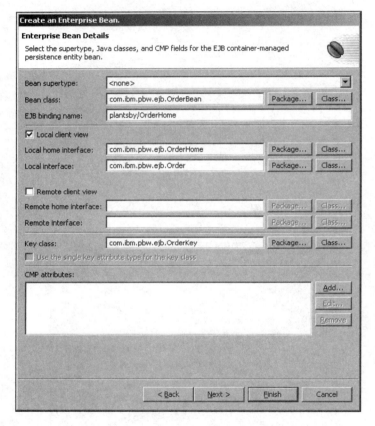

Since EJBs are keyed objects, we'll need a key class. WebSphere Studio suggests a default key class, `OrderKey`, which is fine, so we'll stick with it.

As per the EJB specification, entity beans have container-managed fields, and possibly container-managed relationships. These are defined in the entity bean's deployment descriptor. There are three ways we can define CMP fields:

❑ Through the EJB creation dialog

❑ Through WebSphere Studio's Deployment Descriptor editor

❑ By directly editing the `ejb-jar.xml` deployment descriptor file

We'll add our CMP fields through the creation dialog. We can always go into the Deployment Descriptor editor later if we need to add, change, or delete anything. We'll leave the direct editing the ejb-jar.xml file to those of you who prefer wilderness survival and forging steel by hand.

Adding CMP fields through the dialog is easy, just click the Add button on the Create Enterprise Bean dialog and add the fields through the following dialog:

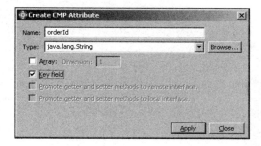

Enter field name and field type. We must also consider the following options and check any that apply:

- ❑ **Array** – check this box if the field is not a single item, but rather an array of items of the same type
- ❑ **Key Field** – check this box if the field is the key for this EJB or a part of the key
- ❑ **Promote getter/setter methods to remote interface** – check this box if a getter and setter should appear in the remote interface for this EJB
- ❑ **Promote getter/setter methods local interface** – same as previous option, except it applies to the local interface.

The Order EJB comprises the following fields:

Field Name	Field Type	Additional Options
orderId	java.lang.String	key field
sellDate	java.lang.String	
customerId	java.lang.String	
billName	java.lang.String	
billAddr1	java.lang.String	
billAddr2	java.lang.String	
billCity	java.lang.String	
billState	java.lang.String	
billZip	java.lang.String	
billPhone	java.lang.String	

Table continued on following page

Field Name	Field Type	Additional Options
shipName	java.lang.String	
shipAddr1	java.lang.String	
shipAddr2	java.lang.String	
shipCity	java.lang.String	
shipState	java.lang.String	
shipZip	java.lang.String	
shipPhone	java.lang.String	
creditCard	java.lang.String	
ccNum	java.lang.String	
ccExpireMonth	java.lang.String	
ccExpireYear	java.lang.String	
cardholder	java.lang.String	
shippingMethod	int	
profit	float	

We can enter each field in turn. Be sure to mark field `orderId` as the key field. After these fields have been defined, close the attribute dialog and click the Finish button on the EJB creation dialog.

The pre-release version of WebSphere Studio we used to build this application failed to generate the OrderKey class that we specified when we initially created this EJB. Because we specified only a single key field, Studio generated the signature of the default create and finder methods on the local home interface implementation using only the same type as the key field:

```
public Order findByPrimaryKey(String orderID) throws javax.ejb.FinderException;
public Order create(String orderID) throws javax.ejb.CreateException;
```

rather than:

```
public Order findByPrimaryKey(OrderKey pKey) throws javax.ejb.FinderException;
public Order create(OrderKey pKey) throws javax.ejb.CreateException;
```

This small oversight should be addressed in WebSphere Studio by the time you are reading this book, since the general release version of Studio will be out by that time. However, if for any reason you find yourself using a level of Studio that exhibits this same key construction behavior, you can apply the following technique to get Studio to do what you want. In the Deployment Descriptor editor, you will find the following set of controls on the Bean tab:

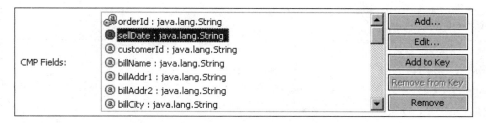

These controls allow you to configure the primary key. To force Studio to build the key class that we specified, simply add an additional field to the primary key, for example sellDate. Studio will then build our specified key class, OrderKey, and rebuild the default create and finder methods. Then simply remove sellDate from the primary key. Studio will then rebuild the OrderKey class – this time based only on our remaining key attribute, orderId. Voila! We have our key class.

While we're thinking about primary keys and home methods, we should add a custom create() method to OrderHome to enable us to create a new Order, passing all necessary values required to have a fully initialized order as input parameters. Let's add the following signature to OrderHome:

```
public Order create(String customerID, String billName, String billAddr1,
                    String billAddr2, String billCity, String billState,
                    String billZip, String billPhone, String shipName,
                    String shipAddr1, String shipAddr2, String shipCity,
                    String shipState, String shipZip, String shipPhone,
                    String creditCard, String ccNum, String ccExpireMonth,
                    String ccExpireYear, String cardHolder, int shippingMethod,
                    java.util.Vector items)
    throws javax.ejb.CreateException;
```

Create OrderItem and OrderIdGenerator EJBs

Following the same basic steps that we took to create the Order bean, create the OrderItem and OrderIdGenerator 2.0 CMP EJBs.

OrderItem has the following attributes:

General Attributes	
Bean class	com.ibm.pbw.ejb.OrderItemBean
JNDI Name	plantsby/OrderItemHome
Local home interface	com.ibm.pbw.ejb.OrderItemHome
Local interface	com.ibm.pbw.ejb.OrderItem
Key class	com.ibm.pbw.ejb.OrderItemKey

Table continued on following page

195

CMP Attributes	
indx (primary key)	int
inventoryId	java.lang.String
name	java.lang.String
pkgInfo	java.lang.String
price	float
cost	float
quantity	int
category	int
sellDate	java.lang.String

We'll also need the following custom `create()` method on the `OrderItemHome` interface:

```
public OrderItem create(Order order, OrderKey orderKey, String inventoryID,
                    String name, String pkgInfo, float price, float cost,
                    int quantity, int category, String sellDate, int indx )
   throws javax.ejb.CreateException;
```

`OrderIdGenerator` has the following attributes:

General Attributes	
Bean class	com.ibm.pbw.ejb.OrderIdGeneratorBean
JNDI Name	plantsby/OrderIdGeneratorHome
Local home interface	com.ibm.pbw.ejb.OrderIdGeneratorHome
Local interface	com.ibm.pbw.ejb.OrderIdGenerator
Key class	com.ibm.pbw.ejb.OrderItemKey
CMP Attributes	
pKey (primary key)	int
orderId	int

Create Order-OrderItem CMR

The container-managed relationship, or CMR, support specified by the EJB 2.0 specification is a very useful capability for use in modeling and generating the implementation code for relationships between 2.0 CMP EJBs. The specification supports one-to-one, one-to-many, and many-to-many relationships. The way it works is that the related bean(s) is exposed as a CMR field – in the same spirit as a CMP field – in the source bean. WebSphere Studio automatically generates a getter and setter for the CMR field. A get or set on the CMR field triggers all necessary underlying events on the related bean(s) to either load it into the container or establish it as part of the relationship with the source bean. This saves us writing a bunch of code by hand.

To define a CMR, open the EJB Deployment Descriptor editor. Switch to **Overview** tab, if not already there. Scroll down until the area labeled **Relationships 2.0** is in view. Click the **Add** button to open the **Relationship** definition dialog:

Select `Order` on the left – this is the "from" side of the relationship. Choose `OrderItem` on the right – this is the "to" side of the relationship. Click the **Next** button to continue:

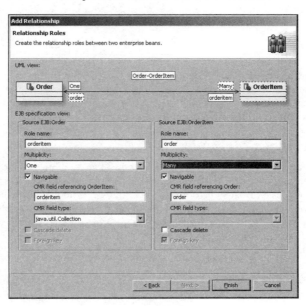

Select **Many** as the multiplicity for `OrderItem`. Note that this makes the CMR field type in `Order` into a collection. Click **Finish**.

Our intention is to relate the underlying relational database tables through a foreign key relationship as depicted in the following diagram:

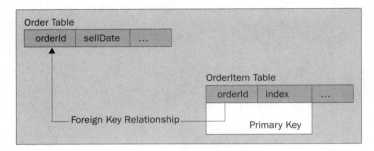

This requires that we make the relationship part of the key. This is done in the EJB Deployment Descriptor editor:

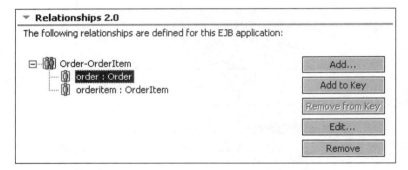

Select the `Order` relationship and click the **Add to Key** button. While this may not seem entirely intuitive, it will define the foreign key from `OrderItem` back to `Order` as part of the primary key of `OrderItem`. This is exactly what we want. This will become clearer once we do the data mapping for our CMP EJBs. We'll do this a little further on in this chapter.

Implement the Business Methods

At this level of our Plants-By-WebSphere design, there is no special business logic, no particular business rules, that we require from our `Order` EJB. We need only the business abstraction itself – a functioning order object. We already introduced the create method signatures for our `Order` and `OrderItem` EJBs. Now we just need to provide the implementations. As we have an EJB relationship (CMR) between these two EJBs, we need to add some additional code in their create methods in order to actually connect the `Order` to its related `OrderItems`.

The basic logic goes like this:

Order

- ❑ Get an `OrderId`
- ❑ Store create parameters in CMP fields
- ❑ Create `OrderItem` collection from `StoreItem` vector
- ❑ Store `OrderItem` collection in CMR field

OrderItem

- ❑ Store `Order` in CMR field

Since our `Order` and `OrderItem` hold a reference to one another, and we have chosen to establish this linkage during creation time, we have a minor complexity on our hands to address. This complexity results from the fact that an EJB does not yet exist during the middle of its `create()` method processing. This is a problem for us because when we create an `OrderItem` EJB, we must pass it a reference to its associated `Order` EJB. The `OrderItem` EJB will update its CMR field with this `Order` EJB reference. When a CMR field is updated, there is some CMR maintenance logic that executes under the covers on behalf of the relationship. In this case, the CMR maintenance logic attempts to reference `Order` EJB. Since we're in the middle of `Order`'s `create()` method, the `Order` EJB does not yet actually exist in the eyes of the EJB container. Since it does not yet exist, no reference to it can yet be made. Attempting to do so will cause an exception. Fortunately the EJB component model accounted for issues like these and includes a "post create" method in the bean-container contract. After `ejbCreate()` returns to the EJB container, the EJB now exists; the container then calls `ejbPostCreate()` to allow the EJB to do any additional initialization, including initialization that involves passing a valid reference to its local interface to other components.

Let's consider the following object interaction diagram, in order to get a better understanding of the logic flow:

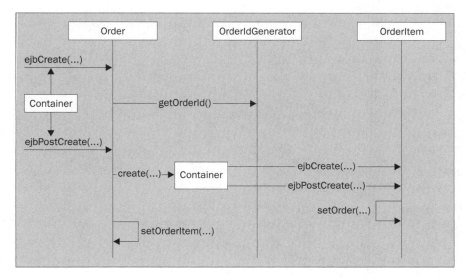

Order's `ejbCreate()` is driven by the EJB container in response to a call on
`OrderHome.create(...)`. In `Order.ejbCreate()`, we get a new `orderId` from the
`OrderIdGenerator`. Order's `ejbPostCreate()` is similarly driven by the EJB container. In
`Order.ejbPostCreate()`, we create the `OrderItem` collection. The EJB container calls
`ejbCreate()` and `ejbPostCreate()` on each `OrderItem` we create. In
`OrderItem.ejbPostCreate()`, we update the CMR field with our `Order` reference. Lastly, we
update Order's CMR field with the fully-formed `OrderItem` collection.

OrderBean.ejbCreate() Code

This code is straightforward and predictable. It simply does three things:

❑   Stores input parameters in CMP fields, using CMP field setter methods

❑   Calls the `OrderIdGenerator` bean to get the next order ID

❑   Builds and returns an `OrderKey`

```
public OrderKey ejbCreate(String customerID, String billName, String billAddr1,
                          String billAddr2, String billCity, String billState,
                          String billZip, String billPhone, String shipName,
                          String shipAddr1, String shipAddr2, String shipCity,
                          String shipState, String shipZip, String shipPhone,
                          String creditCard, String ccNum, String ccExpireMonth,
                          String ccExpireYear, String cardHolder,
                          int shippingMethod, java.util.Vector items)
  throws CreateException  {

  setCustomerID(customerId);
  setBillName(billName);
  setBillAddr1(billAddr1);
  setBillAddr2(billAddr2);
  setBillCity(billCity);
  setBillState(billState);
  setBillZip(billZip);
  setBillPhone(billPhone);
  setShipName(shipName);
  setShipAddr1(shipAddr1);
  setShipAddr2(shipAddr2);
  setShipCity(shipCity);
  setShipState(shipState);
  setShipZip(shipZip);
  setShipPhone(shipPhone);
  setCreditCard(creditCard);
  setCcNum(ccNum);
  setCcExpireMonth(ccExpireMonth);
  setCcExpireYear(ccExpireYear);
  setCardholder(cardHolder);
  setShippingMethod(shippingMethod);

  String sellDate = Long.toString(System.currentTimeMillis());
  //Pad it to 14 characters to sorting works properly
  if (sellDate.length() < 14) {
    StringBuffer sb = new StringBuffer(Util.ZERO_14);
    sb.replace((14 - sellDate.length()), 14, sellDate);
```

```
      sellDate = sb.toString();
   }
   setSellDate(sellDate);

   int orderInt = OrderIdGeneratorHelper.nextId();
   String orderID = Integer.toString(orderInt);
   setOrderId(orderID);
   OrderKey orderKey = new OrderKey(orderID);

   return orderKey;
}
```

The `OrderIdGenerator` EJB is mapped to a relational database table consisting of only a single row. The primary key value of this single row is "1". The `OrderIdGeneratorHelper` class is a simple class that encapsulates the details of accessing the `OrderIdGenerator` EJB and getting the next order ID. This class handles the JNDI lookup on the `OrderIdGeneratorHome`, executes a `findByPrimaryKey()` method on that home to locate the one and only `OrderIdGenerator` EJB instance, then invokes the `nextId()` method on the `OrderIdGenerator` interface to acquire the next available order ID:

```
package com.ibm.pbw.ejb;

public class OrderIdGeneratorHelper {

   static int nextId() {
      int i;
      try {
         javax.naming.InitialContext ctx = new javax.naming.InitialContext();
         OrderIdGeneratorHome orderGeneratorHome = (OrderIdGeneratorHome)
            ctx.lookup("java:comp/env/ejb/OrderIdGeneratorHome");
         OrderIdGenerator orderIdGenerator =
            orderGeneratorHome.findByPrimaryKey(new OrderIdGeneratorKey(1));
         i = orderIdGenerator.nextId();
         return i;

      } catch(Exception e) {
         e.printStackTrace();
         throw new RuntimeException();
      }
   }
}
```

This requires us to add the `nextId()` method to the `OrderIdGenerator` EJB:

```
public int nextId() {
   int i = getOrderId();
   i++;
   setOrderId(i);
   return i;
}
```

OrderBean.ejbPostCreate() Code

This method is where we create the OrderItem EJBs, aggregate them into a collection, then assign the collection to the Order EJB's CMR field. Naturally, we do a JNDI lookup to access the OrderItem EJB home and drive its create() method to create each OrderItem EJB:

```
public void ejbPostCreate(String customerID, String billName,
                          String billAddr1, String billAddr2, String billCity,
                          String billState, String billZip, String billPhone,
                          String shipName, String shipAddr1, String shipAddr2,
                          String shipCity, String shipState, String shipZip,
                          String shipPhone, String creditCard, String ccNum,
                          String ccExpireMonth, String ccExpireYear,
                          String cardHolder, int shippingMethod,
                          Vector items)
    throws CreateException  {

  this.items = (Vector) items.clone();
  Vector orderItems = new Vector();

  OrderKey orderKey = (OrderKey) this.myEntityCtx.getPrimaryKey();

  try {
    javax.naming.InitialContext ctx= new  javax.naming.InitialContext();
    OrderItemHome orderItemHome= (OrderItemHome)
      ctx.lookup("java:comp/env/ejb/OrderItemHome");
    for (int i = 0; i < items.size(); i++) {
      StoreItem si;
      si = (StoreItem) items.elementAt(i);
      OrderItem item= orderItemHome.create(
          (Order) this.myEntityCtx.getEJBLocalObject(), orderKey, si.getId(),
              si.getName(), si.getPkgInfo(), si.getPrice(), si.getCost()
              si.getQuantity(), si.getCategory(), si.getSellDate(), i);
      orderItems.add(item);
    }
    setOrderitem(orderItems);

  } catch (Exception e) {
    throw new EJBException(e);
  }

}
```

OrderItemBean.ejbCreate() Code

This method is straightforward; it simply uses the input parameters to set the OrderItem bean's CMP fields. Remember that the OrderItem key is composed of the CMP field indx and the Order-OrderItem CMR. This created an additional CMP field to hold the foreign key representing the relationship. We must store the orderId value from the orderKey parameter in order to persist the foreign key that makes the relationship actually work:

```
public OrderItemKey ejbCreate(Order order, OrderKey orderKey,
                             java.lang.String inventoryID, java.lang.String name,
                             java.lang.String pkgInfo, float price, float cost,
                             int quantity, int category,
                             java.lang.String sellDate, int indx )
   throws javax.ejb.CreateException {

  setInventoryId(inventoryID);
  setName(name);
  setPkgInfo(pkgInfo);
  setPrice(price);
  setQuantity(quantity);
  setCategory(category);
  setSellDate(sellDate);
  setIndx(indx);
  this.setOrder_orderId(orderKey.orderId);
  return null;

}
```

OrderItemBean.ejbPostCreate() Code

This method's purpose is only to store the input `Order` EJB in `OrderItem`'s CMR field.

```
public void ejbPostCreate(Order order, OrderKey orderKey,
                          java.lang.String inventoryID, java.lang.String name,
                          java.lang.String pkgInfo, float price, float cost,
                          int quantity, int category, java.lang.String sellDate,
                          int indx )
   throws javax.ejb.CreateException {

  this.setOrder(order);
}
```

Create the Inventory EJB

Where there are shopping carts and orders, inventory cannot be far behind. We will build an `Inventory` EJB as our next business abstraction. We can follow the same basic steps as we did for our other 2.0 CMP EJBs, earlier in this chapter. The following attributes describe the essential characteristics of the `Inventory` EJB:

General Attributes	
Bean class	com.ibm.pbw.ejb.InventoryBean
JNDI Name	plantsby/InventoryHome
Local home interface	com.ibm.pbw.ejb.InventoryHome
Local interface	com.ibm.pbw.ejb.Inventory
Key class	com.ibm.pbw.ejb.InventoryKey

Table continued on following page

CMP Attributes	
inventoryId (primary key)	java.lang.String
name	java.lang.String
description	java.lang.String
pkgInfo	java.lang.String
image	java.lang.String
imgBytes	byte Array field (dimension = 1)
price	float
cost	float
category	int
quantity	int

The InventoryHome interface will provide the following create() method signatures:

```
public abstract Inventory create(InventoryKey key, String name, String desc,
                              String pkgInfo, String image, float price,
                              float cost, int quantity, int category)
    throws CreateException;

public Inventory create(StoreItem item) throws javax.ejb.CreateException;
```

With complementary ejbCreate() and ejbPostCreate() methods like so (these are straightforward because there is no CMR relationship to manage):

```
public InventoryKey ejbCreate(InventoryKey key, String name, String desc,
                           String pkgInfo, String image, float price,
                           float cost, int quantity, int category)
    throws CreateException  {

  setInventoryId(key.inventoryId);
  setName(name);
  setDescription(desc);
  setPkgInfo(pkginfo);
  setImage(image);
  setPrice(price);
  setCost(cost);
  setQuantity(quantity);
  setCategory(category);
  return null;
}

public void ejbPostCreate(InventoryKey key, String name, String desc,
                            String pkgInfo, String image, float price,
                            float cost, int quantity, int category)
    throws CreateException  { }
```

```
public InventoryKey ejbCreate(StoreItem item) throws javax.ejb.CreateException {
  setInventoryId(item.getId());
  setName(item.getName());
  setDescription(item.getDescr());
  setPkgInfo(item.getPkgInfo());
  setImage(item.getImageLocation());
  setPrice(item.getPrice());
  setCost(item.getCost());
  setQuantity(item.getQuantity());
  setCategory(item.getCategory());
  return null;
}

public void ejbPostCreate(StoreItem item) throws CreateException {}
```

Now that we have an actual inventory representation, we can wire up the `StoreItem` bean to get its data from an `Inventory` EJB through a new constructor:

```
public StoreItem(Inventory inv) {
  this.id = inv.getInventoryId();
  this.name = inv.getName();
  this.imageLocation = inv.getImage();
  this.price = inv.getPrice();
  this.pkgInfo = inv.getPkgInfo();
  this.descr = inv.getDescription();
  this.quantity = inv.getQuantity();
  this.category = inv.getCategory();
  this.cost = inv.getCost();
}
```

The design requirements for the `Inventory` EJB allow us to get a closer look at another EJB 2.0 feature: the EJB Query Language. The EJB Query language, or EJB QL for short, is a SQL-like language for expressing selection criteria over the domain of 2.0 CMP EJBs. It provides a database-agnostic query language that can be mapped to virtually any relational backend. It is perfectly suited to the task of implementing EJB custom finders. It is also used for implementing `ejbSelect()` methods, which are EJB queries accessible to the bean implementation only.

Our Plants-By-WebSphere design requires the following custom finders:

```
public abstract Collection findByCategory(int category)
    throws FinderException;

public abstract Collectin findByNameLikeness(java.lang.String name)
    throws FinderException;
```

To implement a custom finder an a 2.0 CMP, you must first add a query. Open to the **Bean** tab of the EJB Deployment Descriptor editor, scroll down to find **Queries** and click the **Add** button to open the query creation dialog:

Specify this is a new local find method named `findByCategory` that takes an integer parameter, which will represent the category selection, and returns a collection. Click the Next button to continue.

In the next dialog window we can compose the EJB QL statement that will form the basis of this finder's implementation. Enter the appropriate EJB QL statement and click the Finish button to complete the custom finder:

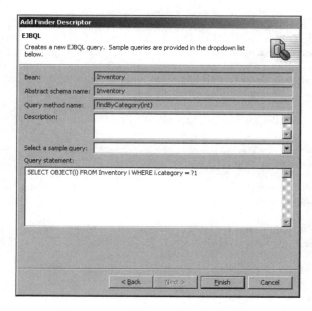

While we're defining custom finders, add this additional finder to `Inventory`:

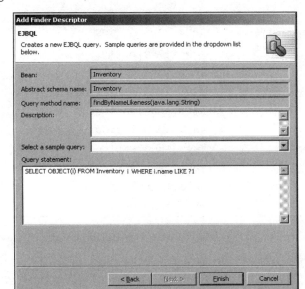

Finally, our `Inventory` bean contains some constants for determining the store category that the inventory item belongs to:

```
public static int FLOWERS    = 0;
public static int FRUIT      = 1;
public static int TREES      = 2;
public static int ACCESSORIES = 3;
```

We'll see these in use later in the chapter when we connect our EJBs up to the web application.

Create the Customer EJB

The `Customer` EJB introduces no new concepts. We can simply build this EJB using the techniques we have already utilized in this chapter to build this additional CMP entity according to the following table of attributes:

General Attributes	
Bean class	com.ibm.pbw.ejb.CustomerBean
JNDI Name	plantsby/CustomerHome
Local home interface	com.ibm.pbw.ejb.CustomerHome
Local interface	com.ibm.pbw.ejb.Customer
Key class	com.ibm.pbw.ejb.CustomerKey

Table continued on following page

CMP Attributes	
customerId (primary key)	java.lang.String
password	java.lang.String
firstName	java.lang.String
lastName	java.lang.String
addr1	java.lang.String
addr2	java.lang.String
city	java.lang.String
state	java.lang.String
zip	java.lang.String
phone	java.lang.String

As with the `Inventory` bean, we'll create customer constructors for the create methods:

```
public Customer create(CustomerKey key, String password, String firstName,
                String lastName, String addr1, String addr2,
                String addrCity, String addrState,
                String addrZip, String phone) throws CreateException;
```

```
public CustomerKey ejbCreate(CustomerKey key, String password, String firstName,
                String lastName, String addr1, String addr2,
                String addrCity, String addrState,
                String addrZip, String phone)
    throws CreateException {

  setCustomerId(key.customerId);
  setPassword(password);
  setFirstName(firstName);
  setLastName(lastName);
  setAddr1(addr1);
  setAddr2(addr2);
  setCity(addrCity);
  setState(addrState);
  setZip(addrZip);
  setPhone(phone);
  return null;
}
```

```
public void ejbPostCreate(CustomerKey key, String password, String firstName,
                String lastName, String addr1, String addr2,
                String addrCity, String addrState,
                String addrZip, String phone) { }
```

There's also an additional business method that will allow a customer's details to be updated:

```
public void update(String firstName, String lastName,
                   String addr1, String addr2,
                   String addrCity, String addrState,
                   String addrZip, String phone) {

  setFirstName(firstName);
  setLastName(lastName);
  setAddr1(addr1);
  setAddr2(addr2);
  setCity(addrCity);
  setState(addrState);
  setZip(addrZip);
  setPhone(phone);
}
```

We will also need to add a constructor to our `CustomerInfo` model to load our model with data from the `Customer` EJB:

```
public CustomerInfo(Customer customer) {

  email = customer.getCustomerID();
  firsName = customer.getFirstName();
  lastName = customer.getLastName();
  addr1 = customer.getAddr1();
  addr2 = customer.getAddr2();
  city = customer.getCity();
  state = customer.getState();
  zipcode = customer.getZip();
  phone = customer.getPhone();
}
```

This completes the work on our `Customer` EJB, which was the last EJB we needed to develop in order to satisfy the model requirements of our Plants-By-WebSphere application MVC design, as described at the start of this chapter.

Create the Catalog EJB

While this chapter has focused primarily on the EJBs required to implement the models introduced in Chapter 4, there is an additional session bean, `Catalog`, which provides a remote, additional abstraction over the `Inventory` entity bean, providing a catalog metaphor. This bean is used in later chapters, such as the web services chapter.

As this bean is just a session abstraction we won't detail the coverage of it here. Its remote interface merely looks like this:

```
package com.ibm.pbw.ejb;
import java.rmi.RemoteException;
import java.util.Vector;

public interface Catalog extends javax.ejb.EJBObject {
```

```
    public StoreItem[] getItems() throws RemoteException;
    public StoreItem[] getItemsByCategory(int category) throws RemoteException;
    public StoreItem[] getItemsLikeName(String name) throws RemoteException;
    public StoreItem getItem(String inventoryID) throws RemoteException;
    public boolean addItem(StoreItem item) throws RemoteException;
    public boolean deleteItem(String inventoryID) throws RemoteException;
    public void setItemName(String inventoryID, String name) throws RemoteException;
    public void setItemDescription(String inventoryID, String desc)
        throws RemoteException;
    public void setItemPkginfo(String inventoryID, String pkginfo)
        throws RemoteException;
    public void setItemCategory(String inventoryID, int category)
        throws RemoteException;
    public void setItemImageFileName(String inventoryID, String imageName)
        throws RemoteException;
    public byte[] getItemImageBytes(String inventoryID) throws RemoteException;
    public void setItemImageBytes(String inventoryID, byte[] imgbytes)
        throws RemoteException;
    public float getItemPrice(String inventoryID) throws RemoteException;
    public void setItemPrice(String inventoryID, float price)
        throws RemoteException;
    public void setItemCost(String inventoryID, float cost) throws RemoteException;
    public void setItemQuantity(String inventoryID, int amount)
        throws RemoteException;
}
```

As you can see it has getters and setters that map to those on the Inventory model.

You can find the complete code for this bean in the source code bundle for this chapter on one of the accompanying CDs.

Map CMP Entities to a Relational Database

CMP entity beans, by their very nature, are designed as persistent objects. That means their state is backed in persistent storage, such as a relational database. WebSphere version 5.0 supports a number of JDBC relational backends. While it is possible to build entity beans that are backed in a variety of different persistent store types, such as a file system or another transaction server type, such as CICS or IMS, you'd have to switch to the bean-managed persistence model (BMP) to implement them. Future plans for WebSphere include direct support for backing CMP entity beans in CICS and IMS transaction systems.

For our application, we will use the bundled Cloudscape relational database. Cloudscape is a simple relational database that uses the file system as a backing store.

Generate a Schema Map

Relational schema mapping is all about specifying which EJB CMP fields map to which relational database table fields. The mapping process will result in generated code, containing SQL statements, which the EJB container will use to perform database operations on the EJB. There are three mapping models from which to choose:

❏ **Top-down**
A top-down mapping creates an EJB-to-table mapping that assumes the EJB name is the table name and that the CMP field names and types are the names and types of the table columns. This option is most useful for applications that will introduce new database tables.

❏ **Meet-in-middle**
A meet-in-middle mapping allows CMP fields to be mapped to existing database tables. The mapping tools allow individual CMP fields to be mapped to individual table columns. The names do not need to match, type conversions are possible through the use of special converter classes, and mapping an EJB to multiple database tables is possible.

❏ **Bottom-up**
A bottom-up mapping creates an EJB and its CMP field names and types based on the definition of an existing database table.

For Plants-By-WebSphere, we will do a top-down mapping, since our tables are new and our mapping is straightforward.

Right-click on the `PlantsByWebSphereEJB` project, then select Generate | EJB to RDB Mapping … from the menu:

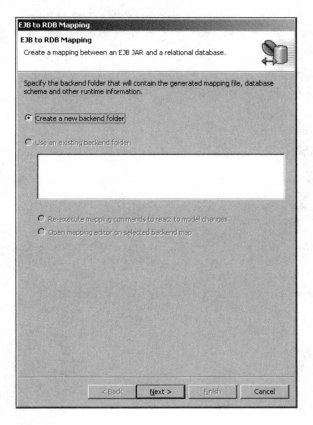

Since this is our first database mapping, our only choice is to create a new backend folder. Click the **Next** button to continue.

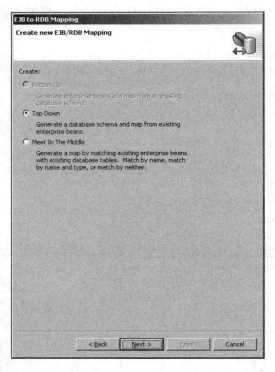

Next choose **Top Down** as our mapping approach, as we just discussed. Click **Next**.

The next dialog window allows us to choose the type of database for which we are generating a mapping. We also specify the database and schema name. Schema name, in case you know it by another term, is the table qualifier that optionally appears in SQL statements – for example, SELECT ... FROM <schema name>.<table name> WHERE ...

You can create multiple mappings for your EJBs – one for each database you intend to use. For example, you might use Cloudscape for unit testing, and DB2 for production. WebSphere supports a number of relational databases, including:

- ❑ DB2
- ❑ Cloudscape
- ❑ Informix
- ❑ Sybase
- ❑ Oracle
- ❑ SQL Server

On this window you may also choose to have DDL generated, which you can use to create the target database tables for your EJBs.

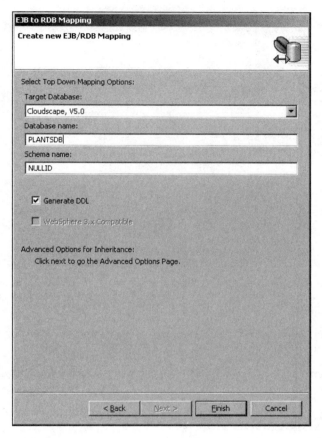

For our purposes, we will map to a Cloudscape database named PLANTSDB. Specify NULLID as the schema name. This is a reserved keyword in WebSphere Studio that means there is to be no schema name used in the table reference of the generated SQL statements. Click Finish to generate the mapping.

At this point, a confession is in order: we actually have an existing PLANTDB database (provided on the CD), which was created through an earlier Plants-By-WebSphere effort. It was created through a top-down mapping process and is ready and primed with inventory data for our use. We'll leverage that database here, so we don't have to repeat the table creation and priming exercise. The top-down mapping will almost perfectly map the fields to columns correctly – the only exception is the generated foreign key field in the ORDERITEM table. The only other rub is that some of the table names are not exactly right. But that's OK; we can explore another WebSphere Studio feature as we fix up these minor mapping inconsistencies. If in fact, our existing database was substantially different, we would have undertaken a "meet-in-middle" mapping.

In the J2EE Navigator view, you will find a back-end folder for our nearly created Cloudscape mapping. The folder includes the table definitions that were generated by the mapping process. Double-click a table name to open an editor:

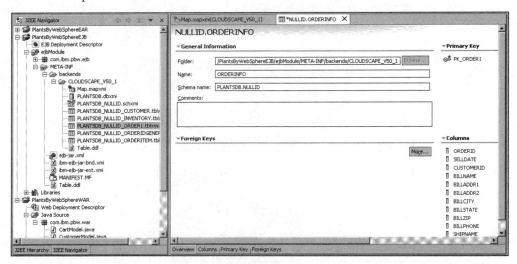

In the editor, change the table name from ORDER1 to ORDERINFO to match our existing PLANTSDB database. Also change the ORDERIDGENERATOR table to ORDERID and ORDERITEM to ORDERITEMS (note the "S" at the end).

Change the name of columns CITY, STATE, and ZIP in the CUSTOMER table to ADDRCITY, ADDRSTATE, and ADDRZIP respectively.

Lastly, change the name of the foreign key field in the ORDERITEMS table from ORDER_ORDERID to just ORDERID.

Declare EJB References

The next necessary step is to define the EJB references. As per the EJB specification, EJB references are the declarative mechanism by which an EJB developer makes it known that one EJB depends on another. Such a dependency requires the dependent EJB gain access to its provider EJB's local or remote home interface. This access is achieved through a JNDI lookup. The EJB reference serves two purposes then:

❑   Informs the application assembler or deployer what other EJBs are required to deploy a particular EJB.

❑   Provides a level of indirection by enabling the bean developer to specify and use a symbolic JNDI lookup name in their EJB, which is resolved lazily during application assembly or installation.

While building the business logic, we'll only declare the external dependencies that our components have. Resolving these dependencies is an application assembly and installation activity, which we will defer until the next chapter.

To declare an EJB reference, let's go to the References tab of the EJB Deployment Descriptor editor. Select the referencing EJB and click the Add button. Let's add the Order EJB's references first.

The Add Reference dialog first asks what kind of reference we want to declare. In the case of the Order EJB, it has references to both the OrderItem and OrderIdGenerator EJBs. As these two EJBs have only local interfaces, we clearly want to use a local EJB reference:

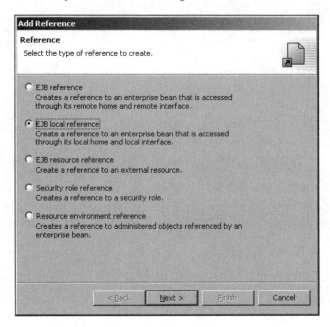

In fact, we would probably always prefer local EJB interfaces – even if remote interfaces are available on the target EJB – because local interfaces always perform better than remote. Local interfaces are perfectly fine as long as our design requirements allow the referencing and referenced EJBs to be co-located in the same application server. If the design requires that these EJBs be distributable across separate application servers, then we would have to specify a remote interface reference. Click the Next button to continue.

The final step in declaring an EJB reference is to identity the EJB type to which we are making reference. The Order bean references OrderIdGenerator bean. We will complete the reference declaration on the following dialog window:

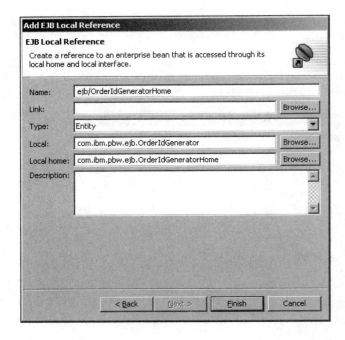

Specify:

- **Name**: `ejb/OrderIdGeneratorHome`
  This is the local name by which the `Order` bean will look up the `OrderIdGenerator` bean's home in JNDI.

- **Type**: `Entity`
  This specifies the EJB type to which this reference refers. It is an assembly hint.

- **Local**: `com.ibm.pbw.ejb.OrderIdGenerator`
  This specifies the bean type to which this reference refers. This is another assembly hint.

- **Local home**: `com.ibm.pbw.ejb.OrderIdGeneratorHome`
  This specifies the bean home type to which this reference refers. This is the final assembly hint.

Click the Finish button to complete this EJB reference declaration.

Add additional local EJB references to our `PlantsByWebSphereEJB` module according to the summary table below:

Bean	Name	Local	LocalHome
Order	ejb/Order ItemHome	com.ibm.pbw.ejb.Order Item	com.ibm.pbw.ejb.Order ItemHome
OrderItem	ejb/Order	com.ibm.pbw.ejb.Order	com.ibm.pbw.ejb.Order Home

Integrate EJBs with Web Module Model Objects

When developing the presentation logic, we were deliberate in not only following a model-view-controller design, but in establishing a façade for the model part of the design. This façade is made up of a simple Java object that represents – or front-ends, if you will – each of our EJBs. This allowed the presentation logic to be built up independently of the business logic development. We introduced these model objects at the beginning of the chapter, so we will simply list them quickly here as a reminder:

- ❑ CartModel
- ❑ OrderModel
- ❑ InventoryModel
- ❑ CustomerModel

Now that we have implemented our business logic as a set of EJBs, it is time to connect them to the model objects.

Implement the Model Code

Since each model object will delegate onto an associated EJB, we will need code that enables the model object to look up the appropriate EJB home in JNDI. We will introduce a specific method in each model object for that purpose. The resulting home reference can be cached for later use. The getShoppingCartHome() method and related code in the CartModel class shows how to do this:

```java
import javax.naming.InitialContext;
import javax.ejb.EJBException;
import java.util.Vector;

public class CartModel {

  private final static String SHOPPINGCART_HOME_NAME =
    "java:comp/env/ejb/plantsby/ShoppingCartHome";

  private static ShoppingCartHome shoppingCartHome;

  private ShoppingCartHome getShoppingCartHome() {
    if ( shoppingCartHome == null ) {
      try {
        InitialContext ctx= new InitialContext();
        shoppingCartHome= (ShoppingCartHome)
        ctx.lookup(SHOPPINGCART_HOME_NAME);

      } catch (Exception e) {
        throw new EJBException(e);
      }
      return shoppingCartHome;
    } else {
      return shoppingCartHome;
    }
  }
}
```

Each model object will have similar JNDI lookup code for its own specific EJB home lookup.

Since a `CartModel` will delegate to exactly one `ShoppingCart` session bean, we can create the session bean in the `CartModel` constructor. The remaining `CartModel` methods do simple delegation onto the session bean:

```
private ShoppingCart shoppingCart;

CartModel() {
  try {
    shoppingCart= getShoppingCartHome().create();
  } catch (Exception e) {
    throw new EJBException(e);
  }
}

public void addItem(StoreItem si) {
  shoppingCart.addItem(si);
}

public Vector getItems() {
  return shoppingCart.getItems();
}
```

InventoryModel

In doing the integration of the `InventoryModel` object with the `Inventory` EJB, we run into a little snafu. The presentation logic uses a `String` type for category, whereas the business logic uses an integer. We cannot possibly over-stress the importance of a rigorous design review process. However, rather than going back and fixing it for the purposes of our development presentation, we opted to leave it in for example's sake, since these kinds of things can really happen in software development. Hey, we're only human (wink)!

So let's add a method to map category strings to integers:

```
private int getCategoryKeyFromString(String category) {

  int icategory;
  if ( category.equals("flowers") ) {
    icategory = Inventory.FLOWERS;
  } else if ( category.equals("fruit") ) {
    icategory = Inventory.FRUIT;
  } else if ( category.equals("trees") ) {
    icategory = Inventory.TREES;
  } else if ( category.equals("accessories") ) {
    icategory = Inventory.ACCESSORIES;
  } else throw new EJBException("category not valid - category = " + category);
    return icategory;
  }
}
```

The `InventoryModel` uses the `StoreItem` class to represent inventory items, so that it does not expose the `Inventory` EJB interface. That means will need additional helper classes to convert an `Inventory` collection to `StoreItems`:

```
private StoreItem InventoryToStoreItem(Inventory inv) {
  return new StoreItem(inv);
}

private Collection InventoryToStoreItems(Collection c) {
  Vector v = new Vector();
  try {
    Iterator i = c.iterator();
    while ( i.hasNext() ) {
      Inventory inv = (Inventory) i.next();
      v.add(InventoryToStoreItem(inv));
    }
    return v;
  } catch (Exception e) {
    throw new EJBException(e);
  }
}
```

The `InventoryModel` offers two finder methods, which do nothing more than delegate to `InventoryHome` finders, then convert the resulting `Inventory` objects to `StoreItem` objects:

```
public Collection findByCategory(String category) {
  try {
    int icategory = getCategoryKeyFromString(category);
    Collection c = getInventoryHome().findByCategory(icategory);
    return InventoryToStoreItems(c);
  } catch (Exception e) {
    throw new EJBException(e);
  }
}

public StoreItem findById(String id) {
  try {
    InventoryKey key = new InventoryKey(id);
    Inventory inv = (Inventory) getInventoryHome().findByPrimaryKey(key);
    return InventoryToStoreItem(inv);
  } catch (Exception e) {
    throw new EJBException(e);
  }
}
```

and of course here's the EJB lookup:

```
private final static String INVENTORY_HOME_NAME=
  "java:comp/env/ejb/plantsby/InventoryHome";

private static InventoryHome inventoryHome;
private InventoryHome getInventoryHome() {
  if ( inventoryHome == null ) {
    try {
      InitialContext ctx = new InitialContext();
      inventoryHome = (InventoryHome) ctx.lookup(INVENTORY_HOME_NAME);
```

```
        } catch (Exception e) {
          e.printStackTrace();
          throw new EJBException(e);
        }
        return inventoryHome;
    } else {
        return inventoryHome;
    }
}
```

OrderModel

The `OrderModel` object has only a single business method, `addOrder()`, which is a simple delegation to the `Order` EJB. Note we have not implement supported for credit cards. We'll just fake it for now. Adding credit-card support is beyond what we'll cover in this chapter:

```
public String addOrder(CustomerInfo c, Vector orderItems) {

    try {
        Order o = getOrderHome().create(c.getEmail(), c.getName(), c.getAddr1(),
                                c.getAddr2(), c.getCity(), c.getState(),
                                c.getZipcode(), c.getPhone(), c.getName(),
                                c.getAddr1(), c.getAddr2(), c.getCity(),
                                c.getState(), c.getZipcode(), c.getPhone(),
                                "NO CREDIT CARD", "NO CC NUMBER",
                                "NO CC MONTH", "NO CC YEAR",
                                "NO CARD HOLDER", 1, // shipping method
                                orderItems);
        return o.getID();
    } catch (Exception e) {
        throw new EJBException(e);
    }
}
```

and the `getOrderHome()` method and support:

```
private final static String ORDER_HOME_NAME =
    "java:comp/env/ejb/plantsby/OrderHome";
private static OrderHome inventoryHome;

private OrderHome getOrderHome() {
    if ( inventoryHome == null ) {
        try {
            InitialContext ctx= new InitialContext();
            inventoryHome= (OrderHome) ctx.lookup(ORDER_HOME_NAME);
        } catch (Exception e) {
            e.printStackTrace();
            throw new EJBException(e);
        }
        return inventoryHome;
    } else {
        return inventoryHome;
    }
}
```

CustomerModel

The customer model has two methods to implement: one to add a customer; one to find one. These methods will primarily use the `Customer` EJB's finder methods. The `addCustomer()` method is the exception: it uses the `Customer` method `update()` to update an existing `Customer` to account for changes the user may have made to their name, address, etc:

```java
public void addCustomer(CustomerInfo i) {
  CustomerKey key = new CustomerKey(i.getEmail());

  try {
    Customer c = getCustomerHome().findByPrimaryKey(key);
    c.update( i.getFirstName(), i.getLastName(),i.getAddr1(), i.getAddr2(),
              i.getCity(), i.getState(), i.getZipcode(), i.getPhone() );

  } catch ( FinderException e ) {
    try {
      Customer c = getCustomerHome().create(key, "PASSWORD", i.getFirstName(),
                                            i.getLastName(), i.getAddr1(),
                                            i.getAddr2(), i.getCity(),
                                            i.getState(),i.getZipcode(),
                                            i.getPhone());
    } catch ( CreateException ex) {
      throw new EJBException("Could not create new customer");
    }
  }
}
```

```java
public CustomerInfo getCustomer(String emailKey) {
  CustomerKey key = new CustomerKey(emailKey);

  try {
    Customer c= getCustomerHome().findByPrimaryKey(key);
    CustomerInfo ci= new CustomerInfo();
    ci.setEmail(c.getCustomerId());
    ci.setFirstName(c.getFirstName());
    ci.setLastName(c.getLastName());
    ci.setAddr1(c.getAddr1());
    ci.setAddr2(c.getAddr2());
    ci.setCity(c.getCity());
    ci.setState(c.getState());
    ci.setZipcode(c.getZip());
    ci.setPhone(c.getPhone());
    return ci;

  } catch ( FinderException e ) {
    throw new EJBException("Could not find customer with key " + emailKey);
  }
}
```

Finally, the EJB lookup:

```
private final static String Customer_HOME_NAME =
  "java:comp/env/ejb/plantsby/CustomerHome";
private static CustomerHome CustomerHome;

private CustomerHome getCustomerHome() {
  if ( CustomerHome == null ) {
    try {
      InitialContext ctx = new InitialContext();
      CustomerHome= (CustomerHome) ctx.lookup(Customer_HOME_NAME);
    } catch (Exception e) {
      e.printStackTrace();
      throw new EJBException(e);
    }
    return CustomerHome;
  } else {
    return CustomerHome;
  }
}
```

Declare EJB References

Finally, and as the last step in connecting our EJBs to the model beans in our web module, let's declare the EJB references we require in PlantsByWebSphereWAR. Do this by opening the Deployment Descriptor editor for the PlantsByWebSphereWAR. Select the Resources tab in the editor.

The screen layout is slightly different because it's a web module, but otherwise it's same idea as when we linked up the EJB references for the EJB module:

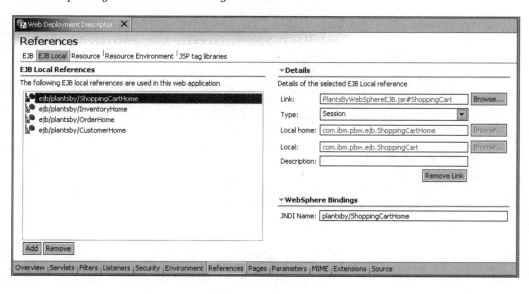

Choose the EJB Local tab, click the Add button Complete the web module reference declarations based on the following table:

Name	Local Home	Local
ejb/plantsby/Shopping CartHome	com.ibm.pbw.ejb.Shopping CartHome	com.ibm.pbw.ejb. ShoppingCart
ejb/plantsby/Inventory Home	com.ibm.pbw.ejb.Inventory Home	com.ibm.pbw.ejb. Inventory
ejb/plantsby/OrderHome	com.ibm.pbw.ejb.OrderHome	com.ibm.pbw.ejb. Order
ejb/plantsby/Customer Home	com.ibm.pbw.ejb.Customer Home	com.ibm.pbw.ejb. Customer

Summary

This marks the end of the business logic development on our example application, Plants-By-WebSphere. In this chapter, we started with the presentation logic we created in Chapter 4. We discussed briefly how component-based application development is a useful organizational model for separating presentation, business, and data logic, and how the EJB component model is especially well suited to the task of implementing business abstractions from that model.

We then focused on the model side of the Plants-By-WebSphere model-view-controller design, walking through the development of several principle EJBs that compose the implementation, step-by-step, including connecting the EJBs back into the presentation logic's model abstract layer.

Hopefully, this chapter has rounded out your picture of one way to partition and implement a common type of Internet application, and more specifically, how to apply WebSphere technology to that job. In the next chapter we'll take the next step in J2EE application development, by exploring the Assembly role and the WebSphere tools that support that task. We will also show you how to configure the WebSphere Studio test environment and take our nascent Plants-By-WebSphere application, now including both presentation and business logic, on a test drive.

6

J2EE Application Assembly and Deployment

At this point, we have completed the development of the presentation and business-logic components of the Plants-By-WebSphere application, using WebSphere Studio. We have seen how the presentation logic is contained in Web Application modules, and the business and data-access logic is contained in Enterprise JavaBean modules. In this chapter, we will focus on assembling these components into a completed Enterprise Application, and deploying that application into a unit test environment, and then a production WebSphere server.

WebSphere 5.0 includes a standalone application assembly tool, and we will provide a brief overview of that tool in this chapter. However, IBM's strategic direction for tools is to use web applications where appropriate, and to host all other tools on the Eclipse platform (as WebSphere Studio is). It is intended that future versions of WebSphere will provide an application assembly tool that is much more consistent with today's WebSphere Studio, and the current application assembly tool will be deprecated. In addition, when creating an application in WebSphere Studio (as we have with Plants-By-WebSphere in the preceding chapters), it is much more consistent and logical to complete the assembly process in the same environment, than it is to export the application to a separate tool for assembly. Therefore this chapter will focus primarily on the application assembly process in WebSphere Studio, instead of the standalone application assembly tool. WebSphere Studio Application Developer edition contains the EJB and J2EE tools, so the examples in this chapter assume that is the edition of Studio being used.

Assembling a J2EE Application

The J2EE specification naturally encourages the adoption of a multi-tier architecture and a strict separation between business logic and the presentation layer. The main component types are web applications, which are saved in a **Web archive** (or **WAR**) file, and **Enterprise JavaBean archives**, which are saved in a JAR file. The application may also contain other module types, including an **application client JAR** file, and a **Resource archive** (**RAR** file).

Each of these archives contains a static deployment descriptor file, defining the content of the archive, and providing a mechanism to pass information from the Component Provider to the Deployer. Reconciling all the individual components, resolving references between the components, and assembling them into a single application is known as, not surprisingly, **Application Assembly**. The resulting archive is saved in an **Enterprise Archive** (**EAR**) file and contains a deployment descriptor of its own, which is used to pass information about the application to the deployment tools and the server runtime:

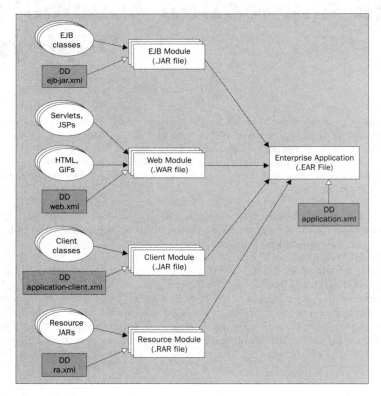

The creation of a J2EE specification-compliant enterprise application can be accomplished using a variety of tools, both command-line and UI-based. The J2EE specification defines the core of what's required in an application, but there are a number of additional pieces of data that are not included in the spec, such as the specification of binding information like JNDI names. The best way to complete the settings is by using one of the WebSphere-specific tools.

There are two such tools:

❑ **WebSphere Studio** can be used for all phases of an application's development, including both its initial creation and the subsequent application assembly.

❑ **WebSphere Application Assembly Tool (AAT)** can be used after development to import other archives and assemble them into a new application. We won't be covering the use of this tool in this chapter because it will likely be deprecated soon, as explained earlier.

We are creating the Plants-By-WebSphere application using WebSphere Studio, so we will focus on the application assembly tasks in that environment. There are two J2EE modules in Plants-By-WebSphere; the presentation logic is contained in `PlantsByWebSphere.war`, and the business logic is contained in `PlantsByWebSphereEJB.jar`.

Note that the J2EE specification does not restrict you to a single instance of each module type in an application; that just happens to be the structure used in this case.

Application Assembly Using WebSphere Studio

WebSphere Studio attempts to create applications in the correct structure from the beginning, to avoid the need to manipulate archive files during the export and assembly steps. There is one important difference between the project structure in Studio, and the archive structure of the eventual application; the assembled application (EAR) file will *contain* the two modules listed above, but the Studio design keeps the two modules as *peers* of the application module.

The reason for this difference is that the constituent modules are actually reusable components; multiple applications can quite easily use different groupings of the same (and other) modules. If the modules were created in Studio as children of a single application module, it would be almost impossible to re-use them in another application. Instead, all modules are created as root projects; the assembly of an enterprise application within Studio is managed logically, and the containment is shown in the Studio **J2EE Perspective**. The physical containment of the other modules will occur automatically when an enterprise archive is exported from Studio to an EAR file.

The following screenshot shows the state of the workbench after the application has been imported. Note that the WAR and EJB JAR modules are shown as children of the EAR project in this view, even though all three projects are actually peers in the underlying file system, and resources view:

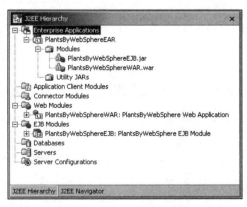

This discussion highlights another important point about application assembly; a portable EAR file must include all required classes and resources, and cannot have Java references to classes defined in other files. In general, the only reference that one application can make to the contents of another application is via a resource reference – even if all you need is to interact with another EJB (for example) as a client, you must have a copy of the client bindings contained within your EAR. The concept of ensuring an application is complete is an important way of scoping the content of the application; you do not need to worry about additional dependencies when installing a J2EE application, because by definition the EAR will contain everything that is required.

As one of its basic design tenets, Studio attempts to direct you down a path that will assemble the application as you create it. Therefore, there is very little composition left to do for the Plants-By-WebSphere application we are creating. The very first project we created in Chapter 4 was the web (or "WAR") project – but as a side effect of that creation, an enterprise (or "EAR") project was created at the same time. Since then, every new addition has added to the enterprise project, meaning the assembly process is already mostly complete.

It is also possible to edit the logical contents of an application module after the initial project creation has been completed. The **J2EE Perspective** can be used to list all application projects, and double-clicking on the project will open the Application editor. The same editor can also be opened by double-clicking on the EAR deployment descriptor for the enterprise project – the `application.xml` file that is located in the `META-INF` directory. Once in the editor, select the module tab, shown in the bottom of the editor view. This will allow you to list, add to, and remove modules from the application:

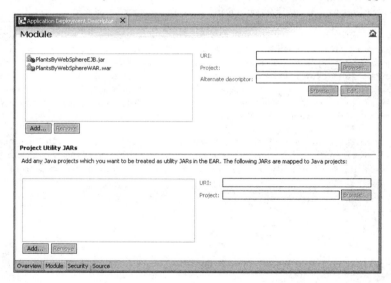

The operation is fast, because you are only manipulating references at this point; for the same reason, it is possible to add a single module to multiple applications.

Having completed the composition of the application, we now need to reconcile the J2EE module deployment descriptors.

The Assembly Process

Application assembly consists of more than just application composition, which is all that's been accomplished in the preceding chapters. In order to generate a consistent application, we need to reconcile the J2EE module deployment descriptors, and complete the WebSphere extensions for those descriptors. The first part of this consists of a number of steps – the J2EE specification requires that the Application Assembler:

❑ Make sure that each component in the application properly describes any dependencies it may have on other components in the application

❑ Assign a context root for each web module included in the J2EE application

❑ Synchronize security role-names across the application

❑ Link the internally satisfied dependencies of all components in every module contained in the application

We will now walk through each of these steps, to complete the Plants-By-WebSphere application.

Resolving Module Dependencies

WebSphere Studio maintains the correct module dependencies for you during development, as long as you have used the JAR dependency editor to define cross-project dependencies. Since each J2EE project module is also a Java project, you may be tempted to just use the Java classpath page in the project preferences to add additional libraries to the classpath. This would only update the classpath used within Studio, however, and would not result in the correct module dependencies being generated into the JAR for use at run time.

The JAR dependency editor (shown below) is an alternative editor for all EJB and web projects. In the J2EE Hierarchy view, select the project you wish to modify, right-click to bring up the context menu, and select Open With | Jar Dependency Editor:

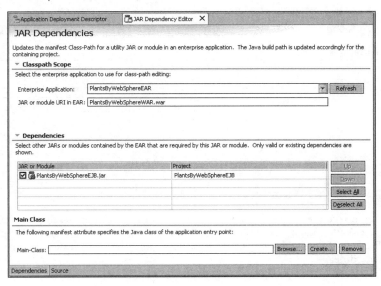

The editor will allow you to select from all modules that exist within the EAR. This will ensure the Java classpath is correct within Studio, and also modify the manifest classpath within the JAR. It is the manifest classpath that allows WebSphere to set the correct classloader dependency chain at runtime. If a module you wish to add a dependency does not appear in the dependent JAR list on this page, it means the JAR is not contained within the EAR; correct that first from the EAR deployment descriptor editor, and then you'll be able to select the dependency for the module.

We need to ensure the `PlantsByWebSphereWAR` project depends on the `PlantsByWebSphereEJB` project. Therefore open the JAR dependency editor on the `PlantsByWebSphereWAR` project, and verify that the EJB project is selected as shown above.

Assign a Context Root

The next requirement during module reconciliation is to assign a context root for each contained web module. The context root is a relative name in the web namespace for the application, and is already defined by this stage when creating the projects in Studio – it is required data (a default is provided) when you create a new web project. The context root we use for Plants-By-WebSphere is /PlantsByWebSphere.

If you wish to modify an existing context root, you can locate the setting in the Module page of the Application Deployment Descriptor editor:

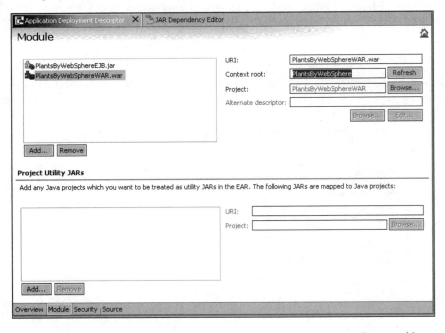

The context root is saved in the deployment descriptor of the enterprise application (the `application.xml` file). Each web module must be given a distinct and non-overlapping name for its context root; Studio validates this, and an error is shown in the task list if duplicate context roots exist in the same EAR module.

Synchronize Security Role Names

The security role names next need to be synchronized across the application. The security roles are initially defined in each of the module deployment descriptors. A security role is a defined with a name and description, and is used to define method permissions for the bean. For each security role defined in the module, you can associate multiple beans, and methods from each bean. Once associated, the execution of those methods is only possible when the caller has permission to run as that role. This abstraction allows the Application Assembler to define method-level permissions, while the Application Deployer only needs to worry about the much smaller list of security roles. We are not going to enable security in the Plants-By-WebSphere application, but we'll provide a brief description now of how to resolve the security roles.

For web applications, the security roles are defined on the Security page of the Deployment Descriptor editor; click the Add button, and then click the new entry in the list to rename it. You next need to associate the security role with the servlets or JSP pages you wish to control. Simply select the desired servlet from the list on the in the Servlets page, and scroll down to the Authorized Roles section. Click the Edit button, and select the role you wish to associate it with the servlet. Here we have defined a WebAppCust role, and associated with the cart JSP page:

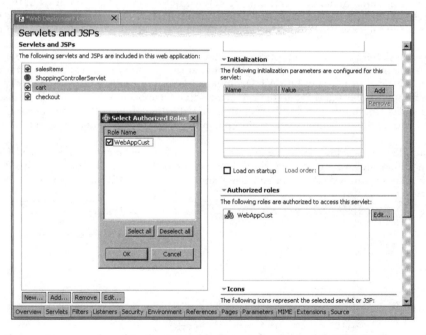

For EJBs, these settings are found in the Assembly Descriptor page of the EJB Deployment Descriptor editor. The first action is to define the security roles you desire. You then move to the Method Permissions section of the page, and click Add. This will bring up a wizard that allows you to associate a specific role with first beans, and then methods. The result of this wizard is shown in the following view; here the Customer role has been defined, and associated with the Catalog.getItemsLkeName(java.lang.String) method:

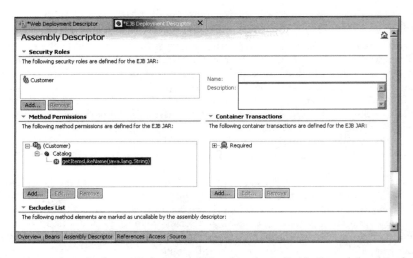

The security roles and method permissions are defined in the individual modules, but these modules are components that may be reused in multiple applications. Therefore you need to reconcile the roles defined in the modules at the application level, in the Enterprise Application deployment descriptor.

The primary task here is to rename role names that are defined in different modules; role names with the same name but different meanings, or different names with the same meanings all need to be reconciled. This can be done in the EAR Deployment Descriptor editor from the Security tab. The **Gather** button will collect and list all the role names that have been defined in all modules in the application. The **Combine** button will bring up a wizard listing all the roles, and allowing one role to be substituted with another. These changes will update the original deployment descriptors.

In the example shown below, there are two similar roles, Customer and WebAppCust. These could be reconciled into a single role name if desired. One the reconciliation is complete you can select the remaining roles shown in the list, and add Users and Groups who will then run in the role listed:

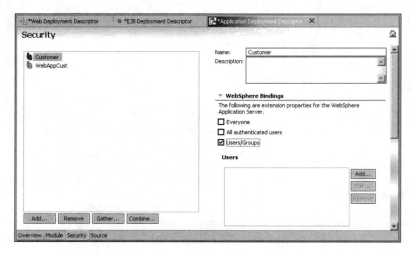

Link the Dependencies

The final stage of reconciling the application is to link the internally satisfied dependencies of all components in every module contained in the application; in other words, to resolve the various references within each module in the application. The fact that inter-component dependencies are resolved via references is what allows the modules to be truly reusable components. Without references, you would end up building an application that was tightly coupled to all other components, and would be correspondingly brittle. With references, it is possible for the module providers to declare a dependency on a certain object or resource, and still defer the definition of those references until application assembly time. References can be defined for EJBs, resources, security roles, and resource environments.

In all module types, the references are defined in the deployment descriptor, and thus exposed in Studio via the associated Deployment Descriptor editor. In a web application, references are defined on the References page of the editor. There are multiple types of references that can be defined, and these are selected from the tabs at the top of the page. Note that the references are defined for the entire web application, and not by servlet. The following example shows the local EJB references for the Plants-By-WebSphere web application:

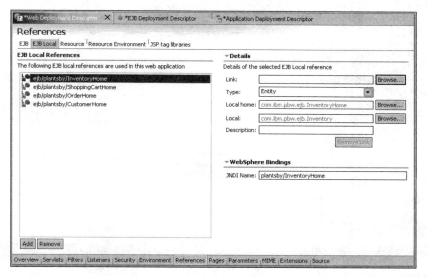

The selected reference is the `InventoryHome` bean. The actual name defined for it, in the list on the left, is `"ejb/plantsby/InventoryHome"`. There is no requirement that EJB reference names start with an `ejb` prefix, but it is a common convention. The reference is used in the `InventoryModel` Java class, looking up the `Inventory` bean. The code looks up the reference via an `InitialContext` object, using the EJB reference name prefixed by `"java:comp/env/"` – in other words, indicating that a computed environment reference should be used.

The local EJB references that need to be defined in the `PlantsByWebSphereWAR` module are:

❑   `ejb/plantsby/ShoppingCartHome`
❑   `ejb/plantsby/CustomerHome`
❑   `ejb/plantsby/InventoryHome`
❑   `ejb/plantsby/OrderHome`

You need to verify that each of these references is completely defined. Open the Web Application editor, and go to the **References** page, and the **EJB local** tab. Ensure that all of the above references are listed correctly. Select each one in turn; if the reference is defined but not resolved, then the **Link** field will be empty. In this case, use the **Browse** button to select the correct EJB to resolve the reference. For example, select the `ejb/plantsby/ShoppingCartHome` entry, and from the browse dialog select the `ShoppingCart` bean.

References within an EJB JAR are defined slightly differently; each reference is defined within the scope of the bean that is using the reference and not the complete module (as was the case for the web application). As a result, the reference support in the EJB editor is slightly more complicated, listing each reference in a tree view by bean. The beans containing the references are those beans using, not providing the reference. For example, the `Catalog` bean uses, and therefore defines a reference to, the `Inventory` bean. The EJB reference support is available via the References page in the EJB Deployment Descriptor editor:

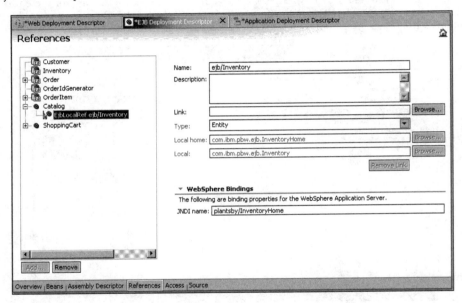

There are several reference types that can be defined:

- ❑ An EJB reference is used to access an EJB's remote home and remote interface.

- ❑ An EJB local reference is used to access an EJB's local home local interface.

- ❑ An EJB resource reference is used to access an external resource, such as a data source, or a mail session. The **Type** field is used to determine the exact type referenced.

- ❑ A Security role reference is used to access a security role.

- ❑ A resource environment reference is used to access an administered object, such as a JMS destination.

The references are often defined by the Component Provider but it is the job of the Application Assembler to confirm the references are all correct. The reference name must match the `String` used in the lookup method in the code. In the Plants-By-WebSphere application, we need the following references. Note that for each component dependency, there must only be one corresponding component in the scope of the application that fulfils the dependency.

EJB	Reference type	Referenced object	Reference name
Order	EJB Local Reference	OrderIdGenerator	ejb/OrderIdGeneratorHome
	EJB Local Reference	OrderItem	ejb/OrderItemHome
Catalog	EJB Local Reference	Inventory	ejb/InventoryHome
OrderItem	EJB Local Reference	Order	ejb/OrderHome

The definition of these references consists of little more than following the above table. For example, to define the reference that `Catalog` requires to access the `Inventory` bean, you follow these steps:

1. Open the EJB Deployment Descriptor editor
2. Select the **References** tab
3. Select the `Catalog` bean
4. Select the **Add** button to open then Add Reference wizard
5. Select the **EJB local reference** option, and then the **Next** button
6. Enter the name you wish to use; in this case it will be `ejb/InventoryHome`
7. Click the **Browse** button next to the link field, and select **Inventory** from the list of beans defined in this project
8. Hit **Finish**

The EJB references that are resolved by other EJBs within the application are linked at application assembly time by the `ejb-link` attribute in the deployment descriptor; for each such link there must be only one matching `ejb-name` in the scope of the entire application. The links are defined for you by Studio in the deployment descriptor editor.

If the reference has been defined but not resolved, then it will appear in the tree view in this editor. However, when selected the **Link** field will be blank. In this case, use the **Browse** button to select the correct EJB to resolve the reference. For example in the `Catalog` bean, select the `ejb/InventoryHome` entry, and from the browse dialog select the `Inventory` bean.

You do not need to define data source links for CMP beans; they access the data source via a CMP connection factory that we will configure later in this chapter.

Deployment Extensions

There are a number of WebSphere-specific extensions to the J2EE specifications, which provide enhanced functionality and control over the runtime behavior. These extensions all have defaults, and are not required to be configured in order to execute the application – but the optimal use of WebSphere is only available by utilizing these extensions. The extensions may be configured during any stage of development and deployment; WebSphere Studio provides editing capability for the extensions, and you can also use the standalone Application Assembly Tool to complete the details.

The extension information is all stored in the module archives as extension documents (which are separate files) to the base deployment descriptors, meaning that the data will remain associated with the module even if it is exported and re-imported into a different application. Despite this separation, the version 5.0 Studio editor provides a single consolidated view of both the specification and extension information. The fact that the settings are an extension to the specification is labeled for clarity, but you do not need to use a separate editor. In this section, we discuss the extensions that are available for web applications, enterprise beans, and other resource types.

Web Application Extensions

When editing the deployment descriptor of a web application, the following extensions are available, each of which will be discussed in more detail below:

- ❑ Web application reloading options
- ❑ Error page selection
- ❑ Additional classpath settings
- ❑ Enablement of directory browsing
- ❑ Whether servlets should be served by class name
- ❑ JSP pre-compilation support
- ❑ Automatic request and response encoding
- ❑ Enablement of automatic filter loading

These options are accessible via the web application Deployment Descriptor editor, on the **Extensions** tab. The extension information is saved as a separate file in the WAR. Although the extensions are edited via the same editor as the standard deployment descriptor settings, the extension information is saved in the file WEB-INF/ibm-web-ext.xmi:

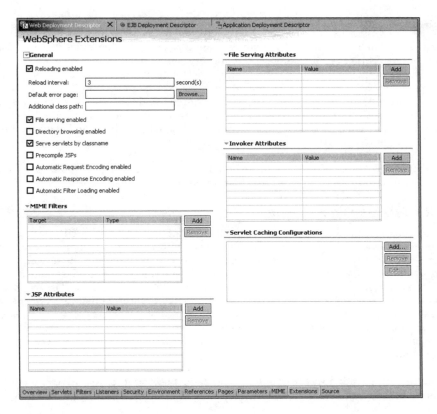

Reloading Options

The reloading options allow you to define if, and how often WebSphere should check the timestamp of the files on the disk, to see if they have been changed. If they have changed, then WebSphere will automatically reload the web application, reloading the changed files in the process. Despite the fact that all the classes in the web application will be reloaded, this is a much faster operation than restarting the entire server. This reload interval is typically set to a low value during development, but can be set to a higher value or even disabled for production use. As we're still developing the Plants-By-WebSphere application, we'll enable this option, with an interval of 3 seconds.

Error Pages

The error page is used as a default setting for the error page to be used, in case of a run-time problem. The standard web deployment descriptor (web.xml) defines a standard set of error pages to be used in response to specific errors, but does not indicate a page to display in case of other errors; this extension provides that. This is an important function that can allow your application to recover gracefully in case of trouble.

File Serving and Directory Browsing

The indication of whether file serving is enabled is another setting that must be reviewed carefully for its use at run time. This capability allows the application server to serve files, such as HTML and GIF file types. The ability to do so is very useful during development of the application, as you do not need to run a separate HTML server (such as the IBM Apache Web Server) in order to test your complete application. During production use however, you may prefer to disable this ability in WebSphere and use a separate web server for file serving, for both performance and security reasons. Directory browsing is a similar setting; its enablement during development can be quite beneficial, but you typically do not want to enable it for a production server.

For the Plants-By-WebSphere application, we do not need the scalability offered by a separate web server, so we will instead serve all files directly from the web container.

Serving Servlets by Class Name

The option to serve servlets by class name enables access of the servlets by a URL listing the implementing class name of the servlets. The alternative to this option is to define aliases for the servlets on the Servlets page; you can create URL mappings from any URL to a specific servlet. Defining the mappings is additional configuration work, but is beneficial to the use of the class names, as it gives you additional flexibility for future development of your application. Surfacing the class names via external URLs means that any changes to the implementation of your application that result in changes to the servlet classes used immediately become visible (as changed URLs) to users of the application. Restricting access to the servlet name also provides greater security, as it does not allow direct access to the class names. We do not need to serve by class name for the Plants-By-WebSphere application, so leave this option unselected.

Pre-compiling a JSP page is a way to avoid making the first user wait for the JSP compilation, by paying the compilation cost on server startup. If you have a lot of JSP files in your application, the delay to the first user may be substantial, and this option provides a mechanism to avoid that. The cost is increased server startup time; something that you may be willing to accept for a production server, but less desirable during development when the JSP files may be changing frequently. We don't need to pre-compile the JSP files for Plants-By-WebSphere during development, so leave the option unselected.

Request and Response Encodings

In WebSphere version 5, the web container no longer automatically sets request and response encodings, and response content types – you are expected to set these values using available methods as defined in the Servlet 2.3 specification. If you choose not to use the character encoding methods, they can enable the automatic request or automatic response encoding. If these options are selected, the encoding is selected by examining the header of the request or response. If these options are not set, the Servlet specification calls for a default encoding of ISO 8859-1. We do not specifically set the encoding in Plants-By-WebSphere, so we need to have the automatic encoding enabled. Select both checkboxes.

Filters

Filters are an important part of the Servlet 2.3 specification. Servlet filtering provides a new type of object called a filter that can transform a request or modify a response. They are normally loaded when they are executed, but selecting the automatic filter loading option will pre-load the filters to optimize run-time performance. We can leave this unselected for Plants-By-WebSphere.

EJB Extensions

There are also WebSphere-specific extensions available for EJBs, which allow you to configure the behavioral characteristics of the bean in the server. These options are all applicable on a per-bean basis, and are visible under the **WebSphere Extensions** heading of the Beans page in the EJB Deployment Descriptor editor once you have selected a bean. As with other metadata, the extension information is saved as a separate file in the JAR. Although the extensions are edited via the same editor as the standard deployment descriptor settings, the extensions information is saved in the file `META-INF/ibm-ejb-jar-ext.xmi`. Each option will be discussed in more detail below:

- ❑ Session timeout settings
- ❑ Activity session type
- ❑ Bean cache settings
- ❑ Local transaction settings
- ❑ Locale invocation selection
- ❑ Data cache settings

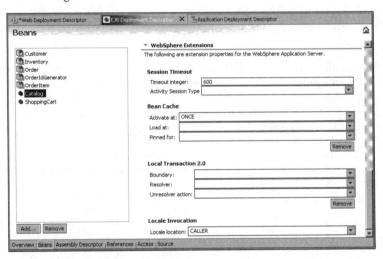

Session Timeout

The **Timeout integer** option only applies to stateful session beans, and allows you to configure the duration in seconds before the session bean times out. This is used to prevent system resources from being exhausted. For each of the Plants-By-WebSphere session beans (`Catalog`, `Login`, `Mailer`, `ReportGenerator`, and `ShoppingCart`), we'll set the timeout to 600 seconds (10 minutes).

Activity Session Type

The **Activity Session Type** option also only applies to session beans. This can be set to **Bean** or **Container**, and allows you to declare who is responsible for starting the activity session; **Bean** means that the application code will start it, and **Container** means the container will do so. Activity sessions are described in more detail in Chapter 9.

Bean Cache Settings

These options apply to entity and stateful session beans, and allow you to configure the local caching of the bean instances within the EJB container – which in turn governs the commit options that are used.

The valid settings for Activate at control when the bean is activated and placed in the cache:

- ❑ ONCE
  The bean is activated when it is first accessed in the server process, and that instance is then saved in the cache; it will be passivated and removed from the cache at the discretion of the container – such as when the cache becomes full.

- ❑ TRANSACTION
  The bean is activated at the start of the transaction, and passivated and removed from the cache at the end of the transaction

- ❑ ACTIVITY_SESSION
  The bean is activated and passivated at the start and end of the activity session. Activity sessions are discussed in more detail in Chapter 9.

The Load at setting specifies when the bean loads its state from the database. The value of this setting implies whether the container has exclusive or shared access to the database:

- ❑ ACTIVATION
  Indicates that the bean is loaded when it is activated (regardless of the Activate at setting) and implies that the container has exclusive access to the database.

- ❑ TRANSACTION
  Indicates that the bean is loaded at the start of a transaction and implies that the container has shared access to the database.

The settings of Activate at and Load at govern which commit options are used. The commit options themselves are described in the Enterprise JavaBeans specification, but the mapping of those options to the WebSphere bean cache settings is:

EJB Commit Option	Activate At	Load at	Description
Commit Option A (implies exclusive DB access)	ONCE	ACTIVATION	This option reduces database I/O (avoids calls to the `ejbLoad()` function) but serializes all transactions accessing the bean instance. Option A can increase memory usage by maintaining more objects in the cache, but could provide better response time if bean instances are not generally accessed concurrently by multiple transactions.

Table continued on following page

JB Commit Option	Activate At	Load at	Description
Commit Option B (implies shared DB access)	ONCE	TRANSACTION	Option B can increase memory usage by maintaining more objects in the cache. However, because each transaction creates its own copy of an object, there can be multiple copies of an instance in memory at any given time (one per transaction), requiring that the database be accessed at each transaction.
Commit Option C (implies shared DB access)	TRANSACTION	TRANSACTION	This option can reduce memory usage by maintaining fewer objects in the cache; however, there can be multiple copies of an instance in memory at any given time (one per transaction). This option can reduce transaction contention for enterprise bean instances that are accessed concurrently but not updated.

The Pinned for option defines how long the bean should be maintained in the cache. The options are ACTIVATION_PERIOD, ACTIVITY_SESSION, TRANSACTION, or BUSINESS_METHOD_ONLY.

The majority of the Plants-By-WebSphere EJBs can use the default activation setting of ONCE for the session beans (Catalog, Login, Mailer, ReportGenerator, and ShoppingCart), as we wish to optimize the response time for these beans by leaving them active (and cached) as much as possible. The entity beans (Customer, Inventory, Order, OrderIdGenerator, and OrderItem) use a setting of TRANSACTION for both Activate at and Load at, which provides for reduced transactional contention – the bean instances are passivated at the conclusion of each transaction. The Mailer bean is the only exception; we need to activate the mailer only once, so set the Load at setting to ACTIVATION, and the Pinned for setting to ACTIVATION_PERIOD.

Local Transaction Settings

The local transaction settings define the behavior when a method runs in what the EJB specification refers to as an "unspecified transaction context". The use of local transactions can provide significant performance benefits in some situations over global transactions. Local transactions are discussed in detail in Chapter 9. There are three local transaction options, Boundary, Resolver, and Unresolver action.

The Boundary setting specifies when a local transaction begins. The options are BeanMethod and ActivitySession. The default behavior is BeanMethod, meaning that the local transaction begins when the method begins and ends when the method ends.

The Resolver options define how the local transaction is to be resolved before the local transaction context ends: by the application through user code or by the EJB container. If this is set to Application, it means your code must either commit or roll back the local transaction. If this does not occur, the run-time environment logs a warning and automatically commits or rolls back the connection as specified by the Unresolved action setting. If the Resolver option is set to ContainerAtBoundary, it means the container takes responsibility for resolving each local transaction. This provides you with a programming model similar to global transactions in which your code simply gets a connection and performs work within it.

The Unresolver action options are Commit or Rollback, and specify the action the container will take if the resources are uncommitted by an application in a local transaction. As described in Chapter 5, The Plants-By-WebSphere application uses only Required as its only transaction policy. This means we do not need to worry about the local transaction behavior for Plants-By-WebSphere. Additional discussion on the transactional semantics is provided in Chapter 9.

Locale Invocation

The locale invocation property allows you to define the locale to be used when executing the bean; the options are CALLER or SERVER, and allow you to influence if the locale-specific settings (such as sorting order, time and date formatting, etc.) of the server or the calling process are to be used. For Plants-By-WebSphere, we will use the caller's locale for every bean.

Data Cache Settings

The data cache settings apply only to entity beans, and allow you to control the lifetime of cached data for an instance of this bean type. This is different from the Bean Cache settings, which control caching of the bean instance itself (not the data). There are two data cache settings: Lifetime in cache, and Lifetime in cache usage.

The Lifetime in cache property defines the duration in seconds for which the data will be cached, but the meaning is determined by the Lifetime in cache usage setting. The minimum value (0) indicates that cached data for a bean instance will not exist beyond the end of the transaction in which it was retrieved. Any non-zero value indicates that the cached data will exist beyond the end of the transaction; this might avoid another retrieval from persistent storage if this same bean instance is used in later transactions. A non-zero value is typically used for beans that are meant to be read-only. Usually, such beans are updated only at predictable intervals, such as every hour or every day at 3 a.m.

The Lifetime in cache usage options are:

❑ CLOCK_TIME
The value of Lifetime in cache represents a particular time of day, in seconds. The value is added to the immediately preceding or following midnight to calculate a future time value, which is then treated as for ELAPSED_TIME. Using CLOCK_TIME enables you to specify that all instances of this bean type are to have their cached data invalidated at, for example, 3 a.m., no matter when they were retrieved. This is important if, for example, the data underlying this bean type is batch-updated at 3 a.m. every day. The selection of midnight (preceding or following) depends on the value of Lifetime in cache. If Lifetime in cache plus the value that represents the preceding midnight is earlier than the current time, the following midnight is used. When you use CLOCK_TIME, the value of Lifetime in cache is not supposed to represent more than 24 hours. If it does, the cache manager subtracts 24 hour increments from it until a value less than or equal to 24 hours is achieved. To invalidate data at midnight, set Lifetime in cache to 0.

❑ WEEK_TIME
The same as for CLOCK_TIME, except that the value of Lifetime in cache is added to the preceding or following Sunday midnight (11:59 PM Saturday plus 1 minute). When WEEK_TIME is used, the value of Lifetime in cache can represent more than 24 hours but not more than 7 days.

❑ ELAPSED_TIME

The value of Lifetime in cache is added to the time at which the transaction in which the bean instance was retrieved is completed. The resulting value becomes the time at which the cached data expires. The value of Lifetime in cache can add up to minutes, hours, days, and so on.

❑ OFF

The value of Lifetime in cache is ignored. Beans of this type are cached only in a transaction-scoped cache. The cached data for this instance expires after the transaction in which it was retrieved is completed.

These options can be summarized like this:

Lifetime in Cache Usage	Sample Lifetime in cache	Description
OFF	n/a	Data is not cached
CLOCK_TIME	10,800	Data cache is invalidated at 3 a.m. (3 * 60 * 60)
WEEK_TIME	270,000	Data cache is invalidated on Wednesday morning at 3 a.m. (3 * 60 * 60) + (3 * 24 * 60 * 60)
ELAPSED_TIME	18,000	Data cache is invalidated 5 hours after the transaction completes (5 * 60 * 60)

The Plants by WebSphere entity beans are not read-only, and because they may have their data updated at any time the data cache settings are left blank (meaning the data is not cached). For example, if reloading the Inventory bean was measured to be an expensive operation, one option would be to split the Inventory bean into two distinct beans, separating the dynamic part of the Inventory bean (such as the quantity field, indicating quantity on hand) from the more static parts of the Inventory bean (such as the description). The new bean containing only static information could then be cached, and the cache invalidated only when the inventory descriptions were likely to be updated (such as once a day).

Deployment Time Binding Information

Having completed the deployment extensions, the only remaining configuration of the application is to complete the binding information. The bindings specify how the actual resource (such as a database) is *bound to* (or associated with) the logical representation of the resource (such as a data source).

Typically the bindings consist of defining JNDI names for each resource. The JNDI names can then be looked up at run time and used to access the concrete implementation of the resource. Before the application can be executed, the binding information defined in the application must be reconciled with the resources defined in the server configuration, and so changes may need to be made in both those areas. If you want to unit test the application, then the binding information can be defined within Studio as part of the unit test server configuration. Alternatively you can install the application into the server using the web-based administration console, and define the information that way. We'll describe both techniques here, although we'll focus on the Studio path.

Define JNDI Names for the Enterprise Beans

The first action is to ensure a JNDI name has been provided for each enterprise bean. The JNDI name is bound to the bean at install time, and used in the implementation of the lookup from the `InitialContext` factory. In Studio the name is entered in the EJB Deployment Descriptor editor, on the Beans tab. Any name can be used here, as long as it is consistent with that used in your application – but it's convention to qualify all the names for a related application into a similar structure; the format used for Plants by WebSphere is "`plantsby/`*Homename*". The JNDI names we're using are therefore:

Enterprise bean	JNDI name
Customer	plantsby/CustomerHome
Inventory	plantsby/InventoryHome
Order	plantsby/OrderHome
OrderIdGenerator	plantsby/OrderIdGeneratorHome
OrderItem	plantsby/OrderItemHome
Catalog	plantsby/CatalogHome
ShoppingCart	plantsby/ShoppingCartHome

Define the Data Sources Used

Next you need to ensure the data sources and database tables have been defined in order to execute the entity beans. The definition of a data source is specific to the database installation that will be used, and we'll describe the use of CloudScape initially. CloudScape is a pure Java, lightweight database that is shipped with WebSphere Application Server; so it is ideal for unit testing purposes. WebSphere has support for multiple database mappings to be defined for each CMP bean; see Chapter 9 for a complete discussion of this support.

> *A pre-populated CloudScape database for Plants-By-WebSphere is included on the CD with this book, as a zip file. To run the sample you need to unzip the file, and then later define the location in the server configuration. We shall be assuming it is unzipped in the* `C:/Wrox/5814/` *directory but it can be anywhere you like.*

Enterprise beans use a data source to access the database; the data source to be used needs to be specified in the entity bean deployment descriptor editor, and later declared and associated with an actual database in the server configuration. Session beans, and beans with bean-managed persistence need to use the JNDI name at run time to look up the data source, but beans with CMP persistence require special configuration. They use a connection factory, which provides access to the data source at run time. You can specify the connection factory on the overview page of the EJB Deployment Descriptor editor, at the bottom of the page. The CMP connection factory binding section allows you to enter the JNDI name that will be a default for all CMP beans in the JAR. It's also possible to override this default for each bean on the Beans page of the editor, but the JAR default will suffice for Plants-By-WebSphere.

You also need to select a container authorization type – this defines who is responsible for authenticating access to the database, the container or the connection factory. We want the authentication to be completed by the connection factory, so select Per_Connection_Factory for each bean.

The following screenshot shows both the JNDI name and data source setting for the Customer bean:

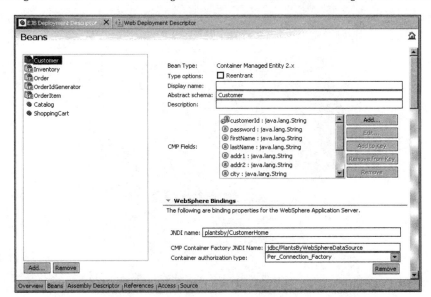

Create the Server Configuration and Data Source

We have now completed assembling the application itself. The next action is to create a server configuration, and add the application to that configuration. If you have not yet created a server configuration (or had one created for you by use of the Run on Server action), then you'll need to create one now. The easiest path is File | New | Other, then Server | Server and Server Configuration, and select the WebSphere version 5.0 | Test Environment:

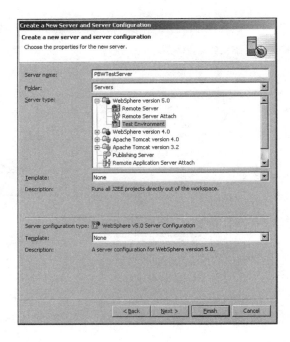

Define the Data Source

We now need to define the data source in our newly created server configuration. Go to the J2EE Hierarchy view, and in the server configurations tree locate the newly created server. Open the Server editor, and go to the Data sources page:

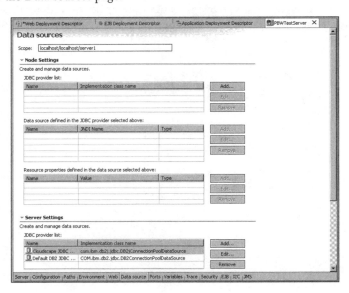

As you can see, we can define JDBC drivers for both the node and individual servers. For our purposes, we'll just use an individual server.

The first step is to ensure you have a JDBC provider defined; there should be pre-defined providers for both Cloudscape and DB2. Select the default CloudScape JDBC provider, and then hit the **Add** button by the data sources table.

As the Plants-By-WebSphere is an EJB 2.0 application, it requires a version 5 data source – select a **Version 5.0 data source**, and hit **Next**:

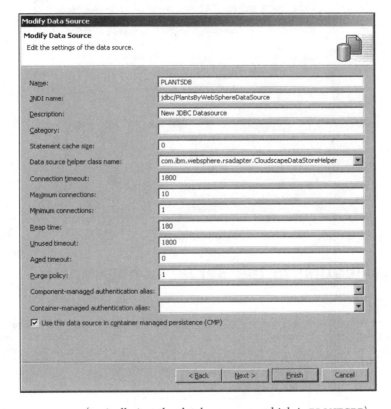

Enter the data source name (typically just the database name, which is PLANTSDB).

The JNDI name is the same as defined in the EJB reference above, which was "jdbc/PlantsByWebSphereDataSource". All other fields can be left as their default values. Hit **Next** to go to the data source properties page.

Cloudscape persists data as a simple directory in the file system, so you need to define in the data source where this will be. Ensure the **databaseName** property is selected, and enter the location of the database as the value of this property. If you extracted the database as described above, then this location will be C:/Wrox/5814/PLANTSDB, but it can be anywhere you have located the database. Remember to use forward slashes in the directory name:

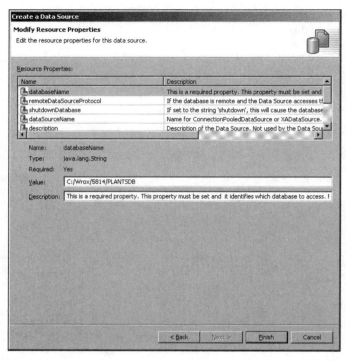

Hit Finish – you have completed creating the data source.

Add the Application to the Server Configuration

The final step before we can test the application is to add it to our newly created server configuration.

From the J2EE Hierarchy view, select the server configuration you created, and bring up the context menu. Select the Add item; all the enterprise applications in your workspace should be listed on the submenu. Select the Plants-By-WebSphere application, and it will be added to your server configuration:

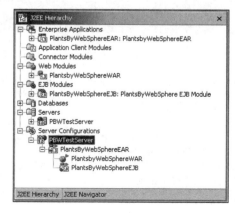

You are now ready to unit test the application in the Studio test environment.

Note that if you are creating an application and wish to quickly test it using a new database, Studio can complete many of the above steps for you automatically (for CMP beans using EJB 2.0 persistence to a CloudScape database). You must first add the application to the server configuration (as described above). Next, go to the Servers view; by default this is available as a tab in the Tasks view area. Select the server, and execute **Create tables and data sources** from the context menu. This action will define the data sources, and also create the CloudScape database for all CMP entity beans that are mapped to CloudScape. We could use this option to test Plants-By-WebSphere, but if you wish to use the pre-populated database you need to define the data source as described above.

Unit Testing the Application

The bulk of the server configuration and application installation can be completed automatically by the Studio unit test environment. If you have not generated the deployment code for your EJBs yet, now is the time to do so. From the J2EE Perspective, select the PlantsByWebSphereEJB project, and run the **Generate | Deploy and RMIC code** menu action. This will generate the Java RMI stubs and ties, plus all the code that the EJB container requires in order to host these EJBs. This includes such things as local/remote home and local/remote interface implementations, as well as artifacts necessary to support CMP persistence.

The creation of the server configuration, and execution of the unit test environment is started simply by selecting an application (typically the web project, although this action can be run from any module, and even some artifacts contained within the modules). So locate the index.html file in the **Web Content** folder for the PlantsByWebSphereWAR project, and from the context menu you can choose one of:

- ❏ Run on Server
  The run action will configure the server, start it, and display the artifact in the embedded Studio web browser.

- ❏ Debug on Server
  The debug action will do the same thing, but start the server JVM in debug mode, meaning you can set breakpoints in the application code.

- ❏ Profile on Server
  The profile action is the same again, but enables profiling of the resultant application.

The first response to this action is to display a dialog, allowing you to specify the server on which the application will be started. Once that's selected, the desired configuration will be generated, and the server started:

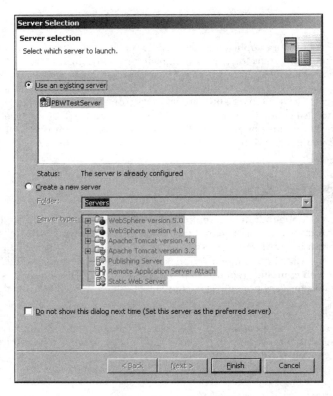

You should now be able to run the complete Plants-By-WebSphere application, in the Studio unit test environment.

Exporting the Application

Having completed your unit test, you'll want to install the application into a standalone server. To do this we'll need an EAR file to install. Therefore, we need to export our enterprise application project.

To do this is quite simple. Just select the PlantsByWebSphereEAR project in one of the J2EE views, right-click and choose Export. From the Export wizard, choose to export the project as an EAR file, then on the next screen, choose where to create the EAR file:

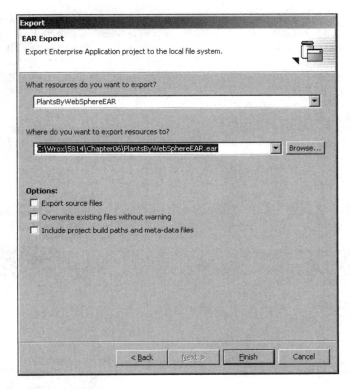

Just hit Finish to complete the process.

Deploying the Application

We will only discuss installation into small, departmental-scale servers here, but WebSphere is fully capable of scaling to a large-scale enterprise environment; see Chapter 11 and 12 for more details.

> **If you have the samples installed that ship with the default installation of WebSphere Application Server, then you will find you already have a PlantsByWebSphere application installed. The application we are developing in this book is somewhat different, so you will need to stop and then uninstall the full blown example application before you can deploy our new created version. Refer to Chapter 14 for more instructions on this process.**

The installation of applications into WebSphere version 5.0 is accomplished via a thin-client web application known at the **Administration Console**. The administration console is simply a web application that is provided with WebSphere 5.0. This allows for consistent administrative access to your applications from any network-connected machine, there's no client software (other than a browser) required.

It is possible to run the admin console in the Studio unit test environment; ensure that the administration console checkbox is selected in the server configuration editor, and then use the Run Administrative Console menu item from the context menu in the Servers view. However, more typically the unit test environment is configured via the Studio editors, and the admin console is only used to configure a standalone WebSphere instance. We'll describe the installation of the Plants-By-WebSphere application using the admin console now, and we'll use the opportunity to explain how to create a DB2 data source at the same time.

You can start the console simply by opening a browser to the remote server's URL; by default the admin console is configured to use a port of 9090, in which case the URL will be of the form http://your_host_name:9090/admin/. When you start the admin console, you are first prompted for a user ID – note that the ID is only used to track changes made to the configuration; it is not secure. You are then taken to the admin console's workspace home page:

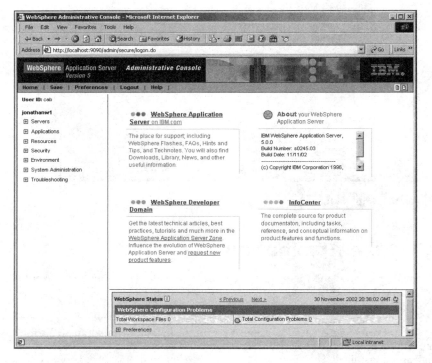

The home page consists of four main components:

❑ The items on the left of the screen show the actions you take, grouped by category.

❑ The central area of the screen is where the bulk of the data entry will occur. We'll walk through these screens below.

❑ The WebSphere Status area in the bottom right of the screen shows the health of the server; any problems detected will be displayed here.

❑ Finally, the menu bar across the top. Any changes you make will not be applied until you select Save from the menu bar, so it's important to remember this task.

Defining a New Data Source

> Again, if you had the default PlantsByWebSphere application installed then you will already have a data source configured. However, because we wish to use an XA-compliant data source, you should first delete the pre-configured data source and follow the steps outlined here to create a new one.

The first action to complete is the creation of the CloudScape data source. In order to support more advanced work in later chapters, we'll describe the creation of an XA-compliant CloudScape data source. Data sources are resources, so expand the **Resources** node on the left, and select **Manage JDBC Providers** and the **New** button on that page:

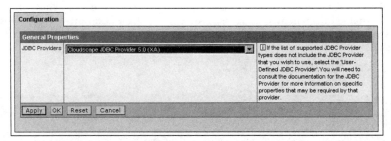

In the drop-down list, select the JDBC provider type you desire; we want **CloudScape JDBC Provider 5.0 (XA)**. Click the **OK** button to continue, and you can complete the definition of the JDBC provider. For most cases, the defaults here are correct, and you can just select **OK** again:

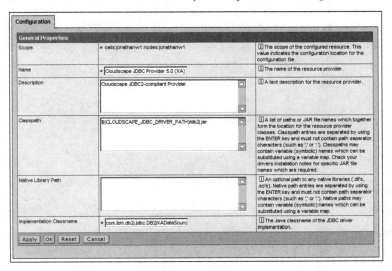

You've now defined the JDBC provider, and it (along with all other defined JDBC providers) will appear in the list shown below:

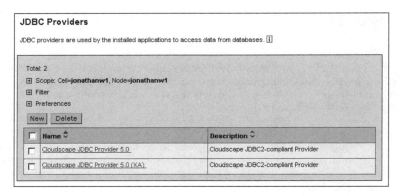

To create the data source, click on the hyperlink name of the new provider. This will take you back to a screen similar to that shown when creating the provider, but with additional options at the bottom. Scroll down, and you'll see a list including "data sources". Select that, and click New on the next screen, and you can configure the new data source as shown below:

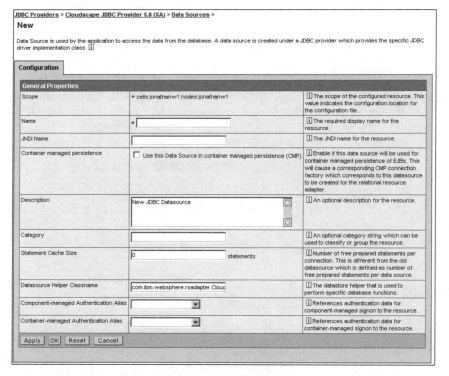

The settings here are very similar to those described previously in the Studio case:

❑ The name is simply used when displaying the data source.

❑ The JNDI name is critical; this is used when installing the application. We will use jdbc/PlantsByWebSphereDataSource.

- ❑ The **Use data source in container managed persistence** checkbox should be selected, to ensure that a CMP connector factory that corresponds to this data source is created for the relational resource adapter.

- ❑ The default data source helper class name should be correct; `com.ibm.websphere.rsadapter.CloudscapeDataStoreHelper`.

Click **OK** to save this data.

The next screen will display the data sources defined in the current provider; the newly created one should be in that list. We now need to configure some properties for the data source, so click the hypertext link that is its name.

As before, this will take you to a screen similar to that used to initially define the data source, but with additional options at the bottom of the screen. Scroll to the bottom, select the option **Custom Properties**, and you'll see the following screen:

⊞ Filter

Total: 8

⊞ Preferences

[New] [Delete]

☐	Name ↕	Value ↕	Description ↕	Required ↕
☐	connectionAttributes	-	Connection attributes specific to Cloudscape. Please see Cloudscape documentation for a complete list of features.	false
☐	createDatabase	-	If set to the string 'create', this will cause a new database of DatabaseName if that database does not already exist. The database is created when a connection object is obtained from the Data Source.	false
☐	dataSourceName	-	Name for ConnectionPooledDataSource or XADataSource. Not used by the data source object. Used for informational purpose only.	false
☐	databaseName	c:\Wrox\5814\PLANTSDB	This is a required property. This property must be set and it identifies which database to access. For example, c:/db/wombat.	true
☐	description	-	Description of the Data Source. Not used by the Data Source object. Used for informational purpose only.	false
☐	enableMultithreadedAccessDetection	false	Indicates whether or not to detect multithreaded access to a Connection and its corresponding Statements, ResultSets, and MetaDatas.	false
☐	remoteDataSourceProtocol	-	If the database is remote and the Data Source accesses the database via client server, set this property to specify what client/server protocol to use. Currently, the only protocol supported is 'rmi'.	false
☐	shutdownDatabase	-	If set to the string 'shutdown', this will cause the database to shutdown when a java.sql.Connection object is obtained from the Data Source. E.g., If the Data Source is an XADataSource, a getXAConnection ().getConnection() is necessary to cause the database to shutdown.	false

Each of the property names and values can be edited by clicking on them. The primary setting we need to change here is the database name, as we did before in Studio, to point to our PLANTSDB location. When complete, click the Save item in the menu bar; after prompting, the new data source will be saved for you as part of the server configuration. Although the administration console user interface is very different from that of the Studio editors, the result is identical; the changes you have made are persisted in a set of XML files that are saved on the server.

Install the Application

We next need to install the application. Expand the Applications node in the main tree view, and select Install New Application. You will first be prompted for the name of the EAR file to install. This file can be anywhere on your local file system, or it may be located on the server you are interacting with. In our case, we'll assume the file is available locally (this should be the EAR file we exported from Studio earlier in the chapter):

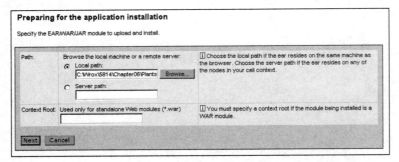

The next page allows us to indicate if default binding information should be generated automatically:

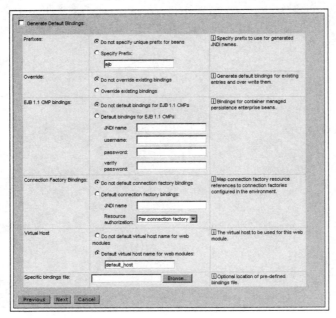

This automatic generation will consist of identifying all the unmapped references (such as `ejb-refs`) in the EAR, and then attempting to resolve them with resources that are defined in the EAR. In order to walk through the details, we'll leave the checkbox de-selected. This also means we do not need to select any of the subsequent fields, which are used to control the defaults when automatic binding is used. The rules used for the defaults are:

❑ EJB JNDI names are generated of the form `prefix/ejb-name`. The default prefix is `ejb`, but can be overridden. The `ejb-name` is as specified in the deployment descriptor's `<ejb-name>` tag.

❑ EJB references are bound as follows: If an `<ejb-link>` is found it will be honored. Otherwise, if a unique bean is found with a matching home (or local home) interface as the referenced bean, the reference will be resolved automatically.

❑ Resource reference bindings are derived from the `<res-ref-name>` tag. Note that this assumes that the `java:comp/env` name is the same as the resource's global JNDI name.

❑ Connection factory bindings (for EJB 2.0 JARs) are generated based on the JNDI name and authorization information provided. This results in the default connection factory being set for each EJB 2.0 JAR file in the application being installed. No bean-level connection factory bindings will be generated.

❑ Data source bindings (for EJB 1.1 JARs) are generated based on the JNDI name, and data source username password options. This results in the default data source being set for each EJB JAR. No bean-level data source bindings are generated.

❑ Message-driven bean (MDB) listener ports are derived from the MDBs by the `<ejb-name>` tag with the string `Port` appended.

❑ For WAR files, the virtual host will be set as `default_host` unless otherwise specified.

The default binding action will suffice for most applications, but is not suitable if:

❑ You want to explicitly control the global JNDI name(s) of one or more EJB files.

❑ You need finer-grained control of data source bindings for CMPs. That is, you have multiple data sources and need more than one global data source.

❑ You must map resource references to global resource JNDI names that are different from the `java:comp/env` name.

Hitting the Next button on this page will start the series of pages known as the **Application Installation wizard**.

> Note that some of the pages are added dynamically, and depending on the choices you make the page numbers may not always be the same.

You can navigate to any page of the wizard directly, by using the hypertext links for each page. Any data that is not completed when you finish the wizard will have defaults provided:

The first page allows you to provide additional options regarding the installation process itself:

- ❏ Pre-compile JSP files if you are deploying an application to a server that will require a quick response the first time a page is hit; but this action will also take some time to complete during the installation. If you are just debugging or testing an application, you may wish not to pre-compile your JSP files.

- ❏ The directory to install the application is the resultant directory for your application; this can be left blank in most cases and the default location of installedApps will be used.

- ❏ The ability to distribute your application refers to the installation of your application into a multi-server networked environment; if you select this, the application will be distributed to all node servers.

- ❏ The binary configuration option allows you to select if a previous set of configuration data saved in the module (such as the data entered in Studio) should be used. If it is not used, then defaults will be provided in most cases.

- ❏ Deploy EJBs allows you to indicate if the EJB deployment code generation action should be run on the server prior to installation. You can deselect this if the EJB deployment code was previously generated (either in Studio, or by using the "EJBDeploy" tool that is shipped with WebSphere). For now, select the button to re-deploy the archive.

- ❏ The application name is just used to identify the application later; the name can be anything.

Step 2 allows you to enter data required for the EJB deployment code generation:

❑ The first two fields allow you to define the classpath and any additional RMIC options required to complete the deploy action.

❑ The database options (type, schema, and name) are only applicable for CMP entity beans, if you have not created a schema map in the JAR. In that case, the settings entered here will be used to create a schema map "top-down" (based on the bean definition) using the database details provided.

We now need to define the JNDI names for each EJB in the application. The JNDI names are used within your application to look up the various home beans from the initial context factory, so it's important to ensure the data entered here is consistent with your application usage:

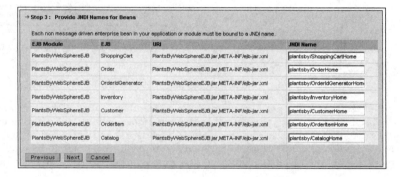

The next action is to define the default data source information for the application, and the JNDI name of the data source to use for the archive. This is the data source that will be used for all CMP beans that do not override the setting on the next page.

> There is a special rule that affects the JNDI name of data sources used by CMP beans. Additional infrastructure is required for a data source to be used by CMP beans, and this modified data source has a slightly different JNDI name; it is given a prefix of **eis/** and a suffix of **_CMP**. For Plants-By-WebSphere, we defined the data source as **jdbc/PlantsByWebSphereDataSource**, but references to it need to use **eis/jdbc/PlantsByWebSphereDataSource_CMP**.

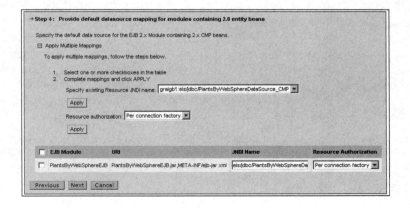

We next have the ability to override the module default for the data source to use, on a bean-by-bean basis. As before, the JNDI name is used within your application to locate the data source:

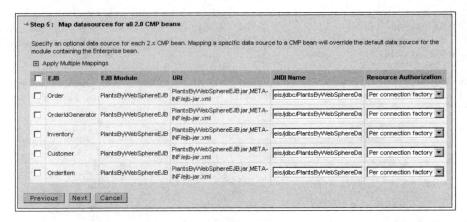

The resource authorization can be per-container or per-connection factory. Container managed authentication is used when you want to control access to a resource, but not by individual ID. In this case, you use the same ID for all access to the resource, and the ID and password declared in the bindings is used. Connection factory resource authentication means that each individual must authenticate themselves to the resource. This must be done by the client code that gets the connection from the factory.

We now move on o completing the EJB references. As described above in the Studio-based support, the references are defined by the bean provider, but the JNDI name of the bean that resolves each reference must be completed. For example, the `Catalog` bean has an `ejb-ref` to `ejb/InventoryHome`, but we now need to bind that reference to the same JNDI name set on Step 3, which was `plantsby/InventoryHome` in this case:

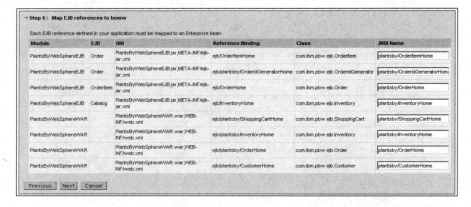

The next page allows you to map virtual hosts for the web application. Virtual hosts allow you to emulate multiple hosts from a single server. We do not need this capability in the Plants-By-WebSphere application:

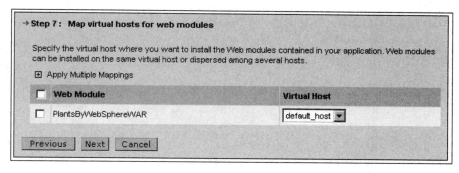

Step 8 in the wizard allows the application to be mapped to multiple servers. This capability is required when you are administering a cluster of servers, and is not required if we are just installing the application onto a single server:

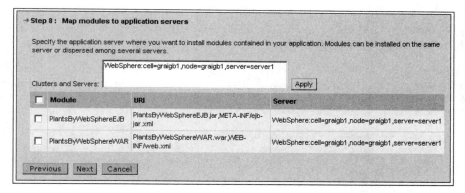

We next need to map any security roles defined in the application to users. As we are not enabling security in the Plants-By-WebSphere application, we can leave these selections blank:

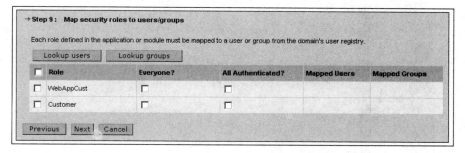

The final data collection page in the wizard verifies the state of all unprotected methods in the application; you can assign a required security role to any such methods, or leave them unprotected:

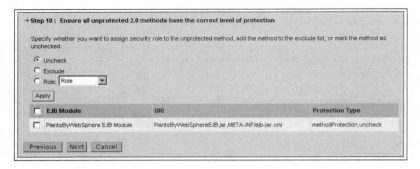

You can now select the final (summary) page in the wizard, and after verifying the data shown click **Finish** to install the application. The server will process the application for a moment or two, and your application will be installed and available from the server. Don't forget to select the **Save** item on the menu, to save the configuration.

> *If your application contained any web services then there would be a couple of additional steps to this wizard – see Chapter 8 for more details.*

The installed application can now be accessed from any browser. The URL will be constructed as http://you_host_name:port/contextroot. By default, the port is 9080, and the context root we assigned for the application was PlantsByWebSphere. These combine to form a URL of http://you_host_name:9080/PlantsByWebSphere, which will result in a page like this:

Summary

The late binding of server-specific information as you assemble and install an application is one of the benefits of the J2EE architecture, and is what allows components of an application to be reused in multiple scenarios. In this chapter we have reviewed the assembly of the web and enterprise bean components into the complete application. The references within the components were resolved, and the complete application was built. This process can be completed using the WebSphere Application Assembly Tool, but for newly created applications it is easier to complete the assembly within Studio, as we did in this chapter. We also reviewed the deployment of an application, and the installation of that application into the Studio unit test server and a production server.

7

EIS Integration and Messaging

So far, we have discussed how to build the presentation and business logic for an application and how to assemble them together. The business logic can be tied to a relational database using entity EJBs to provide object-oriented data access.

In this chapter, we will explore other forms of access, including asynchronous messaging and procedural data access. Asynchronous messaging will be discussed by adding it to the PlantsByWebSphere example application. Procedural access will be discussed from a client point of view, but is not included by example because of the effort required to create an example by hand and the lack of common backends that an example could draw from.

We will also look at the Service-Oriented Architecture. Service-Oriented Architecture provides a means of describing, publishing, locating, and accessing systems in a synchronous and asynchronous manner. It complements the existing J2EE functionality by defining a mechanism that non-J2EE applications can use to access applications deployed in a J2EE environment, as well as providing new means for J2EE applications to communicate. The Service-Oriented Architecture is introduced at the end of this chapter and covered in more detail in Chapter 8.

The integration of back-end systems with J2EE applications can be performed in a number of ways depending on the requirements of the integration. The J2EE architecture provides three technologies useful for Enterprise Information System (EIS) integration. They are:

- ❑ **JDBC**
  Provides both a direct form of access to database information, and an object model form of access using EJBs. This has already been discussed as part of the business logic chapter.

- ❑ **Java Message Service (JMS)**
  Provides a messaging API that allows for asynchronous communications between applications, though synchronous messaging is also possible.

□ **J2EE Connector Architecture**
Provides synchronous integration APIs to a wide range of resource managers.

Asynchronous Messaging

JMS (http://java.sun.com/products/jms/docs.html) provides the ability for an application to send messages to another application without waiting for a reply. There are two forms of message delivery that are supported:

□ **Point-to-Point using message queues**
Allows a peer-to-peer form of communication in which two parties agree to provide the roles of message producer and message consumer, as shown in the figure below:

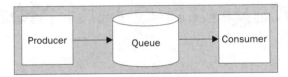

□ **Publish/Subscribe using message topics**
Allows for a one-many communications pattern, shown in the figure below, where a message producer places messages into a topic based on its topic name. Consumers that are interested in that topic can then subscribe to be notified when a message for that topic has arrived:

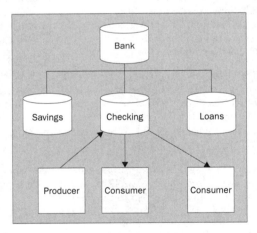

The following sections describe WebSphere's support of messaging followed by an extension of the PlantsByWebSphere application to support order processing using messaging.

WebSphere Messaging Engines

WebSphere provides support for a number of different messaging engines for use within the various WebSphere products. They are:

❑ LightWeight JMS

❑ Embedded JMS

❑ External JMS/MQ

These three messaging engines cover different needs and are discussed in more detail below.

Lightweight JMS

The WebSphere Lightweight JMS engine provides messaging support for development tools – **WebSphere Studio Application Developer** (**WSAD**) in particular – for rapid iterative development use. WSAD uses the lightweight JMS engine to provide messaging support within the unit test environment. However, this does not imply that WSAD cannot be used with the other messaging engines. It can be configured to use any of the three JMS engines. See the *Configuring the Test Environment* section for details on setting up connection factories.

The Lightweight JMS engine provides a close approximation to the J2EE-required JMS functionality; but trades off support for security, persistence, and recoverability, for a quicker startup time. Both point-to-point and publish/subscribe messaging are supported. It will accept durable subscriptions and persistent messages, but they will not be persisted across a server restart. The lightweight JMS engine will also support transactional semantics, but the transaction will not be logged or recoverable across server restart.

The Lightweight JMS provider is designed to be an in-process JMS engine and will not interoperate with the other WebSphere JMS engines. It is installed as part of the WSAD installation.

Embedded JMS

The embedded JMS engine provides a subset of the WebSphere MQ 5.3 and WebSphere MQ Event Broker 2.1 functionality. It is a fully J2EE-compliant messaging engine. JMS provider management is integrated with WebSphere Systems Management. The message engine server is automatically started and stopped as part of the server configuration. Topics and queues can be created as part of the JMS resource configuration. The embedded JMS provider can only be installed if WebSphere MQ is not already installed on the node.

External JMS/MQ

The external JMS engine provides complete functionality for JMS messaging including message queue clustering support. There can only be one WebSphere MQ JMS provider, embedded or external, installed on a node. If WebSphere MQ is installed before the WebSphere Application Server, the external WebSphere MQ already installed will be used. If WebSphere MQ is not installed before WebSphere is installed, the embedded JMS will be installed and can be upgraded to use the full external WebSphere MQ by installing it after WebSphere Application Server is installed.

The WebSphere product family provides additional messaging support in the form of WebSphere MQ Integrator Broker, which provides rule-based message transformation and routing that can be visually composed into message flows.

Other Supported Messaging Providers

In general, WebSphere supports the use of MQ-based JMS providers. Other JMS providers can be used from a client point of view for non-managed connections to a JMS provider, but they cannot replace the functions provided by the WebSphere messaging engines. These non-managed connections are obtained using the same programming model as WebSphere MQ-based JMS connections, but they are not integrated to provide connection-pooling behavior.

WAS expects a JMS provider to have implemented the Application Server Facilities (ASF) of the JMS specification to fully integrate with the runtime (for example, to drive work on message-driven beans). Many JMS providers do not implement this part of the specification.

The Messaging Component Model

Normally, a JMS client sends and receives messages by opening a connection to a JMS queue or topic and then using that connection to transmit a message. However, to asynchronously receive a message in the application server runtime, a thread would have to wait for an incoming message to be received. That is where **Message-Driven Beans (MDB)** come into play. The figure below shows a simple messaging application:

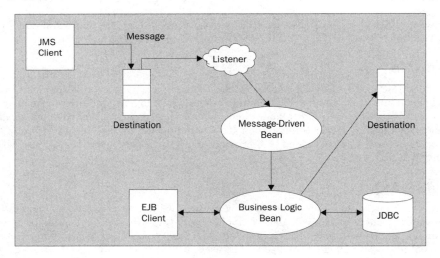

Message-Driven Beans

MDB is an extension to the EJB programming model that allows the container to drive asynchronous work using a component model. Declarations are made in deployment descriptors, which describe the message selector to use and hint at the destination type. The message selector can be used to filter messages that an MDB processes, based on property values. During deployment, this is matched up to a JMS listener port. When a message is received, an MDB instance is driven to service it. The following sections describe how to use WebSphere to build and run a messaging application. The PlantsByWebSphere application will be extended with messaging to support decoupling of order processing from the application.

Designing an Application for Messaging

The first thing to do is identify the JMS resources that the application needs to use. In particular, a decision needs to be made on whether to use point-to-point or publish/subscribe messaging. The choice will also help identify the properties of resources that need to be used within the application, and configured as application deployment descriptors, or within WAS. For this example, a point-to-point queue will be used to deliver notifications to an order-processing subsystem that an order has been received. Pub/sub is not necessary here because the topology will require a single queue and consumer. The order processing subsystem will then take care of processing the order and updating inventory. No message selector will be used to filter incoming messages because all messages will contain an order that needs to be recorded.

It is recommended that we delegate the business processing of incoming messages to another EJB. This provides a clear separation of message handling and business processing, which have different requirements for security, transactions, and scalability. This also enables the business processing to be invoked either by the arrival of incoming messages, or, for example, from a WebSphere J2EE client.

It is important to remember that the client identity that initiated the message does not flow with the message. A run-as identity may be specified to associate an identity with the message request.

Message processing transaction requirements may also be specified. In this case, the processing of the message and placement of the order in the database should occur under the same transaction so that if rollback occurs, the message is not processed. During rollback, the unprocessed message is placed back on the queue to be processed again until the JMS listener threshold is reached or the message is moved (by the JMS provider) to some dead letter queue. The WebSphere JMS/MQ provider provides two queue attributes, backout threshold and backout-requeue queue. The threshold prevents transactional processing loops where a rollback puts a message back on the queue only to be processed and rolled back again. Once the threshold is reached, it is moved to the queue declared by the backout-requeue queue attribute.

One thing to keep in mind while designing and constructing an application using JMS messaging is that WebSphere MQ supports clustering and fail-over of queues if the full WebSphere MQ product (External JMS/MQ provider) is used, but does not support clustering of topics. See the *Managing WebSphere Messaging* section for more details.

Building a Messaging Application

WebSphere Studio Application Developer supports both development and unit testing of MDBs. This section will use messaging to extend the PlantsByWebSphere application to add order fulfilment processing to the existing order-entry capabilities.

The first thing to accomplish is to define the message structure to be passed as a message. For this particular example, we will use a JMS `TextMessage` to carry the order key information. There are other message types that could be used (for details on the JMS specification see http://java.sun.com/products/jms/), but a `TextMessage` is the most commonly used message type. Next, we will divide and conquer using specific EJBs to handle specific message processing functions. A local stateless session EJB will be used to handle sending the order to the fulfillment subsystem. A MDB will be used to receive the message, and fulfillment processing will be handled by a stateless session EJB. Here are the steps for the order sender EJB:

Use the wizard selection panel to create a J2EE enterprise bean in the `PlantsByWebSphereEJB` project. Select Session Bean, and give it a name like OrderSender, with a package name like com.ibm.pbw.ejb, and click Next:

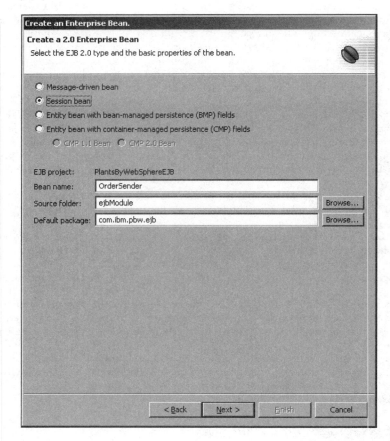

Here, be sure to select a Local client view and uncheck the Remote client view. Since we do not intend to make a remote view available, change the local interface name to OrderSender and the home interface to OrderSenderHome, as shown, and then click Finish:

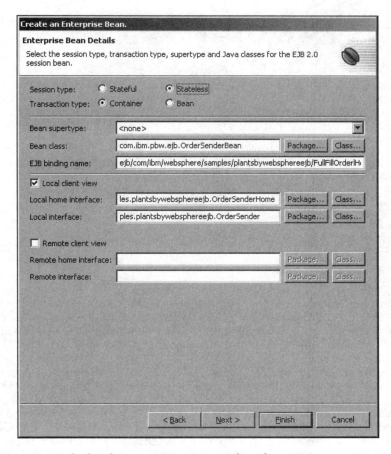

Add a `sendOrder()` method to the `OrderSenderBean` that takes `Order` as an argument. Add business logic to send a JMS TextMessage to the order fulfillment queue. The code should look like the following:

```
public void sendOrder(Order o) {

  try {
    //initiate the order fulfillment process
    Context ctx = Util.getInitialContext();
    QueueConnectionFactory qcf =
                        (QueueConnectionFactory) ctx.lookup(
                        "java:comp/env/jms/ConnectionFactory");
    Queue q = (Queue) ctx.lookup(
                        "java:comp/env/jms/FulfillmentQueue");
    QueueConnection conn = qcf.createQueueConnection();
    QueueSession session = conn.createQueueSession(true,
                        Session.AUTO_ACKNOWLEDGE);
```

```
          QueueSender sender = session.createSender(q);
          //not necessary to start a connection to send a message
          //conn.start();

          //create msg
          String key = ((OrderKey) o.getPrimaryKey()).orderId;
          TextMessage msg = session.createTextMessage(key);

          //send it
          sender.send(msg);

          sender.close();
          session.close();
          conn.close();
      } catch (NamingException e) {
          e.printStackTrace();
      } catch (JMSException e) {
          e.printStackTrace();
      }
  }
```

As you can see, there is a fair amount of coding involved in setting up and managing a standard JMS queue connection for sending a message. First, we must create a connection factory for the queue, then use the factory to create a connection. The connection is then used to create a session, which is used to create a message sender. Finally, a message can be created and sent. WebSphere provides extensions to ease this burden by encapsulating message sender logic in message sender beans.

The connection factory uses the security identity defined by the deployment descriptor or the ID and password provided by the application when the connection is created (if the application chooses to provide them). The credentials are authenticated before processing proceeds. WebSphere provides additional authorization extensions to control access to JMS resources if the embedded JMS provider is used and security is enabled. See was_install\config\integral-jms-authorisations.xml for configuring permissions granted to queues and topics. A cell-based configuration file exists at was_install\config\cells\your_cell_name\integral-jms-authorisations.xml. Be sure to promote the sendOrder() method to the local interface. Set the deployment descriptor container transaction settings for the sendOrder() method to Mandatory, as this will ensure that acceptance of the order by the order fulfillment subsystem will be tied to order entry.

Add a resource reference to the OrderSender EJB deployment descriptor information for the queue connection factory. To do this, edit the deployment descriptor for the module, click the References tab, select the OrderSender bean, and click the Add button. Select EJB resource reference and click Next.

The name must be consistent with the application code used to look up the connection factory. For example, if the code wants to look up java:comp/env/jms/ConnectionFactory, the name of the resource reference must be jms/ConnectionFactory. The type should be javax.jms.QueueConnectionFactory because we are using a queue to send the message. Other resource types include a topic connection factory and a Java 2 Connector connection factory. Set Authentication to Container and Sharing scope can be left as Sharable. Click Finish. See the following figure for an example:

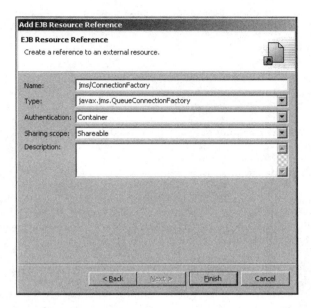

Set the JNDI binding in the deployment descriptor for `jms/ConnectionFactory` to `jms/FulfillmentQCF`. This can be done by selecting the resource and entering the binding in the WebSphere Bindings section. The server configuration will need to be updated to used to set up the connection factory with this JNDI name, as we will see later.

Now add a resource environment reference to the `OrderSender` EJB for the queue. In this case, the **Name** should be `jms/FulfillmentQueue` and the **Type** should be **Queue**.

Set the JNDI binding in the deployment descriptor for `jms/FulfillmentQueue` to `jms/FulfillmentQueue`. The server configuration will need to be updated to create a JMS destination with this JNDI name. This will be handled later.

Now, we need to tie order creation to initiating the order fulfillment process. There are two ways to approach this. One way is to modify the `OrderModel` in the presentation logic to send a message after using the `Order` EJB home to create an order. However, if the `Order` EJB is used to create orders from other locations, then they will need to be modified as well. The alternative is to have the `Order` EJB itself create and send the message. This means that the `Order` EJB will be operating under a two-phase commit transaction protocol. The two-phase commit transaction support allows both order creation and message sending to occur together or not all. Modify the `OrderBean`'s `ejbPostCreate()` method to call the `OrderSender` EJB `sendOrder()` method. The following can be added to the end of the method:

```
        setOrderitem(orderItems);

    OrderSenderHome senderHome = (OrderSenderHome) ctx.lookup(
                        "java:comp/env/ejb/OrderSenderHome");
    OrderSender sender = senderHome.create();
    sender.sendOrder((Order) myEntityCtx.getEJBLocalObject());
    sender.remove();
```

```
    }
  catch (Exception e) {
    throw new EJBException(e);
  }
}
```

Add the `OrderSender` local EJB reference to the deployment descriptor as described in Chapter 5.

At this point, creating an order will not only add a row to the database table represented by the `Order` EJB, it will also send a message to the order fulfillment subsystem using a message queue. This is all done under the same transaction so that order entry and fulfillment process initiation happen together or not at all. However, fulfillment processing happens asynchronously.

We now start on the message consumer side of the application by creating the business logic to process order fulfillment. We will create a `FulfillOrder` stateless session EJB with a `processOrder()` method that handles the business logic for fulfillment. This allows the message processing functionality to be segregated into an `OrderReceiver` MDB.

The business logic for the order fulfillment process will simply be to check that the inventory can satisfy the order and reduce the inventory quantities if the order can be met. However, there may be a case where inventory is less than required by an order. To discontinue processing when inventory does not meet the order requirements, an application exception needs to be created. An exception thrown during order processing will flow back to the order receiver component and it will force the transaction to roll back.

Create an `InsufficientInventoryException` Java class that extends `java.lang.Exception` as part of the `com.ibm.pbw.ejb` package. The constructor should take a `String` as a message argument and call the super-class constructor with the argument:

```
package com.ibm.pbw.ejb;

public class InsufficientInventoryException extends Exception {
   public InsufficientInventoryException(String msg) {
      super(msg);
   }
}
```

Now that we have the exception to pass from the fulfillment process business logic, we can create the bean itself, using the following steps:

Create a stateless session EJB called `FulfillOrder` in the same package as the `OrderSender` EJB. It should use a container transaction type. Add a local client view in addition to the remote client view. The local client view will be used by the `OrderReceiver` MDB for initiating fulfillment processing on an order. The remote client view could be used to initiate order processing manually by a remote client if necessary:

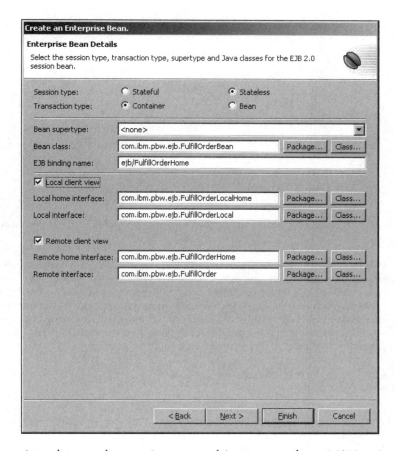

Add two new private data members, `orderHome` and `invHome`, to the `FulfillOrderBean` class. These data members will be used to cache references to `OrderHome` and `InventoryHome` classes. Add a private getter method for each that initializes and returns the private data members. These should be like the following:

```
private InventoryHome getInvHome() {

  try {
    InitialContext ic = new InitialContext();
    if (invHome == null) {
      invHome = (InventoryHome)
        ic.lookup("java:comp/env/ejb/InventoryHome");
    }
    return invHome;

  } catch (NamingException e) {
    return null;
  }
```

```
  }

  private OrderHome getOrderHome() {

    try {
      InitialContext ic = new InitialContext();
      if (orderHome == null) {
        orderHome = (OrderHome)
          ic.lookup("java:comp/env/ejb/OrderHome");
      }
      return orderHome;

    } catch (NamingException e) {
      return null;
    }
  }
```

Add the two local EJB references used by the JNDI lookups to the deployment descriptor as described in Chapter 5.

Add a `processOrder()` method that takes a `String` key argument (the key found in the message) to the `FulfillOrderBean` class and have it throw the `InsufficientInventoryException`. The business logic uses the `orderHome()` to find the order that needs to be processed based on the argument. It then checks the inventory for each item on the order to see if sufficient quantity exists. If there is enough quantity, the inventory count is decremented by the order item count. If not, then processing is stopped and an exception is thrown. It is expected that the caller will roll back the transaction currently in progress when this happens. This example code is part of our continuing example:

```
public void processOrder(String key)
    throws InsufficientInventoryException {

  try {
    Order order = getOrderHome().findByPrimaryKey(new OrderKey(key));
    Iterator items = order.getOrderitem().Iterator();

    while (items.hasNext()) {
      OrderItem oi = (OrderItem)items.next();

      //get inventory info
      Inventory inv = getInvHome().findByPrimaryKey(new
                                  InventoryKey(oi.getId()));

      //check inventory quantity
      if (inv.getQuantity() >= oi.getQuantity()) {
        //decrement inventory count
          inv.setQuantity(inv.getQuantity() - oi.getQuantity());

      } else {
        //stop order processing
        throw new InsufficientInventoryException(
          "requested " + oi.getQuantity() + " have " +
          inv.getQuantity());
      }
    }
  } catch (FinderException e) { }
}
```

In the Outline view, promote the processOrder() method to the remote and local interface.

In the Assembly Descriptor settings of the deployment descriptor, add a Mandatory transaction type for the processOrder() method. This will ensure that it is called within a transaction.

This completes the creation of the business logic for the fulfilment process. We now set up the message handling part of the message consumer by creating a MDB to receive the order message and initiate order fulfilment processing, using the following steps:

Use the wizard selection panel to create a new J2EE Enterprise Bean. Select **Message-driven bean** and enter the **OrderReceiver** as the bean name. Make sure the package and source directory are correct and click **Next**:

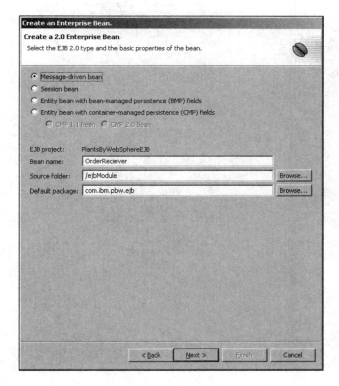

This will display the MDB details page. Ensure **Container Transaction type** is selected. This will enable the message receipt and order fulfillment processing to run under the same transaction. If order fulfillment needs to be rolled back for any reason, the message will be placed back on the queue for reprocessing. Select **Queue** for the **Destination Type**. The selector can be left blank because all messages will be delivered to the MDB for processing. The **ListenerPort** is a binding to a specific connection factory defined in the server configuration. It is not necessary to fill this in, but it does prevent having to specify the binding during deployment if the binding is already known. For rapid iterative development in a WSAD unit test environment, it provides information to automatically generate a server configuration. Give the **ListenerPort** the name **OrderReceiverListenerPort** and click Finish:

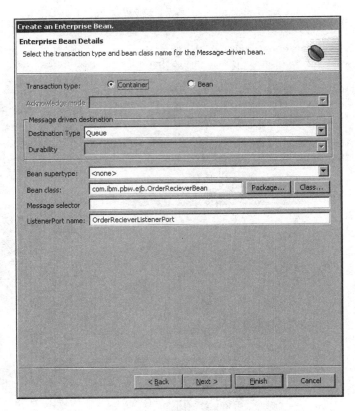

Create a cached reference to `FulfillOrderLocalHome` in the `OrderReceiver` MDB. Declare a private `fulfillOrderLocalHome` member in the `OrderReceiverBean` class and add the following code to the `ejbCreate()` method:

```
public void ejbCreate() {
   try {
      fulfillOrderLocalHome = (FulfillOrderLocalHome)
         Util.getInitialContext()
            .lookup("java:comp/env/ejb/FulfillLocalOrderHome");
   } catch (javax.naming.NamingException e) { }
}
```

Be sure to add a local EJB reference for `ejb/FulfillOrderLocalHome` to the deployment descriptor. For a real application, the exception logic should be filled in with logging information and an `EJBException` would be thrown to let the container know the MDB is not in an acceptable state for additional processing.

Next, edit the `onMessage()` method to receive a `TextMessage` and initiate order processing using the data found in the message. The method should look as shown:

```
public void onMessage(javax.jms.Message msg) {
  TextMessage m = (TextMessage)msg;

  try {
    String orderKey = m.getText();
    FulfillOrderLocal fulfill;
    fulfill = fulfillOrderLocalHome.create();
     fulfill.processOrder(orderKey);
     fulfill.remove();

  } catch (InsufficientInventoryException e) {
    //rollback tran for later processing
    fMessageDrivenCtx.setRollbackOnly();

  } catch (JMSException e) {
  } catch (CreateException e) {
  } catch (RemoveException e) { }
}
```

Under normal circumstances, additional code would be required in the `catch` blocks to deal with the exceptions, such as logging the exceptions and potentially rolling back the transaction. For this example, the error case will be left as an exercise for the reader.

Add the `OrderReceiver onMessage()` method to the required container transaction set in the **Assembly Descriptor** tab of the deployment descriptor. To do this, open the EJB Deployment Descriptor editor and switch to the Assembly Descriptor tab. The container transactions section allows a new container transaction setting to be added via the **Add** button or an existing **Required** transaction setting can be edited using the **Edit** button. Click **Add**, to add a new transaction setting. Select the **OrderReceiver** EJB and click **Next**. Select the **Required** transaction type and the **onMessage()** method and click **Finish**:

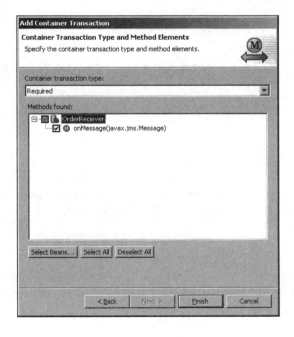

WAS provides an extension that allows methods to run in a local transaction as well, but in most cases a global transaction will be desired. This is used mainly for recovery of dangling resources not contained within a global transaction unit of work (for example, uncommitted updates to a JDBC resource).

To make things more interesting, we will modify the presentation to display the current inventory. This will require updates to the `com.ibm.pbw.ejb.StoreItem`, `com.ibm.pbw.war.InventoryModel`, and `product.jsp`, using the following steps:

Edit the `StoreItem` class. Add a private `int inStock` data member and public getter and setter methods for it. Save the changes.

Edit the `InventoryModel` class and update the methods that create and initialize a `StoreItem` class to also set the `inStock` value:

```
private StoreItem InventoryToStoreItem(Inventory inv) {
  StoreItem si = new StoreItem(inv);
  si.setInStock(inv.getQuantity());
  return si;
}
```

Edit `product.jsp`. Join the cells in the third row of the table then add some text that says, " **items are available in stock**". Place the insert point before the text and use **JSP | Insert Expression** to insert an expression. The value of the expression should be `item.getInStock()`:

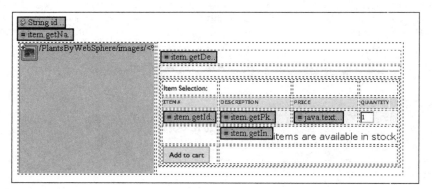

Configuring the Test Environment

Use of the test environment is dependent upon the application scenario being used. The test environment's MQJD Lightweight JMS provider does not support two-phase commit with JMS resources, but a two-phase solution was used for developing the Plants-By-WebSphere application. The *Managing WebSphere Messaging* section discusses how to prepare the WAS for running the Plants-By-WebSphere application. If a single-phase solution is used, this section describes how to configure the test environment.

The server configuration must be edited to configure the queue connection factory, JMS destination, queue names served by the server, and the MDB listener ports. Similar configuration management will be done for the WAS.

To edit the test environment configuration, use the server perspective to display the server configurations that were created earlier. Double-click the WebSphere v5.0 test environment in the **Server Configuration** view to edit it. We need to create an authentication ID to use first. Select the **Security** tab and click the **Add** button for the **JAAS Authentication Entries**. Enter your local ID and password and give the entry an alias name to represent those credentials. Click **OK**.

Select the JMS tab to display the JMS server configuration settings. Click the **Add** button for the **WASQueueConnectionFactory** entries. The name can be whatever name you want to call the connection factory. The JNDI name configured here and the JNDI name declared earlier when the JMS resource reference was created need to match. In this case, use `jms/FulfillmentQCF`. **Description** and **Category** are descriptive fields used for helping to organize the connection factories, but do not affect the runtime.

The **Component-managed authentication alias** and **Container-managed authentication alias** represent the credentials to use depending on what type of authentication was chosen when the JMS resource reference was created. Recall that container authentication was chosen. Therefore, choose the authentication alias created earlier from the **Container-managed authentication alias** drop-down menu. If application authentication was chosen when the resource reference was created, the **Component-managed authentication alias** drop-down menu would be used.

Choose the **Node** and **Server Name** from their drop-down menus. There should only be one choice in the test environment. The rest of the options configure connection pool management and are listed in the figure below. Click **OK**.

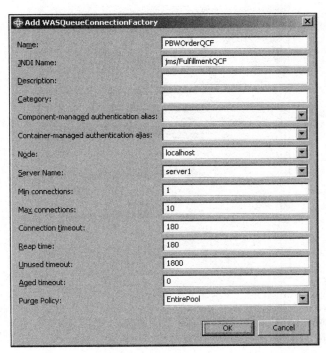

For publisher-subscriber messaging, a topic connection factory would be created instead. As part of creating the topic connection factory, a choice of the JMS server port to be used depends on your needs for transactions or performance:

❑ **Queued Port**
The TCP/IP port number of the listener port used for all point-to-point and publisher-subscriber support.

❑ **Direct Port**
The TCP/IP port number of the listener port used for direct TCP/IP connection (non-transactional, non-persistent, and non-durable subscriptions only) for Pub/Sub support.

Note that MDBs cannot use the direct listener port for publisher-subscriber support. Therefore, any topic connection factory configured with a direct port cannot be used with MDBs.

Now that the connection factory is configured, create the destination. Click the Add button for the WASQueue entries. Set the Name to the name of the queue. By convention, the JMS destination name is the name of the queue prefixed by jms/, but it must match with the JNDI setting used earlier when the JMS destination resource environment reference was created. Select the Node from the drop-down menu and set Persistence to be PERSISTENT. Normally, this would ensure the message survives a crash or shutdown, but the test environment ignores this setting. The Priority settings control message priority, and the Expiry settings control expiration of messages on the queue. This is shown in the figure below. Click OK.

The server needs to be configured to host the destination just configured. Under the JMS Server Properties section of the JMS tab, click the Add button to add a queue name. Enter the name of the Fulfillment destination just created. Be sure the Initial State is START. This will make sure the JMS server is started as part of the server process startup:

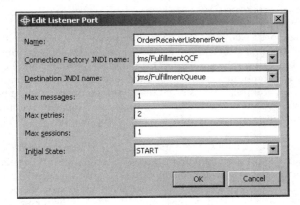

Now create the JMS listener port for the MDB. Switch to the **EJB** tab and click the **Add** button for the **Listener Ports**. Enter a name for the listener port. This name must match the listener port used earlier when the MDB was created or during deployment, it will be necessary to choose a listener port binding for the MDB. The connection factory and destination can be chosen from the drop-down menus. The **Max messages** and **Max sessions** define concurrency settings for the listener port. Set **Max retries** to 2. It defines how many times a message can be processed before the listener is shutdown. This prevents processing loops when something goes wrong. The **Initial State** of **START** will ensure the listener processes messages as soon as the server is started and is shown in the figure below. Click **OK**.

Save the changes to the server configuration.

This completes the set up for messaging support in the Plants-By-WebSphere application. When the Plants-By-WebSphere application is run on the test environment server, it will be possible to order a set of items, note their inventory level, and then return to those item descriptions after the order is submitted and notice the inventory levels they have been decremented. If your order exceeds the inventory level, the fulfilment processing will attempt to process the order twice and then shutdown the listener to prevent a processing loop.

Recall earlier that connection properties can be set for a backout threshold and queue. Setting up another queue and these properties will allow the offending message to be removed from the queue so that other messages can be processed rather than shutting down all message processing.

Container-Managed Messaging

MDBs provide a component-based approach for dealing with inbound message processing. WebSphere Application Server xD provides extensions beyond this to cover container-managed outbound messaging, which in conjunction with J2EE MDBs are collectively called **Message Beans**. The inbound side, covered by MDB support, is abstractly known as Receiver Beans. Sender Beans cover the outbound messaging and convert method calls into outbound messages. Reply support is provided by `ReplySender` and `ReplyReceiver` beans.

Managing WebSphere Messaging

This section describes how to use the WebSphere administration console to manage applications that use messaging. We will use the Plants-By-WebSphere application to walk through the setup and management process. There are two ways to manage messaging for WAS. Management of the embedded JMS engine is integrated with the WAS administration console. WebSphere MQ handles administration of the External JMS/MQ engine. This section only addresses use of the administration console for managing the embedded JMS engine.

It is necessary to understand how the embedded JMS engine is integrated into the application server administration. Systems administration is covered in more detail in Chapter 14. Administration is divided into a hierarchy of artifacts starting at the cell level. A cell contains multiple nodes (machines), and each node can contain multiple server processes. Each server process can contain multiple applications and server components or services. The embedded JMS engine is a JMS server component that controls the JMS engine. Installation of WAS creates a default server configuration that includes the JMS server component. Starting a server process using the default server configuration causes the JMS server component (and therefore, the embedded JMS engine) to be started. Stopping a server process that contains a JMS server component will stop the embedded JMS engine. It is recommended that no more than one JMS server component be started on any given node; or another way to phrase this is that since multiple server processes can be started on a given node, care should be taken to ensure that only one of those is configured to contain a JMS server component.

In general, to use JMS messaging, you must create and use a `QueueConnectionFactory` or `TopicConnectionFactory` for each unique JMS resource reference in an application. It is possible to map multiple JMS resource references within an application to the same configured connection factory, (for example, different security settings). The Plants-By-WebSphere application uses a single queue connection factory, a single queue, and a single MDB, so these must be added to the server configuration.

The administrative console is used to configure the resources and define a physical JNDI name for each. The resources declared in the application's deployment descriptors are retrieved by the application using a logical JNDI name. We cheated a bit earlier when we created bindings to associate the program's logical JNDI name with the physical resource configured in the server, because the physical resources did not exist yet. Normally, the JNDI binding is defined during deployment. To make things easier during deployment, we will create the physical resource to match the binding using the following steps.

In the Administrative Console, expand the Resources tree and click on the WebSphere JMS Provider link. The page provides access to the connection factories and destinations associated with the embedded JMS engine:

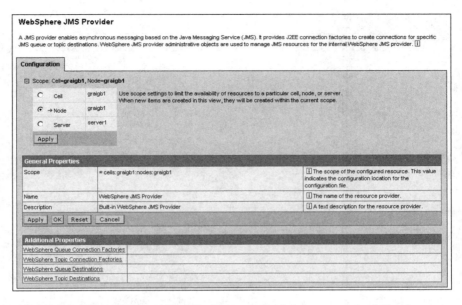

Click on WebSphere Queue Connection Factories to display the currently defined queue connection factories or to prepare to define a new queue connection factory. If the samples were installed with the server, an existing queue connection factory will already exist. We will be creating a separate one:

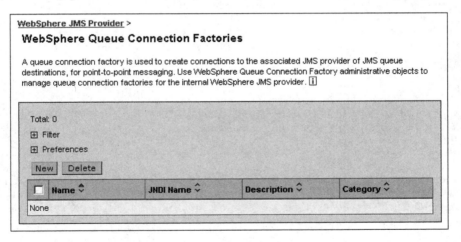

From here, a new queue connection factory can be created by clicking the New button or an existing queue connection factory can be modified. Click New and create a new connection factory, PBWOrderQCF. Use the same settings as described in the *Configuring the Test Environment* section. Be sure to enable XA transactions to ensure that the two-phase commit scenario will be supported:

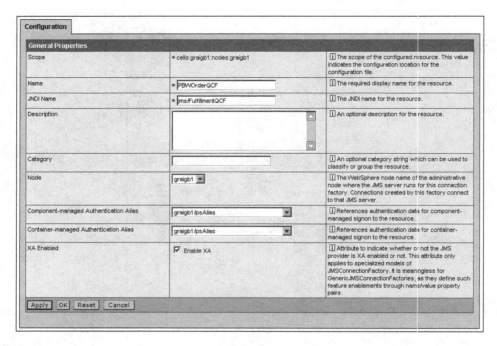

A JMS server may exist on any and every node in the WAS administrative cell (see Chapter 12). The Node defines the JMS server to use for hosting this queue. Under the covers, a QueueConnectionFactory creates remote (TCP) XA MQ connections to the server. A TopicConnectionFactory connection may be QUEUED or DIRECT as described earlier. The latter does not support transactions or persistence, but offers better performance.

> **The embedded JMS Provider does not provide the capability to configure store-and-forward messaging from one messaging server (queue manager) to another. To communicate using JMS, two applications must agree on the JMS Server (node) that they will use.**

In addition to a queue/topic connection factory, you must also define the specific queues and topics, or in general terms, the destination, to be used. From the WebSphere JMS Provider page, click WebSphere Queue Destinations. If the samples were installed, a JMS destination will already exist. We will create a new one:

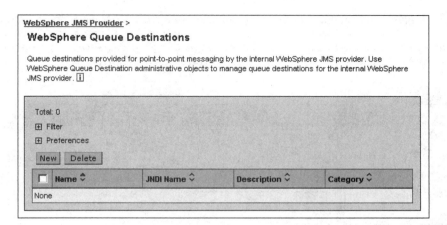

This page allows a new queue or topic to be created by clicking the New button. Clicking an existing queue name can be used to browse or modify existing queues. Queues and topics listed here will be created or modified automatically when the JMS Server starts up. Click New to create a new queue:

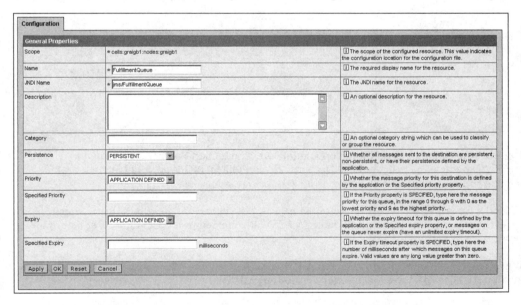

The settings are the same as those in the *Configuring the Test Environment* section. Set the Name to FulfillmentQueue and the JNDI Name to jms/FulfillmentQueue. Set Persistence to PERSISTENT and click OK.

The connection factory and queue setup are now complete.

A separate JMS listener will need to be configured for the MDB to bind to during deployment. Here are the steps:

Expand the **Servers** tree on the left-side navigation panel and click the **Application Servers** link. Click **server1** (or whatever server will be used to deploy the application) on the right-side detail panel. In the **Additional Properties** list, locate **Message Listener Service** and click it. Now locate **Listener Ports** and click it. Click **New** on the Listener Ports detail panel to create a new Listener Port:

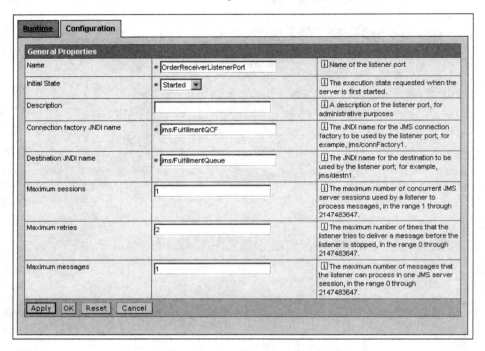

Here, set the **Name** to OrderReceiverListenerPort, **Connection Factory JNDI name** to jms/FulfillmentQCF, **Destination JNDI name** to jms/FulfillmentQueue, and **Maximum retries** to 2 for the reasons described in the *Configuring the Test Environment* section. Click **OK**.

Click the **Save** menu item at the top of the page and save the configuration. This completes the necessary setup to run the application on WAS. You will need to restart your server before these resources will become active.

When deploying our EAR file, there are a few additional configuration steps we need to look out for. First up we need to choose the listener port for our MDB:

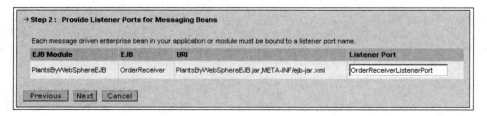

We also have to map the `QueueConnectionFactory` and `Queue`:

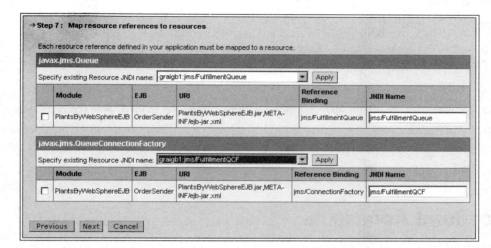

Scalability and Availability

WebSphere messaging provides support for managing the scalability and availability of the messaging server. These are detailed in the sections below.

Queue Manager Availability

The set of circumstances under which a queue manager fails but the node remains available is very limited. While it is possible for an individual disk to fail, in which case another queue manager using another disk might be able to continue, under most circumstances, if the queue manager is down the chances are that the node is down as well. Clustering provides fail-over support, which should prevent the need for multiple cluster managers on a node.

Queue Manager Clustering

With an external MQSeries provider, queue managers may be connected into a queue manager cluster. The queue manager cluster provides:

❑ Simplified systems management

❑ Queue hosting across queue managers in the cluster

❑ Round-robin distribution of messages to each queue manager for load distribution

❑ Fail-over of queue managers in the cluster

Note that workload management is only performed when a Queue Connection Factory is configured to deliver messages to a remote node in the cluster. It will not happen if the queue manager is local. Configuration of the cluster should take into consideration JMS client distribution across nodes in a cell if clustering is desired. In such cases, a separate set of clustered JMS server nodes are used to ensure the client components running within a WAS are not on the same node as the node hosting the queue.

Shared Queues

MQSeries for z/OS provides a feature similar to queue manager clustering called Shared Queues, but it has faster recovery capabilities than its counterpart. A Shared Queue is a Queue that is held in the Coupling Facility, and managed by a set of Queue Managers that form a Queue Sharing Group. The Coupling Facility provides:

❑ Highly available access to the Shared Queue

❑ Tolerance of failure of up to n-1 of the n Queue Managers in the Queue Sharing Group

❑ Alternative Queue Manager access to all messages (including those with in-flight transaction) should a Queue Manager fail

To use Shared Queues, it is necessary to have a Coupling Facility and a DB2 Data Sharing Group.

Procedural Access

The Java 2 Connector Architecture provides a means for integrating EIS backends with a J2EE application server to provide synchronous access. Building a Connector is beyond the scope of this book, but WSAD Integration Edition provides wizards and examples that show how to build one. The following sections discuss issues in using connectors and WebSphere's support for them.

Connectors and Connection Management

The Java 2 Connector Architecture (http://java.sun.com/j2ee/download.html#connectorspec) introduced a new programming pattern that allows a component to cache a handle for a connector for the lifetime of a component. This cached handle pattern is an alternative to the get/use/close pattern, where a client obtains a handle, uses it, and then closes the handle before returning. It may be tempting to use a cached-handle programming pattern as a performance boost. Don't be fooled by this. The run-time code path necessary to do handle re-association on every method invocation can be quite substantial. The recommended pattern is get/use/close.

It's important to note that connections are always used within a containment boundary. If a global transaction is not in place, a local transaction is used. At the completion of the containment boundary, the connection will either be committed or rolled back based on configuration policies.

From a client API usage point of view, Connectors are very similar to JDBC resources. Resources are defined in the deployment descriptor and retrieved using JNDI. The difference between JNDI and Java 2 Connectors is that Connectors can use either a Common Connector Interface (CCI) or a Connector-specific client interface.

Connectors are packaged in Resource Archive (RAR) files. These RAR files can be packaged within an application's EAR file for application-specific access or they can be installed on a server for access by multiple applications. Also, the RAR files contain declarations of required Java 2 Security permissions that must be granted. These permissions are merged with the system-granted permissions at runtime. The WAS allows permissions to be filtered out so that permissions that should not be automatically granted during an application installation will not be granted.

The WAS–IE provides connectors for CICS, IMS, and Host-On-Demand (HOD). These specialized Connectors can be used to drive Container-Managed Persistence (CMP) access to a Connector.

There are some issues to be aware of with the Java 2 Connector Architecture. IBM is actively pursuing resolutions to these within the specification groups and will be providing proprietary workarounds in the meantime:

❏ Although the Java 2 Connector 1.0 and J2EE 1.3 specifications state that an application should not use shareable connections in an unsharable manner, there is no real way for an application server to police programming mistakes. For example, changing the isolation level of a shared connection would probably cause other uses of the connection to fail. This can potentially lead to lost update and deadlock problems that are very difficult to diagnose. Until the specification is updated to provide a mechanism for application servers to police shared connections, it is recommended that connection properties should not be changed for sharable connections.

❏ There are situations where the application server cannot communicate connection event problems back to the connector. This prevents the connector from cleaning up its internal state and notifying the application. WAS provides a proprietary interface that connectors may implement to be notified of problems (until the spec. is cleaned up).

❏ Thread safety of the connector can cause unanticipated exceptions in the programming model. The specification allows for a single active connection handle strategy to be used to implement a thread safe resource adapter. However, this strategy can cause problems with programming model patterns that cache connection handles. Therefore, caching connection handles is not recommended. In addition, it is best to understand the thread safety of the connector being used to make sure it is not used in an unsafe manner.

❏ There are XA recovery issues when a Java 2 Connector RAR file is packaged within a J2EE application. It is recommended that RAR files be packaged outside of the EAR until this is resolved.

Resource Adapters

Resource Adapters can be built by IBM tools to provide access to back-end systems, and driven by CMP entity EJBs that are mapped to them. The Adapters are typically composed from a constructed micro-flow, but may be simple pass-through wrappers to other things such as JDBC connections. The micro-flow describes how to navigate EIS back-end transaction flows and can be built using WSAD-IE.

JMS messaging, Connectors, and Resource Adapters all deal with moving data between an application and some other entity. The distinction between them is starting to blur as asynchronous functionality is moved into the Connector 1.5 specification and interoperability requires standardized messages or data structures. This is where Service-Oriented Architectures start to appear.

Service-Oriented Architecture

Building dynamic e-business applications, which leverage a variety of existing application systems, and deriving a set of new reusable components requires careful planning and a good architectural direction. WAS provides support for the **Service-Oriented Architecture (SOA)**. The SOA concepts and corresponding support in WAS are built upon J2EE and web services concepts and leverage the basic infrastructure of WebSphere.

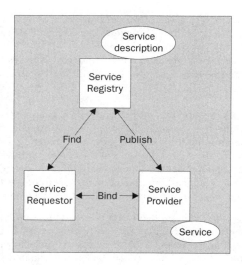

In the diagram above, we see that the SOA is split into a triad of **Service Provider**, **Service Requester**, and **Service Registry**. The Service Provider corresponds to the J2EE developer, assembler, and deployer platform roles. Publishing can be associated with J2EE application deployment. There is no single standard Service Registry yet, but **Universal Description, Discovery, and Integration** (**UDDI**) is as close as you can get for web services. The act of publishing a service not only provides an address or means of locating the service (as in JNDI), but it also provides a description of the service using **Web Services Description Language** (**WSDL**).

This programming-model-agnostic description allows any number of different software platforms to access each other. A client does this by first finding the description of a service, binding to the services location, and using the description to send requests to the service. The details of this will be covered in Chapter 8. The important thing to remember is that web services are for providing access to business functions and data while J2EE is focused on providing technology for implementing new business capabilities.

The Architecture Challenge

The challenge to architects, given the various mechanisms for defining and exposing interfaces is to choose which of these interfaces is appropriate for a given set of business function. In the Plants-By-WebSphere application, we have chosen to expose certain functions in very specific ways, but it is not always easy to anticipate the way in which business logic may be used over time, or the best way to expose it to satisfy those requirements. This section looks at the various ways that business logic can be exposed. The following sections will examine a way to tie them all back together.

First, we could expose this capability as merely a JavaBean or a basic Java interface. This interface would be one that was very efficient and fast. It also would only be useful to Java programmers that had no expectations on qualities of service and were happy to call this through a Java language interface. This is a high-speed, tightly coupled type of interface. The only separation of interface from implementation here is at the Java-language level. Note that the implementation in this case could use JDBC or the Java 2 Connector architecture CCI interface and a CICS application, depending on where the business function really resided.

Next, we could choose to place this business function in with all its inherent qualities of service. The simplest rendering of this would be using a stateless session bean. That stateless session bean could then make calls to the appropriate back-end system.

This stateless session bean then provides the opportunity for remote access, meaning that an RMI/IIOP connection to the application server JVM is possible and appropriate for accessing this service. This makes the service inherently more reusable because it can now be accessed from more environments. In fact, in addition to remote Java access, it now can be accessed from CORBA clients such as C++ or accessed using the ActiveX client, which is part of WAS.

Further, it is possible to provide traditional web service access to this business function. A WSDL interface to this service can easily be created and traditional SOAP/HTTP access is quick to follow. Here then we have some different quality-of-service challenges. The security and transactions story is somewhat more complicated. Inbound transactional context cannot be transferred onto the request on the serverside. However, the declarative model for the stateless session bean is still available as a mechanism to establish quality-of-service attributes. The overhead and translations necessary to access this Java code from a SOAP/HTTP client is obviously more than any of the previously discussed access patterns. Taking the inbound SOAP/HTTP request, demarshaling the request, and finding the proper implementation to dispatch on is more costly than the inbound EJB path.

Additional combinations of technologies can be applied to provide additional ways of accessing this basic set of functions. An MDB could be used to drive the business function as just one more example. Each of the combinations will bring to bear a set of performance overheads, a mechanism for dealing with management, and establishment of the environment in which the business logic is to run. Different combinations are also possible. For example, one can go directly from an inbound SOAP/HTTP request to a JavaBean, skipping the EJB if that quality-of-service attribute is not relevant.

The net result here is that the number of combinations can become significant. Each of these combinations comes with a different set of interfaces, and demands a different programming model for clients using these services.

The Service Bus

It would be nice if there were a consistent means for describing and accessing services in the variety of manners just described. Fortunately, there is one available using WSDL.

WSDL – Another Look

WSDL, as it turns out, is a good way to describe any kind of service. Upon further analysis, the "W" in WSDL is a bit too restrictive. The inventors of WSDL have equipped the language with a smart extensibility mechanism, which allows you to describe any kind of service, be it a web service or some other type of "service".

The following diagram shows the WSDL document architecture:

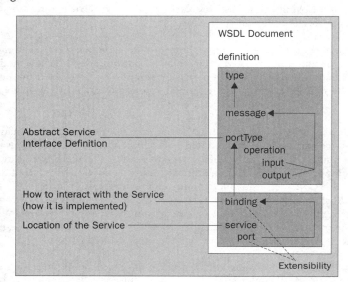

In the top section of the WSDL document, you can see the abstract service interface definition. The service interface in WSDL is called a portType. PortTypes consist of one or more operations with input and output. The input and output are described by messages. Service messages are typed using XML Schema.

The section at the bottom allows you to describe how the service interface is implemented and where you can find it.

The service location is described by a service-provider-specific port extensibility element. The service implementation is described by service-provider specific extensibility elements in the binding section. WebSphere supports the following service-provider-specific bindings: SOAP, Java 2 Connectors, JavaBean, stateless session EJB, flow, and transform. These are some of the same things described in the previous section. Flows and transforms will be described in Chapter 10 when we dig deeper into the workflow capabilities of WebSphere.

So to summarize, we have a mechanism now, WSDL, that lets us describe services as follows:

Data:	XML Schema, Service Message
Interface:	Service Interface
Implementation:	Service Binding
	- SOAP
	- Bean
	- Stateless Session EJB
	- JCA
	- Flow
	- Transform

The Architecture

If we put this together, fold in the idea of a service that can call a service, we get to the bus:

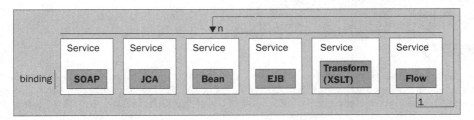

The particular bindings are not important other than to note that a variety can exist, even within the J2EE programming model. This consistent mechanism for expressing the interface to a service, irrespective of the implementation technology or the location of the implementation is a good start. Services calling other services or creating services from services is often called service composition. Further explanation of this will come in Chapter 11.

Some additional factoring and separation of concerns is necessary to complete the SOA. This is explored in the next section.

The Interfaces

Services actually involve a number of interfaces, all of them described in WSDL. The first set of interfaces arises when we split the interfaces into an interface and implementation-binding file. The interface WSDL file contains the interface of the service along with the message and type descriptions. Messages and type descriptions could also be in separate files. The implementation-binding WSDL file contains the binding to the service provider along with its location. These bindings allow any number of implementations of business function to be described. In fact, it is possible that a single implementation can be described by multiple bindings.

Putting it All Together

What we have seen so far in this section is architecture for specifying services that support a number of inbound client types as well as multiple implementation technologies. We have seen WSDL used as the anchor for describing the various interfaces and implementations.

Initially, services can be developed by wrapping existing programs or Connectors. A varied set of inbound bindings can be expressed to allow access for various types of clients to these services. Each binding type comes with some inherent qualities of service and performance overhead. However, the pay-as-you-go strategy is evident here. If local Java access is needed, for example, an inbound binding can be created for that. This binding does not incur the overhead of a binding that would be present in a SOAP inbound binding. This flexibility should encourage the use of service-based architecture because there is no fixed performance penalty inherent in such an architecture.

While this is all good, the service-based approach is not the only architecture to be employed for what happens on the server. Underneath each of the services, we will still find the utilization of the full power of the J2EE programming model. In the next chapter, we will begin to dig into more details on how J2EE and web services complement each other.

Summary

We have walked through an example of integrating systems asynchronously with JMS, and discussed some of the issues related to client use of Connectors and WebSphere's support for them. Integration of databases was covered in Chapter 5. In general, J2EE and WebSphere's support allows integration of numerous back-end datasystems. We have also looked at how using a variety of technologies leads to certain design and access patterns that could be hidden behind a consistent service description. It is now time to dig into web services in more detail.

8

Enabling Business Logic for Web Services

Web Services Description Language (**WSDL** version 1.1, http://www.w3.org/TR/wsdl) is an XML-based description language that has been submitted to W3C as the industry standard for describing web services. It is the result of a cooperative effort between IBM and Microsoft. The power of WSDL is derived from two main architectural principles. The first is its ability to describe a set of business operations. The second is its ability to separate the description into two basic units, a description of the operations and the details of how the operation and the information associated with it are packaged.

Chapter 7 concludes with a description of the Service-Oriented Architecture, which is based on the service description capabilities of WSDL. This chapter describes how WSDL is used in a J2EE environment, including a guided tour of how to enable the `Catalog` EJB in the Plants-By-WebSphere example for access as a web service, as well as how to make a Java client that accesses the service.

The WebSphere platform will support new web services standards and technologies as they appear. WebSphere Application Server (WAS) version 5.0 includes a number of components that support different aspects of web services. The primary focus of this chapter, web services for J2EE, is only one of these components. At the end of this chapter, you'll find a summary of the other web services components included with WAS version 5.0 with resources to continue your learning. A thorough investigation of web services standards and technologies would require a complete book on its own.

WSDL Concepts

This chapter assumes that you're already familiar with XML, and to some extent, the form and function of WSDL. If you don't understand the terms in the following discussion, consider taking an online WSDL tutorial such as that available at http://www.w3schools.com/wsdl/wsdl_intro.asp.

To review, a WSDL document contains the following elements:

❏   `portType`
    The description of the operations and their associated messages

❏   `messages`
    The description of parameters (input and output) and return values

❏   `types`
    The schema for describing XML complex types used in the Messages

❏   `bindings`
    A concrete encoding of the parameters and return values in a specific `portType` that binds the values to a specific protocol that is used to invoke the service

The rest of the WSDL document describes how to invoke an operation in the `portType`, through the following constructs:

❏   **Service**
    Has a name and a list of Ports

❏   **Port**
    The location of the service plus the binding to be used to access the service

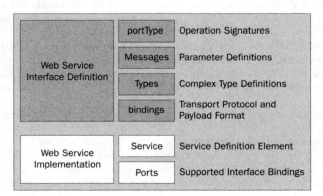

Separating the interface definition into `portType` and `bindings` allows multiple bindings to be created and associated with the same `portType`. This allows the same service interface to be accessible over multiple transports and protocols as used by the Service-Oriented Architecture described in Chapter 7. This is one of the great values of the web services architecture. By describing multiple ways to call a service, the service implementation becomes more reusable by virtue of increased accessibility. Application developers can combine the power of the EJB component model with the accessibility of web services, to produce truly reusable software components.

The protocol most commonly associated with WSDL-based web services is the **Simple Object Access Protocol** (**SOAP**), defined by a W3C memo at http://www.w3.org/TR/SOAP. SOAP is a specification for the format of an XML envelope that contains a value, a set of encoding rules for the values, and a convention for invoking operations remotely. When used with WSDL, the values in the SOAP envelope correspond to WSDL parts, and the remote operations are WSDL operations. Normally, WSDL and SOAP are used together, but it should be noted that SOAP can be used without WSDL and vice versa. For example, SOAP is used without WSDL by the Apache SOAP project (http://xml.apache.org/SOAP). WSDL can be used without SOAP when a protocol other than SOAP is specified in the WSDL binding.

With that introduction to WSDL and SOAP, let's delve more into the J2EE standards and WebSphere features that enable the creation and use of WSDL-described web services.

Web Services Standards for Java and J2EE

In order to use web services from Java, you need to be able to access web services provided by others from Java, as well as create web services others can use from J2EE components.

For a Java or J2EE application to act as a client of a web service, a mapping between the WSDL description of the service and Java is needed. The **Java API for XML-Based RPC** (also known as **JAX-RPC**) defines the mappings between WSDL portTypes and Java interfaces, as well as between Java and XML Schema types. You can learn more about JAX-RPC at http://java.sun.com/xml/jaxrpc/.

You can use a J2EE component to implement a web service. This is accomplished by creating a WSDL description that defines the component's interface and binding information, and then providing the infrastructure in the application server required to accept requests on the service. The J2EE standard for this capability is **Web Services for J2EE** also known as JSR-109. You can learn more about this standard at http://www.jcp.org/en/jsr/detail?id=109.

JAX-RPC addresses the use of WSDL-based web services in a J2SE environment. JSR-109 addresses how JAX-RPC is to be used in a J2EE environment, placing restrictions on JAX-RPC functions that are inappropriate in a managed environment. JSR-109 also specifies the deployment information to be used by J2EE containers to define a web service implementation, as well as the deployment information used by a client in a managed environment to access a web service.

In the case of WebSphere version 5.0, these standards are implemented on a J2EE 1.3-compliant runtime. These standards are expected to be included in J2EE 1.4. Following these standards should lead to portable web services applications and clients that can be used with any J2EE 1.4-compliant product.

The example in this chapter makes the Catalog EJB in the Plants-By-WebSphere application available as a web service so businesses everywhere can access the catalog. After that, a web services client application is developed that accesses the catalog.

Roadmap to the Specifications

Here's a roadmap to the JAX-RPC and JSR-109 specifications that highlight the sections that are of interest and relevance to you as a web services developer. You should start with JSR-109, since it places JAX-RPC in a J2EE perspective. You can think of JSR-109 as the introductory and conceptual material, and JAX-RPC as reference material for detailed information on APIs and mapping.

Web Services for J2EE (JSR-109)

The entire specification is only 74 pages long, and contains a wealth of information, so you might consider reading the entire thing. You can find it at http://www.jcp.org/en/jsr/detail?id=109. Here's an overview:

❑ **Chapters 1-3, Introduction, Objectives, and Overview**
These chapters describe the history, goals, conceptual architecture, benefits, and requirements for the use of web services in J2EE. They also introduce the client and server programming models for web services. The material is presented in an informal manner and is worthwhile reading.

❑ **Chapter 4, The Client Programming Model**
This chapter covers the use of the JAX-RPC client-programming model in a J2EE environment. Be sure to read the *Initial Concepts* section. The remainder of the chapter is client programming model reference material that can be read as needed while developing your web services client.

❑ **Chapter 5, Server Programming Model**
The *Port Component Model Specification* (section 5.3) is essential conceptual material for implementing a web service with a J2EE component. Components currently supported by this standard are stateless session EJBs and JavaBeans in a web container.

❑ **Chapter 6, Handlers**
Handlers can make transformations on messages as they pass in or out of a client or server. The concepts section explains when and why you might want to use them. The remainder discusses the handler APIs. This chapter is advanced material and can be skipped.

❑ **Chapter 7, Deployment Descriptors**
Describes the Developer, Assembler, and Deployer roles for providing, packaging, and interpreting JSR-109 deployment descriptors, as well as annotated DTDs for the new deployment descriptors. This is reference information that is used when developing a web services implementation in J2EE.

❑ **Chapter 8, Deployment**
This is information for implementers of JSR-109, and need not be read unless you need to troubleshoot your web services assembly.

❑ **Chapter 9, Security**
This chapter discusses the existing J2EE security mechanisms and how they apply to web services.

Java API for XML-Based RPC (JAX-RPC)

The JAX-RPC specification is twice as long as JSR-109, and much of the material it contains can be considered reference material for JSR-109. You can find it at http://java.sun.com/xml/jaxrpc/.

❑ **Chapters 1 and 2, Introduction and JAX-RPC Use Case**
Explains terminology and mechanisms used. The material is introductory in nature, and complements the material in this book.

❑ **Chapter 3, Requirements**
Captures the rationale for the specification. It is interesting, but non-essential background material.

❑ **Chapters 4 and 5, WSDL/XML to Java Mappings and Java to XML/WSDL Mappings**
These chapters are essential reference material when you need to understand why certain transformations were made when mapping from Java to WSDL or vice-versa, what exactly can be transformed, which transformations are covered by the specification, and which are left to the vendor.

- **Chapter 6, SOAP Binding**
  Explains the mapping for encoded versus literal use and RPC versus document style. This is the reference information needed primarily when using WSDL that wasn't generated using the JAX-RPC mappings.

- **Chapters 7 and 8, SOAP Message with Attachments and JAX-RPC Core APIs**
  Contain reference information.

- **Chapter 9, Service Client Endpoint Model**
  Discusses the client programming model, including a summary of JSR-109 Chapter 4.

- **Chapter 10, Service Endpoint Model**
  Discusses the J2SE implementation of a web service using a servlet. This model is not supported by JSR-109, so this chapter isn't relevant to WebSphere.

- **Chapters 11, 12, and 13, Service Context, Message Handlers, and JAX-RPC Runtime Services**
  These chapters are largely superceded by JSR-109. Chapters 11 and 12 are useful reference information when you're trying to implement JSR-109 Handlers.

- **Chapter 14, Interoperability**
  Discusses interoperability considerations with web services not hosted by JAX-RPC. This is good information to read before deploying a service for public access.

- **Chapter 15, Extensible Type Mapping**
  Describes the APIs used to register and locate custom serializers and deserializers that enable the use of customer-determined mappings between Java objects and XML. Unfortunately, there is no standard API for the serializers and deserializers themselves – anything you write at this point would be proprietary to a JAX-RPC implementation. For that reason, JSR-109 does not support the use of these JAX-RPC APIs.

- **Chapter 16, Futures**
  This is a one-page chapter summarizing work that remains to be done, including the specification of APIs for portable serializers, deserializers, and stubs. This will further enable vendor-independence of J2EE applications.

- **Chapter 17, References.**
  This extensive list of references, mostly for Java-based XML technologies, is worth perusing.

- **Appendix 18, XML Schema Support**
  Extensive tables list most XML Schema types and whether support is optional or required by JAX-RPC. If support is optional, consult the WebSphere documentation for whether that Schema type is supported, and if so, how.

- **Appendix 19, Serialization Framework**
  This is an implementation case study of interest to JAX-RPC implementers only.

- **Appendix 20, Mapping of XML names**
  This appendix specifies how Java identifiers are mapped to XML names and vice-versa. This identifies the rationale for a particular transformation.

Now that we've reviewed what the J2EE web services standards contain, let's look at the development steps identified by JSR-109 to create a Web service from a J2EE component.

JSR-109 Enablement Process

JSR-109 describes the required steps to make either a stateless session EJB or a JavaBean available as a Web service. These steps can be summarized as follows. Each of these steps is described in more detail in the following sections.

1. Select an existing JavaBean or stateless session EJB you wish to enable.

2. Create a **Service Endpoint Interface** exposing the desired methods of the bean. The Service Endpoint Interface is required by JAX-RPC and is very similar to an EJB remote interface. The Service Endpoint Interface defines the methods that can be invoked on the service. Each method must throw a `java.rmi.RemoteException`, so that a client using the Service Endpoint Interface to invoke an operation on a service can be notified of any communications faults. Also, all parameters on the interface methods must map to XML types as defined by JAX-RPC. These considerations are discussed in detail in the section *Create the Service Endpoint Interface* below.

3. Using tools, generate a WSDL document from the Service Endpoint Interface.

4. Using tools, generate templates for the developer-supplied deployment descriptors required by JSR-109 – the `webservices.xml` file and a mapping file.

5. Complete the deployment descriptors by providing a link to the EJB or JavaBean being enabled.

6. Add the Service Endpoint Interface class, WSDL file, and deployment descriptors to the assembled module (JAR or WAR).

7. Repackage the EAR containing the module.

8. If you are using the initial release of WAS version 5.0 with the Web services Technology Preview (see below), a separate tool called the `endptEnabler` is used to configure the endpoint listener (servlet) for the application. This step is only required for EJBs and will be done automatically during deployment in subsequent updates.

9. Deploy the application. During deployment, the SOAP address in the WSDL file will be updated with the location the service is deployed to.

10. Provide the updated WSDL file to your customers, or publish it to a service registry.

Due to the rapid changes in web services specification and technologies, as well as legal requirements, there are some limitations in the JSR-109 support in the initial release of WAS version 5.0:

❑ JSR-109 web services support for WAS version 5.0 is a separately installable Web Services Technology Preview that can be downloaded from the WebSphere Developer Domain (http://www7b.software.ibm.com/wsdd/downloads/techpreviews.html).

❑ The initial release of WebSphere Studio version 5.0 does not include support for JAX-RPC or JSR-109 based development.

❑ Some assembly and deployment tasks are performed manually.

Due to these limitations, the development and assembly tasks in this chapter are performed from the command line. The arguments used with these tools will be changing as the Technology Preview is being productized, so consult your WebSphere documentation if you encounter differences from this chapter. A future update to WAS version 5.0 and WSAD version 5.0 will provide full support for JSR-109.

The WebSphere Web Services Enablement Process

The following diagram illustrates the process steps identified by JSR-109 that are performed when using WAS to enable an EJB to be a web service:

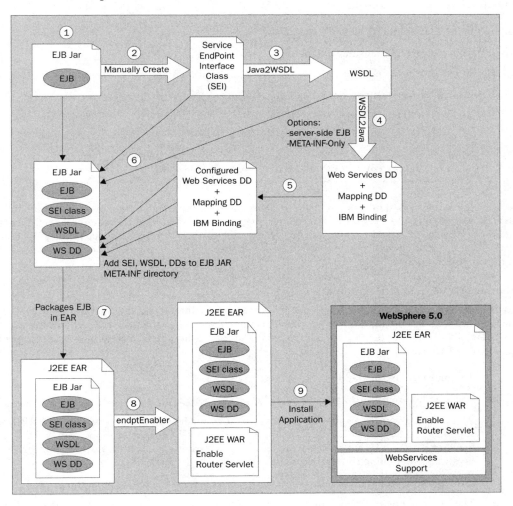

These steps are described in the following sections, followed by a detailed example using the Plants-By-WebSphere `Catalog` EJB.

Select an Implementation Bean

JSR-109 specifies the requirements for selecting an implementation bean. First of all, it must have methods suitable to be mapped to a Service Endpoint Interface, as described in the next step. Next, it must be a stateless implementation, either a stateless session EJB, or a JavaBean without client-specific state. This is because any implementation object might be selected to process a request from any client. If client-specific state is required, a client identifier must be passed as a parameter of the web service operation.

For an EJB, the selected methods must not have a transaction attribute of mandatory. This is because there is no established standard for web services transactions at this time.

For a JavaBean in the web container:

❑   It must have a public default constructor

❑   The exposed methods must be public

❑   It must not save client-specific state between method calls

❑   It must be a public, non-final, non-abstract class

❑   It must not define a finalize() method

> **A word of caution – while WebSphere makes it easy to expose an existing bean as a web service, it may not be appropriate to do so.**

As with any software design creating an appropriate interface for clients is one of the most difficult tasks, it may be better to design a new customer interface tailored to Internet requirements from scratch, and then write a new façade bean to implement it by delegating operations to your business logic. As we work through enabling the Plants-By-WebSphere Catalog EJB later in this chapter, we'll discuss some of these considerations.

Create the Service Endpoint Interface

To enable a bean as a web service, we must first create a Java interface containing just those methods of the bean we want to expose as a web service. This interface is called the **Service Endpoint Interface**. It is similar to the EJB remote interface, and like the EJB remote interface, must follow certain conventions specified by JAX-RPC:

❑   The interface must extend the java.rmi.Remote.

❑   Each method must throw a java.rmi.RemoteException.

❑   All method parameters and return types, including inherited methods must be JAX-RPC-supported Java types, as listed in section 5.1 of the JAX-RPC specification. Probably the biggest restriction is that object references are not permitted unless they are to serializable JavaBeans containing conforming fields.

❑   The interface should not contain constant (public static final) declarations.

❑   The implementation bean, while required to contain methods whose signatures match those in the Service Endpoint Interface, is not required to implement the Service Endpoint Interface.

For an EJB, it is easiest to create the Service Endpoint Interface by copying the remote interface and removing the methods, fields, and parent classes that don't conform to the above requirements.

Generate the WSDL

Every JAX-RPC implementation, including WebSphere, has tooling that reads a Service Endpoint Interface and generates a corresponding WSDL file, following the rules established in JAX-RPC. WebSphere version 5.0 uses the `Java2WSDL` command-line tool for this task.

Create Deployment Descriptor Templates

WebSphere's `WSDL2Java` command-line tool, in addition to other things, will generate templates for the required deployment descriptors from a WSDL document. These templates are automatically filled with deployment information from the WSDL, leaving only a couple of items to be supplied by the developer. The deployment descriptors required by JSR-109 are a `webservices.xml` file and a mapping file that records the mapping between Java names and XML names. An `ibm-webservices-bnd.xml` file is also generated that supports WebSphere-specific functionality such as security configuration.

Complete the Deployment Descriptors

Fill in either the `ejb-link` or `servlet-link` value of the `service-impl-bean` element to link the service to the EJB or JavaBean that implements the service.

Assemble the Module

Add the following files to the J2EE module to enable it for web services:

❑ The Service Endpoint Interface class

❑ The WSDL file

❑ The deployment descriptors, `webservices.xml`, the JAX-RPC mapping descriptor, and the optional `ibm-webservices-bnd.xml`.

Assemble the EAR

Replace the updated module in the EAR.

Enable the Application

If your application contains EJBs, the initial release of WAS version 5.0 requires that the `endptEnabler` command be run on the application to add the HTTP endpoint for the service. This is accomplished by adding a WAR module that configures the web services router servlet. This servlet accepts, demarshals, and dispatches web services requests. This step will be part of deployment in the updated release of WAS version 5.0.

Deploy the Application

The application can be deployed from either the admin console, as shown in Chapter 6, or using the `wsadmin` scripting interface, as described in the WebSphere online help. During deployment, you supply information for the location (URL) of the published service, and choose whether you want the updated WSDL file to be published to the file system. The deployment step fills in the service location element in the WSDL file with the actual location of the service.

Distribute the Application Service Description

The deployed WSDL file is all your customers need to use your service.

Enabling the Catalog EJB as a Web Service

Now let's work through these steps in more detail to provide access to the Plants-By-WebSphere `Catalog` EJB as a web service. The `Catalog` EJB was chosen because it is a stateless session bean and is a realistic example of a business function that would be enabled as a web service. The `StoreItem` bean that represents items in the `Catalog` provides an opportunity to show a `complexType`.

Working with the Sample Code in WebSphere Studio

The following sections showing how to enable the Plants-By-WebSphere sample using WebSphere Studio to edit files and assemble the enablement artifacts into the EAR. For the initial release, some steps require command-line tools to be run outside of Studio.

> **If you are using the initial release of WAS then you will need to install the Web Services Technology Preview before proceeding. You can either download this from DeveloperWorks or it is included on one of the CDs that comes with this book. Follow the instructions to install it.**

In addition, in order to deploy web services-enabled J2EE applications you will need a stand alone installation of WebSphere Application Server. In other words, you cannot use the unit test environment that is part of WSAD.

Creating the PlantsByWebSphereCatalog Service Endpoint Interface

The first step is to create a Service Endpoint Interface that represents the customer's view of the service. The first decision is to determine the name for the Service Endpoint Interface class. The `Java2WSDL` command derives the names of the WSDL `portType` and service from the Service Endpoint Interface name. Knowing this, let's pick `PlantsByWebSphereCatalog` as a name that will be meaningful to a customer when they receive the generated WSDL file.

The next step is to fill in the contents of the `PlantsByWebSphereCatalog` interface. When you have an existing EJB that provides the business logic for the web service, it is logical to use the EJB remote interface as a template, since it is already a Java interface and the methods already throw `java.rmi.RemoteException`.

Let's start by copying the `Catalog.java` remote interface to `PlantsByWebSphereCatalog.java`.

Using Studio locate `Catalog.java` in the `PlantsByWebSphereEJB` project, right-click on it, and select **Copy** then **Paste** it into the same package.

The Name Conflict panel appears to permit you to rename the copied class. Enter `PlantsByWebSphereCatalog` as the new name:

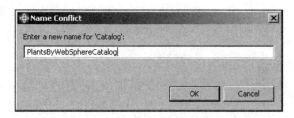

Double-click on the new class to open it in the Java editor:

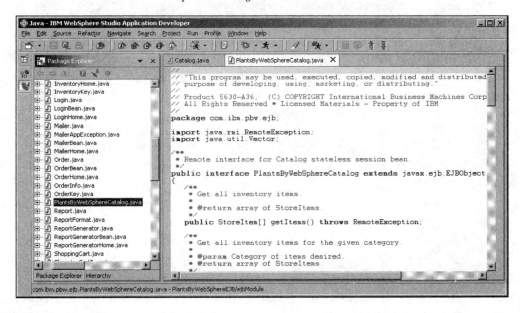

Look at the overall structure of the interface:

```java
package com.ibm.pbw.ejb;

import java.rmi.RemoteException;
import java.util.Vector;

/**
 * Remote interface for Catalog stateless session bean.
 */
public interface PlantsByWebSphereCatalog extends javax.ejb.EJBObject
{
…
}
```

To be compliant with JAX-RPC, the interface must extend `java.rmi.Remote`. Although `javax.ejb.EJBObject` extends `java.rmi.Remote`, it (the `EJBObject`) introduces methods that have parameters of type `java.lang.Object`, which is not permitted by JAX-RPC. Therefore, the interface declaration needs to be changed to extend `java.rmi.Remote`:

```
public interface PlantsByWebSphereCatalog extends java.rmi.Remote
```

Expand the `PlantsByWebSphereCatalog` class to display the methods:

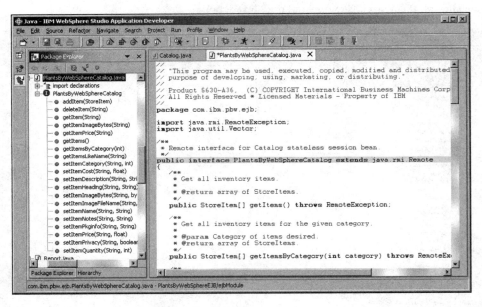

These methods should be reviewed first for suitability as web service operations, and then for whether the parameter types are supported by JAX-RPC.

From examining this interface, it is apparent that it serves a number of different client roles:

❑   A shopping customer who browses the contents of the catalog

❑   A purchasing agent who adds and updates item information

❑   A supplier who queries the current inventory of each item, ships new inventory, and then updates item quantities and costs

Since the latter two roles raise security issues, and we want our enabled catalog to be accessible to everyone, let's eliminate the catalog modification methods from the Service Endpoint Interface and make it read-only.

Delete the unwanted modification methods by holding the *Ctrl* key down and clicking on all the set methods, as well as `addItem()`, and `deleteItem()`. After selecting, press *Delete* and confirm the deletion:

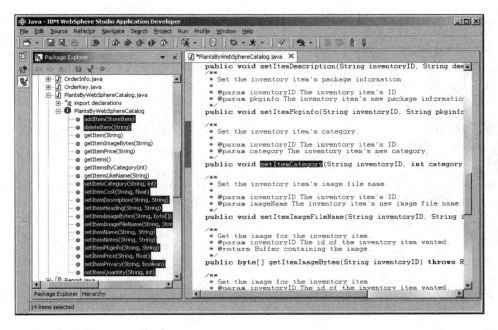

That leaves the following methods:

❑ StoreItem getItem(String id) throws RemoteException;

❑ byte[] getItemImageBytes(String id) throws RemoteException;

❑ float getItemPrice(String id) throws RemoteException;

❑ StoreItem[] getItems() throws RemoteException;

❑ StoreItem[] getItemsByCategory(int category) throws RemoteException;

❑ StoreItem[] getItemsLikeName(String name) throws RemoteException;

> *Note that you can define additional Service Endpoint Interfaces for the* Catalog *EJB that satisfy the requirements of the other client roles. The same EJB can implement multiple web services.*

The next thing to examine is the StoreItem class. Since it is a return type from a web service call, it needs to be represented in XML. JAX-RPC section 5.4 defines the conventions a Java class needs to follow in order to be mapped to XML. To summarize, these conventions are:

❑ The class must have a public default constructor.

❑ The class must not implement (directly or indirectly) the java.rmi.Remote interface. The java.rmi.Remote interface marks an object as able to be referenced by a remote client. Because there is currently no notion of a remote object reference in WSDL, any object passed to or from a Web service must be passed by value. This means that the actual data in the object must be transmitted (serialized) with the invocation.

❑ The class may implement any other Java interface or extend another Java class.

- ❏ The Java type of every public field must be a supported JAX-RPC type. Only public fields are transmitted in XML.

- ❏ The class may contain methods or static, transient, non-public fields, but they are not mapped to XML.

- ❏ The Java class for a JAX-RPC value type may be a JavaBeans class, having non-public fields and public get and set methods to access each bean property. In this case, each property must be a supported JAX-RPC type.

- ❏ The class may, but is not required to, extend java.io.Serializable as long as it meets the above requirements.

Examination of the StoreItem class shows that it follows the JavaBeans pattern, and that all bean properties (String, int, boolean, and float) are supported JAX-RPC types. Let's take a quick look at the properties accessors in StoreItem:

- ❏   `public String getId();`
- ❏   `public String getName();`
- ❏   `public String getHeading();`
- ❏   `public String getDescr();`
- ❏   `public String getPkginfo();`
- ❏   `public String getImage();`
- ❏   `public float getPrice();`
- ❏   `public float getCost();`
- ❏   `public int getQuantity();`
- ❏   `public int getCategory();`

Notice the bean properties include information you might prefer that your customers not have, such as your cost for the item. This illustrates the importance of designing the Service Endpoint Interface as carefully as you would any other publicly exposed interface. If Plants-By-WebSphere were a real enterprise, your development department would likely be designing a PublicStoreItem, and either adding methods to retrieve PublicStoreItems to the CatalogBean EJB, or, more likely, implementing a PublicCatalogBean façade EJB to mediate between the public requests and your internal data.

The methods in the façade EJB would retrieve StoreItems from the catalog and repackage them as PublicStoreItems for public consumption:

```
public PublicStoreItem getItem(String id) {
    Catalog c = ... //reference to Catalog EJB
    StoreItem s = c.getItem(id);
    if (s.isPublic())
       return new PublicStoreItem(s.getID(), s.getName(), s.getDescription(),
                                  s.getImage(), s.getPrice());
    else
```

After the editing is complete, the `PlantsByWebSphereCatalog` Service Endpoint Interface looks like this:

```java
package com.ibm.pbw.ejb;

import java.rmi.RemoteException;

public interface PlantsByWebSphereCatalog extends java.rmi.Remote
{
    /**
     * Get all inventory items.
     * @return array of all StoreItems.
     */
    public StoreItem[] getItems() throws RemoteException;

    /**
     * Get all inventory items for the given category.
     * @param category Category of items desired.
     * @return array of StoreItems in the specified category.
     */
    public StoreItem[] getItemsByCategory(int category) throws
      RemoteException;

    /**
     * Get inventory items that contain a given String within their names.
     * @param name String to search names for.
     * @return array of StoreItems matching name.
     */
    public StoreItem[] getItemsLikeName(String name) throws RemoteException;

    /**
     * Get the Inventory item for the given ID.
     * @param inventoryID - ID of the Inventory item desired.
     * @return StoreItem
     */
    public StoreItem getItem(String inventoryID) throws RemoteException;

    /**
     * Get the Inventory item's price.
     * @param inventoryID - ID of the Inventory item desired.
     * @return the inventory item's price.
     */
    float StoreItem getItemPrice(String inventoryID) throws RemoteException;

    /**
     * Get the image for the inventory item.
     * @param inventoryID The id of the inventory item wanted.
     * @return byte array containing the image.
     */
    public byte[] getItemImageBytes(String inventoryID) throws
      RemoteException;
}
```

Create PlantsByWebSphereCatalog.wsdl

The next step is to convert the `PlantsByWebSphereCatalog` Service Endpoint Interface into a WSDL document. To do this, we need to get set up to run the `Java2WSDL` command-line tool. The `Java2WSDL` command creates a WSDL document from the Service Endpoint Interface class.

Open a command shell, and change directory to the workspace for the
PlantsByWebSphereEJB\ejbModule directory in Studio's workspace directory.

After installing the Technology Preview, the command-line tools are in the WebSphere Application
Server bin directory. Add the bin directory to your PATH environment variable.

Add j2ee.jar in the WebSphere Application Server lib directory and the current directory ("."), to
your classpath environment variable. Since the Java2WSDL command takes a Java class as an option, it
requires that classpath be set up the same as is required to compile the class with the javac command.

Now we can run the Java2WSDL command to generate PlantsByWebSphereCatalog.wsdl:

```
Java2WSDL -implClass com.ibm.pbw.ejb.CatalogBean com.ibm.pbw.ejb.
PlantsByWebSphereCatalog

WSWS3006W: Warning: The -location was not set, the value "file:undefined_location"
is used instead.
```

The -implClass option is used to supply additional information to Java2WSDL to permit the Java
parameter names to be used as the WSDL part names. Since the Java2WSDL command reads the
compiled class file instead of the Java source file for the Service Endpoint Interface, it can't determine
the names of the parameters of the Service Endpoint Interface methods. Without the -implClass
option, the PlantsByWebSphereCatalog.wsdl file would contain WSDL parts named in0, in1, and
so on. This naming scheme isn't helpful to customers that use the WSDL.

The compiled Service Endpoint Interface class doesn't contain parameter names, even when compiled
for debug. However, Java classes, when compiled for debug, do contain parameter names. You use a
Java class that implements methods having the same signature as those in the Service Endpoint
Interface to supply the missing parameter name information. Note that implClass doesn't have to
implement the Service Endpoint Interface, it's sufficient to have methods with matching signatures.

In this example, CatalogBean is the class that implements the methods of the Service Endpoint
Interface. By default, Studio will compile CatalogBean with debug information. If it doesn't, verify
that the **Add variable attributes to generated class files** preference is enabled on the Java compiler
settings panel available by selecting **Window | Preferences | Java | Compiler | Classfile Generation**.

At this point, you have a choice. The following sections examine the internals of the WSDL file you just
created. If you'd prefer to continue with the development steps right away, skip this section for now.

Examining the Service Description

Up until now, you've heard a lot about WSDL, but haven't actually looked inside a WSDL document.
Since we've just created one for the PlantsByWebSphereCatalog service, now's the perfect time to
see what it contains.

You can view the generated PlantsByWebSphereCatalog.wsdl file in Studio by following these steps.

Switch to the XML Perspective by selecting **Window | Open Perspective | XML**.

Navigate to the ejbModule directory that you created the WSDL file in.

Right-click on the `ejbModule` directory and select **Refresh**. The `PlantsByWebSphereCatalog.wsdl` file should appear under `ejbModule`.

Double-click on `PlantsByWebSphereCatalog.wsdl` to display the contents of the file:

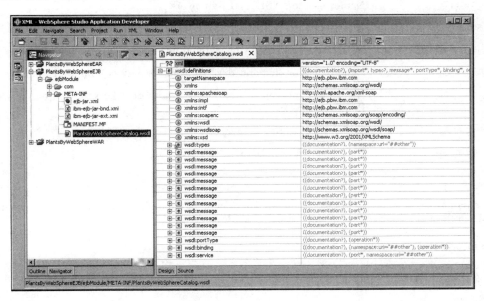

To browse the WSDL file, you can switch between the Design view and Source view by clicking the tabs at the bottom of the XML Editor pane.

Namespace Declarations

A WSDL document contains a set of definitions. The header of a WSDL document declares the XML namespaces that are available for use in the remainder of the document:

```xml
<?xml version="1.0" encoding="UTF-8"?>
<wsdl:definitions
    targetNamespace="http://ejb.pbw.ibm.com"
    xmlns="http://schemas.xmlsoap.org/wsdl/"
    xmlns:apachesoap="http://xml.apache.org/xml-soap"
    xmlns:intf=http://ejb.pbw.ibm.com
    xmlns:impl="http://ejb.pbw.ibm.com"
    xmlns:soapenc="http://schemas.xmlsoap.org/soap/encoding/"
    xmlns:wsdl="http://schemas.xmlsoap.org/wsdl/"
    xmlns:wsdlsoap="http://schemas.xmlsoap.org/wsdl/soap/"
    xmlns:xsd="http://www.w3.org/2001/XMLSchema">
...
</wsdl:definitions>
```

The `targetNamespace`, `http://ejb.pbw.ibm.com`, is derived from the package name of the Service Endpoint Interface by `Java2WSDL`. JAX-RPC does not specify a mapping between Java package names and XML namespaces, but it does require a one-to-one mapping between them.

The table below identifies the meaning of each namespace:

Namespace Prefix	Meaning
default	Namespace for WSDL 1.1 framework
wsdl	Namespace for WSDL 1.1 framework
apachesoap	Namespace for XML types defined by Apache implementations
intf	Namespace for elements derived from the Service Endpoint Interface
impl	Namespace for elements in <wsdl:service> derived from the Service Endpoint Interface
soapenc	SOAP 1.1 encoding namespace
wsdlsoap	Namespace for WSDL 1.1 SOAP binding
xsd	Namespace for XML Schema 2001

These namespace definitions appear in the WSDL document unconditionally, regardless of whether names in these namespaces are actually used in the document.

Service Interface Definition

As shown in the diagram earlier, the service interface portion of the WSDL document defines the interface to the service with four distinct sections:

❑ wsdl:portType
The abstract interface defining the operations that can be invoked on the interface

❑ wsdl:message
Defines the data flowing into and out of each operation in the wsdl:portType

❑ wsdl:type
Defines the types used in the messages

❑ wsdl:binding
Defines the concrete encoding for each operation in the wsdl:portType

The Service Endpoint Interface of the PlantsByWebSphereCatalog is mapped to a portType. Each Java method in the Service Endpoint Interface is mapped to an operation in the portType.

Let's compare and contrast the Java language definition of the getItem() method with the corresponding WSDL operation. First, the WSDL portType:

```
<wsdl:portType name="PlantsByWebSphereCatalog">
...

<wsdl:operation name="getItem" parameterOrder="inventoryID">
  <wsdl:input message="intf:getItemRequest" name="getItemRequest" />
  <wsdl:output message="intf:getItemResponse" name="getItemResponse" />
</wsdl:operation>
...
</wsdl:portType>
```

Then the corresponding Java method:

```
public StoreItem getItem(String inventoryID) throws RemoteException;
```

Both the Java interface and `wsdl:portType` have the same name and both have a rendering of the methods and operations available on the interface.

The Java method signature contains specific types, `StoreItem` and `String`, as you would expect with a programming language. On the other hand, the WSDL interface refers to parameters as a `wsdl:input` message named `getItemRequest()` and return types as a `wsdl:output` message named `getItemResponse()`. The input and output message definitions shown below describe the data transferred to and from the method.

Let's look at the `wsdl:message` definitions for the `getItem()` method:

```
<wsdl:message name="getItemRequest">
    <wsdl:part name="inventoryID" type="xsd:string" />
</wsdl:message>

<wsdl:message name="getItemResponse">
    <wsdl:part name="getItemReturn" type="intf:StoreItem" />
</wsdl:message>
```

Comparing the arguments and result of the Java interface to these `wsdl:messages`, you can see that each parameter on the Java interface is mapped to a `wsdl:part` in a `wsdl:message`. Each `wsdl:part` has a type that is based on the JAX-RPC mapping between Java types and XML.

For more complex or application-specific types, such as the `StoreItem` bean, the `wsdl:part` type is a reference to a type definition elsewhere. For this sample, the `intf:StoreItem` is defined in the `wsdl:types` section as complex types, as shown below:

```
<wsdl:types>
  <schema
    targetNamespace="http://ejb.pbw.ibm.com"
    xmlns="http://www.w3.org/2001/XMLSchema">
   <import namespace="http://schemas.xmlsoap.org/soap/encoding/"/>
   <complexType name="StoreItem">
    <sequence>
     <element name="name" nillable="true" type="xsd:string"/>
     <element name="category" type="xsd:int"/>
     <element name="cost" type="xsd:float"/>
     <element name="public" type="xsd:boolean"/>
     <element name="image" nillable="true" type="xsd:string"/>
     <element name="quantity" type="xsd:int"/>
     <element name="price" type="xsd:float"/>
     <element name="notes" nillable="true" type="xsd:string"/>
     <element name="ID" nillable="true" type="xsd:string"/>
     <element name="pkginfo" nillable="true" type="xsd:string"/>
     <element name="description" nillable="true" type="xsd:string"/>
     <element name="heading" nillable="true" type="xsd:string"/>
    </sequence>
   </complexType>
   <element name="StoreItem" nillable="true" type="impl:StoreItem"/>
  </schema>
```

Note the import of the SOAP encoding namespace. This appears unconditionally to support the use of SOAP 1.1 "section 5" encodings, even though none are used in this complexType. The SOAP encodings are extensions to the standard XML Schema types and support features like sparse arrays and multiple references to a value.

Finally, let's examine a portion of the PlantsByWebSphereCatalogSoapBinding:

```
<wsdl:binding name="PlantsByWebSphereCatalogSoapBinding"
type="intf:PlantsByWebSphereCatalog">
     <wsdlsoap:binding style="rpc"
               transport="http://schemas.xmlsoap.org/soap/http"/>
```

This binding declares a type of intf:PlantsByWebSphereCatalog which as we have already seen is a wsdl:portType. That tells us that this binding is providing a concrete encoding for the PlantsByWebSphereCatalog interface. The type= keyword on the wsdl:binding element describes the wsdl:portType that a binding references.

The next XML fragment in the binding, wsdlsoap:binding, is a WSDL extension element. It is used to further refine the semantics of the invocation of the operations on the interface. In this case, the wsdlsoap elements define information needed to transport the message parts in a SOAP 1.1 envelope on an HTTP transport. The binding style attribute has two choices: rpc or document. Using rpc specifies that each parameter or result will be passed as a separate element in the SOAP message. The alternative style is document style binding. Document style passes the parameters bundled into one or more XML elements.

The Java2WSDL tool has a -style option that lets you specify which style of WSDL to generate from the Service Endpoint Interface. Finally, notice that the header of the binding also contains the definition of the transport over which the Web service invocation will flow. In this sample, it is SOAP over HTTP. Other bindings such as SOAP/JMS are permitted in WSDL, but they are not defined by JAX-RPC.

```
<wsdl:operation name="getItem">
  <wsdlsoap:operation soapAction="" />
      <wsdl:input name="getItemRequest">
         <wsdlsoap:body
                   encodingStyle=http://schemas.xmlsoap.org/soap/encoding/
                   namespace="http://ejb.pbw.ibm.com" use="encoded" />
```

The next element, wsdl:operation, defines which of the operations in the portType are being bound. The wsdlsoap:operation child element provides the binding for the operation to the SOAP protocol. The soapAction attribute is required for client use of SOAP over HTTP bindings. It denotes a value for the SOAPAction HTTP header field. The messages for the operation appear in the wsdl:input and wsdl:output elements. For each message, a wsdlsoap:body element defines how to encode the message parts for transmission.

```
      ...
      </wsdl:input>
      <wsdl:output name="getItemResponse">
         wsdlsoap:body
                   encodingStyle=http://schemas.xmlsoap.org/soap/encoding/
                   namespace="http://ejb.pbw.ibm.com" use="encoded" />
      </wsdl:output>
</wsdl:operation>
...
</wsdl:binding>
```

Note the encodingStyle= attribute on the wsdlsoap:body element. There are two ways to encode the message parts when using the SOAP binding. One is **encoded**, using the SOAP 1.1 "section 5" encoding (named after the section of the SOAP 1.1 specification that defines it), as indicated by the URL http://schemas.xmlsoap.org/soap/encoding/. The second encoding style is **literal**. Knowing the XML schema type for a value may not be sufficient to actually encode it into XML for transmission. A concrete encoding must also be specified to indicate how values are to be encoded and decoded. When the encodingStyle is literal, the parts are transmitted as an XML document.

However, when literal encoding is used to transmit data structures, information may be lost. The primary feature of the encoded encodingStyle is the ability to transmit graphs of objects, maintaining their relationship to one another. This feature is also known as multi-ref. For example, if you have an array containing 10 string references, each pointing to the same String object, literal encoding would transmit the contents of the string 10 times, while encoded encoding would transmit the string value for the first array element, and then for the last nine, transmit references to the first value. In this way, the receiver can reconstruct the same object graph as was sent.

There are four possible combinations of the style and encodingStyle attributes, but (fortunately), only two are commonly used, rpc/encoded for programmatic interfaces that pass individual parameters and maintain their relationships, and doc/literal for exchanging XML documents as messages. The default encoding for WebSphere and JAX-RPC is rpc/encoded, but the industry, prompted by WS-I.org (the Web Services Interoperability consortium founded by IBM and Microsoft), has excluded encoded and recommends doc/literal or rpc/literal.

Contrasting this binding with the wsdl:portType PlantsByWebSphereCatalog reveals one of the greatest strengths of WSDL. Notice how each part of the PlantsByWebSphereCatalog wsdl:portType is repeated in the binding definition and then augmented with WSDL extensions describing the specifics of how to encode each part of the invocation. This enables the binding to precisely describe the encoding to be used when invoking any operation on a given wsdl:portType. More importantly it also enables the web service definition to contain more than one binding for a given portType, because the specifics of how to invoke the service have been separated from what the service interface looks like.

Throughout each section of the WSDL document you can also see use of the wsdl:soap extensions, which in our sample indicate the use of SOAP. The port uses the:

```
<wsdlsoap:address location=/>
```

extension to declare where an implementation of the web service can be found, and the PlantsByWebSphereCatalogSOAPBinding uses the wsdlsoap:binding, wsdlsoap:operation, and wsdlsoap:body extensions to declare that the binding to the web service is going to use SOAP.

Service Implementation Definition

Next let's examine the service implementation section of the service description:

```
<wsdl:service name="PlantsByWebSphereCatalogService">
    <wsdl:port binding="intf:PlantsByWebSphereCatalogSoapBinding
            name="PlantsByWebSphereCatalog">
        <wsdlsoap:address
                location="http://myhost/PlantsByWebSphereCatalog/
                        services/PlantsByWebSphereCatalog"/>
    </wsdl:port>
</wsdl:service>
```

Here you can see that this web service is called `PlantsByWebSphereCatalogService`. It has only one port, called `PlantsByWebSphereCatalog`. This port refers to the `PlantsByWebSphereCatalogSoapBinding` binding that is defined elsewhere in the document. Note that the location of the service implementation is provided by the location URL in the `wsdlsoap:address` element. By combining the target service location and a concrete encoding into a port, we can see how WSDL can be used to enable multi-protocol access to the web service. If there were two bindings defined for this service, there would be two ports defined. Each port provides a separate and distinct access path to the target service, where the access path is defined by the protocol and encoding specified in the binding and the target location specified in the address.

The address location is normally set during deployment of the web service, since that's the time a service implementation is bound to a specific URL. You can also specify the location on the `Java2WSDL` command line using the `-location` argument. Since no location was specified when the `Java2WSDL` command was run earlier, if you view the generated WSDL document, you will see that the location was set to a default location, `"file:undefined_location"`.

Configuring the Web Service

So far, we've selected an implementation EJB, created a Service Endpoint Interface for it that defines the Web services interface for the EJB, and created a WSDL document from the Service Endpoint Interface that describes the service.

The next step is to create and configure the deployment descriptors used by JSR-109 and WebSphere to inform WebSphere that incoming web service requests are to be accepted on a certain URL and routed to the EJB for processing.

Create Deployment Descriptor Templates

Return to the command window and environment you set up in the section titled *Create PlantsByWebSphereCatalog.wsdl* above.

Run the `WSDL2Java` command to generate the templates for the deployment descriptors:

```
WSDL2Java -META-INF-Only -server-side EJB -verbose PlantsByWebSphereCatalog.wsdl

Parsing XML file:  PlantsByWebSphereCatalog.wsdl
Generating META-INF\webservicesclient.xml
Generating META-INF\ibm-webservicesclient-bnd.xml
Generating META-INF\webservices.xml
Generating META-INF\ibm-webservices-bnd.xml
Generating META-INF\PlantsByWebSphereCatalog_mapping.xml
```

The `-META-INF-Only` option tells `WSDL2Java` to generate just deployment descriptors, and not any Java classes. The `-server-side EJB` option indicates that the deployment descriptors should enable an EJB (as opposed to a JavaBean) as a web service. The `-verbose` option displays the names of the generated files.

Notice that the files were generated into a `META-INF` subdirectory, as required by JSR-109 for your EJB JAR. If the current directory isn't the root of the JAR hierarchy, you can change `WSDL2Java`'s output directory with the `-output` option. Also, if you were generating deployment descriptor templates for a JavaBean, they would be placed in a `WEB-INF` subdirectory instead of the `META-INF` subdirectory.

This command generated the following files:

- ❑ `webservicesclient.xml` – required by JSR-109.

- ❑ `PlantsByWebSphereCatalog_mapping.xml` – required by JSR-109. This descriptor contains detailed information about the mapping between Java and XML being used.

- ❑ `ibm-webservices-bnd.xml` – optional for WebSphere, this file contains WebSphere-specific deployment binding information, such as the security configuration for the service.

- ❑ `webservicesclient.xml` – not needed for a web services implementation, but required by JSR-109 for a J2EE application client using the web service in a client container.

- ❑ `ibm-webservicesclient-bnd.xml` – not needed for a web services implementation, optional for an application client to configure WebSphere-specific deployment binding information.

When enabling a WebSphere Application Server component to be a web service, you can delete the generated client deployment descriptor templates. To do so, return to Studio and switch to the XML perspective by selecting Window | Open Perspective | XML.

Navigate to the META-INF directory of the ejbModule.

Right-click on the META-INF directory and select Refresh. The deployment descriptors listed above appear in the Navigator pane:

Delete the two files: `ibm-webservicesclient-bnd.xml` and `webservicesclient.xml`.

You've now created the server-side deployment descriptor templates.

Configure the Deployment Descriptors

Until WSAD is updated to handle the JSR-109 deployment descriptors, you'll have to configure them by hand. This is easier than it sounds. The mapping deployment descriptor records the transformations made by the Java2WSDL and WSDL2Java tools when mapping between Java and XML, and requires no configuration. For the curious, the generated PlantsByWebSphereCatalog_mapping.xml file contains:

```
<?xml version="1.0" encoding="UTF-8"?>
<!DOCTYPE java-wsdl-mapping PUBLIC "-//IBM Corporation, Inc.//
DTD J2EE JAX-RPC mapping 1.0//EN"
"http://www.ibm.com/webservices/dtd/j2ee_jaxrpc_mapping_1_0.dtd">
<java-wsdl-mapping>
  <package-mapping>
    <package-type>com.ibm.pbw.ejb</package-type>
    <namespaceURI>http://ejb.pbw.ibm.com</namespaceURI>
  </package-mapping>
</java-wsdl-mapping>
```

This mapping file specifies that the Java package com.ibm.pbw.ejb corresponds with the XML namespace http://ejb.pbw.ibm.com, something that you've probably already guessed from examining the WSDL file.

> *A note on standards compliance – the initial Tech Preview version of the WebSphere version 5.0 web services only supports describing package to namespace mapping. JSR-109 requires that a number of other mapping items be represented that will be supported in the WebSphere version 5.0 update.*

Configuring the webservices.xml file is almost as easy as configuring the mapping file. The generated template is:

```
<?xml version="1.0" encoding="UTF-8"?>
<!DOCTYPE webservices PUBLIC "-//IBM Corporation, Inc.//
DTD J2EE Web services 1.0//EN"
"http://www.ibm.com/webservices/dtd/j2ee_web_services_1_0.dtd">
<webservices>
  <webservice-description>
    <webservice-description-name>
        PlantsByWebSphereCatalogService
    </webservice-description-name>
    <wsdl-file>META-INF/PlantsByWebSphereCatalog.wsdl</wsdl-file>
    <jaxrpc-mapping-file>
        META-INF/PlantsByWebSphereCatalog_mapping.xml
    </jaxrpc-mapping-file>
    <port-component>
      <port-component-name>PlantsByWebSphereCatalog</port-component-name>
      <wsdl-port>
        <namespaceURI>http://pbw.ibm.com</namespaceURI>
        <localpart>PlantsByWebSphereCatalog</localpart>
      </wsdl-port>
      <service-endpoint-interface>
        com.ibm.pbw.PlantsByWebSphereCatalog
      </service-endpoint-interface>
      <service-impl-bean>
```

```
        <ejb-link>
            ??SET THIS TO ejb-name ELEMENT OF ejb-jar.xml??
        </ejb-link>
      </service-impl-bean>
    </port-component>
  </webservice-description>
</webservices>
```

The string "??SET THIS...??" is all you have to fill in to configure webservices.xml. Copy this value from the ejb-name element in the ejb-jar.xml file that's already in the META-INF directory of the Plants-By-WebSphere EJB JAR:

```
<ejb-name>Catalog</ejb-name>
```

Filling in the ejb-link in webservices.xml with this name tells the application server that calls on the web services are to be routed to the Catalog EJB, and that the Catalog EJB implements methods having the same signature as those of the Service Endpoint Interface.

The completed <ejb-link> element is:

```
<ejb-link>Catalog</ejb-link>
```

To configure webservices.xml in Studio, double-click on webservices.xml in the Navigator to open it in the edit pane. If Studio reports an error on the header, you can safely ignore it. This may occur because the initial version of Studio version 5.0 isn't aware of the JSR-109 deployment descriptors.

Select the Design tab at the bottom of the edit pane, then open the descriptor until you see the ejb-link element:

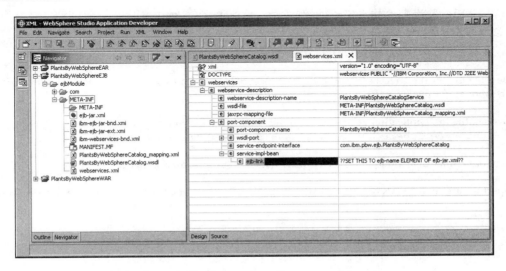

Replace the ejb-link element value with Catalog. Save your changes.

You have now finished configuring the web services deployment descriptors. There are some other interesting elements in `webservices.xml`. They are summarized in the following table:

Element	Description
`webservice-description-name`	The J2EE name for the service. Remember that a service can contain multiple ports.
`wsdl-file`	The relative path of the WSDL file in the module.
`jaxrpc-mapping-file`	The relative path of the mapping file in the module.
`port-component-name`	The J2EE name for the port.
`wsdl-port`	The name of the port in the WSDL file that's being implemented.
`service-endpoint-interface`	The Java Service Endpoint Interface class that corresponds to the `wsdl:portType` of the `wsdl:port`.
`ejb-link`	The EJB that implements this port.

Assemble the EJB JAR and Update the Application EAR

JSR-109 states that the developer is responsible for assembling the web services enablement files into the EJB JAR that contains the EJB, `PlantsByWebSphereEJB.jar`. Correspondingly the following files should be added to `PlantsByWebSphereEJB.jar`:

- ❑   `META-INF\webservices.xml`
- ❑   `META-INF\PlantsByWebSphereCatalog_mapping.xml`
- ❑   `META-INF\PlantsByWebSphereCatalog.wsdl`
- ❑   `META-INF\ibm-webservices-bnd.xml`

The class file for the `PlantsByWebSphereCatalog` Service Endpoint Interface at the relative path corresponding to its Java package.

To assemble the application using Studio, move the WSDL file to the `META-INF` directory, right-click on `PlantsByWebSphereCatalog.wsdl` in the Navigator pane and select **Move**.

From the Folder Selection panel, select the `META-INF` subdirectory and click **OK**.

Export the assembled EAR by selecting **File | Export | EAR file**. Click **Next** to display the EAR Export panel:

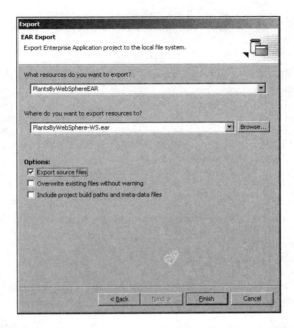

Select the PlantsByWebSphereEAR project under the What Resources do you want to export? field.

Enter the EAR file name in the Where do you want to export resources to? field.

Click Export source files if you wish to have the Java files included in the archive.

Press Finish to create the exported EAR file.

Enable the Web Services Endpoint Listener

For WAS version 5.0 Web Services Technology Preview, an additional step is required to process the web services-enabled EAR file before it is deployed. This step will not be required after the version 5.0 update. This step is to run the `endptEnabler` command to add a servlet configuration to the EAR so that incoming SOAP requests on HTTP are routed to the EJB.

The SOAP runtime in WAS version 5.0 includes a servlet that can be configured to listen for incoming web services requests and route them to the appropriate EJB. The `endptEnabler` command adds a WAR file to the EAR file containing only a `web.xml` deployment descriptor that configures the router servlet appropriately. The Technology Preview install places the `endptEnabler` command in the `bin` subdirectory of the WAS installation directory. `endptEnabler` is an interactive tool run from the command line:

```
endptEnabler
```

```
IBM WebSphere Application Server Release 5
Web services Enterprise Archive Enabler Tool.
Copyright IBM Corp., 1997-2002
```

325

```
Please enter the name of your ear file: PlantsByWebSphere.ear

*** Backing up EAR file to: PlantsByWebSphere.ear~
JSR 109 enabled EJB Jar file at name PlantsByWebSphereEJB.jar
Please enter a file name for your endpoint [PlantsByWebSphereEJB.war]:
Please enter a context root for your endpoint [/PlantsByWebSphereEJB]: PBW
```

The boldfaced text above is entered by the developer. For each JAR file containing `webservices.xml`, you are prompted for two pieces of information: the name of the WAR file to be added to the EAR, and the name of the context root (part of the URL) that will be used to access the service. The complete URL to access the service is:

```
http://host[:port]/context-root/services/port-component-name
```

The `context-root` is specified when running the `endptEnabler`. The `port-component-name` is specified in `webservices.xml`. The `services` component of the URL is constant, as specified by JSR-109. Since the `port-component-name` is `PlantsByWebSphereCatalog`, let's simplify the context root by changing the default to `PBW`.

The `endptEnabler` makes two changes to the EAR file. First, it updates `application.xml` to add the new web module (WAR file):

```xml
<module id="WebModule_1033923424831">
  <web>
    <web-uri>PlantsByWebSphereEJB.war</web-uri>
    <context-root>/PBW</context-root>
  </web>
</module>
```

Here you can see the `context-root` being set as specified and being associated with the new WAR file.

The second change is to add the WAR file to the EAR. The primary content of the WAR is the `web.xml` deployment descriptor:

```xml
<web-app id="WebApp_ID">
  <display-name>WebSphere Web service</display-name>
    <servlet id="Servlet_1033923423118">
      <servlet-name>WSRouterServlet</servlet-name>
      <display-name>Web services Router Servlet</display-name>
      <servlet-class>
          com.ibm.ws.webservices.axis.ws.transport.http.WASWebAxisServlet
      </servlet-class>
    </servlet>
      ...
    <servlet-mapping id="ServletMapping_1033923424772">
      <servlet-name>WSRouterServlet</servlet-name>
      <url-pattern>/services/*</url-pattern>
    </servlet-mapping>
</web-app>
```

The url-pattern says whenever the URL contains PBW/services/, it will be directed to the WSRouterServlet. The WSRouterServlet has the ability to examine the port-component information in the webservices.xml file in PlantsByWebSphereEJB.jar, and route the request to the correct EJB. Putting all this together, the following URL will route your SOAP request to the Catalog EJB:

http://localhost:9080/PBW/services/PlantsByWebSphereCatalog

The context root and port-component-names are automatically included in the SOAP location field in the WSDL port when the application is deployed.

Deploying the Web Services-Enabled Application

> **If you are using the Web Services Technology Preview, deploying and running a JSR-109 compliant web services application requires the *stand-alone* WebSphere Application Server version 5.0 with the Web Services Technology Preview installed.**

When you deploy a WebSphere Application that has been enabled for web services, two extra deployment tasks request information.

Begin deployment by opening the Administration Console and uninstalling the Plants-By-WebSphere application if it's already installed. Then choose Install New Application as shown below and enter the path to the web services-enabled PlantsByWebSphere.ear:

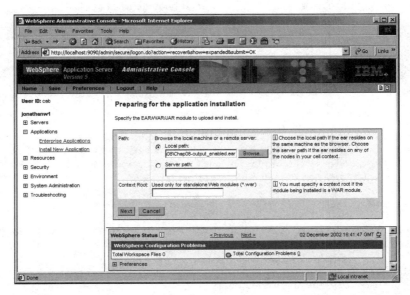

Press Next and proceed as usual for deploying an EJB, as described earlier in Chapter 6.

The first deployment task associated with deploying a web service is the Publish the WSDL file task.

If you're using the initial version of WebSphere Application Server 5.0, you won't see this task unless the Web services Technology Preview has been installed.

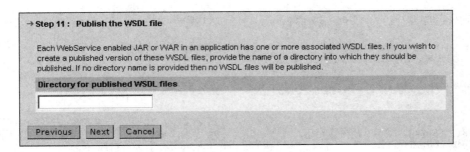

When a web service-enabled module is deployed, the WSDL files in the module are always updated with the location URL for the service and stored in the WebSphere Application Server's configuration directory for that module. If you specify a directory name in the Publish the WSDL file task, the updated WSDL files are also copied to the specified directory in a directory structure representing the modules and services being deployed. You will normally want to specify this directory to obtain WSDL that can be given to your customers to use to access the service. Note that the directory specified must already exist. Specify an existing directory and press Next.

The Get the name of the Server that hosts the web service deployment task appears:

This task prompts for the protocol, host, and port for the location URL to access the web service. The default values are suitable for accessing the server where the EAR file is deployed. If you use an HTTP server such as IHS, an edge server, or other means of accepting and redirecting HTTP requests, you should change the host and port to match the HTTP server.

Finish deployment as usual.

After deployment is finished, the PlantsByWebSphere directory contains the following directory structure and files:

PlantsByWebSphere – the directory you specified to publish to
    PlantsByWebSphere – the application name
        PlantsByWebSphereEJB.jar – the module file name
            PlantsByWebSphereCatalogService – web service description name
                                (from webservices.xml)
                PlantsByWebSphereCatalog.wsdl – the WSDL file for the service

If you look inside the published `PlantsByWebSphereCatalog.wsdl` file you'll find:

```
<wsdlsoap:address
location=http://myhost:9080/PBW/services/PlantsByWebSphereCatalog />
```

You can now give this WSDL document to your customers to use in creating clients to access your service. If you want to publish the WSDL to a UDDI registry, WebSphere Studio Application Developer includes wizards to publish a WSDL file to UDDI.

Restart the server to activate the `PlantsByWebSphereCatalog` web service.

Verifying the Web Service Deployment

After you've deployed the `PlantsByWebSphereCatalog` web service into the application server and restarted, how can you verify the deployment? Let's try typing that URL into a browser and seeing what happens:

The Apache AXIS-based runtime in the application server has intercepted the HTTP request to the URL, recognized that it doesn't contain a SOAP request, and responded with an acknowledgment message showing that the service is alive.

Now append ?wsdl to the URL. Does the result look familiar?

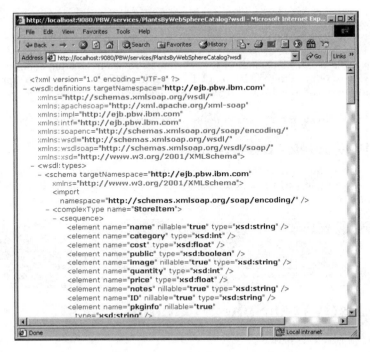

The WSDL for the Catalog service has been published to this specific URL. You can just give this URL to your customers to access the WSDL for your service, instead of giving them the entire WSDL document.

Summary of Business Logic Enablement for Web services

To summarize what you've accomplished so far, we have:

- ❑ Created a Java Service Endpoint Interface representing the Web service
- ❑ Created a WSDL file describing the Java service
- ❑ Created deployment descriptors describing how to map the service implementation to an EJB
- ❑ Assembled and deployed the application
- ❑ Published the WSDL (customers can use this WSDL to develop their own clients on any vendor's platform to access your service)

Creating J2SE and J2EE Web Services Clients

Now let's create a Java client for the `PlantsByWebSphereCatalog` web service, following the JSR-109 and JAX-RPC specifications.

Client Programming Model

The programming model for web services consists of APIs for the client-side programmer specified by JAX-RPC and contained in the Java package `javax.xml.rpc.*`. JAX-RPC provides an abstraction of the WSDL service definition so that the client programmer can interact with a service using late/dynamic binding or early/static binding.

The following abstractions are specified by JAX-RPC:

❑ **ServiceFactory**
An abstract class used to obtain a reference to an implementation of the service when the client is running outside a J2EE container and can't use JNDI to look up the service.

❑ **Service Interface**
A Java interface that represents the WSDL service description. There is a generic service interface, `javax.xml.rpc.Service`, as well as a generated service-specific interface that has methods to directly access the ports in the service. The generated service interface extends `javax.xml.rpc.Service` indicating that it is a JAX-RPC Service.

❑ **Service Endpoint Interface**
The Java representation of a specific WSDL `portType`. This interface extends `java.rmi.Remote` indicating that it can be called remotely over a network.

To use a web service, first use either the `ServiceFactory` or a JNDI lookup to get a reference to the `Service` interface. Then use the service to select the port and obtain a reference to the stub that implements the Service Endpoint Interface. Finally, invoke the operation on the service using the stub.

In the following sections, we examine each of these in more detail.

Locating a Service using JNDI Lookup

In the J2EE environment, JNDI is used to look up the service reference. J2EE components that intend to reference a web service are deployed with a JSR-109 deployment descriptor named `webservicesclient.xml`. This deployment descriptor follows the `java:comp/env` pattern established by J2EE. It contains a mapping of a logical name to the service, so that the calling component does not have to know the actual location of the service in the JNDI namespace. Here's a sample of the client JNDI lookup for the `PlantsByWebSphereCatalog` Service:

```
Context ctx = new InitialContext();

PlantsByWebSphereCatalogService cs = (PlantsByWebSphereCatalogService)
   ctx.lookup("java:comp/env/service/PlantsByWebSphereCatalogService");
```

Locating a Service using ServiceFactory

In the J2SE environment, the client program can't use JNDI to look up the service. In order to accommodate standalone Java clients, JAX-RPC has introduced an abstract class called `ServiceFactory` that provides access to JAX-RPC `Service` implementations, allowing vendor-neutral client code to be written:

```
package javax.xml.rpc;

public abstract class ServiceFactory {

    public static ServiceFactory newInstance() throws ServiceException {...}
    public abstract Service createService(URL wsdlDocumentLocation,
        QName serviceName) throws ServiceException;
...
}
```

The newInstance() method creates an instance of the ServiceFactory. The ServiceFactory implementation class is provided by the JAX-RPC runtime vendor, and extends ServiceFactory. Once the client has an instance of ServiceFactory, they can create a JAX-RPC Service instance using the createService() method. Once the client has a reference to the service, the programming model is identical to the J2EE example above. Here's an example using the ServiceFactory to create an implementation of the PlantsByWebSphereCatalogService:

```
Service cs = ServiceFactory.newInstance().createService(
    new URL("file", "", "PlantsByWebSphereCatalog.wsdl"),
    new QName("http://ejb.pbw.ibm.com", "PlantsByWebSphereCatalogService"));
```

You call createService() with a URL for the WSDL file. In the example code above, the URL file://PlantsByWebSphereCatalog.wsdl identifies the WSDL file. Therefore, when the example client is run, the WSDL file must be in the current directory.

You will normally want to specify a more complete URL for the WSDL file. For example, the ?wsdl URL could have been used to dynamically access the WSDL from the server as follows:

```
Service cs = ServiceFactory.newInstance().createService(
    new URL ("http://myhost:9080/PBW/services/PlantsByWebSphereCatalog?wsdl"),
    new QName("http://ejb.pbw.ibm.com", "PlantsByWebSphereCatalogService"));
```

Using the Generic and Generated Service Interfaces

The result of the JNDI lookup or calling ServiceFactory.createService() is a reference to an object that implements the javax.xml.rpc.Service interface, which in turn is an abstraction of the <wsdl:service> element in the WSDL document. The service in turn serves as a factory for creating stubs connected to specific ports. The Service interface also contains a method that returns the location of the WSDL document used to create *the* Service. The JAX-RPC specification defines the Service interface as follows:

```
package javax.xml.rpc;

public interface Service {

    java.rmi.Remote getPort(QName portName, Class serviceEndpointInterface)
        throws ServiceException;
    java.rmi.Remote getPort(Class serviceEndpointInterface)
        throws ServiceException;
    ...
    java.net.URL getWSDLDocumentLocation();
    QName getServiceName();
    java.util.Iterator getPorts() throws ServiceException;
...
}
```

Both the getPort() methods return a stub that accesses a WSDL port. The stub implements the Service Endpoint Interface and delegates method calls to the remote service. The first getPort() variant, passing the portName in addition to the Service Endpoint Interface class, associates a specific WSDL port with the service. The second form, passing only the Service Endpoint Interface class, permits the JAX-RPC runtime to select an appropriate port (that is, one whose portType matches the Service Endpoint Interface) and configure it for the client's use.

The JAX-RPC specification also requires that tooling generate a service-specific Java interface for the web service. This **generated service interface** provides additional port-specific methods that explicitly expose each port in the WSDL document. For example, running the WSDL2Java command on the PlantsByWebSphereCatalog WSDL produces the following service-specific interface:

```
package com.ibm.pbw;

public interface PlantsByWebSphereCatalogService extends
    javax.xml.rpc.Service {

  public PlantsByWebSphereCatalog getPlantsByWebSphereCatalog() throws
    javax.xml.rpc.ServiceException;

  public PlantsByWebSphereCatalog getPlantsByWebSphereCatalog(
    java.net.URL portAddress) throws javax.xml.rpc.ServiceException;
}
```

These methods return a stub for a specific port without passing any parameters, and without casting the result to a specific Service Endpoint Interface type. The first method uses the soap:location URL in the WSDL to access the service. The second form lets the client override the soap:location URL. If you know at development time that your client program must use a specific WSDL port, then using one of these methods to get a reference to the web service implementation may be faster or more convenient at run time than using the more dynamic binding available in the generic Service interface methods.

> If you're using the Technology Preview, there are some restrictions. JNDI lookup of a service always returns an implementation of the generated service interface that can be cast to the generic service interface if desired. The **ServiceFactory** mechanism for J2SE always returns an implementation of the generic service interface. An implementation of the generated service interface cannot be obtained using the **ServiceFactory**. If you require access to a generated service interface implementation in a J2SE environment, consult the Technology Preview documentation for a workaround.

So far, all we've seen of JAX-RPC is a collection of Java interfaces. You're probably wondering who is supposed to implement all those interfaces. The JAX-RPC standard requires vendors to provide tooling that generates implementations for the generic Service interface, the service-specific interface and the stub for the Service Endpoint Interface. These generated implementation classes are vendor specific and not portable to other JAX-RPC runtime implementations.

Client Programming Model Summary

To summarize, there are three steps the client performs to get a stub that accesses a Web service:

1. Obtain a reference to the service implementation.

2. Select a port from the service. This selection results in a reference to a stub.

3. Invoke the operation on the stub.

Following is an example of obtaining a reference to the `PlantsByWebSphereCatalog` service and invoking the `getItems()` method:

```
Context ctx = new InitialContext();

PlantsByWebSphereCatalogService cs = (PlantsByWebSphereCatalogService)
    ctx.lookup("java:comp/env/service/PlantsByWebSphereCatalogService");

PlantsByWebSphereCatalog c = cs.getPlantsByWebSphereCatalog();

StoreItem[] items = c.getItems();
```

Client Development Process

Now that you're familiar with the JAX-RPC client programming model for web services, let's see how we put all the pieces together. To begin, you must have the WSDL file for the service the client is to access. Then follow these steps to create the client:

1. Run the `WSDL2Java` tool. This will produce the following items:

    ❑   The generated service interface
    ❑   The Service Endpoint Interface
    ❑   Implementations of the Service Endpoint Interface (the stub) and the generated service interface
    ❑   The JSR-109 client deployment descriptor template `webservicesclient.xml`, used when running the client in a container
    ❑   Other runtime support classes used to marshal and demarshal values between Java and XML.

2. Write and compile the client code using the `javax.xml.rpc.*` interfaces, the generated service interface, and the Service Endpoint Interface

3. Compile the classes and assemble the client JAR including all the generated classes.

4. If you're not configuring for a J2EE container, you're done. Otherwise configure the `webservicesclient.xml` deployment descriptor and add it to the JAR.

The following diagram illustrates this process:

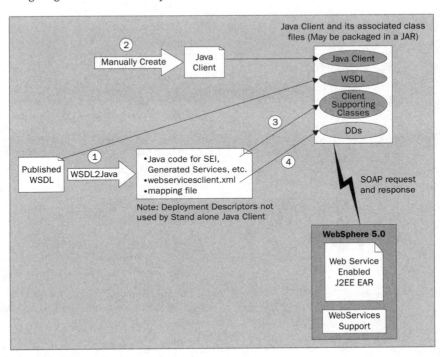

Accessing the PlantsByWebSphere Catalog Service

Now let's work through these steps in more detail to provide access to the
PlantsByWebSphereCatalog web service. All client development begins with a WSDL document.

Generate the Web Service Interfaces and Bindings

Run the WSDL2Java command to generate the client interfaces and bindings files for the client:

```
WSDL2Java -verbose PlantsByWebSphereCatalog.wsdl
Parsing XML file: PlantsByWebSphereCatalog.wsdl
Generating com\ibm\pbw\ejb\StoreItem.java
Generating com\ibm\pbw\ejb\StoreItem_Helper.java
Generating com\ibm\pbw\ejb\StoreItem_Ser.java
Generating com\ibm\pbw\ejb\StoreItem_Deser.java
Generating com\ibm\pbw\ejb\PlantsByWebSphereCatalog.java
Generating com\ibm\pbw\ejb\PlantsByWebSphereCatalogSoapBindingStub.java
Generating com\ibm\pbw\ejb\PlantsByWebSphereCatalogService.java
Generating com\ibm\pbw\ejb\PlantsByWebSphereCatalogServiceLocator.java
Generating META-INF\webservicesclient.xml
Generating META-INF\PlantsByWebSphereCatalog_mapping.xml
Generating META-INF\ibm-webservicesclient-bnd.xml
```

The `-verbose` option displays the files generated by `WSDL2Java`. The purpose of each is shown in the following table:

File	Purpose
`PlantsByWebSphereCatalog.java`	The Service Endpoint Interface, used by the client to invoke operations on the service.
`PlantsByWebSphereCatalogService.java`	The generated service interface, used by the client to access ports of the service.
`StoreItem.java`	A generated JavaBean to provide access to the fields of the `StoreItem` XML complex type.
`webservicesclient.xml`	The template for the JSR-109 J2EE application client deployment descriptor.
`PlantsByWebSphereCatalog_mapping.xml`	The JSR-109 mapping deployment descriptor to be packaged with a J2EE application client.
`ibm-webservicesclient-bnd.xml`	The template for the WebSphere specific binding information for the J2EE application client. Initially used for security configuration.
`PlantsByWebSphereCatalogService Locator.java`	The generated implementation of the Service interface. Client code should not use this class directly.
`PlantsByWebSphereCatalogSoap BindingStub.java`	The generated implementation of the Service Endpoint Interface. Client code should not use this class directly.

`StoreItem_Helper.java`
 	
`StoreItem_Ser.java`
 	
`StoreItem_Deser.java`
	Runtime helper classes for converting `StoreItem` bean to and from XML. Client code should not use these classes directly.

Write the Web Services J2SE Client

Let's start simply with the J2SE client that uses the `ServiceFactory` interface to access the service. Here's the complete code for the client that calls the `Catalog.getItem()` operation to find out more about a wheelbarrow. All of the code to get a reference to a port and call `getItem()` using it is in the `try` block in the `main()` method:

```
import javax.naming.InitialContext;
import javax.xml.rpc.ServiceFactory;
import javax.xml.namespace.QName;
import java.net.URL;
import javax.xml.rpc.Service;
import com.ibm.pbw.ejb.PlantsByWebSphereCatalog;
import com.ibm.pbw.ejb.PlantsByWebSphereCatalogService;
import com.ibm.pbw.ejb.StoreItem;
```

```
//Web services J2SE client for PlantsByWebSphereCatalog Web service.
public class PlantsClient {

  static String wheelbarrowID = "A0011";

  private static void printItem (StoreItem item) {
    System.out.println(item.getName() + "\t $" + item.getPrice());
    System.out.println(item.getDescr ());
    System.out.println("\tQuantity:\t" + item.getQuantity());
  }

  public static void main (String[] args) throws Exception {
    try {
      Service catService = ServiceFactory.newInstance().createService(
        new URL("file", "", "PlantsByWebSphereCatalog.wsdl"),
        new QName("http://ejb.pbw.ibm.com",
        "PlantsByWebSphereCatalogService"));

      PlantsByWebSphereCatalog cat = (PlantsByWebSphereCatalog)
        catService.getPort(new QName("http://ejb.pbw.ibm.com",
        "PlantsByWebSphereCatalog"), PlantsByWebSphereCatalog.class);

      StoreItem item = cat.getItem(wheelbarrowID);
      printItem(item);
    } catch (Exception e) {
      e.printStackTrace();
    }
  }
}
```

The example client has been simplified by telling it the item ID of the wheelbarrow in advance. It's easy to extend the example to call getItems() and browse the entire catalog contents.

Compile and Test the J2SE Client

For the J2SE client, no assembly is required; you can just configure the classpath and compile the client code. The classpath needs to contain the following JAR files:

JAR file	Contents
WAS_HOME\lib\j2ee.jar	J2EE classes, including XML processing APIs
WAS_HOME\lib\jaxrpc.jar	JAX-RPC APIs (used by web services clients and client bindings)
WAS_HOME\lib\xerces.jar	XML manipulation classes, needed by client runtime.
WAS_HOME\lib\axis.jar	Client runtime (used by web services client bindings)
WAS_HOME\lib\ws-commons-logging.jar	Client runtime logging support

Table continued on following page

JAR file	Contents
WAS_HOME\lib\commons-discovery.jar	Client runtime configuration support
WAS_HOME\lib\qname.jar	Contains javax.xml.namespace.QName
WAS_HOME\lib\wsdl4j.jar	Client runtime WSDL utilities
WAS_HOME\lib\webservices.jar	Web services client runtime
WAS_HOME\lib\saaj.jar	Client runtime attachments support

WAS_HOME refers to the WebSphere Application Server 5.0 installation directory. You'll also need to add the path to the files generated by WSDL2Java to the classpath (remember to compile them). You can then compile the J2SE client.

Test the Web Services Client

After checking that the server is running and that the WSDL file is in the current directory, you can execute the stand alone Java client:

```
java PlantsClient
```

```
Wheelbarrow       $29.0
Shiny red wheelbarrow with epoxy coated steel bin and wooden handles. Tire is
solid with thick treads that grip rough, wet surfaces. Large capacity - 3 Cu.Ft.
capacity, 150 Lb. maximum load
        Quantity:      100
```

Monitor the Web Services Messages

Both WebSphere Studio and WebSphere Application Server include tools to monitor SOAP messages being exchanged between client and server. The monitor listens on one TCP/IP port, displays the messages in a window, and forwards to another TCP/IP port.

In order to use the monitor, the client needs to be reconfigured to access the Web service through a port other than 9080. Let's pick port 9088 instead. The easiest way to do this is to edit the client's WSDL document and change the wsdlsoap:address location attribute URL to use port 9088 instead of 9080. Then run WSDL2Java again and recompile the generated bindings.

To run the monitor included with WebSphere Application Server, configure the classpath as shown in the table above and run:

```
java org.apache.axis.utils.tcpmon
```

The TCPMon window opens:

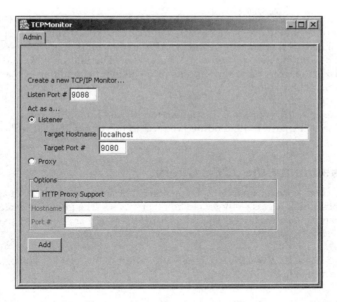

Configure the monitor to listen on port 9088 and forward messages to localhost port 9080 (the port the application server is listening on). Press the Add button to add the Port 9088 tab to the monitor. Select this tab to see the messages. Run the client application again to see the SOAP request and response in the monitor window:

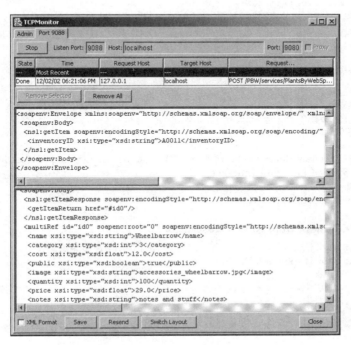

The top pane contains the list of all messages sent and their responses. It shows that one message has been monitored at 06:21:06PM. When there are multiple messages displayed, you can select the one you want to view. The middle pane shows the SOAP request sent by the client. You can see the `getItem` element containing the `inventoryID` part value. The bottom pane shows the response received. You can see the `getItemResponse` message element containing (via a multi-ref), the elements of the `StoreItem` complex type.

While debugging and testing your service, you can modify the text in the request pane and click the **Resend** button. The will transmit the modified request to the server and show the new response in the bottom pane.

Writing and Assembling the J2EE Client

Now let's adapt the client code to run in a J2EE container. This code will work in an application client, or in the web or EJB containers to access web services on other servers. The following example constructs an EAR for the J2EE application client container. The code changes required are to use the JNDI lookup code we saw earlier to get a reference to the service implementation instead of using the `ServiceFactory`.

Start by copying `PlantsClient.java` to a new file called `PlantsClientJNDI.java` and change the client code in the `main()` method from:

```
Service catService = ServiceFactory.newInstance().createService(
    new URL("file", "", "PlantsByWebSphere.wsdl"),
    new QName("http://ejb.pbw.ibm.com", "PlantsByWebSphereCatalogService"));

PlantsByWebSphereCatalog cat = (PlantsByWebSphereCatalog)
    catService.getPort(new QName("http://ejb.pbw.ibm.com",
    "PlantsByWebSphereCatalog"), PlantsByWebSphereCatalog.class);
```

to:

```
InitialContext ctx = new InitialContext();
Service catService = (Service)
    ctx.lookup("java:comp/env/service/PlantsByWebSphereCatalogService");

PlantsByWebSphereCatalog cat = (PlantsByWebSphereCatalog)
    catService.getPort(PlantsByWebSphereCatalog.class);
```

Notice that the J2EE client doesn't refer to any WSDL elements, just the JNDI name for the service and the class for the Service Endpoint Interface.

Compile `PlantsClientJNDI.java`

Configuring the J2EE Client Deployment Descriptor

When you ran `WSDL2Java`, it generated the `META-INF/webservicesclient.xml` file. This deployment descriptor is specified by JSR-109:

```
<?xml version="1.0" encoding="UTF-8"?>
<!DOCTYPE webservicesclient PUBLIC "-//IBM Corporation, Inc.//
    DTD J2EE Web services client 1.0//EN"
"http://www.ibm.com/webservices/dtd/j2ee_web_services_client_1_0.dtd">
```

```
<webservicesclient>
  <service-ref>
    <description>
       WSDL Service PlantsByWebSphereCatalogService
    </description>

    <service-ref-name>
        service/PlantsByWebSphereCatalogService
    </service-ref-name>

    <service-interface>
        com.ibm.pbw.ejb.PlantsByWebSphereCatalogService
    </service-interface>

    <port-component-ref>
        <service-endpoint-interface>
            com.ibm.pbw.ejb.PlantsByWebSphereCatalog
        </service-endpoint-interface>
    </port-component-ref>
  </service-ref>
</webservicesclient>
```

This deployment descriptor does not require any configuration unless you want to change the JNDI name in the `java:comp/env` namespace used to look up the service. This name is specified in the `service-ref-name` element.

Assembling the J2EE Application Client

Next, we need to make a client JAR containing the following files:

- ❏ The client application classes
- ❏ The classes for all the generated Java files
- ❏ The `application-client.xml` deployment descriptor
- ❏ The `MANIFEST.MF` file containing a `Main-Class:` entry
- ❏ The `webservicesclient.xml` deployment descriptor in the `META-INF` subdirectory of the JAR for an application or EJB client, (the `WEB-INF` subdirectory for a client in the WEB container)
- ❏ The JAX-RPC mapping file, `PlantsByWebSphereCatalog_mapping.xml`
- ❏ The WSDL file, which by convention is placed in the `META-INF` directory of the JAR

You can use your favorite assembly tool to create the application client JAR and EAR. The process described in the following sections works from the command line to do the assembly to make the process explicit.

The directory you're working in should currently have the following after running `WSDL2Java`, creating the client class, and compiling all the Java files:

```
PlantsClientJNDI.class
PlantsClientJNDI.java
PlantsByWebSphereCatalog.wsdl
```

```
.\META-INF
   PlantsByWebSphereCatalog_mapping.xml
   ibm-webservicesclient-bnd.xml
   webservicesclient.xml

.\com\ibm\pbw\ejb
   PlantsByWebSphereCatalog.class
   PlantsByWebSphereCatalog.java
   PlantsByWebSphereCatalogService.class
   PlantsByWebSphereCatalogService.java
   PlantsByWebSphereCatalogServiceLocator.class
   PlantsByWebSphereCatalogServiceLocator.java
   PlantsByWebSphereCatalogSoapBindingStub.class
   PlantsByWebSphereCatalogSoapBindingStub.java
   StoreItem.class
   StoreItem.java
   StoreItem_Deser.class
   StoreItem_Deser.java
   StoreItem_Helper.class
   StoreItem_Helper.java
   StoreItem_Ser.class
   StoreItem_Ser.java
```

Now, continue the steps to build the client JAR and EAR.

Move the WSDL file to the META-INF subdirectory.

Create the META-INF\application-client.xml file with the following contents:

```
<?xml version="1.0" encoding="UTF-8"?>

<!DOCTYPE application-client PUBLIC "-//Sun Microsystems, Inc.//DTD J2EE
Application Client 1.3//EN" "http://java.sun.com/dtd/application-client_1_3.dtd">

    <application-client id="Application-client_ID">
        <display-name>PlantsClientJNDI</display-name>
    </application-client>
```

Create a manifest.txt file containing the following line in the current directory:

```
    Main-Class: PlantsClientJNDI
```

This file will be merged into the META-INF\MANIFEST.MF file using the –m option of the jar command to instruct the client container which class has the main method for the application.

Now run the jar command (located in the java\bin directory under the WebSphere installation directory) to update the manifest and create the JAR file:

```
jar –cvmf manifest.txt PlantsClient.jar META-INF\* com PlantsClientJNDI.*
```

That completes the creation of the client JAR. The launchClient command requires an EAR file, so it will take a few more steps to assemble the JAR into an EAR.

Create a `META-INF\application.xml` file with the following contents:

```xml
<?xml version="1.0" encoding="UTF-8"?>
<!DOCTYPE application PUBLIC "-//Sun Microsystems, Inc.//DTD J2EE Application
1.3//EN" "http://java.sun.com/dtd/application_1_3.dtd">
<application id="Application_ID">
     <display-name>WebServices Managed Client Sample</display-name>
     <module id="JavaClientModule_1">
          <java>PlantsClient.jar</java>
     </module>
</application>
```

The purpose of this descriptor is to indicate to the container which JAR in the EAR contains the main class. Finally, create the EAR:

jar cvf PlantsClient.ear META-INF\application.xml PlantsClient.jar

You now have a JSR-109 web services enabled application client EAR. Let's try it out.

Testing the Application Client

Run the application EAR with the `launchClient` command located in the WebSphere Application Service bin directory:

```
launchClient PlantsClient.ear

IBM WebSphere Application Server, Release 5.0
J2EE Application Client Tool
Copyright IBM Corp., 1997-2002
WSCL0012I: Processing command line arguments
WSCL0013I: Initializing the J2EE Application Client Environment
WSCL0035I: Initialization of the J2EE Application Client Environment has completed
WSCL0014I: Invoking the Application Client class PlantsClientJNDI
Wheelbarrow        $29.0
Shiny red wheelbarrow with epoxy coated steel bin and wooden handles. Tire is
solid with thick treads that grip rough, wet surfaces. Large capacity - 3 Cu.Ft.
capacity, 150 Lb. maximum load
          Quantity:      100
```

You have now created a web service from the `Catalog` EJB, and created both J2SE and J2EE clients that access the service. We won't develop the client sample further here, but you can imagine how you might expand the client code to automatically process `Catalog` entries in a variety of ways. You would probably also create web services to handle ordering, customer registration, and so on until Plants-By-WebSphere was a fully web service-enabled enterprise.

Now let's take a look at the rest of the WebSphere web services universe.

Survey of Related IBM Web Services Activities

The web services world is large, changing rapidly, and, to be honest, confusing. It's practically a full-time job just keeping up with current events in the field. This section summarizes some of the IBM WebSphere-related activities in web services and provides references so you can learn more about them on your own.

WebSphere Web Services Components

The components reviewed in this section are included with WAS version 5.0 or the WebSphere Web Services Technology Preview. The information presented here augments that provided in the web services section of Chapter 2.

Apache SOAP

IBM had contributed **Apache SOAP** (http://xml.apache.org/soap) to the open source in 2001. Version 2.2 was included in WAS version 4.0, and support continues for it (at the 2.3 level) in WAS version 5.0. The WebSphere Studio web services support described in Chapter 3 currently uses Apache SOAP. Apache SOAP uses non-standard APIs and was not designed for scalability or performance, so it will be deprecated in future releases of WebSphere.

Apache Axis

Apache **Axis** (http://xml.apache.org/axis) is a follow-on to the Apache SOAP project. It is a redesign for improved scalability, flexibility, and performance. It also implements the JAX-RPC specification. IBM has been a major contributor to Axis. The WebSphere Web Services Technology Preview described in this chapter is based on Axis 1.0. WebSphere Application Server uses Axis "under the covers" as an implementation of the J2EE standards. Axis is not part of the WebSphere programming model, and use of Axis-specific APIs is not supported. There's lots more to learn about Axis; entire books, like *Axis: The Next Generation of Java SOAP* from Wrox Press *ISBN 1-86100-715-9*, have been written about it.

Apache Web Services Invocation Framework (WSIF)

The **Web Services Invocation Framework** was developed by IBM and contributed to the Apache Axis project (http://xml.apache.org/axis). WSIF is included in WAS version 5.0. It is a Dynamic Invocation Interface (DII) designed to closely match WSDL. It has parts, operations, and messages. The power of WSIF is that it can use its internal representation of the WSDL message to transmit the message on a variety of different protocols and transports, not just SOAP/HTTP.

WSIF provider handles the conversion to a specific protocol and transport, and new providers can be written and plugged into the framework. Extensions to WSDL bindings are defined for each new provider to instruct WSIF how to transmit the message. WSIF currently defines WSDL binding extensions and providers for SOAP over JMS, native JMS, direct calls to Java, and direct calls to EJBs.

The role of WSIF is primarily to facilitate the use of protocols and transports other than SOAP/HTTP. Normally WSIF will be configured automatically when a protocol other than SOAP or a transport other than HTTP is required, based on the information in the WSDL file and deployment information. You won't use WSIF directly unless you want to use the WSIF DII as an alternative to the DII defined by JAX-RPC when your application must make calls based on dynamically imported WSDL.

UDDI4J

UDDI4J is a Java class library that provides an API to interact with a UDDI registry. This library is an open source project (http://www.uddi4j.org). There are two versions of the UDDI APIs, 1.0 and 2.0 (see http://www.uddi.org for details), consequently, there are also two versions of UDDI4J bundled with WAS version 5.0. The version 1.0 APIs are included in uddi4j.jar, and the version 2.0 APIs are included in uddi4jv2.jar. You can read more about UDDIJ4 at http://www-106.ibm.com/developerworks/webservices/library/ws-uddi4j2.html.

WSDL4J (JSR-110)

WSDL4J is a Java class library that provides an API to read, write, and modify WSDL files. It is an IBM open source project (http://www-124.ibm.com/developerworks/projects/wsdl4j/) and is in the process of becoming a Java standard under JSR-110, Java APIs for WSDL (http://www.jcp.org/en/jsr/detail?id=110).

Private UDDI Registry

The private UDDI registry is a component of WebSphere Application Server Network Deployment (WASND) that implements a UDDI V2.0 registry for corporate intranet services not intended to be publicly available. It is implemented as an EJB application running on WebSphere Application Server. You can read more about the rationale behind and uses for a private UDDI Registry at http://www-106.ibm.com/developerworks/webservices/library/ws-rpu1.html.

Web Services Gateway

The Web Services Gateway is a runtime component that provides configurable mapping based on WSDL documents. It maps any WSDL-defined service to another service on any available transport channel. It is usually deployed at the firewall and has access to internal services. The Web Services Gateway is a component of WASND. See http://www-106.ibm.com/developerworks/webservices/library/ws-gateway for an introduction. The Web Services Gateway is a dynamic web services application built on the Web Services Invocation Framework discussed above.

The Web Services Gateway provides the following features:

❑ **Service Mapping**
The primary function of the Web Services Gateway is to map an existing WSDL-defined web service to a new web service that appears to be provided by the gateway. The gateway acts as the proxy. External services are imported into the gateway and made available to the enterprise as proxy services internally. Likewise, internal services are imported into the gateway and made available as proxy services externally. These services are also published to the relevant UDDI directories where required.

❑ **Export Mapping**
An internal service can be exported for outside consumption. Given the WSDL file, the gateway will generate a new WSDL file that can be shared with outside requestors. The requestors will use the gateway as the service endpoint.

❑ **Import Services**
Similarly, an external service may be imported and made available as an internal service. This will help the internal service requestors to invoke the service as if it were running on the gateway.

❑ **Transformation**
A request for a service may originate on one protocol, but the service may be invoked in some other protocol by using the transformation function. An internal service available on SOAP over JMS could be invoked using SOAP over HTTP.

❑ **UDDI Publication and lookup**
Gateway facilitates working with the UDDI registry. As you map a service for external consumption using the gateway, you can publish the exported WSDL in the UDDI directories. When the services in the gateway are modified, the UDDI registry is updated with the latest updates.

❑ **Security and Management**
The gateway provides a single point of control, access and validation of web service requests. Authorization is based on the gateway service name and the operation being invoked.

WS-Security

WS-Security is a new web services security standard based on joint work by Microsoft and IBM (http://www-106.ibm.com/developerworks/webservices/library/ws-secure/). It is included with the Web Services Technology Preview for WAS version 5.0. The document at http://www-106.ibm.com/developerworks/webservices/library/ws-secapp/ is a WS-Security application note.

Standards Organizations

Although there are many standards organizations involved with web services, the **Web Services Interoperability Organization** (http://www.ws-i.org) is likely to become the most important. This organization was started by Microsoft and IBM, and currently has hundreds of corporate members. The purpose of WS-I is to publish **profiles** that specify what combinations of other specifications (as well as their versions) work together. Part of the purpose of the WS-I profiles is to clarify existing specifications, for example stating that the SOAP encodings (rpc/encoded) are not permitted in conforming WSDL. WS-I is essential to achieving the objective of "ubiquitous interoperability". At the time of writing, the first WS-I profile is still under development. The Web Services Developer's Kit discussed below, as well as the WebSphere platform, will fully support WS-I profiles in future releases.

DeveloperWorks Web Services Zone

The IBM DeveloperWorks web services web site (http://www-106.ibm.com/developerworks/webservices/) contains a wealth of information about the web services technologies surveyed above. There are white papers, tutorials, and downloads. The most relevant download is the WSDK (Web Services Developer's Kit).

IBM Web Services Developer's Kit

The **Web Services Developer's Kit** (http://www-106.ibm.com/developerworks/webservices/wsdk/) is a free developer-oriented web services development kit. It is intended to promote the programming models and standards used by WebSphere Application Server and WebSphere Studio in a timely, affordable manner while facilitating the development of web services that can be deployed to WebSphere Application Server. Web services technologies that will be added to the WebSphere Programming Model will likely appear in the WSDK first. One important role of the WSDK is to serve as a proof of concept for the WS-I interoperability profiles as they emerge.

AlphaWorks Web Services Technologies

The IBM AlphaWorks web services technologies web site (http://www.alphaworks.ibm.com/webservices) focuses on interesting newly emerging web services technologies. The easiest way to explore these technologies is to download the IBM Web Services Toolkit from http://www.alphaworks.ibm.com/tech/webservicestoolkit. The Toolkit is updated quarterly, and the contents change on a regular basis. There is no guarantee that any of these technologies will ever be included in a product, and, if they are, they may take a year or two to mature and be productized.

Summary

You've now been introduced to the web services core technologies, WSDL and SOAP, and learned about the J2EE standards supporting these technologies and WebSphere's initial incorporation of them.

The J2EE programming model for web services implementations and JAX-RPC programming model for clients will be part of J2EE 1.4, and will become more integrated and pervasive as vendors incorporate and improve their support. This chapter has attempted to strike a balance between teaching you about these important new standards while also giving you enough practical hands-on information so that you can create and use web services today.

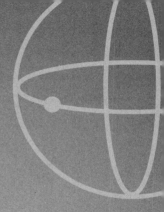

Part 3: Building Enterprise-Enabled Applications

Part 3: Building Enterprise-Enabled Applications

So, what do you do when you need to solve mission-critical enterprise-enabled business problems and the standard J2EE programming model is just not enough? What happens when you need to isolate the rapidly evolving policies of your company from the relatively long development cycles for making application changes; or you need to employ sophisticated sequencing controls in the interaction of your enterprise information services; or you need to introduce more parallelism in your business processes? One choice is that you design solutions for these needs into your application. However, our experience is that these problems can get very complicated and solutions will require a significant investment in time to design, evolve, and maintain. That, of course, is time taken away from solving business problems.

WebSphere offers a variety of services and frameworks for dealing with sophisticated programming needs. This part of the book will take you into these capabilities for building enterprise-enabled applications. We will begin by examining the issues and solutions to complex persistence problems – including those that occur because of trying to scale up the sharing of components in different application scenarios. We will then focus on the WebSphere approach to business rules and process management (modeling and programming). We will round out this part of the book by exploring the WebSphere services for context propagation, asynchronous parallel processing, and internationalization.

All of the features described in this part of the book are only available with the WebSphere Application Server – Enterprise Edition (WASE) of the runtime, and are developed with WebSphere Studio Application Developer – Integration Edition (WSAD-IE) of the tools.

After you complete this part of the book, you will have a good understanding of how much further WebSphere can take you towards solving sophisticated enterprise-scale application problems. More importantly, you will know how program and exploit many of the major features of the WebSphere programming model extensions.

It is not possible to describe how to program everything that WebSphere has to offer. Therefore, we conclude this part with a brief survey of the other features of the WebSphere programming model extensions and solution content that you may be interested in exploring further.

About the Plants-By-WebSphere Sample

This part of the book further extends the Plants-By-WebSphere sample developed in the previous part in Chapter 5. In particular, a workflow is added to the sample that will drive the process for introducing a pricing change to the plant store catalog. The workflow depicted in Chapter 10 presumes a staff role for approving the price change.

The following picture depicts the workflow created in this part of the book:

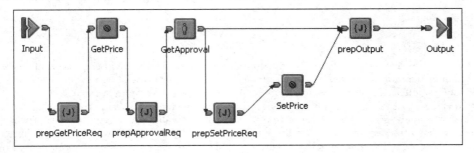

The remaining chapters in this part introduce their own code examples that have been built up outside the Plants-By-WebSphere sample used through the first half of the book. Those examples are discussed in their respective chapters.

9

Advanced EJB Persistence and Optimization

WebSphere Application Server Version 5.0 contains a number of features and optimizations that make the already compelling value of EJB 2.0 applications even more exciting. Container-managed entity beans are the preferred method of data persistence in J2EE 1.3. To the developer, CMP simply means that the EJB container handles interactions with database. However, CMP means a bit more to the vendor that is implementing the container. It means not only that is there a responsibility upon the container vendor, but it also provides a certain amount of opportunity for the vendor to differentiate itself from the competition and to provide additional value to the customer.

This chapter will introduce the value-added features that IBM has provided in its implementation of the EJB container for CMP, including:

- ❑ An introduction to the concept of Access Intent
- ❑ An introduction to the Application Profile service
- ❑ EJB Persistence Support
- ❑ EJB QL extensions
- ❑ Transactions
- ❑ Unit-of-work scoping

> **Beyond basic access intent and local transactions, most of the features discussed in this chapter are part of the Enterprise Edition of the WebSphere Application Server.**

A more detailed summary of features applicable specifically in the base WebSphere Application Server and specifically in the Enterprise Edition is found as part of the *Summary* at the end of this chapter.

Some of these features introduce new programming interfaces and make the applications created with them specific to WebSphere. Other features, however, can be applied to applications declaratively without impacting on the portability.

Access Intent

Entity beans are used in J2EE application architectures as abstractions representing business objects. Entity beans provide an effective way to map the "things" of a business model, often defined by analysts and non-programmers, from something that exists in the "real world" to a construct in source code. Entity bean implementations, and the associated application server runtime support, manage the entity data by interacting with a persistent store such as a relational database. However, the implementation of those entities, done in part by bean providers and in part by the container and the runtime, must decide upon and provide answers to a number of more detailed questions. The answers to these questions may or may not be present in the abstraction being implemented. The answers might lie in the usage of the entity or in the application architecture itself.

A complete entity-relationship diagram of a business model would reveal a number of things about the usage patterns of the data. For example, expectations relating to locking and isolation level might be present, as well as information about result sets and navigation. As the container does much of the work involved in managing an entity bean, you cannot put these hints about usage patterns into the source code.

As it turns out, these facts about the intended usage of the data are often necessary to ensure that a business model can be effectively executed using entity beans. The EJB specification has some accommodation for capturing these facts about the entities and the intended usages involving those entities. For example, settings that can be configured in the deployment descriptor include security roles and method permissions or something as detailed as cascade-delete requirements for relationship management. However, more precise and detailed access intent information is often necessary. This has become even more necessary as we have moved from the EJB 1.1 to the EJB 2.0 model.

EJB 2.0 provides more flexibility and more capability to the bean provider, but also suggests the need for a more precise specification of the various intents. The application server can use this information to govern and regulate the interaction with the resource managers that contain the persistent state data. The persistence mechanisms that manage essential state need additional intent information so they can make proper decisions about concurrency control and resource management.

Access Intent support in WAS 5.0 is centered on capturing this intent information and ensuring that it can be utilized in the runtime. In conjunction with the **Application Profile service**, the WebSphere runtime is able to use the right intents at the right times in the execution sequence to ensure effective and accurate backend interactions.

Access intent is a set of declarative annotations used at run time by WAS to ensure that the optimal calls to the resource managers are made. These policies are named and defined at the module level. An EJB module may have one or many such policies. The Application Profile service enables us to apply multiple policies to a single bean and to determine at execution time which policy to apply based on the run-time context. This lets entity beans be reused in different ways by different applications with necessarily different access intent requirements. The most common example is the need to access an entity bean either optimistically or pessimistically, where optimistic and pessimistic refer to the locking of the underlying rows in the database.

Before diving into the Application Profile service, however, let us first describe the access intent policies that are allowed.

Access Intent Hints

Access intent in WebSphere provides support for the following hints:

- ❑ Access-type
  This indicates whether a component interaction is read or write oriented, and whether or not the component interaction is to be done pessimistically or optimistically. When dealing with EJBs, pessimistic refers to an action on a backend database where a lock is held for the affected data from the time it is first read until the transaction involving the data is complete. Optimistic generally means that the data involved in the transaction is read, but a lock is not held. If the data in the underlying datastore has changed when the transaction is to be finished, a rollback will occur. The pessimistic update hint is further qualified by the following attributes:

  - ❑ Exclusive
    This specifies that the application requires exclusive access to the database rows. The backend should use the most stringent locking scheme available. Specifically this means that it will map down to what is normally called "serializable" on the underlying resource manager.

  - ❑ No collision
    This specifies that the application is designed such that no concurrent transactions will access the same database rows. Therefore, a less stringent locking scheme or in fact no locking at all may be used. Specifically this means that this maps to read-committed on the underlying resource manager.

  - ❑ Weakest lock at load
    This indicates whether a lock upgrade should be attempted. This applies to those resource managers that support read locks; an initial read lock is acquired and later in the transaction the lock is escalated or promoted if an update is performed.

- ❑ Collection scope
  This indicates how long a collection is to be used. This can be set to transaction or ActivitySession. ActivitySession is described in more detail later in this chapter.

- ❑ Collection increment
  This indicates the increment size that should be used for a lazy collection. A lazy collection is a collection that does not hold the complete contents asked for by the caller, but rather maintains the ability to acquire the contents on demand from a cache or database.

- ❑ Read ahead hint
  This is a hint that indicates to the server how deeply the object graph for EJB 2.0 CMR relationships should be read.

❑ Resource manager prefetch increment
This is used by the persistence manager to provide a hints to the database about retrieving data for collections.

These are called hints because, in some cases, the application server runtime will be unable to exactly match the behavior in the hint. This is usually either due to the backend system and restrictions that may exist in the interaction styles allowed or because of conflicts with other hints which may be in effect. More examples will be given as the details are described.

With this brief introduction, let's explore these a bit more before going on to describing how these can be used by applications.

Default Intents

WAS comes with a set of access intent policies that will be enough for you to get started configuring and using CMP 2.0 Entity Beans.

Note that `Resource manager prefetch` *is set to zero for all of these sets of access intents, which lets the database make the best default decision. When we get to the Application Profile service, changing this value is discussed further.*

wsPessimisticUpdate

This set of access intents will provide an update lock at `ejbLoad()` time on the row in the table of the underlying database. This will be useful on a `findByPrimaryKey()` and on single-table finders. This will keep you out of deadlocks more than the other pessimistic options. Specifically, this results in a SELECT FOR UPDATE with whatever isolation level is one level weaker than serializable for a particular database. For Oracle, this is read- committed. For DB2, this is repeatable-read. This setting will connection-share with `wsPessimisticRead`:

```
Access-type                           = pessimistic update
Exclusive                             = false
No collision                          = false
Weakest lock at load                  = false
Collection scope                      = transaction
Collection increment                  = 1
Resource manager prefetch increment   = 0
Read ahead hint                       = null
```

wsPessimisticUpdate-NoCollision

This set of access intents is the same as the previous one, except that it will not generate a SELECT FOR UPDATE on the `findByPrimaryKey()` and other finder methods:

```
Access-type                           = pessimistic update
Exclusive                             = false
No collision                          = true
Weakest lock at load                  = false
Collection scope                      = transaction
Collection increment                  = 25
Resource manager prefetch increment   = 0
Read ahead hint                       = null
```

wsPessimisticUpdate-Exclusive

This set of access intents provides the strongest level of locking. It maps to a serializable isolation level on DB2. This set of access intents should prevent others from inserting rows:

```
Access-type                              = pessimistic update
Exclusive                                = true
No collision                             = false
Weakest lock at load                     = false
Collection scope                         = transaction
Collection increment                     = 1
Resource manager prefetch increment      = 0
Read ahead hint                          = null
```

wsPessimisticUpdate-WeakestLockAtLoad

This set of access intents will potentially upgrade read locks to write locks if the underlying resource manager supports that locking style:

```
Access-type                              = pessimistic update
Exclusive                                = false
No collision                             = false
Weakest lock at load                     = true
Collection scope                         = transaction
Collection increment                     = 25
Resource manager prefetch increment      = 0
Read ahead hint                          = null
```

wsPessimisticRead

This set of access intents will provide a 'repeatable read' semantic. There are no update locks. The runtime will throw an exception if an update is attempted while these policies are in effect:

```
Access-type                              = pessimistic read
Collection scope                         = transaction
Collection increment                     = 25
Resource manager prefetch increment      = 0
Read ahead hint                          = null
```

wsOptimisticUpdate

This set of access intents does not hold a lock. It uses a "read commited" semantic as it applies to the underlying database. Updates are allowed and rollbacks will occur at transaction commit time:

```
Access-type                              = optimistic update
Collection scope                         = transaction
Collection increment                     = 25
Resource manager prefetch increment      = 0
Read ahead hint                          = null
```

wsOptimisticRead

This final set of access intents holds no locks. The runtime, however, will not permit updates:

```
Access-type                            = optimistic read
Collection scope                       = transaction
Collection increment                   = 25
Resource manager prefetch increment    = 0
Read ahead hint                        = null
```

A CMP 2.0 entity bean will run using wsPessimisticUpdate-WeakestLockAtLoad access intent policy unless it is changed in the Application Assembly Tool, which we will demonstrate how to do in the next section.

> *Notice also that the Read ahead hint is always null. This is because these hints are specific to particular CMR relationships and are customized using patterns similar to those described in the next section.*

Applying Access Intent

If no customization of access intent is done, applications with entity beans will default to the wsPessimisticUpdate-WeakestLockAtLoad policy. While this will usually let you start testing an application, it is often not sufficient for use in a production environment. The easiest way to change the access policy used is to use another one of the policies provided in the system. The following example shows setting a specific policy for the Customer entity bean from our Plants-By-WebSphere application.

First, when you right-click on the **Access Intent** item in the AAT, you are given a choice to create a new access intent. This brings you to a window like this:

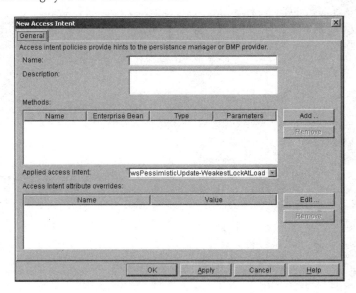

Provide a name for this usage of an access policy. Also, use the pull-down menu to decide which access intent to apply. In our case, we will use the wsOptimisticRead policy:

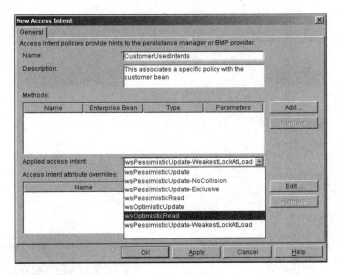

The final task is to describe which methods will use this policy. Access intent policies configured without the benefit of the application profile service (to be described later in this chapter) are applied to the methods of a bean and its home. When the invocation of a method causes the container to read the bean's data from the underlying data store, the access intent policy configured on that method will be used to manage the access and concurrency for that bean instance for the duration of the unit-of-work.

Clicking the Add button under the Methods heading will provide a selection dialogue like this:

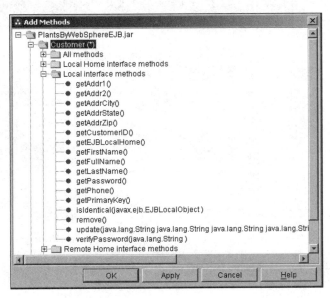

For this first example, we will just pick Customer(*), which indicates that all methods will use the wsOptimisticRead policy. More granular selection is obviously possible. The final display before pressing Apply will the look like this:

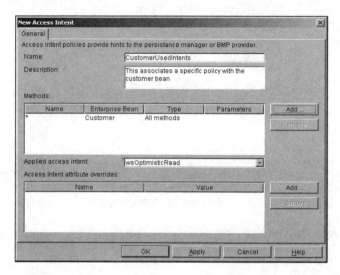

If you want to use a set of access intents for a bean or a set of methods on that bean that had a slight variation form the default, you can override or customize it as shown below. The collection increment is set to 100, but the rest of the default profile will be used as it is:

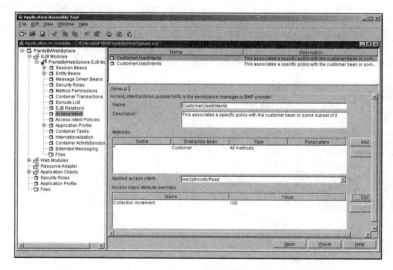

Sometimes it might be necessary to build a completely new access intent policy. This is easy to do in the application assembly tool. Under the Access Intent Policies on the main application assembly tool view, just right-click and you will see the New choice where you should fill in the view as shown:

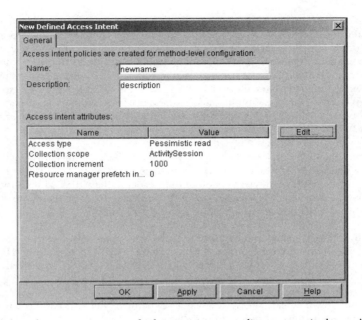

This set of capabilities lets you customize which access intent applies to an entity bean. All of this is done at assembly time and once you have deployed the EJB, the access intent policy that is used to interact with the backend is known, fixed, and used by the runtime. It is part of the extended deployment descriptor information and is found in the `ibm-ejb-jar-ext.xmi` file. The only problem is the "fixed" part. Fortunately, the Application Profile service is going to let us reach another level of flexibility.

Application Profiles

With all of this access intent information now available, properly applying it at the right time during execution is the next thing to understand.

The J2EE 1.3 model for describing information about components (EJBs, servlets, and so forth) involves using deployment descriptors. This is a very good pattern in that it extracts this kind of information into separate XML files that can be changed without changing the underlying component implementations or client programs that use those implementations. This creates a model where component reuse is encouraged. The declarative style can also be beneficial for specifying contractual information that does not fit into the code. Looking at the deployment descriptor of an entity bean, for example, to see what the transactional requirements or expectations are, is very natural to those who have been doing EJB programming for any period of time.

J2EE vendors often necessarily add their own extensions to the base deployment descriptors. WebSphere adds deployment descriptor extensions at the application, module, bean, and method levels for various features that it supports, which complement and augment the base specifications. These are included in separate extension files. In fact, the files `ibm-ejb-jar-ext.xmi` and `ibm-ejb-jar-ext-pme.xmi` represent extensions to the base deployment descriptor that are provided by the base application server and the Enterprise Edition respectively.

The declarative model, however, is largely static. The `ibm-ejb-jar-ext.xmi` extensions support only a single set of extensions per entity bean. The runtime then uses those extensions to make decisions about managing resources and interacting with databases and other resource managers. The problem is that the decisions made for a given deployment of an entity bean, for example, are not always the same. What if the decisions about entity bean resource management should change from application-to-application or from calling client to calling client? For example, what if there were some session beans in the Plants-By-WebSphere application that access the `Customer` entity bean using optimistic transactions, and other session beans in the application that need a pessimistic transaction for the same `Customer` entity?

A simple solution to this is would be to have multiple deployments of our entity bean, each with different statically defined descriptors and extensions. This means that each different usage of a given resource might use a different deployed version of that resource (let's stick with entity beans for this discussion). While this is technically feasible, it is not practicable because the number of combinations needed is untenable and the impact on the caller is too significant.

We could certainly change our deployment tooling and deployment descriptor extensions to have multiple sets of deployment descriptor extensions that need to be used at runtime. However, this is just part of the solution; we still need a way to decide which of these sets of extensions are to be used in any given situation.

The problem should now be clear. We need a way to dynamically alter the information that the runtime uses, based on the usage pattern (profile) of the caller (application).

An **Application Profile** provides a way for applications to suggest to the runtime which among the possible sets of hints should be used for any given server operation. The basic pattern at run time is as follows:

1. Sometime during the execution of the application a label or task name, which is the key to a set of hints, gets attached the thread of execution.

2. Later in the execution sequence, pieces of the runtime that are Application Profile service aware, look on the thread of execution, get the task name if it exists, and use those hints, which are accessed via the task name.

The pattern above deserves a bit more explanation. The next sections goes into detail on this and describes how to set up an application to use the Application Profile service so that the above activities occur during application execution. If these do not occur, we get the default behavior of access intent as described earlier.

The Application Profile Service

The Application Profile service supports configuration, propagation, and presentation of named units of work or tasks. A task designates a unit of work at the business level. In Plants-By-WebSphere, creating a new user, creating a new order, and adding an item to a shopping cart all represent potential tasks, or named units of work. As we will see shortly, a task can be associated with a session bean, session bean method, servlet, servlet method, or J2EE client. A task can be designated wherever the business level unit of work is known and initiated in the runtime system.

The Application Profile service can be used in two ways, programmatically or declaratively.

Bean providers can use the Application Profile service programmatically to tie different ways in which the same bean can operate to a specific task name. The name is a logical label in the code, which is linked by the application assembler via deployment descriptor extensions to a real set of attributes (the profile) that the runtime will use to make decisions. Programmatic use of the Application Profile service might look like this:

```
TaskNameManager tnm = (TaskNameManager) initialContext.lookup(
                        "java:comp/websphere/AppProfile/TaskNameManager");
   //...
   if (someCondition) {
       tnm.setTaskName("someTask");
   } else {
       tnm.setTaskName("someOtherTask");
   //...
```

The above snippet attaches either someTask or someOtherTask to the thread of execution. Exactly how this impacts on access intent will be described later. While bean providers can programmatically put the proper task name onto the thread of execution, it is more flexible to do this work declaratively.

The declarative style is similar to how transactions are managed using the container-managed style. This style of leveraging the Application Profile service is less intrusive from a source-code perspective. This should lead to more intensive and tuned usage of the service. Examples of how to create tasks in the assembly tool and associate them to specific application profiles will be provided in the upcoming section.

The next section will describe how to use Application Profile and the tasks concept, which was described above, to allow dynamic and specialized usage of access intent information. Access intent is the primary use of Application Profile in WAS 5.0.

> *Beyond version 5.0, it is likely that additional usages of Application Profile will be supported. The whole concept of more dynamically applying information about components based on intend usage patterns is one that has great potential and one that is essential if we are to truly create more flexible and reusable components.*

Access Intent Using Application Profile

Now we need to pull it together. How do we use the combination of the access intent support provided by WebSphere and the Application Profile service to control backend interactions in a fine-grained way?

This process of pulling it all together will be described in terms of three activities. These are:

- ❏ Creating the possible profiles
- ❏ Identifying the tasks
- ❏ Mapping the tasks to profiles

This process can be done top-down, bottom-up, or meet-in-the-middle. What is coming in the next sections is a top-down view, but it is clear that different methods of arriving at the answer will be used.

Let's return to some examples to show how this might be done. These examples are somewhat simple to introduce the concept with minimum additional clutter.

Creating Application Profiles

For the example, we will use the Order entity bean from the Plants-By-WebSphere application. Let's assume that we have analyzed all the users of the Order entity bean, such as the Catalog session bean and ReportGenerator session bean, and determined that leveraging different access patterns will be beneficial to overall system performance and throughput. In the example, the Catalog session bean would desire to have access to the Order entity bean using an optimistic update access intent while the ReportGenerator session bean can work best with a specialized access intent that supports the high volume of reading that is part of the business logic of this session bean.

> *The ReportGenerator bean is another session bean from the full-blown Plants-By-WebSphere application. You can find the source for this bean in the source code for Chapter 9 on the CD.*

We start by creating a new Application Profile for eventual use by the Catalog session bean. Select the **Application Profile** of the **EJB Module** and right-click, then select **New** from the pop-up menu. Fill in the name of the profile and a short description as shown and press **Apply**:

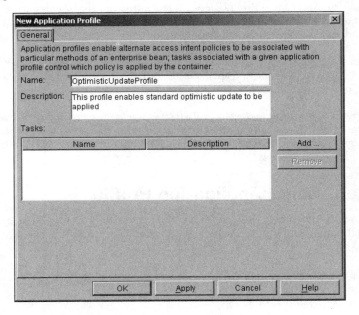

We will come back later to fill in the tasks.

Create the HighVolReadProfile the same way. After this, we have two profiles created, but have not really wired them into the rest of the application yet:

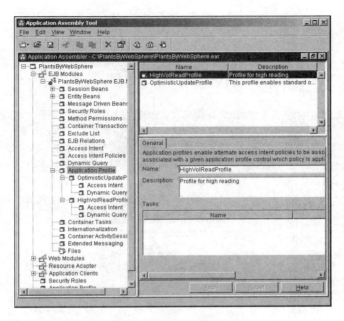

Once these are created, the specific access intents that are desired for this profile can be created. First, select **Access Intent** under the **HighVolReadProfile**, right-click and select **New**.

This will bring up a screen that looks similar to the one from the earlier section where we created an access intent. Because we are now creating the access intent as part of an application profile, the policy can now be applied to an entire entity bean rather than a set of methods. Instead of considering the method that causes the bean's data to load from the backend, the application profiling service will use the application profile associated with the active task to determine the correct access intent.
Below is the screenshot of the completed access intent customization named `HighVolReadIntent` that goes with this `HighVolReadProfile`:

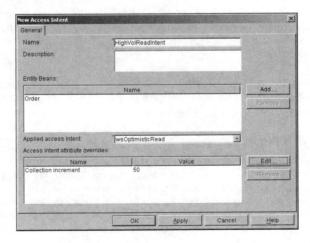

You can see that we have taken the wsOptimisticRead access intent policy set and tuned it using the same style as we learned earlier.

On completing this step, we can create the OptimisticUpdateProfile in the same way, creating the OptimisticUpdateIntent that describes the access intent policy. The assembly tool is shown below with both the profiles ready to be put to use:

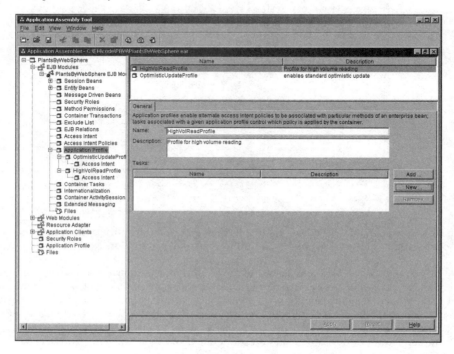

These two profiles are attached to different intents. We have two different ways to access the Order entity bean specified and carried by the application profiles that have just been set up. They are at the application level. Even though they are specific to how we will want to have the Order entity bean interact with the database, they are at the application level. This allows them to be used by the various callers to the Order entity bean.

We have now declared two profiles that can be used when interacting with this entity bean. The next step is to identify the tasks that represent the different callers of this entity bean, which might want to use different profiles to access the entity bean.

Identifying Application Tasks

Tasks represent points in the application where we know a set of interesting and useful things about the application that we want to communicate to the underlying application server. In more concrete teams, this is where we know the intents that we want to use to provide as hints to the runtime. We communicate these hints downstream to give the application server the opportunity to act differently in terms of how it operates. Tasks can be established based on servlets, clients, or EJBs, with the possibility of individual EJB methods having different tasks associated with them.

Getting back to our example, we must create some tasks and map them to specific session bean methods to get the desired effect. Start by creating a task. Right-click on Container Tasks, and click on New. This will bring up the following entry view:

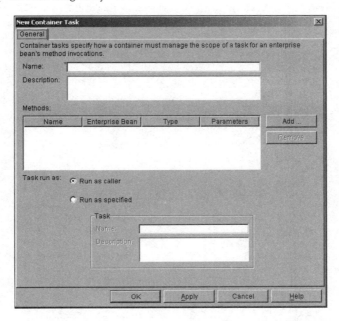

Fill in this view and select the methods that are going initiate the request to do the high volume reading. This time, we will pick specific methods as shown here:

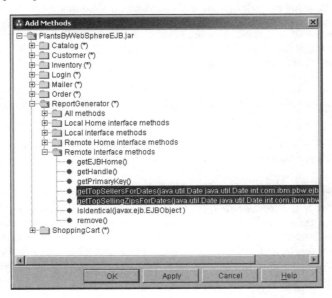

These methods will actually do the high volume reading of the `Order` entity bean.

Shown in the next screenshot is the creation of a task for a couple of methods on the session bean that wish to have the high volume read behavior if possible. Let's name this task `HighVolReadContainerTask` to keep it simple:

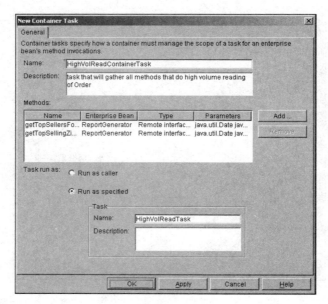

The Run as specified radio button is selected to indicate that this task is to be applied and is not to be overridden by any task that may already be present when the methods are executed. This implicitly suggests that anyone calling the named methods cannot change the task that is used in downstream calls by the runtime. A more comprehensive example might indicate some methods that are to pass through tasks that the caller might have suggested and some patterned like the example, which indicates specific task names for specific methods.

Another one of these tasks is created named `OptimisticUpdateContainerTask` and is mapped to methods on the session bean that drive updates. The same steps just described are repeated and another task is created.

Now that we have defined tasks and we have the profiles, all that is left is to wire them together and inform the system which profiles should be used by which tasks.

Mapping the Tasks and the Application Profiles

Describing the profile to use for specific tasks is probably the easiest of the activities. It consists of simple mapping from the profiles and tasks that we created. While there are a couple of ways to do this, one simple way to begin this process is to go to the Application Profile selection that is at the application level or top level of the `.ear` file that you are working on, and start there. You can see in the following screenshot that you can associate the things we have talked about before. In the example screenshot, we have tied HighVolReadProfile to HighVolReadTask:

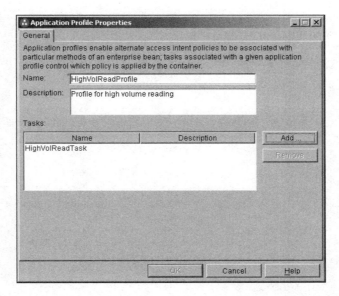

The same step is repeated to map the other task. With both of the mappings complete, we have a view like this:

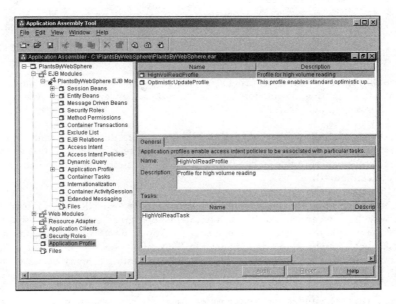

Now we are done going through what it takes to set up and use application profile and access intent. We now have to set up our application to leverage two specific application profiles. The signal to use these profiles comes from the task mappings. The use of the downstream intents is based on the task that is active, and the profile that it points to, when backend interactions are done by the runtime. All that is left is to execute is the application.

When the application is executed, the tasks will be placed onto the thread of execution when the session bean or identified component is executed. This task name then remains on the thread of execution and is leveraged by the runtime when it needs to do operations that involve access intent. Different behaviors from the entity beans can be expected based on the set of access policies that are leveraged.

Pulling these pieces together yields a chart like the one shown below:

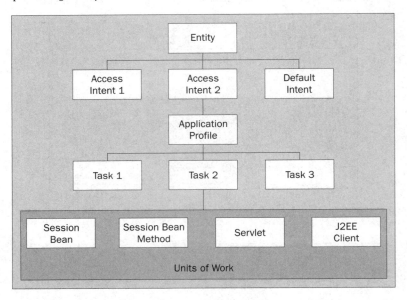

We have been through these concepts using a specific path. This diagram shows the key concepts we have talked about, suggesting the relationships between these concepts, and providing a view of what some of the other paths might be.

A task, as we discussed, pulls together a number of units of work that are the same or similar in terms of the needs they have when it comes to interacting with the backend systems. A task separates units of work from the profiles and provides a level of indirection that simplifies tuning and changing how the applications are configured.

An Application Profile provides a way to link together a task to a specific set of intents. An Application Profile is the way that we can get multiple sets of intents for a given entity bean. What might be a bit confusing is that multiple tasks can be tied to a specific Application Profile. For example, we could have had many tasks that all mapped to a specific profile. This might occur if we have developers identifying units of work and we have someone else during deployment testing actually deciding which tasks best map to which profiles.

Access intents do not map one to one with entities. An entity can have many access intents, which necessitates many Application Profiles. An entity will be configured exactly once per application profile.

A number of new abstractions have been described in this section, which will provide us with a great deal of flexibility in configuring our applications to achieve the maximum efficiency possible.

WebSphere EJB CMP Support

In Chapter 5, we used the "top-down" mapping support for CMP fields, in which a database schema is automatically generated based on the definition of an EJB. This is the easiest way to implement EJB persistence during new development, but it also contains a number of inherent restrictions. The most obvious of these is when you are not creating a new database in reality, but need to map your newly created bean to an existing database. However, there are a number of additional mapping options, which are not available using the top-down approach, and we will review them here.

The WebSphere Studio mapping editor provides the ability to define the specific mapping between individual CMP fields and the database columns. The mapping editor is used to map an entire JAR at once. Nodes in the editor represent the beans and CMP fields that need to be mapped, as there are some scenarios such as container-managed relationships (CMRs) and EJB inheritance that require a complete view of all beans in the JAR. You cannot create mappings that span JARs; if you wish to share mapping information for different beans (in cases such as EJB inheritance), you must have all those beans in the same JAR file.

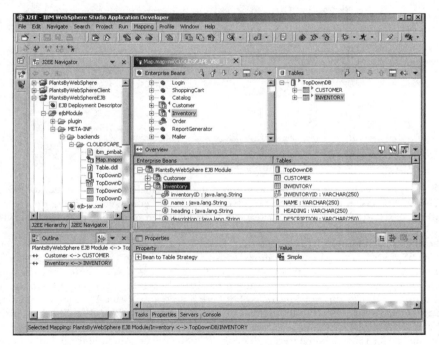

In this view, the underlying model files are seen in the left, in the Navigator view. The mapping editor displays the JAR and the entity beans on the top left-hand side of the editor view, and the database tables and columns on the top right-hand side. Those beans and fields that are mapped have a triangle by their name, and appear in the overview view (bottom-half of the editor) and in the Outline view (bottom-left of the screen). Suppose we wished to change the default mapping of the `Inventory` bean's `INVENTORYID` field, from a `VARCHAR(250)` column to an `INTEGER`, perhaps because we are now going to reuse an existing database, then the following steps should be followed.

371

The first action is to remove the existing mapping for the field; do this by opening the context menu from the INVENTORYID node in the Overview view, and selecting Remove Mapping. Next, we need to update the definition of the INVENTORY table. Select the table in the top-right view, and from the context menu select Open Table Editor. The table editor allows you to make arbitrary changes to the schema – to change the column type, we select the Columns tab at the bottom of the editor, select the column desired, and then make the change using Column type as shown. Now simply save and close the table editor:

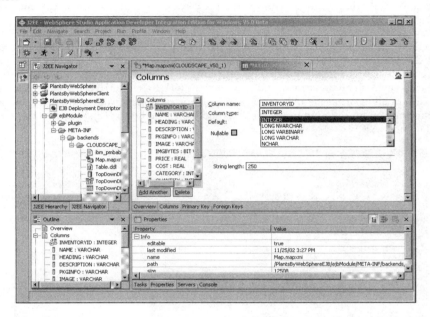

Back in the Mapping editor, you can define the new map by selecting both the inventoryID CMP field and INVENTORYID column nodes, in the top-left and top-right editor views. Bring up the context menu, and select Create Mapping; you will see the results added immediately to the Overview view.

This series of actions highlights several features, most obviously how easy it is to change a mapping using the WebSphere Studio Mapping editor. However, you will also note that the new mapping of a String to an Integer requires a type conversion. This code is generated automatically when the bean is deployed. The implementation details of how a particular CMP field is persisted, are not defined by the specification, and previous versions of WebSphere Studio and VisualAge for Java required a Converter object to be defined to implement this form of type mapping. WebSphere Version 5.0 can exploit the changes in the EJB 2.0 specification, with the result that entity beans with CMP 2.0 style persistence no longer require converters – the correct type-conversion code is now generated in place. Converters are still supported, but are now only required for semantic, or data-value conversion – type conversion is handled automatically.

The ability to change the persistent mapping of a field also highlights the benefits of using CMP entity beans. We have just changed how a bean maps to a column, without having to change any user code, queries, or implementation. You simply have to re-deploy the bean, and the correct code will be generated for you.

EJB Inheritance

EJB inheritance is an IBM extension that is a form of advanced persistence. Inheritance is a fundamental part of object-oriented code, with benefits ranging from simple code reuse, to advanced polymorphic behavior. The behavior of Java objects that use inheritance is a well defined part of the language, but Java objects exist only in memory and do not provide any native form of persistence. Enterprise beans are implemented as Java objects, and as such, the runtime behavior is well defined as well. You can treat an instance of a child class as though it is an instance of the parent class, and you can invoke and override methods defined at various points in the hierarchy. The complex issue is how the type and state of CMP entity beans can be persisted and reloaded again. We will use a simple example to highlight the options:

❑ `Vehicle` – root enterprise bean whose CMP fields include `id` and `dateAcquired`

❑ `Automobile` – inherits from `Vehicle` and adds CMP field `numberOfAirBags`

❑ `RaceCar` – inherits from `Automobile` and adds CMP field `topSpeed`

❑ `Bus` – inherits from `Vehicle` and adds CMP field `maximumPassengers`

❑ `Truck` – inherits from `Vehicle` and adds CMP fields `maximumLoad` and `numberOfWheels`

There are two modes of persistence for EJB inheritance available:

❑ **Single table**
In single-table mapping, each bean type is mapped to the same table. In the Mapping editor, you need to establish a discriminator column for the root bean type, and a distinct value for that column for each bean type. The top-down mapping wizard will also prompt you for these details, on the last page of the wizard. The type of each row is then determined by the value of the discriminator column in that row. This property is set in the Properties view in the EJB Mapping editor, and can be any value you choose, as long as each type is distinct. The benefit of single table mapping is that the data can be queried and reloaded quite efficiently without the need for complex multi-table joins. The cost of this style is that the table definition can grow quite wide, with only a subset of the columns used for each bean type.

The resulting table for the above example, using single-table mapping, would look like this:

Table: `VEHICLE`

ID	DISCRIM	DATE	AIRBAGS	SPEED	MAXPASS	MAXLOAD	WHEELS
12	Vehicle	2002/06/13					
15	Bus	1966/05/22			35		
27	RaceCar	1993/07/05	1	218			
28	RaceCar	1994/11/05	1	235			
42	Truck	1981/08/01				4400	18
52	Automobile	1991/05/14	0				
55	Bus	1999/12/01			28		

❑ **Root/Leaf**

In root/leaf mapping, each type is mapped to a distinct table, but fields defined in the root type(s) are not duplicated. As the name implies, there is a root table, and the table for each derived type only contains the key, and the additional fields defined by that type. Note that queries defined on the root type can result in large joins, due to the need to select all possible fields for all possible types – as a result, queries should generally be defined as low in the hierarchy as possible. The benefit of root/leaf mapping is that each table is smaller, and only contains relevant information. The cost of this style is that the queries needed to load a bean consist of large joins, which can be expensive to run.

The resulting tables for the above example, using root/leaf table mapping, would look like this:

Table: VEHICLE

ID	DISCRIM	DATE
12	Vehicle	2002/06/13
15	Bus	1966/05/22
27	RaceCar	1993/07/05
28	RaceCar	1994/11/05
42	Truck	1981/08/01
52	Automobile	1991/05/14
55	Bus	1999/12/01

Table: RACECAR

ID	SPEED
27	218
28	235

Table: BUS

ID	MAXPASS
15	35
55	28

Table: AUTOMOBILE

ID	AIRBAG
27	1
28	1
52	0

Table: TRUCK

ID	MAXLOAD	WHEEL
42	4400	18

In both mapping models, a series of additional WHERE clauses of database joins are required to implement the persistence pattern you select, but with CMP these mechanics are hidden from you. Your responsibility is to ensure that the schema defined is the one you want, and the bean's mapping to that schema is logically correct. The WebSphere persistence manager and the generated code will then do all the hard work, providing the behavior you want in a way that performs at run time.

You need to define the details of EJB inheritance in two different locations. The basic structure of the inheritance, defining which beans inherit from other beans, is set as part of the EJB deployment descriptor extension. This information can be best changed using the deployment descriptor editor in Studio. The second piece of information is the type of mapping model to use, and the associated data such as a discriminator column and the discriminator values. This data is saved in the mapping document, and changed in the Studio Mapping editor. You can select various beans in the editor, and update the values as properties.

The details of the mappings described above are saved in metadata files that are included with the deployment descriptor in the JAR. As a result, the mapping variants described above are all possible, but the code to implement them does not need to be generated within Studio. The `EJBDeploy` command that can be invoked on the command line, or during the application installation process, has access to the metadata files and will reflect this data during the code and query generation. There are multiple files used to represent the persistence of a single JAR, as described below. As with the mapping editor, the files all represent a complete JAR. The XMI files are all based on an OMG-compliant specification, so you can use a number of tools to browse through them or compare different versions for changes. The files contain a number of links that need to be self-consistent, so it is recommended that you do not manually edit the files; use the Studio editors instead.

The links to the various mapping elements require the use of ID tags within each file, including the deployment descriptor itself. The EJB deployment descriptor DTD does allow for the use of IDs, but the deployment descriptor is not otherwise modified during the mapping of CMP fields. The metadata files saved in the JAR file are:

File name	Description
`META-INF/ejb-jar.xml`	Spec deployment descriptor
`META-INF/ibm-ejb-jar-ext.xmi`	IBM deployment descriptor extensions
`META-INF/ibm-ejb-jar-bnd.xmi`	IBM deployment descriptor bindings
`META-INF/map.mapxmi`	Mapping information for CMP beans
`META-INF/schema/*`	Schema information for CMP beans

Mapping CMP Beans with 2.x Persistence

The above text applies to all CMP beans, but there is additional mapping and support, and a resulting change to the number and structure of the metadata files, when CMP 2.0 persistence is used. Note that an EJB JAR file may be a 2.0 level JAR (meaning, the deployment descriptor uses the 2.0 DTD), but the entity beans within the JAR may use either 1.x or 2.x persistence. It is even possible to mix 1.x and 2.x persistence beans in the same JAR, although that practice is not recommended. There are several differences between the two persistence styles, but the most visible one is the change in the way persistent fields are represented. The 1.x persistence uses public fields in the bean, while 2.x persistence beans have abstract getter and setter methods.

Another important change that comes with WebSphere's support of CMP 2.x beans is the ability to map a single JAR to multiple databases. The whole premise of the CMP design is to separate the implementation of the bean from the mapping to the underlying database, but that mapping has to occur at some point, and from then on the bean implementation is typically bound to a particular schema. With CMP 2.x beans however, you can create multiple mappings to different databases, or even different styles of mappings to the same database – perhaps one mapping for a test database, and another for a production database. When multiple mappings are defined, the metadata files saved in the JAR are modified as follows:

File Name	Description
META-INF/ejb-jar.xml	Spec deployment descriptor
META-INF/ibm-ejb-jar-ext.xmi	IBM deployment descriptor extensions
META-INF/ibm-ejb-jar-bnd.xmi	IBM deployment descriptor bindings
META-INF/backends/id1/map.mapxmi	Mapping information for CMP beans
META-INF/backends/id1/table*.xmi	Schema information for CMP beans
META-INF/backends/id2/map.mapxmi	Mapping infovrmation for CMP beans
META-INF/backends/id2/table*.xmi	Schema information for CMP beans

This approach uses a unique backend ID to store all mapping related metadata that is associated with each backend. Any number of backends can be defined, with as many similarities or differences between them as necessary. The mapping and table editors within Studio understand this structure. The available backends are displayed, and once one is selected, the editors behave as before. The code necessary to execute all included backends is generated when the EJB is deployed, meaning that the current or "active" backend can be changed in the assembly tool without requiring any additional code regeneration. The current backend can also be set at creation time, in the deployment descriptor editor in Studio.

SQLJ Support

An additional mapping option that is available for CMP 2.x beans is the style of database access. The standard approach is to use dynamic access via JDBC, but some advanced databases (such as DB2 Version 8.1) offer substantial performance improvements by using static access via SQLJ. SQLJ is a standard for static SQL usage, but can offer substantial performance benefits over dynamic SQL (such as JDBC). For example, SQLJ provides a SELECT INTO statement that will populate Java variables directly from the results of a SQL statement, avoiding the use of underlying database cursors. The generated code for single-valued EJB finder methods (such as findByPrimaryKey()) will exploit this style, resulting in improved performance. Additional details about SQLJ can be found at http://www.sqlj.org.

The use of SQLJ requires three stages; the SQLJ-specific code needs to be generated, next it needs to be translated into Java, and finally the Java code needs to be profiled against a specific database. The first two of these stages are implemented by the EJB deploy tool. For this, a property can be set in the Properties view of the Mapping editor, indicating that the mapping is to be implemented via SQLJ. This will then be persisted as part of the metadata, and when the code is generated, it will use the static SQL approach. The translation of the SQL into Java code will also occur under the control of the EJB deployment tool, using a translator provided by the database vendor. Finally, the generated code needs to be profiled against a specific database instance. This profiling step allows the database to optimize the interaction and subsequent performance.

Profiling uses a tool provided by the database vendor, and must be run on a machine with live access to the target database. The deployment tool will generate an Ant script that can be run on this machine, to invoke the profiling step. In summary, if you are targeting a database with good SQLJ support, then the tradeoff is simple; in exchange for a slightly more complex build and deployment step requiring live access to the target database, you can substantially improve the performance of your database access (depending on your access patterns).

The entire mapping variations described above, work in conjunction with the access intents described earlier. Each method on the bean may have multiple implementations generated, and the specific implementation used is selected by the WebSphere persistence manager at run time. This is how the dynamic nature of the access intents can be supported, and the use of any or all of the advanced mappings described, does not impede the function of the access intents. Pulling all the options together, it is therefore possible to define a single JAR that contains multiple beans related via EJB inheritance. The persistence of the beans could be spread across multiple tables and loaded via a join at run time, or all beans could be persisted into a single table. The access to the database in either scenario could be via JDBC, or via static SQLJ. Finally, each of these combinations can be used with or without optimistic concurrency, pessimistic locking, read-ahead relationship support, and all the other access intents.

Query Extensions

The EJB 2.0 specification introduces the concept of an EJB Query Language (EJB QL). This provides a standardized mechanism for implementing finders. Finder implementations are now portable across database backends. These implementations are done using the terminology of beans and fields in beans rather than using JDBC statements, which require knowledge of database tables and columns.

This basic EJB QL capability sets the stage for a number of query extensions. These further enhance the power of EJB QL to drive queries to backend systems. Dynamic query changes the point at which queries are executed. This is described first. WebSphere Application Server also introduces a set of extensions to the EJB QL to make it more powerful. This is the second part of the Query Extensions section of this chapter. Finally, a quick look under the covers of WebSphere's query capabilities completes the section.

Dynamic Query

The query function defined by J2EE is a static query capability, that is, queries are defined in the deployment descriptor and each query is associated with either select or finder methods. The EJB QL syntax is used to define queries for entity beans with CMP. The specification means that the bean providers describe queries in terms of container-managed fields instead of database columns. This also implies that the specifications of these finders are portable across different database vendors. With all this capability, what could be lacking?

Statically defined queries mean that all queries need to be defined at development time. Substitution variables are filled into the right-hand side of the operators, using notation such as the ?1 below:

```
SELECT OBJECT(o) FROM OrderBean o WHERE o.total > ?1
```

If we want a query where beans are returned, where the total is greater than some specified minimum and less than some specified maximum, then the following finder would be needed:

```
SELECT OBJECT(o) FROM OrderBean o WHERE o.total > ?1 AND o.total < ?2
```

Each container-managed field in a CMP 2.0 entity bean might participate in queries with various operators being applied in arbitrary combinations. In fact, some highly flexible user interfaces will allow arbitrary queries to be entered against a collection of entity beans. Statically defining all of these queries and placing them in a deployment descriptor at development time could become a very tedious task.

Add CMRs into the picture and the ability to do joins across various fields and the ability to apply predicates in various combinations in this context and it becomes clearer that statically defined queries do have some practical limits.

The **Dynamic Query Service (DQS)**, of WebSphere Application Server Enterprise, introduces an interface that accepts query strings at run time. Using the same parser that transforms EJB QL to the underlying database syntax at development time, the dynamic query service makes those transformations happen at run time. While this is very flexible, there is obviously a runtime overhead incurred. Therefore, a combination of static queries and dynamic queries is the recommended approach.

There are two primary interfaces to DQS located in the com.ibm.ObjectQuery package. One is a remote interface and the other is a local interface.

The remote interface has a method to accept the query string that looks like this:

```
public com.ibm.ObjectQuery.QueryIterator executeQuery(
        java.lang.String queryStatement,
        java.lang.Object[] parameterVars,
        java.util.Properties queryDomain,
        int skipRows,
        int maxRows)
    throws java.rmi.RemoteException, com.ibm.ObjectQuery.QueryException;
```

The local interface for dynamic query looks like this:

```
public com.ibm.ObjectQuery.QueryLocalIterator executeQuery(
        java.lang.String queryStatement,
        java.lang.Object[] parameterVars,
        java.util.Properties queryDomain)
    throws com.ibm.ObjectQuery.QueryException;
```

The five input parameters of the executeQuery() method are as follows:

❑ queryStatement
  A string that contains a query statement:

  ```
  SELECT OBJECT(e) FROM EmpBean e WHERE e.salary < 80000
  ```

❑ parameterVars
  An array of objects used as a value holder for literal values for input parameters, which are numbered starting from 1. An example of a query containing a parameter is:

  ```
  SELECT OBJECT(e) FROM EmpBean e WHERE e.salary = ?1
  ```

❑ queryDomain
A set of pairs of **Abstract Schema Names (ASN)** and EJBHomes or EJBLocalHomes. This second parameter is used only if the ASN name specified in the query statement is not unique across applications. Otherwise, this parameter should be null. An abstract schema name is a standard J2EE artifact for representing types of entity beans in EJB QL queries. It is captured in the standard deployment descriptor.

❑ skipRows and maxRows
These are used to request a subset of results from the complete result collection and control the size of the result set. If skipRows=20, then the result collection will not include the first 20 tuples. maxRows places a limit on the size of the final result collection.

Iterators contain the results of the query. An iterator is an interface over a collection of EJBs, either remote or local, depending on the interface used. Iterators returned from the remote query interface use an **eager policy**, which means that the iterator is fully populated from the results returned by the database when returned to the caller. In database terms, this means that the cursor is drained and closed. Iterators returned from the local query interface support **lazy evaluation** if query optimization allows it. Lazy, in this context, means that the entire result set is not retrieved from the backend system upon query execution, but rather is returned incrementally as the iterator is used.

It is the generally the case that when working with entities, the local query interface will be used. This interface returns local EJBs and is the most efficient. Remote EJBs are returned from the remote interface. This remote interface can be used both locally and remotely. Using it locally is sensible in some cases, most notably those when a reference to the EJB will be exchanged with applications or components that may be running in other servers.

Dynamic Query Example

Let's begin by asserting that we have two beans, EmpBean and DeptBean. EmpBean has attributes named empid, name, salary, bonus, hireDate, hireTime, hireTimestamp, isManager, and dept, where dept is a one-to-one CMR with DeptBean. DeptBean has attributes of deptno, name, budget, emps, and mgr, where emps is a one-to-many CMR to employees, and mgr is a one-to-one CMR back to a specific employee.

This means that each department has many employees and one manager, and that each employee has exactly one department. This is shown below:

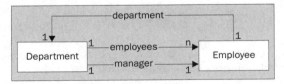

The basic examples are not anything different from what could be placed into static finders. The only thing different is when they execute. They execute at run time using one of the interfaces described in the previous section.

Select method to retrieve all department numbers:

```
SELECT d.deptno
  FROM DeptBean d
```

Select the IDs of employees with employee IDs less than 10:

```
SELECT e.empid
  FROM EmpBean e
  WHERE e.empid < 10
```

Note that the two queries above only return data and not objects, as is allowed by the EJB QL syntax.

The query interfaces are set up to handle the results of the query being either data or objects. The previously described iterator classes actually return a tuple object of class `IQueryTuple`. `IQueryTuple` has a single method on it called `getObject()`, which takes an integer and returns the object that is in that position in the `tuple`. The number of values in a tuple, and the labels for them can be found from the iterator, using methods `getFieldCount()` and `getFieldName(int i)` on the iterator interface.

Printing out the results of the query above should look like this in your code:

```
String query = "SELECT e.empid FROM EmpBean e WHERE e.empid < 10";
QueryLocalIterator it = qb.executeQuery(query, parms, null);
while (it.hasNext() ) {
  IQueryTuple t  = (IQueryTuple) it.next();
  System.out.print( it.getFieldName(1) +"="+ t.getObject(1) );
}
```

Select all employee objects with employee IDs less than 10. The only difference between this query and the previous query is that this query returns EJB objects instead of just the data:

```
SELECT e
  FROM EmpBean e
  WHERE e.empid < 10
```

Select the employee objects that are in department 1. The `emps` relationship is navigated in this example:

```
SELECT e
  FROM DeptBean d,
  IN (d.emps) e
  WHERE d.deptno = 1
```

Select employee objects from department 1 that are managers. This navigates both the `emps` relationship and the `mgr` relationship to determine the result set:

```
SELECT e
  FROM EmpBean e, DeptBean d
  WHERE e.dept.mgr Member OF d.emps AND d.deptno = 1
```

Each of the above queries represents something that can be done in static queries today. The examples here are just a reminder of what static EJB QL can do.

Basic Dynamic Query Summarized

The use of this dynamic run-time query service can make client application development easier and in some cases, potentially even increase overall run-time performances. While a dynamic query, with the same predicate as a static or pre-deployed query, will always be slower, the opportunity for the performance gain comes in the surrounding business logic that might accompany static queries.

Without DQS, applications tend to use static finders that may return more objects than needed by the application. Applications tend to define a findAll() finder method, and if there is not a suitable finder, the application will call the findAll() method. The application then filters out the objects not needed. While functionally this will work, it requires more application code and is expensive, because unneeded data is retrieved from the datastore and unwanted objects are activated. The DQS allows an application to specify more precisely the objects that are to be returned without the needed to define a large number of predefined finder and select methods.

Dynamic query bridges the gap between the finder methods supplied by the bean developer, and the actual needs of a client application. This is especially true for client applications that require unusual search criteria.

Dynamic query reduces the number of finder methods that the bean developer must provide, especially those that are infrequently used. It allows users to develop and test the predefined queries in the finder and select methods by having a test client that takes a predicate and executes it against a bean.

EJB components that are not equipped with a full set of finders can still be successfully reused in the presence of dynamic query. No additional negotiations with the component provider are necessary.

Now that the concept of running standard EJB QL statements dynamically has been described, we can move on to more of the features provided in the context of query that go beyond the basic specification requirements.

Additional Query Extensions

The base query implementation in the WebSphere Application Server and the Dynamic Query Service just described make a powerful combination. This section describes some additional features that complement these already powerful concepts. The first set of features are usable from static queries as well as dynamic queries, while the second set become possible only in the presence of a dynamic query.

Extensions for Static Queries

There are a set of extensions to the EJB 2.0 query service that are applicable to static queries as well as dynamic queries. These are explained in this section.

Delimited Identifiers

This is used to solve keyword problems. It is legal in the WebSphere Query Service to have a statement such as:

```
SELECT x."from" FROM myBean x
```

The word `from` is of course a keyword and would not be accepted if not delimited by the quotes. The standard does not require supporting the use of keywords in this manner.

String Comparisons

The EJB 2.0 specification for EJB QL requires that the "=" and "<>" operators be supported for string comparisons. The WebSphere Query Service supports ">" and "<" as well. An example of this is:

```
SELECT x FROM PersonBean x WHERE x.name > 'Dave'
```

Scalar Functions

A variety of scalar functions are supported by the WebSphere Query Service. Some of these are ABS, SQRT, CONCAT, LENGTH, LOCATE, and SUBSTRING. Other scalar functions are type casting (integer, decimal, char, double, float, smallint, and so on) or deal with date-time expressions (date, days, hour, seconds, year). Casting and date-time scalars only work with a DB2 backend.

ORDER BY

The ORDER BY clause is supported by the WebSphere Query Service. This is a very useful feature and should be available in the EJB 2.1 specification. For example, to find a list of employees who earn less than $30,000 and have the results returned in descending order, the following would be specified as the query:

```
SELECT object(e) FROM EmpBean e
   WHERE e.salary < 30000
   ORDER BY e.salary desc
```

SQL Date/time Expressions

These are supported by WebSphere Query Service and not required by the specification. For example, to find employees who resigned after less than two years on the job, the query would look like this:

```
SELECT object(e) FROM EmpBean e
   WHERE years( e.termDate - e.hireDate) < 2
```

This example requires that `java.sql.*` types (not `java.util.Date`) be mapped to date, time, or timestamp columns. The datastore *must* be DB2 in this case.

Inheritance

VisualAge for Java introduced an inheritance pattern for EJBs. It is a single inheritance model, as that is what Java allows. The depth of the hierarchy is not bounded. This pattern, now also supported by WebSphere Studio is supported by the WebSphere Query Service as well. There is a way to extract objects that are members of a base class and all subclasses, as well as to distinctly extract objects of a particular subclass.

Subqueries, Aggregation, Group By, and Having Clauses

These are all supported by WebSphere and not required by the specification. An example of a subquery that would return objects representing the employees that got the maximum salary could be as follows:

```
SELECT object(e) FROM EmpBean e
   WHERE e.salary = (SELECT max(m.salary) FROM EmpBean m)
```

Notice the inner SELECT statement within the outer SELECT statement.

EXISTS Predicate

The EXISTS predicate tests for the presence or absence of a condition specified by a subselect. The result of EXISTS is true if the subselect returns at least one value, or the path expression evaluates to a non-empty collection. Otherwise, the result is false. NOT can be used to negate an EXISTS. The following example shows how to retrieve all departments that do not have any employees:

```
SELECT OBJECT(d) FROM DeptBean d
   WHERE NOT EXISTS ( SELECT 1 FROM IN (d.emps) e)
```

The "1" is a convention because the content returned by the subselect does not matter; it is the true or false that counts.

Value Object Access

In the snippet below, home is a dependent value object, which is mapped to individual fields in the underlying database:

```
SELECT object(e) FROM EmpBean e
   WHERE  e.home.city = 'Gilroy' AND  e.home.state = 'CA'
```

You *must* use a composer to map home address to columns. This will not work using a default top-down mapping, which uses object serialization, which would serialize dependent objects into a BLOB or other type that would make accessing individual fields impracticable.

Additional Extensions

In some cases, there are extensions that cannot be supported via statically defined queries. This is often because the extensions do not fit into the current description of finders that must go into the deployment descriptor. Rather than introducing specific deployment descriptor extensions for statically defining the following extensions, they are only supported for dynamic queries.

Bean Methods

It is possible for a dynamic query to contain not only attribute or container-managed field getters in the operators, but also any other method that has a return value. It is in this case that the evaluation of these methods needs to be done in object space. **Object space query** means that part, or all, of the query is done by the application server by executing methods against objects. This requires that the objects, to which the method is applied, must be activated. The WebSphere Query Service does support the idea of partial pushdown. This means that a portion of a query can be pushed down into the database and then the result set from that portion of the query is further evaluated in object space. This partial pushdown idea lets the smallest possible set of objects be subjected to activation and object space evaluation. This suggests an economical use of resources while retaining tremendous flexibility in specifying queries.

Partial pushdown does ensure that the query is executed in the most efficient way possible. However, whenever a large set of objects must be activated in the EJB container, the performance cost will be much higher than the cost of just pushing down a query and letting the database do the work. Cases where methods are used in the predicates must be carefully selected.

The real value here is that the methods that participate in a query can encapsulate reasonably complex business logic and that logic can easily participate in the query evaluation. Those participating methods are regular entity bean methods with access to the full J2EE programming model. Complex date calculations are an example of something that might be encapsulated in a method that would then be used as part of a query predicate.

Dependent Value Methods

It is also possible to have arbitrary non-getter and non-setter methods on dependent value classes as part of the query. This means that one can reach into a dependent value and describe a query that includes arbitrary methods within that dependent value. This makes dependent values more powerful and allows them to be used in more situations. This is good if the simplicity and efficiency of dependent values are otherwise appropriate for the application being constructed.

Multiple Element SELECT Clauses

This is a very powerful concept. The EJB 2.0 specification introduces the idea that one can have an EJB QL statement in a SELECT method that returns not an object, but data. For example, a SELECT method could specify:

```
SELECT e.lastname
  FROM EmpBean e
  WHERE e.age > ?1
```

This eliminates the cost of activating the object and is appropriate if all that is needed by the application is some data.

However, it is often the case that more than just as single data element is needed to meet the contract of the presentation logic. The dynamic query capability of WebSphere allows multiple elements to be returned by a select statement. For example:

```
SELECT e.lastname, e.firstname, e.customerNumber
  FROM EmpBean e
  WHERE e.age > ?1
```

The results can then be extracted by leveraging the IQueryTuple object as demonstrated by the previous example. The only difference is that more values are in the tuple as shown here:

```
String query = "SELECT e.lastname, e.firstname, e.customerNUmber FROM EmpBean e
WHERE e.age > ?1";

QueryLocalIterator it = qb.executeQuery(query, parms, null);
while (it.hasNext() ) {
  IQueryTuple t  = (IQueryTuple) it.next();
  System.out.println( it.getFieldName(1) + "=" + t.getObject(1) );
  System.out.println( it.getFieldName(2) + "=" + t.getObject(2) );
  System.out.println( it.getFieldName(3) + "=" + t.getObject(3) );
}
```

This example returns enough data for the application to return what is needed by the presentation logic. It is then common for a selection to be made on the presentation logic that will later be the only object that needs to be activated and transacted on.

Ability to Return Aggregation Values

Static finder and select methods allow objects or CMP values to be returned. Dynamic query allows arbitrary expressions including aggregate values to be returned. To compute MAX and MIN salary for a department, the following dynamic EJB query can be used:

```
SELECT MAX (e.salary), MIN(e.salary) FROM DeptBean d,
   IN (d.emps) e
   WHERE d.deptno=12
```

Additional Examples

Now that all of the query capabilities of WebSphere Application Server Enterprise have been described, a couple of more complex examples can be provided that demonstrate the power of dynamic query. These examples will use the entities department and employee that have been used in some of the previous snippets.

In this example, we show a result set that is a combination of objects (e in this case) and data (e.empid) being returned. This allowed combination was not shown previously:

```
SELECT e, e.empid
   FROM EmpBean e
   WHERE e.empid < 3
```

In this example, the dynamic query uses multiple arbitrary expressions in the SELECT clause:

```
SELECT e.name, e.salary+e.bonus as total_pay, object(e), e.dept.mgr
   FROM EmpBean e
   ORDER BY 2
```

This next dynamic query returns the number of employees in each department:

```
SELECT e.dept.deptno as department_number, count(*) as employee_count
   FROM EmpBean e
   GROUP BY e.dept.deptno
   ORDER BY 1
```

Finally, the example below uses a dynamic query using a method, in this case format(), on a value object which is one of the CMP fields of the EmpBean. This means that, if we looked at the Java class that implements address, we would find a format() method. Here, it is being used directly in the SELECT clause:

```
SELECT e.name, e.address.format()
   FROM EmpBean e
   WHERE e.dept.deptno=12
```

Summarizing Query Extensions

The following table provides a summary of the query topics we have covered in this chapter:

Capability	EJB 2.0 Specification	WebSphere Application Server (base function)	WebSphere Application Server Enterprise
Dynamic Query (local and remote)	no	no	yes
Delimited Identifiers	no	yes	yes
String Comparisons	no	yes	yes
Scalar functions	ABS, SQRT, CONCAT, LENGTH, LOCATE, SUBSTRING	ABS, SQRT, CONCAT, LENGTH, LOCATE, SUBSTRING and additional type conversion, string manipulation and date-time manipulation functions	ABS, SQRT, CONCAT, LENGTH, LOCATE, SUBSTRING and additional type conversion, string manipulation and date-time manipulation functions
Order by	no	yes	yes
SQL date/time expression	no	yes	yes
Inheritance	no	yes	yes
Subqueries, aggregation, group by, and having clauses	no	yes	yes
EXISTS predicate	no	yes	yes
Dependent Value object attribute access	no	yes	yes
Bean method	no	no	yes
Dependent value methods	no	no	yes
Multiple Element Select clauses	no	no	yes
Returning aggregration values	no	no	yes

Unit of Work Options

One of the key features of any application server is support for transactions. Applications use transactions when interacting with resource managers. Transactions are normally started and ended around a set of one or more interactions with a resource manager. These interactions correspond to a **Unit of Work** for which the business demands that, either all changes are made to the backend resource manager or none are made at all. A single transaction can actually involve one or more resource managers. In the case of more than one resource manager, a global transaction is used. A global transaction means that the transaction is coordinated by an external coordinator rather an individual resource manager.

The application server plays this role of coordination for global transactions. When more than one resource manager is involved, this is also referred to as a two-phase commit transaction, requiring both the underlying resource manager and the application server to support specific interaction protocols. A transaction can involve EJBs that are hosted in more than one application server process. When this occurs, it is referred to as a distributed transaction. A distributed two-phase commit transaction involves both resources from multiple resource managers and multiple application server processes. This is the most complex transaction type that application servers will deal with.

The EJB specification defines a set of transactional policies that must be implemented and enforced by the application server. These describe what occurs upon commit and how to signal the beginning and ending of transactions. Individual beans can be set via the deployment descriptor in ways that allow the container to enforce and manage transactional operations. Transactions are important from the perspective of an application builder, and from the perspective of those who are implementing application servers that are J2EE compliant.

It is normally the case that entity beans, and potentially individual methods on entity beans, will be marked with a transaction attribute setting of `Required`, `RequiresNew`, or `Mandatory`. Stateful session beans with session synchronization follow a similar pattern.

Chapter 5 has some further discussion on transactions and transactional demarcation.

Session beans, or other J2EE code that drives these entity beans, may or may not have transactional settings or code specific to transactions. It is common to have a session bean manage the interactions with entity beans. In this case, the session bean can either be set up using the **Bean-Managed Transaction (BMT)** model or the **Container-Managed Transaction (CMT)** model. BMT implies that there is explicit code in the session bean logic to start, commit, and/or roll back transactions. This model involves using the Java Transaction APIs (JTA) directly. In the CMT model, methods on the calling session bean are also marked with transactional settings such as `Required` or `RequiresNew`. This model means that the container will start a transaction or cause the session bean to join an existing transaction without having any explicit transaction API calls in the code. BMT versus CMT is a topic for another discussion. For now, realize that in either case, there is an assumption that downstream entities support transactions.

Resource managers and transactions managers must support the JTA `XAResource` interface to be fully usable in the normal transactional modes described in the previous paragraph. Some resource managers are not fully compliant with the related X/Open XA standards, and are thus incapable of participating in a full two-phase commit distributed transaction. This fact presents a challenge to those wishing to use entity beans and enjoy the benefits of the EJB model as it relates to transactions.

WebSphere defines a fully compliant resource manager to be one that supports XA and full two-phase commit distributed transactions. Fully compliant means that global transactions can involve resources from different resource managers in the same two-phase commit transaction. However, many JDBC drivers and procedural systems do not support full two-phase commit-enabled distributed transactions. Transactions actually work fine for these resource managers and for the transaction settings described above as long as individual transactions do not span resource managers. This is because the transactional semantics required by the application can be honored when only one resource is enlisted in the transaction even when the resource manager does not fully support XA and the two-phase commit protocol. This optimization can be made by the application server.

It is very common, however, to wish to involve multiple resources, each from different resource managers in a single transaction. If the resource managers are not fully compliant, then using global transaction settings will lead to exceptions. Exceptions will arise, indicating that multiple resource managers, that are not two-phase commit compliant, are not allowed in a single global transaction.

Entity beans that are using datastores that are not fully compliant will sometimes have to be marked with transaction attribute settings of `Never`, `NotSupported`, or `Supports`. The EJB 2.0 specification, in section 12.1.6.1 states that:

When the `NotSupported` transaction attribute is assigned to a component interface method, the corresponding enterprise bean class method executes with an unspecified transaction context (See Subsection 17.6.5). This means that the container does not have any well-defined transaction boundaries to drive the `ejbLoad` and `ejbStore` methods on the instance.

It also states in a footnote that the same applies to the `Never` and `Supports` attributes.

The unspecified transaction context mentioned above is the key to the next part of the story. WebSphere Application Server does support these attributes and does document and support a specific behavior in this area where the specification is not specific. We will start by describing this in the next section and then move on to the ActivitySession Service, describing how this further extends WebSphere's support for resource managers that are not fully two-phase commit capable. We will also describe ActivitySession optimization opportunities. Finally, we will describe additional optimizations supported by the WebSphere Application Server that relate to transactions and resource managers.

Local Transactions Support

In the previous section, the use of the word transaction was generally unqualified. In this section, a distinction will be made. A **global transaction** is a transaction such as those we described in previous sections. It is the one that the specification for EJBs refers to when talking about demarcation of unit-of-work boundaries. Generally, it is what is expected when settings like `Required` are used on EJBs. Global transactions are also distributable transactions, meaning they can involve multiple application server processes also.

A **local transaction** then refers to the mechanism by which programmers, either declaratively or otherwise, deal with resource managers that are not fully two-phase commit enabled. Sometimes this involves programming syntax, as we will see in the upcoming section. Other times, local transactions just happen under the covers as part of how the container manages backend interactions. This section will further clarify and delineate the behavior of local transactions and contrast it to the global transaction concept.

The base WebSphere Application Server introduces the concept of **local transaction containment** to define the behavior in what the EJB specification calls the "unspecified transaction context". Local transaction containment support is an aggregating concept, encompassing all resources that might be accessed while in the "unspecified transaction context".

WebSphere defines a **Resource Manager Local Transaction (RMLT)** as a resource adapter's view of a local transaction. A resource adapter is the application server's internal wrapper or layer that talks to an external resource manager such as a database. To a resource adapter, an RMLT represents a unit of recovery on a single connection that is managed by the resource adapter. The resource adapter has interfaces, such as the `javax.resource.cci.LocalTransaction` that enable a bean or the container to request that the resource adapter commit or roll back its RMLT.

In WebSphere, when a method is being executed by the container in an "unspecified transaction context", there will be a **Local Transaction Containment (LTC)** in place. This is the container's view of what is going on when RMLTs are being used. The LTC defines the boundary at which all RMLTs must be complete and how any incomplete RMLTs are resolved. An LTC context is always established by the container in the absence of a global transaction, and thus it is the LTC that defines what really happens in the server when it is in "unspecified transaction context". An LTC is local to a bean instance and is not shared across beans even if those beans are managed by the same container, at least until the concept of ActivitySession is introduced.

To fully describe and elaborate upon what local transactions are meant for, we must begin using some examples assuming that there are no entity beans, assuming that there are no container-managed transactions, and that in fact, we are programming directly to the resource manager using connections and local transactions. There are a couple of styles that are prevalent here and usage will vary depending on whether or not this is a JDBC-based resource or one that is integrated into the server using the Java 2 Connector architecture.

Java 2 Connector Architecture (JCA)

The Java 2 Connector specification introduces the `javax.resource.cci.LocalTransaction` interface, which can be acquired from a connection. Any arbitrary code running in an EJB (session bean), or on the server in general (directly from a servlet perhaps), can make use of the interfaces described here. The key interfaces are:

- ❏ `javax.resource.cci.ConnectionFactory`
- ❏ `javax.resource.cci.Connection`
- ❏ `javax.resource.cci.ConnectionSpec`
- ❏ `javax.resource.cci.LocalTransaction`

These interfaces represent the basics used for acquiring and using connections via JCA Common Client interface (CCI). The CCI interface is used to communicate with Java 2 Connectors, retrieving, updating, creating, or deleting data from the specific backend that the connector encapsulates.

The general starting pattern for direct usage of the CCI involves something such as the following:

```
// Obtain initial Naming Context
  MyContext ic = new InitialContext();
  javax.resource.cci.ConnectionFactory cf =
    (javax.resource.cci.ConnectionFactory)
```

```
        ic.lookup("java:comp/env/myEIS");

// Get a connection
javax.resource.cci.Connection conn =
  (javax.resource.cci.Connection) cf.getConnection();

// Get an interaction
  javax.resource.cci.Interaction interaction = conn.createInteraction();
```

The above code acquires the connection factory, gets a connection, and creates an interaction. The creation of an interaction is usually followed by the creation of Record instances using the RecordFactory create methods.

What is important from a unit-of-work perspective is that the work is scoped inside a local transaction. Somewhere after the initial sequence of code shown above there will be a sequence like this:

```
javax.resource.cci.LocalTransaction localTran =
  conn.getLocalTransaction();

localTran.begin();
  // Run various execute() methods on the Interaction
  interaction.execute(anInteractionSpec,aRecord);
  //...

localTran.commit();
// Or maybe
//...

localTran.rollback();
```

At some point, when the connection is no longer needed, should be a conn.Close() statement to free up the connection.

JDBC Resources

Programming directly to the JDBC interfaces reveals a pattern similar to that described in the JCA section. The java.sql.Connection interface is used to manage the interactions with the JDBC-based resource manager. The following code snippet shows the acquisition of a connection and the subsequent usage of it:

```
private java.sql.DataSource ds;
private java.sql.Connection conn;
private InitialContext ctx;
private Statement stmt;

ctx=new InitialContext();
ds=(DataSource)ctx.lookup("java:comp/env/datasource")
conn=ds.getConnection();          // get a connection
conn.setAutoCommit(false);        // requires user code to commit connection
stmt = conn.createStatement();
```

```
ResultSet rs =
  stmt.executeUpdate("UPDATE X.X SET VALUE = VALUE +10 WHERE \"KEY\"=99");
// additional code could go here dealing with the result set, more
// statements etc..
rs.close();
stmt.close();

if (transactionShouldBeCommitted) {
  conn.commit();
} else {
  conn.rollback();
}
conn.close();
```

The key difference here is that there is no `LocalTransaction` interface, but rather the commit control is based on the presence of a connection. The local transaction is explicitly committed or rolled back through methods on the connection itself.

In both the JCA and JDBC cases, local transactions are used and the container manages these RMLTs using an LTC as described earlier. Remember that the LTC only spans a specific method and must be committed or completed when that method has completed.

The style of programming described here is one that is used outside the context of global transactions. Both the JCA and JDBC styles follow the same pattern. This pattern is prevalent in the presence of resource managers that do not fully support global transactions. It is also used when the overhead of a global transaction is deemed inappropriate. WebSphere takes some specific steps to ensure that this environment is safe with regards to connection and local transaction management. The next section begins describing WebSphere's specific support for these local transaction environments.

WebSphere Settings for Local Transactions

WebSphere has some very specific settings for ensuring proper management of local transaction environments. Some are applicable for the scenarios above and others are predicated upon ActivitySession semantics, which are described later. We will introduce all the settings here and will proceed to further elaborate upon the ActivitySession-related settings in upcoming sections.

There are extensions for EJBs and for both the EJB and web containers. This means that EJBs and servlets allow the following local transaction settings to be configured:

❑ **boundary**
The life of the containment boundary for which all RMLTs may be accessed is controlled by this setting. This can be set to either `ActivitySession` or `BeanMethod`. So far, we have only talked about local transactions outside the context of ActivitySession. The `BeanMethod` setting means that all RMLTs such as those shown in the previous examples must be resolved in the same method in which they were started. The `ActivitySession` setting will be described in upcoming sections of this chapter. The `BeanMethod` setting is the default setting.

❑ **resolution-control**
This indicates which component is responsible for initiating and ending the local transactions. The settings can be `Application` or `ContainerAtBoundary`. The `Application` setting means that specific code must be supplied in the application to start and complete the local transactions. In the JCA example described previously, this means that the `localTransaction.begin()` and `localTransaction.commit()` must be explicitly invoked in the code. `ContainerAtBoundary` on the other hand, implies that the container will actually start and complete the local transactions. This becomes useful in the presence of session beans and entity beans where we want to hide the complexity of dealing directly with the local transaction interfaces. This has additional use in the case where the boundary is set to `ActivitySession`. The default value for this setting depends on the transactional setting for the bean. Beans with CMTs will default the resolution-control setting to `ContainerAtBoundary`, while beans with a BMT setting will default to `Application`.

❑ **unresolved-action**
This can be set to `Commit` or `Rollback`. This indicates to the container what to do with methods containing local transactions, which are unresolved at the end of a method. This setting is looked at only when resolution-control is set to `Application`. A setting for `Rollback`, for example, would cause any unresolved local transactions left at the end of a method to be rolled back by the container. The default value here is `Rollback`.

If you have an EJB that is making direct and explicit calls to backend systems and managing local transactions directly, the following snippet would appear in the deployment descriptor extensions for the bean:

```
<local-transaction>
  <boundary>BeanMethod</boundary>
  <resolution-control>Application</resolution-control>
  <unresolved-action>Rollback</unresolved-action>
  ...
</local-transaction>
```

This shows up in the AAT as follows:

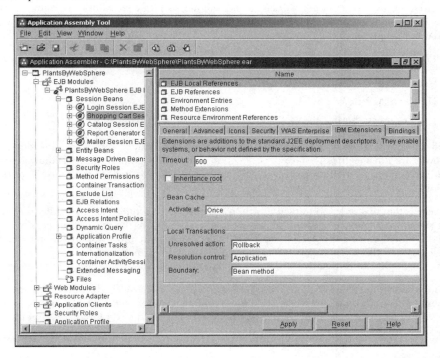

The Local Transactions settings are shown above for a session bean that is managing its own connections.

The WAS local transaction containment support, and its configurability through these three extended deployment descriptors (which are a part of the base application server), give the WAS application programmer who is using this direct style of programming to connections one key advantage: any local transactions that are not committed will be cleaned up by the container. This cleanup will happen according to the resolution control setting described above.

We will describe additional combinations of these settings and additional advantages in upcoming sections.

Container-Managed Interactions

The previous sections on JCA resources and JDBC resources have focused on a very direct and manual interaction style. The code segments that deal with these resource managers are very explicit and certainly not something that is desirable if we can get the container to manage some of this for us. A container-managed entity bean is in fact intended to transparently handle things like connections and transactions. Let's see how the container-managed concept might apply to EJBs that use these resource managers but do not fully support all of the necessary transactional semantics to let the standard global transaction based model assist us.

If an entity bean is marked `NotSupported` in WebSphere, then the local transaction containment support provided by the container will be used. Each method on a container-managed entity bean will have a local transaction containment environment in place during the execution of a method. This means that the programming style for entity beans shown below will work just fine.

1. Find the home for the CMP entity

2. Create a bean using the home

3. Update CMP field x on the bean

4. Update CMP field y on the bean

The good part of this style is that we treat these entities like all other container-managed entities. Transactions are not specifically started, connections are not programmatically acquired, and specific backend interactions are not observable in the Java code. The server does this work of getting connections, starting transactions, and managing the backend interactions.

The concern is that this style of interaction will involve two connections and effectively three local transactions for the sequence above. The first local transaction is for the create and there will be one each for the updates. Now you can see why you might be led back to the more manual interaction model that was previously described. Too many transactions will affect performance of the system. We want better support in the application server for CMP entities backed by these special resource managers.

In the above sequence, there is no global transaction started because the bean is not marked with a transactional setting that will cause the creation of a global transaction. This is good in this case, as there is no need for a global transaction. However, often there is a need to do interactions of the following pattern:

```
Globaltransaction.begin()
  Touch bean1 of type1
  Touch bean2 of type1
GlobalTransaction.commit()
```

If this is the case, then we can mark the `type1` bean with a transactional setting of `Required`, `RequiresNew`, or `Mandatory`. As there is only a single resource manager being enlisted as part of a global transaction, this will work, even though the resource manager does not fully support the necessary transactional protocol. A single connection ends up being used in this case and things are once again looking as we want them.

If we did not demarcate the above sequence with a global transaction then it would still probably work. There are many possible ways to configure applications to use global or local transactions. We cannot cover them all here.

However, not all is yet as flexible as we might want it to be. The following pattern, involving two CMP beans, each of a different type and thus having different connection factories or data sources, neither of which are fully transactional, demonstrates the next level of challenge in this area:

```
CallingMethod begin
  Touch bean1 of type1
  Touch bean2 of type 2
CallingMethod end
```

Now if the beans are set with a transactional setting of Requires, then a global transaction could be started in the code or implicitly started by the calling method. In either case, involving a global transaction, we are heading for trouble. The execution of the method on the second bean will cause an exception to be thrown. This exception will indicate that we cannot have two bean types that do not fully support transactions in a single global transaction. The previous example worked because there was only a single resource manager involved in the transaction, and the global transaction was just a wrapper around what turned out to be a local transaction-based interaction to the backend systems. This example will not work with global transactions.

There are four ways to deal with this apparent problem with container-managed entities. These are:

❑ Go back to the direct programming style of using connections and local transactions, and give up on container-managed entities for these kinds of resources.

❑ Leave out the global transaction and let two separate local transactions run. Handling the exceptions or rollbacks here would be tricky, but doable.

❑ Leverage the ActivitySession service described in the next section instead of the global transaction to get past the error and get more control over the error handling and coordination over the two local transactions.

❑ Leverage Last Participant Support, which is described in an upcoming section.

The third and the fourth options are obviously desirable as they continue to allow us to use a higher level programming model and deal with container-managed entities instead of direct connections to the backend resource managers and have a centralized place to handle potential failures that occur when committing changes to the backend resource manager.

The ActivitySession Service

The **ActivitySession service** of WebSphere Application Server Enterprise introduces interfaces, which allow explicit programmatic or declarative scoping of units of work, which involve multiple non-two-phase capable resource managers. The ActivitySession service extends the WebSphere support for local transactions. An ActivitySession will allow an LTC to live longer than the enterprise-bean method in which it is started.

The ActivitySession service enables a different lifecycle for the EJB from that with existing J2EE mechanisms. ActivitySession becomes a new activation boundary. Normally, an entity EJB will be active in the EJB container for the duration of a transaction and then will be stored and passiviated at the end of a transaction. Subsequent interactions with the same bean will necessitate a reactivation and a reload in the EJB container. The ActivitySession Service changes this when it is active. It separates the load and store timing from the activation and passivation timing. Transactions still control the load and store, but now an ActivitySession controls the activation and passivation. This will be described in more detail, as we get further into this section. For now, realize that this has a number of ramifications and opportunities. From a unit-of-work perspective, you can have zero or more transactions executing within the scope of the ActivitySession. Resources may access data as part of a global transaction or an RMLT. The RMLT boundary can be either determined by the bean method or the ActivitySession. A new set of attributes for ActivitySessions is introduced for EJBs that look like transactional settings in many ways.

There is an <activity-session-type> deployment descriptor extension that can be set to either Bean or Container. This determines whether or not the container should be starting ActivitySessions, or relying upon the application code to do so.

The `<activity-session-attribute>` element can be at the bean or method level and can have the following settings that apply when the `<activity-session-type>` is contained:

- ❑ Supports
  Any received ActivitySession context is retained on the thread of execution for method dispatch. If no ActivitySession is received, none will be created.

- ❑ NotSupported
  Any received ActivitySession context is suspended for the duration of the method and resumed thereafter.

- ❑ Never
  Any received ActivitySession context results in the `InvalidActivityException` being thrown.

- ❑ Required
  Any received ActivitySession context is retained on the thread of execution for method dispatch. If no ActivitySession is received, one is created by the container.

- ❑ RequiresNew
  Any received ActivitySession context is suspended for the duration of the method and resumed thereafter. A new ActivitySession is created for the method invocation.

- ❑ Mandatory
  Any received ActivitySession context is retained on the thread of execution for method dispatch. If no ActivitySession is received, the exception `InvalidActivityException` is thrown.

The `com.ibm.websphere.ActivitySession` package defines the key interfaces that are used to programmatically leverage the ActivitySession service. The primary programming interface is the `UserActivitySession` and the key methods are `beginSession()` and `endSession()`. The `endSession()` method takes a parameter to indicated whether the session is to be check-pointed or reset. This will become clearer in the examples that will follow.

The following screenshot shows specifying ActivitySessions on a CMP entity bean in the AAT:

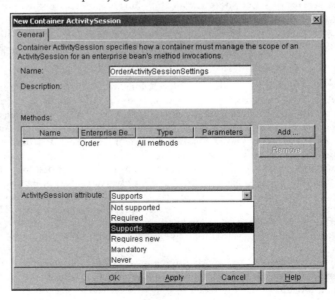

Each method can have a different value. The example above shows all methods on the Order bean's remote interface being set to a value of ActivitySession Supports.

ActivitySession Programming – Implicit Local Transactions

This usage pattern for the ActivitySession Service is the one to consider if you are coming from a global transactions perspective and wish to enjoy the abstraction and simplicity of a global transaction type of model when dealing with resource managers that do not fully support the two-phase commit protocol. The following sequence of code is from a session bean. It uses the ActivitySession Service to scope a number of calls to a container-managed entity bean that is set with the following settings:

❑ Activation policy set to ActivitySession – We will come back to this later with more details on this

❑ The <boundary> for <local-transaction> is set to ActivitySession

❑ The <resolution-control> for <local-transaction> is set to ContainerAtBoundary

❑ The normal transactional policy is set to NotSupported

❑ The <activity-session-type> is set to Container

❑ The <activity-session-attribute> is set to Supports

The session bean itself is set to <activity-session-type> of Bean. The snippet of code starts a session, runs some methods on the entity bean, and ends the session. Ending the session provides each of the registered resources, in this case the bean1 and bean2 instances, the opportunity to complete or commit open RMLTs:

```
InitialContext ctx  = new InitialContext();
UserActivitySession actSess = (UserActivitySession)
  ctx.lookup("java:comp/websphere/UserActivitySession");

actSess.beginSession();        // start the session
  int v1 = bean1.getValueI();
  int v2 = bean2.getValueI();
  int v3 = v1 + v2;
  bean1.increment(v3);
  bean1.setValue(v3);
actSess.endSession(UserActivitySession.EndModeCheckPoint);
```

The snippet above completes with the UserActivitySession.EndModeCheckPoint being the parameter to the endSession() method. This is one of the options for checkpointing and ending an ActivitySession, and most importantly the one that drives forward and completes any work that has been started during the ActivitySession. Each of the resources registered with the ActivitySession has the opportunity to complete or commit whatever outstanding work had been started. Failures encountered during the completion of the ActivitySession, or more properly, the committing of resources registered with the ActivitySession will cause the MixedOutcomeException to be thrown. The caller then can process the data in this exception to determine which resources succeeded and which failed, and write any necessary additional logic to handle inconsistencies.

UserActivitySession.EndModeReset is the other option for ending an ActivitySession. This causes the ActivitySession to reset or return to the last point of consistency.

ActivitySession Programming – Explicit Local Transactions

While the first "programming pattern" for the ActivitySession service keeps us in the container-managed entity space and achieves the maximum level of abstraction for those building J2EE applications, let's revert back to the direct programming style introduced earlier and observe one more problem and demonstrate how ActivitySessions can help us with this problem also.

If you paid careful attention to the example that described how to program directly to connections and directly to local transactions, you would have observed that these examples always showed direct inline usage of the interfaces necessary to manage and manipulate the backend resource managers. A JDBC example, just to restate it for clarity showed:

1. Get a connection

2. Retrieve using the connection

3. Update using the connection

4. Commit the connection

Without ActivitySessions, all four steps above, if they are to be in a single local transaction containment boundary, must be executed from a single method within the controlling J2EE application. The default setting, without ActivitySessions being involved at all, is to have `boundary = BeanMethod` for the local transaction setting.

The above pattern all works fine, but might not be a programming style that is easy to understand or maintain. A better design would involve factoring the steps above into separate methods on the session bean and even providing granular control over connections and local transactions.

Optimally in fact, it would be desirable to have callers (other session beans or perhaps servlets), which would have sequences of code in a method that deals with the resource manager that look something like:

```
x.GetConnection(...);      // Call method to get the connection
x.BeginLT(...);            // Begin the local transaction
x.RetrieveX(...);          // Get some data
x.UpdateX(...);            // Update some values
x.CommitLT(...);           // Commit the local transaction
x.CloseConnection(...);    // Close the connection
```

The above sequence needs to run in an environment where a single ActivitySession covers whichever combination of methods the caller chooses to use. This means that our bean x needs to be configured to run with `boundary = ActivitySession`. This also implies that the calling code, either when the caller is a session bean or when it explicitly demarcates the ActivitySession boundary, can have the method that drives the interactions on x be set to an `<activity-session-attribute>` of `Required`.

This pattern provides additional flexibility over the management of local transactions, enabling the creation of more maintainable and understandable applications, while retaining the advantages of having precise control over backend interactions.

To summarize, the ActivitySession capability of WebSphere Application Server Enterprise provides two more advantages above those provided by the base WAS support for local transactions:

❑   The use of RMLTs (otherwise called local transactions) is restricted, in the J2EE specifications, to single EJB methods. This is because the standard specifications have no scoping device, beyond a container-interposed method boundary, to which an RMLT can be extended. The ActivitySession is a distributed context that can be controlled by a client that provides a longer-than-method boundary over which such RMLTs can extend, reducing the need to use distributed transactions where coordinated operations on multiple resources are not required. This benefit is exploited through the boundary setting. Such extended RMLTs can remain under the control of the application, or remain managed by the container, depending on the use of the resolution control.

❑   For resource managers that do not support XA transaction coordination, the exploitation of ActivitySession scoped LTCs gives a client the same ability to control the completion direction of those resource managers' resource updates as it has for transactional resource managers. A client can start a bean-managed ActivitySession and call its entity beans under that context. Those beans can perform their RMLTs within the scope of that ActivitySession and return without completing the RML(s). The client can control, through the `UserActivitySession` interface, whether those RMLTs should then be committed or rolled back.

Last Participant Support

While the ActivitySession Service provides us power and capabilities for dealing with resource managers that do not support full XA transactions, it does introduce some specific interfaces and requires a specific understanding of the various unit of work patterns that are used to accomplish business tasks. The Last Participant Support feature of WebSphere Application Server Enterprise, offers an additional option for dealing with some of these types of transactions.

The basic transactional capabilities within WebSphere Application Server provide coordination within a global transaction of multiple transactional resources. At transaction commit, if there is more than one resource enlisted in the transaction, or if the transaction has been distributed to another server, a two-phase commit procedure is used. As an optimization, a one-phase protocol is used if there is a single resource in a non-distributed transaction.

There is a clear customer requirement to allow use of these one-phase resources (which include the currently available CICS connector and many other JCA connectors) in transactions that also use true 2PC-capable resources such DB2 and Oracle. **Last Participant Support** satisfies this requirement.

To use Last Participant Support, it is necessary to:

❑   Have WebSphere Application Server Enterprise version 5.0 installed, as this feature only exists in this package

❑   Have all resources involved in the unit of work accessed within a global transaction

❑   Ensure that the transaction is not distributed across multiple application servers (this restriction is expected to be lifted in future releases of WebSphere)

❑   Configure the application to accept heuristic hazards

Heuristic is a term typically used in a transactional situation where a participant transaction manager makes a unilateral decision to commit or rollback, hopefully applying some intelligent heuristic approach to do so. This might happen if a participant transaction manager loses contact with the commit coordinator during commit processing. It knows the commit coordinator will return, but perhaps cannot wait for this happen. If, on a later reconnect, it turns out the participant transaction manager got it wrong, it raises a heuristic exception.

Configuring the application to accept heuristic hazards can be done in the AAT at the application level as shown below:

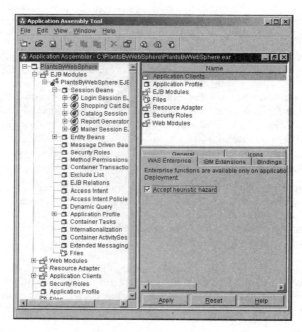

WebSphere Application Server Enterprise Version 5.0 allows resource adapters to be configured as being incapable of accepting 2PC flows. These resource adapters can then be treated exclusively as 1PC resource adapters. Most resource adapter archives should already be properly set. However, if you are building a new resource adapter archive, it can be marked as Local Transaction in the AAT as shown at the bottom of the Resource Adapter screen:

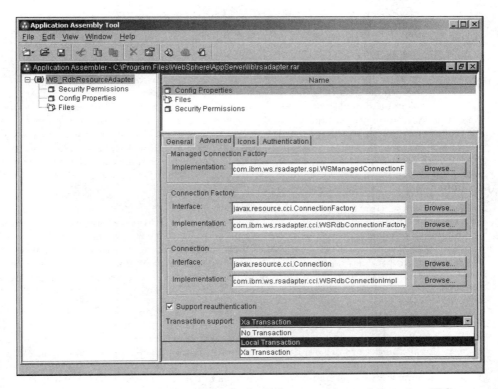

By using these settings, we can now enable a single 1PC resource to participate in a 2PC transaction. This allows normal transactional design and programming techniques to be applied to complex transactions that involve multiple resources, including a single 1PC resource.

What happens inside is that, at transaction commit, the 2PC resources will first be prepared using the 2PC protocol, and if this is successful, the 1PC resource will then be called to commit (one-phase). This gives the mechanism its commonly used name of "Last Participant Support" or LPS, where the single 1PC resource is the last agent to participate. The 2PC resources will then be committed or rolled back depending on the response of the 1PC resource. In the case where more than one 1PC resource is registered in the transaction, it will never get to commit processing. An exception is thrown upon attempting to register the second resource stating that you cannot registered multiple single-phase resources in a global transaction. If you have this requirement, then local transaction and ActivitySessions are your options, not global transactions.

Summarizing Transactions and ActivitySessions

How do we apply all of this functionality and information to our design and implementation of EJB applications? Well, there are some basic rules to follow:

❑ **Global Transactions**
   Global transactions are good in many situations. They provide a consistent and simplified
   unit-of-work scoping mechanism that can be programmatically or declaratively described.
   They should be used whenever multiple operations need to be coordinated, assuming the
   underlying resource managers support the necessary transactional interfaces. Global
   transactions should generally be started either in session beans using BMT or via declaration
   in the session bean deployment descriptors. Using global transactions reduces the complexity
   of the application programming and abstracts away specific transaction programming styles.
   Global transactions cannot be used when it is expected that coordinating resources from
   multiple resource managers do not support full XA transactional semantics. Using Last
   Participant Support, the utility and elegance of global transactions can extend to include
   transactions that involve multiple resource managers where one and no more than one of
   those resource managers does not support full XA semantics.

❑ **Local Transaction Explicit Programming**
   Use local transactions and explicit programming to backend systems, when encapsulation is
   not possible. Local transactions and direct programming to connections is complex. The
   WebSphere Application Server provides the <local-transaction> deployment descriptor
   extensions to provide some additional safety for these kinds of environments. Use
   ActivitySessions to factor these kinds of programs into layers of session beans and methods
   within beans. The ActivitySession can be declared in the deployment descriptor or directly
   programmed to support this explicit local transaction model.

❑ **ActivitySession Programming Model**
   Use this style of interaction when maximum abstraction from resource managers is desired
   and global transactions are not possible or not necessary. Using the ActivitySession-based
   model lets programmers avoid knowledge of the local transaction programming model while
   still enabling a level of grouping of interactions to backend systems that is similar to that
   achievable in the presence of global transactions. The <local-transaction> settings of
   boundary being set to ActivitySession combined with the ActivitySession settings on the bean,
   servlet, or method level enable this style of programming. When a global transaction model is
   possible, but the full recoverable, distributed capability of global transactions is not necessary,
   the ActivitySession model can also be leveraged with expected performance gains.

Additional ActivitySession Service Opportunities

The ActivitySession service has been described so far in terms of unit-of-work scoping and how it can be
leveraged in a variety of situations related to units of work. The ActivitySession Service also has utility as a
performance improving technique within the application server. These situations are described in this section.

The ActivitySession service describes to the EJB container a lifecycle for components that differ from
those that are generally found. Take the following scenario:

1. ActivitySession begins (either declaratively or programmatically)

2. Global Transaction1 begins (either declaratively or programmatically)

3. Entity EJB1 is accessed or updated (forces an activate and load)

4. Entity EJB2 is accessed or updated (forces an activate and load)

5. Global Transaction1 is committed

6. Global Transaction2 is begun

7. Entity EJB1 is accessed or updated (forces a load but not an activate)

8. Entity EJB2 is accessed or updated (forces a load but not an activate)

9. Global Transaction2 is committed

10. ActivitySession ends

Without the ActivitySession in place, the scenario above would involve the loading and activation of EJB1 and EJB2 for each global transaction. With the ActivitySession in place, EJB1 and EJB2 are activated only once and remain activated throughout the course of the ActivitySession. They are reloaded for Global Transaction2, but are not reactivated as they are still in the memory when Global Transaction2 starts. This will improve the performance of the application while maintaining the same transactional control over the underlying resources.

A number of application scenarios exist where a set of objects are activated in one transaction and perhaps updated in another. We are always taught to keep the duration of global transactions short, but this often means more transactions, and thus the possible inefficiency of reactivating objects multiple times to accomplish some piece of business function. ActivitySessions let us keep transactional units of work short while letting us gain the efficiency of relating resources used across multiple transactions.

Setting an EJB to have a passivation lifetime that exceeds a transactional boundary is done in the AAT as shown below:

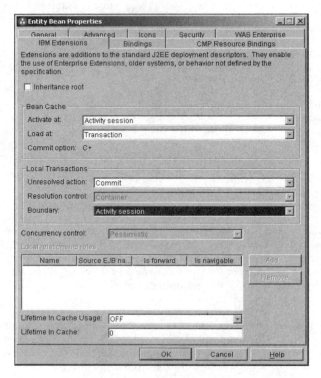

You can see that we have called this **Commit option C+** to indicate that it is like option C, but that the beans will remain activated in the EJB container for the duration of the ActivitySession instead of the normal transaction boundary.

In applications that are driven by servlets or inbound HTTP requests, it is desirable to associate the length of the ActivitySession with the length of the HTTP Session. This is also possible, declaratively, with WebSphere. The following shows how to have an ActivitySession created for each HTTP Session:

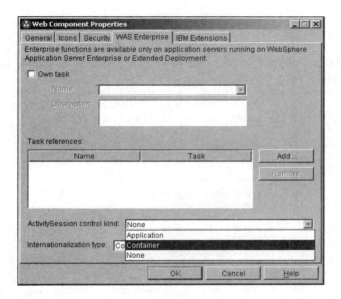

Setting the ActivtySession control kind to Container will cause an ActivitySession to automatically be created for each HTTP session. The default is None. Application means that the programmatic APIs for activity will be honored.

Summary

This chapter has introduced four sets of concepts:

❏ The concept of **Application Profile** and **Access Intent** were introduced. We learned that access intent describes how backend resource managers are used, ensuring effective use of those backend resources, and ensuring that those resource managers are not bottlenecks in the overall application architecture. Application Profile becomes the carrier for Access intent information and lets us dynamically decide, at any desired level of an application architecture, which of the possible access intents should be used downstream. The combination of these two concepts provides significant flexibility and once again should encourage and enable the creation of reusable components. A number of ways to start or approach this powerful combination of features was provided.

❏ The support provided for mapping CMP entities down to relational tables was described. We learned that there are a number of options to consider. Advanced capabilities that enable supporting multiple backends and inheritance patterns are just a couple of examples of what was covered.

❏ The **Dynamic Query Service** and its related capabilities extend the idea of EJB QL, providing a rich set of capabilities for dealing with CMP 2.0 entity beans. Component reuse is more achievable with functions like this, and more efficient programming is likely. This is because very precise queries can be specified that require very little result set processing. After the query, you can just use the beans (or the data) to do business.

❏ Finally, this chapter introduced some **Unit-of-Work** concepts that go beyond the current specifications. In fact, WebSphere goes to great lengths to specify what occurs, transactionally speaking, when the EJB unspecified context is used. The prevalence of resource managers that work in this manner and the possible gains in performance provide the incentive. Advanced features such as ActivitySessions and Last Participant Support further complement the transactional capabilities of WebSphere and provide fine-grained declarative or programmatic control over units of work running the system. ActivitySessions have the additional benefit of being able to allow the EJB container to more efficiently cache EJBs.

The capabilities discussed in this chapter that are provided in the base WebSphere Application Server and those capabilities that are reserved for the Enterprise Edition are listed here:

Capability	WebSphere Application Server	WebSphere Application Server Enterprise Edition
Application Profile	None	Supports Application Profile runtime service and associated assembly tool capabilitiy.
Access Intent	Supports a static assignment of a default set of seven different Access Intent policies to an entity bean. If one of the default policies is not chosen in the AAT, the default of Pessimistic Update with weakest lock at load (wsPessimisticUpdate-WeakestLockAtLoad) is used.	Supports dynamic assignment of Access Intent policies by leveraging application profile. Supports creation of new Access Intent policies to enable customized policies beyond the seven provided.
CMP Field Mapping	Creation of the maps is via WSAD and execution is via the runtime.	No additional support provided in Enterprise Edition.
Dynamic Query	None	Supports full dynamic query.
Query Extensions	Extensions for static queries including string comparison, scalar functions, ORDER BY, SQL date/time expressions, inheritance, subqueries, EXISTS predicate, and value object access.	Extensions for dynamic queries including bean methods, dependent value methods, and multiple element SELECT clauses.
Local Transactions	Support for JCA and JDBC-based local transactions to define what goes on when the transaction context in unspecified per the EJB 2.0 specification.	ActivitySession service actually provides additional control over local transactions.

Capability	WebSphere Application Server	WebSphere Application Server Enterprise Edition
ActivitySession Service	None	Supports bean-managed and container-managed ActivitySessions for both unit of work control and to assist in retaining contained EJBs in the EJB container for durations beyond transaction.

The combination of these four sets of concepts, all provided by the WebSphere Version 5.0 runtime, provides for a lot of possibilities when it comes to leveraging EJB 2.0 beans and CMP beans in particular as part of sophisticated J2EE applications.

10

Enterprise Process Management

As organizations move beyond a first application or first set of applications that are constructed and deployed on application servers, a new set of requirements emerges. These new requirements bring with them an additional set of questions, many of which translate into opportunities and requirements that need to be dealt with by the application server infrastructure. A push towards having a well-factored enterprise architecture of application components becomes necessary to deal with these more complex applications. As this occurs, additional heuristics and guidelines for application architecture are necessary.

Concurrent with understanding the architectural effects of broadening the use of applications servers comes a set of requirements around business logic and business logic factoring. WebSphere Application Server (WAS) provides a number of capabilities that address the challenges of reuse and flexibility.

Broadening the use of application servers in an organization brings to light a number of challenges, such as management of applications and operational requirements. Equally important, however, are the requirements that focus specifically on business logic and business logic factoring. Managing complexity demands that applications be structured for reuse and flexiblity. More large monolithic applications are not the goal. The development and operational costs of large monolithic applications are high. On the other hand, applications that are properly factored for reuse and that leverage the underlying constructs in the middleware will create a base from which more rapid and successful growth of application can occur.

A large servlet/JSP page application as a first application will probably contain a set of logic that is truly independent from the presentation aspects of the application. Often, the application will contain business logic that contains business rules and consists of a series of steps that accomplish a business task. A data-access layer is probably also part of the "first application", providing some encapsulation around interactions to a backend system. Succeeding applications may be created that require some of the same business rules, some of the same business logic, and access to the same business data.

Factoring applications such as these, leveraging session EJBs and entity EJBs, is a first step towards a stronger architecture for reuse. However, even applications that leverage EJBs can be somewhat brittle and monolithic in nature. Specific business logic and business rules may still be "locked" inside a larger component. Constructing new applications that reuse the business rules and many steps in a business logic flow might still prove difficult. Upfront architecture and planning is necessary to achieve the proper set of components. This architecture activity lays the foundation for scaling the usage of application servers in an organzation.

WAS provides a number of additional capabilities that address the challenges of reuse and flexibility and ease the development cost for process and flow-oriented applications.

This chapter will introduce the concept of **Process Choreography** and **Business Rules** as mechanisms for more efficiently creating, running, and changing business processes. These should be valuable tools to architects and developers of reusable components and well structured applications.

Application Structure Revisited

There are many things to think about while constructing an architectural solution for your organization. The combination of J2EE, web services, and the extensions to these capabilities made by the WebSphere Application Server provide a powerful set of tools on which to build your application architecture. This section will describe some basic architectural principles for applications that are aimed at utilizing the underlying run-time capabilities of WAS and allow for solving business problems in the most expedient fashion.

Architectural Origins and Evolution

J2EE applications that run on the application server, especially the first applications produced by an organization, generally start out as either web-based or business component-based. Web-based applications often start out as a set of servlets and JSP pages that do some rudimentary interactions to a backend system. These applications probably originate as part of web-enabling activity. They frequently evolve towards applications that leverage EJBs for encapsulating backend functionality and creating reusable pieces of business logic.

Applications that start life as component-based are those that solve a business problem that may or may not require or support a web-based interface. These applications can be EJB-based on the server and driven by the J2EE client via RMI-IIOP inbound calls. In fact, these applications are usually easy to adapt and to put additional interface layers on as technology evolves and the business demands change. This is because they already have a stronger separation of the business logic, presentation logic, and data logic.

In either case, we arrive at an architecture that ultimately captures a business model. A business model, in the most traditional sense consists of a set of entities and a set of processes that leverage the entities. It represents either how the current business functions or some future desired state. **Business Process Modeling** is about creating the business model. **Business Process Reengineering** is about changing the business processes to be more efficient, effective, automated, or "better" in some way, shape, or form.

Notice that the first definitions of a business model provided above really do not talk about software as much as they do business. This is a key fact and must not be lost sight of as we go forward in this discussion. Ultimately, this is about business, not technology. We will represent and capture the business model in software, but must be driven by the business as we do this, not by the software. This requirement demands that the software infrastructure ultimately is able to capture and represent the business model in an almost effortless way.

Let's go back to the software architecture and explore how to capture and represent business models in software. Enterprise applications include business functionality and an apprpriate means for users to interact with that functionality. The simplest view of an application architecture suggests that we have a presentation layer and a layer which represents the business model, as shown below:

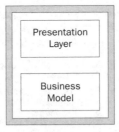

While the diagram appears quite frugal now, we will be expanding on it through the rest of this section.

Implementations of business models have been done in many ways over the years. We have used relational technology to represent the business entities. We have used data-flow and state modeling to graphically capture and subsequently generate software that executes the processes and sub-processes. This separation of the "flow" and the "entities" is very old. There has always been the "data-flow" crowd, the "everything is a state-machine" crowd, and then the "third normal form entity" crowd that would implement most of the business in stored procedures and relational databases if they ruled the day.

All of these styles and others have been practiced successfully for certain kinds of applications. Each of these styles has come with challenges and has given rise to newer and more improved models for development. Object-oriented techniques and component models owe a lot to these early software development methodologies.

J2EE, through EJBs, contains a modern component model for representing both the entities and the "flow" or tasks (session beans) that would be used to implement the business model. While still lacking enough capability to directly translate from the business model to software model, J2EE represents a rich and modern platform on which to implement a business model in software.

Many modern business model implementations expose themselves to the Web and let customers do business through the Web. Simple web presence initially involved static pages, and then evolved towards dynamic content creation via CGI. This gave rise to servlets, JSP pages, and now portals. Presentation now includes web browsers, as well as pervasive devices.

The figure below shows that we have placed some of the J2EE artifacts into our basic structure:

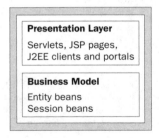

J2EE 1.3 brings a bit more to the table when it comes to accessing and managing the business model. The following diagram shows that we have filled in the picture a bit more, adding in access to backend systems and the ability to take work requests, based on an arriving message.

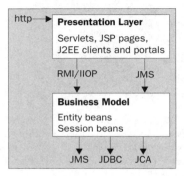

Some of the J2EE 1.3 enhancements over J2EE 1.2 do not involve major new building blocks, but rather evolutions of existing building blocks. Servlet 2.3 and EJB 2.0 are just two examples of existing architectural components that are maturing and evolving. While JMS did exist prior to J2EE 1.3, the emergence of message-driven beans in EJB 2.0 and the JMS provider requirements lets JMS make a bigger impact on architecture than it could previously.

The arrival of web services onto the scene has given provided another power tool for developers wishing to expose pieces of the business model to other applications. As described in Chapter 8, web services interfaces are based on WSDL. WebSphere Studio Application Developer (WASD) provides simple tooling that will allow a session bean to easily be exposed as a web service.

Given this backdrop and perspective, a simple view of a business exposing itself from a web services perspective might look like this:

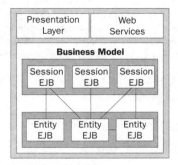

In fact, web services represent the "interface" that external businesses would interact with to do "business". We have a set of technology around WSDL, SOAP, and UDDI that let us represent web services interfaces, an envelope format so we can flow requests over standard protocols, and a way to find the "services" that are needed. Web services leverage XML to pass requests and responses and are capable of using HTTP or other protocols to transport requests. These facts place web services in a position to go beyond older RPC-based distributed systems technologies such as CORBA and DCOM.

The "conceptual" business model described so far and the attendant technologies that enable implementation are a good start on the road to scalable and robust application architecture. However, this is not the end of our story. Additional technologies and constructs can enable further refinement and bring additional value to the architecture and resultant systems. Merely using simple session beans to implement and capture the business processes and flows will become a tedious and complex development activity. It actually can become a costly method of development for solving complex business problems. Building new business processes by assembling and composing existing business processes is desirable and possible, but not easy given only the base capabilities of J2EE 1.3 and web services.

We therefore need to augment our existing view with some additional concepts, which begin to further detail the shape and form of our business model:

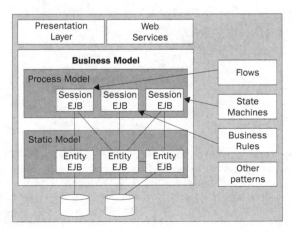

This figure also shows that our business process model or our business processes are really formalizations or clarifications of what is at the session-bean layer. If we were to look at the patterns that exist in the logic of business systems, we would see logic that enables a flow concept or a series of steps that are performed to properly execute a business process. This is represented by the Flows in the diagram. Other patterns also would be observed in business system logic, including business rules, and a state machine pattern. We will dig into the flow patterns and business rules in much more detail later in this chapter and see what WebSphere Application Server Enterprise (WASE) has to enable the construction of these kinds of processes.

We have also added the idea of a static model to the diagram to more formally represent the entities in the business and the relationship between those entities.

We will dig into some of this a bit more later, but the basics should be clear. We have:

❑   Interfaces to the business model in the form of web services and in the form of traditional clients such as servlets/JSP pages or J2EE clients. The web services are represented as WSDL documents and are the entry point for external consumers of the services provided.

❑   Entities in the form of entity beans. These entities are stateful in nature, and the state is persisted to databases or other resource managers.

❑   Processes in the form of session beans, designed to accurately model the actual business flow of the organization.

Before moving on, we must observe that there is also the idea of web services and services in general being leveraged as part of implementing the business model. The following diagram, a variation on the previous diagrams, demonstrates this concept:

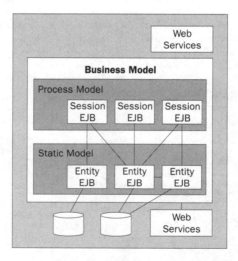

This final picture leverages and builds upon the idea of a service-oriented architecture that was presented in Chapter 7. The diagram above represents using J2EE to build a business model in the middle tier, combined with a service-oriented architecture, which not only exposes business services, but also leverages business services in the formation of new business value. The act of leveraging business services to create new business services is sometimes referred to as **service composition**. The workflow technology that we will describe later in this chapter is meant to enable exactly this kind of composition.

Where to Next?

WAS version 5.0 provides just about every piece of technology that you need to build one of the previously described application architectures. The upcoming sections will further detail some of the advanced capabilities in WASE, which are focused around assisting in the creation of rich, reusable, and robust application architecture.

Business Process Management

Business Process Management (BPM) is about modeling, implementing, and managing the execution of automated business processes. Automated means that the process is driven by an application that orchestrates the interaction of the various human resources and software components that are required to perform the business process. With a few "green field" exceptions, BPM application development generally is a "meet-in-the-middle" process, which comprises these two elements:

❑   A high-level requirements specification of the business functions that an enterprise wants to offer or perform, to achieve a business goal within certain constraints (cost and time limits, quality of service, and so on). Often this requirements specification is derived from the results of a more or less formal business process analysis effort. In other cases, the functions to be provided are dictated by public standards or external partners. In any case, the process specifications are likely to change frequently.

❑   A set of existing application components that encapsulate operational data or perform business functions that need to be integrated into process execution. These components can be legacy applications, packaged applications, new J2EE components, or web services provided by external partners. Since they were not built specifically for use in a particular business process, some adaptation needs to be done to fit these components into the overall process.

The goal of BPM application development is to fill the gap between these two ingredients and make it easier to do the following:

❑   Incorporate existing application components and resources into the process and manage the interactions of human process participants.

❑   Add new business logic and modify previously defined behavior of the process without affecting other components used by the process.

❑   Manage execution of the processes from a business user's perspective. This includes capability to suspend execution of the process or parts of the process if necessary.

❑   Monitor status of the process at any point in time, providing information about progress of the overall process, status of individual process tasks, and resources used by the process.

❑   Analyze business process execution, providing an execution trace of the process that offers sufficient information to analyze performance of one or more processes. This can be used to evaluate process performance, compare it to the objectives defined earlier, and enable process optimization based on lessons learned.

Further background and explanation of business process management would be going into too much detail. It suffices it to say that the challenge in the application server space is to meet these BPM goals in a way that is complementary and appropriate for application server-based business solutions. This really means that we need to expose and present these capabilities in a way that is natural and reasonable to those engaged in J2EE-centered development activities. The preceding statements are actually useful as a manifesto and set of guidelines for any infrastructure base that intends to support BPM. In our case, the infrastructure base is J2EE and web services.

As is usually the case, existing specifications for J2EE 1.3 could be pushed to the limits and used to implement many of the concepts just described. However, to more appropriately address these challenges, additional services and capabilities are called for. Let's see some of the services supported by WASE, starting with **Process Choreography**, and later **Business Rules**.

Process Choreography

The model for execution of a business process is often called a **workflow**. In software, workflow represents the automation of a business process or part of a business process. Sometimes workflow is refered as to just flow, while talking about a specific automated business process. WASE has a new feature called **Process Choreographer**. The workflow capabilities of WebSphere are categorized and measured under this umbrella. Process Choreographer in the runtime involves execution and management of flow-based applications. WebSphere Studio Application Development, Integration Edition (WAS IE) offers tooling that assists developers creating flow-based applications for later execution on the WASE runtime.

WebSphere's support for workflow brings about the true integration of the Java and J2EE worlds with the workflow world. Accessing non-Java artifacts during business processes is possible and simplified through the use of service-oriented architecture. However, when new activities are necessary, they can be constructed in Java using the full power of the J2EE programming model.

Workflow can be depicted graphically using a directed graph. The graph nodes represent individual steps in a flow. The graph edges or connectors describe the execution order of those steps (including conditional and concurrent execution), as well as the data that is needed by the activities. Each of the activities references an "activity implementation", which can be a sub-flow or an elemental operation; for example, a method of an EJB or a web service. People can be assigned to activities if humans perform the respective steps. Actions performed by humans demand that the infrastructure have in place an organizational model and demand that the workflow runtime have access to that. The following figure shows a very simple process as a series of steps shown in WebSphere Studio Application Developer, Integration Edition. Each step executes a different kind of activity just for purposes of demonstration. More refined and complete examples will follow later in this chapter:

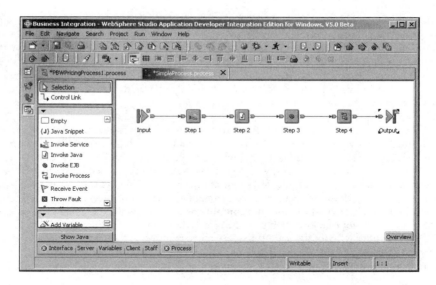

At run time, the business process engine executes instances of business processes, either in memory for short running flows, or with persistent state for long running flows. The individual activity implementations are invoked when needed, the state of the business process is tracked, work items are assigned to people if and when needed, and access to this information is provided via a worklist handler interface and associated GUI. The Process Choreographer capabilities of WebSphere can be used to describe a variety of "executables", from short running scripts involving a couple of service invocations up to long running business processes involving B2B interactions and people.

Many existing IBM products use flows of various types as their execution model – some examples are WebSphere MQ Integrator (formerly MQSeries Integrator), Lotus Workflow, WebSphere Adapters (formerly MQSeries Adapter Offering), Enterprise Access Builder, and MQSeries Workflow. Each of these products is specific to certain environments and certain types of flows. WebSphere MQ Integrator, for example, is optimized to flows that manage the routing and handling of messages in a messaged system.

WebSphere's Process Choreographer adds a general-purpose flow engine (**Business Process Container**) to the application server, which allows for the seamless management and efficient execution of all kinds of flows in the application server. Business processes, a term we will use interchangeably with flows, are deployed as part of EAR files, and are managed by the WAS admininistration console. WebSphere's Process Choreographer is based on a business process engine written in pure Java that was designed with extensibility, flexibility, and performance in mind. With these design principles in place, it is intended that numerous kinds of flows can be executed using this technology to solve many business process problems in a wide variety of environments. The next section provides more details on the possible role for automated business processes.

The Role for Business Processes

Automated business processes can play a key role in architectures, which are based on the application server. This section will elaborate upon some of those architectures, and suggest some of the features that are necessary and available in WebSphere's Process Choreography support. These features make the creation of solutions that conform to the suggested architectures possible.

First, if we look back to our discussion of the business model earlier in this chapter, we will see that the premise was made that the basic elements of the business process are implemented with session beans. The simplest application of flows involves implementing that session bean using flow technology. What happens is that the basic steps necessary to execute a business process are scripted using a flow. This flow probably also involves conditionally calling and leveraging EJBs that are in the solution architecture. These very simple flows are generally short lived in nature and are synchronously executed. These synchronous flows are called **micro-flows** or **non-interruptable processes**.

Secondly, we begin to see more complex business processes being represented by workflow. These processes involve a flow that choreographs or scripts the usage of a number of sub-processes. These sub-processes may also be non-interruptable processes or just traditionally created session beans. What is important is that the system supports the ability to conditionally execute various sub-processes based on business rules. These more complex flows may also run for longer periods of time and are able to live beyond the lifetime of a given server instance. Activities in these flows often contain asynchronous invocations also. These are what would be characterized as **macro-flows** or **interruptable processes**. An interruptable process is shown in the following figure. It shows four major activities and suggests that each activity implementation is a session bean calling some entities. Obviously, actions that are more complex are allowed in the activity implementations. This will be further detailed later in the chapter. The stick figures in the figure represent human-interaction as part of one or more of the activities performed within the business proress:

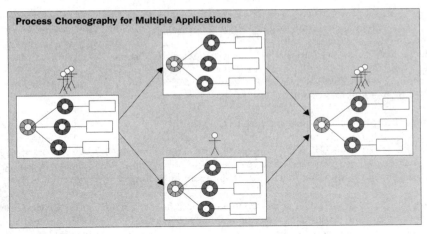

Next, we begin to see these basic short and long-lived business processes taking on various additional roles, leveraging some different features along the way. It is possible that flows will have a series of user-interactions, which are necessary to complete one or more of the steps in the business process. This requires workflows to play a more direct role in the presentation of the business process. The business process then is reacting directly to an ongoing stream of inputs driven by user interactions.

Some business processes will begin executing based on an inbound message rather than some direct invocation from within an existing servlet or session EJB. There is a role for flows in message-oriented applications. The flow continues to drive a series of steps that execute a business process. The difference is that the flow is started by an inbound message. In message-based flows, the results of a flow are also often transmitted with messages as well.

These basic patterns for flow usage begin to suggest some powerful ways to implement the processes that make up our business model. Beyond an individual organization, flows that span businesses or business units should also be considered. The same basic building blocks apply. A business process that spans businesses is called a **public process**. Each step in the public process may indeed involve utilizing some of the patterns we have just described.

With this set of possibilities in place, the details on the more basic elements that make up the business process programming model can be described. This is the topic of the next section.

Business Process Programming Model Concepts

As we have already seen in the previous sections, there are multiple usage scenarios for flows, resulting in flows of quite different capabilities. The capabilities necessary to support these scenarios are described in this section.

Worklist Handler

Starting from an end user's point of view, a specific user is typically involved in flows implementing various business processes, for example, ordering processes, travel expense processes, production processes, and so on. This involvement results in **work assignments** (also called **work items**) for that user being generated by the business process engine during the execution of a specific instance of a business process, and put into the user's **worklist**. That worklist thus contains work assignments from many business processes, which typically are instances of a number of different business process models that implement different external business processes. To efficiently work with assigned work items, an end user requires the ability to query work items, using appropriate filters and sort criteria. In addition, the user needs the ability to "check-out" a work item (claim exclusive access of the associated activity to work on it), and "check it in" (complete it) again when done with it.

The above requires the existence of a generic business process engine API component (often called a worklist handler API), as shown in the figure. We will talk more about this figure as we go along:

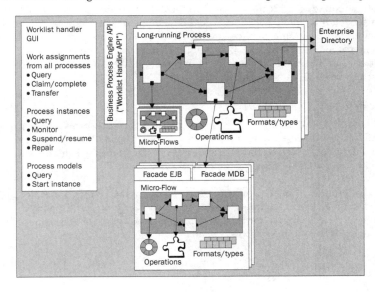

It is important to note that this component needs access to work items from all business process instances from all business process models, including the message and document formats that are associated with them. This "global visibility" of work items is achieved by putting them into a shared relational database, which also allows for efficient filtering and sorting (the use of a relational database is encapsulated by the workflow runtime). The business process engine API and worklist handler GUI also support business process-related functions, for example, to start and monitor business processes.

Interruptable Process

A typical business process in an enterprise involves a mixture of people-based steps that are realized by humans checking-out activities, working on them, and checking them back in, and automatic steps that are realized by invoking (new or existing) services.

People are associated with the business process flow by means of staff queries against the enterprise directory (or a number of such directories). Typically, these directories contain the organizational structure of the enterprise, including responsibilities described by roles. Staff queries determine which people should be performing the people-based steps in a business process. At runtime, work assignments are created for each person or group of people, and put onto the worklists, as described in the previous section.

A particular instance of such a business process runs for a long time, up to weeks or even months. Its execution consists of multiple transactions, which are chained together in a forward recoverable manner, involving transacted messaging. Interruptable business processes, or macro-flows as they are sometimes called, may persist beyond the lifetime of the server process in which they begin execution. If the server shuts down, the current state of the flow is persisted. When the server restarts, the business process engine then resumes execution of the business process instance.

For the invocation of operations associated with automatic steps, there are some choices. Most notable is the distinction between asynchronous invocations (messaging-style) and synchronous invocations (RPC-style).

Operations invoked on behalf of an interruptable process can be private to the flow in the sense that the particular operation requires specific formats and protocols known only by the specific interruptable processes. Examples of thse types of activities would be staff queries or events specific to the flow. In addition to private operations in a flow, other services are used and reused across different flows. These operations invoked by the interruptable process are most often J2EE-based calls, such as those to a session bean or business rule, or are based on a service interface as expressed in WSDL and done according to the service-oriented architecture described in an earlier chapter.

Non-Interruptable Process

The usage of standard invocation protocols as well as standard message formats is very desirable for enterprise-wide flows. However, existing applications typically require their own protocols and formats. In addition, the granularity of the operations provided by existing applications might be too fine for the actual business operation required in an interruptable process.

A non-interruptable process, or micro-flow, can be used to solve these kinds of problems. A non-interruptable process is used to script together a couple of operations, with very little performance overhead. A non-interruptable process runs all steps in the flow in a single unit of work. There is no asynchronous communication done by the business process engine.

As discussed in previous chapters, unit-of-work will normally mean a transaction. However, it is possible that a non-interruptable process could be running in a local transaction or an activity session.

Referring to the figure in the *Worklist Handler* section, the non-interruptable process exposes a business service interface using the service-oriented architecture or an EJB interface. The implementation involves a series of actions that use private formats, appropriate conversion operations, and existing applications available in the application server as needed. Thus, a non-interruptable process is short running, to the order of milliseconds or seconds, and is enclosed by a single transaction. Operations invoked on its behalf can only be of the synchronous RPC style, hence any service bindings used should be synchronous in nature.

Invocation of a non-interruptable process is via façades that are generated automatically by the Process Choreography tooling from the signature of the business process. A façade session EJB provides a `Call()` method with the non-interruptable process's signature. A façade message-driven Bean (MDB) is also provided, which accepts a JMS message in the correct format for the non-interruptable process, and responds with a JMS message on completion of the flow. Further details on these interfaces will be provided later in the chapter.

Compensation

The compensation pattern supports writing business processes, which automatically run activities in the exceptional case where the business process cannot continue. Compensation processing in business process applications supports "undo" processing for actions taken during execution of a business process, for example, restoring the content of business entities manipulated by the process or performing actions that reverse the result of actions performed in the course of the "regular" process. The compensation pattern has two main ingredients: **compensation pairs** and **compensation spheres**.

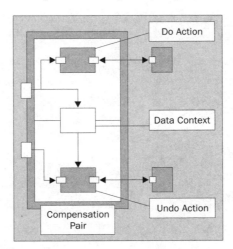

A compensation pair, as shown above, associates a normal activity in a business process, shown as the Do Action with an Undo Action that can be performed to reverse the actions taken in the original activity. When the compensation pair is invoked during normal execution, it invokes the Do Action. The system then stores information that would be later needed to perform the Undo Action. When the compensation pair is invoked after the process has reached a state where it cannot continue forward, it performs the Undo Action, using the previously stored information.

A compensation example would be a business process involving travel booking where steps in the business process would be to acquire a plane ticket, a car reservation, and a hotel reservation. If the business process achieved acquisition of the plane ticket and the car reservation, but could not acquire a hotel reservation, then compensation would begin. The compensation, or undo, actions would have to get refunds for the purchased tickets, cancel reservations, potentially paying penalties, issue notices, and so forth. Data about the purchased tickets and confirmed reservations would be needed during the compensation to accurately carry out the undo actions.

Application developers implementing activities in a flow may define compensation pairs for the actions they implement in the form of operations on business services. Often it is good design practice to design the undo operations while designing a service (for example, place order or cancel order) and design the undo actions for operations on a business service that may be aggregated into another business service. Often, however, business process assemblers will define compensation pairs for operations they use in the context of a business process and collaborate with component providers to implement the services providing the necessary undo operations.

A **compensation sphere** establishes compensation scope and facilitates compensation processing by keeping track of execution status of compensation pairs executed within its scope. The **compensation coordinator** of such a sphere is informed whenever a compensation pair performs an action in the scope of the compensation sphere and provides a "log" of compensation pairs that need to be involved in compensation processing. When compensation processing is initiated, the **compensation executor** uses this information to dynamically build the undo process that needs to be executed to compensate actions that had been performed in the compensation sphere. The major pieces involved with a compensation sphere are shown in the following figure:

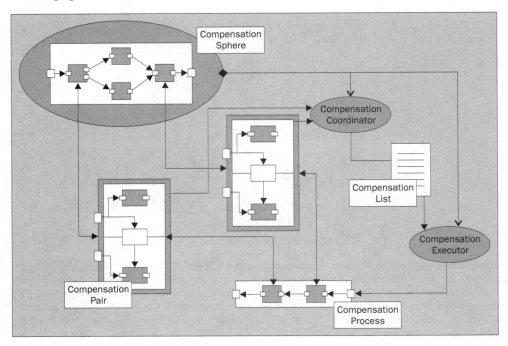

A compensation sphere can encapsulate an interruptable process, which uses compensation pairs as implementations of selected activities. During "regular" execution of the interruptable process, the "do" actions of these pairs are invoked, and compensation pairs store context information and register with the compensation coordinator. When compensation processing is initiated (for example, by a process administrator or due to an exception during execution of the business process model), the compensation executor constructs the "reverse" business process model, which essentially executes the "undo" facets of the compensation pairs that have been executed before compensation processing kicked in.

Comparing how compensation spheres and compensation works to a more traditional two-phase commit global transaction monitor is worth considering. A key difference is that the activities in a process are commited at each step in a process. Furthermore, the "undo" operations often involve activities rather than just rolling back uncommitted changes.

These are the basic flow concepts that are supported by the WAS. These can certainly help to fill out and more quickly create and enrich the business model that we started describing earlier in this chapter.

Creating a Process Application

To better describe and detail the business process capabilities of WASE, a concrete example will be used. This will describe the basic process of creating a business process and become the basis for describing how to unit test and debug a business process within the WSAD-IE tooling. It will also serve as the basis for describing how to start a business process and manage it from the WASE runtime.

Extending PlantsByWebSphere

To demonstrate how to create and run a simple business process application, we will leverage the Plants-By-WebSphere application. Only selected features of the business process capabilities of WASE will be leveraged in the example. Details on some of the additional features will be covered at the end of this section.

The business requirement for the example is to provide an interface that will allow the caller to change the price on items that are sold by the Plants-By-WebSphere business. The requirement is that this interface be provided as a service to ensure that it is accessible from a wide variety of clients. A service in this context is not necessarily a web service, but rather a service in the context of the service-oriented architecture, which was introduced in Chapter 7.

The further requirement states that the application should provide the ability to increase the price on a specified item in inventory by a specified percent. Let's assume we are in the role where we provide any service to those within the Plants-By-WebSphere team, hoping to leverage our catalog capabilities.

The WSDL that represents this basic interface is shown here (we'll create this using the WSAD-IE tooling shortly):

```
<?xml version="1.0" encoding="UTF-8"?>
<definitions name="PriceUpdateServiceInterface"

targetNamespace
  ="http://pbwpricing.pbw.ibm.com/PriceUpdateServiceInterface"
  xmlns=http://schemas.xmlsoap.org/wsdl/
```

```
xmlns:tns
  ="http://pbwpricing.pbw.ibm.com/PriceUpdateServiceInterface"
  xmlns:xsd="http://www.w3.org/2001/XMLSchema">
  <message name="UpdateSingleMsg">
    <part name="ItemID" type="xsd:string"></part>
    <part name="Percent" type="xsd:float"></part>
  </message>
  <portType name="PriceUpdaterIntfc">
    <operation name="UpdateSingleItem">
      <input name="UpdateSingleRequest"
              message="tns:UpdateSingleMsg">
      </input>
    </operation>
  </portType>
</definitions>
```

This interface is completely independent of how it is implemented. Our job is now to implement the `UpdateSingleItem` operation.

UpdateSingleItem Implemented by a Business Process

After an analysis of existing methods provided by the current Plants-By-WebSphere application, it is decided that a business process can implement the `UpdateSingleItem` operation being requested.

Here is the simple workflow that will implement the requested price increase:

1. Input and accept item identifier and percent increase requested

2. Get price of inventory item

3. Set price to current price multiplied by the requested increase

Rather than writing a new session bean or session bean method to do this, we will implement the price increase using a business process, leveraging the Process Choreography feature of WASE. However, a review with the business experts indicated that price increases at PlantsByWebSphere are not done automatically today and that all requests for price increases need to be approved. Today this person uses a manual process to approve price increases. In fact, it was suggested that perhaps that person could run this new application rather than having it initiated externally from elsewhere in the organization.

As it turns out, WASE has the facilities to automate this workflow by using a human interaction as part of the business process. Therefore, the business process to be automated is extended to include the following steps:

1. Input and accept item identifier and percent increase requested

2. Get price of inventory item

3. Seek approval for price increase

4. Set price to current price multiplied by the requested increase

Creating the Business Process in WSAD-IE

This section will step you through creation and implementation of a business process using WSAD-IE.

The basic steps in the tooling to prepare the environment for building our business process are as follows:

1. Create a new service project

2. Create the service interface

3. Create the basic business process

4. Complete the basic steps of the business process

5. Add more Java snippets and control flow

6. Perform additional necessary activities

7. Generate code

We will now go through each of these steps in detail.

Create a New Service Project (PlantsByWebSpherePricingProcess)

First open the Business Integration perspective, select File | New | Service Project. You will get a screen as shown:

Enter `PlantsByWebSpherePricingProcess` as the project name and click Next. Switch to the **Projects** tab, and select the **PlantsByWebSphereEJB** project. This is the name of the project where you have the EJBs that are part of the Plants-By-WebSphere example:

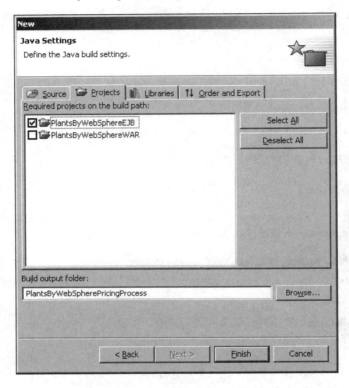

This has given us an empty project, pointed back to the project EJBs from which we can begin to fill in the pieces necessary to implement our business process.

Create the Service Interface

In the Services view on the main screen, right-click on the service project **PlantsByWebSpherePricingProcess**, and select New | Empty Service. The creation wizard will open. Fill in the package name of `com.ibm.pbw.pbwpricing` and the interface name `PriceUpdateServiceInterface` and the rest will automatically appear:

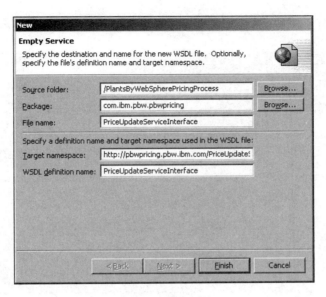

Click on **Finish**, and now there is an empty WSDL file ready to be filled in:

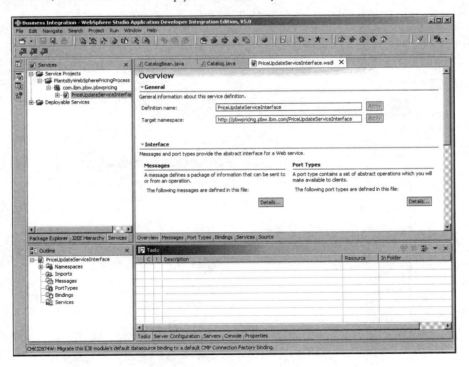

Click on the **Port Types** view and add the `PriceUpdaterIntfc` port and the `UpdateSingle` operation as shown below:

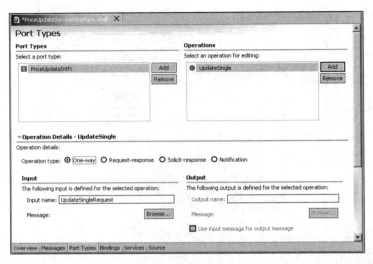

Notice that **One-way** was selected for the **Operation type**, from the bottom of the window. This suggests that the caller of the service submits the request and will not get a synchronous response to the request. Since we have added a human interaction to our business process, it will not be happening synchronously. We are building an interruptable business process as discussed earlier in this chapter.

Now select the **Messages** view and add `UpdateSingleMsg` to the messages. Then add two parts, `ItemID` and `Percent`. Use the **Built-in type** to give them type `xsd:string` and `xsd:float` respectively, as shown:

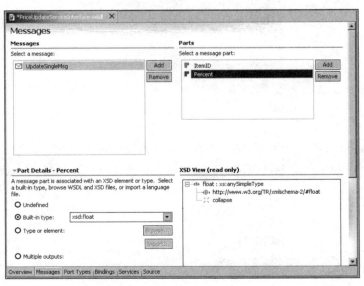

Go back to the **Port Types** and add the `UpdateSingleMsg` to the **Input** part of the screen, using the **Browse** button, as shown below:

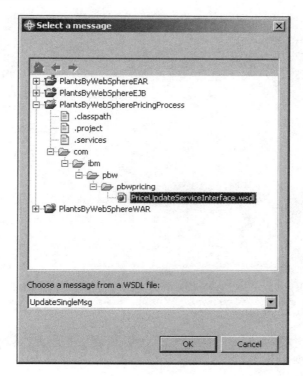

Next, go to the Source view and verify that the WSDL source is the same as that shown earlier in this chapter.

Save your work to this point.

The basic interface for the business process is created and is part of the project. The next step is to create the business process that will implement the interface.

> *This WSDL is independent of business processes and can be created in any convenient way. It does need to be in the WSAD-IE tool, so that we can build the proper service and binding that will implement the interface.*

Create the Basic Business Process

With our `PlantsByWebSpherePricingProcess` service project selected, right-click and select **New | Business Process** and enter the following:

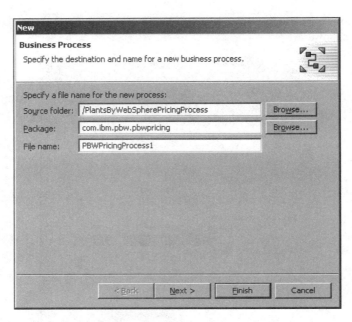

Click Next and the select Use existing WSDL for business process interface. Fill in the Interface file (`PriceUpdateServiceInterface.wsdl`) by using the Browse button. This is telling WASD-IE which WSDL we will be implementing with this business process:

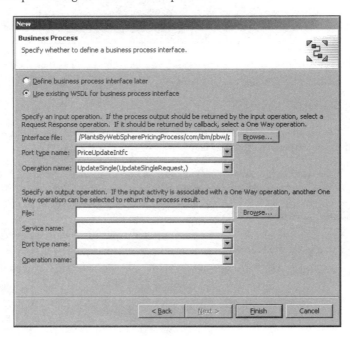

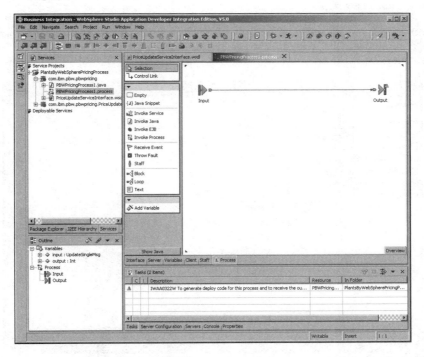

We can now go back to our original design of the process and place our activities onto the palette (remove the control link that connects the input and output). Notice that there are two EJB activities and a staff activity. Right-clicking on them allows you to change the label that appears with them on the display. The result is as shown:

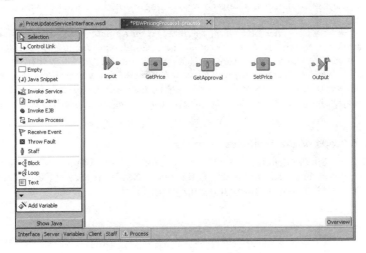

The basic business process is now on the palette. These activities will remain here throughout the development of the example. We will add some intermediary activities and put details behind each of the activities in the upcoming steps.

One other thing that we should do now before we start more detailed implementation is to mark our business process as 'Interruptible'. Click on the Server view of the business process editor and set it to **Run Process as Interruptible**:

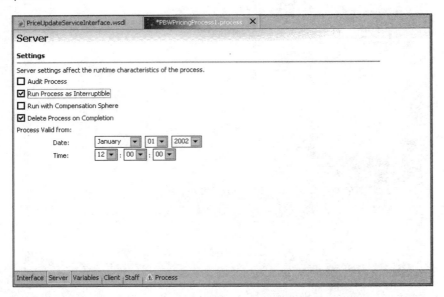

The operation that we created on the `PriceUpdateIntfc`, was marked as `"One-way"`. This fact, combined with the notation above, which checks the box named **Always Run Process as Interruptable,** will ensure that this business runs as a macro-flow. A non-interruptable business process or micro-flow would be marked as `"Request-response"` in the WSDL and correspondingly not check the box above.

> *During the last two steps, we have followed the sequence that started with a WSDL and then created a business process that implements it. This is one of the many possible paths through the development process. Another possible pattern is to create a business process, and then later create a WSDL interface from that process. Which path is followed is a matter of preference, since each results in the same final outputs. For our purposes, the ability to hand the WSDL off to potential users early in the development process is appealing. We are free to continue to refine the way we implement the WSDL through the rest of our steps.*

Complete the Basic Steps of the Business Process

We are now ready to fill in the details behind the steps in our process. We will start with the calls to the EJB. From the process palette, right-click on the first EJB activity (**GetPrice**). Select **Properties**, and from that page, select **Implementation** and start with this empty form:

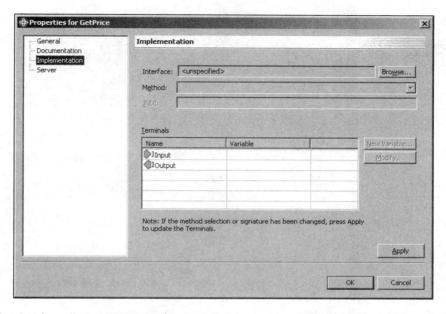

Fill in the class (actually is a EJB method) to be called, by pressing the **Browse** button. From the list displayed (type the first few letters of "catalog" to narrow the list), select the **Catalog** interface, as shown here, and click on **OK**:

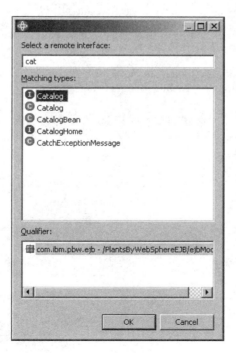

Now we find the method to call. Select the `getItemPrice()` method as shown:

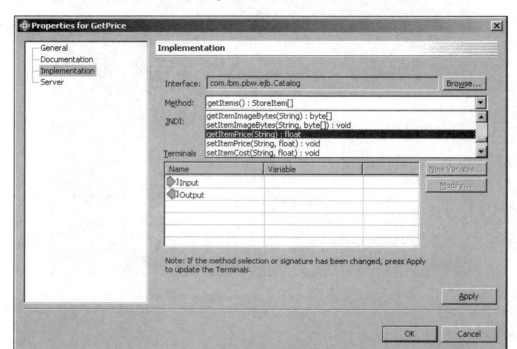

Press Apply. This will generate some WSDL messages for you, under the covers.

Now create new variables for the input, the output, and the exception. First choose the Input parameter and then click on New Variable to give you the following default screen:

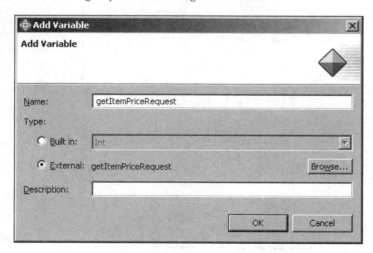

Click on **OK** and you you will return to the earlier screen with the variable name added:

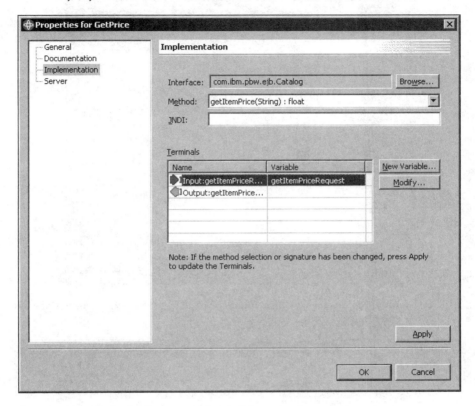

Follow the same steps for the **Output** terminal and click on **Apply**.

At this step in the process, we are to call the `getItemPrice(String)` method on the EJB. We can expect to find a `String` in the variable named `getItemPriceRequest`, and will expect to see a resulting `float` placed into the variable `getItemPriceResponse`.

We also need to fill in the **JNDI:** input field with the JNDI name that represents where the EJBs will be in the running system. For our example, fill in `plantsby/CatalogHome`.

Follow the same pattern for **SetPrice** EJB activity. The completed implementation form for the `setItemPrice` call should look like this:

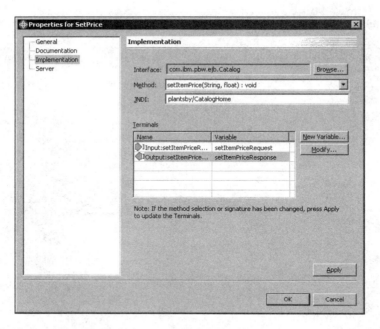

Filling in the **GetApproval** staff node is the next task. So far, we have variables in our business process that handle the requests and responses from the EJB calls:

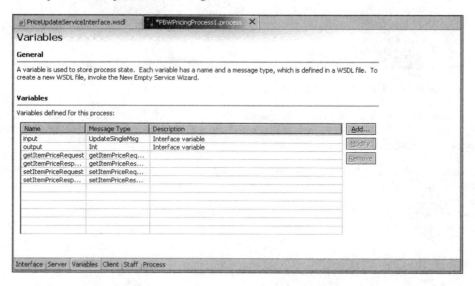

Before moving on to create the variables that our staff node will use, we may need to update the input variable. If it's already set to type `UpdateSingleMsg` *as above then you're OK. If not, use the* **Modify** *button and set the variable type to* **External**, *pointing at* `PriceUpdateServiceInterface.wsdl`.

What we need now is a variable to feed into the staff activity. We can assert that none of the existing messages has enough data to be used as the type for this message. We need to send in a new variable to the **GetApproval** step in our business process, and send the current price of the item, the item ID, and the requested increase. Whoever is going to "approve" or "disapprove" the price increase request needs all the available data from which to make the decision. This data is available from the various variables that we have and can be pulled together into a `getApprovalRequest` variable. First, we need a variable so we will need to define a WSDL message from which we can get a Java type for this variable.

This is our first variable that is not created for us by the system. To create a variable, click on **File | New | Empty Service**. Fill in the details as shown below:

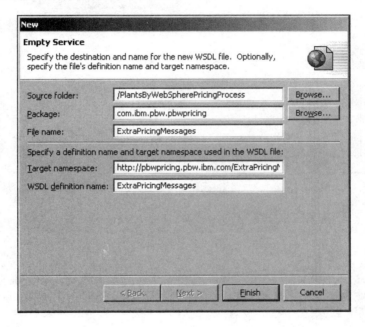

Once it is created, we can select this file and add our message. Under the Messages view, add the `getApprovalRequestMsg` with an `itemID` (`xsd:string`), `existingPrice` (`xsd:float`), and `increasePercent` (`xsd:float`) parts:

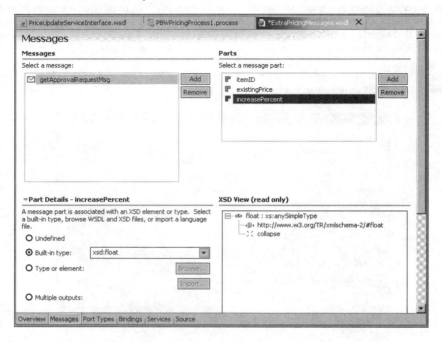

Save, so the new message can be used.

Now we can create a variable, leveraging our new message, to be used by our staff node for input. This means we go back to the process and select the staff node, bring up the Properties menu as before, and select the Data node and add a new variable for input as shown here:

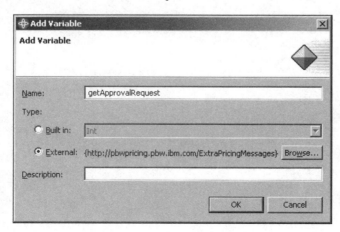

Similarly create a `getApprovalResult` variable for the output and assign it the default Boolean type. After that you should get the following screen:

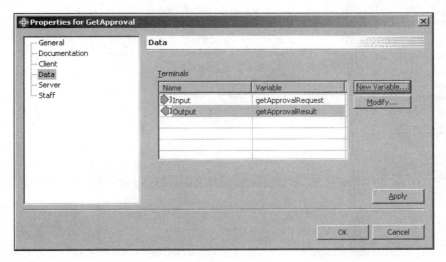

Now we have a variable to feed into the **GetApproval** step. Next, we need to add a small piece of Java code to prepare that input. This input needs to be gathered from the available data at this step in the process.

Add a Java snippet to the canvas with a label, `prepApprovalReq`. Then add the control links as shown:

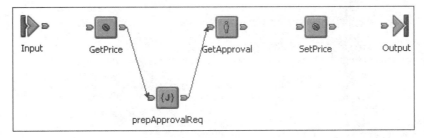

A Java snippet is a piece of Java code that can be used to glue various pieces of the business processes together. For our example, we need to get the three pieces of data from the various variables that already exist to place into the new variable we just added. Fill in the Java snippet by selecting the Java snippet from the canvas, and then press the **Show Java** button. You will get in a window like this:

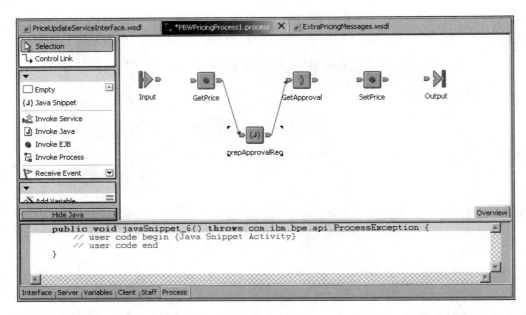

Writing this snippet of Java code is relatively simple. We have a constrained environment where we work with the Java types for the WSDL messages and assign the next variable in the business process to the values from the previously set variables. The code to fill into the snippet is shown here:

```java
public void javaSnippet_6 () throws com.ibm.bpe.api.ProcessException {
    //user code begin {Java Snippet Activity}

    //get a copy of the message we are going to fill in
    GetApprovalRequestMsgMessage msg = getGetApprovalRequest();

    //grab first piece of data from existing variable
    float existingPrice = getGetItemPriceResponse().getResult();

    //grab 2nd piece of data from original input
    float increaseAmt = getInput().getPercent();

    //grab 3rd piece of data form original input
    String itemID = getInput().getItemID();

    //now set this data into our copy of the mesage
    msg.setIncreasePercent(increaseAmt);
    msg.setExistingPrice(existingPrice);
    msg.setItemID(itemID);

    //put the message back into the global data area
    setGetApprovalRequest(msg);

    //user code end
}
```

The number of the snippet you create (`javaSnippet_6`) may vary based on other actions you have already performed in WASD-IE.

Remember that the variables are stored between steps in the process and are available when needed throughout the process. Our job is just to keep the right data going into each step in the process. The WSAD-IE tool is good at helping us along the way. Whenever you are working in the Java editor, you can press *Ctrl-Space* and see a list of choices that match the type you are working with. This helps expedite the snippet coding process.

Make sure there are no syntax errors in the Java snippet. WSAD-IE helps you do this with an added tool. Right-click on errors in the snippet and use the options available in the context menu such as, **Open Declaration, Search**, and so on, to help work your way through this process. Depending on exactly how you created the artifacts, additional imports might be necessary. For our example, you might see an error message about `GetApprovalRequestMsgMessage`. That was the message we defined in a separate WSDL file earlier in this step. There should be an error message in the **Tasks** pane as shown below.

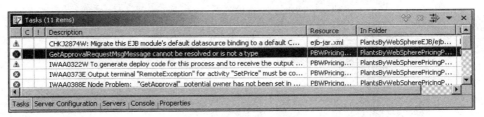

Right-clicking should provide an option of **Quick Fix** to get the proper imports set up. Save the changes and ensure that the error has gone away. If not, right-click on the offending text and choose **Source | Organize Imports**.

We can now complete the staff node in our business process. Right-click on the **GetApproval** activity, and from the **Properties** menu, select the **Staff** option, as shown:

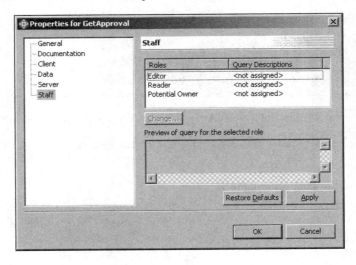

This is where we can assign these staff activities to specific users. Select **Potential Owner** and click on **Change**. The menu that comes up lets us decide who should be performing activities in this business process.

We can assign work items for staff activities to individual users, groups, specific roles, and so on. This selection will then transform into a specific query against a staff plug-in. A staff plug-in is something we will see later when we test this business process at run time.

For our example, we will assign the Potential Owner role. Now all approvals must go through someone that has this user name, Testld1, in the system. Queries that are more complex can be described here. An example would be enabling anyone from a given department to perform the approval:

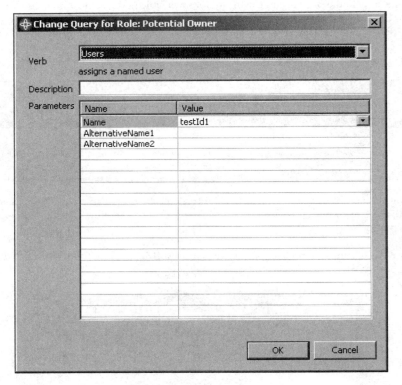

This completes the specification of the staff activity. Make sure you save your work at this point.

The main activities in our business process are now filled in. The next steps are to glue together the remaining activities.

Add More Java Snippets and Control Flow

At this point in the process, the major pieces of the business process are created. What we need next is a few more Java snippets. They will perform the transformations that get the data to the various steps in the process.

The completed process, as far as control links goes, is shown here:

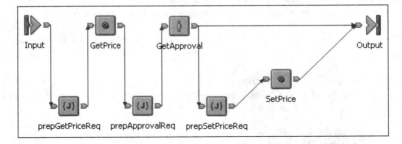

The `prepGetPriceReq` snippet needs this code:

```
public void javaSnippet_7() throws com.ibm.bpe.api.ProcessException {
    //user code begin {Java Snippet Activity}

    //get a copy of the message we are going to fill in
    GetItemPriceRequestMessage msg = getGetItemPriceRequest();

    //get value from input message
    String internalItemID = getInput().getItemID();

    //set value into message
    msg.setInventoryID(internalItemID);

    //set message back into business process
    setGetItemPriceRequest(msg);

    //user code end
}
```

The `prepSetPriceReq` needs this code:

```
public void javaSnippet_8() throws com.ibm.bpe.api.ProcessException {
    // user code begin {Java Snippet Activity}

    //get a copy of the message we are preparing
    SetItemPriceRequestMessage msg = getSetItemPriceRequest();

    //get values we need from existing variables
    float existingPrice = getGetItemPriceResponse().getResult();
    String itemToUpdate = getInput().getItemID();

    //set values into message
    msg.setInventoryID(itemToUpdate);

    //make new price calculation and set result into price
    msg.setPrice(existingPrice * (1 + (getInput().getPercent() / 100)));

    //put the message back as we are ready
    setSetItemPriceRequest(msg);

    //user code end
}
```

Notice the line here where we actually calculate the new price by taking the existing price and doing some multiplication. Other than that, these snippets are taking data that is available in the variables of the business process and getting the right subset of that date to the next step in the business process.

There is one more piece of business logic to consider. If the result of the staff activity is that this price increase is not approved, then we need a path through the business process that will indicate this.

To specify how the control flow after GetApproval should proceed, we need to right-click on the control arrow that goes between GetApproval and prepSetPriceReq. The Properties option should bring up the following display that should be changed as shown:

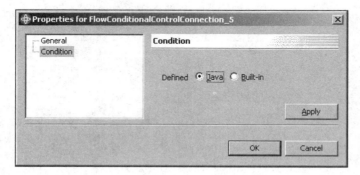

Our condition will be described in Java code. Go back to the main screen and select the same control arrow and we will now see the opportunity to put in some Java code.

The calculation is simply based on the result of our GetApproval step. Place the following code in the Java editor:

```
public boolean controlCondition_FlowNode_5_out_FlowNode_9_in()
    throws com.ibm.bpe.api.ProcessException {
    boolean result = true;

    //user code begin {Condition Expression}
    result = getGetApprovalResult().getValue();

    //user code end
    return result;
}
```

The other control link coming out of GetApproval, which currently goes to Output, needs to be set to otherwise, from the Properties menu, as this is where the business process will proceed if the condition does not evaluate to true. Think of the set of control conditions as a case statement where the true condition is checked first. The change can be made as shown:

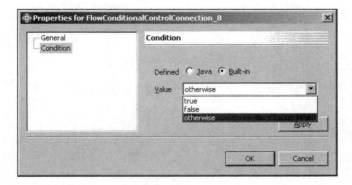

We have only a few more steps to follow to complete our business process.

Perform Additional Necessary Activities

The basics are in place for our process. We need to deal with the business process output and we will be done. The output of a business process that is executed asynchronously also uses a service. What you place underneath this service is pretty much up to you, and probably something that you want to tailor for testing versus what you might want in production. For our simple business process, the desire is to print the ID of the product, the new price, and whether or not the price increase was actually done. This will come out in the console when the business process is executing.

To simplify the process of building this output handler, we will first create a simple Java class. With our project selected, select New | Java | Class, and press Next. Fill in the name of the class as PricerOutput as shown below:

Press Finish and a basic Java editor will open up. Fill in the code as shown:

```
package com.ibm.pbw.pbwpricing;

public class PricerOutput {

    public void PricingComplete(String itemID, float newPrice,
        boolean approved) {

    if (approved) {
      System.out.println("Price uncrease approved");
      System.out.println("ItemID is:");
      System.out.println(itemID);
      System.out.println("New Price is: ");
      System.out.println(newPrice);
    } else {
      System.out.println("Price increase disapproved");
      System.out.println("ItemID is:");
      System.out.println(itemID);
    }
  }
}
```

Now we can build a service from this class to get the output from our business process. With our `PricerOutput.java` selected, right-click and select **New | Service built from**:

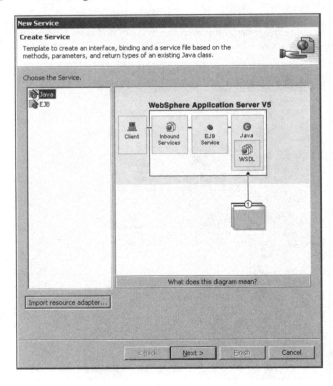

Press **Next** and then select the class and method as shown here:

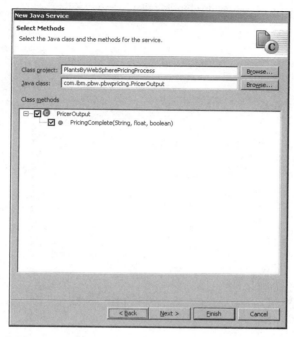

Press **Next** and then arrive here:

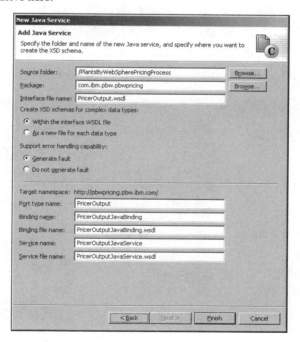

All the default values should be correct and just what we want. Click on Finish and we have now built a service from the Java class, complete with a binding that is ready to use.

Now we can go back to our process and select the Output terminal. From there, we go to the Implementation node from the Properties menu, and fill in the name of the operation that we want to have executed upon completion of our business process. Using the Browse button, pick the new PricerOutput service WSDL file as shown below:

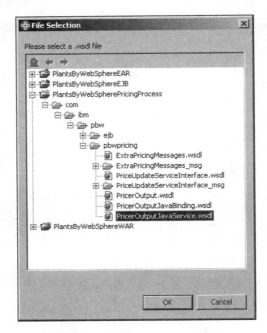

Press OK and this should bring us back to the implementation for Output:

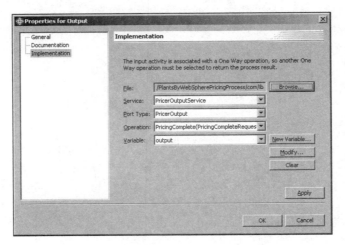

Fill in the rest of the details as shown. As a side effect of this activity, we now have a type for our `output` variable. You can look at the variables now and you should see the output variable to be of type `PricingCompleteRequest`.

In the case of handling the output, we chose the model of bottom up, where we prepared a Java class and then built a service from this Java class. It is also possible to build this service by starting with WSDL and then generating an implementation from the WSDL. This is a matter of choice. In fact, you might have a different service at the end of a business process when it is in production versus when it is in unit test.

As with any activity that is going to be executed, the input to that activity must be prepared. Another Java snippet will help us do that, so we add in **prepOutput**:

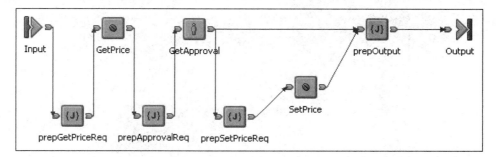

As you can see, we have wired both of the control flows to this snippet before proceeding to the output. Make sure you graphically change the control links. If you do remove the control link between **GetApproval** and **Output** and reestablish a new one between **GetApproval** and **prepOutput**, then you will have to go back and mark it as "otherwise" as was described earlier.

The code to fill in this snippet is:

```
public void javaSnippet_9() throws com.ibm.bpe.api.ProcessException {
    //user code begin {Java Snippet Activity}
    PricingCompleteRequestMessage msg = getOutput();

    //get values I need to fill in the blanks
    boolean approved = getGetApprovalResult().getValue();
    float newPrice = getGetItemPriceResponse().getResult();
    String itemID = getInput().getItemID();

    //set values into message
    msg.setApproved(approved);
    msg.setNewPrice(newPrice);
    msg.setItemID(itemID);

    //put the message back as we are ready
    setOutput(msg);

    //user code end
}
```

We have completed the hard part of creating a business process. Now we have to generate the deployed code, and unit test and debug this business process application. Make sure you save your work.

Generate Code

We have completed our process creation. Right-click on the `PBWPricingProcess1.process` file and select **Enterprise Services | Generate Deploy code**. Select **EJB** for a binding type as shown:

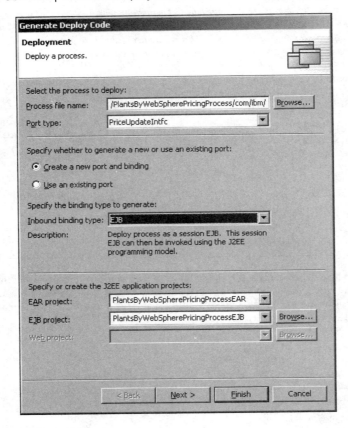

Press **Next**. Take the defaults on this page:

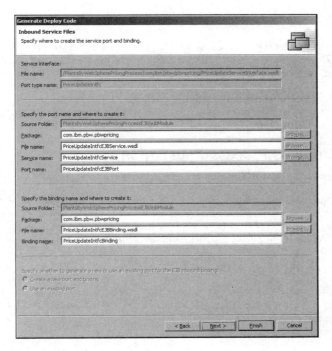

Then make a note of this string on the next page:

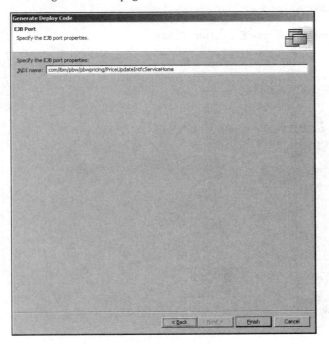

Click on Finish.

We chose the session EJB for our inbound binding. There are three inbound binding choices; Session Bean, JMS – Message-Driven Bean, and SOAP. We will come back later in the chapter to describe the bindings that exist for business processes.

You now have what you need to run in the unit test environment. Select the project and use Export to export the `PlantsByWebSpherePricingProcessEAR`. This will provide you the artifact you need to install the application into the WASE runtime.

Unit Testing a Business Process Application

The WebSphere Studio Application Developer has a rich unit test environment for testing J2EE applications.

WSAD-IE builds upon that base and provides a unit test environment as well. The WSAD-IE test environment allows testing of applications that leverage WASE features as well as all of those supported by the base application server. The WSAD-IE unit-test environment provides the ability to directly unit-test business processes, like the example we created in this chapter.

Runtime and Administration Integration

The exported EAR file from the previous section is nearly a regular EAR file as defined by J2EE. The only thing that is different is that there are artifacts in the EAR file that will be handled by the business process infrastructure during run time.

Before installing the EAR file with the business process in it, the runtime should be properly configured. Other than the normal configuration in the application server, we need to concern ourselves with the business process execution container and the staff plug-ins.

Configuring the Business Process Execution Container

There are three ways to configure the business process execution (BPE) container:

The first way is to configure it during WAS Enterprise installation. This option will create a business process execution container that leverages Cloudscape and the Embedded JMS Provider that ships with WAS. Choose this option if you are going to be testing business processes in a single-user environment:

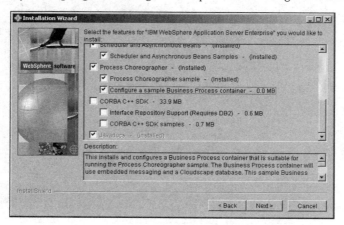

This is found under the custom install option of WebSphere Application Server Enterprise 5.0.

The second method is to use the administration console. Expand the Servers tree in the navigation tree on the left, open the Application Servers link and select your server's link from the main pane and then scroll towards the bottom of the various additional properties, and you will find Business Process Container as shown:

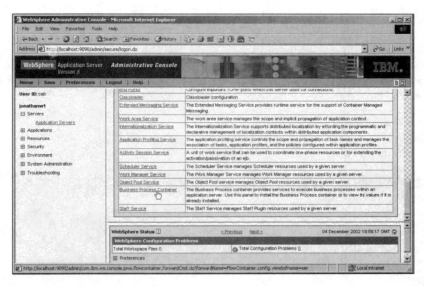

Click on Business Process Container and you will get the following screen:

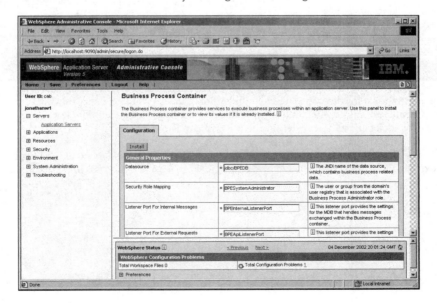

Here you can choose your JMS provider and the queues to be used. You can also choose the database that you want the business process container to use. Various security settings for JMS can also be entered at this point. To install the container, add a JMS user and password and hit the Install button. Note that once you've installed this you can't change any of the values again.

The final path that can be used to install the BPE container is via a `jacl` script, which ships as a sample. Look for the `bpeconfig.jacl` in the `ProcessChoreographer\samples` directory in your WebSphere installation. This script is invoked using the standard `wsadmin` model:

```
wsadmin -f bpeconfig.jacl
```

The script leads you through a series of choices about how to configure the container. Choices about which JMS provider and which database to use are key prompts in the script.

Configuring the Staff Plug-In

Before configuring the staff plug-in, go back to WSAD-IE and look at the properties for PlantsByWebSpherePricingProcess service project, and select the Staff node:

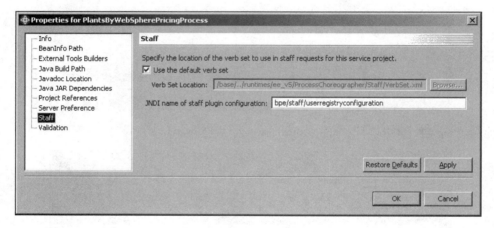

The JNDI name shown for the staff plug-in configuration above is what we need to make sure exists in the runtime environment. This is what links the output of the tooling during run time. For our example, we will use the defaults. A default staff provider for the user registry is provided.

The first screen shows the definition of the staff provider. This includes the name of the plug-in file that is going to execute those staff queries, which we placed into our business process. In our case, we are going to execute those queries against the user registry on a Windows 2000 machine.

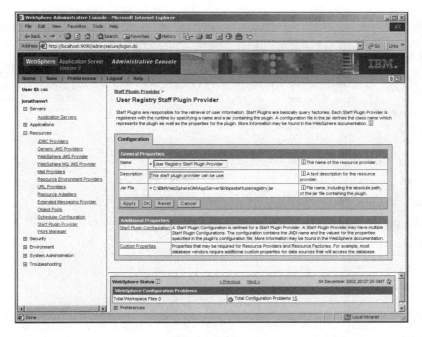

The second screen, shown next, shows the name of the transformation file that will be used to convert the staff queries into something that can be executed by the underlying staff provider:

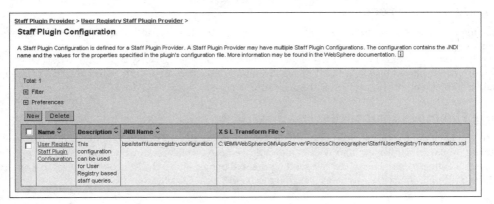

Notice that the JNDI name in the second screenshot matches up with the one shown in the WSAD-IE project page shown earlier.

The Staff Support Service component acts as an intermediary between Staff Queries as defined at application development time and the actual directory infrastructure of a production application server.

Specialized staff plug-ins provide access to specific directories such as LDAP directories or the UserRegistry. They are used to implement abstract staff query verbs for a given deployment environment.

When a business prcoess is deployed, the JNDI name of a specialized plug-in is provided as a deployment descriptor variable. During the business process deployment, the internal Staff Support Service component is invoked to deploy a particular staff query. It converts the staff query extensibility element using a verb conversion XSLT.

Predefined Staff Query Verbs are provided in the context of flow tooling and are utilized by the Staff Support Service component. Each verb defines an abstract Staff Query that can be defined without knowledge about the specific directory infrastructure. The predefined "verbs" used are:

- User
- Group Members
- Department Members
- Role Members
- Manager of Employee
- Person
- Group Search
- Native

> Note, while running business processes that leverage staff support, global security on WebSphere needs to be turned on.

Install Business Processes

Installing business processes into the BPE container happens when you install an EAR file. There are no special steps. You can install business processes using `wsadmin`, the administration console interface, or in any other way that works for you. During any of these, the business process deployment tools will be called transparently as part of installing the J2EE application. Follow the installation instructions described in Chapter 6 to upload our `PlantsByWebSpherePricingProcess.ear` file.

Testing Business Processes

Once you have got the business process installed, you can use the web client to help test and manage business processes. However, before we can do this we need to make sure we set up the correct permissions and user for the process. Recall that we set the potential owner of the GetApproval process to `TestId1`, and that the Staff plug-in user registry was just going to be the local OS registry.

Therefore, when we use the BPE web client, we need to log on with the correct user and permissions to be able to approve the process. To do this we first need to create a new user in the local OS. For Windows 2000 this is condigured through Administrative Tools | Computer Management:

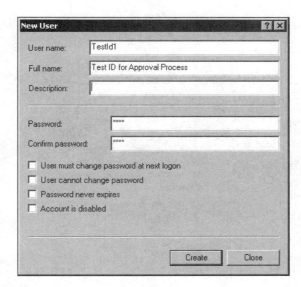

You also need to give this user additional operating system privledges (Act as part of the operating system). This can be set through the Local Security Policy Administrative tool.

Now make sure the security is enabled for the server – refer to Chapter 13 for more details on how to do this.

The BPE web client is located at http://localhost:9080/bpe/webclient. The webclient is intended primarily to enable application developers to easily test business processes. You will first be prompted to log in. This will determine the user and thus if you have permission to control any of the processes. Log-in as TestId1.

A default initial screen is shown next:

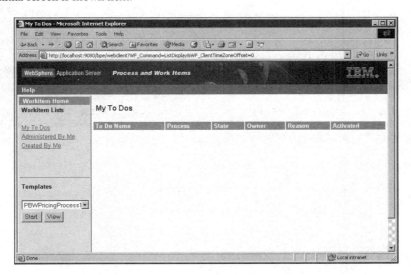

From this client we can create a new instance of a business process by selecting the template and clicking on **Start**. Our screenshot has the default choice shown, as it is the only one on the server being used. From here, we will move on to a screen like this:

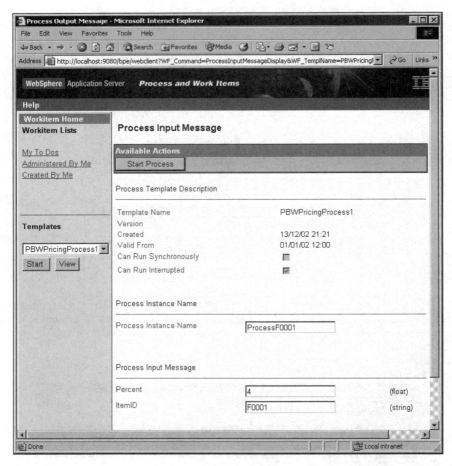

Next, we can actually start the instance of the business process. After entering valid values for the ItemId and Percent that are desired, and then starting the business process, we are lead to a blank My To Dos screen. Refreshing the My To Dos link again, shows our process:

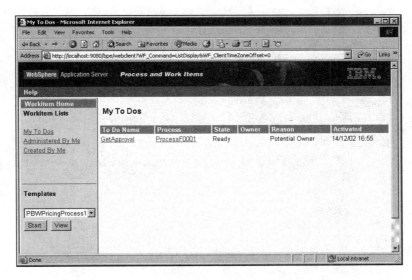

We are interested in the new one that is ready. If we click on it (**GetApproval**), we are lead here:

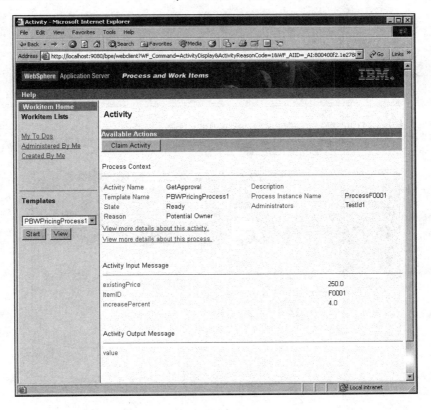

We can claim the activity and then decide if we are going to "approve" this price increase. After pressing **Claim Activity**, we are brought to the following screen:

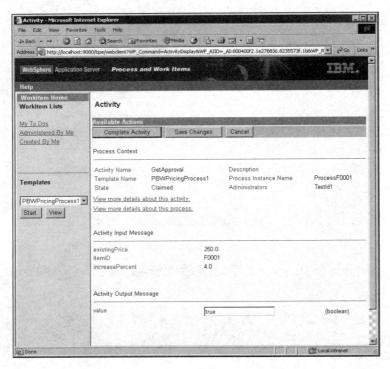

We mark it to **true**, to approve the price increase and then can complete the activity. We could temporarily save our choice, but not complete the business process. However, we can to complete this activity and see if it ends properly. After pressing **Complete Acivity**, we are lead to:

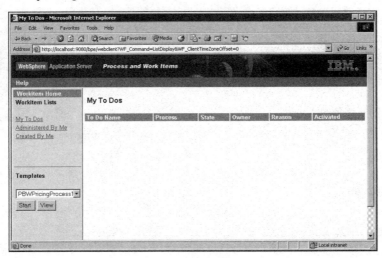

This means that we have completed our workitem and there are no more workitems at this time.

That was a quick tour through configuring the runtime and running business processes in the runtime. The combination of the admin console and the web client for business processes let us easily manage business processes in the WASE environment.

Debugging a Business Process

It is possible that your business processes will not all work the first time you try to execute them in the unit test environment or in the runtime. Debugging business processes can be done using the same debuggers that are used for debugging other J2EE programs in WebSphere. However, in addition to these more traditional debugging capabilities, WSAD-IE comes with a business process debugger. This allows business processes to be debugged at a level of abstraction similar to that used while constructing the business process. The business process debugger is shown below:

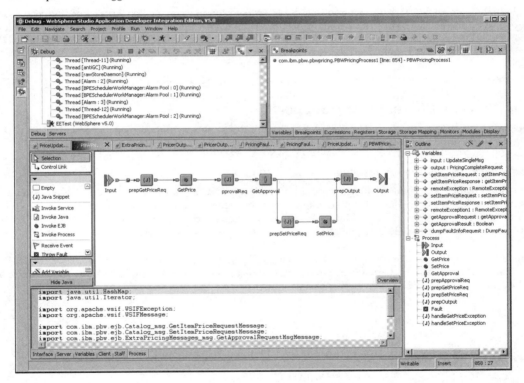

As you can see from the display, debugging takes place at the process level. A breakpoint is set between the Input activity and the prepGetPriceReq activity. From a breakpoint, one can inspect the current values of the variables in the business process. Notice that all of the views available when you develop a business process are available on the debugger, acting as the source for the business process you are debugging.

Basic navigation through the business process uses a series of capabilities to Run the Process, Step Into an activity, Step Over an activity, Step Out of an activity, or Run to Completion. These options are available as icons in the Process Debug window.

These capabilities for debugging processes will let you find problems such as:

❑ Incorrectly wired activities (for example, outputs connected to the wrong inputs)

❑ Incorrect condition branching in transition conditions

❑ Infinite loops in processes

These debugging capabilities become more valuable as processes that are more complex involve sub-processes and complex conditions are built.

If you need to drop into source code level debugging, it can be done at any point in the process using **Step Into Source Code** and **Step Over Source Code** facilities, which are available as icons in the **Process Debug** window.

This debugger will work against an application server that is part of the unit test environment or against any application server that is configured and running on the machine. There is a specific port on the application server and debugger agent process that coordinates the interactions between the debugger interface and the application server. The application server must be configured to run with debug turned on.

Instructions that are more complete are provided with the WSAD-IE help text.

More Process Choreography Support

There is still more to Process Choreography support in WASE. Going into more detail would be beyond the scope of this book. Some of the additional capabilities are summarized here.

Interfacing with Business Processes

In our example, we generated an EJB for our business logic and used a web client to test out our business processes. The web client that was used to test our business process is not intended as the way that production applications will access business processes. Custom-written applications will be created that deal with workitems and handling the initiation and lifecycle of business processes.

In addition to the web client, the WSAD-IE tooling will generate three interfaces to a business process. In addition to these generated artifacts, there is a more direct interface to the business process engine. In total then there are five ways to easily access business processes:

❑ Web client

❑ EJB generated by WSAD-IE

❑ MDB generated by WSAD-IE

❑ SOAP interface generated by WSAD-IE

❑ Direct interface to business process engine

These will be covered one at a time with the exception of the web client, which we have already covered in detail earlier.

❑ **EJB generated by WSAD-IE**
When you select the EJB option, a session bean is generated that can then be called from anywhere in the J2EE server or from any J2EE client. The session bean interface for our example is shown below:

```
public interface PriceUpdaterIntfcService extends javax.ejb.EJBObject {
   /**
   /* UpdateSingle
   /* @generated
   */
   public void UpdateSingle(java.lang.String argItemID, float argPercent)
      throws javax.ejb.EJBException, java.rmi.RemoteException;
}
```

This EJB has an internal implementation that handles the necessary interactions with the business process container. The implementation is obviously different if a non-interruptable business process is called as opposed to the launching of an interruptable business process.

❑ **MDB generated by WSAD-IE**
If we want to launch our business process by sending a JMS message, then we can use this option, which generates a message-driven bean (MDB). Our example business process generates the following MDB interfaces:

```
/**
    * onMessage
    * @generated
    */
   public void onMessage(javax.jms.Message msg) {
     try {
        executeFlowOperation(msg);
     } catch (WSIFException e) {
        e.printStackTrace();
     } catch (javax.jms.JMSException e) {
        e.printStackTrace();
     } catch (ProcessException e) {
        e.printStackTrace();
     } catch (javax.naming.NamingException e) {
        e.printStackTrace();
     } catch (javax.ejb.CreateException e) {
        e.printStackTrace();
     }
   }
```

This is a normal onMessage() method in terms of signature, like that which we would expect to find on any MDB. The implementation has the interesting call to executeFlowOperation() method. This calls a number of other methods internally and handles the calling or initiation of the business process. All you have to do is configure the MDB as part of the business process application, and you can send a message to start a business process.

❑ **SOAP interface generated by WSAD-IE**
The SOAP interface merely creates a SOAP binding and service for our original WSDL file named `PriceUpdaterIntfc`. There is nothing special about this, as it is normal web services capability being leveraged.

❑ **Direct interface to business process engine**
The implementation of the MDB and the EJB session bean interfaces to the business process, are all using an interface from the package `com.ibm.bpe.api`. This package has some key interfaces in it that can be called directly from any Java code that has access to the application server and can call session beans. The `com.ibm.bpe.api.BusinessProcessService` interface is actually another EJB Session bean that wrappers all of the capabilities that one might want to use in calling, initiating and working with business processes. Some of the key methods on the `BusinessProcessService` interface are listed here:

  ❑ `call()`
  Creates and executes a process instance from the specified process template. This is how to start a non-interruptable business process.

  ❑ `claim()`
  Claims a ready activity instance for user processing.

  ❑ `complete()`
  Completes a claimed activity instance.

  ❑ `delete()`
  Deletes the specified top-level process instance and its sub-processes from the database.

  ❑ `getWorkItems()`
  Retrieves workitem assignments for the specified process instance or activity, depending on which variation of the method is used.

  ❑ `initiate()`
  Creates a named process instance. This is how to start an interruptable business process

  ❑ `query()`
  Retrieves selected object properties persistently stored in the business process container configuration database.

  ❑ `sendEvent()`
  Sends the specified event to the specified process instance.

Many of these methods have multiple signatures. You are encouraged to consult the Javadoc that accompanies WASE for more details.

Activity Types

In addition to the staff nodes, Java snippets, and EJB calls that were described in the preceding example, other things can be called as part of an activity implementation. These include:

❑ **Services**
According to the service-oriented architecture, anything that can be expressed as a service can be invoked. This would include calls to external web services, JavaBeans, and JMS calls. The JMS activity in an asynchronous process is worth detailing. If an activity makes an asynchronous JMS call via a service, the business process engine will wait for a response to be received on a reply-to queue, before proceeding to the next step. This pattern fits well into the asynchronous style of long-running business processes.

❑ **Process**

It is an activity that represents a separate business process that is being invoked within a larger one. Unlike the Block activity, the Process activity is a complete process, and can exist on its own outside the primary process, and is used by other processes.

❑ **Events**

The Event activity represents an activity in the business process that waits for one or more external events to happen before continuing. These external events come in through interfaces to the business process via the EJB session bean. We would have seen more methods on our example session bean presented earlier if we had used Events in our business process.

❑ **Blocks**

These constructs let you build more complex business processes. Looping is a distinct activity that you create as a subset of your primary process. The loop will repeat the activities within it as long as the condition within it remains true. This is also known as a "while-do" loop. When a false condition is encountered, the loop is exited, and the next activity in the process is executed. Use the Block activity to simplify your diagram by decomposing your process into individual distinct portions; each representing an entire nested business process that runs within a larger one.

❑ **Loops**

This activity is a specialized form of a Block that can be iterated so that the operation executes more than once during the business process. The execution of the loop is controlled by a conditional expression, and will continue to execute as long as this conditional expression evaluates to true.

❑ **Empty Activity**

An empty activity has no defined implementation and can be used for two reasons; it can act as a placeholder in the design stage to be filled out later, and it can be used when a fault needs to be caught and suppressed.

Compensation

Within the Service activity type is yet another kind of service. This is known as a **Compensation**. The properties panel for a service is shown here:

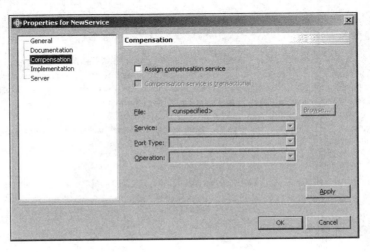

As you can see, there is a compensation selection. This means that for every service that is invoked, a corresponding compensating service can be registered. This means we can register two services for each service icon on our business process.

A "compensatable service" enables compensation for the operations of a primary service, by associating the primary service with an appropriate compensation service. A compensatable service is invoked from within a compensation sphere that has been created by the business process container. When a compensatable service is run, it runs a primary operation and registers information with a compensation coordinator to enable compensation if required. Then, if the business process cannot continue forward, all the registered compensating services are executed.

The use of compensation in business processes is shown in the following figure:

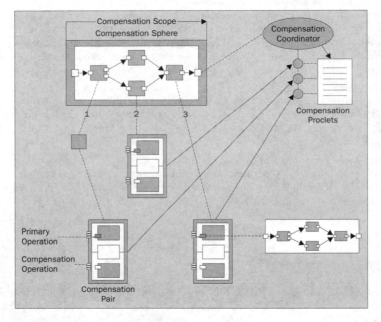

This figure shows a business process that calls several actions, some of which use operations of compensatable services. Each compensation pair runs its primary operation then registers with the compensation coordinator, creating a proclet to be used if compensation is needed. When a business process is started, it creates a new compensation coordinator to start a compensation sphere.

Each compensation pair called as a node of the business process registers with the compensation coordinator, runs its primary operation, and stores the information needed to run its compensation operation if the business process needs to be compensated.

A fault node that is reached at a top-level process (not a sub-process) will cause compensation to be executed. The compensation service invokes proclets in reverse order of the time when their primary services completed.

This completes the description of workflow capabilities within WASE.

Business Rules

The concept of dynamic business policy management is a key feature of WASE. This capability further enhances our ability to implement and maintain business models, with a strong emphasis on maintenance.

Various business policies or rules need constant changing based on external forces such as economic trends. Some examples are pricing algorithms and customer classification into categories for determining customer status, purchase discounts, and so on. Government regulations also change frequently, sometimes back and forth, for things such as tax rates and retirement ages.

Many of these dynamic and policy-driven business processes, which are implemented using application server features, depend on data-driven algorithms. These implementations must be able to cope with the often-changing requirements that are typical in normal business lifecycles. The **Business Rules** facility, also known as **BRBeans**, provides a framework for managing this kind of dynamic business logic.

The primary objectives of BRBeans include:

❑ **Isolation of volatile business logic from application code**
Business logic and application code are implemented separately. Any J2EE application component can leverage business rules. This includes servlets, J2EE clients, and EJBs. Business rules themselves must be implemented as Java classes. Application code interacts with business rule implementations exclusively through well-known interfaces, which maintains this important abstraction.

❑ **Keeping knowledge of business rule implementation external to the application**
Variable business rule data is not embedded in the application calling rule and can be easily accessed with the Rule Management Application. More details on the Rule Management Application will come later in the chapter.

❑ **Administrative maintenance of business logic**
Application behavior can be changed through an administrative process using the Rule Management Application or applications customized for specific business users. The Rule Management Application and application-specific management applications can modify business behavior in two ways:

　❑　By specifying a different rule implementor for a BRBeans rule

　❑　By changing variable business rule data

The rest of our discussion on rules will demonstrate these benefits and provide details on how to leverage the rules capabilities in WASE.

The Role for Rules

Rules provide us with an additional option when implementing business logic. Refering back to the earlier discussion about application structure, there are actually a couple of places where rules can plug in. The most obvious requirement for rules-based capabilities comes in implementing the business model, independent of the presentation logic. The business model is the point in the application architecture where business logic and decision making is occurring. A modified application structure is presented to provide a view as to where rules fit in. It is expected that rules either will be called from session beans within the business model or potentially be accessed directly from the presentation layer applications.

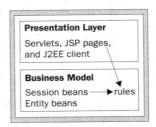

While it is also possible to have rules used to provide a customized view or presentation, our focus in this chapter will deal with rules and how they are used in business logic. The WebSphere Personalization product, which runs on top of the WAS, actually uses the same underlying infrastructure and mechansism as is described in this section. WebSphere Personalization focuses on customized views and presentations.

Rules provide us with a vehicle to separate and independently manage pieces of business logic. Rules can and should be applied in the application architecture in places where business policy is represented in code. If there is a reasonable chance that the business policy can change and a way to create an abstraction of that policy exists, then rules should be considered. One example that we will use periodically in this section is classification of customers into categories such as silver, gold, and platinum, to determine things such as discounts and benefits received. Data that can change might be the threshold of purchases that would put one into the next category. Algorithms that might change could be how the calculation is done. Maybe we give "double counting" during certain times of the year. This is similar to how an airlines changes the way it calculates its frequent flier miles.

In fact, it is often the case that there are a number of rules that apply to do proper classification. Again, in a commercial or retail setting, some times of the year or of a business cycle might require more rules than others to determine how to proceed with the rest of the business logic.

Before diving into the rest of the concepts and details of rules, let us go into some development process thinking. Should rules be created first in the development process and then leveraged as business processes or implemented as part of the business model? Should existing applications be re-engineered to take advantage of rules?

These are questions that do not have a universally correct answer. However, if your organization has a growing set of reusable assets being constructed, then using rules as an architectural factoring mechanism is a true possibility. Just as reusable entity beans and reusable session beans, each with proper interfaces, can be built up over time, a set of reusable rules can be a valuable asset. Rules, and more precisely the rule implementations, are fine-grained reuse opportunities. It may be the case that only higher-level components are the reuse objective and if so, then rules can be considered in the role of implementation technology.

As an implementation technology, rules are about creating flexible applications, where behaviors can be altered at run time, thus avoiding redeployment.

Who changes the rules or the rules data in a system that leverages Business Rules? It is possible that rules can enable a non-programmer class of users to actually alter the behavior of the system. While users can alter system behavior today by providing alternative input data to a running system, rule-based systems allow applications to evolve and respond not only to different data inputs, but to an evolved set of business logic as well. This idea of having a non-programmer changing the behavior of the application in this way is a new "role" or at least an enhanced role. The idea that these kinds of changes can occur without a request to the application development team is appealing. On the other hand, it suggests strongly that the interface used by these non-programmers must be carefully designed and contain rich validation code.

The complete set of possibilities for rules will perhaps become clearer as we dig into the concepts and learn more about creating and deploying rules and applications that leverage those rules.

Rule Programming Concepts

Leveraging the Business Rules support in WebSphere is a simple process. We need to understand a few key concepts before the process of using, creating, and modifying rules can begin. The key concepts to understand are trigger points, Rule Management, Rule Implementor, and the business rules infrastructure that pulls it all together. The following diagram provides a big-picture view as to how these pieces fit together:

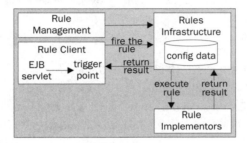

Rule Client and Trigger Point

Let's start with a J2EE application that wants to take advange of rules. The first thing to do is to find the places in the application that have code segments that are desirable to factor out into rules. **Trigger points** are placed in the code at these points instead of the application logic that is being factored into a rule. A trigger point is the place where the call is made into the rules infrastructure.

Underneath the trigger points is the trigger point framework. This framework provides a link to the Rule Infrastructure. The trigger point framework takes the client request and sends it into the infrastructure where the Rule Implementors are selected and executed, and where the results are formulated and formatted. This might sound like a lot of work to do just to execute some business logic. The BRBeans infrastructure also has inbuilt caching. A cache of rules is kept locally, avoiding doing costly rule lookups repeatedly. An administratively controlled setting indicates the frequency of cache refresh.

Part of the trigger point framework involves something called **strategies**. A strategy, in this context, is a mechanism to control the process of triggering a rule, or set of rules. We could assert that these are rules that effect how rules are found, filtered, fired, and combined, but that would further overload the "rule" term. When a trigger point is called, four kinds of strategies are used for customization and modification; they are:

❑ **Finding Strategy**
This strategy controls how the rules are found. The default finding strategy chooses active rules, where the current date is in between the start and end dates of the rule. A precedence setting is used to determine the order in which the rules are returned. Precedence is set using the Rule Management Application. The highest precedence is the lowest value. We will describe the Rule Management Application later in the section entitled *Configuring Rules*. For now, it is sufficient to know that the Rule Management Application is a utility that comes as part of the BRBeans support in WebSphere, and is used by those managing applications that leverage rules.

❑ **Filtering Strategy**
The filtering strategy lets the rules that are found be filtered before firing. A finding strategy can sometimes return many rules. It may or may not be desirable to fire more than one rule for a given trigger point. The values that can be set for the filtering strategy include:

   ❑ Accept Any: Use all rules returned by the finding strategy
   ❑ Accept One: One rule is expected to be found
   ❑ Accept First: Only the first rule found by the framework will be fired
   ❑ Accept Last: Only the last rule found by the framework will be fired

❑ **Combining Strategy**
The combining strategy provides different ways to handle rules' results. The values possible here are:

   ❑ Return All: The results of all fired rules are returned
   ❑ Return First: The result of the first rule fired is returned
   ❑ Return Last: The result of the last rule fired is returned
   ❑ Return AND: The results are combined based on the logical AND operator
   ❑ Return OR: The results are combined based on the logical OR operator
   ❑ Throw Violation: Returns a true if all fired rules are successful

❑ **Firing Strategy**
This strategy determines the order in which rules are fired and the parameters that are passed to each one. The default firing strategy fires the rules in the same order in which they are returned, passing in the same set of parameters to each rule.

Custom strategies can be created if the defaults provided are not what are desired for a particular application or set of applications.

Rules and Rule Implementors

BRBeans supports two kinds of rules: classifier rules and base rules.

Classifier rules return a classification based on the rule logic and available data. Classifier rules can be used to determine the ways in which variables are classified, and are returned in the form of a `java.lang.Object`, which is often just a `java.lang.String`. Classifier rules are triggered with the `TriggerPoint.triggerClassifier()` method.

A classifier rule is used to compute a classification for a particular business situation. The classification returned is required to be a `String`. For instance, a Plants-By-WebSphere customer may be classified into Gold, Silver, and Bronze categories, based on their spending history.

Base rules are the most common type of rule used, and are triggered with the `TriggerPoint.trigger()` method. Base rules return `java.lang.Object`. There are a number of base rules:

❑ **Derivation rule**
A rule that uses an algorithm to return a value. It can return any type of value that makes sense in the business context in which it is used. For example, a derivation rule may calculate a discount or compute the total price of an order.

❑ **Constraint rule**
A rule that confirms that an operation has met all of its obligations, and that a particular constraint has been met. For instance, it may check that a value entered by an external user is within legal bounds. BRBeans provides a special return type: `com.ibm.websphere.brb.ConstraintReturn`, which can be returned by the constraint rule. A `ConstraintReturn` object contains a Boolean value, and if it is false, it can contain information that can be used to produce an external message explaining what constraint was not met.

❑ **Invariant rules**
A rule that ensures that multiple changes made by an operation are properly related to one another.

The state of a rule in the infrastructure is what determines if it can actually be used at run time by a client. Rules can have one of five states:

❑ **In effect**
This means that the BRBeans rule is active and is available for use. This is the state a rule needs to be in so that it can be fired.

❑ **Scheduled**
This state indicates that the rule is set to be in effect as some future date.

❑ **Expired**
This state means that the rule is no longer active and has no future time set for it to take effect.

❑ **Invalid**
This indicates that there are configuration errors in the rule.

❑ **Unavailable**
This state means that the rule is not ready for use.

BRBeans can also be configured with a firing location. A local firing location tells the infrastructure that the client and the Rule Implementor are in the same server. This information allows the infrastructure to make optimizations. It is configurable via the Rule Management Application.

BRBeans Rule Implementors are Java classes that provide implementation for the business logic that can be factored out of the application and placed under the management of BRBeans.

Rule Infrastructure

The **Rule Infrastructure** pulls together the clients that have trigger points and the implementations of rules. The Rule Infrastructure is the rest of the implementation code that makes up the BRBean's implementation in WebSphere. It has the basic machinery for holding the configuration information. It has the logic for executing the strategies that come into the infrastructure through the trigger point framework.

Management Client and Tools

The **Rule Management Application** is a tool that comes as part of WASE. It is used for administering and maintaining BRBeans rules. The tool is an interface into the Rule Infrastructure. It allows the browsing and modification of BRBeans rule configuration data such as rule name, implementation class, start and end date, and initialization parameters.

471

This application is primarily used by developers to test rules and applications that are leveraging rules. End users are unlikely to use this tool.

However, the programming interfaces used by the implementation of the Rule Management Application are also available to be used by developers to build custom Rule Management Applications. These are standard Java and J2EE interfaces. One of the key benefits of business rules is the ability to turn over the management of rules to the business people who know more about what they want to change and when they want to change things. Obviously, exposing these capabilities must be done carefully and opening up control of the entire rules environment is not something that would be commonplace. It is expected that specified business situations will require specific pieces of the rule environment to be exposed. Therefore, programming interfaces are provided so that custom applications can be built.

The Rule Management Application allows the import and export of rule configuration data as XML files. This can be used to move configuration data between various servers in an organization.

Summarizing Rule Concepts

The development process for leveraging business rules involves deciding on trigger points in the code and then ensuring that the necessary Rule Implementors are available. Once these two components are in place, then testing of the application can take place. The Rule Management Application facilitates configuration and testing of BRBeans applications.

The run-time flow for a rule-enabled application is as follows:

1. Client code triggers the rule infrastructure passing in parameters to be used by Rule Implementors.

2. Rule Infrastructure decides which rules are to be fired for the particular trigger point, given the inputs provided by the calling application and what is configured in the configuration data.

3. Rules Infrastructure triggers specific rules, which are linked to Rule Implementors.

4. Rule Implementors run using input information from the trigger point and specific configuration held in the configuration database to execute the rule.

5. Rule Infrastructure takes results from rule firings and prepares a response back to the client code that fired the rule.

These basic concepts should now have us prepared to dig into the programming interfaces to be used.

Basic Rule Usage Interfaces

The basic interface for using a rule is a trigger point. A trigger point is placed in the code wherever a rule needs to be executed. The code for a sample rule firing is shown below. This code could be placed into a servlet, session bean, or J2EE client:

```
/**
 * Trigger a rule to get the customer type (status), based on the amount
 * of money spent.
 * The type will be either gold, silver, or bronze.
```

```
   * @param p_moneySpent The amount of money spent.
   * @return an object containing the type of customer.
   * @throws BusinessRuleBeansException
   */

  public Object checkCustomerType(double p_moneySpent)
      throws BusinessRuleBeansException {

    //firing params on the ruleImplementor
    Double[] params ={new Double(p_moneySpent)};

    //triggerClassifier invoked to find and fire the rule of type Classifier
    Object result=standardTp.triggerClassifier (

      null,              //the target parameter on the RuleImplementor,
                         //which is the target object of the TriggerPoint

      params,            //firing parameter on the RuleImplementor,
                         //which is RuleValueForRange

      classifyCustomersRuleFullyQualifiedName); //the full name of the
                                               //Classifier Rule to find

      return (java.lang.String)result;  // we know it is a string in this case
  }
```

We will actually look at the associated rule and Rule Implementor in the next section.

The example above is one of many types of rule firings. There are a number of interfaces associated with the `TriggerPoint` interface. The types of rule firings include:

❏ **Simple**

A simple trigger point is used to trigger a rule or rules specified by name. This type of trigger point is used by invoking the trigger method on an instance of the `TriggerPoint` class. All rules with the specified name will be triggered and the results combined using the combining strategy specified on the `TriggerPoint` object. This type of trigger point only finds rules that are marked as not being classifiers.

❏ **Classifier**

This type is what was used in the example above. A classifier trigger point is identical to a simple trigger point except that it only finds rules marked as being classifiers. These are rules whose purpose is to determine what sort of business situation is present and return a classification string indicating the result. Usually these rules are used as part of a situational trigger point, but they can be triggered on their own too. This type of trigger point is used by invoking the `triggerClassifier()` method on an instance of the `TriggerPoint` class.

❏ **Situational**

A situational trigger point is used when the rule or rules to be triggered depend on the business situation. It is the most complex of the methods that are available. The complex trigger method, `triggerSituational()`, has a sequence of two steps, the first step to find the classification which is fed into the second step. The second step triggers rules that have the classification equal to the value returned in the first step.

Creating Rules

Rules and Rule Implementors are separated when we speak of BRBeans. Rule Implementors are where the code goes that implements a rule. The "rule" abstraction is aware of a Rule Implementor, but has no code itself.

Rule Implementors are Java classes and must implement the `RuleImplementor` interface. The three main methods on this interfacea are:

❑   `init()`
    This method provides the initial state to the rule implementor and is called by the framework before the rule is fired. The initialization parameters can actually be configured by the Rule Management Application.

❑   `fire()`
    This method implements business logic and returns results. This is the main logic of the rule. This is the method that gets invoked by the Rules Infrastructure.

❑   `getDescription()`
    This method returns a string containing a description of the Rule Implementor.

The following snippet shows a simplified `init()` method of a Rule Implementor:

```
public void init(Object [] parms,  String [ ] dependentRules,
    String userDefinedData, IRuleCopy rule)throws BusinessRuleBeansException {

    //Store the initialization parameters in member variables of the object.

    preferredLevel = ((Integer)parms [0]).intValue();
    goldLevel = ((Integer)parms [1]).intValue();
    platinumLevel = ((Integer)parms [2]).intValue();
    initialized = true;  //set implementor member variable

}
```

We can see from this initialization that there will be three possible results. The values for those three possible results are loaded into the variables `preferredLevel`, `goldLevel`, and `platinumLevel` from the database, which is part of the Rule Infrastructure. These values can be changed independent of the business logic or the application, if the business desired to change them.

The primary method is the `fire()` method and this is shown below:

```
public Object fire(TriggerPoint tp, Object target, IRuleCopy rule,
    java.lang.Object []parms)throws BusinessRuleBeansException {

    String classification = null;
    int amount = 0;
    if (initialized) {  // check implementor member variable
        amount = ((Integer)parms [0 ]).intValue();
        if(amount > = platinumLevel){
        classification = PLATINUM_LEVEL;
    } else if(amount > = goldLevel){
```

```
      classification = GOLD_LEVEL;
    } else if(amount > = preferredLevel){
      classification = PREFERRED_LEVEL;
    } else {
      classification = LEVEL_NA;
    }
    return classification;
}
```

This Rule Implementor simply takes the inbound amount and the amounts established at initialization, and performs some simple logic to determine what classification this particular customer should have at this time.

The Rule Implementor shown above was focused on the primary logic path. A helper class that comes with the Business Rules support, called `com.ibm.websphere.brb.implementor`, should be used while building Rule `Implementors`. This class provides help in checking that the valid number of parameter values are provided so that the required parameters are indeed set to something besides `null`. This helper class throws the `BRBeansIllegalArgumentException`.

Rule Implementors Invocation

When a rule is fired for the first time, the following sequence of events takes place:

❑   An instance of the `RuleImplementor` class is created using the default constructor.

❑   The `init()` method is called, passing the initialization parameters defined for the rule.

❑   The `fire()` method is called to elicit the Rule Implementor's behavior.

It is guaranteed by the rules infrastructure that the `init()` method is called at least once before the `fire()` method is called for the first time. Once the `RuleImplementor` is instantiated, the Rule Infrastructure caches it so that it does not have to be created and initialized again the next time that rule is fired. On subsequent fires, only the `RuleImplementor` instance's `fire()` method is called, not its `init()` method. Hence, the `RuleImplementor` is generally initialized only once, but can be fired many times.

Provided Rule Implementations

Before creating new Rule Implementors, it is important to note that a large number of Rule Implementors are supplied by WAS. These can be used as the implementors for new rules that you define. The following implementors are in the `com.ibm.websphere.brb.implementor` package:

❑   `RuleAND`
    A rule comprising two or more rules that are all fired and their results combined via AND logic.

❑   `RuleOR`
    A rule comprising two or more constraint-type rules that are all fired and the OR logic applied on their results.

❑   `RuleConstant`
    A derivation rule that simply returns a persistent constant.

❑   `RuleConvert`
    A derivation rule used to compute and return the result from a generic conversion performed with the formula $mx + b$.

475

❑ RuleIfThenElse
A rule comprising three rules. First, a constraint-type rule is fired to determine which of the other two rules to fire. If the first rule returns a true ConstraintReturn or a java.lang.Boolean with a value of true, then the second rule is fired, otherwise the third rule is fired.

❑ RuleEqual
A constraint-type rule algorithm that returns a true ConstraintReturn if x = a, where x arrives as a firing parameter and a is either provided as an initialization parameter or as a firing parameter.

❑ RuleGreaterThan
A constraint-type rule algorithm that returns a true ConstraintReturn if x > a, where x arrives as a firing parameter and a is either provided as an initialization parameter or as a firing parameter.

❑ RuleGreaterThanEqual
A constraint-type rule algorithm that returns a true ConstraintReturn if x >= a, where x arrives as a firing parameter and a is either provided as an initialization parameter or as a firing parameter.

❑ RuleLessThan
A constraint-type rule algorithm that returns a true ConstraintReturn if x < a, where x arrives as a firing parameter and a is either provided as an initialization parameter or as a firing parameter.

❑ RuleLessThanEqual
A constraint-type rule algorithm that returns a true ConstraintReturn if x <= a, where x arrives as a firing parameter and a is either provided as an initialization parameter or as a firing parameter.

❑ RuleLink
It rule fires a dependent rule and returns the result of the dependent rule. This implementor is primarily used to give a rule a second name.

❑ RuleIsNull
A constraint-type rule algorithm that returns a true ConstraintReturn if the input is null.

❑ RuleMerger
A rule comprising three or more rules, one of which is a merger rule. All but the merger rule are fired to get a set of results. The merger rule is then fired to arrive at a combined result.

❑ RuleRange
A constraint-type rule algorithm that returns a true ConstraintReturn if a <= x <= b, where x arrives as a firing parameter and a and b are either provided as initialization parameters, or as firing parameters.

❑ RuleRangeNonInclusive
A constraint-type rule algorithm that returns a true ConstraintReturn if a < x < b, where x arrives as a firing parameter and a and b are either provided as initialization parameters, or as firing parameters.

❑ RuleValueForRangeNonInclusive
This rule returns a string value based on where a number falls with respect to a range.

❑ RuleTrue
This always returns a true ConstraintReturn.

❑ RuleFalse
This always returns a false ConstraintReturn.

As you can see, before you start creating Rule Implementors of your own, the existing set of shipped implementors should be leveraged. They provide many of the basics building blocks for putting together a set of simple rules.

Many of these patterns represented by the provided implementors involve dependent rules. When a business rule triggers other business rules as part of its implementation, the rules that are triggered are called dependent rules of the first rule. Dependent rules are specified in the attributes of the top-level rule where the fully qualified name of each dependent rule is listed. When the top-level rule is triggered, an array of dependent rule names is passed to the rule implementor's `init()` *method. They are stored here until they are triggered by the* `fire()` *method.*

Configuring Rules

Rules can be configured and managed using the Rule Management Application or by creating custom applications that leverage the available programming API. This section demonstrates configuration using the Rule Management Application.

The Rule Management Application is launched using the `rulemgmt.bat` file found in the WAS `bin` directory, passing in a properites file that points to the deployment folders for the beans. For example, the properties file for the sample movie BRBeans looks like:

```
host=localhost
port=2809
RuleJndi=brbeans/moviesample/Rule
RuleFolderJndi=brbeans/moviesample/RuleFolder
RuleHelperJndi=brbeans/moviesample/RuleHelper
```

The Rule Management Application is used to configure and maintain the BRBeans that are being used by a WAS environment. The Rule Management Application is used to:

❑ Create a new BRBeans rule definition including:

    ❑ BRBeans rule folder and name

    ❑ BRBeans rule start and end date

    ❑ BRBeans rule type

    ❑ BRBeans rule implementor

    ❑ Initialization parameters for the Rule Implementor

    ❑ Dependent BRBeans rules

❑ Modify a BRBeans rule definition

❑ Export or import BRBeans rule definitions in XML

477

The primary screen for the Rule Management Application is shown first:

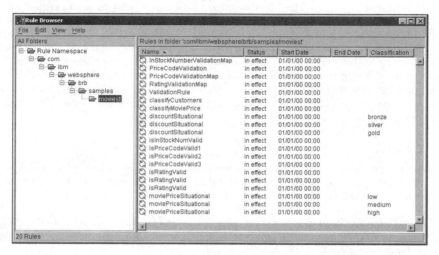

From here, we can see a number of rules organized into rule folders. We can also see some of the key properties of a rule. In our screenshot, all rules are in effect. The classifier rules have a label that shows the nature of the classification for each rule. If we pick our gold classifier rule and look at the properties, we can see a number of additional pieces of information:

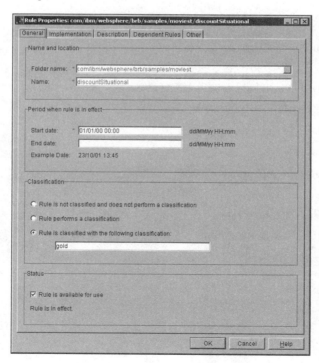

This shows start dates, status, and the nature of the classification. The next screenshot is of the Implementation display:

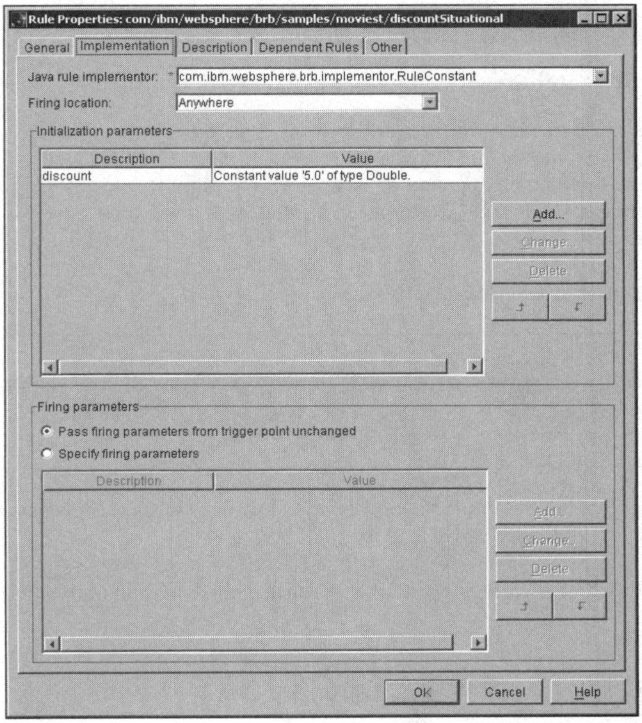

Here we can see the details of how this is implemented, initialized, and fired. The implementation in this case leverages one of the supplied Rule Implementors that come with the WAS.

Putting It Together

We have seen Process Choreography and Business Rules in this chapter. Process Choreography enables us to create new business processes, leveraging the various assets already in our business model. We also have some business rules in our business model, which help our systems react to changes more easily and factor out dynamic algorithms and data-driven code.

Is it possible to leverage the business rules and business processes together? Yes it is. Again, that is how business works so that is how we need the systems that run the business to work. Our sample business process of approving and effecting a price change for a given item in our catalog could be modified to leverage business rules.

Assuming now we have decided that the approval process for simple price changes of some nominal percentage no longer requires approval by a human or employee, as it costs more to approve them than it is worth. The new algorithm now becomes:

1. Input and accept item identifier and and percent price change (could be lowered or raised)

2. Get price of inventory item

3. If the price change is less than x%, then approve it automatically

4. Otherwise drive it thorugh a human interaction for approval

5. Set price to current price multiplied by the requested increase

The challenge is that the x% can change and for some items it might not apply. This is at least what the business policies of the day seem to be. So to put in a solution that will adapt, we will leverage business rules in our business process.

A refactored business process will look like this:

After the request is received and the information on the existing price is retrieved, we will now call a sub-process that will take care of the approval activity.

Instead of a staff activity that always gets put on a worklist, we will add an automated approval process as shown here:

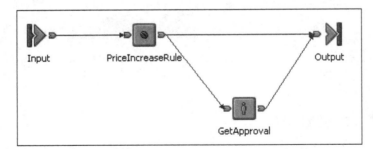

The screenshot shows that the first step is going to the PriceIncreaseRule. This rule will determine if the price is to be increased automatically (the true condition, Step 3 from above), or if human staff activity is required for approval (in case not true, Step 4 from above).

The PriceIncreaseRule is a session EJB that fires a business rule into the Rules Infrastructure. The EJB has a trigger point in it that takes in the current price, the itemID, and the requested increase. The business rule implementor consults the rules database for the currently allowed percentage of increase or decrease.

This models the business requirement and leaves flexibility in the design. A simple servlet application, to be run by someone who has the authority to change the business policy, could change the percentage increase or decrease allowed for automated updates. This can all be done without re-deploying any EJBs or business processes.

If in the future, or even at certain points during the year, if we wish to have more rules fire for that trigger point, such as a rule that would only allow automated price changes on items less than a certain price, it can be done transparently from the EJB and the business process that drives it.

This short example mixes together rules and business process and demonstrates the power of these two features working together.

Summary

Implementing a business model sounds like a relatively simple concept. J2EE 1.3 and the Web Services capabilities provided by WebSphere Application Server, version 5.0 provide many of the basics necessary to begin this kind of task. This chapter has introduced and described some additional concepts and capabilities supported by the WAS that can be used to more productively implement business models. Specifically, we have gone through a few key points in this chapter:

❑   A business model has a static element, which is represented by a set of entities

❑   A business model has a process element

❑   The process model element can benefit from advanced programming concepts described in this chapter as flow-based choreography, including compensation

❑   Business rules assist us in capturing and codifying certain kinds of business processes, especially those that are dynamic in nature

11

Preparing for Enterprise Computing

As you encounter more sophisticated application scenarios, you are going to run into some more complicated and interesting problems. WebSphere offers a set of extended functions to help you prepare your application for large-scale integration and sophisticated application requirements. These include services for:

❑ Handling international user sets

❑ Pass-through parameters

❑ Application initialization

❑ Asynchronous execution

We will describe these services in more detail, as we proceed with the chapter.

These extensions are not part of the J2EE standard – although, IBM has submitted them to the JCP (Java Community Process) for standardization in the future. While using the benefits of these functions, it should be kept in mind that they are non-portable to other vendor's application servers.

About the Examples in this Chapter

The examples introduced in this chapter have not been incorporated into the Plants-By-WebSphere example application. The snippets defined here are taken from the Chapter11Sample application provided on the CD accompanying this book. Nonetheless, we will attempt to describe their utility within the context of the Plants-By-WebSphere scenario.

All of the services described in this chapter will only work with WebSphere Application Server Enterprise (WASE) edition and by extension, should be developed with WebSphere Studio Application Developer-Integration Edition (WSAD-IE). You can import this example into WSAD-IE. You will have to define Java build path variables for the `acwa.jar`, `i18nctx.jar`, `startupbean.jar`, and `asynchbeans.jar` from the `WAS_EE_V5` classpath variables:

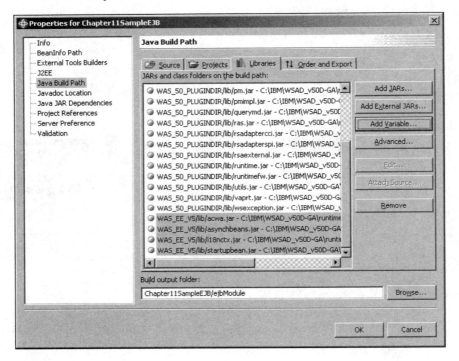

The Internationalization Service

Building applications for use by different countries can add a degree of complexity. Consider, for example, a scenario where you partition your Plants-By-WebSphere application between order processing and inventory management/order fulfillment. Let's say you configure several instances of the order processing applications in different countries (to provide some locality), and drive all these instances against a single central instance of the inventory application (representing your central distribution center).

You will want to process the inventory and order fulfillment in the locale and timezone of the country from which the order is placed. For example, you may want to collate the available item names in a sequence and return it in the customer's language. You may also want to indicate the time of shipment in the timezone and date conventions of the ordering country.

J2EE helps with its support for built-in internationalization, but the support is limited only to servlets on HTTP request and response processing. With this, you can get the locale associated with the HTTP request (allowing you to determine how the client or end user wants to see the information) and set the locale for the response. J2EE does not define any other more comprehensive approach to managing internationalization across J2EE components or the distributed system. More so, the internationalization support described by J2EE will only consider the locale preferences of the end user if the browser (assuming a classic browser-based client) supports and has been configured to define the locale preference of the end user. End users often do not configure this information. WebSphere will compute a default locale if no locale information is provided from the HTTP client using the defined locale of the web container's JVM.

Possibly, you could perform all of the locale-specific processing in your web application – re-sorting the information you get from the inventory system in the locale of the client. However, this could be inefficient. Consider the case where you want to return a partial result – using an iterator to pull the first part of the response from the server and presenting only that subset to the user. Sorting the result at the web application would require obtaining the entire result set from the inventory server before returning the partial result to the end user.

In addition, not all the locale-sensitive information will be used in the response to the user – you may have reasons for filtering it in the intermediate server or using it as part of some other portion of your business logic. In many cases, it would be best to pass the locale information of the client through to the downstream application components.

WebSphere provides an **Internationalization Service** that will automatically propagate locale information on invocation requests between components. This service gives you control over whether to pass the client's locale, or some other locale set by the intermediate application component. The internationalization context is passed implicitly – freeing you from having to pass the locale information as an explicit argument on method requests. This becomes particularly useful if you incorporate intermediate components that are not designed to pass locale information.

The internationalization service implemented by WebSphere has been submitted to the Java Community Process in JSR 150. It is listed at: http://www.jcp.org/jsr/detail/150.jsp.

About the Internationalization Example

The example used in this section to describe the Internationalization service is composed of four parts:

- ❑ **I18Nclient** – is a J2EE client application that drives the various paths of this example to demonstrate the use of the internationalization service. Specifically, it calls a variety of operations on the MidTierCMI and MidTierAMI session beans in the server.

- ❑ **MidTierCMI** – is a session bean deployed in the application server with container-managed internationalization policy.

- ❑ **MidTierAMI** – is a session bean deployed in the application server with application-managed internationalization policy.

- ❑ **FinalTierCMI** – is a session bean deployed in the application server that both the MidTierCMI and MidTierAMI beans call to demonstrate how various policies and programming options affect what context is actually received by the final end-point of cascaded requests.

To run the example, you should install the `Chapter11Sample` application in the application server, and then invoke the client from a command line. At the command prompt:

❑ Make sure that `<WAS_INSTALL_ROOT>`/`bin` is in your path

❑ Invoke the following command:

```
launchClient <WAS_INSTALL_ROOT>/installedapps/<nodename>/Chapter11Sample.ear
             -CCjar=Chapter11SampleI18NClient.jar
```

You will need to substitute `<WAS_INSTALL_ROOT>` with the path to where you have installed the WebSphere Application Server and `<nodename>` with the nodename that you specified during installation (usually taken from your host name, by default).

You can import this example into WSAD-IE. To run this example in the WebSphere EE version 5.0 Test Environment server, you will have to enable the Internationalization Service manually in the `defaultConfiguration.wsc/cells/localhost/nodes/localhost/servers/server1/` `server-pme.xml` document in the **Servers** project. You can find this under the **Servers** perspective. Set the `enable` attribute of the `i18nServer` element to `true`, as highlighted in the screenshot. If necessary, republish your configuration and restart the server:

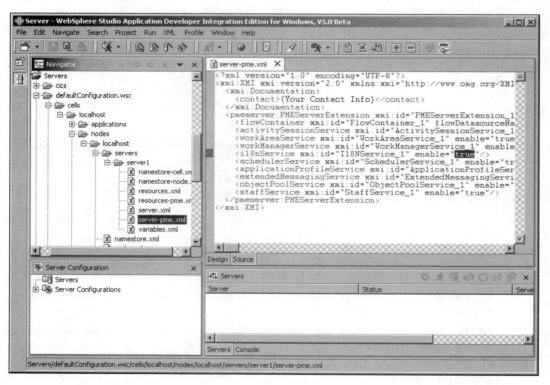

Enabling the Internationalization Service

The internationalization service is provided with the programming model extensions of the Enterprise edition of the WebSphere Application Server. It is disabled by default, but can be enabled through the admin interface. To disable/enable the service, configure the service to begin at server start-up in the Administration console:

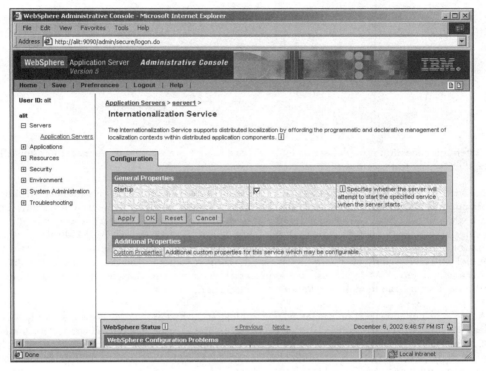

You will find this panel in the Internationalization Service property-group listed in the server configuration panel of the server on which you want this enabled. You will have to enable this on each individual server that you want to run this service. You will have to restart your application server after enabling this configuration option.

The Internationalization Service Architecture

The internationalization service is premised on the idea that work requests operate within an internationalization context. This context identifies both the locale and the timezone of the caller. We sometimes refer to the context as **locale** information, but that is just short-hand for the entire context. The context contains both locale and timezone information. Since, in a distributed object system, any given object can be both the receiver of a request, and the source of a request, the internationalization service goes on to make a distinction between the **caller context** and the **invocation context**. The caller context may be passed through to the invocation context so that the downstream request is performed under the caller's context, or the intermediate object may change it – your object may place different expectations on the objects that it invokes:

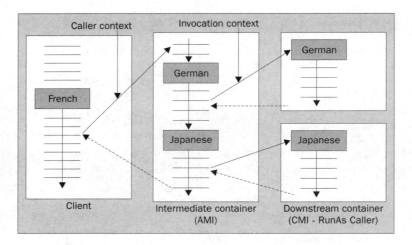

The internationalization provides access to the service itself, from which you can get either the caller context or the invocation context.

The service also makes a distinction between **Container-Managed Internationalization (CMI)** and **Application-Managed Internationalization (AMI)**. You decide which model you want when you deploy your bean, and each bean can select a different model. CMI basically indicates that you expect the container to manage the setting or delegation of internationalization context. AMI indicates that you want to control the setting of context inside your application. You can't have it both ways – if you select CMI an exception will be raised if you attempt to change the context values in your application. This philosophy has been adopted to allow deployers have some control over the behavior your application – they can use CMI to force your bean to make requests with a certain context.

With CMI, the container will set the invocation context according to the policies you set with your bean – either delegating the caller's context through (`runAs-caller`), using the default context for the application server (`runAs-server`), or setting it to a specific context that you configure for your bean (`runAs-specified`). You can set different policies for different methods of your bean (similar to setting `runAs` and permission security policies for your bean).

The internationalization service is composed of three interfaces:

❑ `UserInternationalization`
This is the main representative of the internationalization service. This is analogous to the `UserTransacation` object of the transaction service. You will acquire the `UserInternationalization` object from JNDI. The `UserInternationalization` interface supports the following operations:

    ❑ `getCallerInternationalization()` – returns an `Internationalization` object representing the context received from the caller (or the default context if no context was received from the client or if your program is the client).

    ❑ `getInvocationInternationalization` – returns an `InvocationInternationalization` object representing the context that will be transmitted with any requests from your program.

❏   `Internationalization`
Represents the readable aspects of the internationalization context. An object with this interface is returned from the `UserInternationalization` representing the caller's context. The `Internationalization` interface supports the following operations:

- ❏   `getLocales()` – returns a list (an array) of `java.util.Locales` that are included in the context. The context can contain multiple locales, indicating that the client can accept responses encoded for any of the listed locales, with the preferred locales listed first.

- ❏   `getLocale()` – is like `getLocales` but only returns the first, preferred locale.

- ❏   `getTimeZone()` – returns the `java.util.TimeZone` for the context.

❏   `InvocationInternationalization`
Represents the settable aspects of the `Internationalization` context. An object with this interface is returned from the `UserInternationalization` representing the invocation context. The `InvocationInternationalization` supports the following operations:

- ❏   `setLocales()` – can be used to set the list (an array) of `java.util.Locales` for the context. Multiple locales in the context indicate that any of the specified locales are acceptable to the client, with the preferred locale listed first.

- ❏   `setLocale()` – is shorthand to indicate that only one locale can be supported for the context.

- ❏   `setTimeZone()` – this operation is overloaded and can either take a `java.util.TimeZone` object or a `String` encoding of the time-zone ID for this context.

The following class-diagram illustrates the relationship between these interfaces:

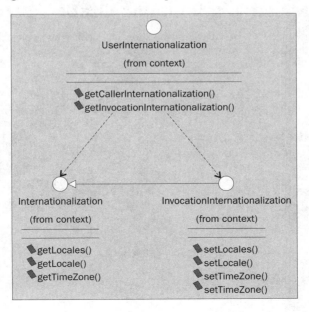

The `UserInternationalization` object gives you access to the service. From that you can get either the caller context (with the `getCallerInternationalization()` operation), or the invocation context (with the `getInvocationInternationalization()` operation). The caller context is represented by the `Internationalization` object – only allowing you to get information in the context. The invocation context is represented by an `InvocationInternationalization` object, which extends the `Internationalization` interface – allowing you to either get or set context information.

Internationalization and Clients

In addition to components (servlets and EJBs) hosted on the application server, the internationalization service also works in full J2EE client containers as well. Thus, you can set the internationalization context that you want to operate within these clients.

Unfortunately, the service does not work in applet clients, nor does it interoperate with other non-WebSphere clients at this point – although, as we stated earlier, the service has been submitted for standardization that should prepare it for such interoperability.

Mapping from HTTP Browsers

J2EE specifies standard support for servlets for obtaining locale information from HTTP requests and setting it in HTTP responses.

The internationalization service can be used in addition to the standard J2EE servlet support for HTTP request and response processing – in essence, to extend the standard J2EE support to enable the propagation and control of internationalization context when communicating with EJBs in your application.

Getting Access to the Internationalization Service

Before you can do anything with the internationalization service in your application, you have to get access to the service itself. This is done by resolving it from the JNDI name space at `"java:comp/websphere/UserInternationalization"`:

```java
package websphere.pro.chapter11.sample;

import com.ibm.websphere.i18n.context.*;
import java.util.Locale;
import javax.ejb.CreateException;
import javax.naming.*;

/**
 * Bean implementation class for Enterprise Bean: MidTierCMI
 */
public class MidTierCMIBean implements javax.ejb.SessionBean {
  private InitialContext jndi = null;
  private UserInternationalization i18nService = null;

  /**
   * ejbCreate
   */
  public void ejbCreate() throws javax.ejb.CreateException {
    try {
```

```
            jndi = new InitialContext();
            i18nService = (UserInternationalization)
            jndi.lookup("java:comp/websphere/UserInternationalization");

        } catch (NamingException e) {
            //The only reason you should ever get this exception is if
            //something is wrong with the naming service, or if the
            //internationalization service has been disabled by the
            //administrator.

            System.out.println("Exception looking up " +
            "internationlization context: " + e.toString());
            e.printStackTrace();
        }
    }
}
```

You only have to get access to the service once, so this is usually done in your component's initialization routine. You should then cache a reference to the service and reuse it on any method request to your component. The reference to the service can be shared across different threads of execution, and will always pick up the context from the thread on which the service is called.

Retrieving the Caller's Internationalization Context

The locale and timezone information for the caller is represented in an **Internationalization Context** that you can obtain from the internationalization service. You can then get the caller's locale(s) and timezone. Callers may supply multiple locales in order of preference. The idea is that, if your server-side application component cannot operate in the first locale specified, then it should operate in one of the other locales – the alternative locales represent the various locales that are acceptable to the caller. If you are not able to operate in any of the locales that are specified, then you run the risk that the caller (or the client user represented by the calling program) will not be able to understand your results. There are no hard rules in this case, but a common convention is to then fail the request rather than return results that cannot be understood.

The internationalization context supports a method for returning an array of locales (the ordered list of locales specified by the client), or just a single locale (the first locale specified in the list). The locale(s) specified by the caller are standard J2SE locales (`java.util.Locale`).

The internationalization context also supports a method for returning the caller's timezone. This is a standard J2SE timezone (`java.util.SimpleTimeZone`):

```
package websphere.pro.chapter11.sample;

import com.ibm.websphere.i18n.context.*;
import java.util.Locale;
import java.util.SimpleTimeZone;
import javax.naming.*;

/**
* Bean implementation class for Enterprise Bean: FinalTierCMI
*/
public class FinalTierCMIBean implements javax.ejb.SessionBean {
```

```
    private InitialContext jndi = null;
    private UserInternationalization i18nService = null;

    public String getReceivedLocale() {

      Internationalization callerI18nCtxt =
        i18nService.getCallerInternationalization();

      Locale callerPreferredLocale = callerI18nCtxt.getLocale();
        SimpleTimeZone callerTimeZone =

      (SimpleTimeZone) callerI18nCtxt.getTimeZone();
      return callerPreferredLocale.toString();
    }
  }
```

There are a number of things you can do knowing the locale and timezone of your caller. The following example demonstrates the use of a `NumberFormat` object to convert price information to the currency convention of the caller's locale:

```
java.text.NumberFormat fmt =
     java.text.NumberFormat.getCurrencyInstance(callerPreferedLocale);

java.lang.String i18nPrice = fmt.format(itemPrice);
```

Setting Downstream (Invocation) Context

If you make calls to other components, the caller's internationalization context will be automatically propagated downstream. However, if you want to have explicit control over the context in the downstream requests, you can create an invocation context and set the locale and timezone information. This context will then become the caller context in the downstream component.

As with the caller's context, you can get an invocation context from the internationalization context. You can set a single locale or a list of locales in preference order. You can also establish the timezone either with the standard J2SE `TimeZone`, or by timezone identity:

```
package websphere.pro.chapter11.sample;

import java.util.Locale;
import javax.ejb.CreateException;
import javax.naming.InitialContext;
import javax.naming.NamingException;

import com.ibm.websphere.i18n.context.InvocationInternationalization;
import com.ibm.websphere.i18n.context.UserInternationalization;

/**
 * Bean implementation class for Enterprise Bean: MidTierAMI
 */

public class MidTierAMIBean implements javax.ejb.SessionBean {
```

```
private InitialContext jndi = null;
private UserInternationalization i18nService = null;

public String sendSetLocale() {

  try {
    InvocationInternationalization invokeI18nCtxt =
            i18nService.getInvocationInternationalization();
    invokeI18nCtxt.setLocale(Locale.JAPAN);
    Object homeObject =
            jndi.lookup("java:comp/env/ejb/FinalTierCMI");
    FinalTierCMIHome i18nCtxtHome =
            (FinalTierCMIHome) javax.rmi.PortableRemoteObject.narrow(
    homeObject,FinalTierCMIHome.class);
    FinalTierCMI termI18nCtxt = i18nCtxtHome.create();
    return termI18nCtxt.getReceivedLocale();

  } catch (NamingException e) {
    System.out.println("Exception looking up " +
                        "internationalization context: "+ e.toString());
    e.printStackTrace();

  } catch (java.rmi.RemoteException e) {
    System.out.println("Remote exception creating " +
                        "TerminalI18NContext: " + e.toString());
    e.printStackTrace();

  } catch (CreateException e) {
    System.out.println("Exception creating " +
                        "TerminalI18NContext: " + e.toString());
    e.printStackTrace();

  } catch (IllegalStateException e) {
    System.out.println("You can not set I18N locale if the bean " +
                        "has been deployed with Container Managed I18N.");
    throw e;
  }
  return null;

  }
}
```

As with the caller's internationalization context, you can also get the locale and timezone of the invocation context. The invocation context is initially set to the values of the caller's context. By separating the caller's context from the invocation context, you can update (or set) the invocation context without affecting the caller's context. Hence, the caller's context cannot be changed.

Modifying the invocation context in your application code is referred to as **Application-Managed Internationalization (AMI)**. The difficulty with managing the internationalization context with AMI is that the invocation policy then becomes hard-coded in the component implementation. If you move that component to another computer, perhaps in another country, you may want to employ a different invocation policy, but will not be able to do so without changing your component implementation.

Container-Managed Internationalization

WebSphere 5.0 introduces support for **Container-Managed Internationalization (CMI)**. Like other similar forms of policy, CMI is a declarative mechanism for setting the invocation policy for internationalization. You can set extended deployment descriptors with your J2EE application that will direct the container on what context to use for downstream requests.

Establishing whether your bean will be application-managed or container-managed is set in with the Application Assembly Tool in the WAS Enterprise extensions of the bean specification:

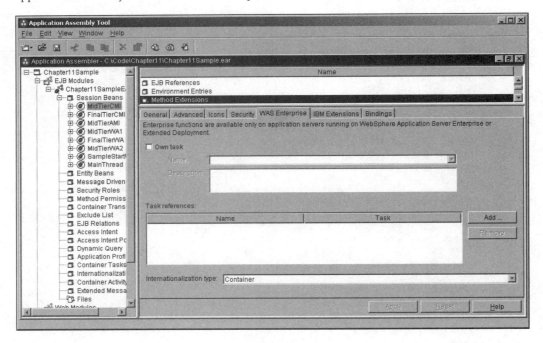

If you have configured your bean to run with CMI, then you can go on to define the internationalization delegation policy – referred to as the "CMI policy" – for each method of your bean.

Valid deployment settings include:

❑ runAs-caller – instructs the container to pass the caller's internationalization context through to downstream requests. This is the default behavior for the container, unless overridden by changes encoded in the component implementation.

❑ runAs-server – instructs the container to pass the server's default internationalization context through to downstream requests. The locale and timezone for the server, on which the component is hosted, will be used in the invocation context.

❑ runAs-specified – instructs the container to pass the specified locale and timezone through to downstream requests. The runAs-specified policy is accompanied with additional descriptors that define the locale (language, optional country code, and optional variant) and timezone identity to use in the invocation context.

The CMI policy can be set differently for each method of the component. By default, unless specified otherwise, the CMI policy will be `runAs-caller`. You can set the CMI policies using the AAT:

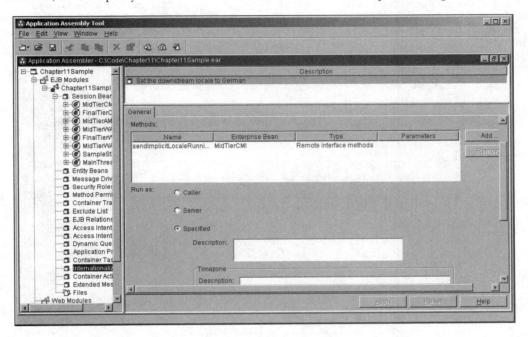

The CMI policy will be applied to all business methods. To be clear, on the servlet side, the `javax.servlet.Servlet.service()` method and the `javax.servlet.http.HTTPServlet.doGet()`, `doPost()`, `doPut()`, `doDelete()`, `doHead()`, `doOptions()`, and `doTrace()` methods, are all subject to the CMI policy you specify in the deployment descriptor for the servlet. In addition, `javax.servlet.Filter.doFilter()` and `javax.servlet.FilterChain.doFilter()` will operate with the deployment policy of the corresponding servlet. With CMI, you do not have to – in fact, you are not expected to do anything in your code. The internationalization locale will be picked up automatically from the servlet request context and propagated to downstream EJBs.

Downstream servlets invoked through the `forward()` or `include()` methods of a `javax.Servlet.RequestDispatcher` are executed under the CMI policy of the calling servlet.

Likewise, any method that you specify in the remote or local interface of an EJB is subject to CMI policy. The CMI policy is applied to both remote and local interfaces in the same manner. The consequence is that, unlike other explicit parameters passed to local methods (which are passed by reference), changing the internationalization context in a local EJB interface will not change the context for the calling servlet or EJB.

In addition, local Java objects called from within a servlet or EJB are executed entirely in the context of the servlet or EJB that called it.

495

Application-Managed Internationalization

With the introduction of CMI, AMI is no longer the default deployment policy for applications in WebSphere 5.0. If you have written code in your application to explicitly set the internationalization context in a prior release of WebSphere, then you must set the deployment policy for those applications to use AMI when porting them on to the 5.0 runtime. As with CMI, you set the deployment policy for AMI in the AAT:

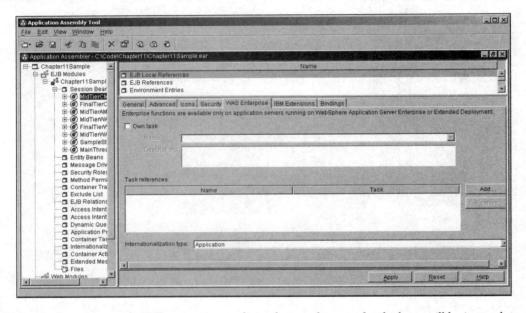

If you deploy a bean with AMI, any `runAs` policies that you have set for the bean will be ignored.

Internationalization and Lifecycle Methods

Lifecycle methods on servlets and EJBs can be called under a variety of situations that may or may not be in the context of a client request. As such, it may or may not be safe to assume an internationalization context, depending on which method and under what circumstances. The following discussion will detail when you can expect internationalization context to be available for use under different methods.

Servlets

The following servlet lifecycle methods will always be executed under the default locale and timezone of the servlet container:

❑ `javax.servlet.Servlet.init()`

❑ `javax.servlet.Servlet.destroy()`

❑ `javax.servlet.ServletContextListener.contextInitialized()`

- ❑ `javax.servlet.ServletContextListener.contextDestroyed()`
- ❑ `javax.servlet.http.HttpSessionActivationListener.sessionDidActivate()`
- ❑ `javax.servlet.http.HttpSessionActivationListener.sessionWillPassivate()`

No assumptions should be made about the internationalization context of the following lifecycle methods:

- ❑ `javax.servlet.ServletContextAttributeListener.attributeAdded()`
- ❑ `javax.servlet.ServletContextAttributeListener.attributeRemoved()`
- ❑ `javax.servlet.ServletContextAttributeListener.attributeReplaced()`
- ❑ `javax.servlet.http.HttpSessionAttributeListener.attributeAdded()`
- ❑ `javax.servlet.http.HttpSessionAttributeListener.attributeRemoved()`
- ❑ `javax.servlet.http.HttpSessionAttributeListener.attributeReplaced()`
- ❑ `javax.servlet.http.HttpSessionBindingListener.valueBound()`
- ❑ `javax.servlet.http.HttpSessionBindingListener.valueUnBound()`

The conditions under which these methods are called are sufficiently ambiguous and varied, that you can never be certain whether they are or are not being called in the context of a client request. Different application servers can further complicate this by driving these methods on different threads.

Stateful Session Beans

For stateful session beans the `setSessionContext()` and `ejbActivate()` methods are invoked with the CMI policy of the corresponding `Home.create()` method.

You can safely assume the CMI policy set for `ejbCreate()`, `afterBegin()`, `beforeCompletion()`, `afterCompletion()` and of course, any bean methods you introduce as set in the AAT.

You cannot assume anything about the CMI policy for `ejbRemove()` as this may be invoked at any time by the container.

The `ejbPassivate()` method will always be invoked with the default internationalization context of the server.

Stateless Session Beans

For stateless session beans, the constructor, and `setSessionContext()`, `ejbCreate()`, and `ejbRemove()` methods are all invoked with the default internationalization context of the server.

CMI policies are only applied to the business methods that you introduce on the EJB interface for stateless session beans – they are not applied to any of the lifecycle methods of your stateless session bean.

Entity Beans

For entity beans, it is unsafe to assume anything about the internationalization context in the constructor, `setEntityContext()`, and `ejbActivate()` methods.

The `unsetEntityContext()` and `ejbPassivate()` methods are always invoked with the default internationalization context of the server.

For all other methods, including the ones declared on the bean interface, it is safe to assume the CMI policy.

Message-Driven Beans

All methods of message-driven beans (MDB) are invoked under the default internationalization context of the server with the exception of the `onMessage()` method. The `onMessage()` method will be invoked with the CMI policy as specified in the deployment descriptors for the MDB, assuming that a context can be propagated with the JMS provider in use.

Web Services Internationalization

To assist in propagating internationalization context for web services, IBM has introduced a proprietary SOAP header for carrying this information. This header is not a standard and therefore, cannot be used for inter-operation with non-WebSphere clients and can only be used between WebSphere clients and servers. Nonetheless, the result is the same as described above for EJB requests. We have chosen to not detail that header here, as it is proprietary and is expected to change as the idea of internationalization propagation is standardized through the various bodies that govern the specifications of web services.

The Work Area Service

Passing information implicitly between application components is a useful idea. It allows you to identify information that has relevance across your application and passes it without having to call it explicitly as an argument to every method request. It also allows you to pass information through otherwise ignorant components.

Work area is a service provided by WebSphere for passing information implicitly on method requests. The principle behind work area is simple. You create a work area in one program (a J2EE client, servlet, or EJB) and fill it with few of application-defined properties. The work area represents a context within a **work scope** – you begin and end that work scope in your program with that context. The work area context, containing the properties that you set, is automatically and implicitly propagated on the downstream requests. The context is then instantiated in the context of the downstream component:

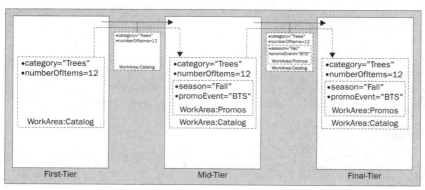

Downstream components can get any number of the properties from the work area context. The work area context continues to be propagated further, on any methods invoked from the intermediate component. Thus, even if the intermediate component does not get any properties from the work area, the downstream components can still get work area information set by the top-most program.

Intermediate objects can extend the work area, adding their own properties, which will then be passed on to downstream components from there.

In some sense, you can think of work areas as contexts for holding global variables – global to the entire distributed system over which you will cascade work. The context is used to scope the variables contained within the work area.

About the Work Area Example

The example used in this section is composed of four parts:

❑   **WorkAreaClient** – is a J2EE client that can be used to drive various operations in this example.

❑   **MidTierWA1** – is a poor choice of names to represent the First-Tier in the diagram above. It is used to create a `Catalog` work area context and to set the `category` and `numberOfItems` properties.

❑   **MidTierWA2** – represents the Mid-Tier in the diagram above. It creates a nested work area context in which it creates the `season` and `promotionalEvent` properties. Beyond that, the `MidTierWA2` object is used to change, remove, and conflict with the protection mode attributes of the property settings created by `MidTierWA1`.

❑   **FinalTierWA** – represents the Final-Tier in the above diagram and demonstrates the actual context received by that tier. It collects up its received context and returns it to the top of the request as an array of strings, which can then be printed by the `WorkAreaClient` for each of the tests that it is coded to perform.

To run the example, you should install the `Chapter11Sample` application in the application server, and then invoke the client from a command line. From a command prompt:

❑   Make sure that `<WAS_INSTALL_ROOT>/bin` is in your path.

❑   Invoke the following command:

```
launchClient <WAS_INSTALL_ROOT>/installedapps/<nodename>/Chapter11Sample.ear
            -CCjar=Chapter11SampleWorkAreaClient.jar
```

You will need to substitute `<WAS_INSTALL_ROOT>` with the path to where you have installed WAS and `<nodename>` with the nodename you specified during installation (usually taken from your host name, by default).

Enabling the Work Area Service

The work area service is provided with the programming model extensions of the Enterprise edition of WAS. It is enabled by default, but can be disabled through the admin interface. To disable/enable the service through the user interface, you can turn to the Work Area Service property page of the application server on which your application will be hosted. In addition to enabling the service, you can also set the maximum send and receive size for work areas – the send size maximum will affect how much data is transmitted from your application server on downstream requests, the receive size maximum will affect how much data will be accepted from upstream requests. The truncation of information for these settings is arbitrary and brutal – potentially truncating property names and/or values. In addition, propagating work area context implicitly will have some effect on network traffic and performance and so you should always use the available work area context prudently:

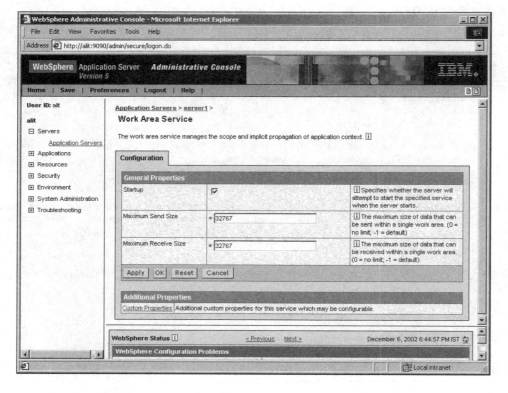

The Work Area Interfaces

The work area service is composed of a single interface, `UserWorkArea`, which extends `java.io.Serializable`, that represents the work area service. You will acquire the `UserWorkArea` object from JNDI. The `UserWorkArea` interface supports the following operations:

❑ `begin()` – takes a string name identifying the work area context that you want to start.

❑ `complete()` – terminates the last work area context opened within this component.

- ❑ getName() – retrieves the name of the outstanding work area context.

- ❑ retrieveAllKeys() – gets the names of all properties in the current work area context.

- ❑ set() – creates or updates a property in the context. This operation is overloaded to allow you to optionally specify the protection mode for the property. Properties are created with the Normal protection mode by default. The set() method can throw a NoWorkArea, NotOriginator, or PropertyReadOnly exception if you attempt to set a property that has already been protected by an upstream owner of the work area, or if you have not created a work area context in which to set the property.

- ❑ get() – returns the specified property, if it exists in the current context.

- ❑ getMode() – returns the protection mode setting for the specified property.

- ❑ remove() – removes the value of the specified property from the current context.

Getting Access to the Work Area Service

As with the internationalization service, you must get access to the work area service itself before you can do anything with work areas. You can get to the work area service from the JNDI name space with "java:comp/websphere/UserWorkArea":

```
package websphere.pro.chapter11.sample.workarea;

import java.rmi.RemoteException;
import javax.ejb.CreateException;
import javax.naming.*;

import com.ibm.websphere.workarea.PropertyModeType;
import com.ibm.websphere.workarea.UserWorkArea;

/**
 * Bean implementation class for Enterprise Bean: MidTierWA1
 */
public class MidTierWA1Bean implements javax.ejb.SessionBean {

    private javax.ejb.SessionContext mySessionCtx;
    private InitialContext jndi;
    private UserWorkArea workArea;

    /**
     * ejbCreate
     */
    public void ejbCreate() throws javax.ejb.CreateException {
        try {
            jndi = new InitialContext();
            workArea = (UserWorkArea)
            jndi.lookup("java:comp/websphere/UserWorkArea");

        } catch (NamingException e) {
            System.out.println("Exception looking up Work Area service: " +
                               e.toString());
            e.printStackTrace();
        }
    }
}
```

You only have to get access to the service once, so this is usually done in your component's initialization routine. You should then cache a reference to the service and reuse it on any method request to your component. The service will always operate on the current context on the thread of execution.

Creating and Terminating Work Area Context

Work areas are created within a execution context that consists of the thread of execution and the specific bean in which the context is created – the context is created when you begin the work area and will remain in effect until you complete it explicitly on the current thread of execution, or until you return from the method where the context was created. Neither work area contexts, nor the changes that you make to them are propagated back upstream to the calling program. The following code demonstrates creating and terminating a work area context:

```
public String[] createAndPassWorkArea() {
  String[] waState = null;

  try {
    workArea.begin("Catalog");
    waState = finalTierWA.getWAState();
    workArea.complete();
  }
}
```

You can specify the name of the work area context when you begin it. The name should be used to identify the context for debugging and tracing. Typically, you can use the name of the entity or the business function you are performing in which the context is created.

The previous code snippet shows beginning and completing the work in the same method. In fact, you can begin and complete the context in separate routines – as long as they are called in the same code path for the thread of execution. If you do not complete the work area context, it will be terminated automatically when the method in which it was created returns.

You can only complete a work area that you begin within your component. Work areas that you create in a component belong to that component on the thread of execution and are terminated when that component returns from executing its request. If you attempt to complete a work area belonging to another component, a com.ibm.websphere.workarea.NotOriginator exception will be thrown.

Setting Work Area Properties

Having a work area context is not very useful unless you have something to put in it. Adding values to the work area is a simple matter of setting properties. A common use of the work area is to place properties about the context in which a business service was requested – such as the type of device the user was using, which might, for example, indicate something about how much or what form of information should be produced for the request. In other cases, you might set the work area context with properties that describe special business conditions that you consider in other parts of your application – in particular, properties that you do not want to pass explicitly on previously designed interfaces. It is entirely up to you to establish an appropriate name convention for your properties – whatever you choose will be what other components will have to look for if they are to retrieve them later, downstream. The following snippet demonstrates setting properties in the work area context:

```
workArea.set("category", "Trees");
workArea.set("numberOfItems", new Integer(12));
```

You can store any Java object type in the work area properties as long as the type implements the class `java.io.Serializable`.

Getting Work Area Properties

A downstream component can retrieve any work area properties passed to it. You do not have to begin a new work area context to retrieve the properties – you just get the property from the work area service:

```
public String[] getWAState() {
   String itemCategory = (String) workArea.get("category");
   Integer totalItems = (Integer) workArea.get("numberOfItems");
   String season = (String) workArea.get("season");
   String event = (String) workArea.get("promotionalEvent");
}
```

Obviously, you do not have to get all the properties contained in the work area. In fact, you do not have to get any of them. Regardless, getting a property does not remove the property from the work area context. The work area context will continue to be propagated further to downstream components.

Nested Work Areas

When a downstream component is invoked, the outstanding work area context is propagated on the request and is then available to the downstream component to access. However, the context really belongs to the upstream component. You cannot change the context that belongs to another component, so if you attempt to change or remove a property in the received component, a `com.ibm.webphsere.workarea.NotOriginator` exception will be thrown.

However, you can create your own work area context within the downstream component. The work area context that you create in the sub-component becomes nested within and inherits the upstream context. You can then create additional properties within the nested context. If you create a property with the same name as an existing property in the received context, you will override the original property value within your own context. The original context property is actually left untouched and will be restored when you complete your nested context:

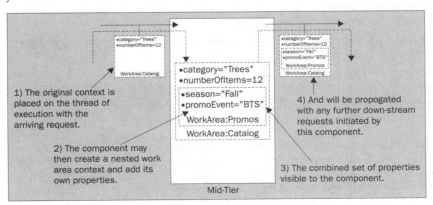

1) The original context is placed on the thread of execution with the arriving request.

2) The component may then create a nested work area context and add its own properties.

3) The combined set of properties visible to the component.

4) And will be propagated with any further down-stream requests initiated by this component.

503

None of the changes you make will be returned back to the upstream component – you cannot communicate changes back to the calling component.

You create a nested work area context in the same way as you created the original context, that is, by beginning the context. Likewise, you can terminate the nested context by completing it, or it will be automatically terminated when you return from your method – even if you have not explicitly completed it. You do not name the context that you are terminating when you issue the complete operation, so the innermost (the most recently) created work area context is terminated.

Terminating the work area context is demonstrated in this snippet:

```
workArea.begin("Catalog");
workArea.set("category", "Trees");
workArea.set("numberOfItems", new Integer(12));
waState = finalTierWA.getWAState();
workArea.complete();
```

Removing Work Area Properties

You can remove any of the properties that you create in your work area. As before, downstream components cannot remove the properties supplied by an upstream component, unless they do so within a nested work area. In other words, a downstream component can create a nested work area, and then remove the inherited property. Of course, this does not actually remove the property from the upstream context – it just renders the property invisible to further downstream components:

```
workArea.remove("numberOfItems");   //removes numberOfItems from received context
workArea.remove("season");          //removes season from nested context
```

Protecting Work Area Properties

There may be cases where you want to introduce a property to the work area context and prevent downstream components from either changing the property value or even removing it. The work area service allows you to control this by setting a protection-mode attribute for any properties you introduce to your work area context. The following protection modes can be set for a work area property:

- ❑ PropertModeType.normal – the downstream components can change or remove the property within their own nested context

- ❑ PropertyModeType.fixed_normal – the downstream components can change the property value in their own nested context, but can not remove it

- ❑ PropertyModeType.read_only – the downstream components can remove the property from their own nested context, but cannot change its value

- ❑ PropertyModeType.fixed_readonly – the downstream components cannot remove nor change the property value, even in their own nested context

You can only set property modes at the time that you set the property. If you are in a downstream component and the received context allows you to set a passed property – that is, the received property has a property mode of either normal or fixed_normal – then you can set the property with a different mode of an equal or more constraining level. In other words:

- ❏ If the received property has a mode of normal, then you can set the property with a mode of normal, read_only, fixed_readonly, or fixed_normal in your nested context.
- ❏ If the received property has a mode of fixed_normal, then you can set the property with a mode of fixed_normal or fixed_readonly in your nested context.
- ❏ If the received property has a mode of read_only or fixed_readonly, then you cannot set the property.

This allows you to even further constrain what downstream components can do to the property in their component. The following snippet demonstrates creating properties with various protection mode attributes:

```
workArea.set("category", "Trees", PropertyModeType.normal);
workArea.set("numberOfItems", new Integer(12), PropertyModeType.read_only);
workArea.set("season", "Winter", PropertyModeType.fixed_normal);
workArea.set("promotionalEvent", "Valentines Day",
             PropertyModeType.fixed_readonly);
```

Work area properties are set to normal mode by default.

The StartUp Service

There are many scenarios in which you want to know when your application has been started and when it has been stopped by the container. That is to say, after an application is deployed to run in a particular container, the application can be administratively started and stopped – the administrator can determine whether the application is allowed to accept requests from its clients (and end users). If an application is stopped by the administrator, the container will not dispatch work to it – it is as if the application is not there. As soon as the administrator starts the application, the container will begin dispatching work to it again.

Knowing when the application is started and stopped gives you the chance to initialize services that you may depend on in your application, and release those resources when the application has been stopped. One common use of this service is to initiate asynchronous work that will execute in the background of your application. We will discuss this further in *The Deferred Execution Service* section of this chapter.

The startup service is a straightforward way of being notified when the application has been started or stopped.

About the StartUp Example

We have included a example startup bean in Chapter11Sample application called SampleStartUp. It does not do much other than to put a message out to the sysout log whenever the application started or stopped, but should give you a template to work from for your own startup beans.

The StartUp Service Interfaces

The startup service is composed of two interfaces:

❑   `com.ibm.websphere.startupservice.AppStartUp` – is the interface your `StartUp` bean must implement. This interface consists of two methods:

     ❑   `start()` – will be called when your application is started. You should implement this method to do whatever you want to do during application startup, and you should return a Boolean value from this operation, where `true` indicates that your application started fine and you want the startup of your application to be completed, and `false` indicates that you encountered an error and do not want your application to start. If you return `false` from this operation, your application will terminate and be put in "stopped" state – an administrator will have to manually start your application again.

     ❑   `stop()` – will be called when your application is stopped. Again, you should implement this operation to do whatever you want when your application is stopped.

❑   `com.ibm.websphere.startupservice.AppStartUpHome` – is the interface your home `StartUp` bean must implement.

The `start()` method is invoked by the WebSphere container when your application is started – including just after a container restart if the application is already in start mode.

The `stop()` method is invoked by the WebSphere container when your application is stopped – including just before the container is shut down if your application is still in start mode.

Neither of these methods will be invoked while the application is in stop mode.

Creating a StartUp Listener

Creating a startup listener is simple. You provide an implementation of the `com.ibm.websphere.startupservice.AppStartUp` interface and deploy that as a stateful session bean in your application. You can implement and deploy multiple startup beans in your application. Simply follow the standard EJB programming model for differentiating these – as you would for differentiating any other session bean.

The following depicts the creation of a `StartUp` bean using WSAD-IE:

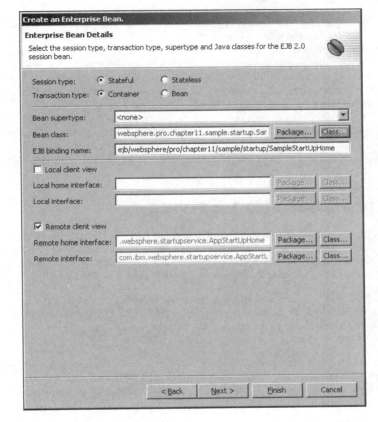

Notice that the bean name and class are customized, while the remote interface and remote home interface are `com.ibm.websphere.startupservice.AppStartUp` and `com.ibm.websphere.startupservice.AppStartUpHome`, respectively. WebSphere will look for this, and the fact that it has been deployed as a stateful session bean as a marker of it being a startup bean.

One other thing worth noting is that WSAD-IE will want to give your bean an EJB binding name that is derived from the package and class name of your remote interface. You will have to go back to the EJB binding name entry field and adjust it to the name you would prefer. This will be important to help avoid colliding with other startup beans you may have included in your application (WebSphere will be able to differentiate between the startup beans included in your application and those included in other applications regardless of what you set this value – just not between multiple startup beans within the same module).

The WebSphere container takes care of the rest. More specifically, WebSphere will detect the presence of session beans in your application that are deployed with the `AppStartUpHome` interface supplied with this service and will automatically treat these as startup beans.

Obviously, you will want to implement the `start()` and `stop()` methods as appropriate to your application.

507

Startup Beans are EJBs

A key feature of the startup service is that the startup bean is an EJB. This is a great benefit to EJB developers, as it ensures that the startup bean will be executed within an execution environment defined by its deployment policies, such as security. However, since the startup bean is invoked by the container (not on behalf of some other application client), you should ensure you deploy with a full set of deployment policies. In particular, you should specify a `RunAsSpecified` security policy to ensure that you execute with the credentials and roles that are appropriate for your application. In other words, if you are going to invoke a method on another EJB during your `start()` method, then you will need the required authority for accessing that bean (however that was configured for that bean). You therefore will need to execute with the credentials of a principal that has that authority – something that you can achieve using the `RunAsSpecified` security policy for your application (see Chapter 13 – *Securing your Enterprise*, for more information on the `RunAsSpecified` security policy.

The Deferred Execution Service

J2EE has had a long-standing constraint that applications should not spawn their own threads. The reasons for this are generally well established – the presence of unmanaged threads in the application server can seriously undermine the ability of the application server to ensure a stable, optimized, and scalable execution environment. (See Chapter 2 for more discussions on multi-threading in an application server).

Prior versions of J2EE did not have a good mechanism for enforcing this constraint, and so it was left to the application developer to apply some diligence. With J2EE 1.3, WebSphere is now able to enforce this constraint by denying applications permission to the threads library (`java.util.Thread` – specifically, for those operations that can be used to start and terminate threads).

Nonetheless, WebSphere extends some leniency by allowing you to request additional permissions. Application administrators can audit this and decide whether to allow applications that request this additional permission to be deployed. The installation will still suffer the consequences of diminished management in the container, if it is deployed with these permissions.

Generally we do not encourage the use of multi-threading your EJBs. Nevertheless, and notwithstanding these constraints, as the sophistication of your application grows so will the need for multi-threading within your application. The most common need for multi-threading stems from scenarios where you need a degree of parallelism in your business processes – for example, performing a risk analysis while you gather product data for a customer account.

The **Deferred Execution Service** is a way to avoid the pitfalls of spawning your own threads with the threads library. The deferred execution service allows you the same benefits of spawning parallel threads of execution, but in a safe fashion – one that can be managed fully by the application server and, by extension, restoring the benefits of managed component application development and execution to applications that need to spawn parallel work.

Deferred execution may sound like a strange way of saying multi-threading. Think of it as a way of deferring the management of work to be executed outside of the main thread to the application server. Work scheduled through the deferred execution service can be executed in parallel (synchronized through the supported rendezvous mechanism – described later in *Joining the Completion of Work*), or entirely asynchronously (without any rendezvous).

The most important point about the deferred execution service, and the thing that differentiates it from the threads library, which is the source of so much concern for J2EE application services, is that the deferred work is managed. That is, the deferred work will execute in a full J2EE execution context under container control, and with context state derived from your main thread of work. You can program the deferred work using the fullness of the J2EE programming model. WebSphere will establish an execution context for the parallel work, monitor any threads created for it, and enable rendezvousing with the results of the work. The deferred work will execute on threads taken from the WebSphere thread pool, and thus avoid the overhead of having to create threads on the fly. Most importantly, WebSphere will account for the work that is performed in these threads in its workload distribution decisions, allowing for better utilization of the application server resources.

About the Deferred Execution Example

The example used in this section is composed of four parts:

- **DefexClient** – is the main deferred execution client that drives the `MainThread` to perform various operations that demonstrate the use of the deferred execution service.

- **MainThread** – this is a stateful session bean and represents the main thread of execution for the example. This bean is used to create work requests with the work manager, to create execution contexts for later execution, create a `WorkListener` and register those work requests, and to terminate outstanding work requests. The `MainThread` maintains a stack of outstanding work objects (one per asynchronous work request), and a vector of all requested work items (each representing a specific request for asynchronous work). These are used for book keeping and to demonstrate the benefits of monitoring work with a `WorkListener`.

- **MyDeferredWork** – is an implementation of `Work` that is used in the entire asynchronous work request examples used here. The `Work` is implemented to simply write the current time out to the `System.out` stream each second for up to 20 seconds. You will have to look in the sysout log to see the results of this work.

- **MySynchWorkListener** – is an implementation of `WorkListener` that is used to monitor the asynchronous work requests in some cases. This listener is implemented to listen only for work-completion requests and to remove the corresponding the `Work` from the outstanding work stack.

To run the example, you should install the `Chapter11Sample` application in the application server, and then invoke the client from a command line. From a command prompt:

- Make sure that `<WAS_INSTALL_ROOT>/bin` is in your path
- Invoke the following command:

```
launchClient <WAS_INSTALL_ROOT>/installedapps/<nodename>/Chapter11Sample.ear
         -CCjar=Chapter11SampleDefexClient.jar
```

You will need to substitute `<WAS_INSTALL_ROOT>` with the path to where you've installed the WebSphere Application Server and `<nodename>` with the nodename you specified during installation (usually taken from your host name, by default).

Main Deferred Execution Components

The deferred execution service is composed of the following components:

- ❑ WorkManager
  This forms the heart of the deferred execution service. It is through the work manager that you will dispatch asynchronous work. The WorkManager supports the following operations:

  - ❑ startWork() – is used to initiate asynchronous work. This operation is heavily overloaded to enable a variety of different ways of controlling the asynchronous work – including with the current execution state or execution state that was captured previously (see the create operation below), with or without a WorkListener, and with or without setting a timeout for when the asynchronous work must be started. If a timeout value is set, the work will be terminated if it has not been started within the specified timeout limit (in milliseconds).

  - ❑ doWork() – is used to initiate synchronous work. This operation is similarly overloaded to enable a variety of different ways of controlling the work. The primary use for this operation is to execute a piece of work under an execution context that was captured earlier – perhaps at a different point in your application.

  - ❑ create() – can be used to create a WorkWithExecutionContext; capturing the current execution context from the calling thread of execution and combining that with the Work that you want associated with that context. The captured WorkWithExecutionContext can be used later with either the startWork() or doWork() operation to initiate that work and the corresponding context in which it was captured.

  - ❑ join() – can be used to block until either any or all of the outstanding asynchronous work has completed. This can be used to idle the main thread while parallel work is completing.

- ❑ Work
  This component represents the work that you want to execute asynchronously. The Work class is derived from java.lang.Runnable, which introduces a run operation. You must implement the Work class and run() method with whatever function you want to execute on the asynchronous thread. The work manager will call the run() method on your Work object when it spawns the thread – having already set the execution context for this thread. The run() method should be implemented as though it is a J2EE client.

  In addition, the Work interface introduces the release() method. The work manager will call this method when it wants to terminate the thread of your Work. You should implement this method to terminate any work that you are performing in the run() method – the run() method should return because of the release() method having been called.

- ❑ WorkItem
  This represents a specific instance of work in some state of execution. An instance of WorkItem will be created and returned from the startWork() method on the work manager to represent the specific thread of asynchronous work created with that operation. The WorkItem supports the following operations:

❑ `getEventTrigger()` – can be used to get a proxy to your `Work` instance for publishing events to it from your application. This operation takes the name of a Java interface. If your `Work` implements that interface, then this operation will return a proxy to your `Work` with that interface. You can then invoke any operation supported by the interface and it will be communicated to your `Work` instance.

❑ `getResult()` – can be used to get access to your `Work` instance to gather the results of its work. You should only invoke this operation after you know the asynchronous `Work` it is performing has completed – accessing the `Work` results at any time prior to its completion could yield unpredictable results.

❑ `getStatus()` – returns the status of your `Work`; one of:

- `WorkEvent.WORK_ACCEPTED` – the `startWork()` request has been accepted and the `Work` has been queued for execution.

- `WorkEvent.WORK_COMPLETED` – the asynchronous work has completed; the `run()` method on your `Work` object has returned.

- `WorkEvent.WORK_REJECTED` – the `startWork()` request has been denied; the `Work` will not be executed.

- `WorkEvent.WORK_STARTED` – the `Work` is running and is at some point of incompletion.

❑ `WorkWithExecutionContext`
This component represents a specific context under which the asynchronous work will be executed. The `WorkWithExecutionContext` can be created with the `create()` method on the work manager. The work manager will capture a snapshot of the current execution context at the point the create call is invoked, and record that along with the supplied `Work` instance in the `WorkWithExecutionContext` instance. This can later be included in a `startWork()` or `doWork()` operation to initiate the contained work asynchronously. The `WorkWithExecutionContext` object supports the following operation:

❑ `getWork()` – this returns the `Work` instance that was captured with this execution context.

❑ `WorkListener`
This is an object that can listen for work events. You can implement your own work listener that supports this interface, and then register an instance of it with the work manager when you start an asynchronous (or synchronous) work request. Your `WorkListener` instance will be notified when the associated `Work` goes through various state transitions. Each state transition is represented with an operation on the `WorkListener` interface:

❑ `workAccepted()` – called when the `Work` request has been accepted and queued for execution

❑ `workRejected()` – called if the `Work` request is rejected

❑ `workStarted()` – called when the `Work` is dispatched on a work thread

❑ `workCompleted()` – called when the `Work` completes; when the `run()` method returns

In all cases, these operations are passed a `WorkEvent` that, in addition to repeating the nature of the state transition, can be used to gain access to more information about the `Work` that is being reported on.

❑ WorkEvent

This represents transitions in the deferred work state. An instance of WorkEvent is created and passed on each WorkListener call and contains information about the Work in question. The WorkEvent supports the following operations:

❑ getException() – can be use to get any exception that was raised by the Work in the run() method during its execution

❑ getStartDuration() – is not supported in the current WebSphere implementation

❑ getType() – identifies the type of the event – WorkItem.getStatus operation above for the complete list

❑ getWork() – returns the Work object in question

These objects are part of a larger package of functions referred to as AsynchBeans (or Asynchronous Beans). The AsynchBeans package covers other services such as a scheduler function, monitoring functions, and an alarm manager. While these functions are useful in complex applications, they are not covered further in this book.

Enabling the Deferred Execution Service

Before you can use the deferred execution service you will need a **work manager** in the application server. The work manager is the point of control for the deferred execution service. WAS-E comes pre-configured with a default work manager. You can use this, or can create as many work managers as you need in your cell. The primary reason for introducing a different work manager is to configure it differently for your specific needs.

Each work manager can be configured with the minimum and maximum threads that will be allocated in the thread pool for asynchronous work, whether the number of threads can be temporarily grown beyond the maximum, which service contexts will be propagated to the asynchronous work, and the JNDI resource name for the work manager, and so on.

You can create a work manager in the admin console under the **Resources** list:

Press **New** to create a new work manager:

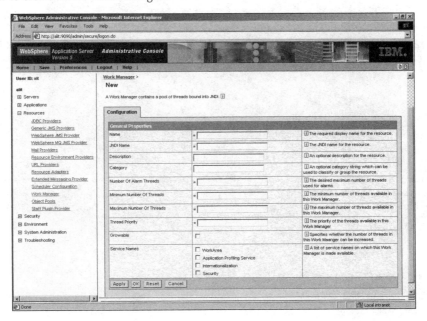

The work manager is a resource, and therefore you will refer to it in your application through a `resource-ref`. That is, you can use whatever JNDI `"java:comp/env"` name you want in your application to refer to your work manager, and then you will map that name to the actual JNDI name of the work manager during deployment. To create a `resource-ref` for the work manager in WSAD-IE you will have to know that the work manager type is `com.ibm.websphere.asynchbeans.WorkManager`. The rest you will derive from the JNDI name of the actual work manager instance you want to use, and the JNDI reference name you used in your application to refer to the work manager. In the example application for this chapter the reference name used in the example application and the actual work manager instance that will be used in the application server are both referred to as `wm/default`.

In WSAD-IE, add a resource reference for your EJB:

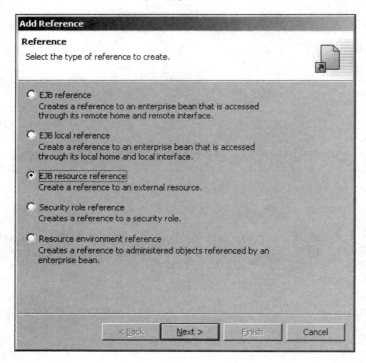

Fill in the reference name you use in your application code (less the `"java:comp/env"` prefix), the type of the resource (`com.ibm.websphere.asynchbeans.WorkManager`), along with the settings for source of authentication to the work manager (the **Container**), and the sharing scope for the resource (**Shareable**):

When you have finished creating the reference, select it and fill in the JNDI name of the work manager resource you will be using (you can do this an the AAT, or at application installation time as well):

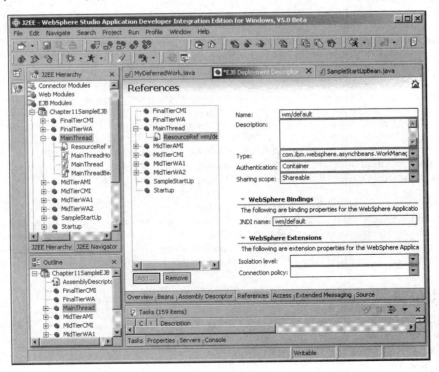

Defining Deferred Work

Any work that you want to defer must be created as an instance of Work. In addition to the release() method introduced by the Work interface, you must implement the run() method of the Runnable interface.

The run() method is where you should implement your work. This method will be called by the work manager on its thread of execution with a J2EE execution context – that is, with a principal identify under which you can make EJB method requests, a java:comp JNDI name space that can be used to look up EJB references, session and RAS information that can be used to record and track problems with your code or correlate your work to other activities in the system, and so on. You should program this method as though you are in a J2EE client. You should not assume the method would contain a transaction context. However, you can begin a transaction, do a JNDI java:comp lookup, find an EJB home, make calls on EJBs – anything that you would normally be allowed to do in a J2EE client application.

The run() method does not take any arguments – you cannot specify any arguments to the work when you spawn it. Therefore, if you need your work to operate on parameters that are set in your main thread, then you must design the work to include settable fields that will capture these parameters as part of the state of the work instance. Your main thread will then have to set these fields in the work before spawning it with the work manager. This will also affect the decision of whether you will spawn a single instance or multiple instances of your work if you want more than one thread executing on it.

For example, if you were to design a Work object that simply initiates a periodic sweep of your customer accounts, but for which you are not collecting any information in the Work state per se, then you could create a single instance of this Work and reuse it on multiple requests to start it asynchronously. If each request takes a long time to complete and you run the risk of having multiple outstanding asynchronous work activities operating with the same instance of Work, then you should be OK – local variables declared in the run operation will be scoped to their respective thread stacks. In effect, your single Work object instance is re-entrant.

If, on the other hand, you want each asynchronous work request to operate on a specific but different subset of customer accounts, and you want to accumulate statistical information about the accounts that were processed by each asynchronous work thread, then you will need a distinct instance of the Work object for each asynchronous request. The Work object should be implemented with attributes that you can set or get outside of the scope of the run() method – the main thread will use these to set the range values before initiating the asynchronous work request, and later will use other attributes to get the statistical information collected during its run after the work has completed.

The release() method will be called to shut down your work if your application or the application server is stopped. This is particularly important if you write a work function that will be long running, for example, if it enters into an unbounded loop. The release() method will be invoked when the server needs you to stop your thread of work. If your main thread does not return within a certain amount of time after the release() method is invoked, the server will abort your thread.

Obtaining a Work Manager

The work manager is used to defer your work. You can obtain a work manager from JNDI with the name you gave it when you created it in the system management facilities:

```
public void ejbCreate() throws javax.ejb.CreateException {

  try {
    jndi = new InitialContext();
    workMgr = (WorkManager) jndi.lookup("java:comp/env/wm/default");
    ...

  } catch (NamingException e) {
    System.out.println("Exception looking up WorkManager: "
                       + e.toString());
    e.printStackTrace();
  }
}
```

Dispatching Parallel Work

The most straightforward way of using the deferred execution service is to spawn an asynchronous thread for your work.

You begin by creating an instance of work that you want to spawn. You can spawn many threads of asynchronous work. Whether you do this with individual instances or with a single instance of your work will depend on the design of your work. If your work is inherently stateless, you can spawn multiple threads of execution on the same `Work` instance. You will have to be careful that your implementation is fully re-entrant. If you have to synchronize to accomplish this, then it will end up serializing the execution of your parallel work, hence undermining the efficiency of parallel processing.

You then register your work with the work manager. It will then spawn an asynchronous thread to run your work:

```
try {
  Work myWork = new MyDeferredWork();
  WorkItem thisWork = workMgr.startWork(myWork);

} catch (WorkException e) {
  //The work could not be registered.
}
```

The `WorkItem` handed back when you register work with the work manager, represents that specific instance of work. You can use that `WorkItem` to find out more information about that work as it proceeds.

The `getStatus()` method can be used to determine what state the work is in – states include `WORK_ACCEPTED`, `WORK_REJECTED`, `WORK_STARTED`, and `WORK_COMPLETED` as defined in the `WorkEvent` object.

The `getResult()` method can be used to get back an instance of the `Work` object that you registered. You can then acquire any state contained within this work through any interfaces that you designed for the `Work` object.

Dispatching Synchronous Work

There may be cases where you want the deferred work to execute synchronously. As before, you can create a `Work` instance and register it with the work manager to be dispatched in a synchronous fashion:

```
workMgr.doWork(myWork);
```

Since synchronous work executes in a blocking fashion there is no `WorkItem` returned from the `doWork()` method – control is simply returned to you when the synchronous work has completed.

Capturing Context

When the work manager dispatches the `run()` method on the `Work` object, it will do so within a J2EE context. That context is obtained from your main thread in one of two ways described.

At the time you register your work with the work manager, it will capture the J2EE context of the thread of your execution, serialize it, and re-establish that context with the deferred work when it is dispatched:

```
WorkItem thisWork = workMgr.startWork(myWork);
```

Alternatively, you can capture a snapshot of the J2EE execution context on your thread of execution (along with the work that you will be registering), and then register this combination of work and context later:

```
WorkWithExecutionContext executionSnapshot = workMgr.create(myWork);
...
//Sometime later, including on some subsequent method request ...

WorkItem thisWork = workMgr.startWork(executionSnapshot);
```

Snapshot execution context can be used with any of the styles of execution described above. If, in either case, the J2EE context that was captured cannot be established on the thread where the work will be executed, then the work will be rejected. You can register to be notified of this with a work listener.

Listening for Work Events

You can register a work listener for any of the work that you spawn. The work listener will be notified when the work transitions go through various states – including, when the work is accepted, rejected, started, or completed. Your work listener must implement the `WorkListener` interface. You can then create an instance and register that with the work manager along with the work:

```
WorkListener myWorkListener = new MySynchWorkListener();

workMgr.doWork(myWork, myWorkListener);
```

The work listener will be invoked on the `workAccepted()`, `workRejected()`, `workStarted()`, and `workCompleted()` methods depending on the transition for the work. These methods are passed a `WorkEvent` object that captures information about the event.

The getType() method on the WorkEvent can be used to find what kind of event is being notified. This information is redundant with the method on which the event was presented.

The getWork() method can be used to get the Work instance for the event. The Work instance will contain whatever state information you have designed into the work.

The getException() method can be used to retrieve any exceptions that may have been raised by the work during its execution.

Joining the Completion of Work

You can join the completion of any work through the work manager. The join() method on the work manager is a blocking call that will not return to you until either the work is joined (one or all of the work items have completed, depending on the conjunction used for the join), or after a specified timeout. If you have spawned more than one thread of work, you can join on any one, or on all of them by including each of the WorkItems for the work that you want to join in the work list.

The timeout is specified in milliseconds, and indicates how long the join will wait for work to complete. If the timeout is 0, then the join will simply peek at the current work state and immediately return. If the timeout is any negative number, then the join will block indefinitely for work to complete.

The following is an example of a join on any of the work items – the join will return when any of the work items listed have completed:

```
public void waitForSomeWorkToEnd(int timeout) {
  ArrayList outstandingWorkList = new ArrayList();

  for (int i=0; i < initiatedWorkItems.size(); i++) {
    if (((WorkItem)initiatedWorkItems.get(i)).getStatus() ==
        WorkEvent.WORK_STARTED)
      outstandingWorkList.add(initiatedWorkItems.get(i));
  }

  if (workMgr.join(outstandingWorkList, WorkManager.JOIN_OR, timeout)) {
    System.out.println("Some work has completed.");
  } else {
    System.out.println("Wait timed out.");
  }
}
```

The following is an example of a join on all of the work items – the join will return when all of the listed work items have completed:

```
public void waitForAllWorkToEnd(int timeout) {
  ArrayList outstandingWorkList = new ArrayList();

  for (int i=0; i < initiatedWorkItems.size(); i++) {
    if (((WorkItem)initiatedWorkItems.get(i)).getStatus() ==
        WorkEvent.WORK_STARTED)
      outstandingWorkList.add(initiatedWorkItems.get(i));
  }

  if (workMgr.join(outstandingWorkList, WorkManager.JOIN_AND, timeout)) {
    System.out.println("All work has completed.");
```

```
    } else {
      System.out.println("Wait timed out.");
    }
  }
```

Collecting the Work Results

Once work has completed, you can collect the results from the Work object. There are no return values from the run() method and therefore you have to provide a means for acquiring the work results through operations that you design on your Work object. You might include, for example, attributes on your Work object that allow you to gather statistical information gathered during its run. When the work completes, you can then call the Work object getter-methods to get the statistical information. You should be careful to re-acquire the Work instance from the WorkItem returned to you when you initiated the startWork() request (or through any of the other avenues for getting the Work object from the work manager – for example, from the WorkEvent that is published when the work completes). The Work instance that you created at the time that you initiated the startWork() request may or may not still be the same instance that the work manager ended up using to do the work – all of the state will be the same, but it may have been serialized and reconstituted in between.

Summary

For many scenarios that you will encounter you should be able to build good, robust applications with the richness of the standard J2EE programming model and services. Doing so goes a long way to ensure that your application will be portable to different application server environments. However, as you progress to deal with increasingly sophisticated and difficult application problems you will likely encounter the need for services that J2EE has not addressed yet. WebSphere provides support for these situations, in part with the services described in this chapter. You should now have a good understanding of:

❑   How to pass internationalization context and arbitrary application-defined context between your EJBs

❑   How to get notified when your application is started and stopped

❑   How to spin asynchronous threads of work from within your application

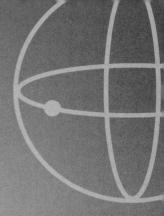

Part 4: WebSphere in Production Deployments

Part 4: WebSphere in Production Deployments

If you have got through the preceding parts of this book, then you should know everything you need to build an application to be hosted on WebSphere Application Server. You are now ready to put your application into a production environment.

This part of the book will help you understand how to set up a WebSphere production environment. It begins by understanding the parts of a WebSphere topology and the variations that you can apply to the structure of your information system. The topology chapter will explain how to put together a network of application servers, deployment managers, edge servers, and HTTP servers to achieve your objectives. It will explain the clustering and other topological constructs used by WebSphere.

The most time and resource consuming aspect of putting an application into production is managing it. We go on, in this part of the book, to explain the administration model for the WebSphere environment. We describe the overall architecture for management, walk you through the administration user interface for many common tasks, and spend an entire chapter describing how to program an administrative application – one that can be used to administer the WebSphere Application Server environment. Through this discussion, we will help differentiate between middleware management and enterprise system management. An appendix has been included at the end of this book with a complete enumeration of the command-line, scripting, and Ant services that are provided by WebSphere.

Of course, no production environment would have any value to you unless you could secure it. While its position within this book might suggest otherwise, security has not been an after-thought in the WebSphere programming model – rather, the security model is built right into the Java and J2EE programming model, and has been incorporated throughout the WebSphere runtime.

Finally, to our own dismay, there is no way we could cover everything there is to say about WebSphere in this one book. We conclude this book with a brief look at the other important features of WebSphere.

12

Deployment Topology

In order to deploy, secure, and administer a WebSphere production environment, it is helpful to first have an idea of the different ways WebSphere can be configured to solve your business needs. While WebSphere runs straight out of the box as a single server, it can be configured and extended into a variety of different multi-server topologies, ranging in span and reach from small to large networks, and ranging in scale and scope to include clustered configurations and EIS integration.

In this chapter, we will take a closer look at the major elements that compose a WebSphere Application Server configuration, plus the objectives and benefits of several common WebSphere topologies. To do this we will walk through several different topics areas:

❑   **WebSphere product packages**
    In this topic area, we will identify the different WebSphere product packages and what they are for.

❑   **Key topography terms**
    Here, we will introduce vocabulary to help us understand the elements that are installed by the different WebSphere packages. We will also use these terms in the topography overviews, which appear at the end of this chapter.

❑   **Application server anatomy**
    In this section, we will take a detour from discussing the application server as a black box, and take a look at its major components. While this information does not pertain strictly to a discussion of topology, we believe an understanding of the application server's major components rounds out your understanding of the application server itself, and may in some ways color your view of how servers inter-relate generally, in multi-server topographies.

❑ **Topography overviews**
Here, we will survey several topographical models in which WebSphere is commonly configured. We will also talk about which of these topographies would make sense for our sample application, Plants-By-WebSphere.

WebSphere Product Packages

WebSphere is not just an IBM application server; it is actually an IBM brand name. Numerous extension and companion products are coming out using the WebSphere name. The core product is the WebSphere Application Server. Other products discussed in this book include:

❑ **WebSphere Programming Model Extensions**
This product extends the application programming model. A number of its features were discussed in Chapter 9, Advanced Persistence, etc.

❑ **WebSphere Network Deployment**
This product enables the configuration and management of multi-server configurations. We'll talk about this subject quite a bit in this chapter. In the next section, we will introduce the elements introduced by this product and describe how they inter-relate.

❑ **WebSphere Edge Server**
This WebSphere extension product is effective for increasing web serving performance, especially in larger configurations. We will briefly introduce this product to help explain one of our later topographies.

Key Topography Terms

To facilitate our discussion, let's introduce a few new terms to create a working vocabulary.

The WebSphere Application Server product introduces these terms:

❑ **App Server**
A single WebSphere application server, which is sometimes referred to as a "base server".

❑ **Admin Console**
This is a special J2EE application that is pre-installed in your WebSphere environment. It provides a browser-based interface through which your app servers and applications are managed. Please note we will discuss the presence of the Admin Console in this chapter, but will defer an explanation of its functions until Chapter 14.

The WebSphere Network Deployment product introduces these additional terms:

❑ **Node**
A logical group of app servers, configured together on the same physical computer system. Note that multiple WebSphere nodes can be configured on the same physical computer system.

❑ **Node Agent**
An administrative process, executing on the same physical computer system as the node it supports. A single Node Agent supports all app servers running on the same node.

❑ **Cell**
A logical group of nodes, configured together in the same network for administrative purposes.

❑ **Cluster**
A logical app server comprising multiple instances of the same app server, usually spanning multiple nodes, and acting as a single unit providing reliability and load balancing.

❑ **Network Deployment Manager**
An app server running an instance of the Admin console that provides administrative control over all other app servers configured together into the same cell.

To illustrate the concepts these terms represent, let us consider some diagrams. Please note we will describe the organization and purpose of these topographical elements in this chapter, but we will defer explanation of how to configure these elements until Chapter 14.

Let's look at a base server first. This is what you get when you install the WebSphere Application Server product. This configuration consists of a single app server installed on some physical computer system. This app server hosts its own instance of the Admin console application, enabling it to be administered through a standard Internet browser. The Admin console is installed automatically in the app server and is used to manage *only* the app server in which it is installed. The following diagram depicts this configuration:

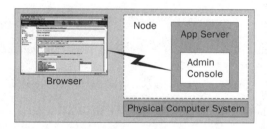

Note in the preceding diagram that the App Server exists in a WebSphere node. Even though we defined a node as a logical collection of app servers on the same physical computer system, even a single app server is in a node – a node of one.

> *For ease in understanding, we have used the term "physical computer system" to represent a collection of hardware operated by a single instance of some operating system. For example, an Intel box operated by Linux or Windows 2000, a Sun server operated by Solaris, etc. Certain hardware platforms, such as IBM P-Series and Z-Series, offer a function commonly referred to as "logical partitioning", which allows a single physical computer system to be sub-divided into multiple logical computer systems, with each logical computer system being operated by a separate operating system instance. A WebSphere node always exists within the boundaries of a computer system, whether that computer system is physical or logical.*

With the WebSphere Application Server product package, you can define as many single servers as you need on the same physical machine. If you have more than one app server installed, each one is independent and administered separately. In other words, they are not centrally administered. For example, two single servers defined on the same physical system would each host their own copy of the Admin console application, each controlled through a separate browser connection:

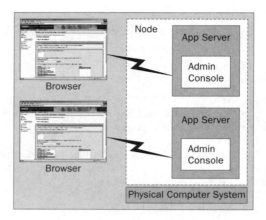

You might start to wonder how to effectively administer a large number of app servers. You'd probably say we were crazy if we suggested that administering each app server through a separate browser connection was the only solution! Fortunately, we're not *that* crazy. This is where WebSphere Network Deployment comes in.

The purpose of the WebSphere Network Deployment product package is twofold:

❑   To enable administration of multiple WebSphere nodes, and the app servers they contain, through a single browser connection

❑   To enable the configuration of servers into clusters for application scale and availability

When you install WebSphere Network Deployment, at first all you get is a single, specialized app server, called the Network Deployment Manager. At first it appears really no different from any other app server, except for its name:

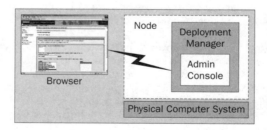

We'll soon see, however, that it plays a unique role within a group of WebSphere nodes, which we call a **cell**.

> **Please note that the Deployment Manager hosts only administrative applications, such as the Admin Console – you cannot target this server for your own applications.**

Another thing to note about the Deployment Manager is that it always exists in its own dedicated node. It is not possible to define other app servers in the Deployment Manager's node. It has its own node largely for isolation purposes because in the WebSphere implementation, server configurations are physically isolated on a per-node basis. We'll talk more about that in just a little bit.

In the following diagram, we see that the Deployment Manager node can be co-located on the same physical computer system as other app server nodes:

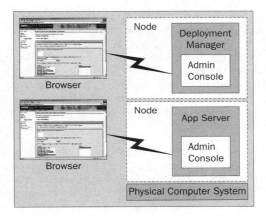

The fact that the Deployment Manager may exist on the same physical computer system as other app servers is evidence that nodes are only logical – in fact you can configure multiple app server nodes on the same physical computer system, too. You might wonder why on earth one would do that. One of the best reasons will not occur until we release the next version of WebSphere – call it WebSphere version X.0. If you had a business reason to run both v5.0 and vX.0 on the same physical system, you would have to separate them by node. You see, each node is essentially a separate installation of WebSphere Application Server.

Naturally, the Deployment Manager can exist on its own physical computer system:

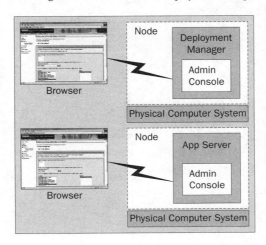

This is our recommendation for increased availability – a point that should become clearer as we describe the organization of a cell.

A cell is a collection of nodes, organized into the same administrative domain. Cells are created by **federating** base server nodes with the Deployment Manager's node. This is done through either a utility program called AddNode or through the Admin console application running in the Deployment Manager. Both of these techniques for adding an existing node to a cell are discussed in greater detail in Chapter 14.

It is important to recognize that a base server is transformed when its node is federated with the Deployment Manager's node. Upon taking this action, the Deployment Manager becomes responsible for providing administrative access to the servers on the newly federated node. The base servers on that node are no longer standalone: no longer separately administered. In fact, the Admin console on each base server is uninstalled. In its place, a Node Agent is activated. Through the Admin console in the Deployment Manager you can access any server in the cell. The Admin function in the Deployment Manager is aware of the other servers in the cell and coordinates administrative actions through each node's Node Agent.

It is because the Deployment Manager is responsible for providing administrative access to all nodes and servers within the cell, that we recommend running the Deployment Manager on its own physical computer system. In a production environment, app server nodes are typically far busier than the Deployment Manager node. This greater activity on an app server node increases the opportunity for failure. Therefore isolating the Deployment Manager to its own physical computer system naturally increases its availability.

OK, so let's consider what our cell would look like after federating our first base server node. The following diagram depicts this trivial cell:

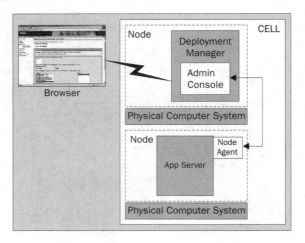

The benefit of grouping servers into cells is that the entire cell can be administered from a single point. This can substantially decrease administrative complexity and facilitates the coordination of administrative actions across a set of app servers.

You can increase the size of your cell by adding additional nodes and app servers. Note that you cannot administratively create a new node. You can only create a new node by installing WebSphere Application Server. If we added another node to our cell, it would look like this:

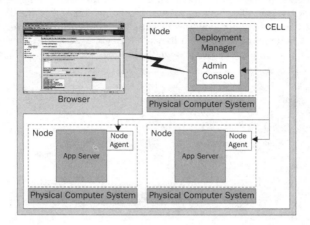

The presence of additional app server nodes makes it possible for us to build a **cluster**. The motivation for configuring a cluster is scale and availability. A cluster is a collection of homogenous servers, with each server having the same configuration and hosting the same applications. When servers are configured into a cluster, WebSphere automatically knows how to distribute work among the servers within that cluster, so from the point of view of the outside world, the cluster appears as a single, logical server. The app servers that compose a cluster may reside on the same node or on different nodes. All nodes must be in the same cell.

The following diagram depicts a server cluster:

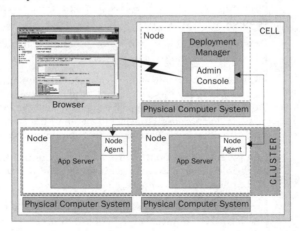

Now that we've built up a basic vocabulary, we're ready for the topography overview coming up later in this chapter, but let's first take that detour we mentioned, inside the application server.

Application Server Anatomy

The WebSphere Application Server environment consists of a number of elements, such as Deployment Managers and Node Agents that work together to deliver the function of this flexible and robust J2EE execution environment. To better appreciate how this application environment works, it helps to understand these elements, and the components from which they are formed. The components depicted in the following diagram are not the only ones present in these elements, but they are among the most significant:

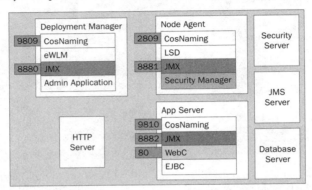

The following table summarizes these components and briefly describes the purpose of each:

Component Name	Component Description
CosNaming	Provides a CosNaming implementation and access to the WebSphere system namespace. The CosNaming NameService is accessible by default through the CORBA Interoperable Name Service (INS) bootstrap port, 2809. The CosNaming service is accessed by J2EE components through JNDI.
eWLM	Provides the workload management function that enables smart workload balancing across clustered servers.
JMX	Provides the communication backbone of the System Management function. Through this component, administrative requests that originate in the Admin application are propagated through the JMX network to those nodes and applications to which the administrative action corresponds. JMX provides access to management components called MBeans.
Admin Application	The J2EE application that provides the administrative function accessible through an Internet browser, and better known as the WebSphere Admin console.
LSD	Provides a CORBA Location Service Daemon. This function routes standard IIOP requests to the correct destination server.
Security Manager	Provides other WebSphere components with a standardized access point to the configured security environment. It typically works in conjunction with a third-party security server.

Component Name	Component Description
WebC	A standard J2EE web container, which hosts J2EE web modules.
EJBC	A standard J2EE EJB container, which hosts J2EE EJB modules.
HTTP Server	WebSphere includes the IBM HTTP Server. This server is useful for serving static web pages. Through use of a WebSphere plug-in, it can route requests for J2EE web components, such as servlets and JSP pages, to WebSphere application servers. WebSphere includes plug-ins for other leading web servers too, such as Apache and Netscape.
Security Server	The WebSphere Security Manager component works either with a provided registry, including native and LDAP registries, or in conjunction with an external security server, for example, Tivoli Access Manager. Please see Chapter 13 for additional discussion of security options.
JMS Server	WebSphere includes an integrated JMS server for J2EE 1.3 compliance, based on IBM's long established MQSeries.
Database Server	WebSphere app servers typically host J2EE applications that require access to your business's data assets. An app server will typically connect to any of a variety of external database servers for that purpose – for example IBM's DB2 relational database.

CosNaming Namespace

A CosNaming namespace is a type of directory in which a J2EE application server may store references to the applications and resources (such as JDBC data sources) configured to it. A client may find an application by looking it up in the directory; similarly an application may find a resource in the directory.

WebSphere features a fully compliant, yet unique, implementation of the CORBA CosNaming standard. CosNaming is required as the mechanism underlying the Java Naming and Directory Interface (JNDI), which is the J2EE API for accessing the directory.

What distinguishes the WebSphere implementation of CosNaming from the standard is that the name service, and the namespace that it represents, is distributed across all WebSphere nodes and servers within the cell. The distributed nature of this name service results in no single point of failure for the name service across the cell; the loss of any particular server does not result in a loss of the name service, or a loss of access to the namespace. Additionally, the namespace is partitioned into different segments, each possessing its own unique characteristics, which will be described in detail later in this section.

The namespace is organized to model the cell-wide topography. Each Node Agent and app server, including the Deployment Manager, houses its own unique view of the namespace. Typically, each node contains namespace entries for only those app servers that are configured on that node. Each app server's namespace contains entries for only those application and resources defined to that app server. Junctions (or links) between nodes and servers are established through use of **corbanames** (part of the INS standard). A corbaname provides a standardized mechanism for establishing remote linkages between naming contexts spanning physical processes. The following diagram depicts the segments in the WebSphere namespace:

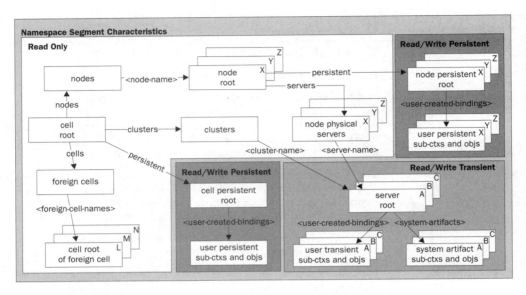

The segments from the preceding diagram are:

❑ **Read only**

This segment exists in each app server and Node Agent. It is built from the information contained in the WebSphere configuration repository. Corbanames are used to establish junctions between remote elements in the cell, such as app servers and Node Agents. For example, following the path /nodes/<node-name>/servers/app server 3 from inside either the Node Agent or app server 1 or 2 would follow the corbaname that addresses the app server 3 namespace. Traversing that junction would result in a remote flow from the current namespace into the namespace of app server 3. The following diagram depicts the namespace binding that establishes this linkage:

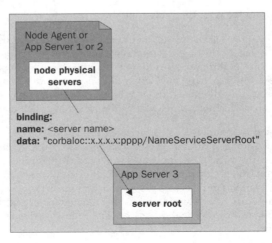

❑ **Read/write persistent**
For applications that require persistent namespace bindings, there is a read/write namespace segment at both the node and cell level, which backs all writes to the file system. The Node Agent and Deployment Manager own the master copy of the node and cell persistent namespace segments respectively. Write requests to these segments are communicated to the Node Agent or Deployment Manager through JMX, then in turn, the Node Agent or Deployment Manager distributes the changes to all other Node Agents and app servers – also through JMX.

❑ **Read/write transient**
The namespace in each app server is read/write. During app server initialization, the app server will bind resource and EJB references into the namespace according to the configuration repository for that app server. Applications accessing the app server's namespace are free to read existing namespace bindings, or create new ones. However, any namespace changes made by the application are not permanent – they are not persisted to any backing store – and are lost when the app server is stopped.

Bootstrapping the NameSpace

To locate an application, a client must connect (or "bootstrap") to the namespace. Bootstrapping refers to the process of obtaining a JNDI initial context, then looking up and accessing J2EE components, typically EJBs. The namespace has several connection points; each is called a **bootstrap address**. Bootstrap addresses exist at the following points within a cell:

❑ Each app server

❑ Each Node Agent

❑ The Deployment Manager

An application may bootstrap into any of these points in order to locate an application and thereby establish initial contact with the application itself. In a larger configuration, it may be difficult for an application to know whether a particular server or node is active at any given point in time. The basic way to insulate a client from the current operational status of any particular node/server pair is to configure the servers into clusters across two or more nodes. Bootstrap into the Deployment Manager and navigate the namespace to the cluster hosting the target application. By always keeping the Deployment Manager up, you have a reliable point of entry into the namespace. Clustering your servers increases application availability: you can lose one node and still have access the function of the application. By looking up the application through the cluster context in the namespace (refer to the *Namespace Segment Characteristics* diagram above) your application will gain access to the application running on of the available nodes; the junctions in the namespace automatically account for the current status of a node and ensure you get routed to an active node if there is one.

The Deployment Manager

The **Deployment Manager** is really just a WebSphere app server that executes the WebSphere Admin application, which itself is merely a J2EE application. The presentation elements of the Admin application are accessed through a standard Internet browser, and are known collectively as the Admin console. The Deployment Manager runs in a separate node, which may run on a separate operating system instance, or be collocated with one or more other nodes hosting app servers.

The Deployment Manager has a CosNaming namespace, accessible through bootstrap port 9809 by default. By bootstrapping an application through the Deployment Manager, an application may gain access to the services of the eWLM component. Through the eWLM component, the Deployment Manager has a view of all server clusters within the administrative domain, and can distribute work across these clustered servers.

The Deployment Manager, through the Admin application, is the center of control for managing the cell-wide WebSphere configuration. The Admin application uses **JMX (Java Management Extensions)**, which is a message-based mechanism for coordinating administrative and operational requests across the WebSphere nodes. Each node, including the Deployment Manager, houses a JMX component. The JMX component listens on port 8880, by default, for SOAP/HTTP requests. JMX can also be configured for access through RMI/IIOP. HTTP is the default because it is easier to configure for firewall access and supports admin clients based on web services. RMI/IIOP is available for building admin clients based on the RMI programming model. RMI/IIOP supports transactional semantics and additional security protocols, such as CORBA's csiV2 – a network interoperable security standard. You can read more about web services and security topics in Chapters 8 and 13 respectively. Through JMX, the Admin application can drive requests to one, several, or all app servers. For example, the JMX flow for starting all app servers on a single node is illustrated below:

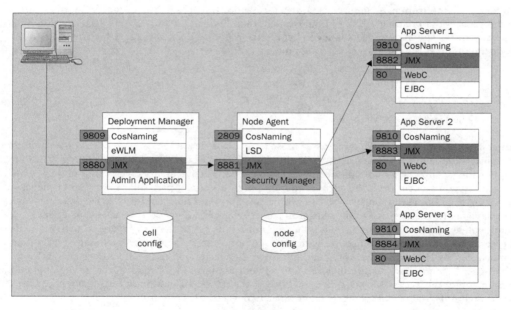

The Admin application is able to coordinate requests through the cell-wide JMX network because the WebSphere topology is known at the Deployment Manager by way of a locally stored, cell-wide configuration repository. The Admin application owns and manages the master copy of this repository. When an administrator makes changes to the cell topology, such as adding a node or server, the master repository is updated and the changes are distributed to the other nodes and servers within the cell. Each node and server has its own local, read-only view of the repository data. This is important, because it eliminates a single point of failure by not requiring app servers to connect to the Deployment Manager to read their current configuration.

The Node Agent

The **Node Agent** is a special process whose primary purpose is to provide node-wide services to the app servers configured on that node. The Node Agent listens on the standard CORBA INS bootstrap port 2809. CORBA IIOP clients booting into the node go to the Node Agent by default. J2EE clients typically use JNDI to access the namespace; the WebSphere JNDI implementation functions as a CORBA IIOP client on behalf of the J2EE client. The Node Agent houses its own copy of the read-only portion of the WebSphere namespace. Navigating through the Node Agent's namespace, an application may walk the namespace into the server of its choice to find those EJB references that it requires to start its processing. These EJB references are actually CORBA Interoperable Object References (IORs) that provide the application with RMI/IIOP access to the referenced EJBs.

The Node Agent keeps track of each of the active servers on its node. The Node Agent provides a **Location Service Daemon (LSD)** that is able to direct RMI/IIOP requests to the correct server. The IORs from the namespace are actually indirect references to EJB home interfaces. According to the EJB specification, an application may use an EJB home interface to create or find EJBs of a particular type, where each EJB type has its own unique home interface. The first use of a home IOR is routed to the Node Agent's LSD, so that the indirection can be resolved to a specific server. This is called "location forwarding" by the CORBA standard. After the home IOR is forwarded to the correct server, the J2EE client's RMI/IIOP requests flow directly to the app server from that point on.

The following diagram depicts this flow:

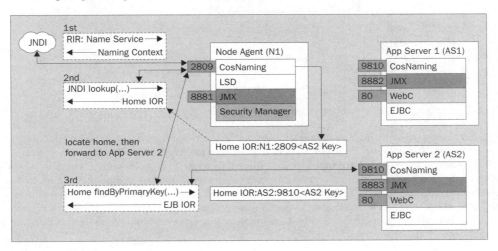

In the preceding diagram, a J2EE client's 1st step is to obtain an initial JNDI context; in the 2nd step, the client looks up an EJB home interface through that context and receives indirect IOR HomeIOR:N1:2809 <AS2 Key> in return. The location information in this IOR points back to the Node Agent (N1), but indicates through the object key (AS2 Key) that the target object resides in AS2. The client's first use of this IOR (3rd step) causes a locate request to flow to the location indicated in the IOR, which is the Node Agent on node N1. Once the locate request arrives at N1, it is passed to the LSD, which in turn, responds with forwarding IOR, HomeIOR:AS2:9810<AS2 Key>, which then enables the client ORB to interact directly with the target application server (AS2) – that's where the findByPrimaryKey() invocation will actually execute in this example.

Please note, the IOR contents depicted in the drawing are for illustrative purposes only and do not reflect the actual format and content of IORs used by WebSphere.

The App Server

So far, all the WebSphere components we have looked at exist for the purpose of supporting the app server. As you would expect, the app server is the place where J2EE applications are deployed and hosted. WebSphere 5.0 supports J2EE 1.3 architecture, so naturally you will find the typical components in the app server necessary to support the programming model: EJB and web containers, Java transaction, connector, and messaging APIs are among the standard components that compose the app server. Additionally you will find various caches and pools, such as connection and thread pools. The following diagram depicts the essential components composing the app server:

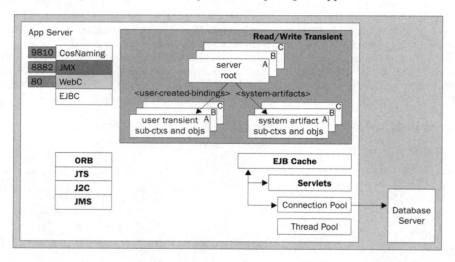

Particularly noteworthy, is the app server's local CosNaming namespace – depicted in the diagram by the box labeled "Read/Write Transient". As described previously, the CosNaming namespace is distributed across the WebSphere topology and linked together with corbanames. The app server's portion of the namespace contains bindings for those resources installed and configured on that server. Programming artifacts such as EJB homes and connection factories are found in the local namespace. By being local, the app server is freed from depending on some external server for directory access to local resources. Since the local namespace is built in memory during server initialization, it is inherently cached, boosting application performance.

The other components depicted in the preceding diagram and previously introduced are:

❑ **EJB Cache** – this is where the EJB container stores in-use EJBs.

❑ **Servlet Cache** – this is where the web container stores in-use servlets.

❑ **Connection Pool** – this is where the app server stores active database connections.

❑ **Thread Pool** – this is where the app server maintains a collection of available threads for executing work.

- ❑ **ORB** – this is the CORBA Object Request Broker. It manages remote method requests on EJBs.

- ❑ **JTS** – this the transaction manager (Java Transaction Service).

- ❑ **JCA** – this is the Java Connector component, providing the basic runtime services required by JCA resource adapters.

- ❑ **JMS** – this is the Java Message Service.

There are a number of other pools, caches, and components, which are not depicted in the preceding diagram that further serve to increase the performance and facility of the WebSphere app server. While we will not describe these other features in detail, we will touch upon the more significant ones briefly:

- ❑ The **Prepared Statement Pool** holds JDBC prepared statements. Combined with pooled connections, this enables the app server to achieve break-neck data access performance.

- ❑ The **Data Cache** holds CMP persistent data. Fed from an underlying database, this cache does wonders to keep CMP entity beans moving fast.

- ❑ **Dynacache** is a flexible caching mechanism used primarily for caching web content. Data delivery from cache has high performance, and is a natural application for web content. Dynacache is the secret behind WebSphere's solid web performance.

- ❑ **Distributed Replication Service (DRS)** is a new service in WebSphere 5.0. It is used for replicating data among clustered servers. Its initial application is for caching and synchronizing stateful data, such as that of HTTP session and stateful session beans. DRS is both a powerful and flexible facility, and is available to your applications.

Workload Management

WebSphere includes powerful **workload management (WLM) capabilities** to leverage clustered servers by dynamically distributing work among the members of the cluster. This delivers significant scalability and availability qualities to WebSphere applications. WLM capabilities exist for both EJB and web component application requests, and there is a separate mechanism for each. This is necessary because of the inherent differences in their respective communication protocols. EJBs, driven by RMI/IIOP requests, use the IOR architecture to deliver special WLM instructions to the WebSphere client-side ORB. Web components are driven by HTTP/HTTPS, which has no provision for delivering WLM instructions; so instead, WLM instructions are configured directly in WebSphere's web server plug-in.

EJB WLM

For RMI/IIOP, the WebSphere WLM function uses the Deployment Manager as the point of control for establishing initial WLM decisions. The Deployment Manager periodically queries the cluster members for their current operational status, so that it can maintain updated routing information for clients who wish to access EJB resources available on that cluster. Clients bootstrap into the Deployment Manager to look up WLM-enabled EJB resources.

The Deployment Manager returns specially tagged IORs for such requests. The additional information in the IOR is a WLM routing table, which includes an initial list of routing choices for use by the client-side ORB. The client-side ORB distributes EJB requests across the servers represented in the routing table. The distribution is round robin by default, but can be adjusted by specifying WLM weights to each of the servers. Servers with heavier weights receive relatively more requests than servers with lesser weights. This allows you to tune your WLM environment based on the size and/or workload mix on the servers in a cluster.

The WebSphere WLM data (routing table) is proprietary: only the WebSphere client ORB recognizes it. There is presently no Java or CORBA standard for conducting workload management. This does not prevent other ORBs from driving requests to a clustered server; it simply means no workload balancing occurs.

The following diagram depicts the run-time flows that occur in a WLM-enabled WebSphere environment:

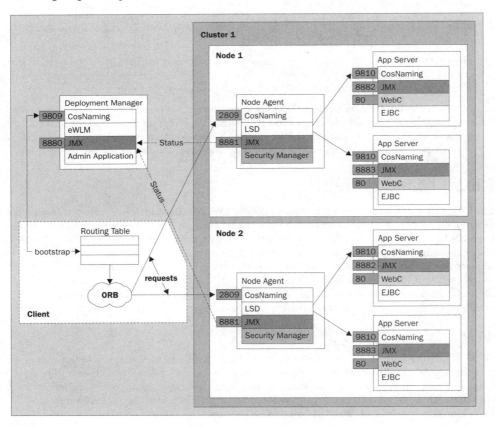

In the diagram, the Deployment Manager receives status information from cluster members in response to its periodic queries. Clients boot into the Deployment Manager to look up EJB resources available on that cluster and receive special WLM routing information carried in the IORs that represent those EJB resources. The client-side ORB uses the routing table information to distribute requests across the cluster.

Dynamic Routing Updates

The operational status of the cluster may change dynamically over time. As the status of the app servers changes, they register and de-register with the Deployment Manager. In addition, the Deployment Manager periodically queries the registered app servers to remain aware of their current operational status. The Deployment Manager uses this knowledge to keep the routing tables updated. It also distributes the routing tables back to the Node Agents on each of the cluster members. This enables each node in the cluster to dynamically modify a client's routing table for requests received by that node.

This is important because the routing table a client acquires by bootstrapping to the Deployment Manager may be retained and utilized by that client for an extended period of time. The possibility exists that the routing table becomes stale or old. Any cluster member can send back an updated routing table in the response messages it returns to the client. This way, the client-side ORB always has the best possible information available for workload routing decisions.

Affinity

Once the client-side ORB sends a request to a particular cluster member, an affinity to that server may be established for a period of time and must be remembered. Such affinities exist for things such as XA-transaction scope and stateful session beans. The IOR architecture is further leveraged to include affinity information, which the client-side ORB recognizes, so that requests are routed to the correct server until the affinity period terminates. For example, if the client starts an XA transaction, the client ORB will route all requests for the same entity bean back to the same server until the transaction completes.

Web Component WLM

Web components can undergo workload balancing as well. Although the HTTP protocol does not lend itself to the dynamic distribution of WLM instructions as IIOP does, the WebSphere plug-in can be configured to map a URL to multiple destinations. It then uses a round robin approach to spread requests across all of the app servers in the mapping. This enables simple, yet effective workload distribution for web requests. Cookies are used to maintain affinity knowledge so HTTP sessions may be routed back to the correct server. Basic operational awareness of the target servers is maintained by monitoring HTTP timeouts; a communication timeout removes a server from the destination list. The following diagram depicts this method of workload balancing:

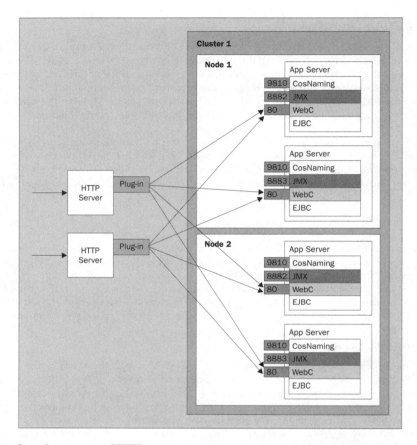

In this preceding diagram two HTTP servers, configured with a WebSphere plug-in, spread work across the same set of app servers. This configuration provides doubly-redundant routing to the same set of applications. The configuration need not be symmetric, as shown in the diagram. Through the WebSphere plug-in you can independently configure each HTTP server to route to only those servers to which you want it to route work.

Overview of Topologies

Now that we have seen the WebSphere server components up close and how they work together, let's now apply these elements to three common WebSphere topologies.

Single-Server Scenarios

The simplest and most prevalent topology in which WebSphere is used is the single-server topology. This includes a single, stand-alone, independent application server instance. This topology shows up in a number of cases, including:

❑ A developer desktop where you need an instance in which to test or assemble application components, or to experiment with the application server to understand how a particular feature works before incorporating that into an application

❑ Individuals who want to try out the application server, perhaps to compare it other competitive application servers

❑ Engineers involved in integration activities – responsible for combing application components to form a progressively more complete application

❑ Small businesses or lines of business within a larger enterprise, needing only the capacity of a single application server for their business needs

> **The objective of the single-server topology is simple: to get you up and running with as little effort as possible. It is the fastest path to getting your first application up and running.**

A common and important variation on this topology is where multiple application servers are executed on the same machine, but independent of each other. We treat this as equivalent to the single-server topology. It is expected that each server instance will be managed independently, often by separate administrators who often double as the owner or user of the app server.

In this topology, everything is administered through an independent configuration file and through direct communication with the application server for operations management function. WebSphere does not impose a dependency on a secondary process for managing the application server in the standalone, single-server topology.

If more than a single-server is operated on a given node, then each server should have its own independent configuration file – independently describing what applications will be hosted on that server instance, what resources will be used by that application server, and so on. There is no attempt to mediate shared resources between the application servers when they are operated as stand-alone servers.

In this topology, configuration is performed by editing the XML files that define the configuration of that server. To perform operations management, the methods on the JMX MBean server, embedded in the application server, are invoked (at least for everything but physically starting the application server process). Both of these are augmented by an Admin application that can be configured to run in the application server – essentially the same 'thin client' administration application used for other scenarios, but by virtue of the configuration confined to operate solely on the application server that it resides on. As an alternative, this same Admin application can be pointed to the configuration of another application server – to edit the configuration file of that server. However, there is no prior knowledge of that other application server.

This is the standard setup you get when you install WebSphere straight out of the box. You get a single app server and basic command-line tools for installing and configuring applications. During installation you specify names for both the app server and the node of which it is a part.

543

The following diagram depicts the single-server configuration:

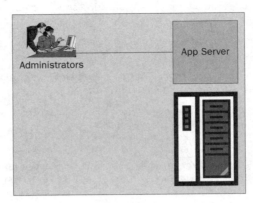

The chief benefit of the single-server topology is that it is easy to set up. It is autonomous, because you administer it directly and by itself. It is the perfect configuration for exploration, development, or entry-level application hosting for a small business or department. This configuration is not sufficient for larger deployments that have application workloads too big for a single-server. This could be from either the number of applications in use or the number of users of those applications or both. Either way, multiple app servers are probably required. These may be installed on the same physical hardware, if that machine offers enough processing power and storage to host the workload.

The alternative is to install app servers on multiple machines, providing increased computational resources. Multiple computers also provide increased availability in case of a system failure. The following diagram depicts these two different approaches:

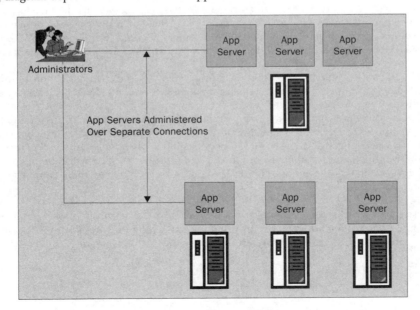

The downside to just adding more app servers is that as the number of app servers increases, it becomes inconvenient and awkward to administer each app server separately – a single point of administration is much more effective as the number of app servers grows. The following section will explore multi-server topologies and centralized administration in greater detail.

Multi-Server Scenarios

As we saw at the end of the last section, you can throw more and more servers at your workload and application portfolio to increase computing capacity and availability; however, that alone is not the approach we recommend for managing multi-server topologies. Central administration is critical to multi-server configurations, and is the reason for organizing app servers into a WebSphere cell. In a cell configuration, all app servers can be administered from a single point of control. Let's look at some typical multi-server scenarios.

Branch Offices

A number of large enterprises are organized around using branches as outlets for their business – bringing their business to the people. Branches tend to look very much like small businesses, requiring their own local computing resources both to reduce latency for high volume functions, and to enable continued business operations when communication to the central organization is cut off temporarily.

These businesses want to install application servers in their respective branch offices to provide local application functions. However, branch offices cannot afford local IT skills – they must completely rely on central operations to manage their IT assets. Further, since the premise of branch computing is to reach a geographically dispersed clientele, those same scales of geography also inhibit the central operations organization from traveling to the branch to provide on-site support. All aspects of administering the branch office systems must be performed remotely. This includes software distribution and installation, configuration and execution control, backup and recovery procedures, and so on.

In addition, the branch must remain autonomous, managing itself automatically when communication with the central operations is cut off temporarily. Fortunately, business procedures in branch offices are not highly dynamic – they do not require massive reconfiguration on an hourly or even daily basis. Any dynamic nature in business processes for these staid bricks-and-mortar institutions is generally measured in weeks or months, often coupled with training for the humans involved in the business process.

Peak workloads can vary throughout the day, or under special economic circumstances. However, these peaks are often moderated by the physical capacity of the branch facilities. In other words, since electronically generated transactions typically bypass the branch and are routed directly to the central operations center, the branch is only involved in transactions that are manually brokered by an agent in the branch.

For example, bank branches only process as many transactions as their tellers are able to handle. Since the branch-based business model generally involves a large ratio of branch offices to central operations, the cost of computing dedicated to each branch ends up being multiplied by the number of branches. There is no pro-rating of shared resources for anything that has to be installed and dedicated to a particular branch. Consequently, the economic model for branch computing is to keep the cost of computing in each branch as small as possible. For example, the computing hardware has very little excess capacity, and companies are generally willing to compromise redundancy to keep their operational costs low.

A vanilla branch configuration will involve a small number (between one and five) of application servers running on one server node. Generally, there is no clustering support used in the branch. The applications used in the branch are designed both to collaborate with centralized applications, and to work off-line. Likewise, the system management facilities must both collaborate with the centralized operations center, enabling full remote control, and be able to continue to work autonomously in off-line mode – being able to re-synchronize themselves automatically when they return to on-line processing.

A small to medium sized community or regional enterprise may consist, typically, of five to fifty branch offices. Each branch typically will have its own app server to provide local access for availability and performance. These app servers will be organized into a cell and centrally administered through a Deployment Manager, running at a central location. All administration for applications and servers is orchestrated from the central location. The following diagram depicts such a configuration, involving three branch offices and a Deployment Manager owned by central IT:

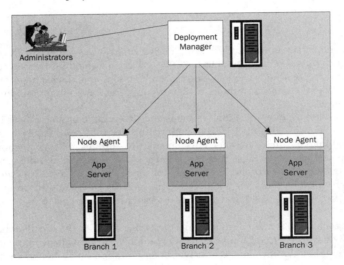

Departmental or Workgroup

Departmental or workgroup computing represents the majority of production topologies in use today. This scenario can exist in both large and small enterprises. Generally it is characterized by a setup that is dedicated to one or a small number of highly related applications all based on the WebSphere runtime. For this reason, the environment is relatively homogenous. In general, any backend systems required by these applications are hosted on other systems, outside the WebSphere cell. They are not subject to management by the WebSphere system management facilities (other than to create bindings to those systems), nor impinging on the computing capacity dedicated for use by WebSphere-based application components.

The departmental or workgroup topology typically involves multiple nodes, or a single high capacity, multi-processor node. Workload across these nodes needs to be balanced. But workload does not need to be balanced against an arbitrary set of general-purpose applications residing on a range of different middleware technologies. Consequently, workload can be balanced against a relatively limited set of variables, mostly stemming from client-generated demand. In this topology, it is often as accurate to base workload balancing decisions on a prior knowledge of the capacity of the nodes as anything else.

This topology may involve from one to twenty nodes, one Deployment Manager, and one Node Agent per node in the cell. The workgroup or departmental topology is administered through a single logical image of the entire workgroup hosted in a Deployment Manager. In many cases, multiple application servers running on the same physical computer can satisfy departmental or workgroup computing, so long as it is sufficiently large. The following diagram depicts an app server workgroup configured and administered as a cell housed on a single large computer:

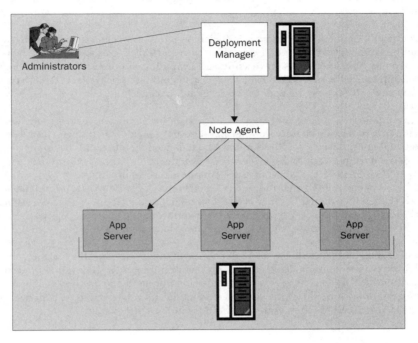

While not geographically dispersed, as in the case of the branch office, a department or workgroup configuration may also want to consider multiple computer systems for increased scale and availability.

> **WebSphere cells can be organized into local or wide-area cells that can be centrally administered for consistency and increased control. However, clustering and firewall configurations must be added to deliver scalability and access.**

Cell configurations are very helpful in consolidating administration and enabling business policies, such as security, to be applied consistently across all app servers within the same cell. Moreover, cells can be used to isolate one WebSphere configuration from another. There are limitations in these topologies, however. The need for increasing application scalability and availability is not naturally met by a group of individual servers – even when centrally administered. Furthermore, these topologies do not address the security and performance issues of applications serving on the Internet.

Scaling Up-and-Out – Enterprise Scenarios

Enterprise topology represents the extremes of cell scaling: vertically or horizontally.

Vertical scaling involves many application server instances – tens or hundreds – on a single logical or physical node. Horizontal scaling involves many nodes in a single cell, any of which may be a vertically scaled node.

You scale vertically to the extent you have sufficient compute-capacity on a single physical machine to support multiple app servers. High-end machines, such as IBM zSeries and pSeries, as well as certain machines made by Sun, and others, have sufficient computing resources to host large numbers of app servers. You still cluster horizontally for increased scale, but also for availability – if you lose one machine, you can still provide the application from another machine.

An enterprise topology will generally involve sharing computing resources between WebSphere-based applications, and applications based on other middleware – including strategic, legacy, proprietary, and standard technologies. Resource utilization must be balanced among all of the applications, based on workloads derived from a variety of sources. For example, an enterprise system may support WebSphere, CICS, SAP, TPF, and proprietary environments. Many different applications may be hosted on these systems supporting traditional 3270 clients, ATM networks and financial switches, APPN or MQ based messaging, IIOP or HTTP-based clients, and so on. The applications may be completely independent of each other, loosely coupled through MQ messaging, web services, or workflow management, or tightly coupled through interdependencies designed into the application.

The levels of scaling and additional execution complexity that represent the enterprise topology require additional features in system management that are not required for workgroup or departmental computing. In particular, clustering servers together for workload balance and availability, building firewall configurations, providing efficient access to application data across wide networks, and integrating EIS resources, are all required capabilities in these topologies.

Clustering

A WebSphere server cluster is a grouping of servers that are administered as individual servers, but represent themselves to application clients as a single logical server. As work is driven onto the server cluster, it is automatically, transparently, and seamlessly distributed across the bank of servers that compose the cluster. This distribution of incoming work requests in this manner is the basis for application scalability on WebSphere.

Note that not all applications can scale this way. Applications that are stateless or have managed affinity can run on a cluster. By "managed affinity" we mean a server affinity that is known to WebSphere, and thus can be managed by WebSphere – for example, a transaction or HTTP session. If an application is stateless, individual requests can be correctly executed on any app server in the cluster. If an application has an affinity, that generally means it has some temporal memory-based resource and must execute in the same process until the application no longer has that affinity. Applications can implicitly establish process affinity through use of transactions and HTTP sessions. WebSphere knows about these affinities and can route requests for such an application back to the correct app server based on the affinity. If an application has other affinities – those not know to WebSphere – such as opening a socket and reading data into memory, then this application cannot execute on a cluster.

Clustered servers can be configured on the same, or across different, network nodes (or machines), so not only can you increase scalability, you can also increase availability by having more servers available on more physical machines. The outage of an individual server or machine does not represent an outage of the application served by the cluster.

True to the WebSphere philosophy, you can organize, spread, and group your servers to meet your specific scale and availability requirements. The following diagram depicts some of these options in effect:

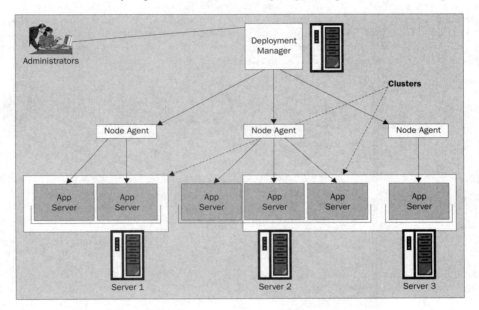

The benefits of clustering are significant:

❑   First, it presents a single logical server to your application clients, freeing them from awareness of the physical topology of your WebSphere cell. For example, the application clients find logical clusters in the namespace – not individual servers.

❑   Second, because clients operate on logical – not physical – definitions, this frees your IT organization from reconfiguring physical resources as requirements and availability dictate. This means that additional servers can be added to or removed from to a cluster without awareness by, or impact on, your application clients.

❑   Third, your application clients are insulated from server failure. The cluster – and the applications deployed on it – remain available to your clients even if individual servers fail and become unavailable. This level of availability is an absolute requirement for mission-critical applications.

❑   Fourth, a WebSphere cluster can be formed from WebSphere servers residing on any platform WebSphere supports. This provides your organization with maximum flexibility and choice in deciding how best to apply available computer resources to satisfy the workload appetite of your client community. This is also helpful for managing application upgrades across a set of servers because you can install it across the cluster's members one at a time.

In the Zone

If you want to allow thousands of customers to access you electronic storefront, but are concerned about the security risks, WebSphere has a common topology for providing safe Internet access.

A sound practice for configuring app servers for Internet access is to setup a **demilitarized zone**, or **DMZ**. The DMZ is established through the use of a firewall pair, which establishes a double-layered protection against intruders. The DMZ is actually the area between the firewalls. In the DMZ, you would typically configure a web server. The left-most firewall (as shown in the following diagram) exposes perhaps only port 80 (default HTTP port) to the Internet, so the DMZ web server can be reached. The right-most firewall exposes ports as required for the DMZ web server to access app servers, other web servers, and possibly other types of server altogether, as dictated by your system architecture:

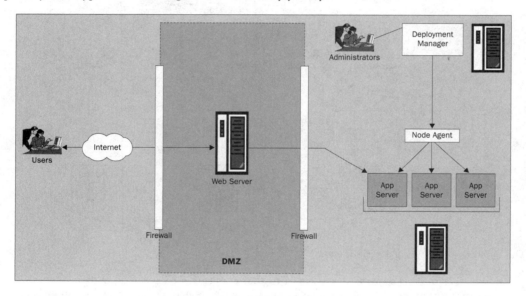

> **Serving only HTTP from inside a DMZ is a common topography for safe Internet access. In this configuration, only DMZ web servers have access to your WebSphere app servers.**

The importance of the DMZ firewall topology is that it is among the safest techniques for enabling Internet access to selected applications, without exposing your entire internal network to the outside. The disadvantage of firewalls, generally, is that by their nature they restrict access. This in turn makes it more difficult to provide access to application clients that require use of communication protocols other than HTTP, such as IIOP and JMS. Advances in firewall technology, such as IIOP firewalls, will increase the ability to provide greater access options, without sacrificing security and control.

Serving to the Edge

An **Edge Server** is a special WebSphere add-on for extending the reach and performance of your enterprise's web presence and applications. "Edge" refers to the area of your WebSphere topology that is closest to your end users, such as where some of your HTTP servers might be found, but farthest away from the servers where your business and data logic is deployed. It is the first point of contact between your enterprise and your customers, business partners, and employees – ultimately the users who access your applications. The trick here is to provide the best access to your users for least cost. This was never an easy goal to achieve. The world of Internet computing, while opening immeasurable possibilities, has also increased network size, bandwidth demand, and the number of devices between users and servers. All this further complicates the tasks required to achieve the goal. The WebSphere Edge Server is an additional tool to help you balance access performance against delivery cost.

The WebSphere Edge Server, installed separately, is a kind of caching proxy server. It can be run in both forward and reverse proxy mode. The following diagram depicts the two common strategies for proxy and content caching across the network:

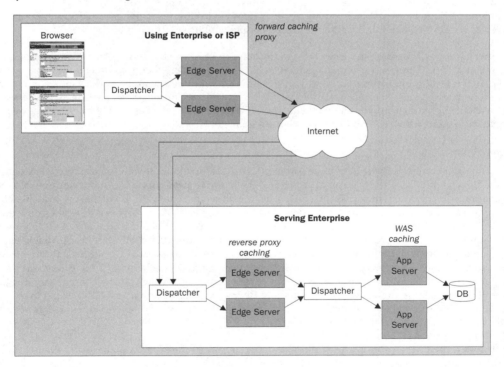

> The WebSphere Edge Server enables you to distribute and cache application content closer to your end users, increasing perceived application performance, while simultaneously offloading work from your mainline application servers.

The most common place to deploy a proxy server is at a network bottleneck. Bottlenecks are often created by slow connections at network gateways. Managing bandwidth at these locations is imperative as your business grows and network traffic continues to increase. The Internet gateway and the branch office connection are two likely bottleneck locations and are therefore prime candidates for a proxy server deployment.

Forward Proxy

Corporations are deploying proxy servers in increasing numbers on their intranets, both in remote locations and on major sub-networks. Proxy servers deployed at major sub-network connections can drastically reduce the traffic on your corporate backbone. At remote offices, which are often connected via slow links to the corporate network, proxy servers can provide a quick mechanism for replicating content, providing better company integration, and increasing network performance – all of which can be achieved without large capital and communications expense.

Many organizations are seeing the value of deploying proxy servers throughout their intranet. Types of deployments that use multiple servers can take advantage of the proxy routing capabilities of the WebSphere Edge Server. Proxy routing allows you to chain proxies together to create a hierarchical caching system that can better serve the various organizations within your enterprise.

Proxy chaining allows multiple Edge servers to cache content locally, setting up a hierarchy of servers for client access. The result is a managed network of proxy servers that is completely transparent to the user. In a typical implementation, smaller, local proxies might be situated near end-user communities, with larger proxies near the firewall and external connections. For most installations, two levels of hierarchy is optimum, but you may benefit from adding more levels, depending on the size of your organization and where the bottlenecks occur on your network.

Reverse Proxy

If you have a content server that has sensitive information that must remain secure, such as a database of credit-card numbers, you can set up a proxy outside the firewall as a stand-in for your content server. When outside clients try to access the content server, they are sent to the proxy server instead. The real content resides on your content server, safely inside the firewall. The proxy server resides outside the firewall, and appears to the client to be the content server. When a client makes a request to your site, the request goes to the proxy server. The proxy server then sends the client's request through a specific passage in the firewall to the content server. The content server passes the result through the passage back to the proxy. The proxy sends the retrieved information to the client, as if the proxy was the actual content server – this is depicted on the bottom of the preceding diagram. If the content server returns an error message, the proxy server can intercept the message and change any URLs listed in the headers before sending the message to the client. This prevents external clients from getting redirection URLs to the internal content server.

In this way, the proxy provides an additional barrier between the secure database and the possibility of malicious attack. In the unlikely event of a successful attack, the perpetrator is more likely to be restricted to only the information involved in a single transaction, as opposed to having access to the entire database. The unauthorized user cannot get to the real content server because the firewall passage allows only the proxy server to have access.

You can use multiple proxy servers within an organization to balance the network load among web servers. This model lets you take advantage of the caching features of the proxy server to create a server pool for load balancing. In this case, the proxy servers can be on either side of the firewall. If you have a web server that receives a high number of requests per day, you could use proxy servers to take the load off the web server and make the network access more efficient. The proxy servers act as go-betweens for client requests to the real server. The proxy servers cache the requested documents. If there is more than one proxy server, DNS can route the requests using a round-robin selection of their IP addresses. The client uses the same URL each time, but the route the request takes might go through a different proxy each time.

The advantage of using multiple proxies to handle requests to one heavily used content server is that the server can handle a heavier load, or the same load more efficiently than it could alone. After an initial start-up period in which the proxies retrieve documents from the content server for the first time, the number of requests to the content server can drop dramatically.

Only CGI requests and occasional new requests must go all the way to the content server. A proxy can handle the rest. For example, suppose that 90% of the requests to your server are not CGI requests (which means they can be cached), and that your content server receives two million hits per day. In this situation, if you connect three reverse proxies, and each of them handles two million hits per day, about six million hits per day would then be possible. The 10% of requests that reach the content server could add up to about 200,000 hits from each proxy per day, or only 600,000 total, which is far more efficient. The number of hits could increase from around two million to six million, and the load on the content server could decrease correspondingly from two million to 600,000. Your actual results would depend upon your situation.

Use of the WebSphere Edge Server can dramatically improve perceived application performance, increase overall network performance, enhance workload balancing, and increase the scope and reach of your applications. This does come at the cost of increased complexity and administrative demand, but the benefits are well worth it.

EIS Integration

The next topographical consideration is most relevant to customers of existing EIS systems, such as users of IBM CICS and IMS transaction monitors. A common requirement for new applications is to leverage and interact with existing application assets.

The Java 2 Connector Architecture (JCA) defines a standard interface for accessing arbitrary backend systems. The unique pluggable nature of JCA connectors enables easy third-party add-ons. Naturally, JCA adapters are available to connect WebSphere to CICS and IMS. You can anticipate availability of JCA adapters from both IBM and other vendors for a growing number of existing application execution environments.

Let's take a closer look at what an EIS integration topology might look like. The following diagram depicts a WebSphere/CICS application integration scenario:

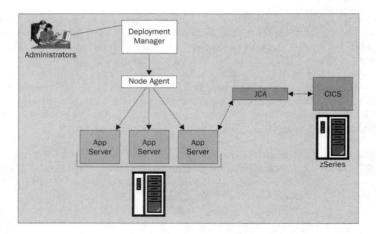

Through JCA adapters, the reach of WebSphere is extended to include access to a number of key application execution environments, including CICS, IMS, and DB2.

While the strength of the J2EE architecture and WebSphere includes the ability to easily integrate EIS applications with new J2EE applications – even across disparate machine architectures and operating systems – WebSphere is uniquely positioned like no other J2EE application server to deliver high performance, highly scalable EIS integration with other IBM application environments through z/OS and OS/390 version of WebSphere.

As the diagram below depicts, WebSphere for z/OS and OS/390, delivers the tremendous benefit of co-locating your J2EE application server with your CICS, IMS, or DB2 server on the same execution platform, which leverages substantial local optimizations:

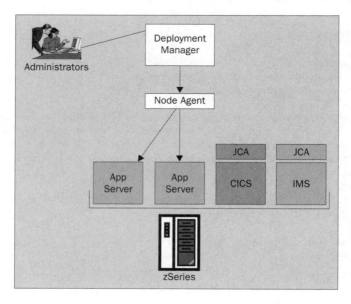

WebSphere and J2EE bring a rich array of tools and capabilities to bear on the task of EIS integration. WebSphere for z/OS and OS/390 offers unique strengths and capabilities for integration with existing CICS, IMS, and DB2 systems. There are many considerations for EIS integration. You can find more information on this topic in Chapter 7.

WebSphere provides unique integration possibilities with your existing EIS infrastructure. You can easily deploy both IBM and third-party JCA connectors for accessing CICS, IMS, SAP, and other EIS systems. You have great flexibility in deciding the best mix of cost and performance. Application server deployments on middle-tier systems (for example Unix), with remote access to your EIS can deliver reasonable performance for moderate access to your EIS at modest cost. Alternatively, WebSphere allows you the option of co-locating your application servers on the same system as your EIS – particularly large scale EIS, such as CICS and IMS on z/OS or OS/390 – delivering significant performance advantages by leveraging local access to the EIS assets.

Large Enterprise Topology

Large enterprises typically have diverse requirements that lead to larger, mixed networks of servers. Often a combination of departmental server groups, Internet-accessible line-of-business servers, and EIS integration, large enterprises demand the highest levels of scale, availability, and control.

WebSphere server networks, by their modular nature and single logical image, are especially well suited to meeting the needs of large enterprises. The following diagram depicts a particular large enterprise configuration, which combines a number of departmental servers with an internet-accessible clustered server, accessing an EIS application on CICS:

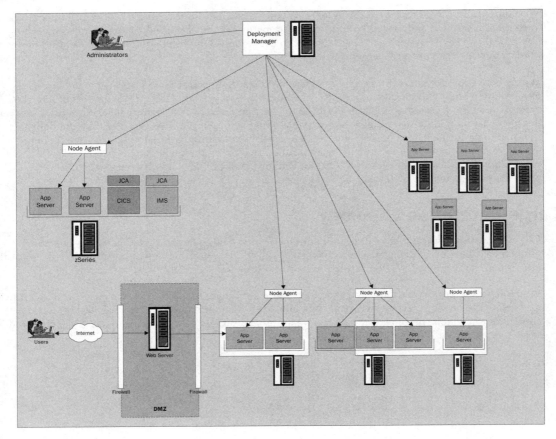

The diversity of WebSphere configuration, advanced administration facilities, and superior EIS integration capability makes it particularly well suited for tackling the needs of the largest enterprise. Moreover, WebSphere clustering delivers the scalability and availability characteristics that enterprise workloads demand.

The benefit of WebSphere to the large enterprise is flexibility. The rich configurability of WebSphere, the breadth of supported platforms, the power and reach of available JCA connectors, and the comprehensive control of WebSphere cell administrative services, all combine to make WebSphere a strong ally in solving the widest array of application deployment and integration requirements.

Plants-By-WebSphere Topology

Now that we've had a fair tour of WebSphere topologies, let's consider our sample application, Plants-By-WebSphere. As usual, when it comes to matching a configuration with business requirements, it all depends! There are a couple things we can easily conclude, however. Since Plants-By-WebSphere is an Internet storefront type application, it is designed to be accessible through the Internet by as many people as possible. So we will need a DMZ to protect our data assets. We'll place an HTTP server in the DMZ and forward all web requests to the presentation logic of Plants-By-WebSphere, running in a WebSphere application server behind the DMZ. We would most likely run a clustered server for availability: if one server or machine goes down, we still have the other one to keep our business running while we recover the failure. In addition, a cluster gives us an easy way to add more processing power to our production environment: we can expend the cluster by adding additional servers on existing or new nodes. The following diagram depicts the topology we would use to support Plants-By-WebSphere in a production environment:

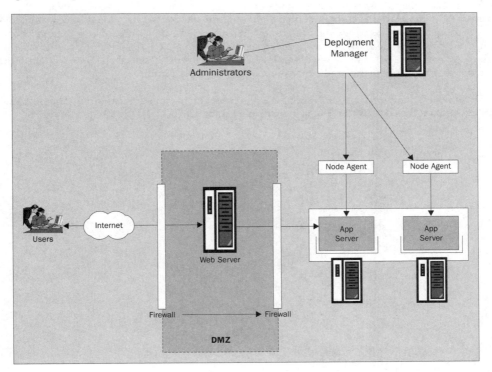

The few factors and considerations we have listed here certainly do not represent to totality of issues that you must face when designing and deploying a production topology – for example, we have not discussed security policy, which we will look at in the next chapter. However, we hope our brief consideration of the configuration characteristics appropriate to support our sample application offers added insight into the subject of topology.

Summary

In this chapter we introduced the WebSphere brand of products, focusing especially on the Application Server and Network Deployment Manager products. We took some time to build up a working vocabulary, consisting of such essential terms as cell, node, server, and cluster. Combining the product names and terms, we constructed some simple WebSphere configurations to clarify the meaning of terms.

We then took a divergence into a short study of a server's anatomy. We saw that it takes a number of components to compose the internals of a J2EE server. While many of these components are easily predicted after reading a J2EE specification, a number of them are unique to the WebSphere implementation, especially the various caches and pools used to boost performance, the segmented CosNaming namespace implementation, and the JMX administrative communication backbone, that flows Admin requests through a network of app servers.

We finished the chapter up with a short study of several common WebSphere topologies. We considered the motivating factors in branch and departmental computing models that would compel us to organize our WebSphere topology differently. We also spent some time looking at larger networking configurations, including firewalls, and edge-of-network caching. We finished up our study by looking at the large-scale problems and saw how WebSphere addresses these issues through server clustering and the ability to host WebSphere applications on large zSeries platforms.

Most production configurations of WebSphere require security and administration. The next two chapters explore these areas of systems management in detail.

13
Securing your Enterprise

Few other topics in the domain of information computing create as much anxiety as that of security. No serious-minded systems analyst would dream of putting their mission-critical business logic and information assets into a production environment without being certain they could be protected from abuse and misuse. A few minutes perusing the CERT advisory board (http://www.cert.org) will leave you thinking twice about where your data has been. How many reports have we seen about viruses, worms, and other nasty vermin bringing down systems or stealing credit card numbers? How many times have you had to re-install Windows because a worm came in through e-mail and wiped out your file system? Who hasn't thought about having to stand in front of their boss having to explain why their web site got hacked?

Yet, if you're like most, the nuances and complexities of securing your systems will seem daunting and elusive. In some sense, this is good – it is often said that "just because you can't think of a way to break into your system, doesn't mean that someone won't find a way". If you're aware of this axiom, then you've already taken the first step towards justifying your paranoia. It is always worth investigating the security of your system. Understanding how the security system works will help you understand where its strengths and weaknesses lie and help you ensure your systems and information remain protected.

WebSphere, in conjunction with Java and the J2EE security model go a long way toward ensuring the protection of your system. Unlike other systems, security has not been added as an after-thought, but rather was architected right into Java and WebSphere from the start. WebSphere and Java are designed to be secure. But as always, you play a key role – whether you're an application developer, assembler, deployer, administrator, or business user, your actions can either undermine or reinforce the safeguards provided by WebSphere. This chapter will provide you with a basic understanding of how the security system in WebSphere works and will provide you some guidance on how to ensure the protection of your system.

Programmatic Security

Our first instinct is to build security into our applications. After all, if your applications are attacked, you're often the first ones to get called. However, as hard as it might be to accept, it is better if you don't – that is, don't encode security policies into your business logic. In many cases, encoding security functions into your application can actually make things worse. We'll illustrate why with some scenarios:

❑ **Multiple User Registries**

Consider a case where you've written a user login function into your application. You prompt the user for their identity (user ID) and a password. You then do a lookup in a database (a user registry) and compare the password to the value stored in the database. First, there is the question of how the database itself is being protected – what is keeping another part of your application, or some other application running on your server from accessing your database; perhaps changing the password values to blanks and thus allowing any user to sign-in as anyone they want?

However, consider further that someone introduces another application into your business that also has its own login function using a completely different user registry. Assuming there is some chance that the same users will need to use both applications at some point then this creates two problems that eventually lead to integrity issues:

❑ The first is that since these are separate registries there is a high probability that each will contain a different password for the same user. This means that the user has to remember two different passwords – maybe even two different user IDs. Given the natural limitations of the human brain, eventually, people will start writing their passwords down somewhere to help them remember them. Of course, whenever you write a secret down you've increased the chances of someone else discovering that secret.

❑ The other problem that occurs in this scenario is that you've doubled the number of registries that have to be administered. If you later discover that one of your users is malicious or poses some other threat that leads you to want to remove them from your system you now have two different places to go to erase their user entry – assuming, of course, that the user held something in common like the same name or address in both registries that allows you to recognize the user in both places. Often, when you're dealing with thousands, or worse, millions of users, this gets increasingly difficult to do – the same user may be identified entirely differently in different user registries, given the opportunity.

❑ **Policy Inflexibility**

Let's say that you've encoded logic in your application that allows the Plant Store Owner and any Cashier to change a Customer order. Later you decide to increase your customer focus and so you replace all of your Cashiers with Customer Representatives and Product Specialists. You will not be able to make this change without also changing your applications. But more importantly, you will likely want to limit access to Customer orders – only allowing Customer Representatives access to the Customer order. This requires sub-setting everyone that was a Cashier, establishing their new roles, and then making sure your application has been re-coded to recognize that distinction.

❑ **Asymmetric Protection**

Next, consider the case that you've provided security in your application, but someone installs another application that does not provide security – and, in this scenario, you both access the same back-end data. This creates an asymmetry in the protection of your data resources – in effect, a weak link. Hackers will eventually find and attack the weaker flank and use that to undermine your well-laid plans. In this case, someone using your application to illegitimately access your backend data will be denied that access. However, that same person can shift over to using the other application and will be granted access. This calls in question why you bothered with the overhead of checking – you could have just gone ahead and given them access as well and possibly have gained some legitimate customers with the additional performance and throughput you might have gained without your protection mechanisms. Before you know, if everyone adopts this same attitude in your organization, you won't have any protection mechanisms in place whatsoever.

All of these scenarios illustrate the pitfalls of embedding security directly into the business logic of your application. However, this does not mean that you should not secure your application. In fact, WebSphere makes it relatively simple to protect your system, but without requiring that you encode security into your applications. WebSphere and J2EE accomplish this through a **declarative security** approach. The WebSphere runtime will enforce security policies that you declare in deployment descriptors about the security needs of your application. Because they are declarative, these policies can easily be changed without having to re-code and re-build your application. Moreover, security policies can be controlled through admin user interfaces and command-line interfaces allowing you to represent aggregations of policy.

This externalization allows security administrators to examine the total set of security policies being enforced by the system and reason about the relative protection of their systems. This approach also allows you to apply security to applications even if the application developer forgets or doesn't know how to include this in their own application (it gets rid of potential asymmetry in the enforcement model).

The Security Model

Before we can discuss the WebSphere security model, we need to start by defining the key terms and security principles on which the model is based. We will then summarize the J2EE and Java security model followed by the full WebSphere security model – showing how this model builds on the J2EE security model.

Protection Domain

Protection domain represents the scope over which the security system will protect resources. This is both a topological statement (the set of resources that can be protected), and a policy enforcement statement (the set of resources that are affected by a given policy statement, and the extent to which those resources are in a position within the network in which those policies can be assured). It is common to talk about the protection domain in terms of a single application server process as this scope is fairly well defined, and the trusted-computing base for the application server is relatively easy to understand. However, this is just one sub-scope within the entire WebSphere-based network of application servers and client processes.

Principal

A principal is any entity in the environment that we want to associate with a verifiable identity. This is most often a person, but it can be other things as well. For example, you may want to give your server process an identity. The server process can then be authenticated to the system and will be allowed or disallowed to perform certain activities based on what that principal (the server process, in this case) has been authorized to do. All principals have a security account in the user registry that retains information about that principal – such as their identity, how they can be authenticated, what groups they belong in, and so on.

Encryption

Converting a piece of data between its clear-text form and an un-readable form (based on a key) is at the basis of the Java, J2EE, and WebSphere security model. Encryption sustains the premise that information can be obscured and cannot be converted back to a readable form without the correct key.

Encryption can be achieved with either symmetric-key algorithms (where the same key is used to encrypt and decrypt the data – also referred to as private-key encryption since the key must be kept private) or public-key algorithms (using two related keys – one for encrypting and the other for decrypting the data). The latter is particularly useful for exchanging information between two parties. The sender can encrypt with one key, and the receiver can decrypt with another key. One key is kept private and the other key can be made public, depending on the effect you're trying to achieve.

Authentication

Authentication is the process of establishing that a principal is who it claims to be. There are a variety of techniques for proving authenticity, but the most common form entails the principal supplying their user ID and password. The user ID establishes who they are claiming to be, and since only they should know their password, then supplying the password is taken as proof of who they are. It's not hard to imagine cases where other people (or processes) have obtained a principal's password. If they do, then they can easily masquerade as that principal – pretending to be that principal by supplying that principal's user ID and password. Thus password-based authentication is often considered to be a relatively weak form of authentication – only as strong as the password is hard to guess, and to the extent the principal has kept their password a secret.

Other forms of authentication, such as certificate-based authentication represent stronger forms of authentication as they require either possessing something physical (like the key to your house), some physical aspect of who you are (such as your finger print, voice, the blood-vessel pattern in your eye, or your signature), or a combination of things, in addition to knowledge of a secret.

Credential

Credential is used in a couple of ways. From an information perspective, your credentials are the attributes about who you are – your title, your degree, your passport, and so on, that give a proof of your knowledge or capabilities. In the information system, a credential is an object that represents the authenticity of a principal. A credential will contain zero or more authentication tokens indicating how the principal represented by the credential was proven to be authentic. Based on the form of the authentication token, you can deduce the relative strength of that authentication. The credential will also contain a set of privilege attributes that could be deduced from the form of authentication performed and the security registry used to authenticate the principal.

Credential Mapping

Credential mapping represents a conversion of a credential representing a principal in one realm to another credential representing that same principal in another realm. This is needed whenever you initiate work that will cross runtime infrastructures associated with different user registries. For example, if your application invokes a servlet and a set of EJBs running in WebSphere against an LDAP-based registry associated with the WebSphere installation, and then calls out to a BAPI transaction running on SAP (which uses its own user registry for defining principals), you will need to perform a credential mapping if you are to continue to be associated with the request as it traverses into SAP. You will want to do this if you want to execute under your own authorization permissions in SAP.

Under other circumstances, the access to BAPI transactions could be performed under the authority of the WebSphere application server, in which case the application server must be authorized in SAP to execute on your behalf (that is, to perform the work that you need done by SAP).

Authorization

Authorization is the process of controlling access to resources based on policies that establish who can do what actions on what resources. Different policies have different levels of granularity. Some policies, for example, may allow that any authenticated user can access any resource in the system. This would be considered a very **coarse-grained** policy.

More common policies state that principals are allowed to perform certain roles – that is, they are allowed to invoke those operations on object types that are associated with that role. These are considered **fine-grained** authorization policies – being specified down to the granularity of individual methods on a class of objects. Even finer than that are policies that are based on the relationship between the principal and the state of the objects they are attempting to access. These are also sometimes referred to as **instance-based** authorization policies as they're dependent on the state of the object instance.

As a general rule, the more fine-grained the policy, the more impact there is on the runtime code-path to the resource. In other words, fine-grained authorization policies generally will have more performance impact than coarse-grained policies. Conversely, coarse-grained policies provide less control over who can do what in the system.

Privilege Attribute

Privilege Attribute states things about the principal; such as what user groups they belong to, and what enterprise role they perform, and so on. This information may be used in authorization policies. For example, an authorization policy may grant a particular group access to a resource. If you are a member of that group, then you will by extension, be granted to that same resource. Ideally, group membership is based on something meaningful in your organization – like the department you are in, or your job title or function, and so on. Being a member of that group essentially claims that you have the privileges of that group.

Message Protection

Message protection describes how messages are protected when communicated between different processes and computers in the network. Different degrees of protection can be associated with a message – ranging from none, to integrity protection, to field or message confidentiality. Integrity protection is basically a mechanism to ensure that nobody in the network can change the contents of a message (although it doesn't necessarily prevent anyone in the network from reading the information in the message). Confidentiality is used to prevent anyone from reading the information in the message. Field-level confidentiality says that only individual fields are hidden from anyone in the network, whereas message-level confidentiality says that the message cannot be read by anyone in the network.

Obviously, in either case, you typically want the end-user – the principal to whom you are sending the message – to be able to read the message you send to them. The message protection system is responsible for protecting the message in such a way that only the intended end user can retrieve it.

Digital Signatures

Digital signatures are a message encoding technique using public-key encryption to form a strong bond between a message and the person that created it (or signed it). Digital signatures are used just like your written signature on a document – they can be taken as some level of endorsement of the document you've signed.

Non-Repudiation

Non-Repudiation is an additional level of security that can be used to prevent an end user from denying that they sent a message, or from denying that they received a message. Most non-repudiation systems involve signing the message with a digital signature, and a heavy dose of auditing. The signature is used to prove that you, and only you, could have sent the document (you cannot repudiate having sent it). Likewise, signing the acknowledgement message can be used to prove that you received it. The audit is used to record these actions, when they occurred, the strength of the encryption mechanisms used in the transaction, characteristics of the key production and management system, and so on – things that will have to be revealed as part of any dispute of repudiation.

Security Architecture

Let us now discuss the J2EE security model. This forms the foundation of the WebSphere security model that we will discuss later in this chapter. The following diagram depicts the elements of the security architecture:

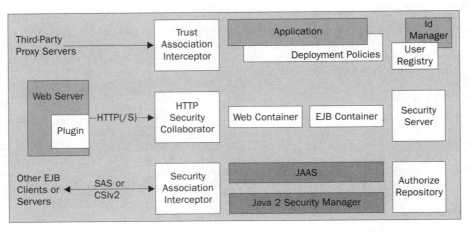

In the diagram above, the Security Association Interceptor protects communication between EJB clients and servers. The WebSphere interceptor supports protection in accordance with either the IBM (also referred to as the Secure Association Service) protocol, or the CORBA standard CSIv2 (Common Secure Interoperation, version 2) protocol over IIOP. This protocol ensures both secure association establishment, and message protection in accordance with the protection policies of the server.

The HTTP Security Collaborator protects HTTP communication. This supports standard HTTP protection mechanisms, including basic-auth, client-certificate, and forms-based authentication and message protection, in accordance with the protection policies of the target application.

The Trust Association Interceptor can be used to integrate the security mechanisms of third-party proxy servers. Tivoli's WebSEAL (part of the Tivoli Access Manager product) can be integrated with WebSphere through the trust association interceptor.

Next, the Java 2 Security Manager forms the foundation of the security system for the WebSphere application server. It provides code-source protection based on J2EE permission settings, and provides the basic security objects used in the system. Java 2 Security Manager permissions can be controlled either with the configuration mechanisms in WebSphere, or through Tivoli Access Manager.

The Java Authentication and Authorization Service (JAAS) is a layer on top of the Java 2 Security Manager to provide authentication services. These are used by the runtime to validate in-bound secure associations, and to establish out-bound secure associations. WebSphere augments the JAAS framework with its own login modules that delegate authentication decisions and the formation of LTPA and SWAM credential tokens to the WebSphere security server. The security server is integral to the WebSphere runtime and will be hosted in the application server, the node agent, or the cell manager depending on your configuration (the placement of this server is automatic).

The web and EJB containers are responsible for enforcing authorization and delegation policies, and performing role-reference mapping in accordance with the deployment policies of your application. The containers will delegate authorization decisions to the permission mechanisms in JAAS, which in turn get authorization policies either from the deployed application or a separate authorization repository.

The application along with its deployment policies forms the top-most layer of the security architecture. Finally, users (principals) and groups are defined in the user registry. The authentication information for principals is also maintained in the user registry and is used to make authentication decisions by the security server. WebSphere bundles the IBM Directory Server that you can use as the user registry, but you can opt to use any of a number of other registries – including a variety of LDAP servers, the native user registry of your local operating system, or your own custom registry. You will manage users and groups (the creation and deletion of these) through the ID Management tools that are provided by your user registry – for example, the native user and group management tools of your operating system if you use a local OS registry.

We will discuss the elements of the security system in more detail throughout this chapter.

Java Security Programming Interfaces

J2EE draws the majority of its security-related programming interfaces from other standard Java extensions and the core Java 2 Security service. The Java 2 Security model introduces the idea of a security manager, security permissions, and the JAAS programming interfaces. We will discuss these in this section.

Java 2 Security

This book is not intended to be a primer on the Java 2 Security model. However, a few aspects of the Java 2 Security programming model are worth highlighting as they are supported in the WebSphere hosting environment.

Principals and Subjects

When WebSphere authenticates a user (or any other entity), it creates a `Principal` object representing that user's authenticity. You can get the authenticated `Principal` associated with a request with the `getUserPrincipal()` or `getCallerPrincipal()` method.

In fact, this `Principal` is actually associated with a JAAS `Subject`, although there are no interfaces for getting a `Subject` from a `Principal`. The `Principal` represents the user's authenticity within a particular authentication domain. The `Subject` represents the user in a more general form – independent of any particular authentication domain. In theory, the same `Subject` may be authenticated in multiple authentication domains concurrently in which case the `Subject` will have several `Principals` – one for each authentication domain.

If you log a user in programmatically through JAAS, using a `javax.security.auth.login.LoginContext`, you can then get from that `LoginContext` the `Subject` that logged-in, and from that any `Principals` that were formed for each of the authentication domains configured to the system.

Java 2 Security Manager

WebSphere uses the Java 2 Security Manager to enforce code-set authorization policies – that is, authorization policies that establish what a Java class is allowed to do. The Java 2 Security Manager operates on the principle of **least-privilege**. This principle requires that a user be given no more privilege than necessary to perform a job. Said a different way, you can only do what the least of the code can do in your context. This is a recursive property that eventually leads to testing the entire code stack on a particular thread of execution. Every piece of code in the call stack must have been granted a permission for any of the code at the top of that stack to perform something that requires permission. So, for example, if you want to read a file in your program, everything that leads to the calling of that program requires you to have permissions.

The purpose of this principle is to keep code that calls your program from gaining access to information and resources that you have, and that the code would itself be denied access to. While this is noble, and in fact critical to maintaining system integrity, it can also be an obstacle. If you offer a service that is designed to perform a particular function, but you require permission to, for example, read a file to accomplish that function, then obviously you will be prevented from performing your function unless the code that calls your service has the permissions that you need.

Java 2 Security offers a way around this problem. Within your program, you can perform a `doPrivileged()` call on a `java.security.AccessController`, passing in the `PrivilegedAction` object that you want to execute. The `PrivilegedAction` object must implement the `run()` operation. The `AccessController` will effectively create a new execution frame on your call stack and then invoke your `run()` operation. The `PrivilegedAction` will then be evaluated in that new execution frame – as though it is executing on a new thread. This can get a little complicated as it essentially requires an additional class for every segment of code that you want to run in this privileged mode. Moreover, the `PrivilegedAction` you introduce also must be granted the permission that your normal class would have – it is now acting as your surrogate.

If you use the `doPrivileged()` operation you are assuming the responsibility for ensuring you don't allow protected information or other resources and actions to be siphoned back to your callers. Consequently, you should use this operation with extreme care. WebSphere makes substantial use of `doPrivileged()` in its runtime to ensure it can continue to operate correctly even if your application hasn't been granted all of the permissions that it needs to do its job.

568

More importantly, WebSphere forces a `doPriviledged()` operation in the call path between EJBs if you make a call between the remote interfaces of EJBs installed in the same application server instance. This is to emulate local-remote transparency. Since the call stack is not transferred between servers, remote EJBs have the built-in equivalent of a `doPrivileged()`. If you write a call to another object in a different server instance, that same call may not work if you relocate that target object to the local server. WebSphere initiates the same `doPrivileged()` between container breaches to help emulate a remote call.

JAAS

The JAAS interfaces can be used to authenticate a new user. This can be used in a couple of different ways. If you simply know that you want to authenticate a real end-user presuming your application is running in a client or somewhere in the vicinity of a real end user, you can use the WebSphere provided `LoginModule()` and initiate a login by creating a default `LoginContext()`.

If you need to do anything more creative – like authenticating a user based on information they supply to you through a set of arguments to a component that you've implemented – then you will have to implement your own `LoginModule` and initialize that in your `LoginContext`. This is done through the standard JAAS interfaces so we won't cover those specifics here.

When a principal is authenticated and a `Subject` and corresponding `Principal` object are formed by WebSphere, it will associate that `Subject` with the execution context for your application. However, when you authenticate a user in your application code, the `Subject` is formed but is not automatically associated with the execution context. However, you can accomplish the same thing by invoking the `doAs()` static operation on the `javax.security.auth.Subject` object. This has the effect of associating the specified Subject with the execution context – the programmatic equivalent of the `RunAs()` deployment descriptor. The Subject associated with the execution context will be used for any down stream requests embodied with the `doAs()` execution block.

The J2EE Security Model

The WebSphere security system is built around the J2EE Security Model. The model is composed of several elements, establishing trust in the user (authentication), and protecting J2EE resources (authorization). The J2EE security model, in turn, is built on the J2SE security. We will discuss all of these in this section.

Establishing Trust in the User

There are several points of entry to a WebSphere-based network. J2EE primarily addresses declarative control for web-based entry to the system – particularly from a web browser. Entry from a traditional browser is primarily controlled with deployment information in the application you are targeting. Establishing trust in the end-user, or authenticating the end user is important for determining whether the end user is who they claim to be.

Since web sites may contain a variety of different kinds of information – not all of which is necessarily sensitive – the J2EE model only requires authentication if the end-user attempts to access a web component that is classified as a protected resource. This is sometimes referred to as **lazy-authentication** – only authenticate when you need to. If a resource is sensitive, it should be identified in a web application security constraint – a deployment descriptor that contains a URL pattern definition and one or more HTTP-methods. The security constraint is discussed further in the section *Protecting J2EE Resources*. If the end user attempts to access a resource that is covered by one of the security constraints, and if the end user has not already been authenticated in their session with the application server, then they will be challenged to authenticate themselves.

You can specify what type of authentication is required using the `<login-config>` deployment descriptor in your web application. The DTD fragment for the `<login-config>` deployment descriptor is:

```
<!ELEMENT login-config (auth-method?, realm-name?, form-login-config?)>
<!ELEMENT auth-method (#PCDATA)>
<!ELEMENT realm-name (#PCDATA)>
<!ELEMENT form-login-config (form-login-page, form-error-page)>
<!ELEMENT form-login-page (#PCDATA)>
<!ELEMENT form-error-page (#PCDATA)>
```

The `<login-config>` element is included within the `<web-app>` tag. Only one `<login-config>` element can be specified per web application thus the same web application cannot support multiple types of authentication challenge.

The `auth-method` defines the authentication method that should be used for the web application and can be one of `BASIC`, `FORM`, `CLIENT-CERT`, or `DIGEST`. However, WebSphere does not support the `DIGEST` form of authentication challenge.

Fortunately, you don't have to worry about the specific form of the deployment descriptor – WebSphere gives you a graphical way of specifying this information in the Application Assembly Tool (AAT). For example, if you want to require basic authentication to the Plants-By-WebSphere site, you can specify this policy in the Plants-By-WebSphere web application:

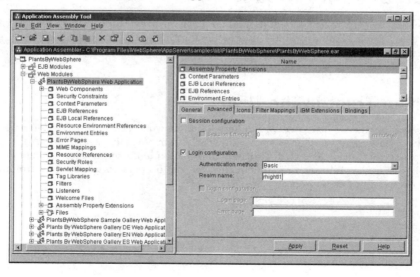

Notice that you have to specify the realm name for the login configuration. It is present here to allow you to select different registries for different applications. However, WebSphere constrains you to only using one realm per cell installation in version 5.0, and so this value is largely ignored in the web application. For clarity, you should set it to a consistent value for all of your applications.

J2EE presumes a reactive model for authenticating users to web applications. The login policy you set for a web application will actually only be executed in response to a user attempting to access a protected resource in the web application. This requires that you set the Security Constraint for one or more components of your web application, including defining the roles that are relevant to your application. Of course, you will want to grant some of your users authority to access the protected resources, and, you will have to enable and configure the security service in the application server that is hosting your application. These tasks are all described later in this chapter.

BASIC Authentication

BASIC indicates `basic-auth` authentication – that is, prompt the user for their user ID and password via a "401 Response code". When this option is enabled, if the user has not already been authenticated in this session, WebSphere will generate a 401 response back to the browser. If the browser does not already have a user ID and password of the current user for the domain in which the application is running, the browser will typically present a login dialog prompt similar to:

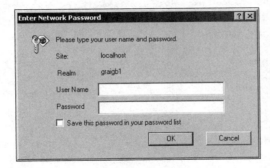

Having acquired the user ID and information for the user in this prompt, the browser will forward that information back to the web site in the `basic-auth` field of the HTTP header.

> **Note that this is sent in clear text, so unless transport-level security is enabled (SSL/TLS) usernames and passwords are vulnerable to packet sniffers.**

WebSphere automatically extracts the information from the HTTP message and use it to authenticate the user. If the authentication fails, WebSphere will automatically re-prompt the user, continuing to do so until either the user authenticates properly, or the user cancels the authentication attempt.

When using this form of authentication, you should also specify the <realm-name> tag to indicate the realm in which the user will be authenticated. This is usually the name of the user registry that you will use in your enterprise.

You should also note that the password is filled into this header in clear-text, and so you should also enable secure HTTP (HTTPS) to protect this information when it flows over the network.

FORM Authentication

FORM indicates a forms-based login – that is, the application will supply a web form that is designed to prompt the user for a user ID and password that will be used to authenticate the user. This allows you to tailor the window that is presented to the user when a login is needed – you can, for example, customize it with your company logo, links to registration pages, help pages, and so forth, to make the login experience for the end user more to your preference. You do need to provide a login form – a servlet or JSP that lays out the form that you want presented.

You will have to specify the `<form-login-config>` tag containing the `<form-login-page>` and `<form-error-page>` sub-tags if you select the FORM type of authentication challenge. The `<form-login-page>` tag is used to specify the web page that you want presented containing the login form, and the `<form-error-page>` is used to specify the page that will be presented if the authentication performed in response to the login form fails.

Again, this can be done through the Application Assembly Tool:

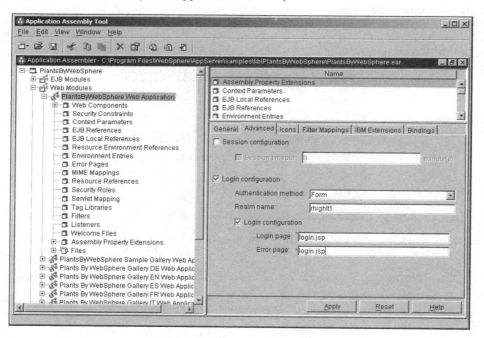

These forms should be implemented to specify a user ID field with the name of j_username and a password field of j_password. The form should be set to post the j_security_check action. The post action and user ID and password fields are highlighted in bold:

```
<table cellpadding="20" cellspacing="0" border="1">
  <tr>
    <td valign="top">
      <form id="existingcustomer" name="existingcustomer"
          action="j_security_check" method="POST">
```

```html
<table cellpadding="5" cellspacing="0" border="0">
  <tr>
    <td class="plantstore" align="center" colspan="2"><b>Yes.</b></td>
  </tr>

  <tr>
    <td class="plantstore_form" align="right"><b>User Name:</b></td>
    <td class="plantstore_form">
      <input class="plantstore_form" type="text"
             size="15" name="j_username" value="j2ee"></td>
  </tr>
  <tr>
    <td class="plantstore_form" align="right"><b>Password:</b></td>
    <td class="plantstore_form"><input class="plantstore_form"
        type="password" size="15" name="j_password" value="j2ee"></td>
  </tr>
  <tr>
    <td align="center" colspan="2"><input class="plantstore_form"
        name="submit" type="submit" value="Sign In"></td>
  </tr>
</table>
</form>
</td>
  <td valign="top">
    <form id="newcustomer" name="newcustomer" action="createuser.do"
          method="POST">
    <table cellpadding="5" cellspacing="0" border="0">

  <tr>
    <td class="plantstore" align="center" colspan="2">
    <b>No. I would like to    sign up for an account.</b></td>
  </tr>

  <tr>
    <td class="plantstore_form" align="right"><b>User Name:</b></td>
    <td class="plantstore_form"><input class="plantstore_form" type="text"
        size="15" name="j_username"></td>
  </tr>

  <tr>
    <td class="plantstore_form" align="right"><b>Password:</b></td>
    <td class="plantstore_form"><input class="plantstore_form"
        type="password" size="15" name="j_password"></td>
  </tr>

  <tr>
    <td class="plantstore_form" align="right"><b>Password (Repeat):</b></td>
    <td class="plantstore_form"><input class="plantstore_form"
        type="password" size="15" name="j_password_2"></td>
  </tr>
  <tr>
    <td align="center" colspan="2"><input class="plantstore_form"
        name="submit" type="submit" value="Create New Account"></td>
  </tr>
```

```
        </table>
      </form>
   </td>
  </tr>
 </table>
```

Notice that this page also allows the user to create a new account for themselves.

CLIENT-CERT Authentication

CLIENT-CERT in the `<auth-method>` indicates that the principal should be authenticated with their X.509 client certificate. This presumes that a client-certificate has been registered for the principal in their browser certificate database.

Protecting J2EE Resources

J2EE resources: JSP pages, servlets, and EJBs are protected in the J2EE model with the declarative Roles-based Authorization Model. The following diagram depicts the overall relationship of J2EE roles in the system:

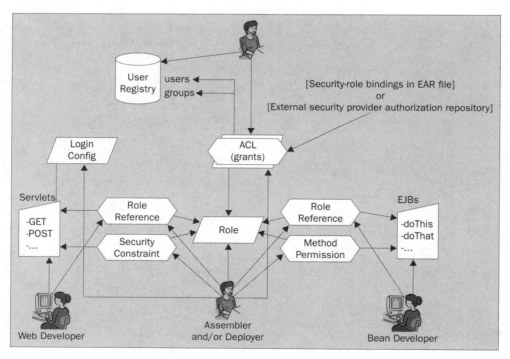

The web and bean developer(s) create their components. They may or may not make explicit reference to role names within their code. If they do, they should declare role references for their components. The application assembler or deployer is then responsible for mapping these references to declared roles in the application. Likewise, the application assembler is responsible for defining security constraints (for web applications), and method-permissions (for EJBs) that define the permissions for their application. There are two ways of granting individual users or groups the roles declared in the application – either through security-role bindings declared in the application itself, or through an external security provider authorization repository. A qualified security administrator should do the granting of authority.

This separation of responsibilities ensures that security policies are kept out of the actual implementation of the application. At the same time it gives the application assembler and/or deployer the opportunity to express security constraints of their application definition. And yet, it enables the enterprise security administrator the flexibility they need to ensure their enterprise policies are being properly enforced and monitored. This model will be discussed in further detail in the following sections.

The Roles-Based Authorization Model

All authorization policies in J2EE are defined in terms of Security Roles. Generally, the application assembler declares roles in enterprise applications through deployment descriptors. Security Roles are represented simply as labels in the descriptor. The DTD for a Security Role is:

```
<!ELEMENT security-role (description?, role-name)>
<!ELEMENT role-name (#PCDATA)>
```

Security Roles should represent relevant actors in the business scenarios supported by the application and for which a security policy may be applied. The assembler may introduce a security role based on hints they get from the developer, and from the business model itself. However, this does not assume the assembler is a security expert. The process itself allows security administrators to adapt the information – the roles and other constraints – to the security policy of the system. You can define the security roles for your web application in the AAT:

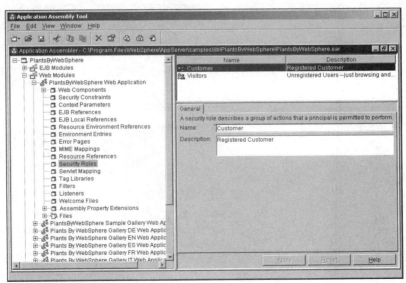

Likewise, you can also define the security roles for your EJB modules in the AAT:

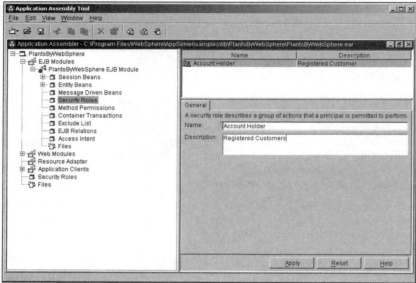

All of the roles defined for both the web application and EJB components in the application will be rolled up to the enterprise application level:

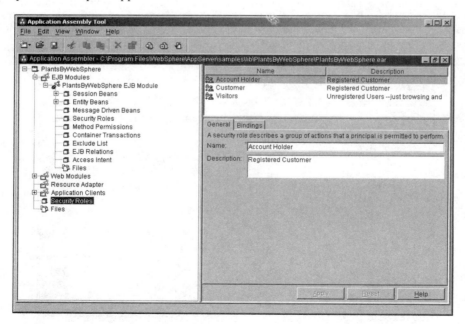

Doing so enables the assembler to resolve any potential conflicts that may have been introduced by any of the components that were assembled in the application. Likewise, they can resolve any similarity that may exist between disparate roles. This becomes particularly useful when an application is assembled from a set of previously defined components – perhaps reused from other applications. Notice, for example, the similarity between 'Account Holder' (introduced by the Customer EJB component), and the 'Customer' (introduced by the web-tier web application component). Having noticed the similarity, the application assembler can then fix up the corresponding components to factor their respective roles down to a common role.

Once the security roles have been defined for the application, the assembler can begin grouping methods and objects and associating those with security roles. The deployment descriptor mechanism for doing this differs between web components and EJB components.

Defining Security Constraints for Web Application Components

The grouping mechanism for web components is the security constraint. The DTD for the security constraint descriptor is:

```
<!ELEMENT security-constraint (display-name?, web-resourcecollection+,
          auth-constraint?, user-data-constraint?)>
<!ELEMENT web-resource-collection (web-resource-name, description?,
          url-pattern*, http-method*)>
<!ELEMENT auth-constraint (description?, role-name*)>
<!ELEMENT user-data-constraint (description?, transport-guarantee)>
<!ELEMENT web-resource-name (#PCDATA)>
<!ELEMENT url-pattern (#PCDATA)>
<!ELEMENT http-method (#PCDATA)>
<!ELEMENT role-name (#PCDATA)>
<!ELEMENT transport-guarantee (#PCDATA)>
```

You can enter this information for your web application in the WebSphere AAT in two parts. In the first part, you create the security constraint and give it a name and indicate what roles are associated with the constraint – that is, what role a requesting principal must possess in order to use any of the resources represented in that constraint. The user must possess at least one of the listed roles. In addition, you specify the data constraint, if any, which must be satisfied. Specifying a data constraint establishes two things.

The first is that secure HTTP must be used to connect to the resource. In fact, WebSphere will automatically redirect a request to an HTTPS port if the request comes in first on an unprotected communication transport and the targeted component is protect by a security constraint that requires integrity or confidentiality. The second is that the HTTPS connection must have been configured to satisfy the constraint – either with integrity or confidentiality, depending on the data constraint setting:

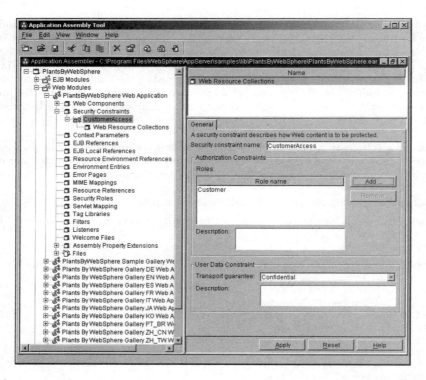

Once you've created the security constraint, you can then create the resource collection for that constraint. This will define which web resources are covered by this constraint. The resource collection is defined as a combination of the URL pattern that represents the web resource, and the HTTP operations governed by that collection.

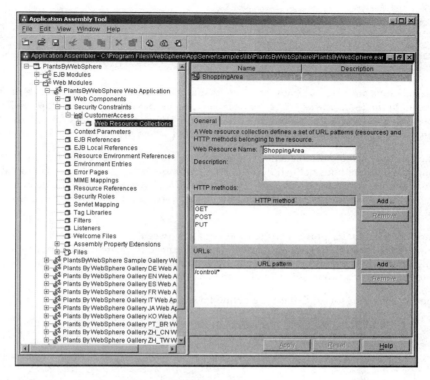

The same resource can be covered by multiple resource collections. If you configure your application in this way then the requesting user must satisfy all of the constraints that govern that resource – the user must be granted at least one role listed in each of the security constraints.

The following rules are taken from the Servlet 2.3 specification to describe the URL patterns that you can define in your web resource collection:

❑ A string beginning with a `'/'` character and ending with a `'/*'` postfix is used for path mapping.

❑ A string beginning with a `'*.'` prefix is used as an extension mapping.

❑ A string containing only the `'/'` character indicates the "default" servlet of the application. In this case the servlet path is the request URI minus the context path and the path info is null.

❑ All other strings are used for exact matches only.

Defining Method Permissions for EJB Components

Associating security roles with EJBs is done with method permission deployment descriptors for EJB components. The DTD for the method permission is:

```
<!ELEMENT method-permission (description?, role-name+, method+)>
<!ELEMENT role-name (#PCDATA)>
<!ELEMENT method (description?, ejb-name, method-intf?, method-name,
         method-params?)>
```

```
<!ELEMENT ejb-name (#PCDATA)>
<!ELEMENT method-intf (#PCDATA)>
<!ELEMENT method-name (#PCDATA)>
<!ELEMENT method-params (method-param*)>
<!ELEMENT method-param (#PCDATA)>
```

Method permissions are a way of stating the role that a user must be granted to invoke the methods on the EJBs listed in the `method-permission`. The method permission can list multiple roles – meaning that the user must possess at least one of the specified roles to access the listed resources. The method permission can also list multiple methods and EJBs – all of which are included in the permission.

The `method-name` can contain the actual name of the intended method, or an asterisk (*). An asterisk is taken to mean all the methods defined in the EJB. A common use of the wildcard is to establish a default. For example, you can specify a method permission for * – this will be the default permission for the bean(s) represented in the permission – and then set more specific overriding permissions for individual methods.

The `method-params` descriptor is used to differentiate between overloaded methods. This element is optional unless the method is overloaded. The roles referenced in the method permission are linked to roles defined in the EJB module. As with web applications, any roles specified for the EJB module are rolled up to the enterprise application level by the AAT.

The method permissions for an EJB can be defined using the AAT.

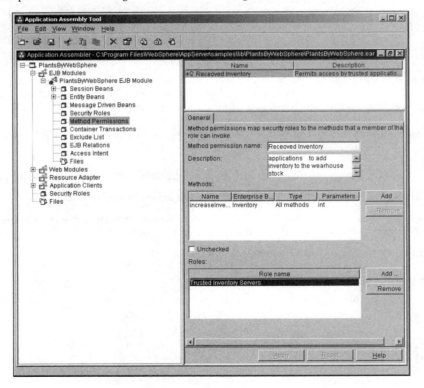

The assembler is expected to provide the deployment information for the application assembly. However, the deployer must ensure the assembler has completed their job. The application installation tool used by WebSphere application deployers will not allow an application to be deployed with incomplete method permissions. That is, if any of the methods in an application are protected with a method permission, then all of the methods must be assigned a method permission.

The AAT simplifies this task in two ways. First, as we stated above, the method permission can specify a `method-name` with an asterisk to mean include all methods of the EJB in the method permission. This makes it easy to include all of the methods of an EJB without having to call out each method individually. Secondly, AAT includes a list of all unspecified methods – that is, all of the methods on any EJB in the module.

The same EJB or method can be included in multiple method permissions. If you define multiple method permissions that collect the same EJB or method then the caller must posses one of the roles listed in any of the method permissions that collect that EJB/method.

You can also indicate that a method is unchecked – that is, no authorization check should be performed on the method. In other words, any principal can access the method, regardless of whether they've been granted any roles:

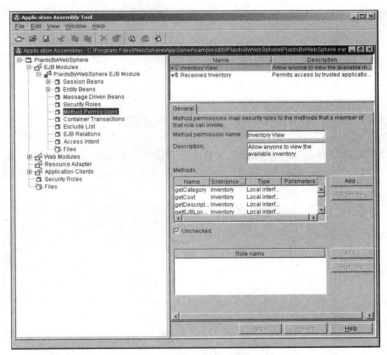

Finally, it is also possible for you to completely prevent access of any sort to a method. This can be done by including the method in an exclude-list deployment descriptor. The DTD for the exclude list is:

```
<!ELEMENT exclude-list (description?, method+)>
```

This can be specified in the AAT.

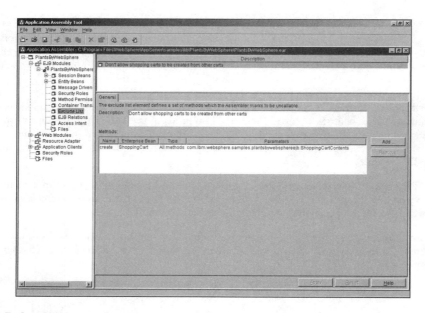

Granting Principals to Roles

For both web application and EJB module components, the process of assigning a user to a specified role is the same. It is possible to specify the users and groups that are assigned to a role in the AAT. This information will be carried in extended deployment information in your application.

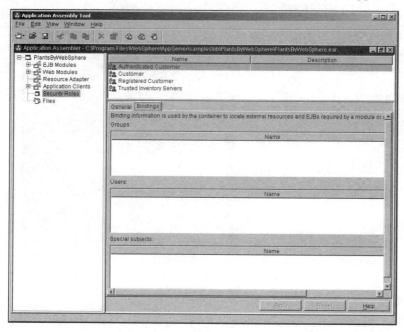

However, this is not the preferred approach as setting these mappings at assembly time is far too static. You can assign users and groups to roles through the security mappings of your enterprise application in the admin console as well. This allows you to grant and revoke access to roles as often as your user community and organization changes – without having to re-deploy your application:

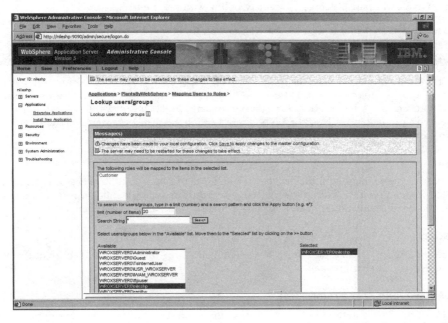

You can get to this panel by selecting your application from the Enterprise Applications collection, scrolling down to Map security roles to users/groups, selecting the role in question, and then pressing the Lookup users or Lookup groups button.

The most efficient model is to assign a user group to a role. In this way you can allow a user access to a role simply by virtue of their inclusion in or exclusion from that user group. You can control that group membership entirely from your user registry administration tools.

Creating and managing users and other principals is performed entirely through your user registry tools. See *User Registry* for more information on this topic.

J2EE Programming Interface

We've stated a couple of times in this chapter that it is generally not a good idea to program security policy into your application. We'll state that one more time before we launch into this section – describing to you how to program security into your application based on the J2EE security interfaces. Programming security into your application reduces the flexibility of the security administrator to set and control policies for your enterprise based on the evolving concerns of your business. Generally security policies evolve more rapidly than the main stream of business processes. Tying security policy to your application implementation means that you have to change and redeploy your application every time a security policy changes. This is not good.

OK, that's out of the way. There are times where you just won't be able to help yourself. This is due in part to security features that may be missing from the WebSphere hosting environment – special circumstances that go beyond the general security system. It could also be the result of a deliberate merger between the business model and the security model of your information system – most often in the form of evaluating the outcome of security policy within the business model.

J2EE provides a short list of interfaces that can be helpful in these circumstances.

Web Application Interfaces

The programming model for servlets in the Servlet 2.3 specification introduces four methods (getAuthType, getRemoteUser, isUserInRole, and getUserPrincipal) for use in servlets. All of these methods are provided on the javax.servlet.http.HTTPServletRequest object. None of these methods are new in J2EE 1.3 or WebSphere version 5.0. They are discussed here only for completeness.

getAuthType

The getAuthType() method indicates the type of authentication used to access this servlet. This can be "BASIC", meaning BasicAuth or user ID and password based authentication; "SSL", meaning client-certificate based authentication; or null, meaning that the user was not authenticated.

getRemoteUser

The getRemoteUser() method returns a String containing the principal identity of the user for which the Servlet is being invoked.

isUserInRole(java.lang.String roleName)

The isUserInRole() method indicates whether the requesting principal has been granted the specified role; the role label is included as an argument to the call. Because the Servlet developer does not know what roles will actually be used in the application assembly, the role label specified with this method is treated as a symbolic label.

This label must be declared in the deployment descriptors for the component as a role-ref. The DTD for the security-role-ref element is:

```
<!ELEMENT security-role-ref (description?, role-name, role-link)>
<!ELEMENT role-link (#PCDATA)>
```

The role-name of the security-role-ref will contain the symbolic label used within the servlet's implementation – in the isUserInRole() call. The role-link then must be mapped by the assembler to a role declared in a security role element elsewhere in the application deployment information. You can specify the security-role-ref mapping in AAT.

The following snippet shows testing whether the calling principal is in the Consumer role:

```
boolean inConsumerRole = req.isUserInRole("Consumer");
```

Notice that the role referenced here is not the same as the roles created (later) for the application. However, Consumer as specified here by the programmer can be taken to be the same thing as a Customer in the application deployment. At assembly time, the assembler (or later the deployer) would be expected to map the Consumer reference to the Customer role in a roleReference deployment statement:

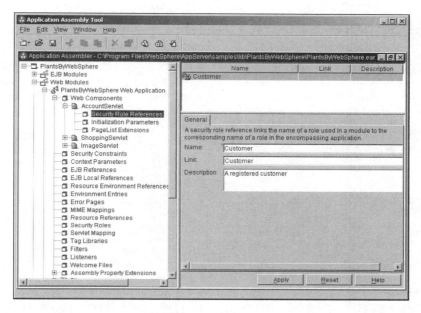

Note that because all referenced roles used in the `isUserInRole` must be declared in the deployment descriptor, the application cannot use variables in this call that would result in a role symbolic label that is not declared in the descriptor. If you manufacture a symbolic role label in your code that is not declared in a corresponding deployment descriptor, then the call to `isUserInRole` will necessarily return `false`.

getUserPrincipal

The `getUserPrincipal()` method returns a Java 2 Security `Principal` object representing the user associated with this Servlet request.

Using this operation is fairly straightforward from within your servlet:

```
java.security.Principal principal =  req.getUserPrincipal ();
String principalName = null;
if ( principal != null )
{
    principalName =  principal.getName ();
}
```

In the above snippet, `req` is the `HTTPServletRequest` passed to your servlet. `GetUserPrincipal` returns the `Principal` associated with the request. You can get the principal's name in a string form with the `getName()` operation.

EJB Application Interfaces

The EJB programming model introduces two methods (`getCallerPrincipal()` and `isCallerInRole()`) in the `javax.ejb.EJBContext` interface. As with servlets, these methods are not new to J2EE 1.3 or WebSphere version 5.0.

The WebSphere Security Model

It is widely accepted that the strongest defense is a 'layered defense'. The WebSphere security model provides a layered defense to protect your resources. What we mean by this is that security policy can be enforced in WebSphere at each container and network boundary. Thus, if someone manages to hack into the router or web server, they will be challenged and restricted at the web container, and again at the EJB container, and again at the data system, and so on.

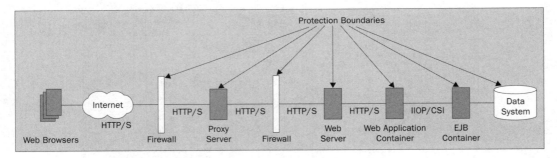

While WebSphere itself is focused on protecting those resources hosted in the WebSphere runtime – JSP pages, servlets, EJBs, and so on – it is designed on open standards and with an eye toward being able to federate with enterprise security providers that can protect your entire system.

As we've indicated earlier, the security system in WebSphere is controlled through security policies that are declared and administered outside the application implementation. Having said that, there are times when you just want to have more control than that embedded in your business logic, or perhaps to overcome existing limitations in the security capabilities of WebSphere. While these are few, they nonetheless can be important.

Two things that you may want in the way of security are instance-based authorization and credential mapping. Neither of these are supported in the version 5.0 of WebSphere and so you will have to code this into your application if you need either of them. See the sections on *Credential Mapping* and *Instance-Based Authorization*, for more discussion on these topics.

Enabling Security

Security in WebSphere is controlled first from a global security switch on the admin console. You need to turn security on before WebSphere will begin protecting its resources. If you do not, WebSphere will allow any request to be invoked on any resource in the system:

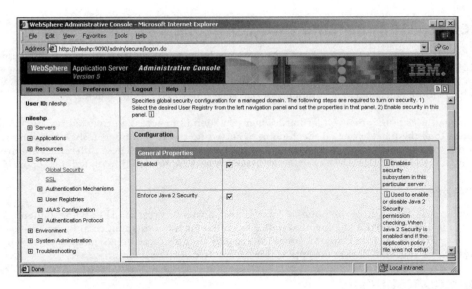

Security is enabled on the Admin console in the Global Security Configuration panel under the Security Center.

Once you've enabled the global security option, then you can begin to define security policies to govern the rest of your system. The following checklist gives you an outline of the activities you should perform to fully enable a secure WebSphere environment for your applications:

❑ Enable the global security configuration option (as indicated above). At the same time you should:

    ❑ Indicate what type of authentication you want to use throughout the system

    ❑ Configure the user registry, level of message protection, and level of trust establishment you want to use (it is generally a good idea to configure your user registry before you attempt to enable global security as the configuration validation may prevent you from turning on security before you've configured the registry)

❑ Ensure sensitive system runtime files are properly protected

❑ Acquire and distribute signed SSL certificates for each of your application servers

❑ Add any additional users to your user registry

❑ As you build your applications, define web resource collections, security constraints, method permissions, and user roles and deploy that information

❑ Configure the data sources and other resources that you will use in your application, setting any credential information the system will need to access those resource managers for your application

❑ Set authorization policies establishing who can access which role

How you perform these tasks will be described in more detail throughout the rest of this chapter.

Challenge Mechanisms and Controls

Before we get too far into the specifics of the system it helps to remember that there are several ways that you may enter a WebSphere network. The most obvious point of entry is from your browser, pointing it to a web site with a specific URL. Other points of entry include fat J2EE or CORBA clients, JMS clients (both consumers and suppliers of messages), and web services clients.

From an end-user point of view it all starts when you attempt to access a protected resource and are prompted to authenticate yourself. Each point of entry into the system offers a slightly different variety of options for authenticating you and using that to protect the system. These differences are driven by the differences in scenarios and expectations that each entry approach is intended to support.

Web Clients

For web applications, where the point of entry is from a web browser via HTTP, the authentication challenge is driven by J2EE deployment policy specified for the web application being accessed. See the *Establishing Trust in the User section* for more information on how these deployment options work. These policies can be specified during the application assembly or deployment processes.

J2EE and CORBA Clients

For EJBs being access from fat J2EE or CORBA clients, the authentication challenge is controlled with configuration options associated with the application server through system management. WebSphere supports two basic authentication protocols over IIOP for J2EE and CORBA clients. The "IBM" protocol is a proprietary protocol used in earlier versions of WebSphere and continues to be supported for backwards compatibility with those versions and products that supported earlier WebSphere clients.

The "CSI" protocol refers to the CORBA Common Secure Interoperation (Version 2 – CSIv2) protocol. This is a standard protocol that is now mandated by the J2EE 1.3 specification for secure interoperation with other vendor application servers. If you will be operating a mixed network of both version 5.0 and a version prior to version 5.0 application servers or clients, then you should select both CSI and SAS protocols. Otherwise, if you will be operating a network of just WebSphere version 5.0 clients and servers, or third-party IIOP-based application servers that support the CSIv2 standard, then you should select just CSI as your active secure association protocol.

You can then configure the specifics for either protocol under the Authentication Protocol tasks:

For the IBM authentication protocol, you have control over the SSL settings to be used for inbound and outbound connections – that is, connections from another client to a WebSphere application server (an inbound connection), and from WebSphere application servers to other servers (outbound connection).

For the CSI authentication protocol, you have control over the inbound and outbound authentication settings, and the inbound and outbound transport (SSL) settings. For inbound authentication, you have control over whether basic authentication (user ID and password), client certificate, and trust associations are allowed or required to the server. In addition, if you specify that trust associations be allowed then you can specify which servers are trusted to assert principal identities:

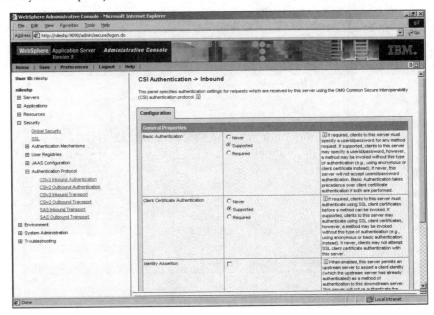

For outbound authentication, you have control over whether the application server can perform `basic-auth` or `client-certificate` based authentication to downstream servers, and whether to propagate identity assertions:

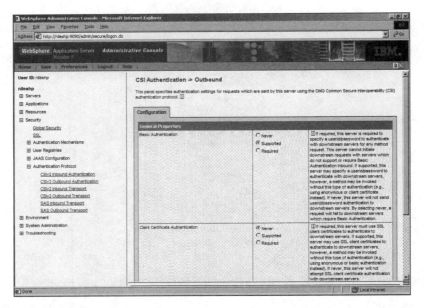

In addition, you can specify whether SSL is required for inbound and outbound connections, and the SSL properties that should be used if SSL is used to connect to the server:

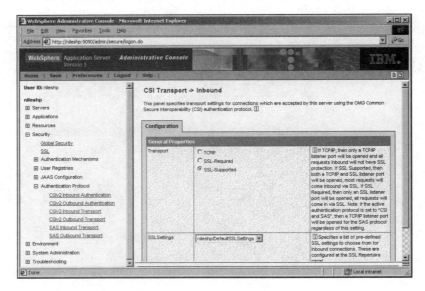

JMS Clients

For JMS clients – both suppliers and consumers of JMS messages – the protection mechanism is relatively simple. The JMS specification itself does not describe a standard security model. WebSphere uses anonymous SSL to protect JMS communication, and then performs a simple topic-based authorization check at each end of the exchange. The identity of the supplier of the message may be transmitted in the JMS message header (derived from the credentials of the requesting principal), but this cannot be used to authenticate the sending principal – the identity by itself is not enough to ensure that was who actually sent the message.

Web Services Clients

For web services clients, the authentication requirements are defined in the WSDL for the web service and established through the same web application controls used for traditional web applications from a web browser, the basic JMS security controls, or the application server-level configuration controls for EJB J2EE or CORBA clients, depending on the actual protocol used for the web service.

User Registry

WebSphere supports multiple user registry mechanisms:

- ❑   Local Operating System (LocalOS)
- ❑   Lightweight Directory Access Protocol (LDAP)
- ❑   Custom Registry

You can select the registry you want to use in your network through the user registry configuration setting in the **Global Security** options in the security center:

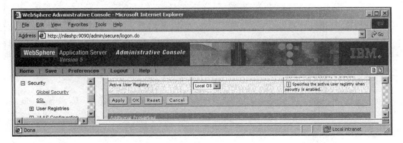

LocalOS User Registry

The LocalOS registry is whatever registry is native to the operating system on which WebSphere is hosted. If this is a single server instance or your entire WebSphere network is hosted on a single computer, then the LocalOS registry is the one associated with that computer. If you are running WebSphere on multiple computers in a cluster or as a multi-tiered topology, the LocalOS registry is the one on the computer on which the security server is hosted – either the local node agent or the cell manager.

If you are running on a Unix platform, WebSphere will authenticate against etc/passwd. If you are running on Windows, WebSphere will authenticate against the localhost or against a Windows domain server, depending on how you have Windows configured. WebSphere will authenticate against the Security Access Facility (SAF – and the underlying SAF provider such as RACF or ACF2) on z/OS.

LocalOS-based authentication has the advantage of reusing your platform's user registry and can thus avoid the necessity to create a new user registry. However, it has the disadvantage that in many cases credentials formed on one host will not be recognized by other hosts in the distributed system, and sometimes not even in other processes on the same host. Thus, if you have a distributed network that spans multiple hosts and your application will be involved in requests that propagate between application servers then LocalOS authentication may not work for you – you will be forced to switch credentials between each server. Each server will have to authenticate itself to the down-stream server to initiate any requests to components hosted on that server.

Client-certificates cannot be used with LocalOS authentication to authenticate end users.

You will have to configure a user ID and password of a principal in your local operating system that has the authority to perform authentication verification when using a LocalOS user registry:

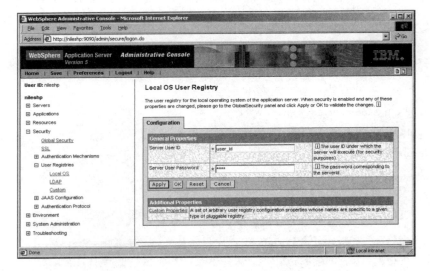

LDAP User Registry

The LDAP registry can be one of several LDAP directories supported by WebSphere, including:

- ❑ IBM Directory Server version 4.1
- ❑ Sun ONE Directory Server version 5.0
- ❑ Lotus Domino Enterprise Server R5.08
- ❑ SecureWay Directory Server R3.21 and later
- ❑ Windows 2000 Active Directory

You select which directory you want to use, and configure how WebSphere controls it through the LDAP user registry settings in the Security Center:

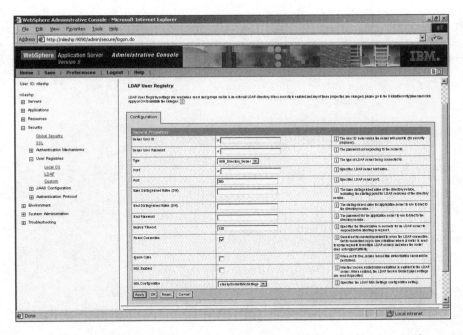

Typically, these LDAP directory servers each have their own schema for how user information in the registry is structured. In addition, you may have extended the native schema for your directory. WebSphere allows you to customize the schema mapping for your directory by specifying where within your schema it should obtain various information it needs to authenticate the user and to derive privilege attributes. These are controlled through the Advanced LDAP Settings in the Security Center:

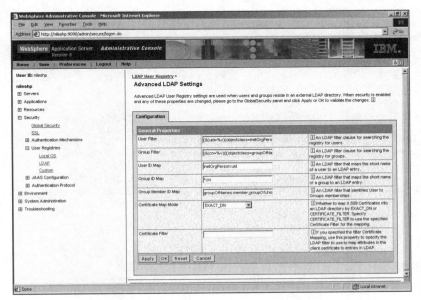

Custom Registry

In some situations, you may have your own user registry that you use in your enterprise. WebSphere does not require that you convert your entire user base over to the operating system registry or even an LDAP directory. If you want to continue to use your existing registry system, you can introduce your own Custom Registry adapter. You do this by creating an implementation of the com.ibm.websphere.security.UserRegistry interface:

```
package com.ibm.websphere.security;

import java.util.*;
import java.rmi.*;
import java.rmi.Remote;
import java.security.cert.X509Certificate;
import com.ibm.WebSphereSecurity.*;

public interface UserRegistry extends java.rmi.Remote {

 public void initialize(java.util.Properties props)
    throws CustomRegistryException, RemoteException;

 public String checkPassword(String user ID, String password)
    throws PasswordCheckFailedException, CustomRegistryException,
         RemoteException;

 public String mapCertificate(X509Certificate[] cert)
    throws CertificateMapNotSupportedException,
         CertificateMapFailedException, CustomRegistryException,
         RemoteException;
 public String getRealm()
    throws CustomRegistryException, RemoteException;

 public List getUsers(String pattern, int limit)
    throws CustomRegistryException, RemoteException;

 public List getUsersForGroup(String groupName, int limit)
    throws EntryNotFoundException, CustomRegistryException, RemoteException;

 public String getUserDisplayName(String userName)
    throws EntryNotFoundException, CustomRegistryException, RemoteException;

 public String getUniqueUser ID(String userName)
    throws EntryNotFoundException, CustomRegistryExceptionRemoteException;

 public String getUserSecurityName(String uniqueUser ID)
    throws EntryNotFoundException, CustomRegistryException, RemoteException;

 public boolean isValidUser(String userName)
    throws CustomRegistryException, RemoteException;

 public List getGroups(String pattern, int limit)
    throws CustomRegistryException, RemoteException;
```

```
    public List getGroupsForUser(String userName, int limit)
        throws EntryNotFoundException, CustomRegistryException, RemoteException;

    public String getGroupDisplayName(String groupName)
        throws EntryNotFoundException, CustomRegistryException, RemoteException;

    public String getUniqueGroupId(String groupName)
        throws EntryNotFoundException, CustomRegistryException, RemoteException;

    public List getUniqueGroupIds(String uniqueUser ID)
        throws EntryNotFoundException, CustomRegistryException, RemoteException;

    public String getGroupSecurityName(String uniqueGroupId)
        throws EntryNotFoundException, CustomRegistryException, RemoteException;

    public boolean isValidGroup(String groupName)
        throws CustomRegistryException, RemoteException;

    public Credential createCredential(String userName)
        throws CustomRegistryException, EntryNotFoundException,
               CreateCredentialNotSupportedException, RemoteException;
}
```

then registering that implementation with WebSphere through the admin console:

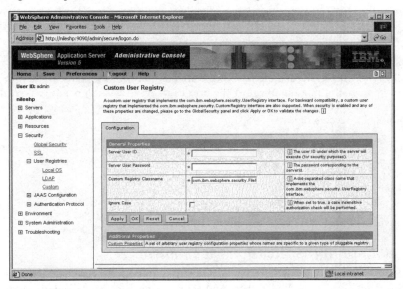

The **Server User ID** and **Server User Password** should be a valid user ID and password in your configured registry. WebSphere will validate this user ID and password when you enable the custom registry setting on the Global Security settings page. If the user ID and password are not valid, WebSphere will not let you configure your registry. Further, these values will be used to validate your authority to bind to that registry every time the application server is started. These checks both ensure your authority to bind to the registry, and to a large extent ensure the correctness of your registry implementation – for example, testing whether the registry's data system can be accessed.

If you build the custom registry implementation using WSAD, you should include the `sas.jar` and `wssec.jar` libraries in your build path.

It is your responsibility to make sure the JAR file containing your registry implementation is distributed onto the WebSphere host on which the security server resides, and that your implementation is available to WebSphere's system classpath. It is easy to place your registry JAR file in the `lib` directory of the application server install root, or you can put the individual classes in a sub-directory of the `classes` directory of the application server install root. If you put classes in the `classes` directory, you should create the appropriate sub-directory structure to represent the package path of your class.

Authentication Mechanisms and Controls

Challenging the user for their authentication information is actually only part of the authentication process. The actual authentication of the user occurs by confirming the authentication information the user supplies. The simplest case to understand is with user ID and password authentication. In this model, the user ID is used to identify the user, and the password is used to confirm the user. The idea is that passwords are secret – only a single end user should know their password, and the password should be sophisticated enough that no one else could guess it. Thus, when you log in only you should be able to state both your user ID and your password. If you know both, then you must be who you claim to be.

To accomplish this, of course, the system needs to also know your user ID and password. This is kept in a user registry. Protecting the user registry then becomes as important to safe-guarding the system as it is for everyone to protect their own password – stealing the passwords in the user registry would allow someone to claim to be anyone in the registry and consequently would allow them access to any of the resources or information the user whose password they stole is able to access.

Once the user is authenticated, a token is created that represents that user's authenticity. The token is cryptographically formatted so that any part of the system that needs to know if the user is authentic can examine the token without re-authenticating the user each time. This too needs to be protected for as long as the token exists and is valid, it can be used to represent the user and used to access the resources to which that user has access rights.

Different user registries and different credential tokens have different levels of strength and scope. For that reason, WebSphere offers different authentication options so that you can select the set of capabilities that best meet your needs. These include:

❑ Simple WebSphere Authentication Mechanism (SWAM)

❑ Lightweight Third-Party Authentication (LTPA)

Simple WebSphere Authentication Mechanism

Simple WebSphere Authentication Mechanism (SWAM) authentication will authenticate the user's user ID and password against the selected registry and form a credential that is optimized for local use. Credential tokens formed by SWAM cannot be propagated between application servers. SWAM is particularly useful if you are operating a single application server instance in standalone mode. In this case the security server will operate within the application server and the credential tokens generally do not need to be delegated to other application servers.

Lightweight Third-Party Authentication

Lightweight Third-Party Authentication (**LTPA**) authentication uses the user registry to authenticate the user and then forms a delegatable credential token. The WebSphere Security Server – which may be hosted in the local application server, the node agent, and/or the cell manager, depending on your topology – acts as a trusted third party to the authentication process.

The benefit of using LTPA is that you can share the same LDAP directory among all of your WebSphere hosts, and consequently pass LTPA credential tokens between application servers to represent the authenticity of the requesting principal. Thus, a user can be authenticated and invoke a component, which in turn invokes a component on another server. The down-stream component will be executed under the authenticity and authority of the user.

LTPA credential tokens are cryptographically formatted by a mutually trusted security server built into WebSphere and in this way are quite secure. However, LTPA credential tokens are not formed with service keys and therefore are not confined to being used with specific application servers. Consequently, LTPA tokens are vulnerable to siphoning attacks and should only be used in environments where you can be confident of what software is running on your systems.

LTPA does support authenticating principals with client certificates.

Authorization and Controls

Once the authenticity of the end user can be established, that user's credentials can be used to determine if they should be allowed access to the resource they are trying to invoke. The authorization system is built on the roles-base authorization model defined by J2EE as described further in the *Protecting J2EE resources* section.

The Topology of the Security System

The classic web application topology consists of any number of browsers, attached through the Internet, via a proxy server, to a web server and on to an enterprise application. The enterprise application is typically connected to a data system. Firewalls will typically isolate the proxy server, creating a demilitarized zone (DMZ) providing a high degree of protection to your company's internal business network:

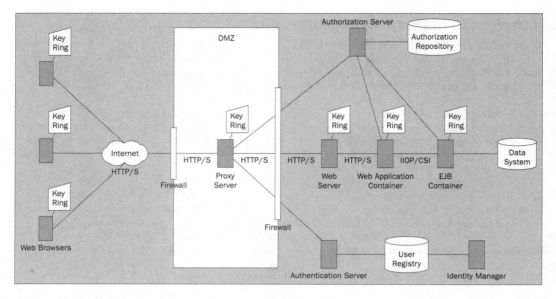

The authorization server is integrated into the WebSphere application server runtime. However, third-party security providers can substitute their own authorization repositories that will generally run in a separate process under their own control. For example, the Tivoli Access Manager can be used with WebSphere and runs as its own process. The authentication server (referred to previously as the WebSphere security server) is built into the application server runtime, and will either be hosted in the application server, in the node agent, or the cell manager depending on your topology. WebSphere determines the location of the authentication server automatically. The Identity Manager represents whatever principal identity management tools come with your selected user registry – with your LDAP server, local Operating System, or custom registry.

Certificates and Transport-Level Protection

HTTP is the dominant protocol through the Internet. For sensitive content, secure-HTTP should be used – HTTP running over a Secure Socket Layer (SSL), or the more standard Transport Layer Security (TLS). Even if you don't use SSL/TLS with a client-certificate to authenticate the end user, you still need to configure the client and server key-rings to work properly. The key-ring represents the certificate-database associated with your client or server. Nearly all mainstream browsers come pre-configured with the root certificates for most of the major commercial certificate authorities, maintained in their embedded key-rings. However, you must have the public root certificate for your servers configured in the browser to establish your willingness to trust the server – sometimes referred to as establishing trust in the target. If you don't have the root certificate then you will have to acquire this and configure it to your browser before you can communicate securely with your servers.

This same principle also applies for communication between servers. For each server that will be a client to another server, the client-server must be configured with the root certificate of the target server. Server certificates are maintained in a key database associated with each server.

The protection of your network relies on the correctness and currency of your server certificates and their corresponding private keys. Protecting these private keys is essential. WebSphere provides a utility, `ikeyman`, for creating certificate/private-key pairs, and importing them to the key ring after your preferred certificate authority has signed them. You may consider forming your own in-house public-key administration capability. However this can be a time- and labor-intensive function, especially if you will be using client-certificate based authentication where you need to create, distribute, and maintain client-certificates and their corresponding key-pairs for each user in your system. You should also consider any of a number of commercial signing authority services.

To create a certificate and key pair, start by bringing up the `ikeyman` utility located in the `bin` directory under the install root. Create or open your own keyring database, and then switch to the **Personal Certificate Requests** content section:

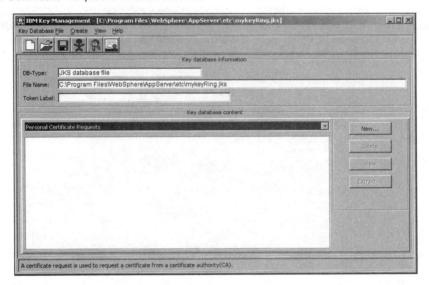

Select **New** to create a new certificate request, and fill in the certificate information.

Notice that the request will be placed in an `.arm` request file. This is a temporary file – it will only be used to prepare your requests to send to a certificate authority. Change the name of this file if you want to separate it from other pending requests.

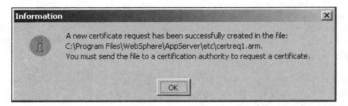

You then need to send your request to your certificate authority (CA) to be signed. How you do this will be specific to your CA's public-key infrastructure – the tools and facilities that they use to manage certificate requests. Later, when you get your certification request back you can import the signed certificate back into your key ring. Start by switching to the Personal Certificates content section:

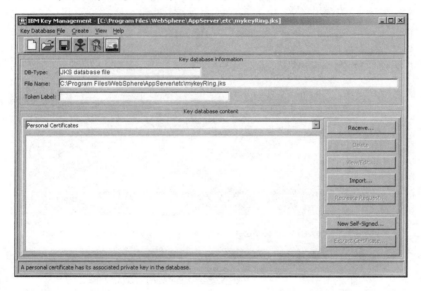

Then press **Receive** and point to the signed certificate file that you got back from your CA:

This will then store the signed certificate in your keyring.

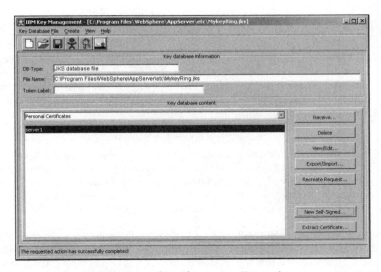

The CORBA Internet Inter-ORB Protocol (IIOP) is generally used to communicate to EJBs hosted in the EJB container. WebSphere version 5.0 introduces support for the CSIv2 protocol for securing IIOP communication. CSIv2, in turn is layered on the SSL/TLS protocol for establishing trust in the target server. Again, the integrity of this communication depends on the correctness and currency of the certificates in the server's keyring.

Connection to your data system should also be protected. Different data systems offer different mechanisms and protocols for connecting, each of these having varying degrees of protection. Most data systems require that you supply a user ID and password for the connection. You can identify the user ID and password for your data sources and resource adapters in the configuration for those resources in the WebSphere admin console. These are specified under an authentication alias associated with the data source or resource adapter:

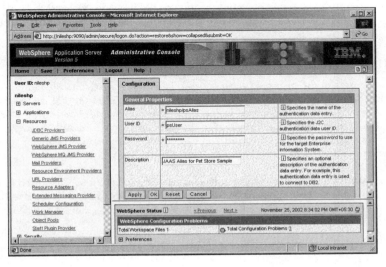

Configuring your DMZ

There are two schools of thought about how to configure your DMZ. Putting your web server in the DMZ allows you to serve static content without the overhead and latency that might come from traversing the intranet firewall. Obviously, if your static content contains sensitive information then you should think twice about hosting it in the DMZ. However, the vast majority of static content is relatively benign. On the other hand, managing the content can be more difficult as it requires traversing the intranet firewall from your content publishing systems.

We tend to prefer to place a proxy server in the DMZ and keep the web server in the intranet. Doing so reduces the problems with content management, and makes it simpler to guard against viruses if someone hacks into the DMZ. As a result, you will have a better chance of surviving a Denial of Service (DoS) attack by compartmentalizing your exposures. This can be further enhanced by combining the proxy server with a network dispatcher (also referred to as an IP sprayer) and multiple proxy servers in the DMZ for bandwidth management and workload-balancing the inbound traffic.

The network dispatcher takes in-bound IP packets and routes them across a number of intermediates (usually proxy-servers). In this way, it is able to distribute the in-bound workload across a number of proxy-servers, and by extension across a number of web servers and or application servers behind the intermediate proxy servers. The network dispatcher is usually smart enough to route requests from the same client back to the same intermediate (and backend) to maintain affinity to the state that has been established for that client in the backend servers.

WebSphere ships both a network dispatcher (Web Traffic Express) and a Caching Proxy Server. The Caching Proxy Server will manage a cache of your content – which can overcome the additional latency imposed by hosting the web server in the intranet.

In either case, whether you prefer to configure your web server or a proxy server in the DMZ, you should also enable Network Address Translation (NAT) in your firewall, and configure different port values for the communication through the Internet firewall and the intranet firewall. For example, when you position a proxy server in the DMZ, if you use the standard port 80 for communication from the Internet to your proxy server, then you should configure the proxy server and the web server to communicate on some other port. Doing so deters traffic that may attempt to route around the proxy server in the DMZ.

Network Authentication

Authenticating the user in the proxy server has several advantages. If your site contains particularly sensitive material you can prevent any traffic from entering your intranet that isn't associated with an authenticated user. If your site has several web servers you can enable sign-on in the proxy – authenticating the user to form a login context in the proxy server that can then be propagated to each of the web servers collected at your site, and you can enforce authorization policies on selected URIs – selectively preventing access into your intranet against protected resources.

The proxy server provided with WebSphere provides all of these functions when used in conjunction with Tivoli's Access Manager for authorization enforcement. The credential token created in the WebSphere Caching Proxy will be propagated through the web server to the WebSphere Application Server.

Credential Propagation and Resource Protection

Even if you don't use a proxy server in your network, WebSphere will ensure that a security context representing the authenticated principal is formed whenever a user accesses a protected resource managed by WebSphere. A credential token is formed representing that principal and associated with any work initiated by that principal in the application server. The credential token is propagated to downstream servers – being validated upon entry to any downstream server to ensure that the credential properly represents the authenticity of the principal that it identifies.

For each protected resource touched by work initiated by that principal, the WebSphere runtime will ensure that the principal is authorized to use that resource in the manner requested. For example, if a principal addresses a URL on their browser that results in invoking a get operation on a servlet, the authorization policies governing the security constraints associated with that servlet are checked to ensure that principal has authority to perform that get operation. Likewise, if that servlet is encoded to invoke an Account EJB with, say, a `getBalance()` operation the runtime will verify that the principal is authorized to access that operation on `Account` objects. The specifics of access control are discussed further in *Protecting J2EE Resources* section.

Protecting the Execution Environment

The integrity of your runtime is fundamentally dependent on the integrity of the execution environment in which it is hosted, this includes the computing system; operating system, file system, and the network system; in essence everything about the physical and logical environment that defines the context for the application server. It is important that you establish a strong set of security policies for your web site, and further that you execute and enforce those policies.

The integrity of the WebSphere hosting environment depends, in particular, on you protecting access to the files and directories containing the WebSphere runtime JARs and configuration files, and your application JARs. You should set the ACLs on these directories so that only a small set of authorized administrators are allowed access to those directories. We suggest that you create a special operating system identity representing the WebSphere runtime, starting WebSphere servers under that identity – of course you'll have to give that WebSphere identity access to its own directories and configuration files.

You can establish the identity under which WebSphere application servers will execute from the Process Execution attributes of the application server definition in the admin console:

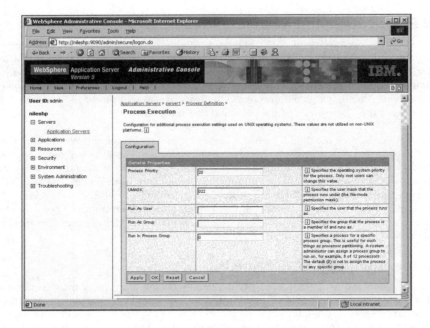

Secure Associations Between Distributed Components

Authenticating the user is about establishing trust in the user – determining whether they are who they claim to be. That is actually only part of the story. Once a user has been authenticated they would prefer not to have to do it again, repeatedly. Somehow their authenticity needs to be conveyed among all the components that care about the user's authenticity – essentially, any component of the system that will be involved in validating that user's authorization to access a resource, that needs to represent the user, or that otherwise needs access to information about the user.

WebSphere conveys the user's authenticity by forming a credential token at the time the principal is authenticated. The credential is cryptographically computed to ensure that a rogue application cannot construct such a token to falsely represent a user on its own. Moreover, once the token is created, WebSphere can pass the token around, examine it, and in doing so determine that the token continues to represent the authenticity of the principal that it identifies. Consider the following scenario:

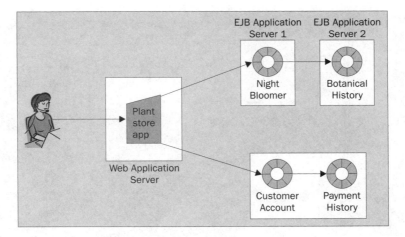

A customer logs in to the Plant Store from home. This is an existing customer with an account with the store and is thus entitled to view the store's inventory of rare and exotic plants. They are interested in buying a Night Bloomer, but want to know that the plant was spliced by a local botanist who is known for raising top rated plants. After confirming the plant's history, the customer puts a hold on the plant so that they can come down and check that the plant is in good shape. The store will check the customer's account to ensure they will be able to pay for the plant before putting it on hold for them.

In this scenario all of the objects presented are protected objects – that is, authenticated users can only access them with the authority for such access.

The WebSphere runtime will ensure the customer is authenticated as soon as they attempt to make a **Request** (1) to a protected object. If they weren't authenticated by an in-network proxy sever, then the WebSphere application server will initiate a **Challenge** (2) to authenticate the user – by the **Login** form (3) included with the plant store application. Then, the login information is **Authenticated** (4) with the **Authentication Server** and a credential token representing that user will be associated (5) with the thread of work for that customer:

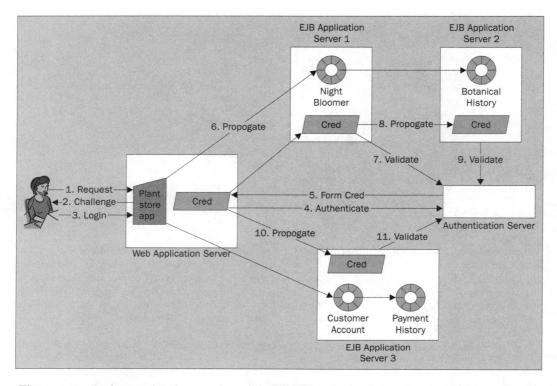

The customer looks into the plant catalog, and finding the Night Bloomer checks its history. This results in an operation being invoked on the Night Bloomer object in EJB Server 1. The WebSphere runtime will **Propagate** (6) the customer's credential to Server 1. Upon arrival, the WebSphere runtime in Server 1 will **Validate** (7) the credential to ensure it is valid, and establish that customer's credential in the server associated with the work initiated for that customer. This continues on downstream as the rest of the work cascades across other servers.

The process of propagating and validating the user's credentials in downstream servers is referred to as *establishing a secure association* for that principal. To make the processing more efficient, WebSphere will maintain a secure session between the application servers on that user's behalf – until the user's involvement in the site is completed. As such, secure associations are stateful.

Identity Assertions

As you might expect, all of the validation that goes into forming a secure association can generate a certain measurable level of overhead in the processing of the credential propagation. WebSphere offers an alternate mechanism to establish associations between servers for the requesting principals – that is, identity assertions. This is also referred to as establishing a trust association for reasons that will become apparent as we describe it:

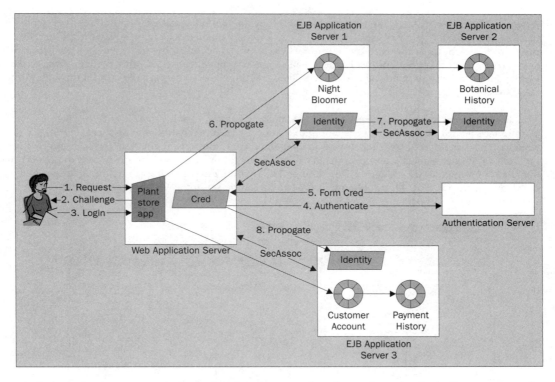

As before, the customer is challenged and authenticated, and a credential is formed representing the principal (1-5). However, when work is initiated on the downstream servers, the identity of the principal is extracted from the credential and propagated to the downstream server. Some time before this point the Web Application Server will have authenticated itself to Server 1, and so forth – each pair of servers will have authenticated with each other and have formed a secure association between them representing their own authenticity. Based on this secure association, and based on trust policies that can be set for the servers, Server 1 will accept an identity assertion initiated by the Web Application Server. That is, Server 1 will accept that the identity that the Web Application Server provides is authentic merely by virtue of the Server 1's trust in the Web Application Server.

An identity assertion is not as secure as a credential propagation. The identity token in the downstream servers cannot be independently verified to represent the authenticity of the principal it identifies. It is theoretically possible for a rogue application to manufacture an identity token and claim the represented identity is authentic. However, if you can trust your servers – more specifically if you can trust the applications deployed to your servers, then the identity assertion model is more efficient than establishing secure associations between servers.

Delegation

Credential propagation as we describe it above is also a form of **delegation** – that is, the credentials used for accessing the plant inventory are then delegated on the downstream request for history information.

Arguably the history for the plants at the Plant Store is not all that sensitive – or, at least, it may not have to be protected on a per user basis. Either by knowing that users have to satisfy the authorization policy of the plant inventory and that customers can only get access to the history if they've been authorized access to a plant, or just because you're not all that concerned about who has access to the history information it may not be necessary to delegate the client principal's identity on through to the downstream object.

You can assign each application server instance its own identity – each server is authenticated to the WebSphere security system and a credential token is formed representing that application server's principal. This is referred to as the **system principal**. In your application you can, for each method or for each component, specify a RunAs deployment descriptor. You can set this descriptor to pass through the client's credential, the server's system credential, or some other specific credential that has been granted a particular role. This deployment descriptor can be set in the WebSphere Application Assembly Tool or WSAD:

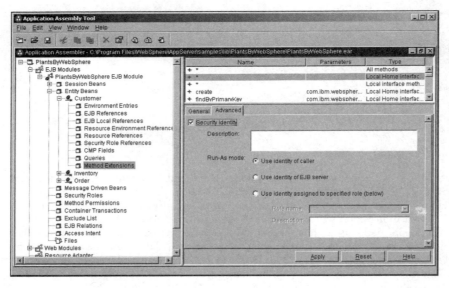

By setting the deployment descriptor to use the server's system credential, all downstream requests within that method will be invoked under the server's identity and any authority granted to the server's principal. On the one hand, this means that the server had better be granted the authority that it needs for downstream resources. On the other hand, this is one way of limiting access to downstream resources except through the component method that has been granted that access. In effect, it can be used to make the calling method a privileged operation. See more about privileged code in the next section.

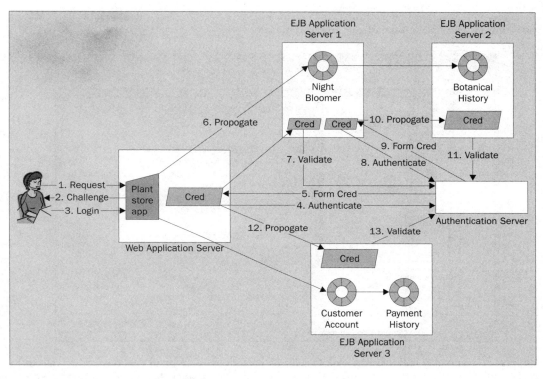

If you are going to run as a specified identity:

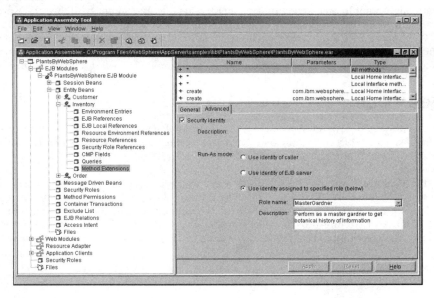

then you must map the specified role to a specific user during deployment, defining their user ID and password for authentication purposes in the application:

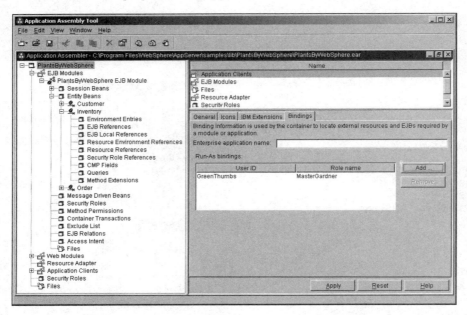

On occasion, you may find that you want to achieve this for only a subset of the downstream calls that you make within a particular method implementation. Let's say, for example, that you were going to access the Customer Account from within the NightBloomer object, in addition to accessing the plant's history. In this case you might want to access the history under the identity and authority of the server-principal, but then you need to access the Customer Account object under the identity and authority of the client principal. WebSphere does not provide you a way of doing this through declarative policy, but you can achieve the affect by (counter to all other recommendations) using the Java 2 Security programming interfaces to invoke the Pedigree History within a doAs() block. This was discussed in *Java 2 Security*.

Privileged Code

The RunAs deployment descriptor, when used to control delegation to the servers with a specified identity, enables a form of privileged execution across components, as we have discussed above. However, often the requirements for privileged execution are more localized.

However, there are times where your application may require more than what these permissions will allow you to do. Resource Adapters, as defined by the Java 2 Connector Architecture are a prime example. It is difficult to write a Resource Adapter without native code or without spawning threads. The Java 2 Connector Architecture specifies a mechanism whereby a Resource Adapter can request additional permissions through the security-permission-spec deployment descriptor:

```
<!ELEMENT security-permission (description?, security-permission-spec)>
<!ELEMENT security-permission-spec (#PCDATA)>
```

The `security-permission-spec` deployment descriptor should be formatted using the Security Policy File syntax as described at:
http://java.sun.com/products/jdk/1.3/docs/guide/security/PolicyFiles.html#FileSyntax.
This descriptor can be defined for your resource adapter in the WebSphere Application Assembly Tool.

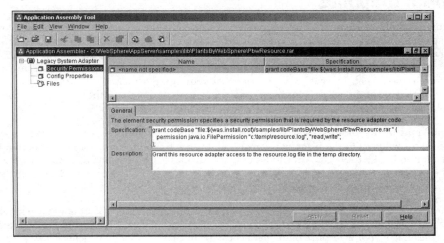

Similarly, you may need additional permissions in your application. It is important that you realize that when you request additional permissions in your application, you are enabling it to violate some of the programming model constraints imposed by the application server. You are, in effect, entering into a realm where the application server can no longer ensure the integrity of your application. You should proceed with caution! You are assuming the responsibility for making sure your application does not contradict controls and activities performed on your behalf by the application server.

You can request additional permissions for your application by including a `was.policy` file in the `META-INF` directory of your EAR file. WebSphere does not provide any tooling to create the permissions you request for your application; however, you construct and edit this file as you would if you were to create a permission file for the Java 2 Security Manager using the `Policytool` provided with the JDK shipped with WebSphere.

This file follows the same general syntax defined for the Security Policy File as referenced above. However, generally you will use relative names for your application code. The substitution variable `"${Application}"` can be used in the `codeBase` to represent your application EAR. For example:

```
grant codeBase "${Application}" {
 permission java.net.SocketPermission "ahost:7777", "connect, accept";
};

grant codeBase "servlet1.war" {
 permission java.net.SocketPermission "localhost:1024-", "accept,listen";
};
```

WebSphere will then merge any permissions requested in the `was.policy` file within your application with the standard J2EE permissions. WebSphere cannot grant all permissions in all cases and will generate a warning and/or error message explaining why in those cases that it is not able to honor a permission request.

Again, not to contradict other recommendations, if you have a reason for requesting permissions within your code, you can do so with the Java 2 Security `doPrivilege()` operation.

Credential Mapping

If you employ multiple security realms or authentication domains in your enterprise then you are likely to run into the problem of having to represent the same principal with different authentication credentials. If you invoke an application at a web site that in turn invokes operations on EJBs or, more likely, transactions in a legacy information system, there is a chance that the work you initiate will span two or more of your security realms. If you want the requesting principal's identity to flow between systems – so that all of the work is initiated (and controlled) under the authority of the requesting principal, then you will have to authenticate that principal to both realms.

A principal may or may not have the same identity in both realms. In any case, the realms will want to establish their own trust in the principal – meaning, they will retain their proof information. Generally, you will want to avoid asking the user to login twice (or more) for the same application work. This is referred to as the *credential-mapping* problem – you need to map the credentials of the principal in one realm to an authentication credential for that same principal in another realm.

WebSphere does not really have any built-in support to fix this problem – at least not in a general fashion. However, there are several solutions you can employ. The first and easiest is to avoid the problem altogether – that is, consolidate your enterprise onto one security realm. This has many benefits all around, not the least of which is to simplify the administration of your security system, and reduce the potential for administration mistakes that could leave your enterprise exposed. However, this is unrealistic for many companies.

Another approach is to employ identity assertions – *trust associations*. In a trust association model, the principal is only actually authenticated to one realm. Their identity is mapped to a corresponding identity in the other realm, and then asserted to other realm. You must have a trust relationship between the two realms – specifically, you must trust that the applications and software stack in one realm will not abuse the identity of the principal; they will properly reflect the accurate identity of the requesting principal all the way through to the second realm. This only works really well if you've coordinated the realms so that principals have the same identity in both realms – this reduces ambiguity over how to identify the principal in the other realm.

WebSphere provides some assistance for this approach with built-in support for identity assertions. But it leaves it to you to establish trust between the realms; certifying the correctness of your applications and the software stack to properly pass on and protect principal identities. Moreover, WebSphere relies on you to determine an appropriate mapping of the principal's identity between the two realms – again, this is made easier if you can coordinate the two realms so that principals have the same identity in both realms; so that no identity mapping is needed.

If you can't perform identity assertions between your realms, then you are left with the prospect of having to implement your own credential mapping in your applications. You will have to define a mapping database to store the user ID and password (or whatever authentication information is needed) to the foreign realm for each principal that you want to map. When you're ready to cross into another realm, you will then look up the user ID and password for your principal, and use that to log in the user under the foreign realm. You will want to use a JAAS login module for the foreign realm. Of course, maintaining the mapping database requires additional administrative effort – not to mention the risk of it being compromised since it contains the passwords of, presumably, a number of key principals. Given the number of issues associated with both maintaining and protecting a credential-mapping database we recommend that you consider any of a number of different security infrastructure vendors that specialize in supporting this type of function.

All told, credential mapping poses a number of concerns. If you can't avoid multiple realms in your enterprise, and you don't want to accept the implications of credential mapping, then consider this final option. Rather than mapping the requesting principal through to the other realm, simply authenticate to the foreign realm with a single identity and perform all downstream work with that one identity or some small subset of identities. WebSphere provides support for this in all of its connection factories – JDBC, J2C, JMS, and EJB.

Instance-Based Authorization

Another common scenario is that you want to control access to individual instances of objects in your application. Consider, for example, the case where you only want customers to be able to access their own accounts. Again, WebSphere does not provide any support in this area – you will have to solve this in your own application. The easiest solution is to encode the logic right into object – for example, do a test in the `Account` object to see if the requesting principal (the customer) is the owner of this account. If not, then exit out of the request. This is awkward for a couple of reasons.

First, you have to include this logic in every method of the object, and remember to include it in any additional methods that you add to the object later – in future versions of the object. Also, the logic has to be right – if you introduce any bug you will have to fix that bug in every method that you copied it to.

To make things worse, often the policy won't be quite that simple. You may want to allow access to the `Account` object by both the account-owner, and other representative employees of your business – such as tellers, or billing adjusters. Of course, the latter could be made a little simpler through the use of the `isCallerInRole` operation on the servlet or EJB context. Finally, you lose a lot of design elegance by having to combine infrastructure issues (security integrity) in with you business logic (unless you rationalize that it is your business to protect your business assets).

A preferred approach is to isolate your authorization logic. One design pattern is to simply call out to a special security routine that you share in common across your application (or maybe even across your organization). This still leaves you with the problem of packaging that routine in your application EAR (or in a common library), and then updating your application whenever the protection policies change. Another approach that will give you a bit more isolation between your business logic (application package) and your policies is to use the Business Rules Beans framework described in Chapter 5).

Conclusions

At this point you should have a fairly comprehensive understanding of the WebSphere security model. WebSphere draws from a combination of the J2EE security model, extensions introduced by WebSphere to fill holes in the J2EE model, and optional third-party security providers, including Tivoli's security services products, to deliver an end-to-end layered defense against intrusion and disruption to your information system. The same plug-points that enable integration with third-party security providers can be leveraged by you to integrate with your own legacy security facilities.

While we have discouraged you from writing security logic into your applications, and have enabled you to avoid this for the most part with built-in and implicit facilities controlled through externally declared policies and administration facilities, we've also enabled a number of programming interfaces that enable you to accomplish some amount of programming where you might need it.

Disclaimer

Understanding the security model and exposures of your information system is key to protecting your information assets. You should now have a much better idea of what you need to do to help ensure the integrity of your system. However, one point that we want to reiterate – if you believe that you've guarded against every possible vulnerability, someone, somewhere, is going to find a weakness that you hadn't considered. Security is dynamic and fluid. You have to be proactive in both monitoring and reinforcing your defenses. The technology by itself will not do it all for you – you need a complete set of security policies, and you have to actively apply those policies; getting the technology to do the work for you, synergistically and efficiently. But the technology is not a substitute for you and your practices.

14

WebSphere Administration

In this chapter, we're going to cover the basic architecture of the middleware management facility built into the WebSphere Application Server and help you understand the role and mechanisms used for controlling the application server and the applications installed on it. We will walk you through the important tasks for setting up a network of one application server and of multiple application servers, for creating a cluster, and for managing your applications on that network of servers. We will discuss some of the key principles for problem detection, analysis, and configuration maintenance. This track will be presented exclusively through demonstrations of the user interface for the management facility.

Enterprise System Management

Before we begin, it is probably worth making one point clear. You may have noticed our use of the term **middleware management**. A fundamental tenet of WebSphere is to distinguish between middleware management and *enterprise system management*. Wherever you see unqualified references made to the term 'system management' within the context of WebSphere it is usually intended to mean middleware management. By that, we mean the facilities that are needed to manage the WebSphere middleware and the applications written to and hosted on the WebSphere Application Server.

The middleware management does not generally concern itself with managing peripheral devices, the operating system, other middleware environments, or even the data and system resources used by the applications hosted on WebSphere. At best, the WebSphere middleware management facility concerns itself with the relationships to these other things.

However, as we all know, an information system is composed of many more things than just the application server and the applications hosted on it. The *application* is really a composition of the client platform, including its operating system and browser, the network used to interconnect the client to the application server, the operating system on which the application server resides, the peripherals and file system it uses, other middleware integrated with the application server, underlying data systems, and so forth. Moreover, other applications hosted by other middleware facilities may often reside on the same computing facilities and so many resources will be shared between WebSphere and non-WebSphere environments.

We presume that enterprise system management is responsible for managing the entirety of the information system. In doing so, we presume the enterprise management system will collaborate with the middleware management facilities of WebSphere – delegating the responsibility for managing the configuration, interconnection, and operational properties of the WebSphere runtime and the applications (or application components) hosted on WebSphere in directions provided by the enterprise management system.

So, why does WebSphere have a middleware management facility at all? Why doesn't it just depend on enterprise management to solve all of its management requirements? The answer is centered on the relationship between the definition of a J2EE enterprise application, the resources it depends on, and the role of WebSphere to provide the best possible scalability and integrity for the applications hosted on it.

For example, WebSphere must have a deep understanding of the servers in a cluster, and the state of that cluster to manage the distribution of workload and recovery across the cluster. By extension, WebSphere must have a good understanding of the application and its resource dependencies. While you might imagine the enterprise management system provides this information to the WebSphere runtime, it is highly specialized to the J2EE model and largely outside the standard models used by the enterprise system for managing everything else. It has to be adjusted as often as the J2EE specification itself changes. It is just better if these relationships are maintained and managed by the middleware itself.

Besides, the separation between middleware management and enterprise management allows WebSphere to deliver an 'out-of-the-box' capability for managing the WebSphere system in simpler scenarios where you may be less concerned about integrating with an encompassing enterprise management system. For example, how often does it concern you that your developer desktop is not integrated into the overall management system of your enterprise? While enterprise management is a critical issue in production environments, most programmers would not be comfortable with having to turn to the central IT operations department in their enterprise to configure a unit test environment on their developer desktop.

WebSphere does have excellent facilities for integrating with the major enterprise management systems available on the market – including Tivoli's Monitor for Web Infrastructure (previously Tivoli Monitor for WebSphere), Computer Associates' Unicenter, Candle's Omegamon, Mercury Interactive's Topaz, Wiley Technology's Introscope, as well as several other vendors' products. A complete list of supported enterprise management products is listed here:

http://www-3.ibm.com/software/webservers/pw/dhtml/wsperformance/performance_bpsolutions.html.

WebSphere Middleware Management Architecture

The WebSphere Middleware Management is essentially composed of these major elements:

- ❑ **JMX Server** – hosts the JMX Model MBeans that represent managed resources in the WebSphere network

- ❑ **Admin Service** – provides for external and remote representation of the JMX Server

- ❑ **Admin Client** – the client library for communicating to an admin service

- ❑ **MBeans and Information Model** – defines the type space for the MBeans introduced by WebSphere

- ❑ **Configuration Repository** – holds the configuration of the managed resources in the WebSphere network

- ❑ **Administration Application and Workspace** – implements the user interface to the middleware management system

- ❑ **Node Agent** – provides localized management control of the application server on a given node; also provides the end-point listener for remote management control from the deployment manager

- ❑ **Deployment Manager** – also referred to as the cell manager; provides centralized control over the resources defined in the topology of the deployment cell

- ❑ **PME Administration Extensions** – extensions to the middleware management system in support of the administrable properties of the programming model extensions (of Enterprise edition)

The picture overleaf depicts these components and their relationships within the WebSphere network. We'll discuss each of these in more detail. In addition, we will discuss the architecture for securing and extending the middleware management system:

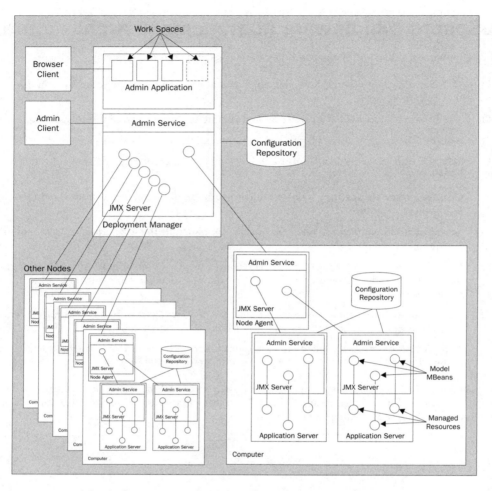

The aggregation of the deployment manager and all of the nodes and application servers collected in a single topology and recorded in the central configuration repository is referred to as a cell. Application servers only ever belong to a single node, and nodes only ever belong to a single cell. However, different nodes and, by extension, different application servers, even in different cells, can be hosted on the same computer.

JMX Server

The WebSphere middleware management system is fundamentally based on the **JMX (Java Management Extension)** standard. Thus, the managed resources of the WebSphere execution environment are represented as JMX Model **MBeans**. MBeans essentially are proxies to the actual managed resource they represent. For example, there is an MBean instance for each application server instance in the system. The JMX specification is described in its entirety at: http://java.sun.com/products/JavaManagement/.

WebSphere makes a strong distinction between operations management and configuration management. Operations management is performed through JMX MBeans. Configuration management is performed through a set of XML documents maintained persistently in the configuration repository (although the configuration repository is itself represented with a Configuration Service MBean). Operations performed on a resource through its MBean proxy may change the operational state of the resource, but will not permanently change its configuration. The next time that resource is initialized with its configuration, it will revert back to the state implied by that configuration. Likewise, a change to a resource's configuration will not be reflected in its MBean state until that resource is actually re-initialized with its configuration (which may be sooner or later depending on the nature of the resource, its ability to accept re-initialization on the fly, and any policies that govern dynamic configuration changes).

Everything in the application server and in the WebSphere network managed by the WebSphere middleware management facility is modeled as an MBean. The full information model is described in detail later. This includes the application server itself, the web and EJB containers' thread pools, and so on. We refer to anything that is represented by an MBean as a **managed resource** – implying that it is a resource that can be managed through the middleware management facility.

Every application server instance comes with an embedded JMX server. The JMX server is where MBeans reside and are managed. You can abstractly think of the JMX server as a container and MBeans as a special component type. The MBeans hosted in the JMX server of a given application server are there to represent the managed resources in that application server – including the application server itself.

In addition, a JMX server resides in the node agent and deployment manager as well. We'll discuss these components in the overall architecture later, but suffice it to say for now that they provide broader levels of management support across a distributed system and facilitate communication of operational commands from the central deployment manager to the application servers deployed in the network.

Admin Service

The standard JMX specification presumes that all MBeans operations will be invoked locally – from within the same JVM as that in which the MBeans are hosted. However, WebSphere is a distributed environment, and even if it weren't you would most likely want to control the application server from some other process – either on the same computer, or more likely from some central location within your network. WebSphere enables remote communication to the JMX server with a pair of JMX connectors – one based on IIOP, and another based on SOAP/HTTP. In the former case, the JMX server is treated as an RMI/IIOP object. In the latter case, the JMX server is treated as a Web Service.

No portion of the middleware management is gained or lost with one connector or the other – they are equally capable of providing communication to the JMX server and the MBeans they host. The difference between the connectors is entirely based on quality of service – exactly the same tradeoffs that exist between IIOP-based versus SOAP/HTTP-based Web Service communication.

The **admin service** is essentially a wrapper to enable remote communication to the JMX server. The admin service provides the end-point listener for both the SOAP and IIOP-based JMX connectors. In addition, the admin service provides support for a JMX router. This router knows how to take a JMX operations request and forward it to whatever JMX server is hosting the actual JMX MBean referenced in the operation request. Admin clients can issue operation requests on the admin service in the deployment manager, and if the specified MBean does not reside in the deployment manager, the router function will forward the request to the admin service in the node agent, which in turn will forward it the application server, and so forth until the MBean referred to in the operation request is located. The operation request is then dispatched on the MBean in the JMX server where it is hosted.

621

Admin Client

The **admin client** provides remote communication to the admin service. It is used in the admin console, commands, and scripting client. If you write any JMX-based admin applications you will use the admin client.

A major difference between WebSphere and other application servers is that IBM has attempted to overcome the limitation of JMX that requires that you be in the same process as the JMX server that you want to operate on by introducing a proxy to the JMX server. WebSphere introduces the notion of an `AdminClient` that hides the fact that you may or may not be in the same process as the JMX server that you want to operate on. The `AdminClient` supports the normal JMX interface, but then takes responsibility for routing JMX requests to the right JMX server where your MBean resides.

When programming management applications in WebSphere, you will mostly be programming to this `AdminClient` interface. The `AdminClient` has the following interface definition:

```java
public interface AdminClient {

    public static final String CONNECTOR_TYPE = "type";
    public static final String CONNECTOR_HOST = "host";
    public static final String CONNECTOR_PORT = "port";
    public static final String CONNECTOR_TYPE_SOAP = "SOAP";
    public static final String CONNECTOR_TYPE_RMI = "RMI";
    public static final String CONNECTOR_TYPE_JMS = "JMS";
    public static final String PROTOCOL_ADAPTOR_TYPE_SNMP = "SNMP";
    public static final String[] CONNECTOR_TYPES =
        { CONNECTOR_TYPE_SOAP, CONNECTOR_TYPE_RMI, PROTOCOL_ADAPTOR_TYPE_SNMP };
    public static final String CONNECTOR_SOAP_CONFIG = "com.ibm.SOAP.ConfigURL";
    public static final String CONNECTOR_SOAP_REQUEST_TIMEOUT =
        "com.ibm.SOAP.requestTimeout";
    public static final String CONNECTOR_SECURITY_ENABLED = "securityEnabled";
    public static final String USERNAME = "username";
    public static final String PASSWORD = "password";

    public void addNotificationListener(ObjectName name,
        NotificationListener listener, NotificationFilter filter,
        Object handback) throws InstanceNotFoundException, ConnectorException;

    public void addNotificationListenerExtended(ObjectName name,
        NotificationListener listener, NotificationFilter filter,
        Object handback) throws ConnectorException;

    public Object getAttribute(ObjectName name, String attribute)
        throws MBeanException, AttributeNotFoundException,
            InstanceNotFoundException, ReflectionException, ConnectorException ;

    public AttributeList getAttributes(ObjectName name, String[] attributes)
        throws InstanceNotFoundException, ReflectionException,
            ConnectorException;

    public java.util.Properties getConnectorProperties();

    public String getDefaultDomain() throws ConnectorException ;

    public String getDomainName() throws ConnectorException ;
```

```
        public Integer getMBeanCount() throws ConnectorException ;

        public MBeanInfo getMBeanInfo(ObjectName name)
          throws InstanceNotFoundException, IntrospectionException,
                ReflectionException, ConnectorException ;

        public ObjectName getServerMBean() throws ConnectorException;

        public String getType();

        public Object invoke(ObjectName name, String operationName, Object params[],
          String signature[]) throws InstanceNotFoundException, MBeanException,
          ReflectionException, ConnectorException ;

        public Session isAlive() throws ConnectorException ;

        public boolean isInstanceOf(ObjectName name, String className)
          throws InstanceNotFoundException, ConnectorException ;

        public boolean isRegistered(ObjectName name) throws ConnectorException ;

        public Set queryNames(ObjectName name, QueryExp query)
          throws ConnectorException ;

        public void reconnect() throws ConnectorNotAvailableException ;

        public void removeNotificationListener(ObjectName name,
          NotificationListener listener) throws InstanceNotFoundException,
          ListenerNotFoundException, ConnectorException;

        public void removeNotificationListenerExtended(NotificationListener listener)
          throws ListenerNotFoundException, ConnectorException;

        public void setAttribute(ObjectName name, Attribute attribute)
          throws InstanceNotFoundException, AttributeNotFoundException,
                InvalidAttributeValueException, MBeanException,
                ReflectionException, ConnectorException ;

        public AttributeList setAttributes(ObjectName name, AttributeList attributes)
          throws InstanceNotFoundException, ReflectionException,
                ConnectorException ;
    }
```

The AdminClient interface is largely the same as the javax.management.MbeanServer interface – the primary difference is the removal of operations that require execution in the JMX server process (in the same JVM address space), and the inclusion of methods to support the connection of the client to the target JMX Server (through its corresponding AdminService).

MBeans and the Information Model

The MBean information model is used to define what types of MBeans can be found in the system. Not every one of these MBean types can be found in every JMX server – a few of them are only relevant in the node agent or deployment manager. Through the JMX connectors and routing function built in to the admin service, you can reference to any JMX MBean wherever MBeans are hosted – in the deployment manager, the node agents, or any of the application servers.

The MBeans in the information model include:

AdminOperations	EJBContainer	MessageDriven Bean	SessionBean
Application	EJBModule	Module	SessionManager
ApplicationManager	EntityBean	NameServer	Stateful SessionBean
AppManagement	J2CConnection Factory	NodeAgent	Stateless SessionBean
CellSync	J2Cresource Adapter	NodeSync	SystemMetrics
Cluster	J2EEResource Factory	Notification Service	ThreadPool
ClusterMgr	J2EEResource Provider	ORB	TraceService
ConfigService	JDBCProvider	Perf	Transaction
ConnectionFactory	JMSDestination	PluginCfg Generator	Transaction Service
DataSource	JMSProvider	PmiRmJmxService	URLProvider
DataSourceCfgHelper	JMSServer	RasLogging Service	WAS40Data Source
DeployedObject	JMXConnector	ResourceAdapter	WebContainer
DeploymentManager	JSP	ResourceAdapter Module	WebModule
Discovery	JVM	SecurityAdmin	WLMAppServer
DynaCache	ListenerPort	Server	WMQQueue Definer
EJB	MailProvider	Servlet	WSGW

As you can see, most of these MBeans represent obvious resources in the system, such as `Cluster`, `ClusterMgr`, `DeploymentManager`, `EJBContainer`, `NodeAgent`, and so on. Other MBeans represent resources within your applications, such as `EJB`, `Servlet`, `WebModule`, etc. Others are a little more esoteric, such as `AdminOperations`, `AppManagement`, and `SystemMetrics`. The full Javadocs for all of these MBeans are included in the WebSphere product under web/mbeanDocs/index.html in the install root directory for the WebSphere Application Server, and can also be accessed from the WebSphere InfoCenter at http://www.ibm.com/software/webservers/appserv/infocenter.html. That's really the best place to get detailed information on each of these MBean types and what you can do with them. We'll detail a couple of them below to give you a sense of what's going on. Before we do, there are a couple of things to be said about MBeans.

MBeans are defined to support a set of attributes, operations, and notifications:

❑   Attributes typically tell you something about the MBean – providing identity information, options that effect operational behavior, relations to other MBeans, or statistical information.

❑   The operations allow you to drive actions on the MBean (and by extension, the resource that the MBean represents).

❑   Notifications are events that you can register for – informing you of significant state changes in the MBean (or the resource that it represents).

The attributes, operations, and notifications that a given MBean supports are defined in an MBean descriptor that is registered with the JMX Server. The descriptor is an XML file that describes the characteristics of the MBean. The Javadoc for MBeans supported by WebSphere is generated from these MBean descriptors.

The AppManagement MBean

The AppManagement MBean allows you to perform a number of application management operations – including installing and uninstalling applications and resource adapters, getting and setting information about the application, and changing which application servers the application is to be hosted on.

The AppManagement MBean has no attributes.

The operations of the AppManagement MBean include:

install Application	setModuleInfo	listModules	removeAllAppsFrom Node
uninstall Application	moveModule	compareSecurity Policy	removeAllAppsFrom Cluster
getApplication Info	export Application	installStandalone RAR	removeAllAppsFrom Server
getModuleInfo	extractDDL	checkIfAppExists	ChangeServerTo Cluster
setApplication Info	list Applications	redeploy Application	ClusterMember Added

The module-related operations – getModuleInfo, setModuleInfo, moveModule, and listModules operate on the J2EE modules defined in the specified application.

The AppManagement MBean resides on the application server and (when configured with one) the deployment manager. The instance on the application server only has visibility to the application server on which it resides, and so you can only install an application on that application server, and cannot move the modules of the application to other application server instances when you're operating on the MBean instance hosted on a given application server. On the other hand, if you operate on the instance in the deployment manager then you can install the application into the cell, and configure it to be hosted on any of the application servers configured in that cell.

The notifications generated by the AppManagement MBean include:

```
websphere.admin.appmgmt
```

The appmgmt notification is fired whenever an application install, uninstall, or update occurs.

The NodeAgent MBean

The `NodeAgent` represents the node agent on each computer (more literally, on each node, as a single computer could have more than one node and therefore more than one node agent – we discuss this further in the *Node Agent* section later in this chapter). The node agent is generally responsible for monitoring all of the application servers that are hosted on that node, and providing remote communication to these servers from the central deployment manager (also discussed later in this chapter). The `NodeAgent` MBean has no attributes.

It supports the following operations:

launchProcess	stopNode	restart

The `launchProcess` operation is used to start an application server. This can be issued with or without specifying a timeout value – indicating the maximum time you are willing to wait for the server to start and initialize.

The `stopNode` operation is used to stop all application servers on the node, including the node agent itself.

The `restart` operation is used to restart the node agent, and optionally to restart any running application servers at the same time. If the option to restart the running applications is not selected, then just the node agent is restarted – the application servers continue to operate normally. If, on the other hand, the option to restart the application servers is selected, then the application servers on that node are stopped gracefully, and then automatically restarted after the node agent is restarted. The node agent will not be shut down until that last application server on that node has fully quiesced and outstanding workload on that server has completed. In addition, this operation can be used to optionally resynch the node configuration with the cell manager as part of the node agent restart.

The notifications emitted by the `NodeAgent` MBean include:

websphere.process.starting	websphere.process.running	websphere.process.stopping
websphere.process.stopped	websphere.process.failed	

Each of these indicates that one of the application servers on the target node is either starting, running, stopping, stopped, or has failed.

The TransactionService MBean

The `TransactionService` MBean represents the transaction service and can be used to collect information about the service – including its current operating attributes and the outstanding in-flight transactions. The `TransactionService` MBean has the following attributes:

transactionLogDirectory	totalTranLifetimeTimeout	clientInactivityTimeout

The `transactionLogDirectory` defines the directory in which the transaction log will be recorded. The `totalTranLifetimeTimeout` indicates, in milliseconds, the maximum amount of time a transaction can take to complete. If any given transaction has not been completed within the time specified in this attribute it will automatically be rolled back by the transaction service. If this attribute is set to zero (0), transactions are not timed – they are left to execute indefinitely.

The `clientInactivityTimeout` indicates, in milliseconds, the maximum time allowed between client requests under a given transaction. If the client takes more than the specified time to initiate another method request in the same transaction, the transaction will automatically be rolled back. If this attribute is set to zero (0), the interval between client requests is not timed.

The `TransactionService` MBean supports the following operations:

printableListOfTransactions	listOfTransactions

The `listOfTransaction` operation returns an array of the outstanding transaction identities, and the `printableListOfTransactions` returns the list as a single string pre-formatted for printing.

The `TransactionService` MBean does not emit any notifications.

This obviously is not a complete specification of the information model for the MBeans in WebSphere. You should consult the Javadoc for the MBean information model in the WebSphere InfoCenter for more detail on the remaining MBeans. However, this short summary should have given you the sense of what MBeans are and what they do. We'll come back to the subject of MBeans during the programming track for this chapter.

Configuration Repository

The configuration repository is where the configuration information is kept persistently. The configuration, of course, describes what application servers are located on which node, on which computer, and in which cell. It also defines what applications are hosted on which servers, which servers are aggregated to form a cluster, what resources are located where, the mapping between application references to those resources and the actual resources, and any behavioral options in effect for each resource.

A configuration repository is created on every node where WebSphere is installed – the repository simply consists of a set of configuration documents stored in a particular directory structure on the file system. In addition, if you've installed the Network Deployment edition, a copy of the configuration documents is maintained on the central deployment manager. The central repository is also maintained in a directory structure on the file system of the deployment management node – collecting a copy of every configuration document for each application server on each node federated in the cell.

Each application server only ever operates on the configuration document held for it in its local file system. In this way, no application server is ever dependent on the central configuration repository to know what applications it is serving, or where the resources are for those applications. In this sense, the repository is a highly distributed and fragmented database. This retains a high degree of independence for each application server – allowing it to operate without the central deployment manager and configuration repository, and by extension avoiding the central repository manager as a single point of failure. On the other hand, this fragmentation would make it difficult for the administrators to understand their system configuration.

To overcome this, WebSphere maintains a copy of all of the repository documents in a central repository on the deployment manager. Any configuration management performed with the deployment manager is done against the repository held with the deployment manager. It is then the responsibility of the deployment manager and the node agents on each node to synchronize their respective copies of the configuration documents.

When you make a change to the configuration of the system with the deployment manager and save those changes they are only saved immediately to the central repository. Those changes won't be propagated out to the individual application servers on their respective nodes until the central repository and the node repository are synchronized. The lag-time between when you save a configuration change and when it actually takes effect on the server depends on a number of things, including the synchronization settings in your configuration, and the state of the server(s) that you are changing – that is, whether it is up or down.

The repositories are synchronized first when you add a node into your cell (see the *Managing a Network of Application Servers* section later in this chapter for more details), and then resynchronized automatically or manually thereafter. A number of options can be set for when and how often the repositories are synchronized. These are controlled through settings on each individual node agent. You can access these options on the admin UI by first selecting System Administration | Cell in the navigation pane of the admin console. This will present the cell configuration notebook:

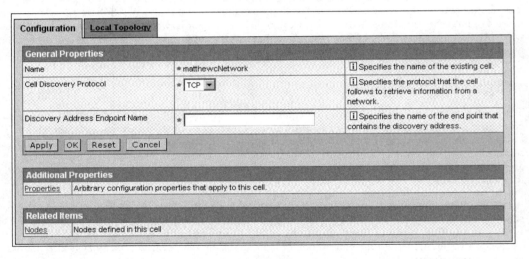

Next, press the Local Topology page tab, and expand the cell topology below that until you can see the node agent server that you want to configure. Notice that the node agent is itself a server (not an *application server*, but nonetheless a *server*), and so you have to expand the servers under the node to locate it. The node agent will always have the name of the node that it represents:

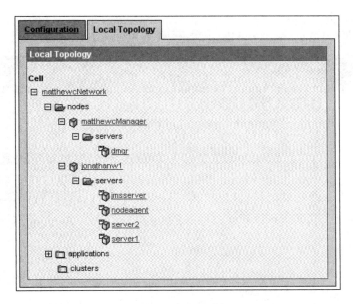

You can then select the node agent server to see the configuration page:

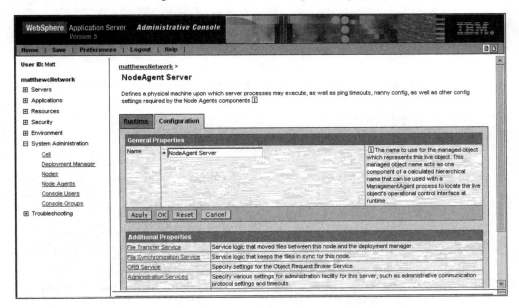

Finally, select the File Synchronization Service to see the options for how and when synchronization between the deployment manager and the node is performed:

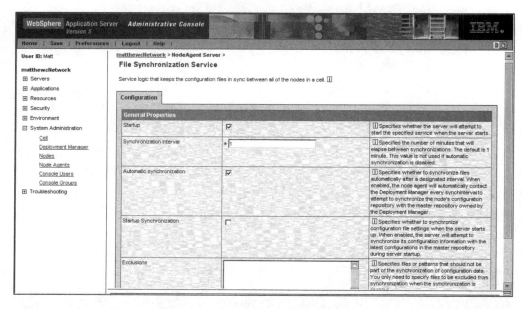

The synchronization options are:

❑ Startup
This option is ignored by the synchronization service – the service is always enabled and operates on the more specific configuration policies listed below.

❑ Synchronization interval
The synchronization interval indicates how frequently (in minutes) resynchronization should be performed if automatic synchronization is selected.

❑ Automatic synchronization
The configuration will automatically be resynchronized between the deployment manager and this node if this option is enabled. If auto-synchronization is enabled, the re-synchronization will occur as often as indicated in the synchronization-interval option above.

> You should think seriously about whether you want auto-synchronization enabled. On the one hand, if you disable it, any configuration changes you make on the deployment manager won't take effect on the application servers affected by that change until you manually force resynchronization. You could find your administrators wondering why their configuration changes are not taking effect. On the other hand, disabling auto-synchronization will help prevent configuration changes from inadvertently changing your production environment. With auto-synch disabled, you have to make the configuration change, save it *and* manually force the re-synchronization. This gives you slightly better control over your production changes.

❑ Startup synchronization
This option instructs the deployment manager to synchronize the configuration for any application server whenever that application server starts.

❑ Publish synchronization
This option instructs the deployment manager to synchronize with the node immediately whenever a configuration change is saved by the administrator at the deployment manager.

❑ Exclusions
This allows you to specify those files that you explicitly don't want synchronized between the deployment manager and the node. You can list file names with or without wildcards (? and *), on separate lines.

The configuration for each application server is held in the file system on each node. The structure of the configuration repository is:

```
cells
    /-- <cell-name>
        /-- nodes
            /-- <node-name>*
                /-- servers
                    /-- <server-name>*
```

Just as you see it in the admin UI.

There is only ever one cell-name – either the name of the local host for standalone servers, or the name of the cell if the node has been federated into a cell.

You will only ever find one node-name listed under nodes on a given node – the name of the local-node. You will find all of the nodes that have been federated into the cell in the same configuration repository on the deployment manager.

All of the application server instances that have been created on this node will be listed under servers.

Each of these directories – cells/<cell-name>, cells/<cell-name>/nodes/<node-name>, and cells/<cell-name>/nodes/<node-name>/servers/<server-name> – contains a set of configuration XML documents. These documents describe the overall configuration for the system.

Administration Application and Workspace

The **Administration application** is a fully conforming J2EE web application that implements the user interface of the middleware management system. This application, as you would expect of a web application, supports a browser-based interface.

This same application is used as the middleware management user interface for all editions of WebSphere. It is hosted in the application server for single, standalone server configurations, or it is hosted in the deployment manager in Network Deployment configurations.

The Admin application is installed in the application server by default. Since it is a standard J2EE application, you can see it in the installed applications of the application server in a single, standalone server configuration:

	Name ⬍	Status ⬍ ⟳
☐	DefaultApplication	➡
☐	PlantsByWebSphere	➡
☐	adminconsole	➡
☐	ivtApp	➡

Like other applications, you can uninstall it. However, if you uninstall it from a single, standalone server configuration you will not be able to install it back using a user interface – you will have to use the command line or script interface to re-install it!

If you convert a single, standalone server configuration into a networked configuration of multiple application servers, the Admin application is typically uninstalled from the application server(s) and only run from the deployment manager.

You will find the Admin application will look slightly different when hosted in the deployment manager. When the Admin application is hosted in a single, standalone server it knows that it essentially only has visibility to the application server on which it is run (see additional comments below for why this isn't entirely true). However, when the Admin application is hosted in the deployment manager, it knows that it has visibility to every application server configured in the deployment cell – even on other nodes. In the latter case, the Admin application adjusts its presentation to show all of the application servers in the deployment cell, and allows you to create clusters of multiple application servers (as you might expect, clusters are not supported in single, standalone server configurations).

Workspaces are a concept that is used within the Admin application to hold configuration changes as you make them. A workspace is created for each administrator user when they login to the admin console the first time. As you navigate around in the admin configuration copies of the configuration documents that you touch (via the admin UI) are cached in your workspace. If you change the configuration, the change is initially only made on the cached copy of the configuration document in your workspace. The changes are not applied to the master repository until you "save" those changes. The Save function is always listed on the system menu bar for the admin UI.

If you change the configuration and press OK, you will be reminded that you have pending changes in the workspace that have not been saved, and will be prompted to initiate the save.

Message(s)
⚠ Changes have been made to your local configuration. Click Save to apply changes to the master configuration.
🗓 The server may need to be restarted for these changes to take effect.

Of course, you may want to hold off on saving your changes if you have other changes you need to make. These additional changes will be collected in the workspace until you do save.

The workspace is retained persistently. If you logout without having saved your changes you will be prompted to do so:

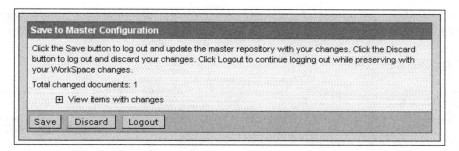

You can proceed to logout without saving, and your workspace will be retained persistently. When you log back in again, you will be given the option of continuing with your unsaved changes:

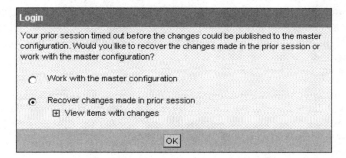

You, of course, can discard your changes at any time without saving them.

Concurrency Model in WebSphere

The base WebSphere Application Server and Network Deployment edition products assume an **optimistic concurrency model**. That means that WebSphere assumes that two administrators will rarely attempt to change the same part of the configuration at the same time. For example, it assumes that normally only one administrator will change the configuration of a given server at a time. WebSphere does monitor for conflicting configuration changes. However, if such a conflict is discovered, the first administrator to save their changes will be fine, and the second administrator will get a choice of either discarding their own changes and starting over again, or overwriting the changes made by the first administrator – setting the configuration to the way the second administrator sees it (even reverting configuration values that the second administrator has not changed).

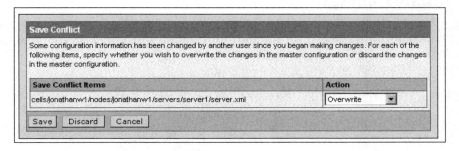

If the second administrator overwrites the changes of the first administrator, the first administrator is not notified of that – they won't discover the overwrite until they re-examine the configuration.

Node Agent

The **Node Agent** is a daemon process that runs on every node federated into the cell. The node agent serves three purposes:

- ❏ The node agent serves as an end point for communication from the deployment manager – principally to enable the synchronization of configuration between the deployment manager and the node. In this capacity, the node agent represents the node and the application server instances configured to the node.

- ❏ The node agent also contains a JMX server and admin service, both to host MBeans that control the state and operation of the node, and as a conduit to communicate operational and monitoring messages between the deployment manager and the individual application servers.

- ❏ The node agent is a monitor and nanny for the application server instances configured on the node. The node agent is responsible for starting application servers on the server, and re-starting them in the rare case they should fail.

The **node** in a WebSphere network is a logical concept – it represents a set of application servers. Its only concrete constraint is that the servers that it represents must co-reside on the same computer – the node agent must be able to monitor the state of the application server processes, to be able to spawn those processes, and if necessary force them to terminate.

Otherwise, you can establish multiple nodes on the same computer – each representing a different set of application server instances. Obviously the node must have a unique name – by default, nodes are assigned the name of the host (as taken from the IP configuration for the computer) on which they're created – and be assigned a unique port address (in the case where more than one node is configured on the same host). A node agent is created for each defined node.

If you don't federate the application server(s) of a given node into the cell, then the node agent is not needed – it will not be instantiated. However, if you federate the node into the cell (using the addNode command), then the node agent for that node will automatically be instantiated. On Windows platforms, you should register the node agent as a service. In this way, the operating system will ensure that the node is automatically started every time you re-boot the system and, more importantly, monitor the node agent process – restarting if the node agent should fail.

Deployment Manager

The deployment manager is only relevant when you have multiple application server instances that you want to control from a single point – it provides a central point of configuration and control for all of the application servers in the cell. The deployment manager represents the cell – a set of application servers and related resources composed in a topology.

In this role the deployment manager has several responsibilities:

- ❏ It manages the central repository for the cell.

- ❏ It synchronizes the configuration captured in the central repository with the node repositories for each node registered in the cell.

❑   It hosts the central JMX server and admin service through which the entire cell can be managed.

❑   It also hosts the central admin application supporting the browser-based admin UI.

The deployment manager is the point of control that you will attach your clients to – browsers, command-line clients, scripting clients, client admin programs – to manage the cell.

Just to reinforce a point that we made earlier – while the deployment manager is a central point of control for the cell, it is not a single point of failure for the operational aspects of the running system. In other words, application servers will continue to come up and service client requests even if the deployment manager is down. The only thing you lose if the deployment manager is down is the ability to centrally administer the network – change configurations, install applications, and so on. Like any of the WebSphere servers, if it should fail you can restart it within a very short period of time.

PME Administration Extensions

Some of the programming model extensions (PMEs) provided in the Enterprise edition of WebSphere have their own administration requirements. For example, you have to administer the task to profile mappings for Application Profiling, you have to administer the rule repository for Business Rules Beans, and so on. The administration support for the PMEs is shipped in Enterprise edition, and plugs in as an extension to the base middleware management facility in WAS and the deployment manager. You continue to use the standard middleware management facilities as described throughout the rest of this chapter, but after installing the Enterprise edition other things just show up on your admin UI and in the information model.

Securing Middleware Management

So, having got this far into the discussion of middleware management for WebSphere, you may have started to wonder how you will protect yourself from the power offered through the administration facility. WebSphere employs the J2EE roles-based security model, along with standard WebSphere authentication mechanisms to protect the middleware. Remember that the Admin UI is a web application. As such, the Admin UI is subject to standard J2EE security policies. This same model is extended to the other admin clients as well – command-line, scripting, and programming clients are subject to the same security requirements.

All of the middleware management functions have been classified as either being monitoring functions, operations functions, or configuration functions. The management facility supports four permissions: Monitor, Operator, Configurator, and Administrator – the permission you must possess to use the corresponding function:

❑   **Monitor**
    You must be granted the Monitor permission to simply look at the configuration and state, or to query performance metrics information about the running system.

❑   **Operator**
    You must be granted the Operator permission to issue operational commands on the running system; for example, to start or stop an application server. The Operator permission implies the Monitor permission – in other words, if you are granted the Operator permission then you can also perform Monitor functions.

❑ **Configurator**
You must be granted the Configurator permission to change the configuration of the system; for example, to create new application servers, change their attributes, or to install applications. The Configurator permission implies the Monitor permission.

❑ **Administrator**
You must be granted the Administrator permission to both perform operations and change the configuration of the system. The Administrator permission implies both the Operator and Configurator (and by extension, Monitor) permissions.

If you want to control access to the management facility you must enable global security. If it is enabled, administrators are registered in the security system like any other authenticated user. You can then grant any user or group any of the four administration permissions through the admin UI.

Individual users can be granted permission under the Console Users selection and groups can be granted permission under the Console Groups selection of the System Administration task navigation:

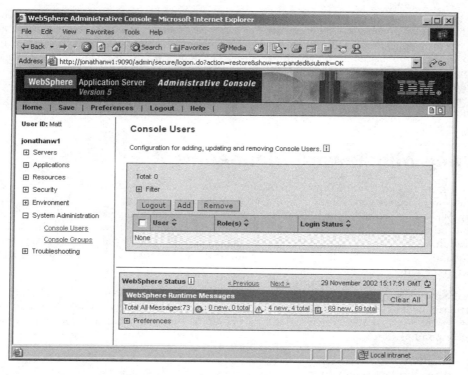

If you have not already granted any permissions to the user, then you need to add that user to the Console Users group. You can then select the permissions that you want to grant that user. The user you define here must be a valid user in the user registry for the WebSphere realm:

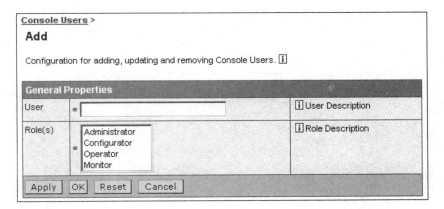

Of course, once you've added the user you must be sure to save your changes. You can always go back later and change the permissions for a given user or group. Setting the permissions for a group is the same, done under the Console Groups selection.

You must already possess the Configurator or Administrator permission to grant permissions to other users, or yourself. By implication, you can downgrade your own permission to Operator or Monitor and thus lose the ability to grant permissions to other users. You should take care to ensure that at least one administrator always has the Administrator and/or Configurator authority or else you could lose the ability to grant, change, or deny anyone else authority to administer the system.

Again, none of this applies unless security is enabled. If it is not, you can grant permissions but they won't be enforced until you do enable security. Likewise, when the system is first configured, and security is enabled, everyone will be granted access to administer the system – until you define at least one administrator (or group) to the console users collection.

With security disabled, you will still be prompted to sign in a user ID when you start the Admin UI. The admin application uses this to correlate you to your workspace.

Managing a Single Standalone Server

In this section, we're going to walk you through a number of common management tasks. The purpose of this is mostly to familiarize you with how administration is performed. We will focus in this section on just a single, standalone application server – one that has not been federated into a cell.

Starting and Stopping the Server

In the single server configuration the application server is the only process (unless you have other application servers running at the same time – the point is each application server is independent; they don't know about each other). No other process executes in the environment that can take responsibility for starting or stopping the application server. Consequently you have to start and stop the application server manually. The easiest way of doing this in Windows is from the Start menu.

You can also start and stop the server from the command line using the `startserver` and `stopserver` commands located in the `\bin` directory of the `\AppServer` install directory. You need to specify the name of the server that you want to start and stop when using this command. The default server created for you when you first install WebSphere is called `server1`. This is also the server that the Start menu items for Start the Server and Stop the Server assume as well:

```
C:\WINNT\System32\cmd.exe                                          _□ x

C:\IBM\WebSphereGM\AppServer\bin>startserver server1
ADMU0116I: Tool information is being logged in file
           C:\IBM\WebSphereGM\AppServer\logs\server1\startServer.log
ADMU3100I: Reading configuration for server: server1
ADMU3200I: Server launched. Waiting for initialization status.
ADMU3000I: Server server1 open for e-business; process id is 564
```

If you have defined other servers, then you will need to use the command-line approach for starting and stopping these servers, specifying the server's name on the request.

Starting the Admin Console

The admin console is presented by the Administration application. This application is installed by default in the application server created when you install the base WebSphere Application Server product. The Admin app is started automatically along with any other applications configured to run in the application server when the application server is started. So starting the admin console is really a matter of pointing your browser to the URL of the Admin application. By implication, you cannot access the admin console if the application server on which it is hosted has not been started (or if the Admin application is not in the configuration of hosted applications for the application server).

As with starting the application server, on Windows the easiest approach to starting the admin console is through the Windows Start menu.

If you start the admin console directly through your own browser instance, you typically find the admin application at: http://localhost:9090/admin/ if you're accessing it from the same computer. Note that the admin console is configured in its own virtual host and so you will have to specify the port address of that node – port 9090, by default, as opposed to 9080 for other applications hosted on that server.

Signing In and Out of the Admin Console

The first thing you will have to do upon accessing the admin console is to login. If security is disabled, you will only have to specify your user ID. This identity is not authenticated or verified against any user registry. If security is disabled, it is presumed that you are trustworthy (the absence of security implies that you don't feel the need to validate the authenticity of your users), and so the login identity is only used to differentiate the workspace that belongs to you. If another user logs-in with your user ID they will be able to see your workspace, so if this bothers you then consider enabling the security system.

If, on the other hand, security has been enabled, you will be prompted for both a user ID and password when logging into the admin console. The user ID and password you enter will be authenticated against the user registry that is configured for the application server.

When leaving the admin console you should log-out. This can be done at any time by pressing the Logout system menu item on the admin console

If you have any outstanding changes in your workspace you will be prompted to save these changes.

Configuring Resources

Before installing an application it is a good idea to install and configure the resources that your application will use in your hosting environment. If you have database and data sources, resource adapters (connectors), JMS implementations, mail providers, or URL or environment providers you can register these in the Resources task section of the Admin UI:

Depending on the resource type the registration and configuration process will differ slightly. As a general rule, the registration process will involve first identifying the resource manager itself, and then one or more connection facilities – data sources, connection factories, queue and topic factories, and so on. The latter are named in JNDI and then can be used later to resolve resource references in the application to these specific named connection facilities.

Follow the specific directions of the resource registration wizard to register a resource.

Configuring the Application Server

You can configure the application server by selecting the server from the **Servers** task section of the Admin UI:

Selecting your server, you will be presented with a notebook page listing all of the common and detailed configuration options that you can set for the server:

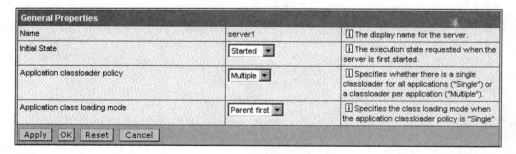

The general attributes of the application server are listed at the top of the page, and the additional more detailed attributes are listed separately in the topics in which they're relevant:

Additional Properties	
Transaction Service	Specify settings for the Transaction Service, as well as manage active transaction locks.
Web Container	Specify thread pool and dynamic cache settings for the container . Also, specify session manager settings such as persistence and tuning parameters, and HTTP transport settings.
EJB Container	Specify cache and datasource information for the container.
Dynamic Cache Service	Specify settings for the Dynamic Cache service of this server.
Logging and Tracing	Specify Logging and Trace settings for this server.
Message Listener Service	Configuration for the Message Listener Service. This service provides the Message Driven Bean (MDB) listening process, whereby MDBs are deployed against ListenerPorts that define the JMS destination to listen upon. These Listener Ports are defined within this service along with settings for its Thread Pool.
ORB Service	Specify settings for the Object Request Broker Service.
Custom Properties	Additional custom properties for this runtime component. Some components may make use of custom configuration properties which can be defined here.
Administration Services	Specify various settings for administration facility for this server, such as administrative communication protocol settings and timeouts.
Diagnostic Trace Service	View and modify the properties of the diagnostic trace service.
Debugging Service	Specify settings for the debugging service, to be used in conjunction with a workspace debugging client application.
IBM Service Logs	Configure the IBM service log, also known as the activity log.
Custom Services	Define custom service classes that will run within this server and their configuration properties.
Server Components	Additional runtime components which are configurable.
Process Definition	A process definition defines the command line information necessary to start/initialize a process.
Performance Monitoring Service	specify settings for performance monitoring, including enabling performance monitoring, selecting the PMI module and setting monitoring levels.
End Points	Configure important TCP/IP ports which this server uses for connections.
Classloader	Classloader configuration

We won't go into all of the configuration options that are available here, but as you can see from the list of available property topics, you have a great deal of control over how the application server behaves. You should spend some time navigating the admin console and getting to know the options that are available to you. The help text for each of the properties goes into more depth, explaining the available values and consequences.

Configuring Additional Application Servers

Even if you are running in a single server configuration, you can create the definition and configuration of more than one application server. This is merely a convenient way of creating other configurations – it is at best a partial substitute for managing multiple application servers. You create additional server configurations by clicking New in the Application Servers task section.

This will then prompt you for basic information about the new server – including the server and node that you want to create the server on. If you are in a single server configuration (without working through a deployment manager), you can only create servers on the same node as the previously existing server:

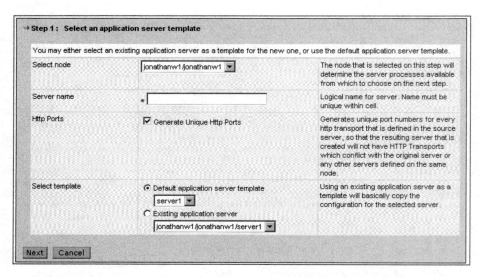

You can use any of the existing servers or defined templates to set the default values of the configuration of the new server. If you create a server using another server's configuration as a starting point, then the entire configuration will be used, including any applications installed on that server – only the server's name will be changed, and any new ports that are generated if the Generate Unique HTTP Ports option is selected.

Templates are base configurations that WebSphere uses to create its own initial servers. As with existing servers, if you use one of the templates you will get whatever configuration is associated with the template.

Once you press Next you will be presented with a summary page and allowed to finalize the creation request:

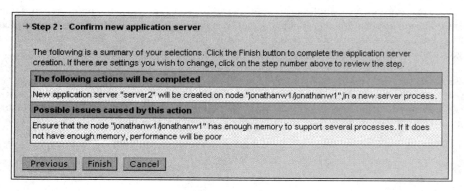

Press Finish to create the new application server.

The configuration you create will be retained in the local host repository on the same computer as your current application server. You will be able to then start another application server instance with the configuration you create. You can then manage that application server's configuration from either server. The WebSphere management facility does not directly prevent one administrator from changing the configuration of the other application server instances. Consequently, if you want to create different application server configurations for multiple application servers within the same installation root and isolate them – say, dedicating each application server configuration to a different administrator, you should do so by placing different permissions on the sub-directories of the individual servers in the file system of your computer.

Installing an Application

One of the most frequent tasks that you will perform is installing an application. This is initiated in the Applications task section under the Install New Application task:

You can install an application from either the computer on which you are running your browser, or from the computer on which the application server is installed. In many cases this will be the same. The Admin application does not allow you to browse the file system on the application server in a single server configuration – you are expected to know the path and EAR file name of the application you want to install if you are installing from the computer of the application server in a single-server configuration.

You can install either a standalone web application (WAR) file or EJB application (JAR) file – either of which will be wrapped implicitly into an enterprise application (EAR) during the installation process – or you can install an enterprise application (EAR) file. If you are installing a standalone web application (WAR), then you must specify the context root for that application. Otherwise, the context root will be taken from the enterprise application for any web applications in the EAR – the context roots are formulated when you assembled the EAR.

Once you've found your application file and pressed Next, if you are installing from your browser's local file system, the application will be uploaded to the application server. You are then prompted for some general installation directions:

643

If you select the **Generate Default Bindings** checkbox then the installation task will fill in default bindings for any incomplete bindings in the application archive. All of the intermediate steps that let you specify the bindings for any un-bound references in the application will be bypassed if this box is checked.

If you want all JNDI names created for EJBs in your application to be prefixed with a tag that distinguishes those names then you can select the **Specify Prefix** radio button. If you leave the radio button on **Do not specify unique prefix for beans** then the JNDI names for EJBs will not be prefixed at all – they will just be given the names as specified in the EJB home for those beans.

The bindings that have already been established for the enterprise application (presumably during application assembly) will be preserved unless you select the **Override existing bindings** radio button. This option is primarily only relevant if you select **Generate Default Bindings**. If you opt not to generate default bindings then you will be given the opportunity to override any of the previously recorded bindings in the EAR during a subsequent step in the installation wizard.

Default bindings for any Enterprise beans in your application that are designated to use the EJB 1.1 CMP semantics will not normally be automatically generated – you will be prompted to supply the binding information for these beans unless you select the **Default bindings for EJB 1.1 CMPs** and fill in the default binding information.

Likewise, default connection factory bindings are not normally generated unless you select the **Default connection factory bindings** radio button and fill in the default binding information:

Default virtual host information is normally filled in for your web applications unless you select the **Do not default virtual host name for web modules** radio button. If you want a different default virtual host filled in you can change the name under the **Default virtual host name for web modules** radio button.

You can pre-define the bindings for any references in your application and store these in a separate bindings file. If you want installation to use this bindings file during the installation of your application then you can specify that under **Specific bindings file**. The installation wizard will use the information in this file in lieu of prompting for that during the installation process.

When you're ready to proceed with the installation you can press the **Next** button. This will take you to the first step of the installation wizard:

- ❑ **Pre-compile JSP** – indicates whether any JSPs in your application should be pre-compiled during the installation process. Pre-compiling your JSPs saves having to compile them during run time.

- ❑ **Directory to Install Application** – if you want your application installed to a specific directory you can fill that directory path in here. You can specify a relative directory path – the directory path will be created relative to the installation root of the application server. Obviously, you need to be careful not to specify a path that would interfere with other directories used by the WebSphere runtime. Or you can specify an absolute directory path to anywhere in the scope of the computer of the application server. If you don't specify a directory, WebSphere installs the application in the \installedApps directory under the WebSphere installation root.

- ❑ **Distribute Application** – tells the Deployment Manager whether to distribute your application binaries to the application server as part of the repository synchronization process. This option is not relevant in a single server configuration.

- ❑ **Use Binary Configuration** – configuration information specific to the application and created during application assembly is kept in two places: in the configuration repository and in the application EAR itself. Setting this option to true instructs the application server runtime to get the configuration information directly from the EAR. This has the advantage that you can re-deploy the application (with a new configuration) by simply updating the EAR file in the repository. This has advantages in a development environment where you'd like to shorten the path to re-deployment. On the other hand, WebSphere may support deploying the same EAR multiple times to different servers (each with a different configuration) in the future. To retain the differences between each deployment, the runtime will have to get this configuration information from the repository. For now, there is little difference. We recommend that you set it to true for development environments, and false for production environments.

- ❑ **Deploy EJBs** – directs the installation wizard on whether to deploy (generate CMP mappings and runtime binding – tie and skeleton – files during installation). This option only affects EARs that contain EJBs that have not already been deployed during the application assembly process.

- ❑ **Application Name** – the name of the application that will be displayed on any UIs representing the application.

- ❑ **Create MBeans for Resources** – if checked, will create an MBean.

- ❑ **Reload Interval** – specifies how often the web components of this application should be re-loaded in the memory of the application server.

The remaining steps of the installation process are optional. They are listed by step title:

Step 2	Provide JNDI Names for Beans
Step 3	Provide default datasource mapping for modules containing 2.0 entity beans
Step 4	Map datasources for all 2.0 CMP beans
Step 5	Map EJB references to beans
Step 6	Map resource references to resources
Step 7	Map virtual hosts for web modules
Step 8	Map modules to application servers
Step 9	Ensure all unprotected 2.0 methods have the correct level of protection
Step 10	Summary

- ❑ **Step 2: Provide JNDI Names for Beans**
  Allows you to change the default JNDI names created for each of the beans supported by your application.

- ❑ **Step 3: Provide default datasource mapping for modules containing 2.0 entity beans**
  This is where you will specify the default data sources that will be assumed by the runtime if no other specific data sources are defined. If you will use any data source other than what's defined for the application in the EAR (during the assembly step), you must have registered the data source with WebSphere before installing this application (actually, before saving the configuration workspace produced during this installation).

- ❑ **Step 4: Map data sources for all 2.0 CMP beans**
  Defines the specific data sources for every Entity bean that uses CMP. If a specific data source is not specified for each bean, then the default data source for the module as specified in Step 3 will be used. If you will use any data source other than what's defined for the application in the EAR (during the assembly step), you must have registered the data source with WebSphere before installing this application (actually, before saving the configuration workspace produced during this installation).

- ❑ **Step 5: Map EJB references to beans**
  Establishes the mapping between the bean references (JNDI `java:comp` names) you use in your application and the actual beans that should be resolved by that name. If you will use any beans in another application, that application must have been installed before you install this application.

❏ **Step 6: Map resource references to resources**
Identifies the mapping between the resource references (JNDI `java:comp` names) you use in your application and the actual resources that should be resolved by that name. If you will use any resources other than what's defined within the application EAR (during the assembly step), you must have created and registered those resources before installing this application.

❏ **Step 7: Map virtual hosts for web modules**
Lets you specify the virtual hosts that you want mapped to each web module in your application. You must have specified any virtual hosts that you want to use before installing this application.

❏ **Step 8: Map modules to application servers**
Is where you identify which application server (or cluster, in the case of installing into a cell deployment manger) you want the application to be hosted on. In a single server configuration you can only configure an application to be hosted on the application server that you're managing.

❏ **Step 9: Ensure all unprotected 2.0 methods have the correct level of protection**
If any methods of your application have not been assigned a role policy during application assembly, this step can be used to assign method permissions. The installation process will not allow you to complete the installation process unless every method has a role policy – either a specific method permission that establishes the role a user must have to access the method, or a specific policy claiming the method is not protected or should not be allowed to any principal.

❏ **Step 10: Summary**
Summarizes the installation options selected for the application. When you press the Finish button on this page the configuration will be updated with the application being installed.

The actual number of steps presented to you will depend on the nature of your application – some applications require more or fewer steps to install. For example, if there were any 1.x EJBs in the application then there may be other steps for establishing how you want those beans mapped. Similarly, if there are any Web Services in your application there will be other steps for resolving the Web Service bindings to your service implementations. On the other hand, if you application does not contain any web application components, or conversely does not contain any EJBs, then those related steps will not be presented to you.

Actually, the configuration is updated in your workspace – you must subsequently save your workspace before the configuration change that represents the inclusion of your application will actually be applied to the configuration repository for the application server.

Starting and Stopping the Application

Once you've installed a new application (and saved the configuration to the local repository), the application will be in the "stopped" state. You can view the states of all applications by selecting the Enterprise Applications task within the Applications topic:

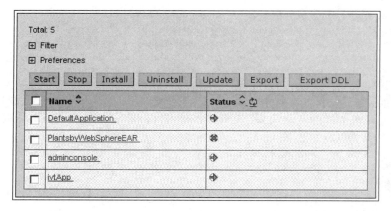

You can start any stopped applications by selecting the checkbox for the application and pressing the Start operation button. Likewise, you can stop any application by selecting the application and pressing the Stop operation button.

Configuring the Application

You can modify the configuration of an application by selecting the application from the Enterprise Applications tasks menu:

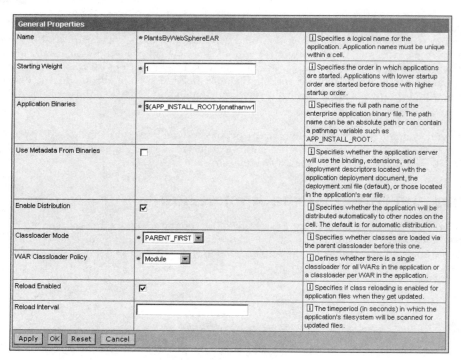

The general properties define the basic characteristics of the application:

❏ **Name** – the display name of the application

❏ **Starting Weight** – the starting weight is used by the application server to determine which order to start the applications in. Applications with the greatest weight are started first, and so forth. Applications with the same weight are started in an unspecified order.

❏ **Application Binaries** – identifies where the binaries for the application are located.

❏ **Use Metadata From Binaries** – indicates whether the application-specific configuration will be taken from the application binaries, or from the configuration repository. This has less relevance in R5.0 of WebSphere, but suggests that WebSphere will support multiple deployments of the same application in the future, and when it does each deployment will have a different set of configuration information (although that will require the configuration information be retrieved from the repository, not from the application binaries).

❏ **Enable Distribution** – WebSphere will automatically distribute the application binaries to the node(s) on which the application is configured if this option is enabled.

❏ **Classloader Mode** – identifies the precedence order that will be used by the class loader for this application. This only applies if the application server has been configured to use a separate class loader per application. Otherwise, the precedence order set for the server takes priority.

❏ **WAR Classloader Policy** – specifies whether a single class loader is used for the entire application, or one per module of the application. This option is ignored if the server configuration indicates that only one class loader is to be used for all applications in the server.

In addition, other properties can be configured for the application. These are organized by topic area:

Additional Properties	
Target Mappings	The mapping of this deployed object (Application or Module) into a target environment (server, cluster, cluster member)
Libraries	A list of library references which specify the usage of global libraries.
Session Management	Session Manager properties specific to this Application
View Deployment Descriptor	View the Deployment Descriptor
Provide JNDI Names for Beans	Provide JNDI Names for Beans
Map resource references to resources	Map resource references to resources
Map EJB references to beans	Map EJB references to beans
Map datasources for all 2.0 CMP beans	Map datasources for all 2.0 CMP beans
Provide default datasource mapping for modules containing 2.0 entity beans	Provide default datasource mapping for modules containing 2.0 entity beans
Map virtual hosts for web modules	Map virtual hosts for web modules
Map modules to application servers	Map modules to application servers

❏ **Target Mappings** – Identifies the server (or cluster, in the case of ND) to which this application is configured to run. Individual modules of the application may be configured to application servers or clusters – see **Map virtual hosts for web modules**.

❏ **Libraries** – shared libraries used by this application.

❏ **Session Management** – defines how HTTP sessions are to be managed for this application.

❑ View Deployment Descriptor – allows browsing of some high-level deployment information for the application, including the JARs and WARs included in the EAR, and the context roots associated with any web applications.

❑ Provide JNDI Names for Beans – specifies the JNDI name for each of the beans in your application. You can change the names of your beans on your deployed application, but you have to be careful of the effect this will have on other applications that may use references to your beans.

❑ Map resource references to resources – defines the JNDI name mappings for each of the resource references in your application. This can be used to change the mappings after the application has been installed.

❑ Map EJB references to beans – allows you to review and update the JNDI name mappings for each of the bean references in your application. You can change the mappings after the application has been installed to make use of different bean implementations.

❑ Map datasources for all 2.0 CMP beans – identifies which data source to use for each of the beans defined in your application.

❑ Provide default data mapping for modules containing 2.0 entity beans – specifies the default data source for your beans. This datasource will be used if you have not specified anything more particular in the Map datasources for all 2.0 CMP beans page above.

❑ Map virtual hosts for web modules – enables you to specify the virtual host for any web modules in your application.

❑ Map modules to application servers – defines which server each module in your application should run on.

Configuring the Problem Determination Facilities

You can control the way the facilities for problem determination (that is, finding and analyzing problems in the WebSphere runtime) work within WebSphere. Open the Troubleshooting task section in the navigation pane. To change the logging behavior, select Logs and Trace task item, and the server that you want to configure – these options are controlled on a server-by-server basis:

Logging and Tracing	
Diagnostic Trace	View and modify the properties of the diagnostic trace service.
JVM Logs	View and modify the settings for the Java Virtual Machine (JVM) System.out and System.err logs.
Process Logs	View or modify settings for specifying the files to which standard out and standard error streams write.
IBM Service Logs	Configure the IBM service log, also known as the activity log.

You can turn on tracing from the Diagnostic Trace page. From here you can specify what level of tracing you want and for which components by defining a series of trace filters. In addition, you can indicate whether you want trace records to be cached in an in-memory buffer, or written out directly. In either case, you specify the file that you want trace records written to – in the case where you've selected the in-memory caching option, records will first be written to the buffer, and then written out to file when the buffer is full. This runs the risk of losing some records if the server should fail, but it is otherwise more efficient as it avoids file I/O in the middle of your transactions. In either case, you should only turn tracing on with some care, as it will impact on the performance of your server.

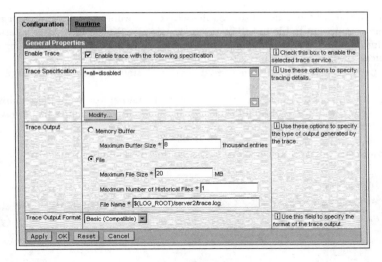

The logs can be configured by selecting **JMV Logs**. This allows you to configure the `System.out` log:

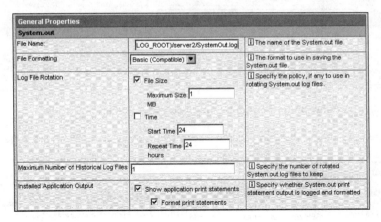

and the `System.err` log:

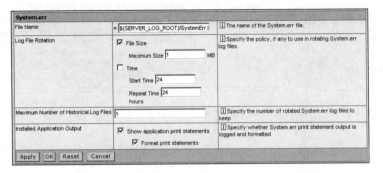

For either you can specify the name of the log file where you want message and error records to be recorded, whether you want to file to roll over at a certain size threshold or after a certain amount of time, the maximum number of files to keep as history (beyond the currently active log file), and whether you want application `println()` output to be piped to the same file (for both `System.out.println()`, and `System.err.println()` statements in your applications).

In addition, for (`System.out`) messages, you can control whether you want the resulting records to be formatted in the style used for WebSphere R4.0, or in an advanced structure that allows for deeper analysis and solution determination.

You can also view the message and error logs by selecting the Runtime page tab:

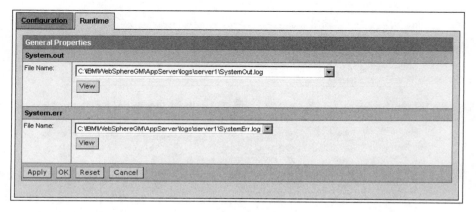

and then pressing the View button for the log that you want to view.

You can change the name of the Stdout and Stderr files by selecting Process Logs.

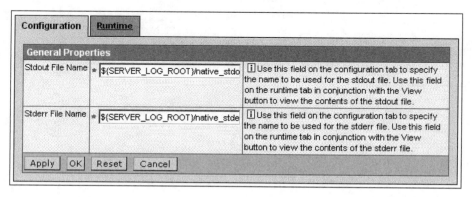

Finally, you can configure the behavior of the IBM service log (also referred to as the 'Activity Log') by selecting IBM Service Logs.

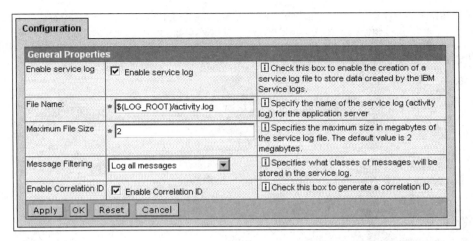

This can be used to specify whether service logging will be performed, the name of the service log, its maximum size, what level of messages will be logged, and whether to enable correlation. If you run into a problem with WebSphere that you want to report to IBM you may be asked to provide this log. The more information captured in this log, the better. However, this does represent another level of background activity that does have some, at least minimal, impact on the performance of your system even if you don't have a problem.

WebSphere will check the validity of your configuration documents every time you save a configuration change. You can specify the level of configuration checking that you want WebSphere do to by selecting in the **Configuration Problems** menu:

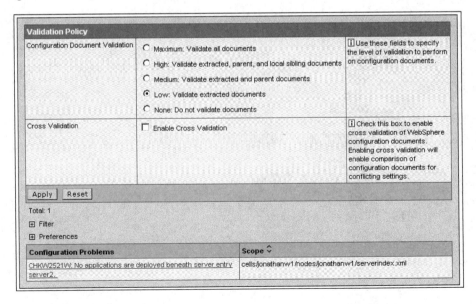

You can direct WebSphere to monitor request metrics (essentially response time measurements on web application and EJB requests). You can configure this by selecting the PMI Request Metrics task. These metrics will then be accumulated and can be obtained through the JMX interfaces for PMI (although they are not displayed in the Tivoli Performance Viewer tool.

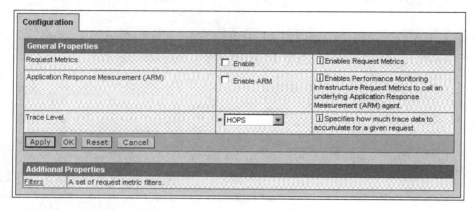

In addition, if you have an Application Response Monitoring (ARM) provider, you can enable ARM tracing. WebSphere will then issue ARM requests through the standard ARM interface.

If you enable PMI Request Metrics, you can filter response time monitoring to only collect information for specific EJBs, specific IP source addresses, or to specific web application URIs.

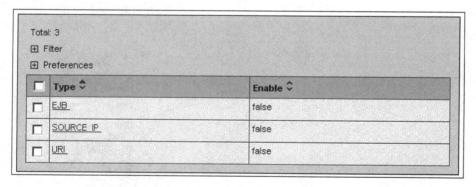

Configuring the Admin Console

You can customize the admin console itself by selecting the Preferences system menu item. These customizations will be unique to you – based in the identity that you logged in to the console with.

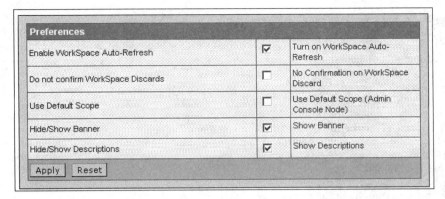

From this page you can control whether your workspace will be automatically refreshed from the master repository as changes occur there. You can suppress the prompt confirming that you want to discard configuration changes in the event that you press the Discard button on the Save Configuration dialog box. The Use Default Scope setting will instruct the admin console to presume the cell and the node on which it is running is the scope of any collections presented by the console, if enabled. You can remove the IBM WebSphere logo banner from the top of you pages, and you can direct WebSphere to either provide detailed description text or to suppress this on configuration object menus.

You can also control how the status window is controlled by opening the Preferences expansion button on the status window:

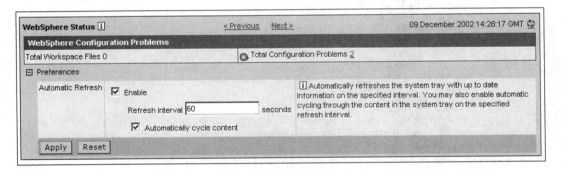

From here you can indicate whether you want the status window refreshed automatically, and how frequently, and whether to cycle between the configuration problems status and the message logs panes.

Managing a Network of Application Servers

Managing a network of application servers is largely the same as managing an individual server. The admin console is almost identical – the primary difference being the addition of clustering task items, and other minor differences that are unique to a networked environment.

Creating a Distributed Network

To create a network of application servers all managed from a common Deployment Manager you have to first install the deployment manager on a particular computer, and then install one or more WebSphere Application Servers. You can install one of these application server images on the same computer as the deployment manager, or you can dedicate the deployment manager computer to only performing deployment. If you install the deployment manager and an application server on the same computer, you will not be able to start both the deployment manager and application server at the same time unless you change the listening ports of one or the other, until you federate the application server to the cell through the addnode command (see below). You can install the application server and the deployment manager in either order – you only have to install the deployment manager before you can form a managed network.

Likewise, you can run any of the application servers in a standalone configuration, including installing applications and setting the configuration for the application server for as long as you want and still federate it into a managed network later.

For each computer on which you have installed an application server that you want to include in the network managed by the deployment manager you have to register that node with the deployment manager. You do this by invoking the addnode command on the computer where your application server is installed.

> **You should ensure the deployment manager is running before issuing the command.**

The syntax of the addnode command is:

```
addNode cell_host [cell_port] [-conntype <type>] [-includeapps]
                  [-startingport <portnumber>] [-noagent] [-quiet] [-nowait]
                  [-logfile <filename>] [-replacelog] [-trace] [-username <uid>]
                  [-password <pwd>] [-help]
```

The only required parameter is the host name or IP address of the computer on which your deployment manager is installed. By default, the addnode command will attempt to contact the deployment manager at the standard port number for the deployment manager – 8879. If you reconfigure the deployment manager to listen at a different port, you will have to specify that port number in this command.

By default, this command will use the SOAP connector to communicate with the deployment manager. If you want it to use another connector then you will have to specify that with the -conntype parameter.

If you have been using the application server(s) on this computer and if you want to continue to support those applications on the application servers after they've been federated into the cell you need to use the -includeapps parameter. This will force the application configuration to be synchronized to the deployment manager as part of the registration process.

If security has been enabled on the deployment manager you will have to specify a user ID and password representing an authentic administrator with authority to change the configuration of the system using the -username and -password parameters.

If you specify the −noagent switch, the node agent will not be automatically started at the completion of this command.

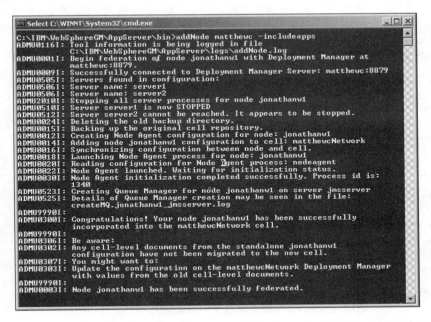

```
Select C:\WINNT\System32\cmd.exe                                    _ □ x
C:\IBM\WebSphereGM\AppServer\bin>addNode matthewc -includeapps
ADMU0116I: Tool information is being logged in file
           C:\IBM\WebSphereGM\AppServer\logs\addNode.log
ADMU0001I: Begin federation of node jonathanw1 with Deployment Manager at
           matthewc:8879.
ADMU0009I: Successfully connected to Deployment Manager Server: matthewc:8879
ADMU0505I: Servers found in configuration:
ADMU0506I: Server name: server1
ADMU0506I: Server name: server2
ADMU2010I: Stopping all server processes for node jonathanw1
ADMU0510I: Server server1 is now STOPPED
ADMU0512I: Server server2 cannot be reached. It appears to be stopped.
ADMU0024I: Deleting the old backup directory.
ADMU0015I: Backing up the original cell repository.
ADMU0012I: Creating Node Agent configuration for node: jonathanw1
ADMU0014I: Adding node jonathanw1 configuration to cell: matthewcNetwork
ADMU0016I: Synchronizing configuration between node and cell.
ADMU0018I: Launching Node Agent process for node: jonathanw1
ADMU0020I: Reading configuration for Node Agent process: nodeagent
ADMU0022I: Node Agent launched. Waiting for initialization status.
ADMU0030I: Node Agent initialization completed successfully. Process id is:
           1340
ADMU0523I: Creating Queue Manager for node jonathanw1 on server jmsserver
ADMU0525I: Details of Queue Manager creation may be seen in the file:
           createMQ.jonathanw1_jmsserver.log
ADMU9990I:
ADMU0300I: Congratulations! Your node jonathanw1 has been successfully
           incorporated into the matthewcNetwork cell.
ADMU9990I:
ADMU0306I: Be aware:
ADMU0302I: Any cell-level documents from the standalone jonathanw1
           configuration have not been migrated to the new cell.
ADMU0307I: You might want to:
ADMU0303I: Update the configuration on the matthewcNetwork Deployment Manager
           with values from the old cell-level documents.
ADMU9990I:
ADMU0003I: Node jonathanw1 has been successfully federated.
```

After issuing this command, the node agent will be started, the node will be registered with the deployment manager, and the configuration will be synchronized between the central repository of the deployment manager and the local repository at the node.

If the admin console application had been installed at the application before being registered into the cell, that application will be deconfigured at the application server, and re-configured to be hosted at the deployment manager.

Note that the addnode process does not merge any of the configuration documents in the cell directory of the application server's configuration repository. This includes

❑ filter.policy – contains the Java 2 Security permissions that an application cannot be granted, even if requested in the app.policy or was.policy files

❑ integral-jms-permissions.xml – grants method permissions to users of JMS queues and topics for the integral JMS provider

❑ namestore.xml – maintains any cell-level name bindings created from the application server

❑ pmirm.xml – the PMI request metric filters established for the cell

❑ resources.xml – configuration information for any resources created/modified for the application sever

❑ variables.xml – environment variables created for the application server

❑ virtualhosts.xml – the virtual hosts definitions used for applications hosted in the application server

Generally, you should re-create any of the information that is contained in these documents through the Admin UI or command-line interfaces of the deployment manager. If you're feeling particularly brave, you can hand edit these in the cell configuration repository under the deployment manager, but be sure to back up your original copies in case you mess them up.

Creating a Cluster from an Existing Server

The biggest reason for forming a cell is to enable central administration of multiple application servers on different computers. One benefit of this is being able to form clusters – multiple application server instances that collectively host the same application. You can create a new cluster composed entirely of new application server instances, or form a cluster from an existing server – adding more application server instances to increase the capacity of the cluster.

To create a cluster, press the New operation on the Clusters page. This will present the new cluster wizard:

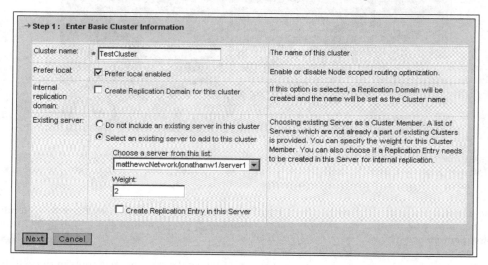

You can then enter the name of the cluster. The Prefer local option instructs the workload manager to select the clustered bean instance that is on the same server process when that is possible.

The Internal replication domain refers to the configuration of the HTTP session replication service. If you want to form a replication group that mirrors the cluster topology, then enable this option and the replication group will be formed automatically to match the cluster configuration.

If you want to form a cluster from an existing application server then select the Existing server option, and specify the name of the server to use.

The weighting value is used by the workload manager to distribute workload proportional to the various weighting values that you give to each application server instance in the cluster.

You can define additional (new) application server instances to include in the cluster in Step 2.

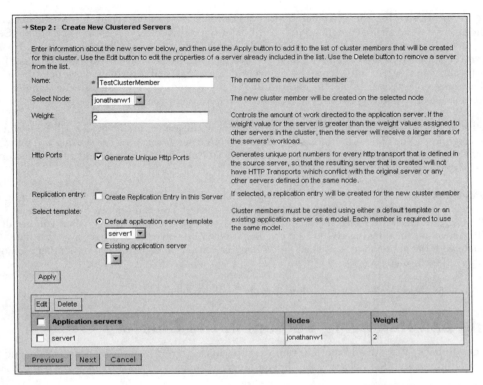

Fill in the application server name, and press the Apply button for each application server instance that you want to add. If you have registered more than one node into the cell, you can select different nodes for each application server instance in the cluster.

You can then review the cluster creation request and press the Finish button to create the configuration change. Remember, as usual, you will need to save your configuration change to the repository.

Once the cluster definition has been created, you can start the cluster by selecting the cluster and pressing the Start button.

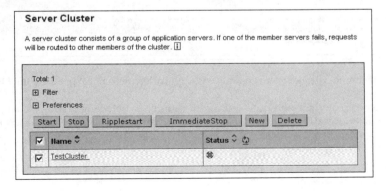

That action will start the cluster and all of the application servers in the cluster (on whatever node the application servers have been defined on). Unlike starting multiple servers on the Application Servers page, all of the servers in the cluster are started in parallel when you start them as a cluster. If you want to start the application servers individually, you can do so from the Application Servers page. You don't have to start every server in the cluster – the workload manager will distribute work over the set of application servers that are available and running at any given time. You can also cause the servers to be started one at a time by pressing the Ripplestart button on the cluster page.

If you start the cluster, the actual initiation of the application servers in the cluster will be performed in the background. You can verify the state of the application servers as they are starting through the Application Servers page. You may have to press the Refresh button to get updated information on the status of these servers.

When you form a cluster out of an existing application server, any applications that were configured to the server are promoted up to being configured to the cluster. You can see this by selecting an application and checking which servers its modules are associated with. In fact, when you install new applications after forming the cluster, the original application server is no longer a server that you can associate with the application – you can only select the cluster (and any other servers that are not members of a cluster).

You can create several clusters, according to your topology needs.

Adding and Removing Servers in the Cluster

You can go back later and add more or remove application servers from the cluster by selecting the cluster definition and then selecting the Cluster Members link:

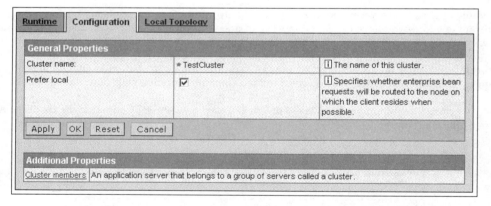

From the cluster members page you can add new application servers by pressing the New button.

You can also remove an application server from the cluster by selecting it and pressing the Delete button. The application server you are deleting must be stopped, which you can do from the same cluster members page.

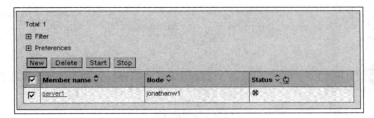

Any applications that are associated with the cluster, including those that were introduced to the cluster as the result of forming the cluster from an existing server continue to be associated with the other servers in the cluster – even if you delete the original application server; the one from which you formed the cluster.

As an aside, you cannot delete the cluster itself if any applications are configured to the cluster – or to any of the application servers in the cluster.

Rippling a Cluster

Once you've created a cluster and installed your applications and have it all running in a production environment, you will likely want to keep the cluster up and running for as long as possible – especially if you operate an around-the-clock global Internet web site. However, there may be advantages to restarting application servers on occasion – for example, if your application leaks a little bit of memory, over time your application server will run out of available resources and stop working. Clusters are enormously resilient. You can stop individual application servers in the cluster and the other servers in the cluster automatically take over whatever workload was being processed by the lost server (assuming they have some amount of additional capacity).

It is a good idea to occasionally take an application server down and then restart it (without taking down the rest of the cluster). Doing so allows the application server to release and clean up any resources that may have been consumed by the server or the applications in the server over a period of time. We call taking one server down and restarting it, followed by the next, and the next through the entire set of application servers **rippling** the cluster. Since only one application server is down at a time, the rest of the cluster continues to operate and service requests from your clients – the outage of individual servers won't be noticeable to them.

WebSphere provides an operation for rippling the cluster. You can drive this operation manually from the clusters page by selecting the cluster and pressing the Ripplestart button.

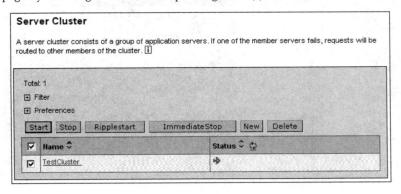

It is often a good idea to build an admin script that ripples all of your clusters periodically – more or less frequently depending on the stability of your applications.

Managing the Programming Model Extensions

The programming model extensions introduce functions that need to be administered. The PME installation image also comes with an extension to the admin console and underlying management facilities. When you install PME you will automatically see these extensions show up in your admin console – either in the standalone server management facility, or in the deployment manager if you are managing a network deployment cell. You have to be sure to install the PME image on the computer that has your deployment manager in the latter case.

The differences introduced by the PME admin extensions show up in five principle ways:

- ❏ Additional configuration topics in the application server definition
- ❏ Additional configuration topics in the application definition
- ❏ Additional resource types (representing the services introduced by PME)
- ❏ Additional options on previous configuration topics
- ❏ Additional sample applications

Configuring the Application Server Extensions

When you first open the Application Server configuration page it will look the same as usual.

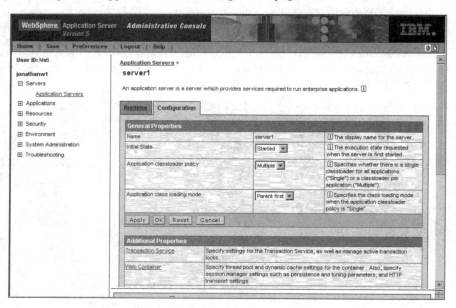

However, after scrolling down, you will notice several new configuration subjects.

Work Area Service	The work area service manages the scope and implicit propagation of application context.
Internationalization Service	The Internationalization Service supports distributed localization by affording the programmatic and declarative management of localization contexts within distributed application components.
Application Profiling Service	The application profiling service controls the scope and propagation of task names and manages the association of tasks, application profiles, and the policies configured within application profiles.
Activity Session Service	A unit of work service that can be used to coordinate one-phase resources or for extending the activation/passivation of an ejb.
Scheduler Service	The Scheduler Service manages Scheduler resources used by a given server.
Work Manager Service	The Work Manager Service manages Work Manager resources used by a given server.
Object Pool Service	The Object Pool service manages Object Pool resources used by a given server.
Business Process Container	The Business Process container provides services to execute business processes within an application server. Use this panel to install the Business Process container or to view its values if it is already installed.
Staff Service	The Staff Service manages Staff Plugin resources used by a given server.

❏ **Work Area Service** – can be used to enable or disable the service in this server instance, and set the maximum send and receive message lengths that will be allowed by the service at this server.

❏ **Internationalization Service** – enables or disables the Internationalization service at this server instance.

❏ **Application Profiling Service** – enables or disables the Application Profile service at this server instance.

❏ **Activity Session Service** – enables or disables the service at this server, and sets the default timeout for activity sessions initiated at this server.

❏ **Scheduler Service** – enables or disables this service at the server.

❏ **Work Manager Service** – enables or disables this service at the server.

❏ **Object Pool Service** – enables or disables the object pooling service at this server.

❏ **Staff Service** – enables or disables staff service at this server.

Generally, all of the programming model extension services are enabled at every application server where the programming model extensions are installed. You should also examine the corresponding configuration controls for these services in the application and in the resource definitions for the service itself.

Configuring the Application Extensions

The application configuration extensions show up within your application's configuration.

Map Extended Messaging resource references to resources	Map Extended Messaging resource references to resources
Last Participant Support Extension	Extension to transaction service to allow a single one-phase resource to participate in a two-phase transaction with one or more two-phase resources.
Application Profile	An application profile is a set of policies that are to be applied during the execution of an enterprise bean and a set of tasks that are associated with that profile.
Provide JNDI Names for Beans	Provide JNDI Names for Beans

❑ **Last Participant Support Extension** – enables support for a mixture of any number of two-phase commit resources and at most one single-phase commit resource in the same transaction. While WebSphere can coordinate one single-phase commit resource in a global transaction along with any number of two-phase commit resources, their inclusion can lead to a slightly higher risk of heuristic outcomes. Thus, you can select to enable this capability for individual applications depending on whether you can accept that additional risk.

❑ **Application Profile** – allows you to create one or more application profiles for this application, and to associate them with one or more Task identities.

Configuring the Resource Extensions

Many of the services introduced by the programming model extensions are treated as independent resource managers – managing the resources of their respective service. Thus, you do the majority of behavior control configuration through the Resources task group.

Work Managers

WebSphere ships with a default work manager – see *The Deferred Execution Service section* of Chapter 11 for more information about work managers. You can change the configuration for this work manager or create other work managers through the Work Manager task.

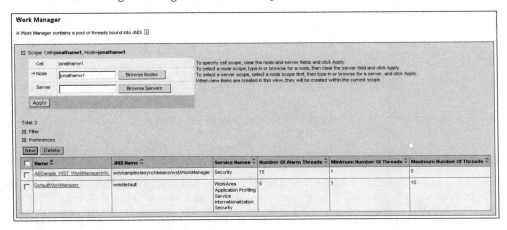

You can control a number of settings for each work manager.

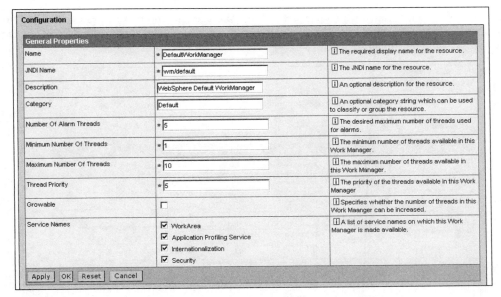

❑   Name – is the name of the work manager as displayed on the admin UI.

❑   JNDI Name – the name by which this work manager is known in the JNDI namespace.

❑   Description – describes the work manager instance; what makes it distinct from other work managers.

❑   Category – is not used by WebSphere; you should leave this blank.

❏ Number Of Alarm Threads – defines the number of alarm threads you want. Typically this will determine the maximum number of asynchronous work activities that can be scheduled to be started at exactly the same time.

❏ Minimum Number Of Threads – establishes the minimum number of threads to hold on stand-by in the thread pool for parallel asynchronous processing.

❏ Maximum Number Of Threads – specifies the maximum number of threads that can be created in the thread pool for parallel asynchronous processing.

❏ Thread Priority – sets the thread priority for the work that is managed by this work manager.

❏ Growable – indicates whether the thread pool can grow temporarily beyond its maximum thread pool size.

❏ Service Names – identifies what services will be involved in setting service contexts on any asynchronous work.

Schedulers

A Scheduler can be created to manage work that has been scheduled to execute on a particular day or time. Scheduled tasks are recorded persistently, and will be executed as scheduled. Scheduled work will be executed by any Scheduler in any application server that shares the same underlying task database (as defined in the configuration for each Scheduler). Work will be distributed to various Schedulers based on which is least loaded at any given time.

Each Scheduler is associated with a particular Work Manager, and derives its work scheduling, thread limit, and priority configurations from that work manager. You will want to create different Schedulers if you want different thread limits and priorities.

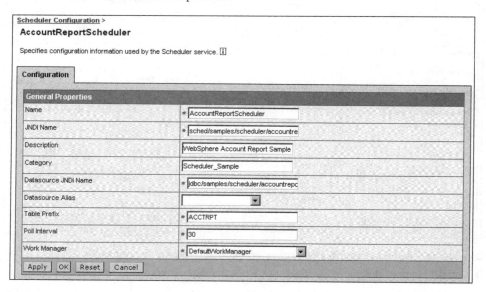

- ❑ **Name** – the name of this Scheduler

- ❑ **JNDI Name** – the JNDI name used to look it up

- ❑ **Description** – a textual description that can be used to communicate about it to other administrators

- ❑ **Category** – is not used by WebSphere; you should leave this blank.

- ❑ **Datasource JNDI Name** – the JNDI name of the datasource that is used to hold the persistent state of this Scheduler; scheduled tasks are recorded persistently to ensure they can be executed at any time in the future, as scheduled, even if the server on which it executes is restarted

- ❑ **Datasource Alias** – the user alias to be authenticated when using this datasource

- ❑ **Table Prefix** – use this to differentiate between different Scheduler entries if sharing the same database amongst multiple Schedulers

- ❑ **Poll Interval** – specifies the frequency with which the Scheduler will look for new task entries in the scheduler database

- ❑ **Work Manager** – the work manager associated with this Scheduler

Object Pools

Object pools are used by applications to create reusable object instances to avoid the overhead of creating new instances. You can configure these pools as a resource through the Admin console.

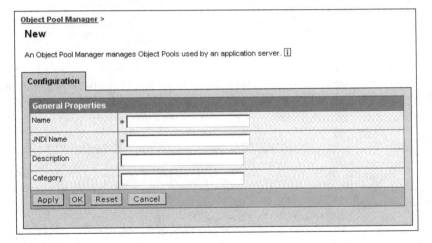

- ❑ **Name** – the displayed name of this object pool

- ❑ **JNDI Name** – the JNDI used to look up the object pool

- ❑ **Description** – a textual description used to communicate about the object pool to other administrators

- ❑ **Category** – is not used by WebSphere; you should leave this blank.

Staff Services

The staff services are a plug-in to the business process manager for mapping the organizational relationships of business processes to individual users and groups defined in the user repository.

A default staff service provider is shipped with WebSphere and can be used with users and groups in an LDAP user registry.

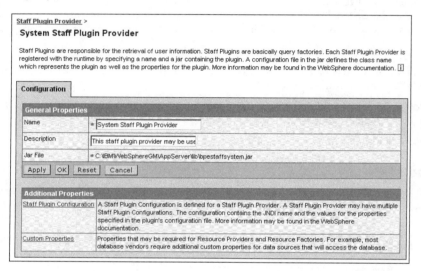

The primary thing you can configure about the staff service is the mapping to the LDAP schema. This is done through an XSL transformation that you define. To change the default mapping, you can create your own XSL file and configure it with the staff service provider:

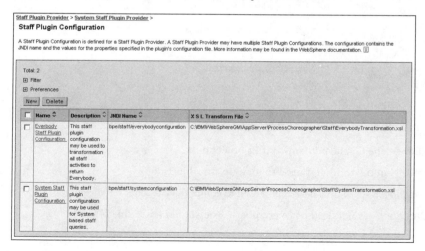

Select the New button to define a different transformation:

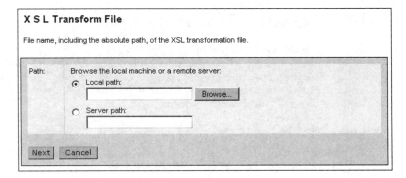

You can then enter the location of the XSL file containing your schema transformations.

Additional Configuration Options

The administration extensions for PME also extend various existing configuration options. The primary example of this is where the Transaction Service configuration for an application server introduces a new option for controlling the logging of heuristic outcomes – something that may be important if a mixture of single-phase and two-phase commit resources are used in the same transaction.

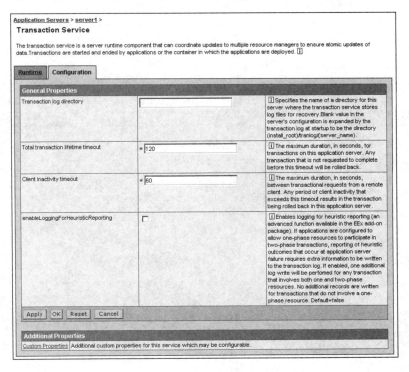

Monitoring Middleware Performance

WebSphere ships a fairly straightforward monitoring tool called the Tivoli Performance Viewer. This viewer can be used to monitor any of the performance data gathered by WebSphere. Before you can monitor any performance data, you must enable the production of performance data in the application server. If you start the TPV without enabling the publication of performance data you will get a warning like the following when you start the performance viewer:

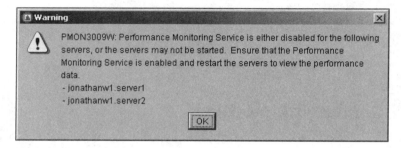

To enable the production of performance data select the **Startup** configuration option on the **Performance Monitoring Server** configuration page of the server that you want to enable. You must restart the server for this change to take affect.

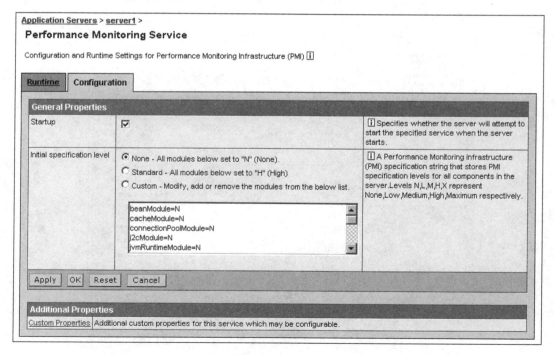

On Windows, you can start the **Tivoli Performance Monitor** from the **Start** menu.

You can control the amount of performance data that is collected from the application server from the performance viewer (superceding the levels set in the application server configuration itself).

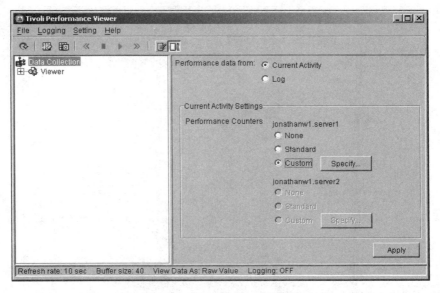

You can select the level of monitoring that can be performed for each resource – ranging from none to maximum, with several points in between. This generally affects what information is gathered:

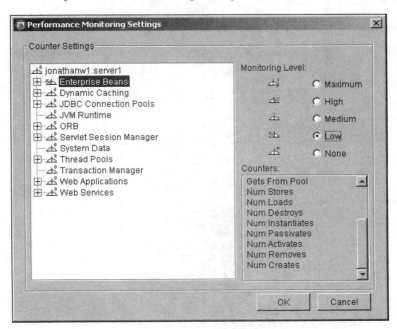

You can then navigate the resource tree to select the resource-types and/or specific resources that you want to monitor. For example, you can monitor all the web components served in the application server:

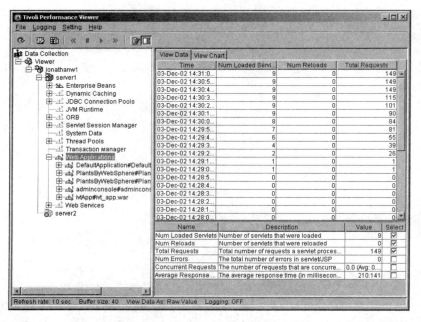

The viewer will present to you the data, collected at the configured interval for the information you've selected to see. You can select to view more information – any of the information that you are collecting based on the monitoring level you set previously.

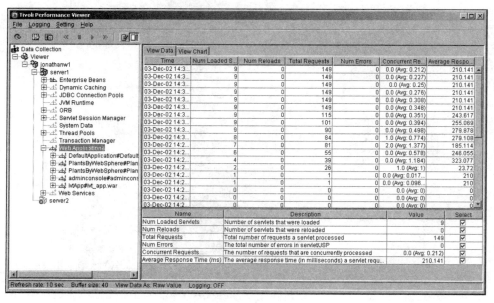

In addition to seeing the information in statistical form, you can also view the same data in graphical form by selecting the View Chart page tab:

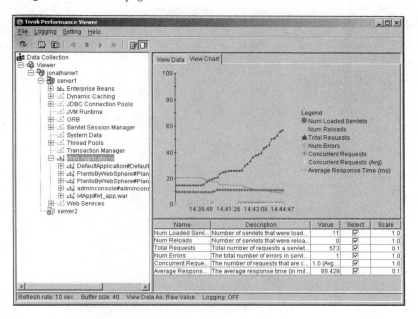

You can also monitor specific resources by navigating the resource tree:

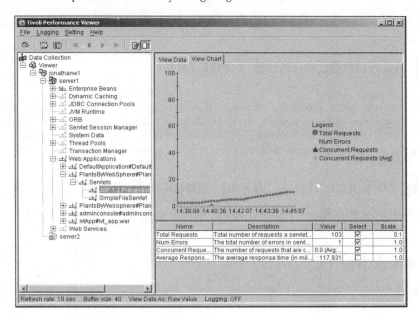

You can also vary the sampling rate from the Settings system menu pull-down.

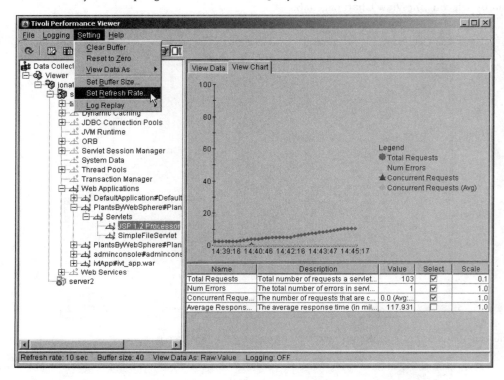

Writing a Management Program

You can gain ultimate control over the WebSphere configuration and operational environment by programming directly to WebSphere's Java management interfaces. These interfaces conform to the **JMX (Java Management Extensions)** standard specification defined for Java. While similar, the information model supported by WebSphere is necessarily different from other application server products on the market (supporting different resources and extensions).

Preparing to Execute a Management Program

Most commonly you will execute your management program from outside any WebSphere server processes – essentially as a client program.

Getting an Admin Client

Before you can anything you have to get an instance of the `AdminClient`. This is done through a static method on the `AdminClientFactory`:

```
private void createAdminClient() {

  Properties connectProps = new Properties();
  connectProps.setProperty(AdminClient.CONNECTOR_TYPE,
    AdminClient.CONNECTOR_TYPE_SOAP);
  connectProps.setProperty(AdminClient.CONNECTOR_HOST, "rhighlt1");
  connectProps.setProperty(AdminClient.CONNECTOR_PORT, "8879");

  try {
    adminClient = AdminClientFactory.createAdminClient(connectProps);
  } catch (ConnectorException e) {
    System.out.println("Exception creating admin client:" + e);
    System.exit(-1);
  }
}
```

Notice that you supply a connection `Properties` object to this operation. The connection properties describe the type of connection you want to create with the target `AdminService` (recall that `AdminService` is a wrapper for the JMX server and the end-point listener for communication from admin clients) – including the address of the target service. This sample hard-codes the address of the service, but obviously you will want to devise a way in which you can get this information as configuration data; perhaps prompted from the end user or derived from other information in your topology.

Identifying MBeans

Remember the JMX MBean system is about performing operations management – starting and stopping servers and applications, setting operational attributes, etc. Operations are performed on MBeans. Thus, nearly all of the operations that you perform require that you identify the MBean that you want to operate on. MBeans are identified by an **ObjectName** – an object containing the fully qualified name of the MBean. The `ObjectName` will consist of a set of attributes that uniquely identify the MBean.

The set of attributes that uniquely identify the MBean are established at the time the MBean is registered and activated. Since the attributes and their values are somewhat arbitrary, it is a bit much to have to know the exact set of attributes for every MBean you want to use. So JMX offers a way in which you can deduce an MBean's object name from a partial list of attribute values. This is done through a query mechanism that returns, at least, a partial list of objects that match the subset of attributes that you supply to the query.

Often, the result set will only contain one MBean – the MBean that you're really interested in. In other cases, it will return a number of MBeans, but it is usually easy to search through this intermediate result to find that one that you really want. Of course, in some cases you may really want the complete set of MBeans returned from the search – even if the result set contains several or many MBeans. Perhaps the query was initiated in response to some action taken by the end administrator and you will be presenting the returned set as a scroll list on the display. In any case, the set of MBeans returned from the query are each represented by a fully qualified object name that uniquely represents each individual MBean in the set. You can use these fully qualified object names as input to other JMX operations. The following code demonstrates a query for getting the fully qualified object name for the MBean representing a particular node agent:

```
String partialName = "WebSphere:type=NodeAgent,node=rhighlt1,*";
ObjectName partialObjectName = new ObjectName(partialName);
ObjectName nodeAgent = null;

Set nodeAgentList = adminClient.queryNames(partialObjectName, null);
```

An object name is created with the partial name of the node agent, and then used as input to the query (`adminClient.queryNames()`) to acquire a set of `ObjectNames` that match that partial name. The `ObjectNames` returned from the query contain fully qualified MBean names.

The second argument to the query (which is `null` in the example) can be a query predicate object (`javax.management.QueryExp`) used to specify predicate to the query operation. You can get a `QueryExp` object from static methods on the `java.management.Query` object.

String-form Names

An `ObjectName` can have a string-form. The string-form of an `ObjectName` has the following syntax:

```
[{<nameSpace> | '*'}':']
    {<attrName>'='<attrValue> {','<attrName>'='<attrValue>}* [',*']} | '*'
```

The `nameSpace` domain is optional – the wildcard * is assumed if no specific name-space is specified, meaning that all of the available name spaces will be examined for the matching attributes. While it may be convenient to wildcard the name space, this is not recommended as it is possible to introduce different MBeans with the same attributes and values with significantly different meanings. For example, you can imagine two different middleware products introducing MBeans representing servers by the name of `"server1"`. But an application server in WebSphere is unlikely to have the same meaning as some other server in another middleware product. The namespace for WebSphere is called, appropriately, `"WebSphere"`. (Notice the capitalization – all tokens in the MBean object name are case-sensitive.)

The namespace is separated from the attribute list by a colon (`:`).

The attribute list is zero or more name-value pairs, separated by commas. The last entry in the list can be a wildcard (*), indicating that no other attributes should be considered when evaluating this name to the actual name of the MBean. If the wildcard is omitted, then an `ObjectName` must contain exactly the attributes specified for it to be considered the same MBean.

Other than the trailing wildcard, no other order is assumed for the attributes in the list – they can be specified and will be presented in any order.

Getting a Node Agent

Building on the query described above, the process of getting a node agent, then, is just a matter of selecting an `ObjectName` from the returned set:

```
private ObjectName getNodeAgent(String nodeName) {

    try {
```

```
        String partialName = "WebSphere:type=NodeAgent,node=" + nodeName + ",*";
        ObjectName partialObjectName = new ObjectName(partialName);
        ObjectName nodeAgent = null;

        Set nodeAgentList = adminClient.queryNames(partialObjectName, null);
        if (!nodeAgentList.isEmpty()) {
          nodeAgent = (ObjectName) nodeAgentList.iterator().next();
        } else {
          System.out.println("Node agent was not found.");
          System.exit(-1);
        }

        return nodeAgent;

      } catch (MalformedObjectNameException e) {
        System.out.println("MalformedObjectNameExc getting the NodeAgent: " + e);
        System.exit(-1);
      } catch (ConnectorException e) {
        System.out.println("ConnectorExc getting the NodeAgent: " + e);
        System.exit(-1);
      }

      return null;

    }
```

Many `ObjectNames` could be returned from the query – if there were many `NodeAgent` type MBeans with the same node name, for example. However, in this case we know that only one node agent is allowed per node, and since we explicitly specified the node name we're interested in, then only one `ObjectName` should be returned – or, at least, we only look for the first name in the set.

Starting a Server

Once you've obtained the node agent, you can use it to start an application server on that node:

```
private void startServer(ObjectName nodeAgent, String serverName) {

    String opName = "launchProcess";
    Object params[] = { serverName };
    String signature[] = { "java.lang.String" };
    boolean launched = false;

    try {
      System.out.println("Starting " + serverName);
      Boolean b = (Boolean) adminClient.invoke(nodeAgent, opName,
                                               params, signature);

      launched = b.booleanValue();
      if (launched) {
        System.out.println(serverName + " was launched");
      } else {
        System.out.println(serverName + " was not launched");
      }
    } catch (Exception e) {
      System.out.println("Exception invoking launchProcess:" + e);
    }
}
```

The server is started by invoking the `launchProcess` operation on the `NodeAgent` object. This operation takes the server name as an argument. Since the `launchProcess` operation is overloaded on the `NodeAgent` MBean (there are two forms of the `launchProcess` operation), you have to provide a signature specification to help differentiate which of the overloaded operations you want to perform.

If you wanted to start the server and only wait a specific amount of time, let's say 20 seconds, before going on to the next thing, you can use the form of `launchProcess` that takes a wait-time as an argument:

```
private void startServer(ObjectName nodeAgent, String serverName) {

    String opName = "launchProcess";
    Object params[] = { serverName, new Integer(20) };
    String signature[] = { "java.lang.String", "java.lang.Integer" };
    boolean launched = false;

    try {
        System.out.println("Starting " + serverName);
        Boolean b = (Boolean) adminClient.invoke(nodeAgent, opName,
                                                 params, signature);
        launched = b.booleanValue();
        if (launched) {
            System.out.println(serverName + " was launched");
        } else {
            System.out.println(serverName + " was not launched in the specified " +
                                            "time.");
        }
    } catch (Exception e) {
        System.out.println("Exception invoking launchProcess:" + e);
    }
}
```

Notice the inclusion of the additional `Integer` argument, and its specification in the signature.

Getting a Server

Getting a server is similar to getting a node, although the MBean `ObjectName` for the server is different:

```
private ObjectName getServer(String nodeName, String serverName) {

    try {
        String query = "WebSphere:type=Server,node=" + nodeName +
                    ",process=" + serverName + ",*";
        ObjectName queryName = new ObjectName(query);
        ObjectName server = null;

        Set s = adminClient.queryNames(queryName, null);
        if (!s.isEmpty()) {
            server = (ObjectName) s.iterator().next();
        } else {
            System.out.println("Server was not found.");
            System.exit(-1);
```

```
        }

        return server;

    } catch (MalformedObjectNameException e) {
        System.out.println(e);
        System.exit(-1);
    } catch (ConnectorException e) {
        System.out.println(e);
        System.exit(-1);
    }
    return null;

}
```

You will discover that the hardest part about using JMX is figuring out the primary attributes of the MBean `ObjectNames`, and the operations and their signatures supported by MBeans. The latter can be got from the Javadocs of MBeans supported by WebSphere. The following is the operation list taken from the Javadoc for the `Server`:

getProductVersion - Gets the XML Version data for the specified product.
> *return type:* java.lang.String
> *parameters:*
> > productID *(java.lang.String)* - ID String for the desired product.

getComponentVersion - Gets the XML Version data for the specified component.
> *return type:* java.lang.String
> *parameters:*
> > componentID *(java.lang.String)* - ID String for the desired component.

getEFixVersion - Gets the XML Version data for the specified efix.
> *return type:* java.lang.String
> *parameters:*
> > efixID *(java.lang.String)* - ID String for the desired efix.

getPTFVersion - Gets the XML Version data for the specified PTF.
> *return type:* java.lang.String
> *parameters:*
> > ptfID *(java.lang.String)* - ID String for the desired PTF.

getExtensionVersion - Gets the XML Version data for the specified extension.
> *return type:* java.lang.String
> *parameters:*
> > extensionID *(java.lang.String)* - ID String for the desired extension.

getVersionsForAllProducts - Gets the XML Version data for the all installed
> products.
> *return type:* java.lang.String;
> *parameters:*

getVersionsForAllComponents - Gets the XML Version data for the all installed

<pre>   components.
            return type: java.lang.String;
            parameters:
</pre>

getVersionsForAllEFixes – Gets the XML Version data for the all installed efixes.
   return type: java.lang.String;
   parameters:

getVersionsForAllPTFs – Gets the XML Version data for the all installed PTFs.
   return type: java.lang.String;
   parameters:

getVersionsForAllExtensions – Gets the XML Version data for the all installed
                              extension.
   return type: java.lang.String;
   parameters:

stop – Stop the server process.
   return type: void
   parameters:

stopImmediate – Stop the server process without going through application
              shutdown.
   return type: void
   parameters:

stop – Stop the server process and callback.
   return type: void
   parameters:
        callback *(java.lang.Boolean)* – perform callback to requester.
        port *(java.lang.Integer)* – port number for callback.

As a general rule you should get operation information about your MBeans from the product Javadoc – at least those that are introduced by WebSphere. If you don't find it in the WebSphere InfoCenter, you should be able to find it in the web/mbeanDocs directory off the product install-root. Launch the index.html file in this directory in your browser and you will see a list of all of the MBeans. You can then navigate to the attribute, operation, and notification specifications for the MBean.

Stopping a Server

Stopping a server is an operation that you can invoke on the Server MBean itself (as opposed to the NodeAgent as in the case of starting the server):

```
private void stopServer(ObjectName server) {

  String opName = "stop";

  try {
    adminClient.invoke(server, opName, null, null);
    System.out.println("server was stopped");
  } catch (Exception e) {
    System.out.println("Exception invoking stop server:" + e);
  }
}
```

In this case, the `stop` operation is overloaded, but one version of its signature does not take any arguments, and so you can pass `null` for the `parameter` and `signature` arguments of the `invoke()` method.

Handling Notifications

You can register a notification listener with the `AdminClient`. This is useful for getting notified of changes in the state of the system – when servers and applications start and stop, when nodes are added and removed, etc. You can register for any of the notifications that any MBean generates – again look at the Javadoc for the MBeans to find out what notifications are produced by that MBean. The following notifications are produced by the `Server` MBean:

- ❑ `j2ee.state.starting` – published by the `Server` MBean when the corresponding server has been started

- ❑ `j2ee.state.running` – indicates that the corresponding server is fully up and running

- ❑ `j2ee.state.stopping` – is published to note that the corresponding server is shutting down

- ❑ `j2ee.state.stopped` – published when the server has fully stopped

To listen for notifications you must create a listener object that implements the `javax.management.NotificationListener` interface, and in doing so implements the `handleNotification()` method:

```
public class PlantsAdminNotifyListener implements NotificationListener {

  public void handleNotification(Notification ntfyObj, Object handback) {
    System.out.println("Notification received:");
    System.out.println("  type = " + ntfyObj.getType());
    System.out.println("  message = " + ntfyObj.getMessage());
    System.out.println("  source = " + ntfyObj.getSource());
    System.out.println("  seqNum = " +
                       Long.toString(ntfyObj.getSequenceNumber()));
    System.out.println("  timeStamp = " + new Date(ntfyObj.getTimeStamp()));
  }
}
```

You can register this notification listener with a specific MBean through the `AdminClient` interface:

```
public void registerNotificationListener(ObjectName nodeAgent) {

  try {
    PlantsAdminNotifyListener notifyListener =
      new PlantsAdminNotifyListener();
    adminClient.addNotificationListener(nodeAgent, notifyListener, null, null);

  } catch(InstanceNotFoundException e) {
    System.out.println("InstanceNotFoundException registering listener:" + e);
  } catch(ConnectorException e) {
    System.out.println("ConnectorException registering listener:" + e);
  }
}
```

At this point, your notification listener (notifyListener in the above example) will be called whenever the NodeAgent you've registered with changes state.

Filtering Notifications

Having registered for notifications, you will receive all notifications – whether you're interested in them or not. You can, however, filter which notifications are handed back to you. This is done with a javax.management.NotificationFilter object. JMX provides pre-defined implementations of NotificationFilters:

❑ javax.management.NotificationFilterSupport
   Allows you to filter notifications by the name of the notification. You can provide full notification name (for example, "websphere.process.running"), or a name prefix (for example, "websphere.process"). By default, all notifications will be disabled with the NotificationFilterSupport until you enable them with by invoking the enableType operation on the filter.

❑ javax.management.AttributeChangeNotificationFilter
   Enables you to filter attribute change notifications by specific attribute name, or attribute name prefix.

These usually provide all of the filtering support you will need. However, if you need to do something else, you can create your own filter implementation, derived from the NotificationFilter interface, and registered in place of any of the pre-defined filters listed above.

The following exemplifies creating a filter, setting its constraints, and registering it along with your notification listener:

```
public void registerNotificationListener(ObjectName nodeAgent) {

    try {
        NotificationFilterSupport myFilter = new NotificationFilterSupport();
        myFilter.enableType("websphere.process.running");

        PlantsAdminNotifyListener notifyListener =
            new PlantsAdminNotifyListener();

        adminClient.addNotificationListener(nodeAgent, notifyListener,
            myFilter, null);
        System.out.println("Notification listener registered.");

    } catch(InstanceNotFoundException e) {
        System.out.println("InstanceNotFoundException registering listener:" + e);
    } catch(ConnectorException e) {
        System.out.println("ConnectorException registering listener:" + e);
    }
}
```

Communicating Handbacks

On occasion, you will want to pass in information, at the time you register for notifications, which is handed back to the notification listener. This can be done with a **Handback** object – an object that you create, and register along with your notification listener, which will be handed back to you on any notifications published to your listener:

```
public void registerNotificationListener(ObjectName nodeAgent) {

   try {
      NotificationFilterSupport myFilter = new NotificationFilterSupport();
      myFilter.enableType("websphere.process.running");
      myFilter.enableType("websphere.process.starting");

      String lookFor = "websphere.process.running";

      adminClient.addNotificationListener(nodeAgent, this, myFilter, lookFor);
      System.out.println("Notification listener registered.");

   } catch(InstanceNotFoundException e) {
      System.out.println("InstanceNotFoundException registering listener:" + e);
   } catch(ConnectorException e) {
      System.out.println("ConnectorException registering listener:" + e);
   }
}
```

The hand-back object can be any valid Java object, including a `String` – as in this example. If you need to make it more complicated then you can create your own object and pass that as well.

Once you've passed the hand-back object on registration, it will be passed back to the notification listener on each notification:

```
public void handleNotification(Notification ntfyObj, Object lookFor) {

   System.out.println("Notification received:");
   System.out.println("   type = " + ntfyObj.getType());
   System.out.println("   message = " + ntfyObj.getMessage());
   System.out.println("   source = " + ntfyObj.getSource());
   System.out.println("   seqNum = " +
                     Long.toString(ntfyObj.getSequenceNumber()));
   System.out.println("   timeStamp = " + new Date(ntfyObj.getTimeStamp()));

   System.out.println(">>> Looking for: " + lookFor.toString());
   if (ntfyObj.getType().startsWith(lookFor.toString())) this.notified = true;
}
```

Remember that the handback handed in is typed to be a Java object. You need to be sure that you test for the proper type before using it in your listener.

Summary

The WebSphere middleware management facility provides you with the means to create a variety of different WebSphere network topologies – of nodes and applications servers and cells – and to construct relationships between the topology of the system and the specific applications that you want to deploy on it. The middleware management facility enables you to define the relationships between your applications and the resources they depend on.

However, it is not the objective of the middleware management facility to manage either your entire system or the resources that your application depends on. For this, you will want to make use of an enterprise management facility such as those provided by Tivoli, Candle, BMC, Wiley, Mercury, and others. You can use the rich set of programming interfaces that WebSphere provides to introduce your own management scripts and programs to automate various aspects of management. These will be described in the next chapter.

15

WebSphere Summary

Recent market feedback suggests that most people underutilize the power of their application servers. Customers often limit themselves to only building web front-ends – essentially using the application server as a *glorified web server*. They overlook and ignore the potential of the application server for building transactional business logic, or for integrating their independent lines of business. Interviews suggest that the primary reason for this is inadequate skill and experience – not enough programmers have learned how to build effective J2EE applications. If this is true for you also then it suggests that you're not getting all of the value out your application server; but more importantly it also suggests that you're spending your valuable time and skills on unnecessary tasks.

Application servers are workhorses. Don't underestimate the power that an application server can offer as the foundation for all of your business computing requirements. Application servers are as fundamental to your information systems infrastructure as databases and messaging systems. Think of the application server as a modern transaction monitor, as a hub for integrating your business, and a platform for building dynamic business processes.

Good middleware design incorporates three key principles: **precision** to work well; **tolerance** to work with varying conditions; and **strength** to keep working under stress. WebSphere is designed to blend the precision needed to run your business efficiently, the tolerance needed to handle your specific computing requirements, and the strength needed to handle your largest workload demands.

After reading this book you should have the skill that you need to build applications that harness the power of the application server. To recap a few key points made in this book:

❑ WebSphere supports four basic models of e-business computing ranging from traditional multi-tiered distributed computing, to web-based computing, to enterprise integration and business management, to service-oriented computing. Within this we define some ten fundamental component design patterns. We suggest that you spend some time examining the published material about patterns for e-business for guidance on how to assemble your application for your specific deployment needs.

❑ WebSphere is fundamentally a J2EE 1.3 conforming application server based on the Java language standards. WebSphere also extends beyond the J2EE standards to support and incorporate the broad set of web services standards.

❑ The WebSphere family is partitioned to differentiate support for the open standards and support for the extensions that are most commonly needed to build sophisticated and powerful enterprise solutions. This differentiation helps you distinguish between building a conforming application that can be easily ported to other compliant J2EE application servers, and building applications that are tailored to solving the complex problems that you may be facing in your enterprise. In fact, most of the WAS Enterprise functions were derived from direct work between IBM research and development labs and customers – these services are already proven to be critical to the success of customer applications even before they're delivered as part of the WebSphere product. While the extensions introduced by WAS Enterprise edition may be proprietary, IBM is introducing many of these extensions for standardization and so while your investment in these extensions may be motivated now by immediate needs in your enterprise, you may be able to re-gain the ability to port these if and when other application server vendors adopt those same standards.

❑ In addition to differentiating between standard vs. extended programming features, the WebSphere family also differentiates between a single, stand-alone server configuration and a multi-server, centrally administered configuration with the WAS Network Deployment edition. The ND edition enables you to federate multiple application servers on different computers in to a single network, which you can administer from a single console. You can aggregate multiple servers in to a cluster – allowing you to distribute the workload of any application deployed to the cluster over many different processes or computers.

❑ WebSphere Studio Application Developer is an essential part of the WebSphere experience. You can create conforming applications to run on WebSphere with other development tools, but WSAD is designed with specific knowledge of the WebSphere Application Server. Chief amongst these synergies is the integration of the WebSphere Application Sever as the unit-test environment for WSAD. You can build and test your application without ever leaving the WSAD integrated development environment. Changes you make to your application are automatically re-deployed to the runtime test environment. You can use the Universal Test Client to quickly exercise the functions you create. The unit-test application server is the same application server implementation that you will be using in production and so your test results will accurately reflect the correctness of your application.

❑ The Enterprise programming model extensions introduced in the WAS Enterprise edition are complemented by a corresponding set of tools extensions in WSAD and delivered in the WSAD Integration edition version of the tools product. Like the base WSAD product, the unit test environment of the WSAD IE tool is the WebSphere Application Server – extended in this case with the Enterprise edition runtime services. This will ensure your test results are valid to your production environment.

❑ The development process for creating applications to be hosted on the application server has been divided into multiple steps to enable different roles to contribute their expertise to the end solution. As the bean developer your responsibility is to formulate the design of the application, and to codify your knowledge of the business domain and application requirements. In doing so, you can express any constraints and assumptions that you've built into your application components. The Assembler is responsible for aggregating your components with components from other bean developers into a cohesive solution. The Deployer is responsible for mapping the application components to the specifics of the enterprise computing environment, including mapping the abstract persistence schema of the application components to the concrete schema of the database design in your information system. The Administrator is responsible installing the application and managing it in the information system – ensuring that is configured and balanced for maximum efficiency.

❑ Building client presentation using JSP pages and servlets is fundamental to web-enabling your application. It is important to maintain a clear separation of concerns between the presentation logic (defining how your application will interact with end users) and business logic (a model and encoding of the business functions and controls that your application uses). This separation can be enhanced with the use of model wrappers that allow for parallel development of your presentation logic and business logic.

❑ WebSphere encourages the use of EJBs for capturing basic business functions. In particular, you should use container-managed persistence for your entity beans. The EJB 2.0 specification has introduced enhancements that dramatically improve the utility and appropriateness of entity beans for business logic. With its broad knowledge of everything else that is going on in the execution environment, including what other applications are installed, what access intent policies different clients are operating with, and the interrelationships between different beans, along with its use of internal data caches, the EJB container in WebSphere can generally achieve a higher degree of throughput and more efficient resource utilization than you could independently within your own bean implementation of persistence. As a general rule of thumb, you should implement entity beans with local interfaces, and use session beans to provide remote access to business functions that operate on those entity beans.

❑ Session beans that capture the business services of your application can then be promoted into web services that can be exposed to and exploited by other lines of business within your enterprise, or optionally by other businesses that you work with.

❑ Web services can also be used within your application to encapsulate the boundaries to other information systems in your enterprise that you want to integrate with WebSphere. The web services encapsulation boundary, as represented by the Web Services Definition Language (WSDL), is used to build Java 2 Connector adapters, and within those micro-flows can be used to orchestrate multiple interactions with the external information system to compose a higher-order realization of that integration.

❑ Asynchronous messaging has also come front and center to enterprise application design for WebSphere. Version 5.0 of WebSphere ships with an embedded JMS message provider supporting point-to-point (queue-oriented) and publish-subscribe (topic-oriented) messaging with or without persistence. Message-driven beans, as defined in EJB 2.0, allow you to easily integrate messaging with your EJBs – driving EJB requests from a given in-bound message queue, or a notification topic that you want to subscribe to.

❑   WebSphere has even further enhanced the benefits of container-managed persistence with the introduction of deployment policies that capture the intent of the bean methods and your client usage patterns through access intents. These policies can be used by the container to optimize the management of your components – locking the state of your beans in the underlying data system in a way that allows for maximum concurrent access to the state of your enterprise information while maintaining the integrity of your business data. This capability is extended even further with the use of application profiles that recognize the different ways in which your application clients might use your beans for different purposes. Application profiling allows the management of your beans to be tailored to each client scenario.

❑   The WebSphere EJB programming model has been extended to allow you to invoke queries on collections of EJBs entirely in object-space dynamically encoded in your application – the component-oriented equivalent of dynamic-SQL. The query engine performs these queries efficiently be re-writing the component-oriented query request to push-down as much of the query as possible into the underlying data system – using metadata generated during application deployment to map between the component-oriented semantics of your external object design and the concrete schema of your underlying data system.

❑   Transaction and activity-session unit-of-work scopes are expanded and clarified by WebSphere. The semantics of unspecified and local transactions and their relationships to global transaction and sessions are tightened up by WebSphere – removing some of the ambiguity that exists in the J2EE specifications around these scoping mechanisms. WebSphere introduces the idea of an activity-session providing a broader unit-of-work scope than can be normally achieved with global transactions – allowing you to provide some level of coordination among resources that are not normally able to participate in two-phase commit protocols.

❑   Business process management promises to leverage the foundations being established with the formulation of business applications on WebSphere to greatly enhance the productivity of business managers and the influence they have over their business. Business process management allows a business manager to gain advantage by first giving them the tools to formalize the model of their business processes – an activity that can have benefit all by itself in the way that it can provide insight into their business – but also by allowing them to use that model to drive the integration and flow of otherwise disparate business activities across their entire organization. Having gained that much advantage, business process management extends that even further by giving business managers the ability to manipulate their business processes – extending and modifying those processes to help them respond to new or changing business opportunities.

❑   From a programming perspective, business process management is a composition technology – helping you be more productive in integrating your components to meet the requirements placed on you by the business. The business process engine operates on a new component model, called a *process-definition*, which can be created using a graphical wiring tablet in WSAD IE. The tool enables rapid development and maintenance of process definitions that choreograph the integration of your business services – using web services interfaces. Thus, any web service in your enterprise (whether hosted by WebSphere or not) can be integrated into your business processes. The business process engine also allows you to define compensating transactions that allow you to define very long running business process (transactions) that avoid the normal temporal constraints of a two-phase, ACID transaction, and yet still retain the ability to be recovered in the event of a failure in the transaction.

❑ IBM, working with Microsoft and BEA, formulated the Business Process Execution Language for Web Services (BPEL4WS) standard for specifying process definitions. BPEL4WS is derived from the combination of the Web Services Flow Language (WSFL), already supported by the WebSphere workflow engine, and elements of the XLang specification written by Microsoft. Business processes that you define with the WAS-E workflow engine now should port easily to the BPEL4WS standard in the future.

❑ The Business Rules Framework is a powerful mechanism for maintaining a separation of concerns between your relatively stable business functions and business rules and policies that are much more prone to change often. The framework allows you isolate the dynamic aspects of your logic, and yet maintain a high degree of consistency with fundamental concepts in your business design. For example, the business rules framework allows you to select different rules for classifications of your customers (Gold, Silver, Bronze) and apply the rule-results to the same conditional logic.

❑ The Enterprise edition of WAS targets a set of other services at those situations you are likely to encounter as you increase the reach and complexity of the work you are trying to perform. These services include support for propagating internationalization context (locale and timezone information) between different parts of your distributed system; the ability to define application context that will be implicitly propagated across your application components; the ability to be notified when your application is open or closed for business; and support for spawning parallel work within your application.

❑ WebSphere can be deployed in a number of different configurations – ranging from a single, standalone server through to a multi-machine network of clustered servers. An important element in any robust production configuration is the placement and configuration of a Demilitarized Zone (DMZ) to protect your applications from intrusion attacks from the Internet; and the placement of proxy servers at the edge of your enterprise or your network (edge servers) for offloading frequent access to web content (content caching).

❑ Hopefully we've all learned the importance of securing our applications. The strategy that you will use to secure your application must be considered up front during the design phases of your application development. Having said that, WebSphere makes it possible, and in fact encourages you to avoid encoding security functions in your application – rather you should employ policy declarations to express your security needs, and then use external security tools to satisfy those needs. The WebSphere runtime will enforce the synthesis of your policy declarations and the control policies set by your security administration tools in the execution environment of your applications. If you don't want to use, or don't have a set of external security management tools, WebSphere provides a set of tools that can be used out of the box for your entry scenarios.

❑ Configuring your WebSphere network, installing and configuring your applications, and monitoring and managing your operational system can be performed through the WebSphere middleware management facilities. WebSphere employs a single comprehensive management architecture for all editions of WebSphere. This consistency shows through in all topologies – from single, standalone configurations through multi-node clustered configurations, and even into WebSphere for zOS. WebSphere honors the distinction between middleware management and enterprise system management. Middleware management provides the facilities needed to manage the WebSphere middleware environment and your applications hosted on it. Enterprise system management is about managing your entire enterprise information system – including both the WebSphere middleware environment and the facilities that you use in your enterprise to host other applications that are not based on WebSphere. While maintaining this distinction, WebSphere also can be plugged into your enterprise system management environment – acting as an agent to the WebSphere middleware environment.

❑ In addition, WebSphere offers a rich set of tools and facilities for servicing the WebSphere runtime and the applications hosted on the runtime. These include logging interfaces that you can use within your application, log-analysis tools, performance monitoring tools, and first-failure data capture facilities. In the event of a significant problem, you can quickly gather logs and other service data to send to IBM with the collector tool.

❑ The WebSphere middleware management system offers command-line and scripting interfaces and Ant tasks that you can use within your environment to automate your administrative procedures.

❑ The WebSphere middleware management system is built around the Java Management Extensions (JMX) programming standard. JMX programming interfaces and extensions are exposed to system management application and product developers to control the configuration, monitoring, and operations management of WebSphere. The WebSphere middleware management console facility is itself built on these interfaces.

❑ A large portion of the breadth of services and capability of WebSphere are discussed in this book. Nonetheless, it has not been possible to cover everything. WebSphere supports other facilities for container-managed messaging; gatewaying of web services for mediation, filtering and limiting exposure to internal business services on the Internet; a Universal Description, Discovery, and Integration (UDDI) registry for private network scenarios; and a C++ ORB server for use in situations where you may be transitioning from another ORB vendor or a C++ legacy application and need to stage the conversion to a J2EE environment.

In summary, WebSphere offers you a tremendous opportunity to build efficient, flexible, and durable applications. You have the domain knowledge to understand what is required of your application. Through this book you should have acquired the skill that you need to build applications that exploit WebSphere. What you need now is experience. There's only one way to gain that.

The WebSphere Application Server incorporates four decades of accumulated knowledge about information computing: transaction processing; distributed computing; connection management; resource utilization and virtualization; query processing; web-based computing; data and systems security; object-oriented and component-based programming; message-oriented middleware; parallel-processing and clustering for performance, through-put, high-availability and failover; service-oriented architecture; business process management; MVC presentation architecture; caching and data coherency; rules processing, internationalization, systems management and administration; serviceability and autonomics – all based on extensible, open systems standards and coupled with a rich set of integrated, visual, and intelligent tools that are a showcase of technological coalescence in their own right. WebSphere is a finely engineered global freight hauler. All you have to do is load it up with the business applications you want delivered and put your foot down on the throttle – it'll take you where you want to go.

Command-Line Utilities

WebSphere offers a number of command-line utilities for use with the standalone server, and with a networked deployment manager for managing the WebSphere runtime.

Application Server Commands

The application server command-line utilities are located in the \bin directory of the installation root for the WebSphere Application Server and include the following commands:

- addNode
- removeNode
- startNode
- stopNode
- syncNode
- startServer
- stopServer
- serverStatus
- backupConfig
- restoreConfig
- versionInfo

addNode

The **addNode** command is used to register the current node into a federated cell. The addNode command has the following syntax:

```
addNode <cell_host> [<cell_port>] [-conntype <type>] [-includeapps]
                    [-startingport <portnumber>] [-noagent] [-quiet] [-nowait]
                    [-logfile <filename>] [-replacelog] [-trace] [-newtracefile]
                    [-timeout <seconds>] [-username <uid>] [-password <pwd>]
                    [-help]
```

The cell_host is the IP address or host name of the computer hosting the deployment manager representing the cell. You will only have to specify the cell_port if you have changed the default port value of the targeted deployment manager. If global security has been enabled at the deployment manager, you will have to specify a valid user ID and password for an administrator with authority to change the configuration of the system in the username and password parameters.

You can use the startingport as a hint to what port values you want the addNode command to use in creating port values for the endpoints in the node agent. Port values will be generated starting at the startingport value.

removeNode

The **removeNode** command is used to de-register the node from the cell. The removeNode has the following syntax:

```
removeNode [-force] [-quiet] [-nowait] [-logfile <filename>]
           [-replacelog] [-trace] [-timeout <seconds>]
           [-statusport <portnumber>] [-conntype <type>]
           [-username <uid>] [-password <pwd>] [-help]
```

The node agent knows the cell that it is currently part of so that does not have to specified as a parameter. As with the addNode, if security is enabled at the deployment manager you have to specify the username and password parameters for a legitimate administrator with authority to make configuration changes.

The force parameter forces the node configuration to be cleaned up locally, even if the deployment manager can't be contacted.

startNode

The **startNode** command is used to start the node agent. You will only have to do this if you have federated the node into a cell, and the node agent is not automatically started as a service. It is generally better to register the node agent as a service of the operating system. In that way, the operating system will ensure the node agent is always running – re-starting it automatically in the event that it is inadvertently stopped. The syntax for startNode is:

```
startNode [-nowait] [-quiet] [-logfile <filename>] [-replacelog]
          [-trace] [-script [<script filename>]] [-timeout <seconds>]
          [-statusport <portnumber> ] [-username <name>] [-password <password>]
          [-J-<javaoption>] [-help]
```

If you specify the `script` parameter, the `startNode` command will generate a script file representing the `startNode` command. This is a convenient way of capturing the command and its arguments for later batch processing.

stopNode

The **stopNode** operation stops the node agent on the local host. The syntax for the `stopNode` command is:

```
stopNode [-nowait] [-quiet] [-logfile <filename>] [-replacelog]
         [-trace] [-timeout <seconds>] [-statusport <portnumber>]
         [-conntype <connector type>] [-port <portnumber>]
         [-username <name>] [-password <password>] [-help]
```

The `nowait` switch can be specified to instruct the `stopNode` command to return immediately – leaving the stop operation to execute and complete in the background.

The `port` parameter can be used to specify the port number of the node agent if you know it. This saves the `stopNode` command from having to look the port number up in the configuration documents, thus making the command operate more efficiently.

syncNode

The **syncNode** command can be used to force the node agent to synchronize the node repository with the cell repository. You should use this command if you suspect the repositories have become out of sync. The `syncNode` command has the following syntax:

```
syncNode <cell_host> [<cell_port>] [-conntype <type>] [-stopservers]
                     [-restart] [-quiet] [-nowait] [-logfile <filename>]
                     [-replacelog] [-trace] [-timeout <seconds>]
                     [-statusport <portnumber>] [-username <uid>] [-password <pwd>]
                     [-help]
```

The `stopservers` switch instructs the `syncNode` command to stop all of the application servers on this node before synchronizing. The servers will then be automatically restarted if the `restart` switch is specified.

startServer

The **startServer** command will start an individual application server on the node. The syntax of the command is:

```
startServer <server> [-nowait] [-quiet] [-logfile <filename>] [-replacelog]
                     [-trace]   [-timeout <seconds>]
                     [-statusport <portnumber>] [-J-<javaoption>]
                     [-username <name>] [-password <password>] [-help]
```

The `server` parameter is the name of the server you want to start as specified in the configuration for that server.

stopServer

The **stopServer** command can be used to stop a given server on the node. The syntax of the `stopServer` command is:

```
stopServer <server> [-nowait] [-quiet] [-logfile <filename>] [-replacelog]
                     [-trace] [-timeout <seconds>] [-statusport <portnumber>]
                     [-conntype <type>] [-port <portnumber>]
                     [-username <name>] [-password <password>] [-help]
```

The `logfile` parameter can be used to specify where you want information about the stop server command written. If you specify the `replacelog` switch, the log file will be overwritten. Otherwise, the log information is appended to the end of the file.

serverStatus

The **serverStatus** command is used to get information about the status of the servers on this node. The syntax of the command is:

```
serverStatus {<server_name> | -all} [-logfile <filename>] [-replacelog]
                                     [quiet] [-trace] [-username <uid>]
                                     [-password <pwd>] [-help]
```

You can either request the status of a given server, specified by `server_name`, or get the status of all of the servers on the node, using the `all` switch.

backupConfig

The **backupConfig** command is used to back up the node configuration repository and saves it to a zip file. The syntax of the `backupConfig` command is:

```
backupConfig [<backup_file>] [-nostop] [-quiet]
             [-logfile <filename>] [-replacelog] [-trace]
             [-username <uid>] [-password <pwd>] [-help]
```

You can specify the name of the zip file you want the backup written to in the `backup_file` parameter. Otherwise, the `backupConfig` command will generate a backup file name for you – usually something that involves a constant and the current date plus an additional suffix to help differentiate it from other backups that may have occurred on this date.

If you invoke this command from the `bin` directory of your application server install root, unless the `-nostop` switch is specified, any running servers on the node will be stopped by this command prior to saving the configuration. This ensures that the configuration documents are not locked by the application server(s), and will not attempt to change the configuration while it is being backed-up. You will have to restart the servers after the backup is complete. If you specify `-nostop`, the servers will not be stopped beforehand.

If you have network deployment installed, and if you invoke this command from the `bin` directory of the network deployment installation root, then only the deployment manager will be stopped during the backup – the application servers will continue to operate with their local configuration repository.

The `backupConfig` command does not capture anything outside the repository. It does not, for example, capture your application binaries if they are stored outside the repository. Nor does it capture application data stored elsewhere. As such, the `backupConfig` command is not a substitute for a comprehensive system backup facility.

restoreConfig

The **restoreConfig** will restore the configuration captured in a previous `backupConfig` command. The syntax of the command is:

```
restoreConfig <backup_file> [-nostop] [-quiet]
                            [-logfile <filename>] [-replacelog] [-trace]
                            [-username <uid>] [-password <pwd>] [-help]
```

You must specify a backup zip file that was created from a prior `backupConfig` command in the `backup_file` parameter. If the `restoreConfig` command is invoked from the base application server installation root it will stop all running application servers before restoring the configuration repository. This ensures there are no sharing or read conflicts between the application servers and the restore processing. If the command is invoked from the deployment manager installation root, it will only stop the deployment manager – leaving the application servers to operate from their local configuration repositories.

versionInfo

The **versionInfo** command is used to get information about the current version of WebSphere installed on the local computer. The syntax of the command is:

```
versionInfo [-format {text | html}] [-file <output file>] [-long]
            [-efixes] [-efixDetail] [-ptf] [-ptfDetail] [-components]
            [-componentDetail][-help]
```

You will get basic information about the version of the application server installation from this command. By default, this information will be presented in text format. If you want the information formatted as an HTML document you can use the `format html` parameter. If you want the output placed in a file, you can use the `file` parameter and specify the file that you want used. If you want verbose information you can use the `long` switch. If you want details about the individual components of WebSphere, specify the `components` switch. Using the `componentDetail` switch will give you detailed information about the components. Using the `efixes` or `ptf` switches will get you information about any eFixes or PTFs that have been installed, respectively. Likewise, the `efixDetail` and `ptfDetail` switches will get you detailed information about and eFixes or PTFs that have been installed, respectively.

Deployment Manager Commands

The deployment manager commands are located in the `\bin` directory of the Network Deployment installation root. The deployment manager commands include:

- ❏ `startManager`
- ❏ `stopManager`
- ❏ `cleanupNode`

699

In addition to the server-level commands that are applicable to the deployment manager: `backupConfig`, `restoreConfig`, `serverStatus`, `startServer`, `stopServer`, and `versionInfo`.

startManager

The **startManager** starts the deployment manager. The syntax of this command is:

```
startManager [-nowait] [-quiet] [-logfile <filename>] [-replacelog]
             [-trace] [-script [<script filename>]] [-timeout <seconds>]
             [-statusport <portnumber>] [-J-<javaoption>]
             [-username <name>] [-password <password>] [-help]
```

If you want to specify any other JVM options you can do so with the **J** parameter.

stopManager

The **stopManager** stops the deployment manager. The syntax of the `stopManager` command is:

```
stopManager [-nowait] [-quiet] [-logfile <filename>] [-replacelog]
            [-trace] [-timeout <seconds>] [-statusport <portnumber>]
            [-conntype <type>] [-port <portnumber>]
            [-username <name>] [-password <password>] [-help]
```

The `quiet` switch can be used to suppress normal messages from being presented on the console.

cleanupNode

The **cleanupNode** command can be used to clear out any information about a node for the configuration repository. The syntax is:

```
cleanupNode <node_name> [cell_host] [cell_port] [-quiet] [-nowait]
            [-logfile <filename>] [-replacelog] [-trace]
            [-username <uid>] [-password <pwd>] [-help]
```

The `cleanupNode` can be useful if you've simply removed a computer from you network. It can also be used if you use the force switch with the `removeNode` command to force a node to be de-registered when communication could not be achieved between the node agent and the deployment manager.

Other Commands

Beyond that, there are a sundry other command line commands available to both the base app server and the deployment manager that are worth noting. These include:

- ❑ `assembly`
- ❑ `collector`
- ❑ `dumpNameSpace`
- ❑ `EARexpander`
- ❑ `ejbdeploy`

- ❏ genPluginCfg
- ❏ ikeyman
- ❏ JspBatchCompiler
- ❏ showlog
- ❏ waslogbr

assembly

The **assembly** command starts the application assembly tool. The `assembly` command takes no arguments.

collector

The **collector** command starts the collector tool. The collector tool will collect a variety of information about your configuration and execution environment that can be used to help diagnose a problem you might have with your system. You should run this tool and provide the resulting JAR file to IBM when opening a service request.

The collector command takes no arguments:

```
collector [-help]
```

This command cannot be invoked from any directory under the installation root for WebSphere. You should create a new temporary directory in your file system and run this command from there:

```
C:\>mkdir temp
C:\>cd temp
C:\temp>"c:\Program Files\WebSphere\AppServer\bin\collector"
```

This will create a collection JAR called something like `rhighlt1-BASE-WASenv.jar`.

dumpNameSpace

The **dumpNameSpace** command can be used to dump out the JNDI name space – listing the names and their bindings, recursively for each sub-context of the root. The syntax of this command is:

```
dumpNameSpace [-host <bootstrapHost>] [-port <bootstrapPort>]
              [factory <factoryClass>] [-root <rootLocation>]
              [-url <resourceLocation>] [startAt <startingContext>]
              [-format <formatStyle>] [-report <reportLength>]
              [-traceString <traceFilterString>]
```

Where:

- ❏ `bootstrapHost` is the host that you want to bootstrap from. Every WebSphere server – including application servers, node agents, and deployment managers host a bootstrap service. You can point this command utility to any host containing a valid WebSphere process – or any other (non-WebSphere) server containing a valid CORBA bootstrap service. Of course, the bootstrap service must be started before issuing this command. This will default to the `localhost`.

701

❑ portNumber is the port number of your bootstrap service. By default this is 9810 for application servers, 9809 for the deployment manager, or 2809 for the node agent, however; you can set this to whatever port number has been configured for your bootstrap service. You can find bootstrap port values under the BOOTSTRAP_ADDRESS of the endpoints page of whichever server you want to target – using the admin UI, for example.

❑ factoryClass is the Java class name of the JNDI InitialContext factory. By default this is com.ibm.websphere.naming.WsnInitialContextFactory. You should not have to change this – if you do, be sure that the context factory is compatible with the name space that you want to view.

❑ rootLocation is the root of the name space that you want to view. This can be one of "cell", "server", "node", "host", "legacy", "tree", or "default". These keys have slightly different uses for different versions of WebSphere, and only "default" is applicable to non-WebSphere namespaces.

❑ startingContext is the starting sub-context (from the rootLocation) that you want to start. Do not specify this as an absolute context – in other words, there should not be a leading slash (/) in the starting context name. For example: –startContext servers/nodeagent is valid, but –startContext /servers/nodeagent will cause a problem.

❑ resourceLocation is a URL for the name service. This should take on the URL form defined by the CORBA bootstrapping service – for example:

```
corbaloc::rhighlt1:9810/NameServiceServerRoot
```

If you use the –url parameter, you would not specify the –host or –port parameters as these are inferred by the URL. The port you use here will depend on the bootstrap port configured for the source of your bootstrapping service.

❑ formatStyle indicates how you want names formed in the report. This can be either "jndi" or "ins". If you select a form style of JNDI (the default), compound names (those containing an ID and type field) are composed as a single string. If you select an INS, the compound name will be concatenated with an intervening period (.) – per the CORBA Interoperable Naming Service (INS) rules.

❑ reportLength indicates whether you want summary or detailed information for each binding. This can be "short" (summary information; the default), or "long" (detailed information).

❑ traceFilterString is a trace filter string that will affect what gets traced during the execution of this command.

EARExpander

The **EARExpander** utility can be used to expand an EAR file – un-zipping its contents in a directory structure in the file system. The syntax of this command is:

```
EARExpander -ear <earFile> -operationDir <targetDirectory>
            -operation {expand | collapse} [-expansionFlags {all | war}]
```

Specify the EAR file that you want to work with in the earFile parameter. This should be path-qualified to refer to the absolute or relative location of the EAR file. The targetDirectory should specify the target directory for your expanded EAR. The operation parameter tells the utility to either expand the EAR file to the target directory, or collapse the target directory to the specified EAR.

ejbdeploy

The **ejbdeploy** utility will generate the schema mappings and bindings for your enterprise application. This is a necessary step before you can use your application in the application server. There are a variety of ways in which you can initiate the deployment of your application – including in the WebSphere Studio Application Developer tool, as an Ant task, and during application installation. This command-line utility enables you to do deployment as a manual activity from the commandline.

The syntax of this command is:

```
ejbdeploy <inputJar> <workingDirectory> <outputJar>
        [-keep] [-cp <classpath>] [-codegen] [-dbname <database>]
        [-dbschema <databaseSchema>] [-dbvendor <databaseVendor>] [-35] [-sqlj]
        [-debug] [-rmic <rmicOptions>] [-ignoreErrors] [-quiet] [-nowarn]
        [-noinform] [-trace]
```

The inputJar is the JAR or EAR file (including qualified path name) that you want to deploy. The workingDirectory is a temporary directory that the ejbdeploy utility can use to hold temporary and intermediate files that it generates. If the keep switch is specified, then this directory will be kept after the utility is done – otherwise, it may remove the files that it generates in this directory. The outputJar is the name of the JAR or EAR file that you want produced from this deployment process. If you specify a JAR in the inputJar parameter, then you must specify a JAR in the outputJar parameter. Likewise, if you specify an EAR in the inputJar, then you must specify an EAR in the outputJar.

You can specify any additional classpath that you need during deployment in the cp parameter. If you specify the codegen switch, the ejbdeploy utility will only generate code during this process – it will not compile that code or run the RMIC compiler to produce the stubs and ties for the EJBs in your application.

If you will be following a top-down pattern, you should specify the database parameter for the database you want created, the databaseSchema for the schema you want created, and the databaseVendor to specify the type and version of relational database product that you want to target in your application. Valid databaseVendor values include: SQL92, SQL99, DB2UDBWIN_V71, DB2UDBWIN_V72, DB2UDBOS390_V6, DB2UDBOS390_V7, DB2UDBISERIES, ORACLE_V8, ORACLE_V9I, INFORMIX_V73, INFORMIX_V92, INFORMIX_V93, SYBASE_V1192, SYBASE_V1200, SYBASE_V1250, MSSQLSERVER_V7, MSSQLSERVER_2000, and CLOUDSCAPE_V50.

If you want the utility to generate mappings in the manner used for WebSphere version 3.5, you can specify the 35 switch. The default mappings are much improved so you should only use this switch if you're having a particular problem with compatibility.

You can direct the utility to generate to SQLJ instead of JDBC by specifying the sqlj switch. There may be some performance advantages to using SQLJ in some cases.

Specifying the debug switch instructs the deploy utility to generate debug information in the deployed application.

The rmic parameter can be used to pass in options to the RMIC compiler. These options should be enclosed in quotes to keep them together, and separate them from other parameters and switches recognized by this command utility.

The `ignoreErrors` switch instructs the utility to proceed with the deployment even if errors are encountered. Otherwise, the utility will stop deployment if it encounters any errors. The `quiet` switch instructs the utility to suppress warning and informational messages during the deployment process. Likewise, the `nowarn` and `noinform` switches suppress warning and information messages, respectively. The `trace` switch will cause this utility to generate trace messages.

GenPluginCfg

The **GenPluginCfg** command utility can be used to generate the web server plug-in configuration documents. The syntax of this command is:

```
GenPluginCfg [-config.root <configrootDirectory>] [-cell.name <cellName>]
             [-node.name <nodeName>] [-server.name <serverName>]
             [-output.file.name <targetFile>] [-debug <enableDebug>]
```

Note that this command, unlike other commands, use a dotted-name convention for switch names.

Where:

- ❑ `configrootDirectory` is the root directory of the configuration repository.
- ❑ `cellName` is the name of your cell. Use this parameter if you're generating a plug-in configuration for a network deployment installation – will generate the plug-in for the entire cell.
- ❑ `nodeName` is the name of your node. Use this parameter if you want to generate a configuration for only one node in a network deployment installation.
- ❑ `serverName` is the name of your application server. Use this parameter only for a single-server installation.
- ❑ `targetFile` is the name of the configuration file (and directory location) you want to generate. If you don't specify this parameter, the utility will generate the configuration in the `plugin-cfg.xml` file under the configuration root.
- ❑ `enableDebug` is either "yes" or "no" indicating whether you want debugging enabled.

ikeyman

The **ikeyman** command starts the IBM Key Management utility. Use this utility for creating or managing X.509 certificate key-files – both for creating initial certificate and private-key pairs. The syntax of this command is:

```
ikeyman
```

This command accepts no arguments.

JspBatchCompiler

The **JspBatchCompiler** command utility can be used to pre-compile JSPs of an installed application. The syntax of this command is:

```
JspBatchCompiler -enterpriseapp.name <appName>
                 [-webmodule.name <warName>][-cell.name <cellName>]
                 [-node.name <nodeName>] [-server.name <serverName>]
                 [-filename <jspName>] [-keepgenerated <enableKeepGenerated>]
                 [-verbose <enableVerbose>]
                 [-deprecation <enableDeprecation>]
```

This command must be used with enterprise applications that you've already installed. You specify the enterprise application containing the JSP pages that you want compiled in the appName parameter. If your application contains multiple WARs, and if you want the JSP pages of only a specific WAR file compiled then you can specify that WAR file in the warName parameter. Otherwise, the JSP pages in all of the WARs in the EARs will be compiled.

You usually have to supply the cellName, nodeName, and serverName on which your application is installed. These parameters will default, but the default values are usually insufficient to find your application.

If you only want to compile a specific JSP specify the jspName parameter. Otherwise, all of the JSP pages will be compiled.

The enableKeepGenerated parameter is either "true" or "false" indicating whether you want to keep the generated intermediate (servlet source) files produced by this compilation process.

If you want the servlet compiler to generated deprecation warnings then specify "true" for the enableDeprecation parameter.

Specify the verbose switch if you want detailed information messages produced during this command processing.

showlog

The **showlog** command utility will convert the (binary) contents of a specified log into a text format that can be used in an editor or other text processor. The syntax of this command is:

```
showlog <binaryFilename> [<outputFilename>]
```

The binaryFilename parameter should be the name of the activity.log, in the \logs subdirectory of the WebSphere installation location. Alternately, you can supply a fully qualified file and path name to the log that you want converted.

The outputFilename parameter should be specified if you want the output of the conversion written to a specific file. Otherwise, the converted text will be written to the standard out stream.

waslogbr

The **waslogbr** command starts the log browser. The syntax of this command is:

```
waslogbr [<logfile>]
```

The logfile parameter is optional, and should specify the fully qualified name of the log file that you want to browse. If this is not specified then the browser will start by opening the activity.log in the \logs sub-directory of the WebSphere installation root.

Writing Management Scripts

WebSphere supports scripting of administrative operations through the **wsadmin** command utility. The syntax for starting the wsadmin command utility is:

```
wsadmin [-c <command>] [-p <properties_file_name>]
        [-profile <profile_script_name>] [-f <script_file_name>]
        [-lang <language>] [-wsadmin_classpath <classpath>]
        [-conntype <type>] [-host <host_name>] [-port <port_number>]
        [-user <userid>] [-password <password>] [<script parameters>]
```

You can execute a single script command with the c parameter. You should supply a single script statement with this option.

You can execute an entire script contained within its own file with the f parameter. Specify the script file with this option. We'll come back to this in a bit.

You can create a common script – referred to as a **profile script** – that you want always executed in front of anything else you run. You can create a profile script, and specify it with the profile parameter. This is useful, for example, for setting up standard path statements, recording activities, and so forth.

If you have special classpath needs within your script, you can extend the classpath with the wsadmin_classpath parameter.

Any parameters you need to pass into the script should be specified last – they will be passed into the script as specified on the command line.

By default wsadmin operates with the Jacl language. This is the only language supported by WebSphere at this time, but we expect this will be expanded in the future to include other languages such as Jython and JavaScript. You will be able to specify the scripting language you prefer to write with in the lang parameter.

A common use of the wsadmin command utility is to run it as a shell. Simply specifying wsadmin without the c or f parameters will bring up the shell:

```
c:\Program Files\WebSphere\AppServer\bin>wsadmin
WASX7029I: For help, enter: "$H WASX7209I: Connected to process "server1" on node
rhight1 using SOAP connector;
The type of process is: UnManagedProcess
elp help"
wsadmin>
```

This, of course, assumes you know the Jacl language. WebSphere provides basic information on programming in Jacl in the InfoCenter. Another document worth looking at is at: http://www.usenix.org/publications/library/proceedings/tcl97/full_papers/lam/lam.pdf. Beyond that, the first thing you will want to know is the $Help object – this object can be used to get information about the other predefined objects introduced by WebSphere. It can also be used to discover the attributes, operations, notifications and other details of the MBeans registered in the WebSphere environment.

To get information about a particular MBean you can use the `all` operation on the `$Help` object, passing in a fully qualified MBean `ObjectName`. For this and any other operation that requires an `ObjectName`, you can generate a fully qualified name using the `completeObjectName` parameter of the `$AdminControl` object. The command:

```
wsadmin> $Help all [$AdminControl completeObjectName
            "WebSphere:type=Server,process=server1,*"]
```

will return all of the object information about the server MBean representing `server1`. Notice the use of square brackets – these are used to enclose a sub-expression in the Jacl language.

The other key objects to know about are:

❏ `$AdminControl` – supports operations that can be performed on specified MBeans

❏ `$AdminConfig` – introduces operations that manage the configuration of the application server or cell

❏ `$AdminApp` – supports application management operations

AdminControl

The `AdminControl` command supports the following operations:

Operation	Argument(s)	Usage
completeObjectName	\<name-template\>	Returns a string version of `ObjectName` that best matches the template name.
getAttribute	\<name-string\> \<attribute-name\>	Returns the value of the attribute for the MBean best matching the template name.
getAttribute_jmx	\<ObjectName\> \<attribute-name\>	Returns the value of the attribute for the specified `ObjectName`.
getAttributes	\<name-string\> \<attribute-name-list\>	Returns a string of name-value pairs.
getAttributes_jmx	\<ObjectName\> \<attribute-name-list\>	Returns a list of attribute values; one for each of the attribute names listed.
getCell	none	Returns the cell name of the connected server.
getConfigId	\<name-template\>	Returns a config ID for the corresponding configuration object, if any. The resulting identity is used with the `AdminConfig` object.

Table continued on following page

Operation	Argument(s)	Usage
getDefaultDomain	none	Returns "WebSphere".
getDomainName	none	Returns "WebSphere".
getHost	none	Returns a string representation of connected host.
getMBeanCount	none	Returns the number of MBeans registered in WebSphere.
getMBeanInfo_jmx	\<ObjectName>	Returns MBeanInfo for the specified MBean.
getNode	none	Returns node name of the connected server.
getPort	none	Returns the port in use.
getPropertiesForDataSource	\<config-id>	Returns the properties that may be used in testing the connection to the specified data source.
getType	none	Returns the connection type in use.
help	[\<operation>]	Gets help information. Will provide a summary of all operations supported if no arguments are provided. Otherwise, will returns specific information about the specified operation.
invoke	\<name-string> \<operation> [\<args> [\<signature>]]	Invokes the specified operation on the MBean identified by \<name-string>. If the operation takes arguments, you can specify those as \<args>. If the operation is overloaded, you must qualify which form to use by supplying a \<signature>.
invoke_jmx	\<ObjectName> \<operation> \<args> \<signature>	Invokes the specified operation on the specified MBean. You must supply an \<args> Java Object array (null if the operation does not take any arguments), and \<signature> Java Object array (null if the operation does not take any arguments). The results of the invoked operation, if any, are returned from this request.
isRegistered	\<name-string>	Returns true (1) if supplied MBean \<name-string> is registered.
isRegistered_jmx	\<ObjectName>	Returns true (1) if supplied \<ObjectName> is registered.
makeObjectName	\<name-string>	Returns an ObjectName object built with the given string.

Operation	Argument(s)	Usage
queryNames	\<name-string\> \<QueryExp\>	Returns the set of ObjectNames that match the \<QueryExp\> on the MBean specified by \<name-string\>. The \<QueryExp\> is a javax.management.QueryEval generated from a Query object.
queryNames_jmx	\<ObjectName\> \<QueryExp\>	Returns the set of ObjectNames that match the \<QueryExp\> on the specified MBean. The \<QueryExp\> is a javax.management.QueryEval generated from a Query object.
reconnect	none	Reconnects with the server if the server should have gone down for some reason.
setAttribute	\<name-string\> \<attribute\>	Sets the \<attribute\> on the specified MBean. \<attribute\> is a javax.management.Attribute object.
setAttribute_jmx	\<ObjectName\> \<attribute\>	Sets the \<attribute\> on the specified MBean. \<attribute\> is a javax.management.Attribute object.
setAttributes	\<name-string\> \<attributes\>	Sets the \<attributes\> on the specified MBean. \<attributes\> is an array of javax.management.Attribute objects.
setAttributes_jmx	\<ObjectName\> \<attributes\>	Sets the \<attributse\> on the specified MBean. \<attributes\> is an array of javax.management.Attribute objects.
startServer	\<server\> [\<node-name\>] [\<wait-time\>]	Starts the specified \<server\>. You must specify the \<node-name\> when operating on a deployment manager. The \<wait-time\> (in seconds) is optional.
stopServer	\<server\> [\<node-name\>]	Stops the specified \<server\>. You must specify the \<node-name\> when operating on a deployment manager.
testConnection	\<datasource-config-id\>	Tests the connection to a DataSource object.
trace	\<trace-spec\>	Sets the wsadmin trace specification.

The \<name-template\> argument is a partially qualified name-string representing the MBean. For example:

```
"type=Server,process=server1,*"
```

is sufficient for identifying the application server named server1.

The <name-string> argument is a fully qualified name-string representing the MBean. A fully qualified name contains a complete list of keys and values that identify the MBean object – as registered from the MBean when it was created. Each MBean may be registered with a different set of name keys and so it is usually difficult to guess (or even type out) the fully qualified MBean name. For example, the fully qualified name for a server might look like:

```
WebSphere:name=server1,process=server1,platform=common,node=rhighlt1,version=5.0,t
ype=Server,mbeanIdentifier=cells/rhighlt1/nodes/rhighlt1/servers/server1/server.xm
l#Server_1,cell=rhighlt1,processType=UnManagedProcess
```

The easiest way of forming this is with the $AdminControl completeObjectName <name-template> command. For example:

```
set server1 [$AdminControl completeObjectName "type=Server,process=server1,*"]
```

The <ObjectName> argument is a javax.management.ObjectName object. The easiest way of forming this is with the $AdminControl makeObjectName <name-string> command. For example:

```
set server1name [$AdminControl makeObjectName $server1]
```

Starting a Server

Starting a server can be done with the startServer operation.

```
wsadmin> $AdminControl startServer server1 rhighlt1
WASX7262I: Start completed for server "server1" on node "rhighlt1"
```

will start server1 on node rhighlt1.

Stopping a Server

Stopping a server be done with the stopServer operation:

```
wsadmin> $AdminControl stopServer server1 rhighlt1
WASX7337I: Invoked stop for server "server1" Waiting for stop completion.
WASX7264I: Stop completed for server "server1" on node "rhighlt1"
```

will stop server1 on node rhighlt1.

AdminConfig

The operations supported by `AdminConfig` are:

Operation	Argument(s)	Usage
attributes	`<type>`	Shows the attributes for a given type.
checkin	`<documentURI>` `<filename>` `<digest>`	Checks a file into the config repository at the specified URI. This should be the same digest returned from the extract operation.
convertToCluster	`<server-name>` `<cluster-name>`	Converts a server to be the first member of a new server cluster.
create	`<type>` `<parent>` `<attributes>` `[<parent-attribute-name>]`	Creates a configuration object, given a type, a parent, and a list of attributes, and optionally an attribute name for the new object.
CreateCluster Member	`<cluster-name>` `<node-name>` `<member-attributes>` `<template-id>`	Creates a new server that is a member of an existing cluster.
createDocument	`<documentURI>` `<filename>`	Creates a new document in the config repository.
createUsingTempl ate	`<type>` `<parent>` `<attributes>` `<template-object>`	Creates an object using a particular template type – the `<template-object>` should be produced from the `listTemplates` operation.
defaults	`<type>`	Displays the default values for attributes of a given type of MBean.
deleteDocument	`<documentURI>`	Deletes a document from the config repository.
existsDocument	`<documentURI>`	Tests for the existence of a document in the config repository.
extract	`<documentURI>` `<filename>`	Extracts a file from the config repository.
getCrossDocumentV alidationEnabled	None	Returns true if cross-document validation is enabled
getid	`<containment-string>`	Show the config ID of an object, given a string version of its containment.

Table continued on following page

Operation	Argument(s)	Usage
getObjectName	<config-id>	Given a config ID, returns a string version of the `ObjectName` for the corresponding running MBean, if any.
getSaveMode	None	Returns the mode used when "save" is invoked.
GetValidation Level	None	Returns the validation used when files are extracted from the repository.
getValidationSev erityResult	<severity>	Returns the number of messages of a given severity from the most recent validation. `<severity>` is a numeric value.
hasChanges	None	Returns true if unsaved configuration changes exist.
help	None	Shows help information.
InstallResource Adapter	<rar-filename> <node> <options>	Installs a J2C resource adapter with the given RAR file name and an option string in the node.
list	<type> [<scope>]	Lists all configuration objects of a given type.
listTemplates	<type> [<match>]	Lists all available configuration templates of a given type. Will be subsetted to those templates whose name contains the <match> string, if specified.
modify	<config-id> <attributes>	Change specified attributes of a given configuration object.
parents	<type>	Show the objects that contain a given type.
queryChanges	None	Returns a list of unsaved files.
remove	<config-id>	Removes the specified configuration object.
required	<type>	Displays the required attributes of a given type.
reset	None	Discard unsaved configuration changes
save	None	Commit unsaved changes to the configuration repository.
setCrossDocumentV alidationEnabled	None	Sets the cross-document validation enabled mode.

Operation	Argument(s)	Usage
setSaveMode	rollbackOnConflict | overwriteOnConflict	Changes the mode used when "save" is invoked.
setValidationLev el	none | low | medium | high | highest	Sets the validation used when files are extracted from the repository.
show	`<config-id>` `[<attr-list>]`	Shows the attributes of a given configuration object. If `<attr-list>` is provided, then only show those attributes in the list.
showall	`<config-id>` `[<attr-list>]`	Recursively show the attributes of a given configuration object, and all the objects contained within each attribute.
showAttribute	`<config-id>` `<attribute>`	Displays only the value for the single attribute specified.
types	None	Shows the possible types for configuration.
validate	None	Invokes validation on the repository (as controlled by the Validation Level – see setValidationLevel).

The `<type>` argument is the class name of a registered MBean. For example:

```
wsadmin> $AdminConfig attributes Server
```

The `<documentURI>` is the name of a configuration document in the repository. For example:

```
wsadmin> $AdminConfig existsDocument
            /cells/rhighlt1Network/nodes/rhighlt1/servers/server1/server.xml
```

The `<containment-string>` refers to an MBean in the system, represented by its configuration path. For example:

```
wsadmin> $AdminConfig getid /Node:rhighlt1/Server:server1/
```

You should think of the $AdminConfig object being used two ways – one to modify the configuration of the network, and the other to extract and check-in documents in the configuration repository. The former involves operations like convertToCluster, create, getObjectName, modify, save, show, reset, etc. The latter involves operations like checkin, createDocument, extract, remove, etc.

Modifying the configuration allows you to change the configuration documents without actually having to extract and check-in the actual documents – WebSphere will make the document changes for you. Similar to the Admin UI, when you make a configuration change with these operations, the changes are saved in a workspace and won't change the actual repository until you save.

Handling documents in the repository allows you to get or put the entire configuration document, or any other document held in the repository. Don't forget, if you make any changes to the configuration or repository, including creating new documents in the repository, these changes only actually change your workspace – you must invoke the save operation to write these changes back into the repository.

AdminApp

The AdminApp object supports the following operations:

Operation	Argument(s)	Usage
DeleteUserAndGroup Entries	\<appname\>	Deletes all the user/group information for all the roles and all the username/ password information for run-as roles for a given application.
edit	\<appname\> \<options\>	Edits the properties of an application.
editInteractive	\<appname\> [\<options\>]	Edits the properties of an application interactively.
export	\<appname\> \<filename\>	Exports application to a file.
exportDDL	\<appname\> \<filename\>	Exports DDL from application to a directory.
help	[\<operation\>]	Shows help information. Will list a summary of operations if no arguments are specified. Otherwise, will provide detailed information of the operation specified.
install	\<filename\> \<options\>	Installs an application, given a file name and an option string.
installInteractive	\<filename\> [\<options\>]	Installs an application in interactive mode, given a file name and an option string.
list	none	Lists all installed applications.
listModules	\<appname\>	List the modules in a specified application.
options	[\<filename\>]	Shows the options available, either for a given file, or in general.

Operation	Argument(s)	Usage
taskInfo	\<filename\> \<task\>	Shows detailed information pertaining to a given install task for a given file. The following are valid tasks for this operation: MapRolesToUsers, MapRunAsRolesToUsers, CorrectUseSystemIdentity, BindJndiForEJBNonMessageBinding, BindJndiForEJBMessageBinding, MapEJBRefToEJB, MapResRefToEJB, MapResEnvRefToRes, DataSourceFor10EJBModules, DataSourceFor20EJBModules, DataSourceFor10CMPBeans, DataSourceFor20CMPBeans, MapWebModToVH, MapModulesToServers, EnsureMethodProtectionFor10EJB, EnsureMethodProtectionFor20EJB, CorrectOracleIsolationLevel, AppDeploymentOptions, EJBDeployOptions.
uninstall	\<appname\>	Uninstalls the specified application.
updateAccessIDs	\<appname\> \<all\>	Updates the user/group binding information with accessID from user registry for a given application. If \<all\> is true (1), all users and groups will be updated in the bindings. If \<all\> if false (0), only new users and groups (those not previously specified in the bindings) will be updated. **Note**: Using this operation has security tradeoffs that should be understood. Read the *Granting Principals to Roles* section in *Chapter 13* to understand these implications better.

Options

The valid options for any of the $AdminApp operations listed above include:

Option	Description
appname \<appname\>	The name of the application.

Table continued on following page

Option	Description
BindJndiForEJBMessageBinding { <ejbmodulename> <ejbname> <uri> <lpjndiname> }+	The listener port JNDI name you want given to your Message Bean.
BindJndiForEJBNonMessageBinding { <ejbmodulename> <ejbname> <uri> <ejbjndiname> }+	The JNDI name you want given to your (non-MDB) EJB.
cell <cellname>	The name of the cell.
cluster <clustername>	The name of the cluster.
contextroot <contextrootname>	The context root for the web application.
CorrectOracleIsolationLevel { <modulename> <referencebinding> <jndiname> <isolationlevel> }+	The isolation level for Oracle data sources.
CorrectUseSystemIdentity { <ejbname> <ejbmodulename> <uri> <methodsignature> <role> <username> <password> }+	The run-as-role policy to use.
DataSourceFor10CMPBeans { <ejbmodulename> <ejbname> <uri> <dsjndiname> <username> <password> }+	The data source to use for a specific 1.x CMP EJB.
DataSourceFor20CMPBeans { <ejbmodulename> <ejbname> <uri> <dsjndiname> <resauthpolicy> }+	The data source to use for a specific 2.0 CMP EJB. The resauthpolicy can one of: "per connection factory" or "container".
DataSourceFor10EJBModules { <ejbmodulename> <uri> <dsjndiname> <username> <password> }+	The default data source to use for the 1.x EJBs in the specified module.
DataSourceFor20EJBModules { <ejbmodulename> <uri> <dsjndiname> <resauthpolicy> }+	The default data source to use for the 2.0 EJBs in the specified module. The resauthpolicy can one of: "per connection factory", "container".
defaultbinding.cf.jndi <cfjndiname>	The JNDI name of the default connection factory.
defaultbinding.cf.resauth <resauthpolicy>	The resauth policy to assume for the default connection factory.
defaultbinding.datasource.jndi <dsjndiname>	The JNDI name of the default data source.
defaultbinding.datasource.password <password>	The password to assume for the default data source.
defaultbinding.datasource.username <username>	The username to assume for the default data source.
defaultbinding.ejbjndi.prefix <jndiprefix>	The default JNDI prefix to assume for EJBs.

Option	Description
defaultbinding.force	Use to force the default bindings to be used in place of the existing bindings.
defaultbinding.strategy.file <filename>	The name of the default bindings file.
defaultbinding.virtual.host <virtualhost>	The default virtual host.
depl.extension.reg <filename>	The deployment extensions property file.
deployejb	Deploy the EJBs in the application during installation.
deployejb.classpath <classpath>	Additional classpaths to use for EJB deploy.
deployejb.dbschema <dbschemaname>	The schema to use for EJB deploy
deployejb.dbtype <dbtype>	The DB type for the EJB deploy. Can be one of: CLOUDSCAPE_V50, DB2UDB_V72, DB2UDBOS390_V6, DB2UDBAS400_V4R5, INFORMIX_V73, INFORMIX_V92, MSSQLSERVER_V7, MSSQLSERVER_2000, ORACLE_V8, ORACLE_V9I, SYBASE_1200
deployejb.rmic <rmicoptions>	The RMIC options to use for EJB deploy.
distributeApp	Whether to distribute the application binaries.
EnsureMethodProtectionFor10EJB { <ejbmodulename> <uri> <protectpolicy> }+	Ensure 1.x EJBs in the application are protected. The protection policy can be one of: "methodProtection.uncheck", "methodProtection.exclude", or blank ("").
EnsureMethodProtectionFor20EJB { <ejbmodulename> <uri> <protectpolicy> }+	Ensure 2.0 EJBs in the application are protected. The protection policy can be one of: "methodProtection.uncheck" or "methodProtection.exclude".
installdir <install-directory>	The directory to install the application.
MapEJBRefToEJB { <modulename> <ejbname> <uri> <ejbreference> <targetclassname> <targetejbjndiname> }+	Maps the EJB reference to an EJB JNDI name.
MapModulesToServers { <modulename> <uri> <servername> }+	Maps individual modules of the application to specific application servers (overriding the server option).

Table continued on following page

717

Option	Description
MapResEnvRefToRes { <modulename> <ejbname> <uri> <resenvreference> <resenvtype> <resenvjndiname> }+	Maps resource environment references in your application to environment resources in the configuration.
MapResRefToEJB { <modulename> <ejbname> <uri> <resreference> <restype> <resjndiname> }+	Maps the resource references in your application to resources in the configuration.
MapRolesToUsers { <role> <isEveryone> <isAllauthnusers> <username> <groupname> }+	Maps the roles in your application to users or groups. You should specify either "Yes" or "No" for isEveryone and isAllauthnusers. Setting isEveryone to Yes indicates the role is granted to everyone; isAllauthnusers should be set to No and the username and groupname should be blank. Setting isAllauthnusers to Yes indicates the role is granted to all authenticated users; isEveryone should be set to No and the username and groupname should be blank. You can specify multiple users and groups by separating them by | and surrounding the list in double-quotes.
MapRunAsRolesToUsers { <role> <username> <password> }+	Maps the run-as-role policy in your application to a specified user principal.
MapWebModToVH { <webmodulename> <uri> <virtualhostname> }+	Maps web modules in your application to defined virtual hosts.
nocreateMBeansForResources	Do not create MBeans for resources (including JSPs, servlets, EJBs, etc.) in your application.
node <nodename>	The name of the node.
nodeployejb	Do not deploy the EJBs in your application.
nodistributeApp	Do not distribute your application binaries to the servers on which they're configured.
nopreCompileJSPs	Do not pre-compile the JSPs in your application.
noreloadEnabled	Do not enable servlet re-loading.
nousedefaultbindings	Do not use default bindings.

Option	Description
nouseMetaDataFromBinary	Do not use the configuration information from the application binaries (use only the configuration information stored for the application in the configuration repository).
preCompileJSPs	Pre-compile the JSPs in your application.
reloadEnabled	Enable servlet re-loading.
reloadInterval \<interval\>	The re-load interval.
server \<servername\>	The server name.
update	Updates the installed application with a new version of the EAR.
update.ignore.new	Ignore bindings from the new EAR.
update.ignore.old	Replace the existing bindings with those in the new EAR.
usedefaultbindings	Use default bindings.
useMetaDataFromBinary	Use the configuration information stored in the application binaries (overriding the configuration information stored in the configuration repository for the application).
verbose	Provide additional information during the operation.

Required fields are <u>underlined</u> in the table above. To leave a field blank you specify it as a double-quoted empty string (""). You must put double-quotes around any field entries that contain blanks.

Options are always entered with a leading "-" (dash). For example:

```
$AdminApp install "C:/Program Files/WebSphere/AppServer/samples/lib/PlantsByWebSp
here/PlantsByWebSphere.ear" {-cell rhighlt1Network -node rhighlt1 -usedefaultbind
ings -server server2}
```

The following example demonstrates a couple of options listed above:

```
$AdminApp install "C:/Program
Files/WebSphere/AppServer/samples/lib/PlantsByWebSphere/PlantsByWebSphere.ear" {-
BindJndiForEJBNonMessageBinding {{"PlantsByWebSphere EJB Module" ShoppingCart
PlantsByWebSphereEJB.jar,META-INF/ejb-jar.xml plantsby/ShoppingCartHome}} -
DataSourceFor20CMPBeans {{"PlantsByWebSphere EJB Module" Inventory
PlantsByWebSphereEJB.jar,META-INF/ejb-jar.xml
eis/jdbc/PlantsByWebSphereDataSource_CMP container}}}
```

The -BindJndiForEJBNonMessageBinding option binds the JNDI name for the ShoppingCart bean in the "PlantsByWebSphere EJB Module". The URI for this is PlantsByWebSphereEJB.jar,meta_inf/ejb-jar.xml. The EJB will be bound with a JNDI name of plantsby/ShoppingCartHome.

The -DataSourceFor20CMPBeans establishes the data source for the Inventory bean in the "PlantsByWebSphere EJB Module". The URI for this is PlantsByWebSphereEJB.jar,meta_inf/ejb-jar.xml. The data source for this bean is eis/jdbc/PlantsByWebSphereDataSource_CMP, and the last argument instructs the container to authenticate with the data source on behalf of the application.

Ant Tasks

If you're not already familiar with Ant, we highly recommend that you get to know it. Ant is an open source build facility that you can get from the Apache organization. It is similar to any of the 'make' utilities that are common in the marketplace. However, Ant is based on Java and can be easily extended with Java classes.

> *http://jakarta.apache.org/ant/index.html is a good source of information about Ant.*

Ant works from an XML file that describes the tasks that you want performed during the build – similar to rules in a make file. Each Ant task has a pseudo-DTD that describes the parameters that you can pass into the task – each parameter corresponding to an attribute of the task's Class object. The attributes of the XML task element are set on the Ant Task class. The task is then invoked with the execute() operation.

The WebSphere samples are built using Ant. For an example of an Ant build file, look into the samples/lib/source/PlantsByWebSphere/build.xml file in the WebSphere installation directory.

The following Ant tasks are supported by WebSphere:

Task	Description
wsadmin	Executes the WebSphere command-line administration tool with the specified arguments.
wsDefaultBindings	Enables you to generate default IBM WebSphere bindings for the specified EAR file.
wsejbdeploy	Executes the WebSphere EJB deploy tool on the specified JAR file with the specified options.
wsInstallApp	Lets you to install a new application into a WebSphere server or cell.
WsJspC	Compiles a directory full of JSP files into .class files.
wsListApps	Lists all the applications installed on a WebSphere server or cell.
wsNLSEcho	An echo extension task to display translated messages.

Task	Description
wsServerStatus	Enables you to get status on a server instance or all server instances.
wsStartApp	Allows you to start an existing or newly installed application on a WebSphere server or cell.
wsStartServer	Helps you to start a standalone server instance.
wsStopApp	Lets you to stop an existing or newly installed application on a WebSphere server or cell.
wsStopServer	Enables you to stop a standalone server instance.
wsUninstallApp	Lets you to uninstall an existing application from a WebSphere server or cell.
wsValidateModule	Performs validation of the deployment descriptor, extensions, and bindings documents of an EAR, WAR, EJB JAR, or application client JAR.

wsadmin

The **wsadmin** task can be used to invoke any wsadmin command-line script. The task element has the following XML syntax:

```
<wsadmin { command=<wsadmincmd> | script=<wsadminscript> } [lang=<scriptlang>]
         [wasHome=<wasinstalldir>] [properties=<JVMsyspropsfile>]
         [profile=<scriptprofile>] [conntype=<type>] [host=<hostaddr>]
         [port=<portnumber>] [user=<username>] [password=<passwd>] >
    <arg value=<argvalue> />
    <arg value=<argvalue> />
    ...
</wsadmin>
```

Where:

❏   <wsadmincmd> is the command that you want processed by wsadmin.

❏   <wsadminscript> is the script file that you want processed by wsadmin. You must specify either <wsadminscsript> or <wsadmincmd>.

❏   <scriptlang> is the language in which the command or script is written. WebSphere currently only supports the Jacl language. Support for Jython and Javascript expected in the future.

❏   <wasinstalldir> is the installation directory for WebSphere. This should be the installation directory for the App Server when installing in a single server environment, and should be the installation directory for the Deployment Manager when installing against the deployment manager in a networked cell environment.

❏   <JVMsyspropsfile> is the name of a file containing system properties that you want to pass into the JVM for this task.

- ❏ `<scriptprofile>` is a profile script that you want run before the command or script is performed.

- ❏ `<type>` is the type of connection you want to make to the `AdminService` for this task. This can be SOAP or IIOP.

- ❏ `<hostaddr>` is the host name or IP address of the `AdminService` that you want to connect to.

- ❏ `<portnumber>` is the port number of the SOAP or IIOP listener of the `AdminService` that you want to connect to.

- ❏ `<username>` is your user ID. This is only needed if security has been enabled. If so, you must have been granted the authority to perform whatever is contained your script.

- ❏ `<passwd>` is your password – corresponding to the user ID you supplied in `<username>`.

- ❏ `<argvalue>` is any argument value you want/need to pass in to the script. You should specify as many `<arg value=<argvalue> />` statements are you there are arguments in your script.

This task will invoke the `wsadmin` command utility, passing in the parameters that you've specified above, including either the command (as a `-c` parameter) or the script file (as a `-f` parameter).

You must add the following statement to your Ant `build.xml` file to use this task:

```
<taskdef name="wsadmin" classname="com.ibm.websphere.ant.tasks.WsAdmin"/>
```

The following demonstrates invoking a `wsadmin` script from an Ant task:

```
<target name="installResources" depends="init"
    description="Install the PBW JDBC and JMS resources via wsadmin">
    <echo> " Installing Plants JDBC/JMS resources on WAS Node ${node} " </echo>
    <input
        message="Please enter the database type [db2 or oracle]:"
        property="dbtype"
    />
    <input
        message="Please enter the database username:"
        property="dbuser"
    />
    <input
        message="Please enter the database password:"
        property="dbpass"
    />
    <input
        message="Please enter the Oracle database hostname:"
        property="dboraclehost"
        onlyIfDbtypeEquals="oracle"
    />
    <input
        message="Please enter the Oracle database SID:"
        property="dboraclesid"
        onlyIfDbtypeEquals="oracle"
    />
```

```
    <input
        message="Please enter the fullpath to the JDBC driver db2java.zip or
                 classes12.zip (e.g. c:/sqllib/java/db2java.zip)"
        property="basepath"
    />
    <path id="base.path" path="${basepath}"/>
    <pathconvert dirsep="/" property="dbdriverpath" refid="base.path"/>
    <echo> "Database Classpath path converted ${dbdriverpath}" </echo>

    <echo> "Creating Plants JDBC Datasource"</echo>
    <wsadmin script="createPlantsRDBMSResources.jacl">
            <arg value="${dbtype}"/>
            <arg value="${node}"/>
            <arg value="${dbdriverpath}"/>
            <arg value="${dbuser}"/>
            <arg value="${dbpass}"/>
            <arg value="${dboraclehost}"/>
            <arg value="${dboraclesid}"/>
    </wsadmin>

    <echo> "Creating Plants JMS Queues and Topics"</echo>
    <wsadmin script="createPlantsJMSResources.jacl">
            <arg value="${node}"/>
    </wsadmin>
</target>
```

This is part of a larger Ant task that could be used to deploy and install the Plants-By-WebSphere
application to an application server, for example in a test environment. This task target shows
prompting for the JDBC and JMS resources used by Plants-By-Websphere, and then firing the
createPlantsRDBMSResrource and subsequently the createPlantsJMSResrouces Jacl scripts.

wsDefaultBindings

The **wsDefaultBindings** task can be used to create default bindings for an application. This task element
has the following XML syntax:

```
<wsDefaultBindings ear=<earfilename> outputFile=<outputfilename>
                   [defaultDataSource=<defDSname>] [dbUser=<dbusername>]
                   [dbPassword=<dbpasswd>] [defaultConnectionFactory=<defCFname>]
                   [resAuth={PerConnFact | Container}]
                   [ejbJndiPrefix=<jndiprefix>]
                   [virtualHost=<vhname>] [forceBindings={true | false}]
                   [strategy=<genstrategy>] [exportFile=<expstratfilename>] />
```

Where:

❏   <earfilename> is the filename of the EAR that you want to deploy.

❏   <outputfilename> is the name of the deployed EAR that you want produced from this task.

❏   <defDSname> is the JNDI name of the default data source that you want used.

❏   <dbusername> is the default user name that you want used to access the database.

- ❏ `<dbpasswd>` is the password for the default user name for accessing the database.
- ❏ `<defCFname>` is the JNDI name of the default connection factory you want used.
- ❏ `<jndiprefix>` is the JNDI prefix that you want appended in front of any resources defined within this application.
- ❏ `<vhname>` is the default virtual host name.
- ❏ `<genstrategy>` is an external binding strategy file that may provide additional information about how to produce binding information for this application.
- ❏ `<expstratfilename>` is the name of a binding strategy file that you want generated from this task. The resulting strategy file will capture the specifics of any assumptions or directions used in this task. Generating a strategy file may be useful for future invocations of this task – perhaps for re-deployment, or as input to other similar binding activities.

This task will produce the bindings information for your application – similar to what would be produced during the installation process. If you don't specify a binding strategy file, this task will generate binding names that are derived from the referenced objects and resources. If names won't work for your application, can provide specific binding information in a strategy file.

This is only part of the deployment process – you should use the `wsEjbDeploy` task to generate the EJB stubs, skeletons, and schema mapping files for your application.

You must add the following statement to your Ant `build.xml` file to use this task:

```
<taskdef name="wsDefaultBindings"
         classname="com.ibm.websphere.ant.tasks.DefaultBindings"/>
```

Deploy-gen Strategy File

The `<genstrategy>` attribute refers to an external `deploy-gen` strategy file that provides more details about the deployment process. The `deploy-gen` strategy file is an XML file with the following DTD:

```
<!ELEMENT dfltbndngs (global-bindings?,module-bindings?) >

<!ELEMENT global-bindings (data-source?,connection-factory?,virtual-host?)>
<!ELEMENT connection-factory (jndi-name,res-auth)>

<!ELEMENT module-bindings (ejb-jar-binding | war-binding | java-binding )+ >
<!ELEMENT ejb-jar-binding (jar-name, data-source?,connection-factory?,
                           ejb-bindings?,resource-ref-bindings?,
                           resource-env-ref-bindings? )>
<!ELEMENT war-binding (jar-name,virtual-host?,resource-ref-bindings?,
                       resource-env-ref-bindings?)>
<!ELEMENT java-binding (jar-name,resource-ref-bindings?,
                        resource-env-ref-bindings?)>
<!ELEMENT ejb-binding (ejb-name,jndi-name?,data-source?,connection-factory?,
                       resource-ref-bindings?,
                       resource-env-ref-bindings?,listener-port?)>
<!ELEMENT resource-env-ref-bindings (resource-env-ref-binding)+>
<!ELEMENT resource-env-ref-binding (resource-env-ref-name,jndi-name)>
```

```
<!ELEMENT resource-ref-bindings (resource-ref-binding)+>
<!ELEMENT resource-ref-binding (resource-ref-name,jndi-name)>
<!ELEMENT data-source (jndi-name,user?,password?)>
<!ELEMENT ejb-bindings (ejb-binding)+>
<!ELEMENT ejb-name (#PCDATA)>
<!ELEMENT jar-name (#PCDATA)>
<!ELEMENT jndi-name (#PCDATA)>
<!ELEMENT listener-port (#PCDATA)>
<!ELEMENT password (#PCDATA)>
<!ELEMENT res-auth (#PCDATA)>
<!ELEMENT resource-env-ref-name (#PCDATA)>
<!ELEMENT resource-ref-name (#PCDATA)>
<!ELEMENT user (#PCDATA)>
<!ELEMENT virtual-host (#PCDATA)>
```

For example, the following `strategy.xml` document might be used to set the virtual host and some binding information for Plants-By-WebSphere:

```
<?xml version="1.0" encoding="UTF-8"?>
<!DOCTYPE dfltbndngs SYSTEM "dfltbndngs.dtd" >
<dfltbndngs>
  <global-bindings>
    <virtual-host>default_host</virtual-host>
  </global-bindings>
  <module-bindings>
    <ejb-jar-binding>
      <jar-name>PlantsByWebSphereEAR.jar</jar-name>
      <data-source>
        <jndi-name>eis/jdbc/PlantsByWebSphereDataSource_CMP</jndi-name>
      </data-source>
      <ejb-bindings>
        <ejb-binding>
          <ejb-name>Catelog</ejb-name>
          <jndi-name>plantsby/CatalogHome</jndi-name>
        </ejb-binding>
      </ejb-bindings>
    </ejb-jar-binding>
  </module-bindings>
</dfltbndngs>
```

This DTD is stored in `properties/dfltbndngs.dtd` under the WAS installation root.

If you're going to be doing a lot of deployment, it is generally a good idea to create a strategy file that details the specifics of your deployment. You can then re-deploy the same application with the same strategy file, or make minor modifications to deploy other similar applications.

A common technique is to create a deployment strategy file for every application you put in to your production environment and save these in a source control system along with the application. That way you have a record of exactly how the application was deployed. This can be used for auditing purposes, as well as a control mechanism for future re-deployments of the application.

wsejbdeploy

The **wsejbdeploy** task can be used to deploy an application EAR – that is, promote and resolve deployment information and optionally generate the stubs, skeletons, and schema-mapping files for the application. The wsejbdeploy task element has the following XML syntax:

```
<wsejbdeploy inputJar=<injarfile> outputJar=<outjarfile>
            [wasHome=<wasinstalldir>] [workingDirectory=<tempdir>]
            [classpath=<classpath>] [classpathref=<antclasspath>]
            [codegen=<enablecodegen>] [dbname=<databasename>]
            [dbschema=<databaseschema>] [dbvendor=<databasevendor>]
            [dynamic=<enabledynamicquery>] [keepGenerated=<enablekeepGenerated>]
            [quiet=<enablequiet>] [noValidate=<enablenoValidate>]
            [noWarnings=<enablenoWarnings>] [noInform=<enablenoInform>]
            [rmicOptions=<rmicopts>] [compatible35=<enablecompatible35>]
            [sqlj=<enablesqlj>] [failonerror=<enablefailonerror>]
            [trace=<enabletrace>] />
```

Where:

❑　<injarfile> is the JAR, WAR, or EAR file that you want to deploy.

❑　<outjarfile> is the EAR file that should be produced from the deployment.

❑　<wasinstalldir> is the installation directory for WebSphere. This should be the installation directory for the App Server when installing in a single server environment, and should be the installation directory for the Deployment Manager when installing against the deployment manager in a networked cell environment.

❑　<tempdir> is a temporary working directory. Make sure you specify a directory that does not contain any files that you want to keep.

❑　<enablekeepGenerated> is either "true" or "false" indicated whether to keep the working directory.

❑　<classpath> is any additional classpath that is needed to compile the JSP pages.

❑　<antclasspath> is the same as classpath, except expressed as an ANT reference path.

❑　<enablecodegen> is either "true" or "false" indicating whether you want stub, skeleton, or schema-mapping code to be generated from this deployment processing.

❑　<databasename> is the name of the database you want created when you install this application (used in top-down deployment).

❑　<databaseschema> is the name of the database schema you want created when you install this application (used in top-down deployment).

❑　<databasevendor> is the database identity/vendor you want to use with this application. This will be used to customize the SQL statement that will be generated – considering the access intent and other deployment policies set in the application.

❑　<enabledynamicquery> is either "true" or "false" indicating whether you use the dynamic query service (only available with the programming model extensions in the Enterprise edition). This directs the deployment task to generate the metadata for the dynamic query service.

- ❑ `<enablequiet>` is either "`true`" or "`false`" indicating whether you want the deploy process to suppress information and warning messages (only producing error messages).

- ❑ `<enablenoValidate>` is either "`true`" or "`false`" indicating whether you want to suppress validation.

- ❑ `<enablenoWarnings>` is either "`true`" or "`false`" indicating whether you want to suppress warning messages.

- ❑ `<enablenoInform>` is either "`true`" or "`false`" indicating whether you want to support informational messages.

- ❑ `<rmicopts>` is a list of additional options you want passed into the RMIC processor. These options should be enclosed in quotes.

- ❑ `<enablecompatible35>` is either "`true`" or "`false`" indicating whether you want the deployed EAR to be compatible with WebSphere R3.5.

- ❑ `<enablesqlj>` is either "`true`" or "`false`" indicating whether you want to use a SQLJ adapter for CMP beans.

- ❑ `<enablefailonerror>` is either "`true`" or "`false`" indicating whether you want to stop deployment if any errors are encountered.

- ❑ `<enabletrace>` is either "`true`" or "`false`" indicating whether you want to trace the deployment process.

You need to add the following to your `build.xml` before you can use this task:

```
<taskdef name="wsejbdeploy" classname="com.ibm.websphere.ant.tasks.WsEjbDeploy"/>
```

wsInstallApp

The **wsInstallApp** task will install a deployed application into the runtime. The `wsInstallApp` task element has the following XML syntax:

```
<wsInstallApp ear=<earfilename> [wasHome=<wasinstalldir>]
              [options=<installoptions>] [properties=<JVMsyspropsfile>]
              [profile=<scriptprofile>] [conntype=<type>] [host=<hostaddr>]
              [port=<portnumber>] [user=<username>] [password=<passwd>] />
```

Where:

- ❑ `<earfilename>` is the name (and path location) of the EAR file that you want to install.

- ❑ `<wasinstalldir>` is the installation directory for WebSphere. This should be installation directory for the App Server when installing in a single server environment, and should be the installation directory for the Deployment Manager when installing against the deployment manager in a networked cell environment.

- ❑ `<installoptions>` are any of the installation options that you might normally pass to the `$AdminApp` install operation. These options should be enclosed in quotes so that they will be handled as a single XML attribute.

❑ `<JVMsyspropsfile>` is the name of a file containing system properties that you want to pass into the JVM for this task.

❑ `<scriptprofile>` is a profile script that you want run before the installation step is performed.

❑ `<type>` is the type of connection you want to make to the `AdminService` for this installation task. This can be SOAP or IIOP.

❑ `<hostaddr>` is the host name or IP address of the `AdminService` where you want to install the application.

❑ `<portnumber>` is the port number of the SOAP or IIOP listener of the `AdminService` where you want to install the application.

❑ `<username>` is your user ID. This is only needed if security has been enabled. If so, you must have been granted the authority to modify the configuration with the installation of this application.

❑ `<passwd>` is your password – corresponding to the user ID you supplied in `<username>`.

The `InstallApp` task is useful if you want to install your application after it has been compiled, Jar'ed, and deploy-gen'ed – for example, if you want to initiate a simple build-verification test on your application after it has been built.

You need to add the following to your `build.xml` before you can use this task:

```
<taskdef name="wsInstallApp"
         classname="com.ibm.websphere.ant.tasks.InstallApplication"/>
```

The following demonstrates the installation of the Plants-By-WebSphere application using this Ant task:

```
<target name="installApp" depends="init" description="Install the PBW ear file">
   <wsInstallApp
      ear="${PlantsByWebSphere.ear}"
      options="-appname PlantsByWebSphere -useMetaDataFromBinary yes
               -deployejb yes -usedefaultbindings"
   />
</target>
```

wsJspC

The **wsJspC** task can be used to pre-compile the JSP pages in your application. Pre-compiling your JSP pages increases the size of your application EAR, slightly, but improves the performance of your application – your JSP pages have to be compiled on the first request that involves them if they haven't already been compiled.

The `JspC` task element has the following syntax:

```
<wsjspc src=<sourcedir> toDir=<targetdir> [wasHome=<wasinstalldir>]
        [classpath=<classpath>] [classpathref=<antclasspath>] />
```

Where:

- ❏ <sourcedir> is the directory containing your JSP source files.

- ❏ <targetdir> is the directory where you want the compiled JSPs to be placed.

- ❏ <wasinstalldir> is the installation directory for WebSphere. This should be the installation directory for the App Server when installing in a single server environment, and should be the installation directory for the Deployment Manager when installing against the deployment manager in a networked cell environment.

- ❏ <classpath> is any additional classpath that is needed to compile the JSP pages.

- ❏ <antclasspath> is the same as classpath, except expressed as an ANT reference path.

Add the following statement to your Ant build.xml if you want to use this task.

```
<taskdef name="wsjspc" classname="com.ibm.websphere.ant.tasks.JspC"/>
```

wsListApps

The **wsListApps** task will list all of the applications installed on the application server or in a cell. This task has the following syntax:

```
<wsListApps [wasHome=<wasinstalldir>] [options=<installoptions>]
    [properties=<JVMsyspropsfile>] [profile=<scriptprofile>]
    [conntype=<type>] [host=<hostaddr>] [port=<portnumber>]
    [user=<username>] [password=<passwd>]  />
```

Where:

- ❏ <wasinstalldir> is the installation directory for WebSphere. This should be the installation directory for the App Server when installing in a single server environment, and should be the installation directory for the Deployment Manager when installing against the deployment manager in a networked cell environment.

- ❏ <JVMsyspropsfile> is the name of a file containing system properties that you want to pass into the JVM for this task.

- ❏ <scriptprofile> is a profile script that you want run before this step is performed.

- ❏ <type> is the type of connection you want to make to the AdminService for this task. This can be "SOAP" or "IIOP".

- ❏ <hostaddr> is the host name or IP address of the AdminService for this task.

- ❏ <portnumber> is the port number of the SOAP or IIOP listener of the AdminService for this task.

- ❏ <username> is your user ID. This is only needed if security has been enabled. If so, you must have been granted the authority to view the configuration of your cell or application server.

- ❏ <passwd> is your password – corresponding to the user ID you supplied in <username>.

Add the following statement to your Ant `build.xml` if you want to use this task.

```
<taskdef name="wsListApps"
         classname="com.ibm.websphere.ant.tasks.ListApplications"/>
```

wsNLSEcho

The **wsNLSEcho** task can be used to display messages from a resource bundle. The syntax for this task is:

```
<wsNLSEcho message=<defaultMessage> [key=<messageKey>]
           [bundle=<resourceBundle>] [replace=<subvalues>] />
```

Where:

- ❑   `<defaultMessage>` is the default message that you want presented in the case none could be found in the resource bundle by the given key.

- ❑   `<messageKey>` is the key of the message that you want to obtain from the resource bundle.

- ❑   `<resourceBundle>` is the name of the resource bundle you want to use. Typically the resource bundle is identified here in its neutral form – the system will append the locale information of the local process to obtain the translated string for your locale.

- ❑   `<subvalues>` is a list of value (strings), separated by the characters ";;". Each substitution value will be assigned to a position within the string in accordance with the ordinal identified in the message. This follows the same conventions as are used in `java.text.MessageFormat`.

This task extends the standard Ant `Echo` task by adding support for internationalization based on the standard Java resource bundle facility.

Add the following statement to your Ant `build.xml` if you want to use this task:

```
<taskdef name="wsNLSEcho" classname="com.ibm.websphere.ant.tasks.NLSEcho"/>
```

wsServerStatus

The **wsServerStatus** task can be used to get the operational status of a given server. The syntax of this task is:

```
<wsServerStatus { server=<serverName> | [all=<enableall>] } [quiet=<enablequiet>]
                [trace=<enabletrace>] [cell=<cellName>] [node=<nodeName>]
                [timeout=<requestTimeout>] [statusPort=<statusportnumber>]
                [wasHome=<wasinstalldir>] [failonerror=<enablefailonerror>] />
```

Where:

- ❑   `<serverName>` is the name of the server that you want to query.

- ❑   `<enableall>` is "true" or "false" indicating whether you want to display the status of all servers.

❏   <enablequiet> is "true" or "false" indicating whether you want to suppress all warning and informational messages from this task.

❏   <enabletrace> is "true" or "false" indicating whether you want to trace the execution of this task.

❏   <cellName> is the name of the cell for the server you are testing.

❏   <nodename> is the name of the node for the server you are testing.

❏   <requestTimeout> is the maximum time (in seconds) that you're willing to wait for this task to complete. If this attribute is not specified, the task will take as long as needed to get a status result.

❏   <statusportnumber> is the port to send status reports to.

❏   <wasinstalldir> is the installation directory for WebSphere. This should be the installation directory for the App Server when installing in a single server environment, and should be the installation directory for the Deployment Manager when installing against the deployment manager in a networked cell environment.

❏   <enablefailonerror> is "true" or "false" indicating whether you want this task to terminate immediately if it encounters any errors.

Add the following statement to your Ant build.xml if you want to use this task:

```
<taskdef name="wsServerStatus"
         classname="com.ibm.websphere.ant.tasks.ServerStatus"/>
```

wsStartApp

The **wsStartApp** task can be used to start an application. This task has the following syntax:

```
<wsStartApp application=<appname> [wasHome=<wasinstalldir>]
     [server=<serverName>] [node=<nodeName>] [properties=<JVMsyspropsfile>]
     [profile=<scriptprofile>] [conntype=<type>] [host=<hostaddr>]
     [port=<portnumber>] [user=<username>] [password=<passwd>] />
```

Where:

❏   <appname> is the name of the application that you want to start.

❏   <wasinstalldir> is the installation directory for WebSphere. This should be the installation directory for the App Server when installing in a single server environment, and should be the installation directory for the Deployment Manager when installing against the deployment manager in a networked cell environment.

❏   <serverName> is the name of the server hosting the application that you want to start.

❏   <nodeName> is the name of the node hosting the application that you want to start.

❏   <JVMsyspropsfile> is the name of a file containing system properties that you want to pass into the JVM for this task.

❏   <scriptprofile> is a profile script that you want run before this step is performed.

- ❑ `<type>` is the type of connection you want to make to the `AdminService` for this task. This can be "SOAP" or "IIOP".

- ❑ `<hostaddr>` is the host name or IP address of the `AdminService` for this task.

- ❑ `<portnumber>` is the port number of the SOAP or IIOP listener of the `AdminService` for this task.

- ❑ `<username>` is your user ID. This is only needed if security has been enabled. If so, you must have been granted the authority to operate on resources in the system.

- ❑ `<passwd>` is your password – corresponding to the user ID you supplied in `<username>`.

Add the following statement to your Ant `build.xml` if you want to use this task:

```
<taskdef name="wsStartApplication"
         classname="com.ibm.websphere.ant.tasks.StartApplication"/>
```

The following demonstrates starting the `PlantsByWebSphere` application using this Ant task:

```
<target name="startPlants" depends="init"
        description="Starts the PlantsByWebSphere application in WebSphere">
  <wsStartApplication application="PlantsByWebSphere" />
</target>
```

wsStartServer

The `wsStartServer` task can be used to start an application. This task has the following syntax:

```
<wsStartServer server=<serverName> [wasHome=<wasinstalldir>]
               [noWait=<enablenoWait>] [quiet=<enablequiet>]
               [logFile=<logfilename>] [replaceLog=<enablereplaceLog>]
               [trace=<enabletrace>] [script=<scriptfile>]
               [timeout=<timeoutseconds>] [failonerror=<enablefailonerror>]
               [statusPort=<statusportnumber>] [username=<username>]
               [password=<passwd>] />
```

Where:

- ❑ `<serverName>` is the name of the server that you want to start.

- ❑ `<wasinstalldir>` is the installation directory for WebSphere. This should be the installation directory for the App Server when installing in a single server environment, and should be the installation directory for the Deployment Manager when installing against the deployment manager in a networked cell environment.

- ❑ `<enablenoWait>` is "true" or "false" indicating whether to wait for the server to start.

- ❑ `<enablequiet>` is "true" or "false" indicating whether to suppress warning and informational messages from this task.

- ❑ `<logfilename>` is the name of the log file you want used to record the server start process.

- ❏ <enablereplaceLog> is "true" or "false" indicating whether to replace the log file, or append to the end of the log file.

- ❏ <scriptfile> is the name of a script file that you want to execute during server startup.

- ❏ <timeoutseconds> the amount of time, in seconds, to wait for the server to start. If the server has not started in this number of seconds, the task will return control to the caller. The request to start the server will proceed in the background.

- ❏ <enablefailonerror> is "true" or "false" indicating whether you want this task to terminate immediately if it encounters any errors.

- ❏ <statusportnumber> the port you want this command-line client to use receive status about the server's startup results.

- ❏ <username> is your user ID. This is only needed if security has been enabled. If so, you must have been granted the authority to operate on the resources in the system.

- ❏ <passwd> is your password – corresponding to the user ID you supplied in <username>.

Add the following statement to your Ant build.xml if you want to use this task:

```
<taskdef name="wsStartServer"
         classname="com.ibm.websphere.ant.tasks.StartServer"/>
```

The following depicts starting server1 using this Ant task:

```
<target name="startWebSphere" depends="init"
        description="Start the WebSphere app server1">
  <wsStartServer server="server1" />
</target>
```

wsStopApp

The **wsStopApp** task can be used to stop an application. This task has the following syntax:

```
<wsStopApp application=<appname> [wasHome=<wasinstalldir>]
           [server=<serverName>] [node=<nodeName>] [properties=<JVMsyspropsfile>]
           [profile=<scriptprofile>] [conntype=<type>] [host=<hostaddr>]
           [port=<portnumber>] [user=<username>] [password=<passwd>] />
```

Where:

- ❏ <appname> is the name of the application that you want to stop.

- ❏ <wasinstalldir> is the installation directory for WebSphere. This should be the installation directory for the App Server when installing in a single server environment, and should be the installation directory for the Deployment Manager when installing against the deployment manager in a networked cell environment.

- ❏ <serverName> is the name of the server hosting the application that you want to stop.

- ❏ <nodeName> is the name of the node hosting the application that you want to stop.

❑ <JVMsyspropsfile> is the name of a file containing system properties that you want to pass into the JVM for this task.

❑ <scriptprofile> is a profile script that you want run before this step is performed.

❑ <type> is the type of connection you want to make to the AdminService for this task. This can be "SOAP" or "IIOP".

❑ <hostaddr> is the host name or IP address of the AdminService for this task.

❑ <portnumber> is the port number of the SOAP or IIOP listener of the AdminService for this task.

❑ <username> is your user ID. This is only needed if security has been enabled. If so, you must have been granted the authority to operate on resources in the system.

❑ <passwd> is your password – corresponding to the user ID you supplied in <username>.

Add the following statement to your Ant build.xml if you want to use this task:

```
<taskdef name="wsStopApplication"
         classname="com.ibm.websphere.ant.tasks.StopApplication"/>
```

The following demonstrates stopping the Plants-By-WebSphere application using this Ant task:

```
<target name="stopPlants" depends="init"
        description="Stops the PlantsByWebSphere application in WebSphere">
   <wsStopApplication application="PlantsByWebSphere" />
</target>
```

wsStopServer

The **wsStopServer** task can be used to start an application. This task has the following syntax:

```
<wsStopServer server=<serverName> [wasHome=<wasinstalldir>]
              [noWait=<enablenoWait>] [quiet=<enablequiet>]
              [logFile=<logfilename>] [replaceLog=<enablereplaceLog>]
              [trace=<enabletrace>] [timeout=<timeoutseconds>]
              [failonerror=<enablefailonerror>][conntype=<type>] [host=<hostaddr>]
              [port=<portnumber>] [statusPort=<statusportnumber>]
              [username=<username>] [password=<passwd>] />
```

Where:

❑ <serverName> is the name of the server that you want to stop.

❑ <wasinstalldir> is the installation directory for WebSphere. This should be the installation directory for the App Server when installing in a single server environment, and should be the installation directory for the Deployment Manager when installing against the deployment manager in a networked cell environment.

❑ <enablenoWait> is "true" or "false" indicating whether to wait for the server to stop.

- ❏ <enablequiet> is "true" or "false" indicating whether to suppress warning and informational messages from this task.

- ❏ <logfilename> is the name of the log file you want used to record the server stop process.

- ❏ <enablereplaceLog> is "true" or "false" indicating whether to replace the log file, or append to the end of the log file.

- ❏ <timeoutseconds> the amount of time, in seconds, to wait for the server to stop. If the server has not stopped in this number of seconds, the task will return control to the caller. The request to stop the server will proceed in the background.

- ❏ <enablefailonerror> is "true" or "false" indicating whether you want this task to terminate immediately if it encounters any errors.

- ❏ <type> is the type of connection you want to make to the AdminService for this task. This can be "SOAP" or "IIOP".

- ❏ <hostaddr> is the host name or IP address of the AdminService for this task.

- ❏ <portnumber> is the port number of the SOAP or IIOP listener of the AdminService for this task.

- ❏ <statusportnumber> the port you want this command-line client to use receive status about the server's startup results.

- ❏ <username> is your user ID. This is only needed if security has been enabled. If so, you must have been granted the authority to operate on the resources in the system.

- ❏ <passwd> is your password – corresponding to the user ID you supplied in <username>.

Add the following statement to your Ant build.xml if you want to use this task:

```
<taskdef name="wsStopServer"
         classname="com.ibm.websphere.ant.tasks.StopServer"/>
```

The following depicts stopping server1 using this Ant task:

```
<target name="stopWebSphere" depends="init"
        description="Stop the WebSphere app server1">
  <wsStopServer server="server1" />
</target>
```

wsUninstallApp

The **wsUninstallApp** task can be used to uninstall an application. The syntax of this task is:

```
<wsUninstallApp application=<appName> [wasHome=<wasinstalldir>]
                [options=<uninstalloptions>] [properties=<JVMsyspropsfile>]
                [profile=<scriptprofile>] [conntype=<type>] [host=<hostaddr>]
                [port=<portnumber>] [user=<username>] [password=<passwd>] />
```

Where:

- ❑ <appname> is the name of the application that you want to uninstall.

- ❑ <wasinstalldir> is the installation directory for WebSphere. This should be the installation directory for the App Server when installing in a single server environment, and should be the installation directory for the Deployment Manager when installing against the deployment manager in a networked cell environment.

- ❑ <uninstalloptions> are any of the uninstallation options that you might normally pass to the $AdminApp uninstall operation. These options should be enclosed in quotes so that they will be handled as a single XML attribute.

- ❑ <JVMsyspropsfile> is the name of a file containing system properties that you want to pass into the JVM for this task.

- ❑ <scriptprofile> is a profile script that you want run before the uninstallation step is performed.

- ❑ <type> is the type of connection you want to make to the AdminService for this task. This can be SOAP or IIOP.

- ❑ <hostaddr> is the host name or IP address of the AdminService.

- ❑ <portnumber> is the port number of the SOAP or IIOP listener of the.

- ❑ <username> is your user ID. This is only needed if security has been enabled. If so, you must have been granted the authority to modify the configuration with the uninstallation of this application.

- ❑ <passwd> is your password – corresponding to the user ID you supplied in <username>.

You need to add the following to your build.xml before you can use this task:

```
<taskdef name="wsUninstallApp"
         classname="com.ibm.websphere.ant.tasks.UninstallApplication"/>
```

wsValidateModule

The **wsValidateModule** can be used to validate the modules of an EAR file. This task has the following syntax:

```
<wsValidateModule  src=<srcfilename> />
```

Where:

<srcfilename> is the directory path and filename of the EAR file that you want validated.

You need to add the following to your build.xml before you can use this task:

```
<taskdef name="wsValidateModule"
         ="com.ibm.websphere.ant.tasks.ModuleValidator"/>
```

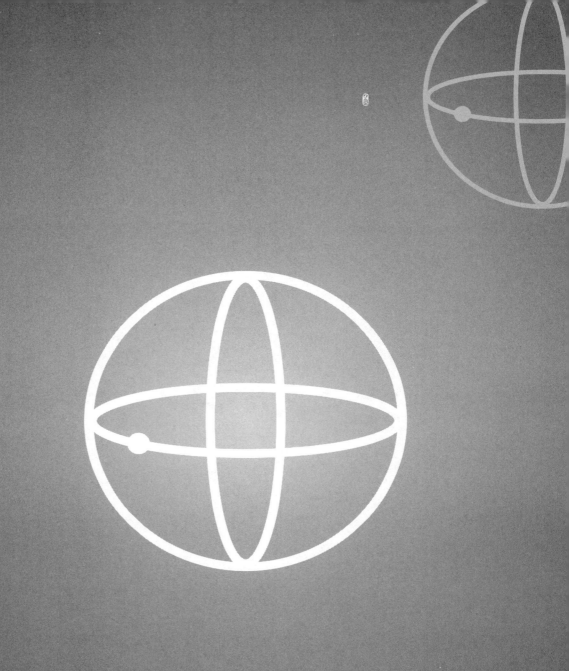

Index

A Guide to the Index

The index is arranged hierarchically, in alphabetical order, with symbols preceding the letter A. Most second-level entries and many third-level entries also occur as first-level entries. This is to ensure that users will find the information they require however they choose to search for it.

X

Z

ASPToday - Your free daily ASP Resource . . .

A discount off your ASPToday subscription with this voucher!!! see below for more details.

Expand your knowledge of ASP.NET with ASPToday.com - Wrox's code source for ASP and .NET applications, with free daily articles!

Every working day, we publish free Wrox content on the web:

- Free daily article
- Free daily tips
- Case studies and reference materials
- Index and full text search
- Downloadable code samples
- 11 Categories
- Written by programmers for programmers

And for just-in-time, practical solutions to real-world problems, subscribe to our Living Book - our 600+ strong archive of code-heavy, useable articles.

Find it all and more at http://www.asptoday.com

This voucher entitles you to a discount off your annual ASPToday subscription; to claim your reduced rate please visit:

http://www.asptoday.com/special-offers/

If you have any questions please contact customersupport@wrox.com

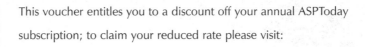

p2p.wrox.com
The programmer's resource centre

A unique free service from Wrox Press
With the aim of helping programmers to help each other

Wrox Press aims to provide timely and practical information to today's programmer. P2P is a list server offering a host of targeted mailing lists where you can share knowledge with your fellow programmers and find solutions to your problems. Whatever the level of your programming knowledge, and whatever technology you use, P2P can provide you with the information you need.

ASP
Support for beginners and professionals, including a resource page with hundreds of links, and a popular ASP.NET mailing list.

DATABASES
For database programmers, offering support on SQL Server, mySQL, and Oracle.

MOBILE
Software development for the mobile market is growing rapidly. We provide lists for the several current standards, including WAP, Windows CE, and Symbian.

JAVA
A complete set of Java lists, covering beginners, professionals, and server-side programmers (including JSP, servlets, and EJBs)

.NET
Microsoft's new OS platform, covering topics such as ASP.NET, C#, and general .NET discussion.

VISUAL BASIC
Covers all aspects of VB programming, from programming Office macros to creating components for the .NET platform.

WEB DESIGN
As web page requirements become more complex, programmer's are taking a more important role in creating web sites. For these programmers, we offer lists covering technologies such as Flash, Coldfusion, and JavaScript.

XML
Covering all aspects of XML, including XSLT and schemas.

OPEN SOURCE
Many Open Source topics covered including PHP, Apache, Perl, Linux, Python, and more.

FOREIGN LANGUAGE
Several lists dedicated to Spanish and German speaking programmers; categories include: NET, Java, XML, PHP, and XML.

How to subscribe:
Simply visit the P2P site, at http://p2p.wrox.com/

Wrox Press

Web Services

A selection of related titles from our Web Services Series

Professional Java Web Services
ISBN:1-86100-375-7
Professional Java Web Services concisely explains the important technologies and specifications behind web services. The book outlines the architecture of web services, and the latest information on implementing web services.

Professional C# Web Services: Building Web Services with .NET Remoting and ASP.NET
ISBN: 1-86100-439-7
This book covers building web services and web service clients with both ASP.NET and .NET Remoting. We also look at the generic protocols used by web services: SOAP and WSDL.

Professional XML Web Services
ISBN: 1-86100-509-1
The technologies presented in this book provide the foundations of web services computing, which is set to revolutionize distributed computing, as we know it.

Professional ASP.NET Web Services
ISBN: 1-86100-545-8
This book will show you how to create high-quality web services using ASP.NET.

Early Adopter Hailstorm
ISBN: 1-86100-608-X
Hailstorm Preview of Version 1.0 - Using SOAP and XPath to talk to Hailstorm - Hailstorm Data Manipulation Language (HSDL) - Practical Case Studies.

Professional Java SOAP
ISBN: 1-86100-610-1
Organized in three parts: Distributed Application Protocols, Sample Application, and Web Service, this book is for all Java developers and system archictects.

Programmer to Programmer™

Registration Code: 58140P9X1T0ZY901

Wrox writes books for you. Any suggestions, or ideas about how you want
information given in your ideal book will be studied by our team.
Your comments are always valued at Wrox.

Free phone in USA 800-USE-WROX
Fax (312) 893 8001

UK Tel.: (0121) 687 4100   Fax: (0121) 687 4101

Professional IBM WebSphere 5.0 Application Server – Registration Card

Name _____

Address _____

_____

_____

City _____ State/Region _____

Country _____ Postcode/Zip _____

E-Mail _____

Occupation _____

How did you hear about this book?

☐ Book review (name) _____

☐ Advertisement (name) _____

☐ Recommendation _____

☐ Catalog _____

☐ Other _____

Where did you buy this book?

☐ Bookstore (name) _____ City _____

☐ Computer store (name) _____

☐ Mail order _____

☐ Other _____

What influenced you in the purchase of this book?

☐ Cover Design ☐ Contents ☐ Other (please specify):

How did you rate the overall content of this book?

☐ Excellent ☐ Good ☐ Average ☐ Poor

What did you find most useful about this book? _____

_____

What did you find least useful about this book? _____

_____

Please add any additional comments. _____

_____

What other subjects will you buy a computer book on soon?

_____

What is the best computer book you have used this year?

_____

Note: This information will only be used to keep you updated
about new Wrox Press titles and will not be used for
any other purpose or passed to any other third party.

5814   Check here if you DO NOT want to receive support for this book ■   5814

Programmer to Programmer™

Note: If you post the bounce back card below in the UK, please send it to:

Wrox Press Limited, Arden House, 1102 Warwick Road,
Acocks Green, Birmingham B27 6HB. UK.

Computer Book Publishers

BUSINESS REPLY MAIL

FIRST CLASS MAIL   PERMIT#64   CHICAGO, IL

POSTAGE WILL BE PAID BY ADDRESSEE

WROX PRESS INC.,
29 S. LA SALLE ST.,
SUITE 520
CHICAGO IL 60603-USA